INTRODUCTION TO AMERICAN EDUCATION

INTRODUCTION TO AMERICAN EDUCATION

A HUMAN RELATIONS APPROACH

by

GEORGE HENDERSON

With a Foreword by Lloyd P. Williams

Norman
University of Oklahoma Press

By George Henderson

Foundations of American Education (with William B. Ragan) (New York, 1970)
Teachers Should Care (with Robert F. Bibens) (New York, 1970)
America's Other Children: Public Schools Outside Suburbia (editor) (Norman, 1972)
To live in Freedom: Human Relations Today and Tomorrow (Norman, 1972)
Education for Peace: Focus on Mankind (editor) (Washington, D.C., 1973)
Human Relations: From Theory to Practice (Norman, 1974)
Human Relations in the Military: Problems and Programs (Chicago, 1975)
A Religious Foundation of Human Relations: Beyond Games (Norman, 1977)
Introduction to American Education: A Human Relations Approach (Norman, 1978)

Library of Congress Cataloging in Publication Data

Henderson, George, 1932–
Introduction to American education.

Includes bibliographies.
1. Educational sociology—United States. I. Title.
LC191.H43   370.19′3   77–18609
ISBN 0–8061–1458–4

*To William B. Ragan, a humane teacher
and a profound scholar*

FOREWORD

The disordered condition of modern life gives all thoughtful persons pause. Without planning or intention we have become captives of a highly complex and interdependent society. These qualities of life are not in themselves bad, but the instability of our times in conjunction with the technological possibilities for mutual destruction make them potentially lethal.

Both internally and internationally the threats to stable and just society in these waning years of the twentieth century are immense. Internally we suffer from several seemingly relentless cultural pressures. Racial conflict is endemic in American life; sometimes open, frequently covert, it continues to bedevil the nation and to defy democratic resolution generation after generation. Urban congestion carries us every day closer to urban chaos as our cities become increasingly unliveable. Nonfunctional government seems pervasive in the American system from the city council to the national government, and this ossification in varying degrees permeates not only all levels of government but also all three major branches of government. The legislative branches are often incapable of serving the public need; the judiciary is often lost in a maze of procedural trivia; and the executive is often paralyzed by lack of authority or courage or integrity, or perhaps some combination thereof. Crime is rampant and rising. And not the least of our concerns is inflation abetted by the near exhaustion of some major resources and the accompanying industrial pollution and exploitive destruction of much of our environment.

Internationally our burden overlaps many of the foregoing problems and in addition sees the world subject to explosive population increase, a kind of sociological inundation that can immobilize us. The absence of effective international government keeps the community of nations in a continuing state of anarchy, a fact that is doubly serious in light of the possibilities for nuclear war. International traffic in drugs, the multinational corporation more often interested in profits than in economic stability or justice, and the systematic destruction of the air and oceans all threaten us.

Confronted with problems of such magnitude some give up, whereas others seek solutions in Utopia or perhaps in revolution. None of these alternatives commends itself to Professor George Henderson, for he seeks a resolution of them through the minds and hearts of humanity. He considers a wide range of problems, always analyzing thoughtfully, although sometimes hitting hard at the lethargy or inertia of persons and institutions that have proved intractable to twentieth century needs. Regretting that democracy has not always worked, Professor Henderson nevertheless comes out on the side of the democratic alternative. Yet he holds no simplistic assurance that we shall necessarily solve these problems. The cultural bet is on the intelligence of the common person, but that intelligence must be used. The reflective citizen does well, however, to note that the democratic alternative is open to us now, but how much longer it will be open is problematical. Certainly it is not open indefinitely if modern trends continue. With the right kind of realistic, effective education, with teachers trained to understand and to face objectively the problems before us, modern citizens may find ways to control the world, and with greater or equal importance, ways to control themselves as well. The heart of Professor Henderson's argument is that we can build a better nation and a better world through education if we promote that kind of understanding that leads us to render justice to all. Cultivation of humanistic sensibility is essential, although all too often it is neglected. The serious student will find in the following pages a provocative appraisal of our problems and prospects—promises and threats—both educationally and socially. This analysis is not an exercise in romantic idealism, but rather the tone is one of realism culminating in a hopeful consideration of the future.

That the author dedicates this book to William B. Ragan is not only an expression of friendship but also indicative of the hope that democracy entails. In his long career as teacher and scholar, William Ragan never wavered in his conviction that human intelligence is ultimately capable of facing and solving the problems of the world. George Henderson continues to work in that tradition, and in so doing encourages us all.

LLOYD P. WILLIAMS

PREFACE

Although this book is written primarily for students interested in pursuing careers as elementary and secondary school teachers, it should also be of value to experienced teachers. The major foci are on social science *concepts* pertaining to American education, but attention is also paid to activities that will assist individuals to get in touch with their *feelings* about these concepts as well as to examine their *attitudes* toward teaching. This then is not a book to be passively read; it is a human relations process in which to become actively involved. The following features of the book should be especially noted:

An interdisciplinary approach. Materials are taken from several areas in the field of education plus the social sciences—especially sociology, psychology, and anthropology. This is done in order to give the reader a broad view of the major sociocultural forces affecting American education. Students who specialize in a particular area will have an opportunity in other courses to explore some of these topics in even greater detail.

Emphasis on current problems. We are living in a very exciting period in history. Educational models that once served us well are being altered to fit the postmodern world in which we live. In highlighting specific problems I have tried to vividly illustrate the difficulty in effectively planning curricula for today's students. Special emphases are placed on human rights issues, e.g., racism, sexism, cultural pluralism, and student rights. But more than educational problems are discussed;

techniques, strategies, and programs for abating the problems are integral dimensions of this text.

A spiral arrangement of content. Each of the four sections in the book begins with a brief reading designed to spark the readers' thoughts. Many of the topics discussed briefly in early chapters are covered more fully in later ones. This process of expanding on urban/rural school problems and possible solutions is in harmony with the psychological principle that growth and learning are continuous.

Capricious use of sex pronouns. Throughout the book, the words "he," "she," "him," and "her" are used capriciously and in most instances interchangeably to designate both sexes. Such usage may seem awkward to the reader. Perhaps someday discrimination based on sex will also be awkward.

In summary, this book is written for courses generally entitled "Introduction to Education," "Introduction to Teaching," and "Social Foundations of Education." But it is more than a book about negative school conditions; I also suggest ways to humanize instruction within the nation's elementary and secondary schools. Too frequently, educators design and implement programs without relating them to hard data. Teachers and administrators who want to understand more clearly the community forces affecting students may find the data presented in this book to be helpful.

The design of the book is intentional—it combines *cognitive* information with examples of *affective* approaches to teaching and learning. I firmly believe that the *process* of interaction within the school is as important as the academic *content*. It is a truism that until students feel good about themselves, they are not likely to learn basic course materials. This applies to teachers and administrators too.

Portions of this book first appeared in *Foundations of American Education* (Harper & Row, 1970), co-authored with William B. Ragan. Many of my ideas and concepts grew out of my association with Bill Ragan. His counsel was greatly missed as I wrote this manuscript. Above all else, I have tried to write a suitable memorial to him.

I am indebted to Ronald Berman and Kendyll Stansbury for allowing me to revise and reprint portions of their timely essays. Nor should I forget to commend Eve Shank, Larry Bishop, Connie Bleck, and Delores Lee; their typing transformed by scribbling into legible words. Finally, I consider it an honor to have Lloyd Williams, a superb teacher and an insightful scholar, to set the tone for this book.

CONTENTS

LIST OF TABLES
FIGURES
& CHARTS

TABLES

FIGURES

CHARTS

PART I
BASIC
FOUNDATIONS

WHEN I WAS
A LITTLE
MUCHACHO*

Piri Thomas

*Reprinted from *Civil Rights Digest*, Vol. 6, No. 2, 1974, pp. 13–14.

I sent my mind back into time to recall my days as a child growing up in El Barrio in New York City. I can remember the anguish of living amidst poverty. But I can also remember the beautiful freedom of being able to speak Spanish in my home and in the streets. It was a most uptight feeling I went through finding out that in the schools, Spanish was a taboo language—as if the school had added another commandment to the existing Biblical ten: "Thou shalt speak no other language except English."

I can remember my *madre* first taking me to school, leaving me in a classroom, and the only identification I had with that room was other children who looked like me—also dark-skinned and Puerto Rican. The teacher said something to me and I looked very blank-faced as I struggled hard to understand the meaning of her alien language. With a great sense of controlled impatience, she gritted her teeth and pointed a long white finger towards an empty desk. I smiled politely and whispered a courage-filled, *"Muchas gracias."* She smiled sort of tightly and said what sounded like, "We speak on-lee Engleesh here."

It was with great difficulty that I was able to put words phonetically together in English. But learn I did, all the time wondering why I couldn't learn in the language with which I had been familar since the moment I left my mother's womb.

I cannot count the times, as the year passed, that whenever I or other Puerto Rican boys and girls would take a seventh-inning stretch from English and converse among ourselves in Spanish, some teacher would remind us of the great American culture and that the "ugg-dy, ugg-dy" language we were speaking was going to be a handicap to us in America. If we were to grow up to be good Americans, then English had to be our forte (whatever that word meant).

It was *mucho* tough, running into all those kinds of racism and still trying to relate to wearing white shirts and red ties on auditorium day and pledging allegiance to the flag of the United States of America, singing at the top of our lungs the National Anthem, and learning the history of America. We learned about George Washington and Betsy Ross, about England with its King George, and France with its Lafayette, and on and on—never once hearing about the history, culture, roots, and heritage of Puerto Rico.

My God, I felt at times I could only identify with a fire hydrant and hot and cold running cockroaches. We were fed the diet of "You too can become the President of the United States." I wonder how they were able to keep a straight face.

The history the books taught us was geared toward the white children, who must have grown up with a sense of superiority in learning that whites had invented everything from a needle to the last star in the universe; that whites had painted all kinds of great masterpieces, from the paintings of Cro-Magnon man in his prehistoric caves to the ones hanging on the walls of the world's greatest museums. And whites had written all the literature, from a few scratches on some stone tablets eons ago up to "Popeye the Sailor Man"—including a particular piece of literature that somehow was felt to be relevant to us, known as "Little Black Sambo."

Any inquiries by us Puerto Ricans as to our background and heritage were usually answered with reference to the greatness of Spain, with its goldcrazed conquerors such as Pizarro and Cortez. These were the very men who had ripped off culture and destroyed contributions to the arts and sciences created by human beings from South and Central America and Mexico. Another answer given to us, in our quest for our Puerto Rican background, was plain and simple: "We don't know much about Puerto Rico." Or, "You people are very primitive, and really the best thing in the world that has happened to Puerto Rico is that its people are now citizens of the United States."

But it was hard to accept that, because we Puerto Ricans felt no citizenship. We had had no choice as to what country we belonged to. It is certainly true that for human beings

3

to know where they are going, they must first know where they come from. There is no doubt that English is important to know in the United States, but so is Spanish and so is any other language. Language and culture do not belong to any one country or ethnic group. It is like music or art; it belongs to the world, to all human beings.

For children, school in Puerto Rico is actually an extension of the home. The teachers not only love to teach, but love the children they are teaching and are like mothers and fathers to the children. In Puerto Rico, children are taught in the home to respect their teachers and are given respect in return.

In Puerto Rico teaching is an honored profession, and there is a day set aside as a holiday to pay homage to teachers. In this country teachers can be anyone who has had the means to become a teacher—regardless of the fact that they may be racist, bigoted, or hung up in similar neurotic ways. The system, not caring that teaching is such a responsibility, is turning its back on the untold damage done to the minds and lives of children who pass through the hands of uncaring or indifferent, racist teachers.

I couldn't help thinking of one such teacher who was part of a large group of teachers where I was conducting a seminar on sensitivity training. When I spoke of a teacher's responsibility and the importance of blending love for the children with their education, this pitiful woman glared at me in obvious bigotry and damn-near snarled, "I don't have to love them. All I have to do is teach them."

Obviously, she was not talking about white children but about Puerto Ricans, Blacks, Asian Americans, and American Indians—any child that was not as white as she. I remember silently staring at her for long moment and, with *mucho* control, quietly saying, "Why don't you get a job washing dishes? At least if you drop a dish, it is not a child's heart and mind you will be shattering."

1.
HISTORICAL AND IDEOLOGICAL FOUNDATIONS

This chapter is not intended as a substitute for a systematic course in the history and philosophy of American education. It is designed merely to document the thesis that schools have generally tended to reflect the needs, circumstances, and aspirations of their patrons during various periods of history.

A brief summary of the forces that have influenced the development of American schools does not imply that history repeats itself. The circumstances that demand changes in school programs today are not comparable to those that brought about educational innovations in earlier years. (For instance, the modern elementary school building providing one instructional area for several hundred pupils is a far cry from the one-room school of the past.) Although traces of the ideas of Johann H. Pestalozzi, Francis W. Parker, John Dewey, and other educational reformers can be found in modern schools, these ideas have been modified by more recent research and experimentation.

A study of the social forces that have brought about changes in the American school over the years will, however, help the student to understand the reasons why a changing society calls for continuous educational reform.

EDUCATION IN THE AMERICAN COLONIES

The Old Deluder Satan Act, passed by the General Court (legislature) of the Massachusetts Bay Colony in 1647, was the first legislation in America requiring the establish-

ment of schools. This law was designed to make the education of children a public rather than a private enterprise. As a matter of fact, the same legislative body had already taken an important step five years earlier when it had established the new principle that the education of children is a proper subject for legal control. (The 1642 act empowered local officers to find out whether parents and schoolmasters were teaching the children to read and to levy fines on those who failed to report to them.) The idea of public, organized education, however, was something new in American thinking about education. More than two hundred years passed, moreover, before the idea had been effectively implemented by the establishment of public school systems in all the states.

The idea that local governments should be responsible for providing schools was not entirely original when our Puritan forefathers enunciated it. Like many American ideas and practices in the field of education, it had its origin in Europe. In his famous document addressed to the mayors and aldermen of German cities, Martin Luther urged in 1524 that the task of educating the young should immediately be taken hold of by the city officials lest they " . . . be obliged to feel in vain the pangs of remorse forever."[1] It seems likely that the Puritans in the Massachusetts Bay Colony were familiar with Luther's ideas.

The Religious Motive

The Old Deluder Satan Act required each town with fifty or more families to provide a

5

teacher to instruct in reading and writing, and each town with one hundred or more families to establish a grammar school. The religious motive for education that prevailed in New England and the middle colonies is clearly revealed in this act, the preamble to which began with the main reason for requiring towns to establish schools: "It being one chief project of the old deluder Satan to keep men from the knowledge of the Scriptures."

Discipline. Discipline in colonial schools was in harmony with the Puritan theology that children were conceived in iniquity and born in sin; that they were possessed by the Devil and that only by the most severe beating could the Devil be persuaded to depart from them. Thus it was a moral obligation of parents and teachers to "beat the Devil out of Children." The whipping post was a familiar item of furniture in colonial classrooms and anyone passing a school house could hear constant wails of anguish from children. Indeed, college students were not exempt from brutal discipline:

Thomas Sargent, a Harvard student, convicted in 1674 of speaking blasphemous words, was publicly beaten in the library before all the scholars; but the solemn punishment was preceded and followed by prayer by the president, under whose supervision it was inflicted.[2]

Yet we are told that children were often as rebellious in those days as they are now; there were "sit-down strikes" and "lockouts" of teachers.

Discipline in colonial schools can be understood only when one considers the climate of opinion of the time. Government was regarded as ruling over rather than as serving people; there was no confidence in the ability of common people to participate in government; the rights of individuals depended on the class into which they were born. Harsh and cruel punishments were inflicted on adults and children alike in the world outside the school. There was no concern for the need of children for play; they were to become virtuous by performing unpleasant tasks; and fear was the only method known for maintaining order in school. Unmindful of the changes in the cli-

mate of public opinion that have taken place since colonial days, some people today express the opinion that all the problems relating to rebellious youth would suddenly disappear if parents would just use this harsh type of discipline with their children. Fortunately numerous competent authorities in the field of child development have evolved more humane and more effective methods of dealing with children.

Textbooks and teachers. *The New England Primer*, which was the most-used book in colonial schools for more than a hundred years, was a religious book in the strict, narrow sense of Calvinistic theology. It contained a list of the books in the Old and the New Testaments, the Lord's Prayer, the Apostles' Creed, the Ten Commandments, and the Shorter Catechism. Pupils started reading by learning the alphabet by means of rhymes beginning with "In Adam's fall we sinned all" and ending with "Zacheas he did climb a tree his Lord to see." The principal qualifications required of the colonial teacher were to be sound in the doctrines of the church and a good disciplinarian. Teachers generally "boarded around" in the homes of their pupils; frequently they were paid in Indian corn, rye, barley, or tobacco. They led the singing at church, read the sermon in the absence of the minister, dug the graves, and did odd jobs in the community to supplement their income.

The New England colonies (with the exception of Rhode Island) adopted the Massachusetts type of school. The population of the middle colonies, on the other hand, was made up of people of many different religious denominations; there was little chance to establish a church-state system like that in Massachusetts. Each church provided its own educational program. Whatever education was available to people as a whole was limited, narrow, and inadequate. Legislatures in these colonies showed little interest in education. Some schools were established in the southern colonies by grants from interested individuals, but generally the plantation owners and government officials feared that education would bring disobedience and heresy to indentured servants and slaves. Governor William Berkeley wrote in 1671 that he thanked God that there were no free schools in Virginia and hoped there would be none for a hundred years.

Changing Circumstances in Colonial America

According to one authority, "The passage of the Massachusetts Act of 1647 was followed by a period of educational decline in that colony."[3] The reasons for this decline are not difficult to understand when one examines the changing circumstances of colonial life. When towns established schools in Massachusetts, the people lived in compact villages; when the danger of attack by the Indians was diminished as a consequence of King Phillip's War, the colonists spread out and set up more schools. The first town schools in Massachusetts were under the strict domination of the Calvinists. When other Protestant groups began to establish places of worship, they founded their own sectarian schools. Thus the educational program was weakened by a multiplicity of competing schools. Sectarian schools became obstacles to the establishment of free, public, secular programs of education and remained so for more than two hundred years.

The rise of the school district system also weakened education during colonial times and for many years to follow. By the middle of the eighteenth century, the practice of dividing townships into school districts had become common throughout New England. The people who lived in outlying parts of townships demanded that the control of the schools be left in their hands. The small school districts were not able to maintain good schools and local disputes arose over the selection of school committeemen, teachers, and school sites. The school district system was to spread throughout the United States; indeed, it remains an obstacle to educational progress in rural areas even today.

THE PUBLIC SCHOOL REVIVAL

The desire of many early national leaders to establish public school systems in all the states met with opposition from religious sects, private schools, and taxpayers. During the middle years of the nineteenth century, the public school revival succeeded in overcoming these obstacles. Actually a series of movements, the revival involved persuading voters to cast their ballots for increased school appropriations, establishing state departments of education, providing programs of teacher education, and expanding and enriching the curriculum. It represented an awakening of the American conscience concerning the importance of educating children and youth, and its contribution to the strength of the nation in the years that have followed can hardly be overestimated.[4]

Credit for the success of the public school revival cannot be assigned to any one section of the country. Massachusetts, as I have noted, was first to establish many important agencies for public education. Developments on the frontier also were influential. When new states were formed in the territory west of the Appalachians, property qualifications for voting and holding offices were omitted from state constitutions; the number of offices to be filled by popular elections was increased; and the basis for representation in state legislatures was changed from wealth to population. These reforms represented increasing confidence in the ability of people to participate in government. When the right to vote was extended, the agitation for free public schools increased.

The ideas of Pestalozzi, the example of the systems of public education in Prussia and other German states, and the infant school, the Sunday School, and the monitorial system imported from England were important factors in the success of the public school revival. Perhaps the most important factor in its success was the prodigious labor of intelligent leaders in the various states. These leaders were not all educators. One of the most influential was Samuel Gompers (1850–1924), who was elected president of the American Federation of Labor thirty-seven times. He saw in the public school a means by which all children, regardless of the circumstances into which they were born, could develop their talents to the fullest degree possible and bring into the life of the nation a force that would make for a larger degree of freedom. Without the support of organized labor, it is doubtful that the battle for free public schools could have been won at the time.

Horace Mann (1796–1859) left a promising career as an attorney and statesman and became an effective leader in the battle for public education. He had a definite plan for state systems of public education. He also had the eloquence and logic to awaken an apathetic public to an appreciation of public education as the foundation of democracy. When the first permanent state board of education was established in Massachusetts in 1837, Horace Mann became its secretary—a position now generally known as State Superintendent of Public Instruction. He was instrumental in the establishment of the first public institution for the education of teachers at Lexington, Massachusetts, in 1839. Selling his law library and donating the money to this institution, he explained, "The bar is no longer my forum. I have abandoned jurisprudence and betaken myself to the larger sphere of mind and morals. . . . I have faith in the improvability of the race—in their accelerating improvability."

Other leaders in the battle for public schools included James G. Carter of Massachusetts, Henry Barnard of Connecticut, Calvin H. Wiley of North Carolina, and Caleb Mills of Indiana.

The battle for tax-supported high schools began during the first quarter of the nineteenth century. The first public high school for boys was established in Boston in 1821, followed in 1826 by a public high school for girls. The number of high schools grew rapidly after 1874, when the famous *Kalamazoo* case in Michigan established the legality of taxing people for their support. Thus at long last the American people had established a system of public education extending from the first grade through the college and university.

EXPANSION AND REFORM

The early history of American public education falls rather readily into two definite periods. The colonial period began in 1647 and, of course, ended in 1776 when the thirteen colonies declared themselves independent. The dominant motive for education during this period was religious. The national period then followed for a century, until the end of Reconstruction in 1876. This period of expansion, during which the country survived the supreme test of the Civil War, proved that we were a nation. The dominant motive for education was political, and impelled largely by this motive, political and educational leaders established public school systems in all the states.

After 1876 the boundaries between periods became less distinct and the motives for education became more complicated. Political and educational movements tended to become links in an endless chain rather than entirely new phenomena belonging to specific periods in history. The United States entered a period of rapid expansion in area, population, industrial and agricultural production, and influence in world affairs. The expansion was halted during the Great Depression of the 1930s, but it was resumed during World War II and has been increasing in tempo ever since.

Since 1876 thirteen states have been admitted to the Union. The first official census taken in 1790 placed the population of the United States at 3,929,214. We had 100 million people by 1917, 131 million by 1940, 175 million in 1959, and 200 million in 1968. The Gross National Product (GNP) increased from $157 billion in 1947 to $370 billion in 1957, $733 billion in 1967, and $1.5 trillion in 1975. Since science and technology have made the world smaller in terms of travel time, our national needs have become more closely mingled with the needs of all people. Americans could at one time be concerned primarily with circumstances in only one of the thirteen independent states. Now they have to be concerned with circumstances in a nation of fifty states, and they must be concerned with the problems of a global society.

The rapid expansion of the United States brought prosperity, but it also brought conditions that spurred reform movements: Social and economic forces and the energy and initiative of individuals were building a powerful nation, but progress was not always measured in terms of human welfare. The exploitation of human and natural resources, the slums and sweatshops, child labor, and the unwholesome influence of money in politics brought with them the demand for reform.[5]

Reform as a goal has dominated American political history, particularly since 1876. It was the theme of the famous "Cross of Gold" ad-

Chart 1. Selected List of Educational Events

Date	Event	Significance
1630–1730	Puritan experience Latin grammar school	Academic curriculum emphasizing Latin and Bible reading
1730–1830	Academy	Included some commercial subjects for the middle class
1827	Massachusetts law	Started the public high school movement
1830s–1840s	Common school movement	Led by Horace Mann, developed publicly financed, nonsectarian schools
1862	Morrill Act	Gave impetus to agricultural education by support at the college level
1874	Kalamazoo case	Decided that public funds could be used for secondary education
1892	Committee of Ten	Concluded that the academic, college oriented curriculum was the most appropriate for the secondary level
1918	Seven Cardinal Principles	Broadened the secondary curriculum to include "citizenship education"
1930s	Eight-Year Study	Concluded that progressive education was as good as or superior to traditional education
1959	Conant reports	Recommended a return to more academic rigor in the curriculum

dress delivered at the 1896 Democratic Convention by William Jennings Bryan; it was reflected in the efforts of Grover Cleveland to bring about tariff reform; it motivated the energetic efforts of Theodore Roosevelt to reduce the power of "malefactors of great wealth"; it was the mainspring of Franklin D. Roosevelt's "New Deal"; and it reached new heights in Lyndon B. Johnson's "Great Society." When Frederick Lewis Allen wrote a book that described the reforms of the first half of the twentieth century, he called it *The Big Change*. He emphasized that we have tried to make our economic system provide a maximum of security for all by using the method of evolution rather than that of revolution. He suggested: "When the ship of state was not behaving as it should, one did not need to scrap it and build another, but by a series of adjustments and improvements, repair it while keeping it running—provided the ship's crew

were forever alert, forever inspecting it and tinkering with it." [6]

"Expansion" and "reform" are appropriate terms to describe developments in public education during the years since public schools were established in all the states. Enrollments in public and private elementary and secondary schools increased from 9.8 million in 1880, to 32.3 million in 1934, to 45 million in 1975. Enrollments in secondary schools alone increased from 700,000 in 1900, to 7 million in 1950, to 15 million in 1975. The total cost of public and private elementary and secondary schools increased from $214 million in 1900, to $5.8 billion in 1950, to $75 billion in 1975.

Other significant developments have included the establishment of land-grant colleges, the addition of kindergartens and junior colleges to many public school systems, the addition of many new subjects to the curriculum, changing the two-year normal school to a four-year college for the preparation of teachers, the consolidation of schools, the establishment of schools or colleges of education at universities, the development of the profession of school administration, and the increased participation of the federal government in financing public education at all levels.

Although public schools expanded rapidly in number and type, they were slow to respond to demands for reform in the education they were providing. Many factors operated to entrench the formal, regimented type of school program. One of these was the mechanistic, stimulus-response psychology that regarded repetition as the best means of learning and the reproduction of the words of the textbook or the teacher as the proof of learning. Another factor was the influence of the example of the factory on school practice. This rather strange trend has been vividly described as follows:

The subject matter was analyzed for the teacher into minute parts, each of which was different from every other part. . . . A pupil was put through many machines. At the end of each operation he was inspected by someone other than the teacher. This person with a series of educational calipers determined whether the pupil was properly machined to standard form.[7]

Educational reforms gained momentum during the 1960s. The public has been made more aware than ever of both innovations in education and the need for them. More people than ever before are concerned with what is happening in the schools. An increasing amount of time and space is being devoted to "the revolution in the schools" in newspapers and magazines, in books and pamphlets, and in radio and television programs. But educational reform has actually been going on for many centuries—at least since the time of Plato (428–348 B.C.). Many principles that are firmly established in educational theory today were enunciated by educational reformers of previous centuries. For example the extensive use of material objects to help children gain an understanding of concepts in the "new" mathematics and the "new" science programs of today was anticipated by Johann Amos Comenius (1592–1670) when he insisted that the proper order of learning must be things, ideas, then words. The reader can and should gain perspective on current educational re-

forms by examining the ideas of Erasmus, Rousseau, Pestalozzi, Herbart, Froebel, and other European pioneers who helped to lay the foundations for modern educational reforms. Here, however, we must limit our discussion to a few of the reforms undertaken in this country since public school systems have been established in all the states.

Two Influential Educators

Francis W. Parker (1837–1902) was principal of the Cook County Normal School in Chicago from 1883 to 1890. He conceived it to be the function of the normal school to help teachers learn to use the methods of democracy, so that they could "set the souls of children free." He reorganized the teacher education program so that the child became the center of interest; introduced the practice of cooperative planning of the school program by parents, teachers, pupils, and administrators; made the use of textbooks supplementary to a variety of learning activities closely related to the life of the community; encouraged spontaneous expression on the part of pupils; regarded effective living in the present as the best preparation for future living; and demonstrated that competence in the use of basic skills could be achieved by a program that emphasized their use in meaningful situations. Parker's work undoubtedly was influenced by the ideas of Froebel, who said: "To learn a thing in life and through doing is much more developing, cultivating, and strengthening, than to learn it merely through the verbal communication of ideas."[8]

John Dewey (1859–1952) regarded education as a social process—helping children to share in the inherited resources of the human race and to use their powers for social ends. He regarded education as a continuous process, beginning almost at birth and proceeding gradually as the individual participates in the life about him. He believed that education must begin with insight into the child's capacities, interests, and habits, but he also emphasized the social side of education. He taught that the only true education was that which stimulated the child's powers by the demands of the social situation in which the child found himself or herself. In other words, Dewey regarded the school as a form of community life; he said that it should be as real and vital a part of a child's life as the home, the neighborhood, and the playground and that the influence of the school should flow into the life of the community. He defined subject matter as anything that helped a student solve a problem; thus he was more interested in the social contributions of science than he was in the search for knowledge for its own sake.

Four Theories

Four theories of education that have influenced the development of the American school are perennialism, essentialism, reconstructionism, and progressivism.

Perennialism. According to this theory education should teach the eternal verities. Human nature never changes; therefore good education should not change either. Adjustment to the world as it actually exists is not a proper goal of education; real-life situations have no place in the school program; the school exists to discipline the rational powers and develop the intellect of the child; and this can best be done by confronting him or her with the "Great Ideas" developed in western civilization.

Essentialism. Adherents of this theory maintain that an educated person is one who has mastered the fundamental fields of knowledge; that education should be made up of the timeless basic academic disciplines. The Council for Basic Education is currently the leading advocate of essentialism.

Reconstructionism. This theory holds that education should be the principal means for building a better social order; that the schools should take the lead in building the widest possible consensus relating to the values that should motivate the reconstruction of the social order; and that the overarching purpose of American education should be to help in the development of a world civilization.

Progressivism. This theory can perhaps be best understood by paraphrasing its essentials as stated by the Progressive Education Association itself. They include: (1) the dominant ideals of our democratic society provide the basic direction for American education; (2) these ideals should be continuously reinterpreted and refined; (3) every child should have adequate opportunity for achieving his or her fullest potential through education; (4) education should make students aware that social changes demand reforms in education; (5) it is only through living and working together that optimal development of personality can be achieved; (6) the physical and mental health of children should be a major concern of the school; (7) children should be provided with opportunities for self-expression at all stages of development and in many diverse areas of experience; and (8) children should have increasing freedom to direct their own behavior as their knowledge and experience increase.[9]

The Progressive Education Association was founded in 1919 by a group of leading citizens, most of them not professionally connected with education. During the 1920s a number of professional educators, including John Dewey and William Heard Kilpatrick, joined and became active in it. The total membership never was large, but it included many people of great knowledge and vigor. Although the association did not even approach gaining control of American schools, the many activities it engaged in gave it a considerable influence on educational theory and practice in this country. For instance it initiated and stimulated the workshop technique now widely used in teacher education. During the 1930s it sponsored what is perhaps the most widely known of its activities. This was an experiment known as the Eight-Year Study, involving thirty selected secondary schools and 250 accredited colleges and universities. In order to free the schools (half of them public high schools) for creative experimentation, the colleges and universities were persuaded to waive their technical admission requirements for graduates of the thirty schools and accept them on the basis of their achievement in broad fields and on their scholastic aptitude and intelligence rating.

A thorough study of how well these students actually did at college was conducted later by a commission headed by Wilford M. Aikin. The study revealed that the grades of these progressive-school graduates were higher during the first three years of college than were those of a control group of graduates of traditional-curriculum high schools. The

progressive-school graduades showed a slight
lead in every subject except foreign languages.
They also wrote more, talked more, took a
livelier interest in politics and social problems,
went to more dances, and had more dates.[10]

In the 1940s progressive education was subjected to an increasing amount of criticism.
The public tended to blame progressive
theories for what seemed to be inadequacies in
educating youth in the fundamentals. Defenders of progressive education retorted that any
such inadequacies as did exist should be attributed to the widespread persistence of traditional education. In any case the membership
of the Progressive Education Association
steadily declined, and the association was dis-
banded in 1955. Nevertheless, during the
thirty-six years it existed the association made
many lasting contributions and raised many
issues that are still very relevant.

The Tests and Measurement Movement

The development of standardized objective
tests to explore individual differences began
with the work of Sir Francis Galton in the
1860s. Although proclaimed the founder of
individual psychology, Galton never produced
a successful test of intelligence. With the publication of the Binet Scale in 1905, the movement was well underway. In this country James
M. Cattell published his study of "mental
tests"—a term he coined in 1890. Joseph M.
Rice devised a spelling scale, the first educational achievement test, in 1894. After World
War I, Arthur S. Otis, Lewis M. Terman, and
Edward L. Thorndike developed tests that had
broader application to classroom practice.
During the first decade of the twentieth century, courses in tests and measurement were
set up at Columbia University, the University
of Chicago, and Stanford University. During
the next decade centers for the distribution of
tests and the interpretation of test scores were
established at universities in Oklahoma, Indiana, and Minnesota. Currently, the major IQ
tests include the Stanford-Benet scales, the
Wechsler Adult Intelligence Scale (WAIS), the
Wechsler Intelligence Scale for Children-
Revised (WISC-R) and the Wechsler Preschool and Primary Scale of Intelligence
(WPPSI).

The earlier tests were used primarily to
measure individual differences in the rather
general aspects of intelligence, achievement,
and personality traits. But the number of types
of tests has increased rapidly, and tests have
also become more specific and more widely
used. As the use of tests has increased, charges
that test results are being misused have also
increased. As a matter of fact the testing controversy has been building up for the past
quarter of a century. Tests now stand accused
by many of increasing the likelihood of a controlled curriculum and of unduly emphasizing
simple recall at the expense of thinking and
reasoning.

Newspapers and popular magazines have
carried articles with sensational titles such as
"The Evils of School Testing Techniques,"
"The Scandal of Educational Testing," and
"Testing Versus Your Child." *The Tyranny of
Testing* was the title Banesh Hoffman gave his
book in which he severely criticized standardized achievement tests that tend to penalize
the bright and imaginative child and to reward
the child who conforms.[11] Five departments of
the National Education Association (NEA)
cooperated in the production of a pamphlet
that emphasized the child's right to be different
and raised the question: "If the individual pupil
counts, is good or evil to be found in a barrage
of standardized tests, college board examinations, searches for talent, state-wide examinations, and national survey tests?"[12] Some
writers have asserted that the malfunctioning
of testing lies with the users of the tests rather
than with the designers of the tests. Some have
suggested that teachers and school administrators need more adequate preparation in the
nature and uses of tests. Others have attempted to answer the criticisms by evolving
procedures for testing educational outcomes
involving more than the simple recall of information. The issue is likely to be settled in
the U. S. Supreme Court.

VARIOUS PURPOSES OF EDUCATION

A closed society attempts to govern all human
activity in conformity to one body of principles
existing at a given time; an open society permits individuals and groups to hold contrasting
views. In an open society each individual has a
moral obligation to base the beliefs that guide
his or her behavior on an intelligent evaluation
of all relevant facts.

The scope of this book does not include a

Chart 2. Major Educational Philosophies

Basic Philosophies	Subject-Matter Emphasis	Preferred Methods	Approaches to Behavior	Scope of the Curriculum
Idealism	Subject matter of the mind; literature, religion, intellectual history	Recitation; lecture; discussion; "seeing" ideas	Imitation of the ideal	Emphasis upon the past: stable and predetermined by authority
Realism	Physical world of things: precise, definite, and measurable answers— mathematics, science	Demonstration; factual recitation; lectures and drill for precision	Rules and laws of conduct for objective recall	Emphasis upon the past: stable, and quantitative structure
Scholasticism and classical humanism	Subject matter for the intellect and spirit: language, mathematics, doctrine	Formal drill; catechism; recitation; lecture	Discipline the mind; discipline to reason	Emphasis upon the past: stable and unchanging
Experimentalism	Human experiences: social problems, scientific problems	Problem solving: analysis; criticism; organization; try out ideas; discovery	Cooperative decisions relative to consequences	Emphasis upon the present: changing; relating to past and future
Existentialism	Individual choice: art, music, literature, religion, moral ethics	Appeal to the total: commitment; personal responsibility	Caring, self-responsibility	Changing individually from present and past toward the future

SOURCE: J. Minor Gwynn and John B. Chase, Jr., *Curriculum Principles and Social Trends* (New York: Macmillan, 1969), p. 46. Copyright © 1969 by The Macmillan Company. Reprinted by permission of The Macmillan Company.

detailed discussion of specific philosophies of education—realism, idealism, experimentalism, and so on. (See Chart 2.) Most education majors will take a systematic course in the philosophy of education that will give a comprehensive treatment of this very broad topic. Nevertheless, there are inextricable links between philosophy and purpose. As we consider purpose, it will be apparent that philosophy cannot be ignored. Indeed since philosophy is one of the sources of purpose, we turn now to a brief discussion of it in that role.

We shall explore four current views of the central purpose of American education: learning the basic disciplines; becoming adequate persons, developing the rational powers, and creating a world civilization. These purposes are not mutually exclusive, of course, but they can be treated separately in terms of their principal emphases.

The Teacher's Philosophy of Education

Decisions made by the teacher emerge from her conviction about the worth of each individual, the quality of human nature, the nature of the good life, and the role that the school should play in a democratic society. These convictions constitute her philosophy of education—her educational objectives—at any given time. Her philosophy of education, however, is a living, growing one; as she gains greater insight into the results of her work in terms of richer lives for individuals and a better society for tomorrow, her philosophy of education matures. A broader, less personal source of educational objectives is the realities and ideals of contemporary American society.

The purposes of education take into consideration what children should learn. Recent curriculum improvement projects have therefore drawn heavily on subject-matter specialists for suggestions concerning the contribution their disciplines can make to the achievement of the purposes of education. What children can learn is also an important consideration. Studies of children and of the learning process are therefore important sources of the purposes of education.

There are basic differences among Americans about the purposes of education and the roles that schools should play, just as there are differences about religion, politics, medicine, and styles of clothing. There also are, however, widespread agreements. For instance according to Myron Lieberman, the American people as a whole believe that "the purposes of education are the development of critical thinking, effective communication, creative skills, and social, civic, and occupational competence."[13]

The disagreements center on the problem of what central overall purposes should receive major emphasis. They also arise from differing interpretations of what is an end and a means. For example those who argue that the one overarching purpose of education must be the creation of a world civilization would no doubt admit that the teaching of world geography serves as a means to that end. Those who argue that the development of the rational

powers is the central purpose of education recognize that this is not the exclusive purpose of education. Those who propose the development of adequate persons as the new focus in education include a rich and available perceptual field—that is, knowledge of various kinds—as one of the characteristics of the adequate person. One cannot be both adequate and stupid at the same time, but our knowledge must have a personal meaning for us if it is to affect our behavior and be available to help us understand the events that take place in our environment.

LEARNING THE BASIC DISCIPLINES

The rationale of those who believe that learning the basic disciplines is the principal function of eduation (essentialism) has been outlined by Philip Phenix. He maintains that educators should understand the kinds of meaning that have proved effective in the development of civilizations, that these meanings may be found in the various scholarly disciplines, and that these realms of meaning indicate the kinds of understanding a person must have if he or she is to function well within the civilized community.[14]

Separate Subjects Versus the Unified Program

The case for organizing learning experiences around basic subjects has been presented by Carl F. Hansen in a book about the Amidon School in Washington. He lists the basic academic subjects for elementary schools as reading, composition, grammar, spelling, speech, mathematics, science, geography, history, art, and music. His fundamental thesis is:

It should be common practice for teachers to assign problems for study, to encourage independent research, to elicit creative work in the arts and sciences. But these should not overwhlem and push aside order and substance in basic subjects as does the unit-dominated curriculum.[15]

He says that the unit method of curriculum organization has become "the Frankenstein's monster of the classroom" and that the core program is "wide, undefined, shifting, and soft."[16]

Whether or not the Amidon School was actually a successful demonstration in basic education (as Hansen describes it in his subtitle) is not the point here. The broad educational issues are: (1) What are the basic academic disciplines that can make significant contributions to the achievements of the purposes of elementary and secondary schools? (2) How can learning experiences be organized so that these disciplines can make their maximum contributions? (3) Are these disciplines the means or the ends of education?

The basic academic disciplines. If one accepts the premise that it is the central purpose of elementary and secondary schools to teach the basic academic disciplines, the list suggested by Hansen is too narrow. Social studies programs, for instance, now usually draw materials from history, geography, political science, economics, sociology, and anthropology. Indeed it has been suggested that the broad framework of a coordinated social studies program should be developed by a team including specialists from each of these disciplines plus a psychologist and a curriculum planner.[17]

Organization of learning experiences. It is not feasible for an elementary or secondary school to offer separate courses in the six social sciences; there would be little time left for other subjects. Even if the school day, week, and year were lengthened there would not be room for twenty academic subjects in the kindergarten.[18] One alternative is the "ladder" system of grade placement in which history is taught at one grade level, geography at another, and the other social sciences are left for senior high school or college. A second alternative is the "spiral" system of grade placement, in which the social studies curriculum is built around themes, drawing materials from all the social sciences at the primary level and revisiting these themes or concepts in increasingly more difficult and complex forms at higher grade levels.

Both research and prevailing practice support the spiral system. Studies of child development indicate that growth and learning are continuous—that new learnings are built on earlier learnings. Therefore concepts are not fully developed at any one grade level; they are introduced early in the school program and take on new, expanded, and more complex meanings at later levels. Children do not wait until they are in senior high school to become interested in economics; after all, they have experienced many economic aspects of living from their earliest years. This is also true of mathematics, geometry, and physics. These views are now widely accepted. A survey of the states several years ago revealed that only two of the fifty were planning to return to the separate subjects organization in the social studies.[19] The same trend toward a unified program has been evident in other curriculum areas.

The means and ends of education. Whether or not the basic academic disciplines have important contributions to make at all levels of the school program is not an educational issue. What is an issue is how the basic facts are regarded. Are they ends in themselves or means? The prevailing opinion now is that they are tools to be used in the solution of problems rather than ends in themselves. William Van Til has described the real "basics" in education, the goals we set out to achieve using the study of basic subjects as one of the effective means.

Let us not be misled by the oversimplifiers who would restrict education to rote learning of the three R's without recognizing that skills must be taught meaningfully and applied to problems which grow out of social realities, needs, and values; who would have the child study a cultural heritage without relating it to his surrounding society and his life as a learner, without exercising critical thought and applying human values. . . . True intellectual development draws upon the cultural heritage in order to use it thoughtfully in dealing with issues real to the learner and important to society.[20]

BECOMING ADEQUATE PERSONS

The authors of the 1962 Yearbook of the Association for Supervision and Curriculum Development (ASCD) suggest as a new focus for education the production of adequate persons. The authors—Earl C. Kelley, Carl R. Rogers, Abraham H. Maslow, and Arthur W.

Combs—stated that the production of such persons must be the primary goal of education. They raise this intriguing question: "Who can say what kind of world we might create if we could learn to increase our production of adequate persons?"[21] The book describes the adequate, self-actualizing person in terms of characteristic ways of seeing oneself and the world, listing and explaining the following characteristics: (1) a positive view of self, (2) openness to experience and acceptance, (3) identification with others, and (4) a rich and available perceptual field. The book also presents new school practices suggested by these concepts of the adequate, fully functioning person.

A positive view of self. A person with a positive view of self is not a person who never recognizes any of his faults or weaknesses; he generally regards himself as a person who is liked, wanted, accepted, and able. When he looks objectively at himself he decides that although he is not perfect, he is able to face life with confidence. As Kelley says, he sees himself as "enough." The person with a positive view of self is less disturbed by criticism, more likely to remain calm in the midst of stress and strain, and less likely to carry around abnormal doubts and fears that would prevent him from living life to its fullest.

A positive image of self is gained from experience; a child comes to view herself as capable, wanted, and liked by being treated by others in a way that indicates they believe she is that kind of person. The school therefore has as much responsibility for helping children develop a positive view of self as it has for teaching school subjects. Indeed there is a high correlation between school achievement and a positive view of self. The school can foster the development of such a positive view by giving attention to the classroom climate, respecting the uniqueness of each pupil, individualizing instruction, and pacing school tasks in harmony with the rates of learning of different children.

Openness to experience. A person with a closed mind is wedded to a single dogma; he rejects all evidence from experience that conflicts with his rigid set of beliefs. "Mankind," wrote John Dewey, "likes to think in terms of extreme opposites. It is given to formulating its beliefs in terms of either-or's, between which it recognizes no intermediate possibilities."[22] Extremely ethnocentric individuals live within codes of behavior of their own groups and are unable to profit from the experience of other groups.

The person who is open to experience has a much wider source of data on which to base decisions. Openness to experience, like the development of a positive image of self, is learned from experience. Teachers can help pupils learn to be more open to experience, to be willing to gain new ideas, and to learn to face new problems. Teaching for openness and creativity helps pupils to develop new goals for learning and to explore a great variety of materials.

Combs states the case for openness to experience as follows:

Truly adequate people possess perceptual fields maximally open to experience. That is to say, their perceptual fields are capable of change and adjustment in such fashion as to make fullest possible use of their experience."[23]

Identification with others. The adequate person is capable of expanding her concept of self to include others; she is unable to think of self apart from significant others with whom she has been associated or with whom she shares ideas and purposes. Identification with others is learned; it is a part of growing from immaturity to maturity. The very young child is egocentric: she is interested primarily in herself, and her desire to be first in everything makes it difficult for her to get along harmoniously in a group. She first learns to play harmoniously with one other child of approximately her own age; she then learns to identify with increasingly larger groups. The truly adequate person eventually learns to identify with all people, even with those who differ from her in color, creed, and nationality. Combs points out that identification, like the self-concept, is learned:

The more positive the individual's feelings about self, the easier it is to identify with an even broader sample of mankind. The capacity for identification appears to be a product of an essentially positive view of self and of successful, satisfying experiences in interaction with other people. Here is a place where a child's experiences in school can be made to count.[24]

It is appropriate in this context to mention a new estimate of human nature that has been emphasized by some biologists and psychologists. It has been customary in the past to blame human nature for conflicts between groups and nations: "Human nature being what it is, nothing else can be expected." There is evidence, however, that human nature contains no specific war instinct, that the aggressive tendency in our make-up is not an unvarying instinct, and that it can be molded into the most varied forms. The best hope for mankind—indeed the only real hope—lies in developing the science of human relations. As long as environmental forces continue to mold men and women into viciously competitive animals, as long as people continue to exalt change in everything but themselves, human misery and war will remain distinct possibilities.[25]

A rich and available perceptual field.   As I have noted earlier, the American system of universal, public education was established in this country because our forefathers realized that the success of popular government depended on enlightened citizens. Today the minimum level of what one must know in order to understand the forces and events that affect his or her well-being increases year by year; the future belongs to the well-informed person. It should not be assumed, therefore, that emphasis on the production of adequate persons as the primary goal of education minimizes the importance of information.

A rich and available perceptual field involves a great deal more than mere exposure to the contents of the basic disciplines. Perceptions are gained not only from formal schooling but also from informal sources and from first-hand involvement in human relations. Each individual selects from the myriad stimuli to which he is exposed. He selects them in terms of his previous experiences, his interests, and his purposes: "The deeper, more personally significant the perception, moreover, the more likely it is to affect behavior."[26]

There is a considerable amount of evidence that the way a thing is learned determines its future usefulness to the learner. Combs explains this principle as follows:

Something more than confrontation with events is necessary to insure inclusion of perceptions in the field and their availability on later occasions. This availability seems dependent upon at least two factors: (a) the individual's discovery of personal meaning, and (b) the satisfaction of need.[27]

Gertrude Noar has raised this pertinent question: "What kinds of learning experiences do children need besides reading, writing, figuring, and reciting?" She includes in her answers (1) creating a self-concept that permits the pupil to like himself and others, (2) learning human relations skills, and (3) providing status-building experiences for minority group children.[28]

DEVELOPING THE RATIONAL POWERS

In 1961 the Educational Policies Commission (EPC) of the NEA published a pamphlet in which the development of the rational powers of the individual was presented as the central purpose of American education. The publication mentions the seven cardinal principles evolved by an NEA committee and published in 1918: health, command of the fundamental processes, worthy home membership, vocational competence, effective citizenship, worthy use of leisure, and ethical character. It calls attention to another list published in 1938 by the Educational Policies Commission: self-realization, human relationship, economic efficiency, and civic responsibility.

The EPC admits that these are all desirable objectives, but maintains that "neither the schools nor the pupils have the time or energy to engage in all the activities which will fully achieve all these goals. . . . The school seeks rather to equip the pupil to achieve them himself." The Commission therefore suggests that the central purpose of American education is the development of the rational powers of the individual—helping students to learn to think clearly. The rational powers are listed as recalling and imagining, classifying and generalizing, comparing and evaluating, analyzing and synthesizing, and deducting and inferring.

The twenty-one-page pamphlet presents an excellent summary of the principles on which modern educational theory and practice are based: (1) Americans regard education as a means for improving themselves and their society; (2) the schools are charged with fostering the development of individual capacities that will enable each human being to become the best person he or she is capable of becoming; (3) a free society must create circumstances in which all individuals may have opportunity and encouragement to attain freedom of the mind; (4) the development and use of the rational powers are indispensable to a full and worthy life; (5) students who feel inadequate, insecure, or unduly apprehensive are hampered in their learning; (6) good teaching can help students to learn to think clearly; (7) human beings have already transformed their world by using their minds.

The fascinating series of events through which new materials and new teaching procedures have been introduced into elementary and secondary school programs in recent years will be discussed in later chapters. It can be said by way of summary that the current curriculum reform movement has been proceeding from the national level down to the local school system; that attention has been sharply focused on single subjects; that projects at the national level have been generously supported by funds from the federal government and from foundations; and that scholars from the various disciplines at the universities have been involved in planning the precollegiate curriculum as never before.

The emphasis in all of these programs has been on teaching the student to think. The search has been for something more lasting than the memorization of isolated bits of information; the purpose has been to provide the kind of education that would enable the student to become self-propelling during a lifetime of learning. For example, as John W. Renner and William B. Ragan have put it: "Recent curriculum developments in elemenatry-school science encourage the learner to develop his rational powers which are the essence of the ability to think." [29]

In the EPC statement, however, there is evidence of confused thinking about the purposes and the means of education. For instance immediately after the list of rational powers is the statement, "These processes enable one to apply logic and the available evidence to his ideas, attitudes, and action, and to pursue better whatever goals he may have." [30] Following this is an explanation of how the use of the rational powers helps in the achievement of the objectives of the seven cardinal principles already listed. The statement would have been more consistent if the title of the pamphlet had been "The Importance of Developing the Rational Powers as a Means of Achieving the Purposes of American Education."

CREATING A WORLD CIVILIZATION

The title of this section reflects a fourth view of the central purpose of American education, reconstructionism. Theodore Brameld has expressed this view as follows:

I hold with the strongest conviction of which I am capable that our schools and colleges, abroad as well as in America, require one overarching purpose, by comparison with which all others, bar none, are of subordinate importance. This purpose is to channel and release the full resource of education in behalf of the creation of world civilization—a world civilization capable both of preventing destruction and of providing the peace and abundance that men everywhere crave. [31]

The schools have always been charged with the responsibility of developing intelligent citizens of the United States. Today they have the additional obligation of developing citizens of the world. This responsibility is not one that educators sought in order to broaden the scope of an already overcrowded curriculum; it is one that has been forced upon the schools by the realities of the world in which we live. Science and technology have reduced the size of the world in terms of communication and travel time. Each individual's community is in a real sense now a world community. Events that take place in China, Russia, or Africa are likely to have more impact on the lives of individuals living anywhere in the United States today than events that took place at the state capital had on the lives of our grandparents. Technology has been dictating to the schools, and the schools have had to respond, regardless of the philosophies of their personnel.

One Overarching Purpose

The schools have, of course, traditionally provided opportunities for students to gain information about various countries in the world through instruction in history and geography.

But information is not enough in terms of bringing the full resource of education to bear on the problem of creating a world civilization. This would involve placing greater emphasis on the forces that operate to cause conflict among nations and the agencies at work to promote peaceful settlement of disputes, providing more opportunities for pupils to engage in cooperative enterprises, helping pupils develop attitudes that permit them to identify with people who differ from themselves, and using much more effective methods and materials.

Teaching for World Understanding

Teaching for world understanding generally consists of (1) helping students to understand that conflict is a part of life that must be reckoned with, (2) helping them to understand its costs to individuals and nations, (3) helping them to realize how much cooperation there is at the community, national, and international levels, (4) providing opportunities to practice the skills of cooperative living, (5) helping them to understand that war is not inevitable, (6) providing them with information about humanity's long struggle for a peaceful world society, (7) helping them to understand the economic and social interdependence of nations, and (8) helping them to develop an appreciation of the worth of individuals of all races and nationalities.

Teaching world affairs, like teaching anything else, must take into consideration not only what children *should* learn but also what they *can* learn. Leonard S. Kenworthy has suggested content and activities that are appropriate for the preschool and primary grades, the middle grades, and the upper grades. Stories about the Christ of the Andes statue (celebrating the end of hostilities between Chile and Argentina) or the Peace Arch and gardens between the United States and Canada provide tangible evidences of international cooperation easily understood by children in the primary grades. The long history of collaboration between nations in health and other fields provides appropriate content for the middle grades. By the time children reach the upper grades they are generally ready for a detailed study of the organization and achievements of the United Nations.[32]

John Jarolimek suggests the central role that teaching for international understanding must play in the school curriculum: "War, peace, and depression have all been strong influences in curriculum building; today it is international relations which is dominating the attention of the nation. Consequently, social studies programs are being planned to equip the young citizen to deal thoughtfully and intelligently with problems of international import."[33]

He points out that motivation for teaching world understanding emerges from (1) the fear of total destruction, (2) the desire to settle differences through peaceful means, (3) the economic interdependence of nations, and (4) the desire to help all peoples of the world obtain for themselves a full share of freedom and abundance. He lists objectives, activities, and criteria for selecting countries to be studied at the various grade levels and sources of materials relating to the teaching of world affairs.

The Project on the Instructional Program of the Public Schools suggests ten broad concepts or themes around which the program in international understanding might be built for Grades 1–12. These are: nationalism, the population increase, the desire for peace, the power conflict, similarities and differences among cultures, the balance among aspects of society, national characteristics and stereotypes, United States foreign policy, foreign assistance, and international organizations.[34]

OUR DOMESTIC ASPIRATIONS

The struggle for human freedom is as old as civilization itself. But this desire to have a share in shaping their own destiny has always been a particularly compelling motive for Americans. The right to do so, indeed, is one of the basic principles of our society. A system of education open to all American children and youth will help to realize this American dream.

Education and the Achievement of Social Ideals

Schools have always been expected to assist other social agencies in furthering the social ideals of the people who support them. Napoleon recognized this when he said, "There cannot be a firmly established political state unless there is a teaching body with definitely recognized principles." Thomas Jefferson, James Madison, James Monroe, and many other leaders in early American political life urged the necessity of education as a basis for the success of a democracy.

A series of articles by ten distinguished Americans appeared in 1959 in *Life* magazine and the *New York Times* dealing with the theme of "the national purpose." They raised such questions as: What shall Americans do with the greatness of their nation? What is the national purpose of the United States? Have Americans lost, at least temporarily, their sense of national purpose? These articles, published in book form in the next year, created a great deal of national concern and debate.[35]

Goals for Americans, a report of the President's Commission on Natonal Goals, gave an explicit description of the nature of our basic aspirations and the steps that needed to be taken to achieve them.[36] The goals included concern for the individual, equality of educational opportunity, a democratic economy, and a peaceful world order. The program advocated doubling expenditures for education, sharply reducing discrimination on the basis of color, and strengthening the United Nations.

There are, then, various purposes that are rather widely accepted in this country. Nevertheless, we often admit to confusion about them. Perhaps what this admission really means is that we are unwilling to face the difficult task of putting them into practice.

But we must face that task. We must realize that democracy is not merely a set of beliefs; it is a process that can be practiced in any group—nation, family, or classroom. In the classroom we must strive to achieve the particular form of education that supports a democratic society. Such education promotes the continuous growth of students so that they can join fully and freely in the shared purposes of their society; so that they will never stop expanding their horizons; so that they can develop their innate capacity for becoming adequate, self-actualizing persons; in short, so that they can become fully human in the world in which they are growing up.

The Methods of Democracy

Democracy is a way to work out human relationships, a way to work together in group situations, a way to exercise control over group action. (Other methods of arranging relationships include force, domination, and laissez faire.) Although research has provided much evidence that democratic procedures in school situations work out better in the long run, many professional educators nevertheless object to the actual use of the term democratic in relation to teaching and administration. They contend that the term is frequently used as a rug under which inefficient or manipulative practices are swept. They deplore in general what they call fuzzy, quasi-religious prating about democracy. (Interestingly, such educators usually admit that their opponents are able to "discuss" other topics but insist that they are only "prating" when democracy is the topic.)

Cavils about terminology are not important, however. The main point is that it is imperative, if the schools are indeed to serve as instruments for preserving and improving the democratic way of life, that teachers and administrators make greater efforts to discover and use the methods of democracy. Nor should we be deterred by the fact that some who talk about democracy are not practicing it.

The hallmarks of democratic procedures are not difficult to identify; indeed, capable teachers have been using many of them for decades. Recent curriculum projects have supplied new models for their application, and recent research in the area of human growth and development has provided new insights into their psychological foundations. These democratic methods fall into a number of categories. Some focus on teacher-pupil relations; others focus on pupil-pupil relations; still others involve administrative procedures, drawing up curricula, and the like. It is impossible here to discuss more than a few. Therefore I have selected four types of procedures that seem particularly important in their day-to-day effect on pupils. Two are of a rather specific nature: learning by discovery, and growth through involvement in decision-making. The others are broader in implications and practice: the search for equality of opportunity, and respect for the individual.

Learning by discovery. Authoritarian procedures, whether in government or in education, eventually dig their own graves by suppressing all ideas except those of individuals who are in authority. Authoritarian teaching is

Chart 3. Instructional Learning Model

	Instructional Strategy (What the teacher does)	Learning Strategy (What the pupil does)
1. Task orientation	Uses a variety of media in presenting introductory information. Gaps in knowledge, missing links, and discrepancies are made evident.	Attends, notices, and thinks for the purpose of identifying and making notation of unclear, ambiguous, conflicting, or contradictory ideas, concepts, events, or situations.
2. Preliminary investigation	Helps pupils to be information seekers and to recognize problematic situations.	Collects, inspects, and classifies data for the purpose of finding problems for possible investigation.
3. Analysis and definition	Guides pupils in preparing problem statements and hypotheses.	Recognizes, states, restates, and prepares in final form significant problems.
4. Inquiry, ideation, and hypothesizing	Assists pupils in framing inquiry type questions, provides time for ideation pertaining to the solution of posed problems.	Prepares inquiry type questions, poses possible solution to selected problems, states hypothesis.
5. Exploration and investigation	Provides time, encouragement, and resources for exploration and investigation.	Identifies and makes use of available resources to obtain information needed to solve problems.
6. Solutions formulated and examined	Provides instruction and guidance in the use of evaluative skills.	States alternative solutions; conducts examination, comparison, and evaluation.
7. Inference and synthesis	Gives time and assistance for the purpose of going beyond the given solution to draw new and original conclusions through inference and futuristic projection of thought.	Engages in hunching, speculation, and guessing for the purpose of futuristically projecting the possible effect of problem solutions.

SOURCE: Robert Eberle, "Problem-Solving Modes of Classroom Instruction," *Educational Leadership*, 30 (May, 1973), 728. Reprinted with permission.

a one-way process—always from the teacher or the textbook to the pupils. The obvious— and almost insuperable—difficulty is that pupils simply are not interested in merely memorizing ready-made answers fed to them by the teacher and the textbook; thus teachers using such methods are compelled to spend much time and thought inventing all sorts of devices intended to arouse interest.

In an attempt to solve this problem, the learning by discovery method was developed. Its advantages have been described thus: "If we help boys and girls learn the process of discovering knowledge and ways of working for themselves, we need not give our energies to finding fascinating ways to hold their attention or whip up their enthusiasm. The strong urge to pursue learning comes from within." [37] Helping children learn to use the method of discovery—of finding their own solutions to problems—requires a concept of the role of facts in the educative process that is different from the one frequently held by teachers.

Facts are important, of course, but they are tools used to solve problems rather than ends in themselves. John Dewey expressed this idea when he said that subject matter is anything that is used by a child in the solution of a problem.

Curriculum improvement projects are developing materials and techniques designed to produce something more lasting than the memorization of bits of information. Indeed, the goal is no less than a process of education that will help children and youth become self-propelling during a lifetime of learning in a rapidly changing world. Learning by discovery thus represents the kind of education that supports a democratic society, the kind of education that deserves the most heartfelt support of those who believe in democracy.

Growth through involvement in decision making. Plans developed by one person or a few people in authority and handed down to others as decrees seldom work out well in the long run. First, people who have had no part in formulating plans usually do not fully understand what is expected of them. Second, people work with more enthusiasm when they regard the plans as "our" plans rather than as "their" plans. Only through participating in decision making can teachers grow professionally. Only through sharing in the planning of activities can pupils develop the qualities of initiative, cooperation, and concern for the welfare of the group that are essential to the success of a democratic society.

The teacher in a democratic classroom makes certain that every pupil takes a responsible part in the life and work of the classroom. Pupils are involved in formulating plans, in working them out, and in evaluating results. The teacher makes a careful appraisal of the readiness of each pupil for assuming certain responsibilities; the teacher encourages timid pupils to participate in classroom activities. Pupils help in establishing rules for the orderly transaction of the work of the class. There is a free exchange of ideas, and members of the class take turns serving as a group leaders.

The search for equality of opportunity. The course of American history has been motivated largely by the search for a social system that would allow every individual to advance as far as his or her ability and effort permit—with no artificial barriers based on race, religion, sex, or socioeconomic status. The public school has been regarded as the principal instrument through which this democratic ideal would be achieved.

Most Americans believe in the democratic principles of respect for the worth of every human being and equality of opportunity. Nevertheless, these ideals have not been applied in reality to most women, poor whites, Blacks, Puerto Ricans, Mexican-Americans, and American Indians. The children of all these groups are described as "disadvantaged" because they are all denied the economic and psychological advantages enjoyed by other American children. Disadvantaged subcultures have long presented a problem in America, but only recently has the problem received widespread attention. The Educational Policies Commission has put it this way: "For many years this problem was permitted to persist. It did not generate that unrest which in a democracy precedes the making of changes

in major public policies. Today, conditions are different; unrest is widespread and critical." [38]

The increasing concentration of the poor and unskilled in rural towns and central cities and the increasing unwillingness of disadvantaged people to tolerate the hopelessness of their efforts to get ahead—symbolized by protests and violence in the streets—have brought the disparity between ideals and practices to the attention of many Americans and caused them to look to the schools for help in eliminating what is now recognized to be an intolerable condition.

Many children with great potential for learning never have an opportunity to develop this potential through education because of the low income of their parents. Studies have been done that indicate that, when one considers only the group in the upper quarter of intellectual ability, 75 per cent of upper-middle and upper class youths finish four years of college, whereas only 25 per cent of working-class and lower-lower class youths do so.

If elementary and secondary schools are to provide equality of opportunity for culturally disadvantaged children and youths, they must be staffed by teachers who understand the handicaps these children labor under when they enter school: different vocabularly, negative image of self, distrust of school because it is an institution for middle-class children, and little exposure to books or reading in the home. Yet numerous surveys reveal that by and large preparation for working with disadvantaged children is a neglected area in teacher education programs.

Children from impoverished homes are not the only ones who need curriculum adaptations in terms of their abilities and backgrounds. Minimum grade standards, rigid promotion policies, and narrow, book-centered curricula stand in the way of helping all children develop whatever talents they have to the fullest extent possible. A school program that provides opportunities for only the intellectual elite is undemocratic; a program that does not challenge the more capable pupils is also undemocratic.

Respect for the individual. A democracy thrives on diversity; dictatorships therefore attempt to impose uniformity. Teaching procedures in a democracy are judged in terms of their effect on the children involved. The democratic principle of respect for the worth of the individual is involved in all progressive curricula reforms and innovations.

The right of the child to be different imposes many obligations on the teacher. Teachers who respect this right do not expect all children to learn at the same rate. They provide opportunities for slower pupils to experience success in terms of their ability, they challenge brighter pupils to achieve as much as their ability permits, and they permit individuals to spend some time working on individual projects in line with their interests and purposes.

INTRODUCTION TO PERSONAL GROWTH EXERCISES

The exercises appearing at the end of each chapter are presented as an aid to teachers who want to get in touch with some of their feelings, beliefs, values, and behavior. They are not designed to follow specific chapters and can therefore be tried out at any time. The exception to this statement is the last exercise, which is an evaluation of the course.

It is a truism that until people in the helping professions understand and accept themselves, they are not likely to understand and accept others. Some of the things these exercises reveal to you will not be new learnings; rather, they will reinforce old knowledge. However, some of the things revealed will be new and ego-deflating and/or ego-inflating. None of the exercises are designed to embarrass you, and most of them can be self-administered.

The important point is that you get better acquainted with the best friend that you can ever have—yourself. The decision to change or maintain your beliefs, values, and behavior should, I believe, be a personal decision—made free of coercion. For optimum results you should be honest when answering questions and engaging in the selected exercises.

A SURVEY OF HUMAN RELATIONS ISSUES

This questionnaire is designed to probe your opinions about several issues confronting teachers and administrators.

Instructions

Read carefully each statement. Indicate your feeling about each statement by putting a check (✔) in the appropriate column. Be sure to check after each statement. After you have completed the survey, you may want to compare your opinions with those of a close friend.

	Agree Very Much	Agree Pretty Much	Agree A Little	Disagree A Little	Disagree Pretty Much	Disagree Very Much
1. Everyone in America should have an equal opportunity to get ahead without regard to sex, race, ethnic background, or religion.	☐	☐	☐	☐	☐	☐
2. Any child who wants to learn badly enough can be taught.	☐	☐	☐	☐	☐	☐
3. The best safeguard of a democracy is the solid stability of social traditions, such as the maintenance of male and female sex roles.	☐	☐	☐	☐	☐	☐

	Agree Very Much	Agree Pretty Much	Disagree A Little	Disagree A Little	Disagree Pretty Much	Disagree Very Much

4. Public school desegregation threatens one of the basic principles of democracy: the right of each citizen to choose his or her own associates.

☐ ☐ ☐ ☐ ☐ ☐

5. Most teachers are poorly prepared to provide drug and alcohol abuse education.

☐ ☐ ☐ ☐ ☐ ☐

6. Although the IQ scores of nonwhites on the average are lower than the IQs of whites, this gap is due mainly to differing opportunities rather than heredity.

☐ ☐ ☐ ☐ ☐ ☐

7. It doesn't take much skill to be a good teacher. If you understand kids, you can teach them.

☐ ☐ ☐ ☐ ☐ ☐

8. The emphasis upon creating sex-free school materials is a waste of valuable time and resources.

☐ ☐ ☐ ☐ ☐ ☐

9. Teachers should not join unions because such behavior is not professional.

☐ ☐ ☐ ☐ ☐ ☐

10. Teachers and admnistrators should be paid according to how well their students score on standardized tests.

☐ ☐ ☐ ☐ ☐ ☐

11. There is little difference between rural and urban schools; both are inadequately financed.

☐ ☐ ☐ ☐ ☐ ☐

12. The more effective teachers love all their students—they do not have favorites.

☐ ☐ ☐ ☐ ☐ ☐

13. All Americans should be allowed to live anywhere they can afford the rent.

☐ ☐ ☐ ☐ ☐ ☐

14. Multi-lingual education is a waste of time, it is more important that all students learn English.

☐ ☐ ☐ ☐ ☐ ☐

15. It is more difficult to maintain discipline if the teacher does not have the power to use corporal punishment.

☐ ☐ ☐ ☐ ☐ ☐

16. Although some radical nonwhite leaders try to make people think otherwise, the majority of nonwhites do not want desegregated public schools; the majority of nonwhites want separate but equal facilities.

☐ ☐ ☐ ☐ ☐ ☐

	Agree Very Much	Agree Pretty Much	Agree A Little	Disagree A Little	Disagree Pretty Much	Disagree Very Much

17. We should go back to stressing the basics in education and abandon the frills that have been added.

☐ ☐ ☐ ☐ ☐ ☐

18. There will always be poor people in America; this is mainly because some groups are genetically inferior.

☐ ☐ ☐ ☐ ☐ ☐

19. The women's equality laws are unfair to women who must now compete on equal terms with men.

☐ ☐ ☐ ☐ ☐ ☐

20. People should help each other in time of need.

☐ ☐ ☐ ☐ ☐ ☐

21. The primary aim of education is to prepare students to secure jobs.

☐ ☐ ☐ ☐ ☐ ☐

22. All social conflict is destructive.

☐ ☐ ☐ ☐ ☐ ☐

23. Class size does not affect the manner in which students interact with each other.

☐ ☐ ☐ ☐ ☐ ☐

24. Desegregation will lead to a permanent lowering of standards in the public schools.

☐ ☐ ☐ ☐ ☐ ☐

25. Whether a child can learn depends on his/her biological make-up; what he/she learns depends on his/her culture.

☐ ☐ ☐ ☐ ☐ ☐

26. Teaching is an art, not a science.

☐ ☐ ☐ ☐ ☐ ☐

27. With all the emphasis on civil rights for ethnic minorities and women, white males are now being discriminated against.

☐ ☐ ☐ ☐ ☐ ☐

28. Drug abuse is mainly a problem in the inner cities.

☐ ☐ ☐ ☐ ☐ ☐

29. Teachers assigned to inner city schools should receive special hazardous duty pay.

☐ ☐ ☐ ☐ ☐ ☐

30. I would be willing to have a member of another race as my son-in-law.

☐ ☐ ☐ ☐ ☐ ☐

31. Minority groups are happier and have more freedom in their own neighborhoods.

☐ ☐ ☐ ☐ ☐ ☐

32. White people have higher standards of living than nonwhites because of their initiative.

☐ ☐ ☐ ☐ ☐ ☐

	Agree Very Much	Agree Pretty Much	Agree A Little	Disagree A Little	Disagree Pretty Much	Disagree Very Much
33. The news media greatly exaggerate the extent of drug and alcohol abuse among teenagers.	☐	☐	☐	☐	☐	☐
34. Group aptitude tests tend to have a culture bias which operates against students from culturally impoverished environments.	☐	☐	☐	☐	☐	☐
35. The overall education test scores show a gradual rise in national scores.	☐	☐	☐	☐	☐	☐
36. School boards should assume more control in selecting textbooks for classroom use.	☐	☐	☐	☐	☐	☐
37. Racial assimilation is more in keeping with our democratic ideals than cultural pluralism.	☐	☐	☐	☐	☐	☐
38. Fostering knowledge and understanding of human rights should be part of the public school curricula.	☐	☐	☐	☐	☐	☐
39. The educational innovations and reforms in the 1950s and 1960s drastically altered the nature of American education.	☐	☐	☐	☐	☐	☐
40. Parents should be invited into schools by principals so that the community can be actively involved in the educational process.	☐	☐	☐	☐	☐	☐
41. Good teachers are also good listeners.	☐	☐	☐	☐	☐	☐
42. Sensitivity training should be used in in-service training of teachers and administrators.	☐	☐	☐	☐	☐	☐
43. Desirable change in attitudes toward racial and sexual equality are not likely to occur as long as radical leaders are pushing change as a moral issue.	☐	☐	☐	☐	☐	☐
44. It is not necessary that students be allowed to plan classroom activities—this is what teachers are paid to do.	☐	☐	☐	☐	☐	☐
45. It is more difficult to teach in central city schools than in suburban schools.	☐	☐	☐	☐	☐	☐
46. Teaching is still viewed by the general public as a high prestige occupation.	☐	☐	☐	☐	☐	☐
47. Corporal punishment should be abolished in all school districts.	☐	☐	☐	☐	☐	☐

	Agree Very Much	Agree Pretty Much	Agree A Little	Disagree A Little	Disagree Pretty Much	Disagree Very Much
48. Anyone who wants to work badly enough can find a good job.	☐	☐	☐	☐	☐	☐
49. What is taught is more important than how it is taught.	☐	☐	☐	☐	☐	☐
50. Children should have the same rights as adults.	☐	☐	☐	☐	☐	☐

ADDITIONAL READINGS

Anderson, Lewis F. *History of Common School Education.* New York, Henry Holt, 1909.

Beck, Robert H. *A Social History of Education.* Englewood Cliffs, N. J., Prentice-Hall, 1965

Binder, Frederick M., ed. *Education in the History of Western Civilization.* New York, Macmillan, 1970.

Bowyer, Carlton H. *Philosophical Perspectives for Education.* Glenview, Ill, Scott, Foresman, 1970.

Brameld, Theodore B. *Pattterns of Educational Philosophy: A Divergence and Convergence in Culturological Perspective.* New York, Holt, Rinehart & Winston, 1971.

Broudy, Harry S. *Building of Philosophy of Education.* 2d Ed. Englewood Cliffs, N. J., Prentice-Hall, 1961.

Butts, Robert F. *The Education of the West: A Formative Chapter in the History of Civilization.* New York, McGraw-Hill, 1973.

Cohen, Sol, ed. *Education in the United States: A Documentary History.* New York, Random House, 1973.

Craig, Robert P., ed. *Issues in Philosophy and Education.* New York, MSS Information Corp., 1973.

Derr, Richard L. *A Taxonomy of Social Purposes of Public Schools: A Handbook.* New York, McKay, 1973.

Downey, Meriel E. *Theory and Practice of Education.* New York, Harper & Row, 1975.

Dupuis, Adrian M. *Philosophy of Education in Historical Perspective.* Chicago, Rand McNally, 1966.

Greene, Maxine *Teacher as Stranger: Educational Philosophy for the Modern Age.* Belmont, Cal., Wadsworth, 1973.

Jeffreys, Montagu V. C. *Education: Its Nature and Purpose.* New York, Barnes & Noble, 1971.

McClellan, James E. *Philosophy of Education.* Englewood Cliffs, N. J., Prentice-Hall, 1976.

Marshall, John P. *The Teacher and His Philosophy.* Lincoln, Neb., Professional Educators Publications, 1973.

Mayer, Frederick. *Foundations of Education.* Columbus, Ohio, Charles E. Merrill, 1963.

Parker, Don H. *Schooling for What?* New York, McGraw-Hill, 1970.

Pulliam, John D. *History of Education in America.* Columbus, Ohio, Charles E. Merrill, 1968.

Shermis, S. Samuel. *Philosophic Foundations of Education.* New York, Van Nostrand Reinhold, 1967.

Smith, Wilson, ed. *Theories of Education in Early America, 1655–1819.* Indianapolis, Bobbs-Merrill, 1973.

NOTES

1. John D. Russell and Charles H. Judd, *The American Educational System* (Boston, Houghton Mifflin, 1940), 19–21.

2. Edgar W. Knight, *Education in the United States*, rev. ed. (Boston, Ginn, 1951).

3. *Ibid.*, 108.

4. William B. Ragan, *Modern Elementary School Curriculum*, 3d ed. (New York, Holt, 1961), 10.

5. *Ibid.*, 14.

6. Frederick L. Allen, *The Big Change* (New York, Harper & Row, 1952), 105.

7. L. Thomas Hopkins, *Interaction: The Democratic Process* (Boston, Heath, 1941), 403–405.

8. Knight, *Education*, 520.

9. The Progressive Education Association, "Progressive Education: Its Philosophy and Challenge," *Progressive Education* (May, 1941).

10. Knight, *Education*, 651–655.

11. Banesh Hoffman, *The Tyranny of Testing* (New York, Crowell-Collier, 1962).

12. American Association of School Administrators, *Labels and Fingerprints* (Washington, D.C., National Education Association, 1961).

13. Myron Lieberman, *The Future of Public Education* (Chicago, University of Chicago Press, 1960), 17.

14. Philip Phenix, *Realms of Meaning* (New York, McGraw-Hill, 1964), 28–29.

15. Carl F. Hansen, *The Amidon Elementary School: A Successful Demonstration in Basic Education* (Englewood Cliffs, N.J., Prentice-Hall, 1962), 9.

16. *Ibid.*, 11–12.

17. Paul R. Hanna et al., *Geography in the Teaching of Social Studies Concepts and Skills* (Boston, Houghton Mifflin, 1966), 50.

18. John I. Goodlad, "Changing Curriculum in America's Schools," *Saturday Review* (November 16, 1963), 65.

19. John D. McAulay, "What the States are Doing: Elementary Social Studies," *Pennsylvania News and Views* (March, 1964), 3.

20. William Van Til, "What are the Real 'Basics' in Education?" *Childhood Education* (November, 1962), 107–109.

21. Association for Supervision and Curriculum Development, *Perceiving—Behaving—Becoming*, (Washington, D.C., ASCD, 1962), 62.

22. John Dewey, *Experience and Education* (New York, Macmillian, 1938), 1.

23. ASCD, *Perceiving—Behaving—Becoming*, 141.

24. *Ibid.*, 56.

25. See William B. Ragan and John D. McAulay, *Social Studies for Today's Children* (New York, Appleton-Century-Crofts, 1964), 50–51.

26. ASCD, *Perceiving—Behaving—Becoming*, 61.

27. *Ibid.*, 60.

28. Gertrude Noar, "Information Is Not Enough," in August Kerber and Wilfred Smith (eds.), *Educational Issues in a Changing Society*, rev. ed. (Detroit, Wayne State University Press, 1964), 117–119.

29. John W. Renner and William B. Ragan, *Teaching Science in the Elementary School* (New York, Harper & Row, 1968), 299.

30. Educational Policies Commission, *The Central Purpose of American Education* (Washington, D.C., National Education Association, 1961), 5.

31. Theodore Brameld, "World Civilization, the Galvanizing Purpose of Public Education," in Stanley Elam (ed.), *New Dimensions for Educational Progress* (Bloomington, Ind., Phi Delta Kappa, 1962), 11–12.

32. Leonard S. Kenworthy, *Introducing Children to the World* (New York, Harper & Row, 1956), chap. 13.

33. John Jarolimek, *Social Studies in Elementary Education*, 2d ed. (New York, Macmillan, 1963), chap. 15.

34. Project on the Instructional Program of the Public Schools, *Education in a Changing Society* (Washington, D.C., National Education Association, 1963), chap. 9.

35. John K. Jessup et al., *The National Purpose* (New York, Holt, Rinehart & Winston, 1960).

36. President's Commission on National Goals, *Goals for Americans* (Englewood Cliffs, N.J., Prentice-Hall, 1960).

37. Lucile Lindberg, "Learning Through Searching," *Childhood Education*, 38 (October, 1961), 58–60.

38. Educational Policies Commission, *American Education and the Search for Equal Opportunity* (Washington, D.C., National Education Association, 1965), 3.

2.
SOCIAL AND PSYCHOLOGICAL FORCES

Altering educational programs to meet new conditions of living is a task that has confronted each new generation for centuries. Since 1945, however, changes have occurred with incredible speed. Thus the task of reforming education now presents a formidable challenge. In addition more Americans than ever before realize that drastic reforms in education are necessary. They understand that children now in school will spend their adult years in a radically different society. Indeed it is not an exaggeration to say that education will determine the outcome of the race between civilization and catastrophe. It is apparent that educational reforms must keep pace with changes in society.

SOCIETY

If we are to understand school as a miniature society it is necessary to understand its prototype. Human nature is the raw material out of which *homo sapiens* fashions societies. Technically, a description of human nature begins with the needs of human beings. Each living creature has certain innate needs. Some biology instructors say that when we list the needs of an organism we have described it. The activities of each person's lifetime evolve around his or her efforts to satisfy basic needs. Failure results in suffering and sometimes death.

Innate Needs

Humans are peculiar in terms of the number, variety, and complexity of their innate needs.

Consider the following examples of human needs. We need food, shelter, and protection from wild animals and microbes. We need communication and association with other people. We need love and some kind of family relationship with other people. We need an explanation of the universe. We even need a theory of our needs.

Corresponding to each of the innate needs is a tendency to perform actions that will get us what we need. At this juncture it is important to note that unlike nonhuman animals, most human behaviors are learned—not instinctual. Instinctual tendencies to behave in certain need-satisfying ways are definite and precise. A chicken, for instance, begins pecking for its living as it is hatched. It does not learn to peck.

When humans get things they need, they usually feel satisfied. For each innate need there is a corresponding desire. Some of our desires are vague yearnings—we know that we want something but cannot "put our fingers on it." When our desires are not satisfied we tend to experience discomfort or pain. Such discomfort or pain may be physiological or psychological. As a rule, a feeling of pleasure indicates need satisfaction and, conversely, an unpleasant feeling indicates that a need is not being met. Words of caution are in order. Our feelings are not always accurate guides to our needs (medicine might taste bad but be quite helpful).

An individual's attempt to satisfy all of his or her needs will result in varied activities, both humane and inhumane. Civilization has been gradually built up through the endless, cumulative efforts of each generation to satisfy its basic needs. These efforts arrange themselves around certain universal institutions, including the family, the state, the school, and the church.

The Human Pecking Order

From time to time historians have argued with much fervor that human nature changes greatly from century to century. While egoinflating, this is not the case. Our "savage" ancestors who roamed half naked through Europe, Africa, South America, and Asia had just as much innate intelligence as we have. While the centuries have added to our inventions, our innate intelligence has undergone little change. In short, the tools our minds work with have improved considerably, but not our minds. For example, Cro-Magnon people who inhabited Europe for twenty-five to thirty thousand years and became extinct approximately ten thousand years ago had stone implements and drew pictures of the animals they hunted. Most anthropologists believe that the cranial capacity of Cro-Magnons and their drawings imply that they were at least our intellectual equals. Had they been brought up from early childhood in our civilization there is ample evidence to indicate that they could have used our cultural objects as well (or as poorly) as we do. The human tragedy to be culled from this analogy is that humans have yet to build a world (or educational institution) that is more humane than savage.

The assumption that our ancestors were just as innately good as we are is based on Weismann's law: *acquired characteristics are not transmitted through the germ cells*. The human relations implications of this law are profound. This means that cultural changes which take place in an individual's society during his or her lifetime cannot be genetically transmitted to his or her offspring. Educating parents in the best institutions does not produce babies with more innate cultural knowledge. It makes no difference how many generations of parents are educated. Acquired characteristics must be relearned by each successive generation. Frequently, Weismann's law is difficult for parents and teachers to comprehend. Human parents and teachers tend to be impatient with the trial-and-error methods of learning which characterize their children, especially parents

and teachers of children from "good" families.

While the innate traits of human nature are common to all human beings, none of these traits is exactly alike in any two individuals. Each person has varying degrees of need and, relatedly, exhibits varying behaviors for need satisfaction. As to the quality of intellect, individual differences range from idiots to geniuses. Psychologists have devised serviceable but questionable instruments for measuring the intelligence of individuals. The relative quality of a person's intellect is expressed in terms of intelligence quotient (IQ). An IQ of 100 is average. According to research, members of societies group around this average in a normal curve of distribution. That is, there is a fixed percentage of the population for each grade of intelligence.

The notion that different social classes differ with respect to traits of human nature, especially intelligence, is an erroneous and elitist view of humankind. Historically members of the under classes have been defined as inferior to the top classes in morality and mentality. In Western thought we owe much to Aristotle and Plato, who maintained that slaves and the common people were as much below the ruling class in native intelligence as nonhumans are below human beings. Similar ideas have been perpetuated throughout the centuries, and today it is not uncommon to hear poverty-stricken people referred to as "animals," "brutes," and "inferior." Along with this mythology goes the belief that affluent, upper-class people are very intelligent. The illogic concludes that the latter group is successful because of intelligence, whereas the former group is poor because of lack of intelligence. Missing in this explanation are the opportunity structures which facilitate or impede achievement of social and economic aspirations.

Technological Change

It is also foolish to dwell excessively on the "great race" theory; that is, the belief that different races differ significantly in terms of intellectual ability. Rather, there are ample reasons to assume that the various races are approximately equal in native endowments of the mind. For one thing, there are no pure races—all nations are mixed races. Furthermore, the so-called "advanced" or "developed" cultures were recently backward, while the so-called "underdeveloped" or "Third World" cultures were once the advanced nations. This does not suggest that people of African, Asian, or Hispanic stocks have degenerated biologically during the last two thousand years. Rather it shows that unless nations continuously maintain and, where necessary, improve technological aspects of their cultures, they will undergo technological stagnation. Consider the following illustrations: The Spaniards used gunpowder (invented by the Chinese) to destroy the Aztec civilization. The Japanese have only recently borrowed technological aspects of Western civilization, and they have regained the world prominence they lost thousands of years ago. These illustrations have much to do with cultural conditions and nothing to do with biological inferiority or superiority. The decline of Greek, Roman, and African cultures, or the German shift from the intellectualism of the early nineteenth century to militarism in the early twentieth century are additional illustrations. Change is the only constant condition characterizing societies.

Science and technology are, of course, two of the principal causes of the constantly accelerating rate of change. In an expanding process, each invention opens the way for several others; each research study leads to other related studies; each innovation lays the foundation for more elaborate innovations. Many of the resulting changes in the culture are so drastic that it is difficult for us to understand them and difficult therefore to sense fully their implications for educational programs. For instance the release of the energy stored in the atom created, as one writer put it, "a blanket of obsolescence not only over the methods and the products of man but over man himself."[1] The launching of Sputnik I opened an era that has been aptly called the "postmodern world."[2]

SIGNIFICANT TRENDS IN OUR SOCIETY

It is apparent that an understanding of the ever-changing American society is essential to an understanding of the changes that are taking place—and should take place—in education.

Education always has been and always will be influenced by time, place, and circumstances. The social trends that affect the tasks the schools are expected to perform are too numerous and too complex to be treated in detail here. Thus only a few of the more significant trends are now analyzed.

Our Affluent Society

We live in a tremendously wealthy society. Here is an illustration: Imagine all the people in the world compressed into a village with a population of one thousand persons. Only sixty inhabitants of the village would be Americans, but these fortunate few would enjoy fully half the total income of the village. The other 940 people would definitely have the short end of the stick—they would have to make do with the other half. Our wealth is great not only in relative terms but also in absolute ones—and it is increasing. The Gross National Product (GNP) of the United States was $157 billion in 1947, $370 billion in 1957, $730 billion in 1967, and $1.5 trillion in 1975. Per capita income increased from $600 a year in 1900, to $2,000 in 1957, to $6,155 in 1975. Some comparative GNP figures make such statistics more meaningful. In 1975 our GNP was $1.5 trillion, but France's was $225 billion, the United Kingdom's was $175 billion, Brazil's was $77 billion, and Nigeria's was $14 billion. We have in fact moved from an economy of scarcity to an economy of abundance. Until recently our main problem was to produce enough goods to go around. Now our problem is the proper distribution of the goods that are pouring from our farms and factories in ever increasing volume.

This picture of prosperity and abundance is marred by the threatening fact that all Americans do not share in it. For instance the year 1976 was a prosperous one for the country, but in that year 26 million Americans lived in poverty. This was so even though poverty was defined as an urban family of four persons with an annual income of less than $5,500 or a single person with an annual income of less than $2,700. Most of these poverty-stricken Americans constitute a subculture made up of people without the education or technical skills to admit them to the mainstream of American life and work. It is inconsistent with our democratic ideals of equality of opportunity and the worth of every human being to have allowed such a subculture to be formed and to allow it to continue. This is what Gunnar Myrdal, the eminent Swedish economist, had in mind when he said, "There is an ugly smell rising from the basement of the stately American mansion."[3] Can anyone deny that this waste of the talents of our disadvantaged minorities is the social problem that should lie heaviest on our consciences?

The Urban Crisis

Poverty and substandard educational opportunities in the United States are by no means confined to urban communities; discrimination and prejudice against those who are different from the majority are by no means directed only at Blacks and other minority ethnic groups. (Any American boy or girl who has completed grade school in a rural community and moved to an urban community to attend high school knows how difficult it is to become a member of the in-group.) Nevertheless, poverty in the cities presents perhaps a more difficult problem than rural poverty. Discrimination on ethnic and sex grounds is more difficult to deal with than discrimination on social grounds, and it also has become a problem whose results are more acute in the cities.

There are many reasons for the urban crisis, most of them of quite recent origin. As a matter of fact the big city itself is a relatively new development on the American scene. It was not until 1820 that any American city had a population of 100,000; we now have one city of more than 7 million and five others of more than 1 million each. Three-fourths of the school children and school teachers of the United States are in metropolitan schools. The Bureau of the Census now uses the term "Standard Metropolitan Statistical Area" (SMSA) to mean either a city of 50,000 inhabitants or more, or twin cities with a combined population of at least 50,000. This area may also include surrounding counties that are economically and socially integrated. There were 272 SMSAs in the United States in 1975.

As technology has invaded the farms, the rural poor have moved to the central cities. At the same time those who could afford to do so have moved from the cities to the suburbs. Chicago is a good example of the results of this trend. In 1940, 3,115,000 whites and only 282,000 nonwhites lived in that city; by 1970 the whites had dropped to 2,579,000 and the nonwhites had increased to 980,000. In 1940 the suburbs of Chicago had 1,148,000 whites and 25,000 nonwhites; by 1970 the suburbs had 3,464,803 whites and 147,181 nonwhites. In Detroit families living within six miles of the central business district gained 10 per cent in median income between 1951 and 1975; families living in the suburbs gained 80 per cent in median income during the same period. The trend has also produced proportions like these in the schools: in Washington, D.C., 93 per cent of the elementary school pupils are nonwhite; in Detroit, Chicago, Baltimore, and Philadelphia the figure is almost 80 per cent.

It is widely recognized that it will take the combined and coordinated efforts of many agencies to solve the urban crisis, but the schools are expected to play a major role. It is generally acknowledged that the schools cannot fulfill this role by trying to impose educational programs designed for middle-class children on children whose home environments have not prepared them for such programs. In an attempt to resolve this dilemma, expedients such as integration and compensatory programs specifically designed for disadvantaged children have been evolved and tried.

Nevertheless, the efforts to provide equality of educational opportunity for children in rural and city slums have, for the most part, failed. Integration has not proceeded as rapidly as it was expected to, and it has been beset by many unforeseen problems. Compensatory education programs such as Head Start have to some extent made up for the absence of opportunities for learning in the home, but children who have been in such programs have generally fallen behind when they entered schools with no provisions for differentiated instruction. It can be said that education in the rural and urban slums still presents a dismal picture characterized by old buildings, poorly prepared teachers, and a high percentage of dropouts.

THE ROLE OF CULTURE

A study of the social foundations of education serves two purposes. First, it provides a broad understanding of how the culture influences human development. More specifically it identifies the social problems that influence the tasks education must perform. This chapter is concerned with the first of these purposes; later chapters will explore the second purpose.

Since the time of Rousseau, educational theorists and practitioners have never ceased debating the principal function of education: Should it be planned to benefit primarily the child or the society? Rousseau initiated a revolution in educational thought with *Émile* (1762) in which he said, "God makes all things good; man meddles with them and they become evil."[4] One of the main theories he advanced in this novel about the upbringing of a boy is that education should change with the various stages in a child's development. Profoundly influenced by Rousseau, educational reformers began developing educational programs based primarily on the interests, purposes, and normal activities of children. For instance Pestalozzi's school at Yverdon, Switzerland (1805), John Dewey's at the University of Chicago (1896), Junius L. Meriam's at the University of Missouri (1904), and Ellsworth Collings' in McDonald County, Missouri (1917), were all "child-centered" schools.[5] The importance of using information about how children develop, grow, and learn as a basis for planning educational programs continues to be recognized. An almost staggering amount of such information is available. In one publication, about two thousand studies in child psychology—most of them done between 1953 and 1963—are reviewed.[6]

It is almost a truism now to say that the nature and needs of children must be taken into consideration in planning school programs. But there are broader ramifications that are not so self-evident. Child development does not take place in a vacuum; the ideas, habits, attitudes, and behavior patterns of the individual are acquired from interacting with the culture in which the child lives. It is now generally acknowledged, in other words, that it is oversimplifying to say that the school program should be based entirely on a single factor such as the interests and purposes of children, the major functions of social life, or the development of the rational powers of the individual. The more balanced approach that now seems desirable has been described by many experts, one of whom puts it this way: "No one area is sufficient for curriculum planning today. A combination of the three basic areas—organized knowledge, society, and the individual—seems to offer the best hope for curriculum improvement."[7] Teacher education programs usually do include a study of these three basic areas.

The Socialization Process

The *culture* is the environment that humans themselves have made. It includes the distinctive ways of carrying on life processes: the artifacts, ideas, values, language, attitudes, and customs of a particular time and place. The culture is influenced to some extent by geography, resources, climate, and the history of a particular society. It is influenced to an even greater extent by knowledge, which is the source of technological progress. As knowledge and skills increase, the culture changes; new ways of carrying on life processes are incorporated into it. Young people, therefore, do not simply repeat the life processes of their parents; they learn to live according to the demands of the latest developmental stage of the culture. The strain that inevitably develops between youth and their elders as a result of cultural conflicts is commonly called the "generation gap."[8]

Each child is born into a culture, but he or she must learn the behavior patterns needed to live effectively with others in the culture. The changes that take place in children and young people as they acquire the knowledge and skills necessary for living harmoniously and effectively with other individuals and groups are called *social development*; the help they receive from parents, siblings, peer groups, schools, churches, and other educative agencies is called *social education*.

Diversity of Cultures Within American Society

Ours is a society of great cultural diversity. Although all segments of our population share certain common elements in life patterns and basic beliefs, there are also significant differences in the attitudes, interests, goals, and even dialects that children internalize by interacting with their families and subcultures. Respect for individual differences and the desire to provide opportunities for every individual to learn, to realize his or her potential, and to find a place in society according to his or her ability and efforts have long been recognized as the essence of our democratic aspirations. Diversity is both permitted and prized in an open society, at least up to a certain limit; in a closed society behavior patterns are not matters of personal choice—they are dictated by the state. As early as 1835, Alexis de Tocqueville noted, "The American relies on personal interest to accomplish his ends and gives free scope to the unguided strength and common sense of the people; the Russian centers all the authority in a single arm."

The process of socialization, however, is complicated by the diversity of cultures in our society. (One glaring example is our failure to provide adequate educational opportunities for the children of the lower socioeconomic classes; this result of our public policy—or lack of policy—has finally begun to lie heavily on our consciences.) John Dewey's remarks in this connection are as pertinent today as when he made them in 1916:

> A democracy is more than a form of government; it is primarily a mode of associated living, of conjoint communicated experience. The extension in space of the number of individuals who participate in an interest so that each has to refer his own action to that of others, and to consider the action of others to give point and direction to his own, is equivalent to the breaking down of those barriers of class, race and national territory which keep men from perceiving the full import of their activities. [9]

Among the barriers—the cultural differences—which children bring to school with them are those arising from differences between masculine and feminine roles, rural and urban backgrounds, ethnic groups, and social classes.

Masculine and feminine roles.   Until recently, in our culture—as in almost all cultures—men and women were expected to play different roles. One of the first lessons children learned from those about them was that their behavior must accord with that generally considered appropriate to their sex. A boy was frowned upon if he took on too many feminine characteristics; a girl was handicapped if she was not feminine in dress, speech, and behavior. The terms "sissy" and "tomboy" vividly reflected the common attitude toward a boy or

girl who did not seem to possess enough of the proper sex-role attributes. One of the basic aspects of the socialization process was the belief in the necessity for a child to internalize sex-appropriate patterns of behavior. Gradually, sex stereotyping in terms of male and female academic and employment norms are disappearing.

Rural and urban backgrounds.   Though they are not so striking as they used to be, there still are differences in language, attitudes, and interests between rural and urban children. Some school systems, therefore, run a type of orientation program designed to acquaint rural children moving to cities with urban cultural resources and patterns of living. As I have mentioned, acquiring urban patterns of behavior is generally a painful process for rural children.

Ethnic groups.   This term refers to groups of different national or racial origins. The population of the United States is composed of people with a great variety of ethnic backgrounds; nearly everyone can trace his or her ancestry back to some country across the seas. These ethnic groups have enriched our culture with their own particular types of music, food, customs, and dress. Americans are proud of the fact that our nation has been a melting pot, assimilating people who came here from many different nations. There is evidence that the schools have played a leading role in this accomplishment. [10]

However, it usually takes two or more generations for the members of a new group to be sufficiently absorbed into the life of the community so that they lose their separate identity; some groups never achieve assimilation. The assimilation of the more recent immigrant groups seems to be problematical; most of them are of the lower socioeconomic class in our large cities, and they tend to maintain their own patterns of beliefs, attitudes, and behavior.

Social classes.   Many studies have been made of the influence of social class on educational opportunities. These studies justify the conclusions that there are rather clearly defined social classes in the United States, that the social class to which the parents belong determines to a great extent a child's educational attainments, and that there are circumstances that make it difficult for an individual to advance from one social class to another on the basis of capability and effort.

Our system is not, of course, a caste system. The difference between caste and class has been described thus:

The rules of caste demand that an individual be born, live, and die in one caste. Social mobility in a class system permits an individual during his lifetime to move up or down through the several social strata. A man may be born lower-class but in time climb into the upper ranges of society, although, ordinarily, a person stays in the class into which he was born.[11]

Nevertheless, for some in our society the effects of the system are disturbingly similar to those of a true caste system. For example, education is generally regarded as the principal means of promoting social mobility, but our society has erected serious barriers to acquiring a good education and thus to improvement of life chances for many of our youth. Indeed, the lowering of these and other barriers has become one of the major goals of our domestic policy. As the President's Commission on National Goals said in 1960: "Vestiges of religious prejudices, handicaps to women, and, most important, discrimination on the basis of race must be recognized as morally wrong, economically wasteful, and in many cases dangerous. In this decade we must sharply lower these last stubborn barriers."[12]

Family income is closely associated with class structure in this country. Education is generally regarded as the means to the better-paying jobs; nevertheless there is evidence that in 1975, although 52 per cent of the white high school graduates had clerical jobs, only 30 per cent of the nonwhite graduates held such jobs. Furthermore, 25 per cent of the nonwhite graduates were employed in service occupations, but only 12 per cent of the whites were. The results are apparent in statistics like these: In 1975, 15 per cent of the Blacks and Puerto Ricans in New York had incomes under $3,000 a year; only 8 per cent of the whites had incomes that low. In 1975 the average income of Blacks in the United States was only 60 per cent of the average income of whites.

The schools cannot be expected to provide all the levers for social mobility. The social and economic structures that surround the children, particularly families and community agencies, must also contribute. But it is the business of the school to help children make the most of their individual capacities so that their life chances will be enhanced. Two informed observers have said that "even the most staunchly loyal professional educator with a knowledge of the urban situation would hesitate to claim that big-city schools are adequately performing the task that is squarely and particularly theirs to do."[13]

Many factors contribute to effective teaching, but it is generally recognized that truly effective teachers are those who seek to understand their pupils. A very important aspect of understanding children is understanding the life styles of the social classes from which they come. Pupils from different social classes have different manners, beliefs, and language and behavior patterns acquired through the social pressures of home and community. To be specific, teachers must understand that children from impoverished homes come to school with many handicaps and that they need a school program designed to compensate for the lack of educational opportunities in the home and community.

THE SOCIAL DEVELOPMENT OF CHILDREN

Information about child development has accumulated so rapidly that intellectual development, physical development, emotional development, and social development are now separate areas of research. The studies that treat each of these areas in greater depth than is feasible in one course or one book on child development are invaluable; nevertheless, it is important to realize that no one phase takes place independently of the others. Physical defects and poor health frequently interfere with academic achievement; the effective use of language is closely related to social relationships; the emotionally disturbed child is not likely to do well in school; and as every parent knows, acceptance by the peer group is an important factor in a child's success in school.

Although there has been a trend in recent years to emphasize the importance of intellectual development—the development of the rational powers—many specialists in the psychology of cognition recognize that education involves more than this. Robert M. Gagné, whose book is restricted to what may be termed "intellectual" development, states:

The reader must be made aware, also, that there are some problems of great importance to education which cannot be solved by applying a knowledge of the principles of learning as they are here described. For example, there are many aspects of the personal interaction between a teacher and his students that do not pertain, in a strict sense, to the acquisition of skills and knowledges that typically form the content of the curriculum. These varieties of interaction include those of motivating, persuading, and the establishment of attitudes and values. The development of such human dispositions as these is of tremendous importance to education as a system of modern society. [14]

Social development is an important phase of growing into the culture—of becoming fully human. Children must learn to live in a veritable sea of human relationships as they engage in the activities of ever enlarging groups of people. Their life outside the school provides many opportunities for social development, but the school can be their most effective social laboratory; at least it can be when the school environment is structured to meet their social needs and release their social potential.

Measurement of Children's Social Development

The measurement of children's intellectual development, particularly as it applies to learning school subjects, has been developed to a high level of proficiency. For instance a score of 4.3 on a standardized achievement test in reading can be interpreted to mean that a pupil is reading at the level of the third month of the fourth year in school in terms of national norms in reading. Moreover, these measurement instruments are well known and widely used in most schools. A great deal of progress also has been made in the identification of the stages through which a child progresses in other aspects of mental development, such as concept development. [15]

Comparable progress has not been made in the measurement of social development, although there have been many attempts. For example, Edgar Doll developed the Vineland Social Maturity Scale, which consists of a series of rating scales arranged in a developmental sequence and grouped according to the ages at which certain behavior traits generally appear in children. The sociogram is a device that can serve as an effective starting point for the study of students' progress in gaining acceptance by their peers, but it must be used in connection with other methods of evaluating social development. These instruments are by no means as well known or as commonly used as those used for evaluating intellectual development. [16]

Benjamin S. Bloom, whose research reveals the tremendous importance of the first few years of the child's life, concludes that: (1) many of the changes in human characteristics that take place with increasing age can be explained in terms of environmental variations, (2) because there is a lack of direct measures of the influence of variations in the environment on changes in human characteristics, we must be content with considering only the influence of extreme differences in the environment, and (3) there is a need for the development of more precise measures of the influence of the environment. [17]

Factors in Children's Social Development

The social behavior of children can be observed and recorded, and these records can be used as indications of growth in such important characteristics as the recognition of the rights of self and others, the ability to make friends, the ability to cooperate with others, and the ability to exercise leadership in a group situation. The summary that follows is not inclusive, but it can be useful in recognizing the social characteristics of children at various stages of development.

1. The quantity and quality of relationships in the home influence the child's patterns of social behavior that tend to persist when he or she enters school.

2. The child's principal source of social experience during his or her first few years is free play. Until the age of two, the child's play is solitary; even when other children are in the same room, little interaction takes place.

3. Between the ages of three and five there is likely to be an increase in social play. The

Table 1. Number of Public School Pupils, by State (in thousands)

State or other area	Fall, 1962	Fall, 1964	Fall, 1966	Fall, 1968	Fall, 1970	Fall, 1972	Fall, 1974	Fall, 1975[1]
Total United States	38,837	41,416	43,055	44,962	45,903	45,753	45,056	44,700
Alabama	812	821	873	832	805	733	764	757
Alaska	50	56	62	72	80	85	87	86
Arizona	353	366	383	411	440	485	487	483
Arkansas	436	448	451	453	463	461	455	451
California	3,755	4,140	358	4,582	4,633	4,501	4,428	4,394
Colorado	438	476	499	524	550	574	568	563
Connecticut	520	560	597	632	662	665	660	655
Deleware	92	105	113	125	133	134	131	129
District of Columbia	133	141	147	149	146	140	132	130
Florida	1,094	1,184	1,260	1,356	1,428	1,514	1,557	1,544
Georgia	991	1,042	1,074	1,103	1,099	1,090	1,082	1,072
Hawaii	152	158	166	172	181	182	177	175
Idaho	167	173	175	179	182	185	188	186
Illinois	1,890	2,043	2,159	2,274	2,357	2,349	2,296	2,278
Indiana	1,029	1,100	1,155	1,205	1,232	1,221	1,187	1,177
Iowa	598	620	636	658	660	646	618	616
Kansas	502	605	516	522	512	475	450	446
Kentucky	647	663	675	699	717	715	701	695
Louisiana	760	786	821	865	842	846	841	833
Maine	213	218	222	232	245	250	251	248
Maryland	668	736	741	859	916	921	894	887
Massachusetts	943	993	1,083	1,113	1,168	1,203	1,200	1,200
Michigan	1,792	1,919	2,015	2,124	2,181	2,198	2,138	2,121
Minnesota	773	788	835	895	921	910	890	884
Mississippi	563	579	581	582	534	526	514	509
Missouri	858	948	964	1,056	1,040	1,030	1,002	994
Montana	157	165	168	173	177	180	172	171
Nebraska	301	317	319	329	329	329	319	316
Nevada	80	100	108	118	128	132	137	136
New Hampshire	116	125	134	146	159	168	172	171
New Jersey	1,159	1,255	1,326	1,422	1,482	1,510	1,470	1,458
New Mexico	239	260	271	273	281	285	282	280
New York	2,943	3,130	3,249	3,411	3,477	3,524	3,436	3,411
North Carolina	1,140	1,179	1,184	1,195	1,192	1,161	1,178	1,169
North Dakota	142	148	148	149	147	142	133	132
Ohio	2,082	2,230	2,320	2,384	2,426	2,423	2,330	2,314
Oklahoma	563	600	598	604	627	607	596	591
Oregon	413	441	474	490	480	472	477	473
Pennsylvania	2,059	2,212	2,211	2,310	2,358	2,361	2,278	2,261
Rhode Island	143	151	160	173	188	190	179	177
South Carolina	611	633	642	649	638	624	627	622
South Dakota	160	164	168	167	166	162	154	153
Tennessee	838	864	874	884	900	892	873	865
Texas	2,291	2,464	2,563	2,704	2,840	2,738	2,785	2,762
Utah	258	283	292	301	304	306	306	304
Vermont	78	82	88	100	103	107	105	104
Virginia	906	969	1,003	1,056	1,079	1,069	1,073	1,084
Washington	685	719	753	804	818	791	786	779
West Virginia	436	436	421	410	400	410	404	401
Wisconsin	767	831	890	954	994	995	974	968
Wyoming	83	88	85	86	87	86	87	85
Outlying areas:	634	662	701	711	734	780	786	783
American Samoa	6	7	8	8	9	8	10	10
Canal Zone	13	13	13	14	13	13	11	11
Guam	15	16	18	21	25	27	28	28
Puerto Rico	592	618	651	668	687	711	713	710
Virgin Islands	8	9	11	–	–	21	23	24

[1] Estimated

NOTE.—State and area figures may not add up to total figures because of rounding.

SOURCE: U.S. Department of Health, Education and Welfare, National Center for Education Statistics, *Fall Statistics of Public Schools.*

first playmates are provided by the immediate neighborhood; the child's desire for playmates is so strong that he or she may resort to imaginary playmates if there are none in the neighborhood.

4. If circumstances in the home and neighborhood have been favorable, children will be experienced in cooperative play by the time they enter school. They will have lost some of their self-centeredness; they will be able to share and take turns; they will be able to serve as a leader part of the time.

5. Young children generally are more concerned with the approval of parents and teachers than they are with the approval of other children. After they have been in school a few years, their interest in the approval of their classmates increases and their interest in the approval of adults decreases.

6. The social climate in the classroom has an important influence on the social behavior of children. The autocratic climate tends to produce expressions of hostility, demands for attention, and sharp criticisms of the work of other pupils. The laissez faire climate is the least effective type found in classrooms in experimental studies; the children tend to get in each others' way, and very little is accomplished. The democratic climate produces the most favorable results; pupils are more inclined to stay with tasks whether the teacher is present or not, form more favorable attitudes toward other pupils, and develop valuable social skills.

A Larger Task for the Schools

If they are to be effective in producing citizens who have the insights and skills needed in the preservation of a free society, the schools must be concerned not only with what the pupils know, but also with what kind of persons they are becoming in their interaction with others. The free society puts more responsibility on the individual—on inner controls of behavior and on ability to participate in decision making—than any other kind of society does. The school in a free society must therefore accept as one of its important functions the continuation of the socialization process that began in the family and the neighborhood.

This function of the school in a free society is by no means fully understood or universally accepted in this country. Those who want to limit the schools to the teaching of the basic subjects assert that the school is not a social club—that the process of socialization should be left to the home and other agencies. An increasing number of Americans, including most parents, are looking to the school for contributions in the areas of human relations, citizenship, and personal-social adjustment. A larger number of school patrons are demanding a return solely to the three Rs.

According to the 1977 *Gallup Poll of the Public's Attitudes Toward the Public Schools*, an overwhelming majority of Americans familiar with it favor the back-to-basics movement. And to the chagrin of many educators, this movement is defined in terms of reading, writing, and arithmetic. In terms of the educational process, back to basics usually is described as "respect for teachers," "good manners," "obedience," "respect for elders," and "structured classrooms." The decline in national test scores and media reports of illiterate high school graduates have given impetus to such a movement.

An obvious danger in the back-to-basics movement is the desire of some persons to reduce the number of social studies, arts, and humanities classes in a school's curriculum and to substitute newly designed competency-oriented classes. On closer, less emotional analysis the major issue is not whether the so-called frill subjects should be abandoned for basic subjects. Rather, the major issue is whether teachers of all subjects—required and elective—will devise more effective ways to teach the three Rs. This will necessitate utilizing and, where needed, designing materials which appeal to the broadest range of student interests and abilities. Teachers should overlook neither commercial television, an underutilized electronic resource, nor student creativity, an underutilized human resource.

Acculturation and Cultural Conflict

Thus far our examination of the relationship between the culture and education has bened primarily with the *socialization* process, that is, with the problems involved in helping the child internalize the culture into which he or she was born. *Acculturation* is a somewhat different process; it involves a changeover from one culture to another. This is generally a difficult process even for parents who have already achieved the organization of their behavior patterns in the culture in which they grew up. For their children, who are still trying to internalize one culture when they are expected to take on the ways of a brand-new culture, the transition is even more difficult. *Cultural conflict* is the term frequently used to denote the frustrations an individual experiences in such circumstances.

It has become increasingly difficult during recent decades for metropolitan areas in the United States to provide adequate educational opportunities and life chances for children from immigrant families. Factors that complicate the problems include the following illustrations:

Mass Migrations to the Cities

There were 500 persons of Puerto Rican birth in New York City in 1910, 7,000 in 1920, 45,000 in 1930, and 812,000 of Puerto Rican birth or parentage in 1970. Glazer has characterized the situation of the Puerto Ricans in New York as follows:

Something new, then, has been added to the New York scene—an ethnic group that will not assimilate to the same degree as others have, but will resemble the strangers who lived in ancient Greek cities, or the ancient Greeks who set up colonies around the Mediterranean.[18]

Conflicts in Social Roles of Parents

Parents play an important role in helping children internalize the culture in which they live. However, the social behavior the in-migrant child learns from her parents is usually not in tune with the new social environment. The typical Puerto Rican mother, for example, keeps her daughters under strict control, does not allow them to go out on the streets, and forbids them to talk with other people. The girls therefore grow up without developing the ability to relate to others. As Sophie L. Elam points out, "It is important in working with Puerto Rican parents to help them find ways to protect their children without completely depriving them of social interchange."[19]

The Language Barrier

Language is an important tool used in interacting with others. The in-migrant child often lacks this tool for adjustment to new people, a new area, and a new culture. He brings to school a nonstandard form of English learned from parents, relatives, and friends. His acculturation depends to a great extent on learning to speak the standard dialect of the school and the larger community fluently. There are difficulties involved in this process, of course, but some teachers tend to magnify them. After all, it has been demonstrated that children can learn to speak a second language, such as Spanish or Chinese, at any early age; thus they can surely learn to speak a second dialect. (As a matter of fact, most adults in our society find that they use different dialects when speaking to different people—a university professor, a service station attendant, or a young child.) Arnold B. Cheyney, who has provided many practical suggestions for teaching language to culturally disadvantaged children, has said, "I believe the idea that home conditions are an insurmountable barrier to effective language instruction is a myth we have comfortably hidden behind all too long."[20]

NEWER INSIGHTS INTO HUMAN BEHAVIOR

It is not merely a brain or an isolated set of nervous tissues, but rather a whole child that confronts the teacher. For this very good reason, student teachers are told that they must teach "the whole child." Each child comes to school with good and bad habits, with misinformation as well as accurate knowledge, with loosely formulated goals, and sometimes with obvious impediments. In addition he or she may be ill-nourished or well-fed, energetic or listless, placid or tense. It is this extremely complex mass of characteristics that teachers must attempt to shape and mold into a productive adult.

Every individual's development is limited by

both heredity and environment. Broadly speaking, heredity determines whether the child will learn, and environment determines what the child will learn. The usual direction of intellectual development is first the expression of behaviors that evolve out of physical maturation and later the expression of behaviors that grow out of group acculturation experiences.[21]

Perceptual Development

As early as he is able to comprehend, the child is taught to perceive the world around him. This phenomenon has given rise to the expression that many people "look at" but few "see" the same things. "Seeing" cultural objects and giving them the same meanings is the result of learning within social (group) settings. This *perceptual development* takes place through the senses—vision, hearing, touch, taste, smell. Most psychological studies conclude that the major portion of an individual's development occurs within the first five years of his life. This development is, of course, especially related to the home.

Homes vary in their suitability for the development of cognitive skills. Home environments in depressed rural communities and urban neighborhoods are noticeably deficient. Living quarters are overcrowded, the noise level is generally high, and the result is continual interpersonal strain. In addition amenities such as games, toys, books, magazines, and furniture are scarce or even nonexistent, creating a very limited visual environment. Another condition of intellectual development is the amount of interaction between parents and child. Parent-child interaction is greatly reduced in most depressed-area homes. Frequently the mother must play two roles, serving both as the main wage earner and as the housekeeper. If the family is large, the interaction is further reduced between parents and children. Reduced interaction of this type results in less intellectual stimulation of the child.

The most important aspect of intellectual growth is verbal communication. School learning is heavily dependent on language skills. Adults in middle-class homes use words freely and teach them to the child constantly, both indirectly and directly. Middle-class parents encourage their children to say words aloud, correct them when they apply words to the wrong objects or events, and reward them when they learn correct usages. This type of feedback, which is essential to the learning of language, is more readily available to relatively affluent children.[22]

As a child develops complex language patterns, he becomes more able to perceive aspects of his environment, to abstract relevant portions, and to commit them to memory. Through language he can grasp such important concepts as "past," "present," and "future." Symbols and their implications allow him to compare and differentiate material and nonmaterial cultural items. The ability to order and reorder the physical environment also allows him to change his self-conceptions. In other words the fundamental difference between human and animal behavior is that human beings can talk and animals cannot.

Self-Conception

Because they possess language and high intelligence, humans are able to think about their bodies, their behavior, and the impression they make on other persons. Only the human being is able to become an object to himself or herself. The notion of self grows out of interaction and communication with other persons. In short, the self is a social product. Three conditions are necessary for the formation of a self-concept. Charles Horton Cooley explained this process in his concept of "the looking-glass self": An individual gets a reflected view of herself from the actions of others toward her.[23] First the individual must imagine how she is judged by other persons around her. These judgments may be explicit, as when a teacher tells a student she is a terrible scholar; or they may be implicit, as when a student interprets her teacher's frown as a sign of disapproval.

The second condition for formation of a self-concept is the individual's ability to judge her reflection of self against a set of norms that she and others hold in reference to how she should behave and what characteristics she should have.

Finally, if she meets or exceeds these standards, she is likely to feel proud; if she does not, she is likely to feel ashamed. The social

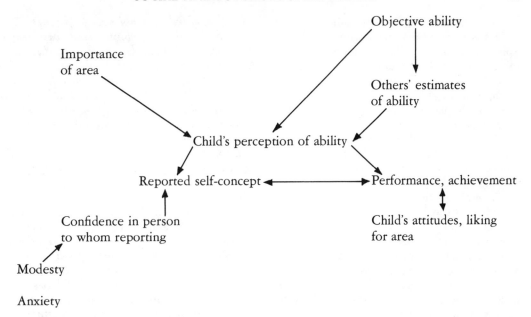

Figure 1. Factors Relating Children's Self-Concepts and School Achievements.

self therefore refers to the way a person views herself in relation to others and the way she perceives her role expectations and the roles of others. As might be expected, students in the classroom constantly seek to achieve positive feedback from their teachers.

Self-concept is the organization of qualities that the individual attributes to himself in varying situations.[24] An individual's behavior is largely determined by his pictures of himself. In reference to school, a student's behavior is largely determined by his academic self-conception. For example students who believe that they are weak, bad, or stupid will behave accordingly. Arthur T. Jersild has described such a situation:

When a person resists learning that may be beneficial to him he is, in effect, trying to protect or to shield an unhealthy condition. But more broadly speaking, he is not actually protecting something unhealthy as such; he is trying to safeguard his picture of himself, his self-concept, the illusions concerning himself which he has built and which give him trouble.[25]

In the early days of experimentation in education, much time and energy were devoted to seeking the best method of teaching. Implicit in this approach was the belief that what was learned was a direct consequence of what was taught. Only lately have educators begun to realize that method as such is only one variable in a complex learning pattern that has attitudinal as well as instructional determinants. In short, learning appears to be related to the learner's membership in various subgroups, her readiness to learn, and the degree of significance she perceives in the materials being presented. Recently another step has been taken in recognition of the relevance of the thoughts that students think about themselves—the self-concepts or self-images they have come to hold. The beginnings of this focus can be traced back to experiments in genetic, experimental, and clinical psychologies.

Internal dialogue that reflects the self-conception of students includes their questions:

What type of student am I?

How do I compare with other students?

What do other people think of me?

Answers to these questions affect both continuity of mental functioning and progressive personal development. Negative or positive responses tell students:

This is what I am.

This is how I compare with others.

This is what others think of me.

Specifically, for the child who wants to succeed in school, the school-task-related questions become:

Can I do it?

Am I adequate?

Do teachers like me?

What is school all about?

The thoughts of a once-reluctant student who managed to succeed might go as follows:

Can I do it?

The teachers think I can.

Perhaps I can.

I can!

How, one might ask, does the student develop a positive attitude toward school? In addition to receiving passing grades, she picks up verbal cues and physical gestures that, when decoded, mean "You can succeed." Consider the psychological impact of the following types of classroom prompting: "Well done." "Think this time." "Wrong again." "Let's look at this together." "You wouldn't understand." "Be careful." "Now isn't that a stupid question?" Test scores and the remarks of administrators and teachers cause children to think of themselves as being trustworthy, responsible, and competent, or unwanted, unattractive, and stupid. Eventually their behavior falls into line with their thinking.

Maturation

Certain motor behavior patterns are common in all children. Experimental evidence indicates that physical maturation determines the rate and pattern of mental growth. Little skill development is possible until the child has matured sufficiently to engage in a particular activity. Each child's developmental pattern is unique. The internal growth process of body organs and functions is called *maturation*. Specific organs do not function until minimum growth has taken place. For example a child does not walk until his or her legs and other parts that coordinate walking movements are able to function properly; a child does not learn to read until his or her nervous system has developed sufficiently for language capacity, eye control, ability to concentrate, and other related body functions.

Most of the tasks which we set for the child are complex activities combining many basic sensory-motor skills. If basic skills necessary to this complex of abilities are lacking, the total activity may break down. Consider the problem of laterality. If laterality is not established in the child and if the directionality resulting from laterality has not been developed, then certain relationships in space will be meaningless. . . . It is fruitless to attempt to teach the child the complex activities involved in reading as long as he continues to lack this basic skill. [26]

For many children, teachers may have to devise artificial means of providing additional practice in sensory-motor skills. This would include providing students with ladders to climb, fences to walk, or bicycles to ride. Improvements in these and related basic skills help children master the more complex activities of reading, writing, and arithmetic.

The age at which children are "ready" to read and write is determined by their developmental level—neuromuscular, physical, and intellectual—and by their earlier experiences. [27] Children with physical and social handicaps tend to be slower in learning school assignments, but all children tend to move in their learning from the concrete to the abstract. Therefore they should be actively involved with materials, substances, tools, and situations.

Piaget demonstrated that the very young child is easily and quickly confused by apparent changes in sizes of objects. [28] The preschool child has not yet learned some of the basic physical constants of his environment. That is, he does not know that the weight, volume, length, or quantity of objects remains constant despite changes in their shapes or the contexts in which they appear. Thus a three-year-old will acknowledge that two identical jars contain the same number of cookies, but if the cookies in one jar are emptied into a taller jar, he is likely to decide that the taller jar contains more cookies. His understanding of the concept is not yet stable and abstract.

Bruner emphasized four factors related to maturation: linguistic skills are best taught at an early age; mental growth is based not on gradual increases of associations or stimulus-response connections, but rather on sudden sharp rises and stops as certain capacities develop; children are in a state of readiness at an earlier age than previously had been thought; and the emphasis in education should be on skills and areas related to learning skills, with curriculum leading to self-reward sequences.[29] Bruner stressed the importance of children learning to learn in a nonlinear, or spiral, manner.

B. F. Skinner noted that grades, medals, diplomas, and other awards are reinforcers that facilitate learning.[30] Young children who succeed in playing games, solving puzzles, and building simple objects receive positive learning reinforcement. In short, an act of approval on the part of the teacher can, if repeated, lead to more complex forms of behavior. Teaching machines are based on this principle. For optimum learning to occur, furthermore, the process must minimize the threat of punishment.

Achievement Motivation

Student desires for better grades and higher test scores have very little relation to the types of tests administered or whether they are national tests. Personal achievement has multiple origins, including fear of failure, desire for social prestige, and anxiety created by parental pressures.[31] Social constraints or group definitions of acceptable behaviors, plus individual abilities, are the primary factors influencing a student's motivation for academic achievement. For some students achievement in school is an avenue to high prestige and social status. For others it is a sign of nonconformtiy.

At least four basic factors determine the level of achievement a student will accept.[32] First, each student must have an appraisal of her capacities and limitations. A student is likely to seek to become a scholar if she believes that it is within her capacity. But if she imagines herself to have extremely limited intellectual ability, she will not expect to become a Phi Beta Kappa.

Second, each student must be aware of what levels of achievement are possible. It is not enough to tell a student that she can achieve great heights. The specific criteria of achievement must be defined, for example an "A" average, the dean's list, the National Honor Society. To be meaningful achievement must relate to concrete goals that allow the student to evaluate her performances.

Third, each student must be prepared to experience success and failure. A highly motivated, successful student raises her goals higher and higher until she perceives that she has reached her full potential. Conversely, a poorly motivated, failing student progressively reduces her goals in order to protect herself against further failure. Consistent failures will cause her to drop out of school.

Finally, each student must have an acceptable position or status within her group. If her peer group encourages academic achievement, then she will try to get minimum passing or higher grades. A nonacademically oriented peer group will have a dampening effect on academic achievement. Motivation makes learning possible. If a student does not have academic achievement needs, she is not likely to perform well in scholastic tasks.

The activities of the teacher are, of course, important in sustaining or curtailing achievement motivation. Praise and blame, rewards and punishment, and rivalry are the major techniques used. Studies indicate that praise tends to stimulate average and below-average students but has less effect on superior students. Blame usually lowers the achievements of all students. Rewards and punishment, if not used properly, can be very ineffective. Punishment can breed antagonism, resentment, and avoidance of learning tasks to which it is attached, whereas rewards are most effective when they are commensurate with the performance. Rivalry between individuals is the least desirable technique for building the achievement motivation of low-performing students. Self-rivalry—competition with one's own records—tends to be the most efficient way to secure optimum effort from all students.

Most students have intrinsic motives for learning, such as satisfaction in the successful termination of an activity. They are attracted by curiosity to things that are unclear or unfinished. Rewards come from satisfying that curiosity. Other intrinsic motives for learning are the needs to achieve competence, to cope with the environment, and to be good at something. These drives are related to the need for approval by others. The student must feel that his or her needs are shared by the teacher and that they have common objectives. Obviously an understanding of childhood and adolescence gives valuable insight into motives for academic achievement.

DEVELOPMENT OF SOCIAL BEHAVIOR

Although social development begins slowly at birth, it is greatly accelerated during the preschool and elementary school years when a child's interaction with his or her peers becomes more frequent and intense. As preschool children grow older, demands for socialization cause them to spend less time in nonsocial, individualistic activities. They gradually learn to repress egocentric behaviors in favor of group-approved responses. The social-psychological processes of interaction through which the individual learns the habits, beliefs, values, and skills for effective group participation are known as *socialization*. As we shall see, the periods of socialization are overlapping. The major function of socialization is to transform an untrained human organism into an effective member of a society. The most important elements of socialization take place during childhood. In a complex modern society, the individual is subjected to many diverse socializing influences, many of which may not be consistent with one another.

Preschool Behaviors

Social conflicts tend to decrease and friendly interactions increase during *early childhood* (ages two through five), when children form their first friendships. The patterns of friendship change markedly with age changes. For example between the ages of two and three the number of friends increases; after this age the major change is in the closeness of attachment to a few peers.

A socially oriented and responsive preschool child seeks out companions and has a variety of contacts with them. In the course of learning the modes of social interaction, such a child has both satisfying and frustrating experiences, and consequently, exhibits social responses that seem to be contradictory. For example, preschool friends tend to argue more frequently with each other than children who rarely associate with one another.[33]

The very young child cannot play hide-and-seek because she cannot understand the concept of being hidden but yet present. Nor can she play simple games that involve taking turns and making choices because she cannot understand these concepts. Similarly she is unable to distinguish between reality and fantasy. Feeling extremely little in a world filled with big people, she is thrilled when she succeeds in controlling a situation or learning new concepts. Her gradually emerging sense of self binds her to her parents and immediate family members.

During this period varying modes of popularity and leadership patterns emerge. By the time they reach kindergarten, most children have a fairly definite idea of other children with whom they would like to play. Some children are constantly sought out by others for playmates; others are rejected and avoided by their peers. Some children quickly assume leadership roles; others are content to be followers. Obvious styles of leadership emerge: "statesmen" control others by using subtle, indirect techniques, whereas "bullies" use force to get others to obey them. The drift toward group activities is often threatened by what seems to be an endless number of minor conflicts. On the whole, however, the interactions of preschool children are characterized by cooperation and friendship.

Elementary School Behaviors

Unlike preschool friendships, which are casual, unstable, and transient, elementary school relationships become more intense, stable, and lasting. With the exception of his parents and perhaps some of his teachers, the child's closest friends are his agemates. Indeed his classmates are his most important socialization agents. Elementary school is the first group experience outside the home in which membership is mandatory for all children. This shift from rather informal home situations to formal group experiences may be the greatest shift in role expectation the child will ever encounter. Within a relatively short period of time he must learn to share the attention and supervision of one adult with unknown children and to respond to demands for conformity (e.g., take your seat, stay in line, put your paper away).

Middle childhood (ages six through twelve)

is dominated by "gang" activities. Gangs at this stage are usually informal groups with rapid turnover in membership. Middle-class children between the ages of ten and fourteen are likely to join highly structured, formal groups such as YMCA, YWCA, Boy Scouts, and Girl Scouts. The middle childhood period is the beginning of learning to play appropriate sex-roles. Differences in the behavior of men and women have some biological basis, of course, but they are largely produced by teaching appropriate role expectations to boys and girls. Despite women's liberation efforts, boys are taught not to be "sissies" and girls are conditioned not to be "tomboys." This delineation of sexual identity also leads to different reading and vocational interests. The importance of middle childhood can be underscored by noting that the child's choice of extracurricular games, dress, speech, and food are heavily influenced by peer choices during this period.

Preadolescence (ages ten through twelve) is characterized by many conditions, including a growth spurt, awakening sexuality, and (as noted above) an increase in peer group relationships. Except for infancy the body undergoes the most rapid changes in size and shape during this period. Children aged ten, eleven, and twelve begin to "look down on" little children. Along with these changes, the reproductive system starts to mature, causing sex-linked physical characteristics to begin to appear; girls develop obvious breasts and begin to produce feminine hormones; boys get more muscular and begin to produce masculine hormones. This is hardly the period of "latency" early psychologists imagined it to be.

During this period friends tend to resemble each other in social class, chronological age, physical maturity, and race. Racial and religious attitudes are developed. Studies indicate that attitudes toward children of various religious faiths develop more slowly than racial attitudes, largely because perceptual differentiations are more difficult to make on religious grounds. Seeking to conform to group expectations, children tend to echo their dislike for children of other religious or racial backgrounds. Protestant children, for example, ritualistically dislike Jewish children; white children dislike nonwhite children.

This is also the time, however, when positive contacts can alter prejudicial attitudes. Social values are transmitted both within and outside of the classroom, but the classroom influence is extremely important. In a classroom where social class, sex, racial, and religious intolerance are encouraged, intolerant children will result. The reverse, of course, is also true. Thus the behaviors of adolescents are conditioned by early childhood experiences.

Adolescent Behaviors

Adolescence has often been described as the impossible period between childhood and adulthood. And it is true that to a great extent adolescents are marginal people. Being denied many of the rights of either children or adults, they are nevertheless expected to fulfill many of the obligations of both groups—to remain obedient to their parents, to control their sex impulses, and still to select a vocation and otherwise begin to act as adults. This is a period in which young people need association with the opposite sex; they also need to evolve their own theory of life. Adolescents identify most strongly with their own peers and form cliques. Members of cliques usually come from the same racial and socioeconomic backgrounds, and therefore have much the same interests and social values. Cliques are dominant forces because they are based on personal compatibility, congeniality, and mutual admiration. College-bound youths, for example, tend to associate with other college-bound youths; high school dropouts tend to associate with others who are planning to drop out or who have dropped out.

The peer group gives rewards and punishments to its members on account of their moral behavior. Those who are honest, responsible, loyal, kind, and self-controlled tend to be rewarded. It is not moral qualities alone, however, that determine whether a child will be rewarded or punished by his peer group. Operating in addition to the moral qualities are such non-moral qualities as diffuse geniality, and skill in games, which sometimes overshadow the moral qualities in determining the status of a child in a peer group. In general, though, the forming of stable, positive relationships with the peer group is indicative of sound character development, while inability to make friends may indicate the opposite. [34]

Most adolescent groups reinforce and strengthen the values that members have acquired from their parents. In other words, peer groups are less originators than reinforcers of values and behaviors developed in the family. However, in some areas, such as dress and the use of slang, peer groups aid adolescents in achieving independence from adults. By sticking together and behaving alike, they are able to insulate themselves from outside pressures to abandon nonadult-conforming behaviors.

During the junior high or middle school years, girls and boys are noticeably different in their levels of biological and social maturity. Girls usually are quite advanced biologically and show considerable interest in the opposite sex, but their male agemates are less developed in both areas. This is especially true of eighth and ninth graders, among whom the girls have more problems centering on social life and heterosexual behavior than the boys do. Around the tenth grade boys begin catching up with girls in biological and social maturity. Dating then becomes a central concern for both sexes. Along with the problem of getting dates come issues involved in "making out," that is, issues raised by the necessity to define the outer limits of heterosexual and homosexual relationships. In general adolescent girls engage in much less premarital sexual intercourse than boys, but standards of acceptable sexual behavior vary with social class. For example studies indicate that masturbation is quite widely tolerated and practiced among middle-class boys, whereas sexual intercourse is a much more frequent outlet among lower-class boys.

Contrary to some opinions, most adolescents do not view their parents as unnecessary authoritarians. Rather they consider them as necessary teachers of moral and ethical values. Thus most adolescents grow up to behave like their parents in particular and like members of the larger society in general. In a recent study, Muzafer and Carolyn Sherif clearly demonstrated the extent to which all adolescents are affected by the values of middle-class-oriented adults:

There is one clear and striking generalization about the high school youth which holds in all areas and despite their differing backgrounds: Their values and goals earmark them all as youth exposed to the American ideology of success and wanting the tangible symbols of that success. There were no differences between the youth in different areas with respect to desires for material goods. In addition to comfortable housing, the symbols of success for these adolescents include a car in every garage, a telephone, television set, transistor radio, fashionable clothing, time to enjoy them, and money to provide them. It is obvious, however, that the present accessibility of these items differed enormously for youth in the different areas. . . .

Youth in areas of low, middle, and high rank did have different scales for evaluating success in a variety of activities essential to acquiring the desired standard of living. Their latitudes of acceptance differed even for the financial achievement necessary to support it. Relative to these latitudes of acceptance, and especially relative to their parents' accomplishments, school youth in low rank areas appear as more ambitious than those in high rank areas.

The differences in absolute level of goals in different activities are significant, but more striking are the differential opportunities available in the different areas for achieving these goals. . . . [35]

The significance of peer groups in relation to an adolescent living in rural poverty or an urban slum, his activities within a school situation, and his feelings about society are accentuated in school. For the lower-class student, school is a negative microcosm of the community; racial, academic, sex, and social segregation are commonplace. In any case, young adolescents tend to exhibit patterns of behavior that will be characteristic of them during their later adolescence and their adult life.

GOALS FOR PERSONAL DEVELOPMENT

This form is to help you think about various aspects of your relationships with other persons and your skills in group situations. It gives you a chance to set your own goals for development and measure your progress. The steps in using it are:

1. Read through the list of activities and decide which ones you are doing all right, which ones you should do more, and which ones you should do less. Mark each item in the appropriate place.

2. Some goals that are not listed may be more important to you than those listed. Write such goals on the blank lines.

3. Go back over the whole list and circle the numbers of three or four activities which you would like to improve at this time.

Communication skills	Doing all right	Need to do it more	Need to do it less
1. Amount of talking in class	☐	☐	☐
2. Being brief and concise	☐	☐	☐
3. Being forceful	☐	☐	☐
4. Drawing others out	☐	☐	☐
5. Listening alertly	☐	☐	☐
6. Thinking before I talk	☐	☐	☐
7. Keeping my remarks on the topic	☐	☐	☐
8. _____	☐	☐	☐

Observation skills			
1. Noting tension in groups	☐	☐	☐
2. Noting who talks to whom	☐	☐	☐
3. Noting interest level of class members	☐	☐	☐
4. Sensing feelings of individuals	☐	☐	☐
5. Noting who is being "left out"	☐	☐	☐
6. Noting reaction to my comments	☐	☐	☐
7. Noting when someone avoids a topic	☐	☐	☐
8. _____	☐	☐	☐

Problem-solving skills			
1. Stating problems or goals	☐	☐	☐
2. Asking for ideas, opinions	☐	☐	☐
3. Giving ideas	☐	☐	☐
4. Evaluating ideas critically	☐	☐	☐

	Doing all right	Need to do it more	Need to do it less
5. Summarizing discussion	☐	☐	☐
6. Clarifying issues	☐	☐	☐
7. _____	☐	☐	☐

Morale-building skills

1. Showing interest	☐	☐	☐
2. Working to keep people from being ignored	☐	☐	☐
3. Harmonizing, helping people reach agreement	☐	☐	☐
4. Reducing tension	☐	☐	☐
5. Upholding rights of individuals in the face of group pressure	☐	☐	☐
6. Expressing praise or appreciation	☐	☐	☐
7. _____	☐	☐	☐

Emotional expressiveness

1. Telling others what I feel	☐	☐	☐
2. Hiding my emotions	☐	☐	☐
3. Disagreeing openly	☐	☐	☐
4. Expressing warm feelings	☐	☐	☐
5. Expressing gratitude	☐	☐	☐
6. Being sarcastic	☐	☐	☐
7. _____	☐	☐	☐

Ability to face and accept emotional situations

1. Being able to face conflict and anger	☐	☐	☐

	Doing all right	Need to do it more	Need to do it less
2. Being able to face closeness and affection	☐	☐	☐
3. Being able to face disappointment	☐	☐	☐
4. Being able to stand silence	☐	☐	☐
5. Being able to stand tension	☐	☐	☐
6. _____	☐	☐	☐

Social relationships

	Doing all right	Need to do it more	Need to do it less
1. Competing to outdo others	☐	☐	☐
2. Acting dominant toward others	☐	☐	☐
3. Trusting others	☐	☐	☐
4. Being helpful	☐	☐	☐
5. Being protective	☐	☐	☐
6. Calling attention to oneself	☐	☐	☐
7. Being able to stand up for myself	☐	☐	☐
8. _____	☐	☐	☐

General

	Doing all right	Need to do it more	Need to do it less
1. Understanding why I do what I do (insight)	☐	☐	☐
2. Encouraging comments on my own behavior (feedback)	☐	☐	☐
3. Accepting help willingly	☐	☐	☐
4. Making my mind up firmly	☐	☐	☐
5. Criticizing myself	☐	☐	☐
6. Waiting patiently	☐	☐	☐
7. Reading and thinking alone	☐	☐	☐
8. _____	☐	☐	☐

ADDITIONAL READINGS

Battle, Jean A. *Culture and Education for the Contemporary World.* Columbus, Ohio, Charles E. Merrill, 1969.

Beck, Helen L. *Don't Push Me, I'm No Computer: How Pressures to "Achieve" Harm Pre-School Children.* New York, McGraw-Hill, 1973.

Bee, Helen L. *Social Issues in Developmental Psychology.* New York, Harper & Row, 1974.

Bloom, Benjamin S. *Human Characteristics and Social Learning.* New York, McGraw-Hill, 1976.

Brunk, Jason W. *Child and Adolescent Development.* New York, Wiley, 1975.

Butts, Robert F. *A Cultural History of Western Education: Its Social and Intellectual Foundations.* New York, McGraw-Hill, 1955.

Cass, John E. *The Role of the Teacher in the Nursery School.* New York, Pergamon Press, 1975.

Carnoy, Martin. *Education as Cultural Imperialism.* New York, David McKay, 1974.

Erikson, Erik H. *Childhood and Society.* New York, W. W. Norton, 1950.

Flinchum, Betty M. *Motor Development in Early Childhood: A Guide for Motor Education with Ages 2 to 6.* Saint Louis, Mosby, 1975.

Gilbert, Arthur. *Prime Time: Children's Early Learning Years.* New York, Citation Press, 1973.

Henderson, George. *To Live in Freedom: Human Relations Today and Tomorrow.* Norman, University of Oklahoma Press, 1972.

Hildebrand, Verna. *Introduction to Early Childhood Education.* 2d ed. New York, Macmillan, 1976.

Kushel, Gerald. *Fact and Folklore: Social and Psychological Foundations of Teaching.* New York, Wiley, 1974.

Landes, Ruth. *Culture in American Education: Anthropological Approaches to Minority and Dominant Groups in the Schools.* New York, Wiley, 1965.

Margolin, Edythe. *Young Children: Their Curriculum and Learning Processes.* New York, Macmillan, 1976.

Miller, Harry L. and Roger R. Woock. *Social Foundations of Urban Education*, 2d ed. Hinsdale, Ill., Dryden Press, 1973.

Piaget, Jean. *The Origins of Intelligence in Children.* New York, International University Press, 1952.

Reichart, Sandford. *Change and the Teacher: The Philosophy of Social Phenomenon.* New York, Crowell, 1969.

Sarason, Seymour B. *The Culture of the School and the Problem of Change.* Boston, Allyn & Bacon, 1972.

NOTES

1. Norman Cousins, *Modern Man is Obsolete* (New York, Viking Press, 1946), 8.

2. Peter F. Drucker, *Landmarks of Tomorrow* (New York, Harper & Row, 1959), ix.

3. R. F. Peck and R. J. Havighurst, *The Psychology of Character Development* (New York, John Wiley & Sons, 1960), 139.

4. Jean Jacques Rousseau, *Émile* (Trans. by Barbara Foxley, London, Dent, 1955), p 5.

5. See Ragan, *Modern Elementary Curriculum*, 166.

6. National Society for the Study of Education, *Child Psychology* (Chicago, University of Chicago Press, 1963).

7. Donald F. Cay, *Curriculum Design for Learning* (Indianapolis, Bobbs-Merrill, 1965).

8. For a more detailed analysis of this phenomenon see Margaret Mead, "The Generation Gap," *Science* (April 11, 1969).

9. John Dewey, *Democracy and Education* (New York, Macmillan, 1916), 101.

10. Henry Steele Commager, *Our Schools Have Kept Us Free* (Washington, D.C., National Education Association, 1962).

11. W. Lloyd Warner, Robert J. Havighurst, and Martin B. Loeb, *Who Shall Be Educated* (New York, Harper & Row, 1944), 19.

12. President's Commission on National Goals, *Goals for Americans* (Englewood Cliffs, N.J., Prentice-Hall, 1960), 3.

13. Harry L. Miller and Marjorie B. Smiley, *Education in the Metropolis* (New York, The Free Press, 1967), 13.

14. Robert M. Gagné, *The Conditions of Learning* (New York, Holt, Rinehart & Winston, 1965), 23.

15. See Ragan, *Modern Elementary Schools*, 50–57.

16. *Ibid.*, 58, 467–470.

17. Benjamin S. Bloom, *Stability and Change in Human Charateristics* (New York, John Wiley & Sons, 1964), 9–10.

18. Nathan Glazer, "The Puerto Ricans," in Miller and Smiley, *Education in the Metropolis*, 105.

19. Sophie L. Elam, "Acculturation and Learning Problems of Puerto Rican Children," in E. T. Keach, R. Fulton, and W. E. Gardner (eds.), *Education and Social Crisis* (New York, John Wiley & Sons, 1967), 232.

20. Arnold B. Cheyney, *Teaching Culturally Disadvantaged in the Elementary School* (Columbus, Ohio, Charles E. Merrill, 1967), 58.

21. See Warren R. Baller (ed.), *Readings in the*

Psychology of Human Growth and Development (New York, Holt, Rinehart & Winston, 1962), part III.

22. *Ibid.*

23. Charles H. Cooley, *Human Nature and the Social Order* (New York, Charles Scribner's Sons, 1902).

24. See Edon E. Snyder, "Self-Concept Theory: An Approach to Understanding Behavior of Disadvantaged Pupils," *Clearing House*, 40 (December, 1965), 242–246.

25. Arthur T. Jersild, *In Search of Self* (New York, Columbia University Teachers College, 1952), 114.

26. Newell C. Kephart, *The Slow Learner in the Classroom* (Columbus, Ohio, Charles E. Merrill, 1960), 32.

27. Evelyn Goodenough Pitcher et al., *Helping Young Children Learn* (Columbus, Ohio, Charles E. Merrill, 1966), 100.

28. Jean Piaget, *The Construction of Reality for the Child* (New York, Basic Books, 1954).

29. Jerome S. Bruner, *Toward a Theory of Instruction* (New York, Belknap, 1966).

30. B. F. Skinner, *Science and Human Behavior* (New York, Macmillan, 1953).

31. John W. McDavid and Herbert Harari, *Social Psychology: Individuals, Groups, Societies* (New York, Harper & Row, 1968), 60.

32. David Krech, Richard S. Crutchfield, and Egerton L. Ballachey, *Individual in Society* (New York, McGraw-Hill, 1963), 80–81.

33. Paul H. Mussen, *The Psychological Development of the Child* (Englewood Cliffs, N.J., Prentice-Hall, 1963), 88.

34. Peck and Havighurst, *Character Development*, 139.

35. Muzafer Sherif and Carolyn W. Sherif, *Reference Groups* (New York, Harper & Row, 1964), 199–221.

3.
COMMUNITY
FORCES

In this chapter we shall consider first what happens to the family during rural and urban revolutions. Then we shall discuss the changing economic foundations of education. Finally we shall discuss poverty.

Each year America becomes more urban. More than two-thirds of the population now live in urbanized areas. "Urbanization" is a complex and difficult process to define. The definitions given by a particular author are merely a way of categorizing a given community. There are, in short, no single best or innate definitions of "rural," "urban," and "urbanization." Even the United States censuses have periodically undergone official changes in definitions.

THE SHIFT FROM RURAL LIVING

Urban revolution, a term coined by V. Gordon Childe, refers to changes brought about by the great discoveries and inventions between 4000 and 3000 B.C.[1] The new trades and techniques demanded specialists, and once a person became specialized, he became dependent on other people. Another consequence of this revolution has been the growth of cities populated by nonproducers of food. *Rural revolution* refers to the changes villagers face during the process of becoming urban dwellers.[2] This revolution is the result of suddenly precipitated changes in styles of life affecting a considerable portion of a culture. One of the major problems during this transition is how to make life more satisfying for the remaining villagers while aiding the urban adjustment of the rural migrants. Technically the problem is how to assimilate great numbers of rural people into complex industrial communities. Modern cities, unlike the preindustrial ones, are dependent on extremely advanced technology and are extremely sensitive to malfunctions of many types. Furthermore, impersonal group interactions are becoming increasingly prevalent.

The migration of Americans from nonmetropolitan to metropolitan areas appears to have peaked. Between 1970 and 1974 only two of the largest metropolitan areas (Washington, D. C. and San Francisco-Oakland-San Jose) grew by as much as 3 per cent. Furthermore, the decline in the farm population dropped from 4.8 per cent per year in the 1960s to 1.8 per cent in the 1970s. The Mountain States and the South are gaining in population. More Blacks in particular are moving to the South, while fewer Blacks living in the South are moving to the North.

Changing Family Relationships

The shift of populations from the farm to the city has altered family members' relationships and activities. Instead of large, extended families that include many relatives, most urban families are isolated conjugal units, consisting only of husband, wife, and children. Other changes include the decline of male dominance and the rise in the importance of women; an increase in mobility, resulting in social distance between family members and less emphasis on a family homestead; and the transfer of work from the home to the factory, accompanied by money wages and specialization of labor.

The rural child shares in the work of the family and is given considerable responsibility at any early age; the urban child devotes most of his time and energy to play activities and is introduced to adult tasks and responsibility slowly and relatively late in childhood. In the semipatriarchal atmosphere of the rural home, the child is expected to be "seen and not heard," but generally the urban child is allowed more self-expression and in nonlower-class homes is a main participant in adult conversations.

Family settings differ greatly, then, in the following ways: (1) the demands for responsibility made on children, that is, the number and kinds of duties expected of them; (2) the emotionally positive behaviors of mothers to children, such as praise, absence of physical punishment, and general warmth; (3) the degree of control demanded over aggression toward peers both inside and outside the family; (4) the degree of aggression and obedience toward parents; (5) the extent to which the mother does the caretaking of babies; (6) the extent of her caretaking of older children; (7) the degree of the mother's emotional stability. . . . [3]

Since the skills needed in modern technology require extensive formal education, few parents can effectively train their children for economic roles. In most communities specialized agencies, mainly the school, provide better education for children than the family can. Some school districts, for example, have gradually expanded their elementary programs to include counselors who help young people solve their personal problems and select vocations. Elementary school counselors are able to give students a wide variety of information that is not available to the average parent. Indeed, much of this special information is needed to help the young person adjust to the complexities of urban life. Nevertheless, this type of assistance undermines the interdependence of parents and children.

The urbanization of great numbers of people also modifies the way they are housed. The shift away from single-family dwelling units with their surrounding yards, gardens, and sometimes even orchards or fields to smaller houses and yards and to apartments in large buildings restricts space for free movement for the entire family. Although urban children are taught to be quiet so that they will not disturb other families, their recreational activities are not easily confined to a small house or an apartment. There is little space for privacy or for development of hobbies, indoors or out. More disruptive strains on family life include divorce, desertion, and death. More than one million divorces—compared with two million marriages—are granted in America each year, causing some social scientists to project that the time is almost here when two out of every three marriages will end in divorce. (The divorce rate is higher among childless couples than among those with children.) In addition many marriages are ended by desertion or death.

It is interesting to note that the children who still live in rural America are becoming urbanized not merely through mail-order catalogs, newspapers, films, and television but also through the structure and programs of their schools. Rural public schools are imitating urban schools in their remedial programs, the content of their courses, their administrative organization, and their selection of personnel.

Functions of the Family

The modern family has relinquished some of its traditional functions and gained importance in others. The family has lost most of its economic production functions and is now mainly a unit of economic consumption. The protective functions have declined, giving way to institutions outside the home. The socialization function is being shared largely with the school. However, the family is still the primary agent in passing on social skills: The child is almost totally in the care of the parents during the first few years of life when the basic characteristics of personality are being formed. The sex-regulation and reproductive functions have shown little change; although norms are changing, sexual intercourse is still considered proper only within marriage, and every society depends primarily on the family for producing children. Child-bearing and child care also remain primary functions of the family. The status function continues, as families prepare children to retain their inherited social positions and, in some cases, to aspire to higher ones. A most important function is the affectional one; in general, this function of the family has increased.

Suburbia

The suburbs have been the most rapidly growing urban communities in the United States in the past two decades. Concurrent with the growth of the suburbs is a change in the ethnic and social class composition of the central city. The white urban middle classes who have moved to the suburbs have been largely replaced by Black, Chicano, and Puerto Rican migrants. About half the jobs in an urban area exist to meet needs that arise because of the presence of the urban dwellers. As people move to the suburbs, many jobs go with them. Industries also move outward when the central city ceases to be the only source of their labor supply. These changes have created acute problems for the central cities. Their tax bases have shrunk with the loss of industry, business, and middle-class homeowners; but demands for city services have not decreased proportionately.

Between 1970 and 1975, suburban areas gained 12.7 million persons; while losing 7.3 million. Thus during this period there was a net gain of 5.4 million persons in the suburbs. On the other hand, central cities lost 13 million persons and gained only 6 million—a net loss of 7 million persons. The average income of families who moved out of cities was higher than for families who moved to cities during this period. In some of the older suburbs adjacent to big cities—such as Detroit, Los Angeles, Atlanta, Chicago, and St. Louis—Blacks have become the majority.

What has happened to the central cities is now, in fact, occurring in many of the older suburbs and small cities. They too have begun to decay at the center as residents of old neighborhoods have moved out in search of more spacious, convenient, and prestigious places to live. Many urban poor whites are leapfrogging to the newer suburbs, where they settle near the centers of the communities; as they do, they frequently convert these neighborhoods into slums and semislums. A number of lower-class minority group people,

mainly Blacks, are waiting patiently for housing to open up in the suburbs.

It is often assumed that the flight of the middle class to the suburbs, urban sprawl, poor housing, racial hostility, and other urban problems exist chiefly in the large cities. Actually, studies have shown that these problems are sometimes found in a greater degree in the suburbs, which are often seething with unrecognized problems. The difference is that in the large cities there is national concern and protest about conditions that do not receive publicity in the suburbs. This can be explained partially by the existence of political forces, especially those in the large cities that are highly organized and have articulate special-interest constituencies, and by a larger number of problem-oriented professionals.

SOCIAL STRATIFICATION

An individual's socioeconomic status determines his or her peer, school, and community contacts. Socioeconomic status is a broad concept; it encompasses not only social class but also education, occupation, income and several other factors. *Low socioeconomic status* describes a consistent pattern of life: low level of education, unskilled or semiskilled work, small income, and living in a poor residential area. (*High socioeconomic status* of course means that all the elements are reversed.)

Determinants of Social Class

A child's social class is defined by the position the parents hold in society. From before birth until after death an individual's opportunities and rewards are affected by class position. Social stratification is a condition in which a mass society is differentiated by layer upon layer of population qualities. A *stratified society* has been defined as "one in which the population has been separated into categories that are unequal in social evaluation. The greater the inequality among categories or the less the likelihood of their becoming equal, the more highly stratified the society is said to be."[4] People can be stratified according to any quality that is recognized by members of the society. That is, before groups of people can be said to be unequal they must have in common

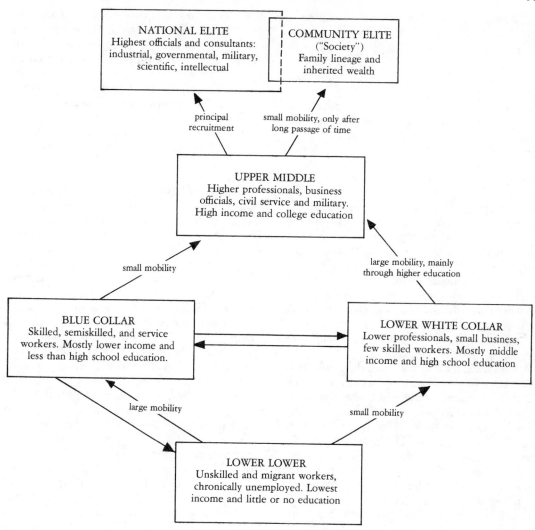

Figure 2. Stratification and Generational Mobility in the United States.

SOURCE: Leonard Broom and Philip Selznick, *Sociology*, 3d ed. (New York, Harper, 1963), Fig. VI:13, p. 214. Reprinted by permission.

some property or factor that can be differentiated. Therefore when a society is said to be stratified, it is so in terms of a referent—a factor in each stratum that can be graded either by some type of measurement or by judgment. The major dimensions that underline the American social class structure are prestige, occupation, possessions or income, class consciousness, value orientations, and power.

The terms "social stratum" and "social class" are in most cases synonymous. Harold L. Hodgkinson defines social class as any group

of people who feel socially involved with one another and who feel that in some way they are different from others who are not members of the group.[5] W. Lloyd Warner is as responsible as anyone for stimulating research into social class in America.[6] His six-fold scale of class strata—upper-upper, lower-upper, upper-middle, lower-middle, upper-lower, lower-lower—has become much used in both scientific and nonscientific contexts.

Although rural areas do not lack social class features, it is in the city where the class system appears in its most elaborate form, where social status implies extreme differences in "cultural" appreciation and in political and economic opportunities. Even though no single, objective criterion determines class status, above average income tends to remove a person from the lowest level. But upper-class people sometimes have relatively low incomes; conversely, some persons with high incomes are excluded from the upper classes (e.g., known criminals). In the United States occupation is the most important source of status.

An individual's social status can change for better or for worse. *Social mobility* refers to the movement of people between positions. Loss of status (*downward mobility*) usually comes about through improper behavior, that is, by acts that do not conform to the code of a social class. Movements up the status ladder (*upward mobility*) usually result from achievement. A rise from the top of lower class to the bottom of middle class is the least difficult upward move.

A high school education and the acquisition of certain social and employment skills are the usual prerequisites to securing a lower-middle class position. To move from the lower-middle to the upper-middle class is much more difficult, since increased ability may not result in social mobility. Upper-middle class positions are awarded in competition where factors other than ability (whom you know, not necessarily what you know) play a decisive role. Equally important is the fact that in many instances the number of applicants exceeds the number of available positions. The number of available positions decreases toward the top of the social class pyramid, but so too does the number of qualified competitors.

Effects of Social Class

We have noted that social class is mainly inherited (*ascribed status*). Even in the most mobile society, change in ascribed status is rarer than its retention. The opportunities for rising to a higher class through selective competition (*achieved status*) are limited. Effective family control over opportunities excludes most nonfamily-member competitors who have different racial, religious, or ethnic characteristics. Children of a high social class, for example, have a distinct advantage over outsiders: They are adequately prepared to move into the positions held by their parents. Access to formal education is clearly related to social class. The upper groups enjoy better educational facilities that permit them to develop their innate abilities. Social class is a nearly irreversible determinant of success in the competition for education and jobs.

August B. Hollingshead, studying the relation between adolescents' social behavior and their class position, found that upper- and middle-class children are taught not to be aggressive, to have "good" manners, to study hard, to attend Sunday School, and to avoid making friends with lower-class children.[7] In contrast, the child in the lower class learns that she and her family are held in contempt by boys and girls in the higher classes. Frequently she comes to resent her family and her dependence upon it for food, money, clothing, and shelter. Hollingshead concluded that social class values and patterns of behavior learned in family and surrounding neighborhood subcultures not only provide the stage upon which the child acts but also provide her with ways of acting and of defining the action.

As the child participates in various social situations, she learns to act in certain ways, to regard herself either as a valued member of the group or as an unwanted participant. The social class of an individual greatly limits her way of eating, what she wears, her choice of friends, selection of occupation, types of recreation, use of money, and conceptions of right and wrong. Hodgkinson noted that child-rearing practices also differ between middle- and lower-class families.[8] Fewer middle-class children are breast fed, and they are weaned earlier from either bottle or breast. Lower-class families are more lenient in their training and in their demands that a child assume responsibility. Some social scientists believe—with a large body of data for substantiation—that whether one is consciously aware of it or not, his or her every activity, no matter how independent he or she may feel, is greatly influenced and conditioned by early childhood training, growth, and development.

DOMINANT TRENDS IN AMERICAN LIFE

We have discussed two broad aspects of American life: the shift from rural to urban living and social stratification. We now turn to some of the dominant trends in life in this country that are directly related to urban living and social classes.

The Labor Force

In 1900 more than 6 in 10 boys and 1 in 10 girls aged 14 to 19 were in the labor force. Today children have ceased to be an important part of the labor force. They no longer have a credit value in the family economy; instead, they are considered expensive deficits who must be totally cared for. Also families have fewer children today than in 1900. In 1975 the average size of the family was 3.5; in 1890 it was 4.5; and in 1790 it was 5.4. Women have replaced children in the labor force: In 1975 they became 46 per cent of it. This trend partially reflects rising consumption standards which demand more money than many husbands can earn.

The nonwhite labor force, largely Black, differs greatly from the white labor force in age, sex, educational, and employment characteristics. Unemployment and underemployment are consistently higher among nonwhites. Although nonwhite representation is increasing in both white collar and blue collar jobs, the largest gains are in manual and lower white collar jobs. It may be wise to consider lower-class whites as a group separate from but somewhat similar to lower-class nonwhites. Certainly both groups have low socioeconomic status. Yet largely because of their skin color, upwardly mobile whites are able to disappear into white middle-class cultures, whereas most upwardly aspiring nonwhites are unable to do so.

Another point bearing closer analysis when comparing unemployed and underemployed whites and nonwhites is the weaker psychological rationalization now available to nonwhites, whereas rationalization has become somewhat easier for poor whites. In the past nonwhites could more easily justify their lack of income by pointing to conditions of discrimination and segregation than could lower-class whites. Recent civil rights gains have narrowed the opportunity gap between lower-class whites and nonwhites, removing some of the discrimination against nonwhites but at the same time causing many lower-class whites to feel discriminated against.

Styles of Life

The average American family today has four times the income of the average family in 1900. (The difference is less when adjusted for changes in the value of money.) Along with this increase has come more money for luxuries and recreation. Considerably more of the average family's budget is spent on leisure-time activities; in fact, nearly 5 per cent of Americans' personal income after taxes is spent on recreation and recreational equipment. One in 10 Americans, however, does not share in this mass leisure. This group is so poverty-stricken that they cannot even be called relatively deprived—they are completely deprived. In the mass media, school textbooks, and other contacts poverty-stricken people learn how the more fortunate live; the contrast with their own existence confirms their plight. Low-income children growing up under these conditions are not the bright-eyed, enthusiastic scholars children from affluent or comfortable backgrounds are likely to be.

Education as a humanization process includes learning certain social roles that allow for satisfactory cultural adjustments. As an individual changes culture, he often changes his social role. This type of adjustment begins at birth and ends at death. Therefore, education for social adjustments is not a process in which an individual participates for the first time on entering school. His family, peer groups, mass media, and all of the other informal and formal units of interpersonal behavior are vital parts of the education process. In terms of compulsory attendance, the role of the school is very significant in the total socialization process.

We might quite logically expect formal education systems in America to epitomize *democratic education*: "Democratic education recognizes as its enduring purpose the fullest development of the individual within the framework of society."[9] This ideal, however, is seldom attained in practice. Indeed, most schools perpetuate rather than ameliorate the cultural differences between the poor and the affluent. Cultural differences show up significantly in articulation of vowels, complexity of remarks and vocabulary, and recognition of words. According to one authority, the cognitive style of the deprived child is typically:

1. *Physical and visual rather than aural.*

2. *Content-centered rather than form-centered.*
3. *Externally oriented rather than introspective.*
4. *Problem-centered rather than abstract-centered.*
5. *Inductive rather than deductive.*
6. *Spatial rather than temporal.*
7. *Slow, careful, patient, perserving (in areas of importance), rather than quick, clever, facile, flexible.*[10]

Preschool experiences determine a child's readiness for middle-class-oriented education experiences. Few low-income students are given the readiness at home that will allow them to succeed in school. Equally important is the fact that the low-income child is likely not only to have lower verbal achievement and educational aspirations but also to attend school where most of the students reflect similar low achievement and aspirations. The slum school climate, therefore, is conducive to perpetuating cultures of poverty. Furthermore, because the low income child remains isolated from the mainstream of life in the dominant society, the world of the school is inexplicable to him. This alien world usually clashes with his values; certainly it fails to open up new vistas of the American dream of equal opportunity.

Social Importance of Education

Even though fewer individuals today amass great fortunes than was common in the nineteenth century, research indicates that there is as much economic opportunity in this country today as there was a century ago. But the ability to take advantage of economic opportunity is based to a great extent on education. This is especially true in the technical and service professions, which have grown at a rate that far exceeds the growth in population. The number of executive positions, for example, is increasing so rapidly that the number of children born into middle-class families does not meet the need. As a result some of these positions will be filled by people from the lower class.

Education has become the main road to technical and professional occupations. A college education is necessary for most upper-middle-class occupations, and a high school education is required for lower-middle-class occupations, such as clerical, sales, and technical jobs. The amount of education, in other words, is a good indicator of an individual's potential for achieving a particular socioeconomic status. At least it serves as a variable that affects other factors such as choice of occupation, spouse, and place of residence.

Social class and education interact in at least two ways. First, to get a higher education takes money plus motivation. Upper-class youths have money; they also have family tradition and social encouragement. The upper-class or upper-middle-class youth asks, "What college are you going to?" Lower-middle-class and perhaps upper-lower-class youths ask one another, "What will you do after graduation?" The lower-lower-class youth asks, "How soon can I quit school?" Second, one's amount and kind of education affect the class rank he will secure. Education is one of the main levers of the ambitious. Higher education brings not only occupational skill but also changes in tastes, interests, goals, etiquette, speech—in one's total way of life.[11]

Although family background is a criterion for securing upper-upper-class status, education is an adequate substitute for family background at the intermediate social class levels. Social class determines life opportunities, affects personality development, influences social participation, and assigns responsibilities and privileges. Many differences commonly attributed to race, religion, and ethnic group are actually social class differences. For example there are fewer differences in life styles between middle-class Blacks and middle-class whites than most people imagine.

POVERTY

Poverty is characterized by conditions of not enough—not enough money, food, clothes, adequate housing, prestige, or hope. Generally, when affluent people go without soap, hot water, light, food, medicine, and recreation it is because they elect to do so. When poverty-stricken people go without these items, it is usually because they have no choice. Therein lies a major difference between the poor and the affluent. The former is controlled by the economic system and the latter controls the economic system.

Poverty has a familiar smell—a smell of rotting garbage and sour foods. It is the smell of children's urine and unwashed bodies. Above all else it is the smell of people wasting away physically, socially, and psychologically. Urban poverty is much more visible than rural poverty. Dilapidated buildings, garbage-strewn alleys, and rats are all too often the dominant characteristics of urban slums. These conditions tend to blur the memory of clean, wellkept buildings which also characterize many urban poor neighborhoods. While it is difficult to change the negative image of the urban slum, it is almost impossible to erase the idyllic picture of rural poverty.

Tourists driving through the countryside are likely to define the blight they see as "quaint," "picturesque," or "Americana." Nearly 40 per cent of rural Americans are poverty-stricken. In some rural communities, welfare has become a way of life. Small children grow up aspiring not to finish high school but, instead, to get their own welfare case number.

In terms of life-styles, there is much similarity between the so-called city slickers and country bumpkins. Both share and are influenced by the products of urbanization. Both have been enculturated in a country that has a strong rural bias against cities.

Rural Communities

The words "urban" and "rural" represent a continuum along which types of communities are not always clearly distinguished. The criterion of size—less than 2,500 people—is hardly an adequate indication of what life is like in a rural community. Villages are much like towns, towns shade into cities, and cities into metropolitan regions. Rural isolation and its concomitant social characteristics that were found in abundance at the beginning of the nineteenth century have all but disappeared. There are still a few semi-isolated rural communities (most of them marked by extreme poverty), but as a whole urban and rural communities do not represent totally different localities. In a real sense the entire American population is urban.

Rural people—one-fourth of the nation's population—can be divided into two groups: those living in the open country and those living in villages. Farmers who live on and produce from the land make up the bulk of the opencountry (rural-farm) group. Also included in this category are nonfarming people—ministers, livestock truckers, creamery operators—whose primary social and business associations are with farmers and village residents. Even though some villages may have manufacturing plants, their major source of wealth can be traced to an interdependent relationship with the farming periphery. There are no completely independent communities.

In rural communities people are surrounded by nature and are more likely to work out of doors with animals and machines. Children play freely with natural play materials such as earth, flowers, rocks, and branches of trees. In addition, they can run, climb, jump, and swim without constantly being stopped by fences, buildings, and traffic.

Although 25 per cent of Americans live in rural areas, less than one-fourth of them earn their livelihood from agriculture. Over three-fourths of the rural residents have nonfarm employment—a tenth of the United States labor force produces all of the country's food.

The average successful farm represents an investment of more than $90,000 in land, building, and machinery. Lacking this kind of money for investment, one-fourth of all farmers are small, marginal businessmen and businesswomen who gross less than $6,000 per year. While the per capita farm income has been increasing, it does not approximate that of nonfarm groups. Three-fifths of the farm poor are too old, too inadequately educated, or too handicapped to transfer to other occupations, even if provided job retraining. As they retire or move away, their lands are added to other farms. This accounts for the fact that each year the number of farmers decreases, while the average size of farms increases.

The largest number of rural poor are concentrated in the Appalachian regions; the Ozark and Ouachita Mountain areas of Missouri, Arkansas, and Oklahoma; the northern counties of Minnesota, Wisconsin, and Michigan; northern New England; and the Delta and Piedmont area in the South.

Rural areas lag behind urban areas in structural adequacy of housing. The 1970 census revealed that more than 80 per cent of the urban residents lived in structurally sound houses with complete plumbing, while less than 60 per cent of rural residents had equally good housing. Even though rural areas accounted for approximately 30 per cent of all housing units, nearly half the units lacked structural soundness or complete plumbing. Thirty per cent of the rural homes had complete baths compared with 97 per cent of urban homes. Over 20 per cent of the rural homes did not have running water, while only one per cent of the urban homes lacked running water. Nearly one out of every five rural homes did not have both hot and cold running water compared with nineteen out of twenty urban homes that had both.

Other housing disparities can be found in the number of consumer goods—televisions, telephones, and automobiles—owned by rural and urban residents. Although the lack of certain consumer goods such as televisions and automobiles does not mean families are impoverished, it does indicate that most rural families have not achieved a level of living comparable to most urban families. Yet there are five urban poor persons for every three rural poor. Both central cities and rural areas share the distinction of having the highest proportions of males fourteen years or over in the labor force, and the highest unemployment rates. It seems that moving from the farm to the central city merely changes the location of the unemployment. Migrant workers epitomize the plight of poverty-stricken Americans.

Migrant workers. Hispanics comprise approximately 70 per cent of the more than 500,000 migrant workers, each of whom earns less than $2,500 per year. Life for migrants is seasonal: a day here, a week there. For example, migrants pick citrus fruits in California and Florida, beans and tomatoes in Texas, cherries and blueberries in Michigan, sugar beets in Kansas, cucumbers in South Carolina, and potatoes in Idaho and Maine.

They almost always sleep in dilapidated structures that lack adequate heat, refrigeration, and sanitary facilities. They play in garbage-strewn grounds and drink polluted water. Communites in which migrants work tend to lack even minimally adequate medical care and health services. Most migrants and their families are infected with intestinal para-

sites, have chronic skin infections and dental problems, and many have chronically infected ears that can result in partial deafness.

It is not unusual for a migrant child to attend schools in three or more states during a single school year. Thus a major problem for the public schools is the correct placement of migrant children. Without adequate data, most schools do little to provide a top quality education for migrant children. Ninety per cent of the more than one million children in migrant families never enter high school, and only 10 per cent of those who do graduate. Most migrant children drop out of school after fourth or fifth grade and join their parents and relatives in the fields.

In 1966 Congress recognized the special needs of children of migratory workers by passing an amendment (Public Law 89–750) to Title I of the Elementary and Secondary Education Act of 1965 (ESEA). Specifically, Public Law 89–750 gives the U.S. Office of Education authority and funds to improve educational programs and to offer supplementary services for migrant children. In 1974 Congress passed Public Law 93–380 which extended the migrant program to include children of migratory fishermen. Health care (medical examinations and treatment), nutrition (free meals), psychological services, and prevocational training and counseling comprise the major thrust of the migrant children program.

The Migrant Student Record Transfer System (MSRTS), which is located in Little Rock, Arkansas, collects and stores in its computers the academic records of migrant children. MSRTS is able to disseminate its information within twenty-four hours to any school system with connecting computer terminals. This service allows concerned school districts to place their migrant enrollees better.

Federal funding for migrant education increased from $9.5 million in 1967 to $145 million in 1977. Even so, most migrant students are three to four years behind their age mates in school achievement.

The migrant poor have become a nagging conscience for America. As long as large numbers of Americans live in abject poverty, our bragging about technological excellence rings hollow. In our affluence poverty is a bitter irony. Critics of capitalism chide the United States for being able to send the first men to the moon, discover medical cures for perennial diseases, and produce the most cars, but fail to abolish poverty. Because the norm is affluence, to be poor in America is to be one of the most economically deprived persons in the world.

Urban Communities

Because of distinctive patterns of growth, many large cities consist of three separate cities within one: an "old" city, a "middle-aged" city, and a "new" city.[12]

Old city. Built before community building codes and zoning regulations, most of the structures in this area originally did not have modern plumbing, lighting, or heating facilities. Houses with wooden foundation posts and narrow (thirty feet) lots add to the irregularity of the streets; industrial and commercial establishments are scattered capriciously throughout residential neighborhoods. The majority of old city residents live in dilapidated, insect- and rodent-invested multiple-family dwellings. Streets are congested and parking space is insufficient; school and recreation facilities are inadequate. This area is occupied by predominantly low-income whites and nonwhites, with the majority being nonwhite. Old city is sometimes referred to as inner-city. (Diminishing energy sources are causing many cities to rebuild the inner-city in hopes of luring commuters back as permanent residents.)

Middle-aged city. Most of the structures in this area were built under some kind of building code and are physically sound. Yet as in the old city, most of the buildings—mainly multiple-dwelling units—were built on narrow lots (many with less than six feet of yard space between them). By comparison, middle-aged city is better developed than old city. However, it too is characterized by congested streets, insufficient parking space, and inadequate education and recreation facilities. Middle-aged city is occupied by predominantly lower-middle-income whites and nonwhites, with the majority being nonwhite. As this area undergoes racial and economic changes, it usually becomes a part of the inner city.

New city. Built after 1930 under both building and zoning codes, most of the structures in the new city are in very good repair. Nearest to the suburbs, this area is primarily a single-family residential district. Compared with the old and middle-aged cities, the new city has larger lots, fewer congested streets, and more nearly adequate recreation and school facilities. This area is occupied by predominantly upper-middle-income white residents.

Since 1950 many urban neighborhoods have seen a large exodus of white residents, along with a still larger in-migration of nonwhites, especially Blacks. Sociologists call this phenomenon an *ecological invasion*. But more than racial composition is changing in the cities. Mainly because of urban renewal and state highway expansions, urban neighborhoods are changing from middle-class white to middle-class nonwhite to lower-class nonwhite. As middle-aged city neighborhoods change in occupancy to lower-class residents, large and structurally sound single-family dwellings are converted to multiple-family uses. Soon they too begin to deteriorate. Maintenance (plumbing, wiring, heating, plaster, and painting) is generally neglected. Renters blame the slum landlords; the landlords blame the renters. Most frequently landlords fail to comply with city property maintenance regulations. On the other hand, when landlords do attempt to prevent their properties from deteriorating, their efforts often are negated by tenants who fail to maintain the premises. Along with the physical changes go an increase in adult and juvenile crime rates and changes in such interrelated factors as unemployment and underemployment, school dropouts, population per household, and number of broken homes.

Public housing projects are being built in an effort to alleviate slum conditions. Critics of public housing contend that these projects correct only the physical aspects of slums; they replace the blight with new landscaping and architecture, but the major problem, the slum-dwellers themselves, remains unaffected. When this happens, a massive public housing project is, in effect, merely transferring a slum environment from, say, twenty square blocks to twenty stories. In fact, federally sponsored housing programs intensify concentrations of the poor within the central cities. Fortunately the trend is away from large public housing projects and toward scattered-

site housing, consisting of single family and
duplex dwellings for the poor.

Negative Life Themes

A major disadvantage of being poverty-
stricken is the negative definition that individuals, whatever their incomes, attach to poverty. The words to the song "Dead-End Street"
are only too well understood by many of the
poor:

They say this a big rich town,
But I live in the poorest part.
I know I'm on a dead-end street
In a city without a heart.

I learned to fight before I was six—
The only way I could get along.
When You're raised on a dead-end street
You've gotta be tough and strong.

All the guys go get in trouble—
That's how it's always been.
When the odds are all against you,
How can you win?

The song accurately reflects the despair, lone-
liness, and cynicism of the slums—the cultural
and social impoverishment that comes from
economic deprivation. Children who grow up
in such an atmosphere in turn become unskilled and unemployed adults. Thus the cycle
of poverty continually renews itself.

Out of poverty comes insecurity. Prolonged
conditions of insecurity lead to feelings of
alienation. These anomic aspects of alienation shown in the beliefs of the poor have been
described. The individual believes that (1)
community leaders are indifferent to and detached from his needs, (2) his social conditions
and those of people like him are getting progressively worse, (3) life is meaningless, and
(4) his immediate circle of relationships is not
comfortable or supportive.[13] The life themes
of the poor also include a preference for
fatalism and an orientation to the present.
Feeling helpless in an unpredictable world, the
poor resort to a live for today philosophy that
leaves little room for projecting long-range
goals such as completing educational courses.
Dropping out of school and getting a job seem
to make more sense to them.

Defeatist attitudes partially explain why the
poor pay more for consumer goods. Rather

than shop around for bargains, they pay more
not only for their few luxuries but also for their
necessities—housing, food, clothing. Neighborhood merchants realize large profits by
offering slum dwellers credit for goods that
have high marks-ups and hidden installment,
finance, and service charges. As for the programs that do enable the poor to save
money—for example public housing, surplus
goods, food stamps, free legal aid—many
poverty-stricken people do not make use of
them. Bureaucratic red tape and social workers frighten them, and the means test used in
determining the need for public aid is often
degrading or time-consuming or both.

Within the perspective of middle-class rewards and punishments, it is economically bad
to be poor and it is socially bad to be a member of a racial minority group. There are
ample studies to support the contention that
poverty-stricken minority-group people are
by far the most economically and socially disadvantaged.

What about all the social-action programs
that have been initiated? Minority groups have
made gains, of course, but even the most ardent supporters of the programs admit that so
far the improvements in employment, housing, and education have been almost entirely
limited to lower-middle-income minorities.
Many informed people believe it will be a
number of years before significant gains begin
to filter down to poverty-stricken minority
groups. Indeed our antipoverty efforts have
been more successful in recruiting previously
underemployed slum-dwellers. It is depress-
ingly apparent that the vicious circle of inferior education, low-paying jobs, and segregated neighborhoods (difficult enough for racial minorities to get out of) is becoming even
more difficult to escape. Racial ghettos are
inexorably expanding, and public schools are
inexorably becoming more segregated.

Blacks

Seldom have writers been able to capture the
feeling of life from the Black person's viewpoint as objectively but sensitively as Whitney
M. Young, Jr., in *To Be Equal*.[14] The Black
child begins life with much higher odds against
him. He is more likely to die in infancy than
the white baby. If the Black baby lives, the
chances of losing his mother in childbirth are

relatively high; the maternal mortality rate is four times as high as for white mothers. The Black baby is born into a family that lives in the inner city (over 70 percent of the Black population does), usually in the Black ghetto. It is a family that is larger than its white counterpart, and it is crowded into housing that is dilapidated—quarters structurally unsound or unable to keep out cold, rain, snow, rats, or pests. With more mouths to feed, more babies to clothe, and more needs to satisfy, the Black family is forced to exist on a median family income of barely half the median white family income. When the Black youngster goes to school, he is usually aware that he is starting down a path that has proved no avenue to adequate living, much less to fame or fortune. And because Black children are generally taught in slum schools, usually with inferior teachers, equipment, and facilities, the real gap between Black and white students of the same age often approaches five or six years.

Most Blacks look at all these conditions, but not all of them see the same social implications. For some the conditions require a change; for others the status quo is fine. The conflicts that center on color do not lead to a single response: Many Blacks withdraw, others clown, others assume proud mannerisms, and still others become aggressive or highly suspicious of nonblacks. Those who run to a pride in blackness do not find Utopia. Once inside the winner's circle of blackness, a veil of racial discrimination seems to enshroud both the light-skinned and the dark-skinned "victors." This invisible veil, as Ralph Ellison pointed out, is not physical invisibility:

That invisibility to which I refer occurs because of a peculiar disposition of the eyes of those with whom I come in contact. A matter of the construction of their inner eyes, those eyes with which they look through their physical eyes upon reality. . . . It is sometimes advantageous to be unseen, although it is most often rather wearing on the nerves. . . . You ache with the need to convince yourself that you do exist in the real world, that you're a part of all the sound and anguish, and you strike out with your fists, you curse and you swear to make them recognize you. And, alas, it's seldom successful.[15]

In most communities heavily populated by Blacks, low- and middle-income groups live in extremely close proximity to each other. This situation is not caused primarily by a natural selection process but by *de facto* housing segregation. Consequently, the plight of poverty-stricken Blacks is distorted if only census data are considered. Black "haves" appear less affluent and the "have nots" seem less disadvantaged than they actually are. There is, in short, a much wider gap between Black middle and lower classes than is apparent. Both groups closely approximate their white counterparts in income and living styles.

Now let us consider the fact that most Blacks are marginal in the dominant white culture.[16] Add to this disadvantage by making them marginal compared with their white socioeconomic counterparts. Finally, make poverty-stricken Blacks marginal compared with surrounding middle-income Blacks. When all these facts coalesce, one will have a picture of poverty-stricken Blacks—a minority group within a minority group. Marginality therefore is characterized by the following conditions: (1) There must be a situation that places two cultures (or subcultures) in lasting contact. (2) One culture must be dominant in terms of power and reward potential. This is the nonmarginal of the two cultures; its members are not particularly influenced by or attracted to the marginal culture. (3) The boundaries between the two cultures are sufficiently defined for the members of the marginal culture to internalize the patterns of the dominant group and not be satisfied with the "inferior" group. Although not all poverty-stricken Blacks are marginal people, many exhibit marginal characteristics, such as high juvenile delinquency and adult crime rates. It is likely that those who are marginal have become victims of aspirations that they will never achieve and hopes that they will never satisfy. (See, for example, the Appendix.)

Whites

Investigation of the nature of urban communities, has made evident the existence of a substantial poverty-stricken white population. A large number of the urban poor whites came from the rural Appalachian mountain areas of Kentucky, Tennessee, West Virginia, Arkansas, Georgia, and Alabama.[17] For years the emigration rate from these states to other parts of the country has been very high. During the 1950s, 1.5 million people left the Appalachians; most of whom became economically secure. Like their Black counterparts, they moved to northern cities primarily for economic reasons. They were attracted by the growing northern industries as contrasted with a comparatively stagnant southern economy.

Most studies indicate that the southern whites moved to urban communities in order to improve their economic conditions, but recent documentation of those who failed to achieve middle classness illustrates a seemingly low respect for money. A few writers have observed the lower-class southern white's lack of commitment to the thrift theme that permeates our country's basic middle-class orientation. They usually do not put anything away for a rainy day. Money for them appears to be inordinately easy come and easier to go. Mountain people usually return "home" not because they have accumulated enough money to buy a small farm or business but, instead, because they are broke. Home is the migrant's place of origin in the South; home folks are those with similar rural backgrounds.

Primary group relationships.   The southern migrant brings to the city rural culture patterns vastly different from those found in urban communities. Often the migrant's behavior is so different from that of indigenous urban residents that conflict rather than assimilation is the dominant pattern of adjustment. Both groups, when thrown into sudden contact, have been known to experience severe *culture shock*;[18] that is, they are unprepared to interact in a positive manner with members of the other culture.

The central focus of Appalachian whites is the family. Having strong family and kinship ties, they often practice voluntary segregation in the urban place of residence. Family cohesiveness is a shield against the large, overpowering, and impersonal city. Clustering together gives southern white migrants a sense of protection against the many disorganizing experiences rural newcomers find in big cities. This voluntary togetherness provides an outlet for their basic needs for recognition, affection, and security.

Both objective research and subjective novels reveal a harsh, authoritarian relationship between the father and children in low-income southern white families.[19] Out of this relationship come awe and fear, but seldom love. Traditionally, the father is the disciplinarian and the mother is the emotional (love) center of the Appalachian family. But as more mothers find employment ouside the home, these roles are being filled by parent surrogates.

Health conditions.   Except during religious services, southern whites normally do not openly express fear, pain, or hardship. This suppression of emotions causes some observers mistakenly to stereotype mountain people as having an unlimited amount of strength and patience. In reality they have a very limiting set of folkways. Taught not to express fear or pain and believing that illness is quite unavoidable, poor whites—like poor nonwhites—fail to take preventive health measures or use health-care social agencies. Low-income mothers, for example, are not likely to have their children immunized in free health programs; the mothers themselves do not take advantage of free medical services. Symptoms of illness are often ignored. Money is more likely to be spent for daily needs than for abstract preventive medical care. Only when an illness is quite severe does the poor person begin even self-medication. (The poor tend to have well-stocked home medicine chests.) When self-help has proved useless, friends and relatives are called in. If they are of no avail, then paraprofessionals like druggists or spiritual healers are most often consulted. Only after all home remedy measures have failed will the poverty-stricken sick person consult a medical doctor. Private doctors and free clinic personnel are much too cold and businesslike for the rather frightened and unsophisticated poor white patients, at least until they are so sick that they are desperate.

Educational goals.   The lack of cultural aspirations to formal education makes difficult the successful urban adjustment of low-income southern whites. "A little readin' and writin'" seems sufficient for most of them. Only a few urban schools have been able to reach out effectively and pull in southern white parents in order to raise the educational goals of their children. The parents do not seem to be against the educational system; they are indifferent to it. Their children enter school ready to drop out and susceptible to being pushed out. The heterogeneity of the student population, the large size of the physical plants, and the more or less sterile decorum of urban schools quickly crush what little emotional security southern white students have on first entering school. The formality in schools is likely to accentuate their shyness and reticence.

Some teachers have observed that unlike low-income Black students, who tend to become verbally or physically aggressive, southern white students tend to withdraw and become passive when angered. "They are like vegetables. They just sit and stare. And if the pressure becomes too great, they merely get up and leave," a puzzled Detroit teacher commented at a workshop. Many southern white students respond in this manner because they do not internalize a dialogue that convinces them that they are active school participants. School is something that is happening to them, and not for them. In a "Poor Scholar's Soliloquy," some of the past negative effects of a rigid curriculum on the motivation and achievement of urban school students with rural backgrounds are vividly portrayed:

No, I'm not very good in school. This is my second year in the seventh grade and I'm bigger and taller than the other kids. They like me all right, though, even if I don't say much in the schoolroom because outside I can tell them how to do a lot of things. They tag me around and that sort of makes up for what goes on in school.

I don't know why teachers don't like me. They never have very much. Seems like they don't think you know anything unless they can name the book it comes out of. I've got a lot of books in my room at home—books like Popular Science Mechanical Encyclopedia, and the Sear's and Ward's catalogues, but I don't very often just sit down and read them through like they make us do in school. I use my books when I want to find something out, like whenever Mom buys anything secondhand I look it up in Sears or Wards first and tell her if she's getting stung or not. I can use the index in a hurry to find the things that I want.

In school, though, we've got to learn whatever is in the book and I just can't memorize the stuff. Last year I stayed after school every night for two weeks trying to learn the names of the Presidents. Of course I knew some of them like Washington and Jefferson and Lincoln, but there must have been thirty altogether and I never did get them straight.

I'm not too sorry though because the kids who learned the Presidents had to turn right around and learn all the Vice Presidents. I am taking the seventh grade over but our teacher this year isn't so interested in the names of the Presidents. She has us trying to learn the names of all the great American inventors. . . .

Dad says I can quit school when I'm fifteen and I'm sort of anxious to because there are a lot of things I want to learn how to do and my uncle says, I'm not getting any younger.[20]

Teachers who believe that such students are innately incapable of memorizing facts because they cannot memorize the names of presidents, vice presidents, and inventors might be surprised to learn that the same student have memorized the names of famous athletes and hundreds of cars. Once the basic skills of reading and writing are learned, school loses its functional value for such pupils. Many youths state that they do not need a high school diploma in order to get a job somewhere; "somewhere," of course, usually means in an unskilled or semiskilled capacity.

As most cities and rural communities become ever more populated with disadvantaged white and nonwhite families, their educational offerings become less relevant for the students. One reason is that what has been called "meaningless education" is not related to their community and adjustment patterns.[21] Nor is education an automatic income equalizer even when nonwhites do stay in school. Nonwhite high school graduates earn much less than their white classmates. However, current efforts by local, state, and federal agencies are narrowing the gap.

The negative effects of poverty are evident in children who come to school tired and hungry, from a home barren of reading materials and lacking in contact with the world beyond the immediate neighborhood. Their preschool conditioning usually does not include being taught to respond to oral or written stimuli, and they must rely on less complex visual stimuli. They are likely to point, push, shove or grimace instead of using verbal skills. They may even be unprepared to sit quietly in a classroom. The ability to sit and listen does not come automatically with maturation but, rather, with a child's experiences in a "sitting" atmosphere. Many of those who can sit quietly at their desks are severely limited in their ability to solve middle-class abstract reasoning problems, and of those few who can, the majority are not in one school long enough to complete a planned sequence of work.

Middle- and upper-class children generally view school as an extension of home, whereas lower-class children view school as an environment separate from, and often antagonistic to, the home. To the lower-class child—regardless of race—home is home and school is school, and it is difficult for educators to cause the two to meet in his mind. For example the elementary school readers often are so culturally biased that stories in them simply do not make sense to most nonwhite students. Most of these children, and some of their parents, have not been farther from their homes than twenty-five blocks. Many have not seen a motion picture, eaten in a restaurant, or ridden in a bus; nor have they lived in a situation where a mother and father work together to rear a family. It is little wonder that they find it difficult to identify with the white middle-class Dicks and Janes in the typical reading books. (Only since the Detroit Public Schools Series in 1962, for example, have Black characters appeared in first-grade basic readers used in American schools. Within the past few years, several publishers have issued multiracial readers.)

Many college textbooks focus exclusively on the educational problems of Blacks and whites, ignoring Mexican-Americans, Puerto Ricans, Asian-Americans, and American Indians. Although there are about 25 million Blacks in this country, there also are 7 million Mexican-Americans, 2 million Asian-Americans, 1.7 million Puerto Ricans, and 800,000 American Indians. Nearly all of the negative conditions characteristic of Blacks also characterize other minority groups, but there are cultural differences among the groups. We now briefly discuss these minority groups that are too frequently ignored.

Mexican-Americans

Mexican-American students reflect a variety of cultural patterns, including those created by their parental heritage and the length of time their families have been American citizens. Second- and third-generation descendants of early Spanish settlers are usually affluent, but second- and third-generation descendants of

agricultural workers tend to be poverty-stricken. There is still a third group: first-generation children of *braceros*—farm workers who have recently migrated from Mexico. The first two groups are likely to be Americanized; they have little knowledge of their Spanish heritage and they speak little or no Spanish. Children of migrant workers speak fluent Spanish and hold tightly to Mexican customs and traditions.[22] All groups are discriminated against by the *Anglos*—the white American majority. Indeed, in some communities Mexican-Americans are the victims of more discrimination and segregation than Blacks.

Mexican-Americans, like American Indians, Asian-Americans, and Puerto Ricans, are truly marginal people. Culturally they are neither Black nor white. Their marginality affects individual searches for identity. In most schools the curriculum does not include material with which the Mexican-Americans can positively identify. In history classes, for instance, they become the villains who massacred the courageous Americans at the Alamo. Most elementary and secondary schools inflict the final blow on the cultural identity of Mexican-American children by forcing them to leave their ancestral language at the schoolhouse door.[23] Many students react by adopting a defense mechanism called *ethnic self-hatred*.[24]

Some studies of Mexican-American students in junior and senior high schools conclude that in many instances the negative self-images adopted by Mexican-Americans are simply coping devices. Recent studies also illustrate the detrimental effects of negative definitions that teachers and administrators hold of the students. Students become aware of the negative views and, in some instances, role-play as people with negative self-images in order to minimize conflicts in school. Submissive acts—"playing dumb"—are ways Chicano pupils manage to coexist with the Anglos.

Most of the 1.7 million or so Mexican-American school children in the Southwest have suffered academic failure because of the unwillingness or inability of schools to build a curriculum around their Spanish-speaking background. Yet as early as the 1920s researchers became aware that Mexican-American students are better able to achieve in reading and other school-related tasks when they are taught first in Spanish. Recently, a few school districts in the Southwest have implemented bilingual classroom instruction. Projects in San Antonio, Tucson, and Albuquerque are proving that *cultural difference does not mean cultural inferiority.*

Puerto Ricans

Like the children of other minority groups, Puerto Rican students are frequently plagued by problems revolving around acculturation, language difficulties, and economic barriers. Furthermore, Puerto Rican parents give little or no parental support to the schools—they are preoccupied with the problems of learning English, finding housing, securing employment, and otherwise trying to survive.[25] When they do turn their attention to the schools, they feel powerless to improve them, controlled as they are by white administrators and teachers. In some communities Puerto Ricans are joining Blacks in trying to achieve educational and other gains.

Puerto Rican children are taught very early to respect their elders by bowing their heads. In the schools, however, teachers insist that pupils look at them when giving verbal responses. Other illustrations of cultural differences include the Puerto Rican pattern of little physical contact between the adolescent boy and male adults. Thus, in the classroom boys jerk away when male teachers try to touch them. Still other teachers fail to understand that in some families illness in the home requires everyone to remain home until the sick person's health is restored. Ignorance of such differing cultural norms, or the inability to understand them, results in unjustly labeling students as belligerent or docile or not interested in school. Many teachers not only do not understand cultural differences, they also are insensitive to and often shocked by the accelerated social maturity of slum-dwelling children. Slum children become socially mature at an early age in order to survive.[26] By the time the average slum child is ten or twelve, she has seen too much and done too much. Sex, violence, and crime are all familiar to her.

The Hispanic-American population—native and foreign born—continues to grow at a tremendous rate. New York City and its surrounding communities have been the ports of entry for most of these immigrants. Contrary to popular notion, Puerto Ricans and Mexican-Americans are not the only large Hispanic groups in the United States. A sizeable number of legal and illegal immigrants have come from Argentina, Bolivia, Columbia, Cuba, the Dominican Republic, Ecuador, Peru, and Venezuela. Even though the U. S. Census Bureau will conduct its first complete count of Hispanic Americans in 1979, exact figures will not be available for several years. Part of the difficulty in accurately counting and classifying Hispanic immigrants is due to the tendency of non-Puerto Rican Hispanics to list themselves as Puerto Ricans in order to gain full rights as American citizens. (Puerto Ricans are American citizens by virtue of the Jones Act of 1917.) Since only a few census takers or school officials are able to distinguish the various Spanish dialects, this deception is seldom caught. In addition to the official count, New York City alone has between 750,000 to 1,000,000 illegal immigrants.

The more effective teachers and administrators seek to understand their own prejudices and cultural limitations before trying to understand and help people from other backgrounds. Much of the turmoil and dissension in recent years in rural and big city schools has arisen because too many administrators and teachers have found the concepts "culturally deprived," "disadvantaged," and "different" to be convenient alibis for failing to provide equal educational opportunities.

American Indians

Currently, American Indians are at the bottom of the economic ladder. They have the highest rates of unemployment and school dropouts, live in the poorest housing, and in some parts of the country are accorded the lowest social status.[27] These conditions reflect both what white Americans have done to the Indians and what the Indians have not been able to do for themselves.

Unable to realize that we have not an Indian problem but rather an *American problem* we have established government-controlled Indian bureaus, reservations, and assistance programs. Each of these short-sighted solutions has contributed to the psychological emasculation of Indian men, the demoralization of Indian women, and the alienation of Indian children. In other words, most government programs have failed to assist Indians in their efforts to maintain individual dignity and cultural identity while achieving success in the larger society. Yet with missionary zeal, white Anglo-Saxons continue their ill-fated efforts to Americanize the Indians.

Half the Native American population lives on 56 million acres of reservations in 26 states. Part of their frustration is revealed in the following statistics. Indians have 90 million fewer acres of land today than in 1887. Their average life expectancy is 45 years. Nearly 60 per cent of the adult Native American population has less than an eighth-grade education. Infant mortality is more than 10 points above the national average. The majority of Native American families have annual incomes below $5,000; 75 per cent have annual incomes below $4,000. Indian unemployment is almost 10 times the national average.

Feeling trapped and powerless in a world controlled by non-Indians, most rural and urban Indians have not become militant, but instead have withdrawn. Overgeneralizing from this group, representatives of non-Indian cultures pass on stereotypes about shiftless and drunken Indians. There is a saying in some towns, "If you hire an Indian, never pay him the first day if you want him to come back the second day. He'll take the money and drink it but not come back to work." It is not only what is said about Indians that is detrimental but also what is not said. Until the 1970 United States census, Native Americans were not even listed as an identifiable ethnic group. Little wonder then that from time to time a few automobiles owned by Indians display bumper stickers that say "Custer had it coming."

Conflicts between white and Indian cultures are found on reservations, in small towns, and in big cities. The strains show up in many ways, including juvenile delinquency, adult crime, and alcoholism. Such social pathologies are but symptoms of man's inhumanity to his fellow man. Historically, non-Indians have looked at Indian tribes but have failed to see the deplorable social, psychological, and physical deprivations. White teachers in particular tend to think that because an exceptional Indian student has managed to succeed, the others should also.

One-third of the 280,000 Indian children in schools are in federally operated institutions. Indian schools range from trailers on Navajo reservations to large off-reservation boarding schools. The dropout rate for Indians is twice the national average, their level of educational attainment is half the national average, and their test scores are far below those of other students. Generally, the longer Indian children stay in school, the further behind they get.[28] This *cumulative deficit* partially explains why Indian high school graduates earn 75 per cent less than the national average.

The Bureau of Indian Affairs is trying to increase the number of Indians in teaching and administrative positions so that Indian children will have more models to look up to. As school districts improve the quality of education for Indians, they also are teaching that cultural pluralism is not making nonwhite children white, but instead is allowing them to maintain their own cultural identities. The deficiencies in Indian education reinforce the growing need for teachers, administrators, and literature that better reflect a multiethnic society.

Asian-Americans

Most Asian-Americans (Japanese-Americans, Chinese-Americans, and Filipinos) live in Hawaii, California, Washington, Illinois, and New York. Each of these groups is beginning to react overtly to patronizing and racist behaviors.

Many non-Orientals still think of Chinese-Americans and Japanese-Americans as people who work primarily in laundries and gardens. In academic circles the equally patronizing stereotype of the earnest, bespectacled young Oriental scholar is replacing the older stereotype of the pig-tailed coolie. The new stereotype has grown out of the national reputations achieved by such men as I. M. Pei and Minoru Yamasaki, architects; Gerald Tsai, head of the Manhattan Fund; Tsung Dao Lee and Chen Ning Yang, winners of the Nobel Prize in physics; Samuel I. Hayakawa, president emeritus of San Francisco State University; Daniel Inouye, U.S. senator from Hawaii; Toyohiko Takami, dermatologist; and Hideyo Noguchi, bacteriologist.[29]

The plight of poverty-stricken Asian-

Americans is vividly captured in San Francisco Chinatown statistics: More than one-third of Chinatown's families are poverty-stricken; three-fourths of all housing units are substandard; rents have tripled in the past five years; more than half the adults have only a grade-school education; one-third of core city residents are more than sixty-five years old; juvenile delinquency is increasing; and the suicide rate is three times the national average.

The educational problems of Asian-Americans are compounded by language problems and basic philosophical differences: Asian children are taught to respect older people, deal with others peacefully, observe proper manners, and remember that making money is not the only purpose of education. Non-Asian schools frequently subscribe to a different set of values. Thus racial desegregation of the public schools is opposed by many Asian-American parents who want to maintain their own communities and cultural values.

FEEDBACK EXERCISE

Ask a friend to answer the following questions about you.

Do you see me as one who:

1. Is proud of his/her social background?
2. Not ashamed of his/her ethnic group?
3. Proud of her/his sex?
4. Expresses herself/himself clearly and concisely?
5. Dresses appropriately for most occasions?
6. Contributes to conversations without cutting others off?
7. Accepts constructive criticism without becoming defensive?
8. Has a clearly thought out philosophy of life?
9. Is more theory-oriented than people-oriented?
10. Takes the lead in challenging bullies?
11. Knows how to relax and enjoy her/himself?
12. Works effectively with small children?
13. Enjoys being with people of various ethnic and social class backgrounds?
14. Makes strangers feel at home?
15. Avoids ridiculing other people's life styles?
16. Is hard to understand?
17. Runs away when faced with a major problem?
18. Is able to laugh at her/himself?
19. Yields to group pressure?
20. Would rather make money than friends?
21. Sticks blindly to her/his point when arguing?
22. Has the desire and interest to be a very good teacher?

ADDITIONAL READINGS

Bathurst, Effie G. *Where Children Live Affects Curriculum*. Washington, D.C., U.S. Government Printing Office, 1950.

Drucker, Peter F. *The Age of Discontinuity: Guidelines to Our Changing Society*. New York, Harper & Row, 1969.

Easthope, Gary. *Community, Hierarchy, and Open Education*. London, Routledge & K. Paul, 1975.

Goldfield, David R. and James B. Lane, eds. *The Enduring Ghetto: Sources and Readings*. Philadelphia, J.B. Lippincott, 1973.

Henderson, George, ed. *America's Other Children: Public Schools Outside Suburbia*. Norman, University of Oklahoma Press, 1971.

Hyman, Herbert H., et al. *The Enduring Effects of Education*. Chicago, University of Chicago Press, 1975.

Jencks, Christopher, et al. *Inequality: A Reassessment of the Effect of Family and Schooling in America*. New York, Basic Books, 1972.

Juster, Francis T., ed. *Education, Income, and Human Behavior*. New York, McGraw-Hill, 1975.

Mindel, Charles H. and Robert W. Habenstein, eds. *Ethnic Families in America*. New York, Elsevier, 1976.

Owen, John D. *School Inequality and the Welfare State*. Baltimore, Johns Hopkins University Press, 1974.

Pettigrew, Thomas F., ed. *Racial Discrimination in the United States*. New York, Harper & Row, 1975.

Walter, John P., et al. *Deprived Urban Youth: An Economic and Cross-Cultural Analysis of the United States, Columbia, and Peru*. New York, Praeger, 1975.

White, Burton L. and Jean C. Watts. *Experience and Environment: Major Influences on the Development of the Young Child*. Englewood Cliffs, N.J., Prentice-Hall, 1973.

Zeigler, Luther and Karl F. Johnson. *The Politics of Education in the States*. Indianapolis, Bobbs-Merrill, 1972.

NOTES

1. J. O. Brew, "The Metal Ages: Copper, Bronze, and Iron," in H. L. Shapiro (ed.), *Man, Culture, and Society* (New York, Oxford University Press, 1956), 111–138.

2. Joel M. Halpern, "The Rural Revolution," *Transactions of the New York Academy of Science*, 28 (1965), 60–73.

3. William W. Lambert and Wallace E. Lambert, *Social Psychology* (Englewood Cliffs, N.J., Prentice-Hall, 1964), 13.

4. Bernard Barber, *Social Stratification: A Comparative Analysis of Structure and Process* (New York, Harcourt, Brace & World, 1957), 52.

5. Harold L. Hodgkinson, *Education in Social and Cultural Perspectives* (Englewood Cliffs, N.J., Prentice-Hall, 1962), 12.

6. W. Lloyd Warner et al., *Social Class in America* (Chicago, Science Research Associates, 1949), 86.

7. August B. Hollingshead, *Elmtown's Youth* (New York, John Wiley & Sons, 1949).

8. Hodgkinson, *Perspectives*, 23–24.

9. Deborah P. Wolfe, "Curriculum Adaptations for the Culturally Deprived," *Journal of Negro Education*, 31 (Spring, 1952), 139.

10. Frank Riessman, *The Culturally Deprived Child* (New York, Harper & Row, 1962), 73.

11. Paul B. Horton, *Sociology and the Health Sciences* (New York, McGraw-Hill, 1965), 234.

12. For a comprehensive analysis of the cities-within-a-city approach see Maurice F. Parkins, *Neighborhood Conservation: A Pilot Study* (Detroit, Detroit City Planning Commission, 1958).

13. David Hunter, *The Slums: Challenge and Response* (New York, Macmillan, 1962), 89.

14. Whitney M. Young, Jr., *To Be Equal* (New York, McGraw Hill, 1964), 67–68.

15. Ralph Ellison, *Invisible Man* (New York, New American Library, 1964), 7–8.

16. At one time or another adolescents, career women, migrants, chiropractors, bilingual persons, monks, the hard of hearing, middle-income groups, Catholics, factory foremen, druggists, and sociologists have all been situationally marginal. See J. W. Mann, "Group Relations of the Marginal Personality," *Human Relations*, 11 (1958), 77–92.

17. See W. D. Weatherford and E. Brewer, *Life and Religion in Southern Appalachia* (New York, Friendship, 1962).

18. George Henderson, "Poor Southern Whites: A Neglected Urban Problem," *Journal of Secondary Education*, 41 (March, 1966), 111–114.

19. See Harriette Arnow, *The Dollmaker* (New York, Macmillan, 1954); Henry Hill Collins, Jr., *America's Own Refugees* (Princeton, N.J., Princeton University Press, 1957).

20. Stephen M. Corey, "Poor Scholar's Soliloquy," *Childhood Education*, 20 (January, 1944), 219–220.

21. Dave Berkman, "You Can't Make Them Learn," *Atlantic Monthly*, 210 (September, 1962), 62–67.

22. See Luis F. Hernandez, "The Culturally Disadvantaged Mexican-American Student," *Journal of Secondary Education*, 42 (February, 1967), 59–65; (March, 1967), 123–128.

23. Frank M. Cordasco, "The Challenge of the Non-English Speaking Child in New York," New York, Board of Education, 1958.

24. Hernandez, "Mexican American Student," 60.

25. J. Cayce Morrison, "The Puerto Rican Study (1953–1957): A Report on the Education Adjustment of Puerto Rican Pupils in the Puplic Schools of the City of New York," New York, Board of Education, 1958.

26. See Patricia Cayo Sexton, *Spanish Harlem* (New York, Harper & Row, 1955).

27. Fred Harris, "American Indians—New Destiny," *Congressional Record—Senate*, April 21, 1966, 8311. Little has changed since 1966.

28. Rosalie H. Wax, "The Warrior Dropouts," *Trans-action* (May, 1967), 40–46.

29. George Henderson, *To Live in Freedom: Human Relations Today and Tomorrow* (Norman, University of Oklahoma Press, 1972), 134.

4.
SCHOOLS
IN TRANSITION

Other chapters in this book deal with the impact on the school of rapid changes in the culture and with the processes of socialization and acculturation through which young people learn to achieve self-realization through participation in ever enlarging groups of people. This chapter focuses on the influences of social and cultural forces on the teaching-learning process. It examines the effect of these forces on the teacher, who must balance them against the professional tasks to be performed.

There is increasing agreement that teaching is a task for professionals. A professional person is one whose preparation has been so extensive and so rigorous that he or she has knowledge and skills not possessed by others; a person whose work is so technical and important that society requires him or her to have legal authorization; and a person whose behavior is controlled by a code of ethics determined by members of his or her profession.

EFFORTS TO IMPROVE TEACHING

There is increasing recognition that the work of the teacher is intimately related to the release of human potentials and a better future for all. Current efforts to improve the quality of teaching in our schools have emerged from this better understanding of the important tasks performed by teachers. (See Table 2.) These tasks are exacting; indeed, they require high-level competence comparable to that of the surgeon or the engineer. Some of the more important of them are (1) engendering interest in the world of ideas, (2) developing problem-

solving abilities, (3) maintaining discipline, (4) creating an intellectually stimulating classroom atmosphere, (5) keeping several different groups working productively in the classroom, (6) recognizing and making provision for individual differences, and (7) using evaluation procedures that measure more than mere recall of information.

The history of American education is replete with examples of efforts to improve instruction. The period since 1960 has been particularly fruitful in the development of new approaches. Thus the student who wants to understand the meaning of the "revolution in instruction" must examine many publications, including articles in educational journals that specialize in various phases of teaching and books like the *Handbook of Research on Teaching*, which contains thirty-one articles relating to the problem.[1]

Efforts to develop a theory of instruction. There has been an interesting trend during the last two decades toward developing theories in educational administration, curriculum, and instruction. The development of a theory of instruction can be taken to mean the development of a set of principles that seem to predict or account for events much more accurately than mere chance; it implies that instead of following hit-or-miss methods, the teacher can operate in accordance with carefully developed procedures. Jerome S. Bruner has stated that a valid theory of instruction must be concerned with the factors that predispose a child to learn effectively, the optimal structuring of knowledge, the optimal sequence re-

Table 2. Major Problems with Which Public Schools Must Deal: 1970 to 1977

Possible Problems	Percent of Respondents Citing Problems				
	1970	1972	1974	1975	1977
Lack of discipline	18	23	23	23	26
Integration/segregation/busing	17	18	16	15	13
Lack of proper financial support	17	19	13	14	12
Difficulty getting "good" teachers	12	14	11	11	11
Poor curriculum	6	5	3	5	10
Use of drugs	11	4	13	9	7
Parent's lack of interest	3	6	6	2	5
Size of school/classes	—	10	6	10	5
Teacher's lack of interest	—	—	—	—	5
Mismanagement of funds/programs	—	—	—	—	4
Pupils' lack of interest	(1)	—	2	3	3
Crime/vandalism	—	—	—	4	3
Lack of proper facilities	11	5	3	3	2
Transportation	2	—	—	—	2
Parents' involvement in school activities	—	—	—	—	2
There are no problems	5	2	3	5	4
Miscellaneous	6	9	13	5	5
Don't know/no answer	18	12	17	10	16

[1] Less than 1%.

NOTE—Totals add to more than 100% because of multiple answers.

SOURCES: Phi Delta Kappa, Inc., *The Gallup Polls of Attitudes Toward Education, 1963–73*, and *Phi Delta Kappan*, September 1974, December 1975, and September 1977.

quired for learning, and the nature and pacing of rewards and punishments. "You take the child where you find him and give him the structure that is economical, productive and powerful for him and that allows him to grow."[2]

Efforts to define the professional role of the teacher. The term "role" can be defined as the set of expectations applied to a person who occupies a particular position in a social system or in an organization. Techniques of role analysis have been developed by social psychologists; they are proving useful in the effort to improve instruction in classrooms. It is becoming apparent that the teacher cannot be expected to achieve maximum proficiency in the performance of her truly profession- al tasks—the ones that cannot be done by others—unless there is a more precise defini- tion of these tasks than has generally existed in the past. The advantages of role analysis have been stated as follows:

The concept of role provides a natural basis upon which to view teaching behavior. It is task- oriented; it is function-oriented. It is behavior- oriented not in a general sense but in terms of the job to be done. It is concerned with behavior rele- vant to the effects desired. Thus it is a useful tool in the hands of teachers and students of teaching.[3]

The need for giving more attention to role analysis and role expectations is evident when we examine teacher education programs, the role expectations of some school systems, and procedures for evaluating teaching effective- ness. As a matter of fact, the development of teacher education programs in terms of the actual professional tasks teachers are expected to perform in school systems has been called "An Unstudied Problem in Education."[4] (Sur- veys of teacher education programs have re- vealed, for example, that preparation for work- ing with culturally disadvantaged youngsters is a neglected area in teacher education. Another problem that needs study is the time that must be spent on nonteaching chores, estimated to be 26 per cent of the teacher's working day in many school systems. Policing playgrounds and hallways, supervising lunchrooms, collecting money for a variety of purposes, and making out complicated attendance reports take valuable time from the professional tasks for which the teacher was employed and which he alone can perform.)

From time to time a debate flares up over the professional status of teaching. By most standards teaching is a profession. Specifically, it is a profession which has the following characteristics:

1. Possesses a unique body of knowledge, skills, techniques, and attitudes not possessed by other occupational groups.

2. Assumes responsibility for assuring the competence of its members for admission to practice and continuation in professional status.

3. Maintains national accrediting bodies to enforce predetermined quality levels for programs preparing its members.

4. Achieves unity through effective professional organizations.

5. Promotes, in the interest of society, quality educational opportunities for all students.

6. Advances and protects the welfare of its members, who in turn are expected to adhere to a code of ethics.

Until recently efforts to evaluate teacher effectiveness were based on *traits* theory; it was assumed that all effective teachers possessed certain traits in common. An extensive study of the measurement and prediction of teacher effectiveness listed fifteen traits as essential to successful teaching: buoyancy, considerateness, cooperativeness, dependability, emotional stability, ethicalness, expressiveness, flexibility, forcefulness, judgment, mental alertness, objectivity, personal magnetism, physical energy and drive, and scholarliness.[5] Aside from the difficulty of obtaining objective evidence of the presence or absence of these traits, it is apparent that they are desirable attributes for any person in any type of occupation; they are not traits unique to successful teachers.

More recent efforts to evaluate teacher effectiveness have emphasized the identification of the professional roles of teachers and the effective performance of these roles—performance evaluation instead of traits evaluation. Efforts are also being made to determine the effects certain styles or patterns of teaching have on pupil performance. The ultimate criterion of teacher effectiveness is, of course, the effect that the teacher has on the behavior of pupils. It is no longer accepted that this effect cannot be evaluated until the pupils have lived their entire lives.

THE SOCIAL CONTEXT OF TEACHING

Effective teaching, then, presents difficult and technical challenges even when it is viewed only in terms of the kinds of classroom behavior that produce desired changes in the behavior of students. But teaching does not take place in a neat classroom vacuum; it is always influenced by the social relationships in which the teachers are involved. (It is also influenced, of course, by the social relationships in which the pupils are involved. They are considered elsewhere in this book.)

Changes in the culture have been so rapid in recent decades that it has become difficult for teachers to understand the full implications of the social context in which their work is embedded. This chapter analyzes four of the most important social relationships in which teachers participate and which affect their work: their relationship to American society, to the teaching profession, to the community in which they work, and to the local school system.

The Teacher in American Society

Teaching is inevitably influenced by time, place and circumstances. Teaching in the second half of the twentieth century, in the United States of America, in an interdependent, urban society differs in important ways from teaching at different times, in different cultures, under different circumstances. The thesis that teaching is expected to help shape the future of American life is presented elsewhere in this book; this chapter is concerned with the ways in which American society in turn shapes the teaching-learning process.

Social realities affecting teachers. The
most potent social reality affecting the work of
the teacher is the fact that we live in a dynamic
rather than a static society. The role of the
teacher in our society used to be defined in
terms of the teacher's responsibility for trans-
mitting the culture as a social heritage from the
past. Today, however, the impact on individuals of new forces in the culture is so dramatic
that education for social change is a necessity.
Helping students make satisfactory adjustments to a dynamic society is much more
difficult than helping them make adjustments
to a relatively static society.

The major social realities of contemporary
American society are discussed in detail elsewhere in this text. Thus only a brief statement
of their effect on the work of the teacher is
necessary now. The threat of a world war, the
armaments race, the plight of underdeveloped
nations, the population explosion, and the intense desire for a peaceful world mean that
today's teachers must educate for international
understanding. The prejudices that exist and
the discriminations that are practiced against
women and minority groups in our society
produce disunity and friction at home and distrust of the sincerity of our professed beliefs
abroad. These stern realities mean that intercultural education is a responsibility that
teachers must assume. The rapidly increasing
rural-urban migration of recent decades has
confronted American cities with problems of
education—to say nothing of problems involving housing, jobs, sanitation, and safety—that
they were not prepared to handle. Providing
the kind of learning situations which can profit
children who live in rural poverty and city
slums is another obligation placed on teachers
by the realities of the society in which we live.

Value systems affecting the teacher. As
mentioned earlier, it is possible to identify certain ideals to which a vast majority of Americans subscribe, and it is possible to develop
teaching procedures that harmonize with these
basic ideals. These ideals for the most part cut
across the various subcultures in our society.
Nevertheless, in attempting to implement
them, we must take into account our diverse
value systems; for example, lower class, middle class, upper class; native American and
immigrant; traditional and emergent. This diversity is, of course, one of the sources of the

---

AMERICAN SOCIETY

Realities	*Ideals*
Dynamic	Basic values
Interdependent	Divergent value systems
Urban	Changing values
Industrialized	
Affluent	
Unsolved problems	

THE TEACHING PROFESSION

Magnitude—Organizations—Prestige—Income

LOCAL STRUCTURE OF THE SCHOOL

The Community

⬇

The Board of Education

⬇

The Superintendent

⬇

The Principal

⬇

Teachers

⬇

Pupils

Figure 3. The Social Context of Teaching.

---

strength of our nation. As noted historian Arthur L. Schlesinger has put it: "Freedom implies humility, not absolutism; it implies not
the tyranny of the one but the tolerance of the
many. Against the monolithic world, free men
affirm the pluralistic world. Against the world
of coercion, let us affirm the world of choice."[6]

Diverse value systems also, however, present problems for the teacher. Here is a specific
example, the case of an intelligent but unruly
Korean-American boy: "Unaware of the ven-
eration accorded by Koreans to the head of the
household, school representatives tried persis-
tently to reach the mother. Finally, when the
father was approached in the manner to which
he was accustomed, he cooperated with the
school in controlling the child."[7]

The vast majority of American teachers are
imbued with middle-class values: politeness,
respect for the property of others, industry,

sportsmanship, and ambition. But lower-class children have a different set of values; the result is that they feel alienated from the school, and many intellectually capable ones drop out. This represents a tremendous waste of human talent that is needed in our society. The teacher, therefore, is challenged to acquire a better understanding of the values of lower-class children and to help culturally disadvantaged children win acceptance in the social system of the classroom and make academic gains in line with their mental capacities.

There is another dichotomy of cultural values with which the teacher must deal: traditional versus emergent values. As our society has moved from an economy of scarcity to an economy of abundance and from an agrarian society to an industrialized society, some traditional values growing out of the Puritan ethic have changed or at least been reinterpreted. For example:

In order to provide for its own growth, business must constantly persuade people to consume ever larger quantities of nonessentials. As a result, abstinence is retreating before consumption, thrift before installment buying. . . . Self-reliance is giving way to groupmindedness.[8]

There seems to be some evidence that educators tend to be less traditional in their value systems than the general public. Teachers are generally less traditional than administrators, but administrators are still less traditional than school board members, who lean strongly toward traditional values. These value conflicts affect teachers when they engage in curriculum development, decide what instructional methods to use, participate in the selection of textbooks and teaching aids, and decide how much relative emphasis to place on group enterprises and individual efforts.

What the teacher can do about cultural values. The teacher cannot be completely neutral about the basic values of democracy as opposed to those of authoritarianism. She should live by and foster democratic values— respect for individual personality, cooperation toward the common welfare, faith in human intelligence. She should not attempt to compel pupils to accept her own opinions; she should reject all efforts to create mental strait jackets;

and she should not try to impose any party line, either right or left, on her pupils.

The teacher should consciously try to synthesize the best elements from conflicting value systems so that she can reach more children in more ways. Her job is to stimulate young and growing minds—to prod them to think and to formulate and live by their own value systems. Her responsibility is to guide pupils in the use of the method of inquiry so that their values will not be determined by pressure groups or by the fluency in expression of those around them. Young people are entitled to build their own beliefs on the basis of facts, theories, and experiences. Teachers must help young people to locate, use, and evaluate information about contemporary problems and to form judgments about them; they must not compel any particular judgments.

The Teacher as a Member of a Profession

The teacher is a part of an enterprise of tremendous magnitude. During the school year 1975–1976, more than 70,000,000 Americans were engaged as full-time students, teachers, or administrators in the nation's public and private schools at all levels; another 136,000 were serving as school board members or college or university trustees. This constituted about 30 per cent of the population of the United States. When we add those groups engaged in the production and distribution of textbooks and other supplies and equipment, in school building and school transportation enterprises, and in other school-related occupations, the nation's educational enterprise involves perhaps 40 per cent of the people.

Professional organizations. Countless people have labored for many years to develop professional educational organizations. These organizations have been responsible for much that has been accomplished in improving both the general performance of teachers and the conditions under which they work. The organizations provide services that include (1) disseminating information throughout the profession, (2) conducting and promoting research, (3) sponsoring improvements in teacher education, (4) seeking adequate salaries and reasonable teaching loads, (5) defending the basic freedoms of teachers, (6) informing the public about the achievements and needs of the schools, (7) influencing public policy relating to education, and (8) developing a code of ethics for the teaching profession.

The National Education Association (NEA) had its beginnings in Philadelphia in 1857, when the National Teachers Association was established. The National Education Association of the United States was chartered by an act of Congress in 1906; the present name was adopted in 1907. It has more than 1.7 million members in 59 state and territory and 9,000 locally affiliated associations. The organization has departments representing almost every professional group interested in education. The NEA sponsors Future Teachers of America for high school students interested in teaching as a career and Student NEA for college students preparing to teach.

The American Federation of Teachers (AFT) was founded in 1916; it now has more than 480,000 members in more than 2,200 local organizations. It has experienced appreciable increases in membership in recent years, especially in large cities. It vigorously promotes integration within the schools, supports equality of educational opportunities, and opposes merit-rating salary plans. Although it is affiliated with AFL-CIO, it is a legal entity in its own right.

Officials of the NEA and the AFT have agreed to pursue a merger. Despite philosophical differences, it is quite possible that in the near future the organizations will complete the merger. If this happens, the nation's strongest educational unit will be created.

The occupational prestige of teaching. Teacher morale is generally recognized as an important factor in effective teaching. When morale is high, teachers work with enthusiasm, obtain satisfaction from their job, and achieve satisfactory results; when morale is low, teaching becomes drudgery, teachers receive little satisfaction from their job, and their achievements are far below their potential. Even though most teachers are convinced, as they should be, that the long-term effects of their work are vital, they may become discouraged if they see no tangible evidence that their work is so regarded by others. Capable young men and women are reluctant to enter a profession that ranks low in social prestige and financial re-

wards when compared with other professions. The importance of occupational status has been described as follows:

The influence of occupational status on the practitioners is both pervasive and fundamental. It affects who will enter the occupation and what specializations within it they will seek. It affects the quantity and quality of the work that is done, the job satisfactions of the practitioners, and the dress, manners, outlook and moral ideas of the practitioners. [9]

Much has been written about teacher stereotypes. W. W. Charters presented the most extreme model of such a stereotype under the title, "The Teacher in the Sacred Community." [10] He pointed out that educational sociologists writing during the 1930s had in mind a special type of community—a small town or village relatively untouched by industrialization, where the cultural values were homogeneous or dominated by a single controlling group. Teachers were pictured as the victims of strict controls imposed by the community. The only status they had in the community was their occupational status; contractual provisions precluded courtship or marriage, at least by female teachers. The male teacher was highly visible in the small town, but always as "the teacher"; the only escape he had from this identity was to leave town, and this was prohibited except during summer vacations.

There are, perhaps, a few small towns and villages in which teachers are still subjected to strict controls, but considering that two-thirds of all teachers now work in metropolitan areas and that most of them—both men and women—are or have been married, the Charters' picture is far from an accurate portrayal of the position of the teacher in American society today. Unfortunately, the idea that entering the teaching profession means being subjected to petty regulations and the scrutiny of prying eyes still persists.

Teacher's salaries. It has been difficult to convince our people that teaching is one of the major professions; that it requires rigorous preparation, technical skills, and professional competence comparable to the requirements for a successful practitioner in any of the major professions; and that teachers need higher

Table 3. Average Starting Salaries: Teachers v. Private Industry, 1968–1975

	1968–1969	1974–1975
Beginning men and women teachers with bachelor's degree (school systems with enrollments of 6,000 or more)	$5,941	$ 8,000
Men with bachelor's degree		
Engineering	$9,312	$11,940
Chemistry	8,520	11,160
Accounting	8,424	11,472
Mathematics-statistics	8,412	10,440
Economics-finance	7,800	10,104
Sales-marketing	7,620	10,080
Business administration	7,560	9,324
Liberal arts	7,368	8,940
Women with bachelor's degree		
Engineering-technical research	$9,672	$11,424
Chemistry	8,532	10,536
Mathematics-statistics	8,484	10,056
Accounting	8,304	10,416
General business	7,104	9,300
Liberal arts	6,264	9,024

SOURCE: *Research Bulletin*, National Education Association, 1976.

salaries if our schools are to compete successfully with other occupations for the services of capable young men and women. Although teachers' salaries have been increasing, beginning salaries are still far below those of other occupations that require four years of college preparation.[11]

Teachers' salaries have increased during the 1970s. The average annual salary of classroom teachers in 1975–1976 was $13,400; the figure for 1968–1969 was $9,121. But the percentage of the Gross National Product (GNP) that is spent for teachers' salaries has not increased significantly during the 1970s. The amount spent for this purpose in 1975–1976 was $3.5 billion—about 4 per cent of the GNP.

The Teacher as a Member of the Community

Teachers generally are active participants in the life of the community. Nationwide surveys have indicated that about 90 per cent of teachers are church members, compared with about 60 per cent of the total population, and that 9 out of every 10 voted in the last presidential election.

It is generally recognized that classroom teachers are the most effective public relations agents connected with the school system. But aside from the public relations service, many personal and professional rewards come to teachers who understand the communities in which they work and who participate in community activities. Contacts with the great variety of personalities found in the local community enrich the life of the teacher, and participation in the on-going activities of the community provides a means of self-realization. Most important of all, however, is the professional advantage that comes from understanding the community forces affecting the development, achievement and behavior of pupils in school.

From the standpoint of community expectations, the "serving" status of the teacher has been overemphasized. The frequently reiterated theme that teaching is a public service, paid for at public expense, can become the rationale for loading teachers down with so many community responsibilities that little time and energy are left for the truly professional tasks that have been identified in the

Table 4. Average Salaries of Instructional Staff, by State

State or other area	Adjusted dollars (1974–75 purchasing power)[2]		
	1959–60	1969–70	1974–75[3]
United States	**$9,121**	**$12,123**	**$12,070**
Alabama	7,055	9,537	9,503
Alaska	12,091	15,076	16,906
Arizona	9,854	12,308	11,168
Arkansas	5,808	8,839	[4] 9,021
California	[5] 11,634	13,687	14,915
Colorado	8,809	10,834	11,554
Connecticut	10,591	12,891	12,051
Delaware	[5] 10,224	12,754	12,110
District of Columbia	11,070	15,188	14,716
Florida	8,955	11,794	10,780
Georgia	[6] 6,882	10,110	10,641
Hawaii	9,501	13,479	13,665
Idaho	7,432	9,952	9,573
Illinois	10,249	13,645	13,469
Indiana	9,769	13,120	11,358
Iowa	[5] 7,104	11,245	10,598
Kansas	[5] 7,844	10,712	9,770
Kentucky	5,865	10,456	9,240
Louisiana	8,775	9,902	9,800
Maine	6,512	11,052	13,202
Maryland	9,796	13,556	13,282
Massachusetts	[7] 9,775	12,583	12,468
Michigan	9,967	13,385	14,224
Minnesota	9,299	13,655	12,851
Mississippi	5,842	8,245	8,338
Missouri	[7] 7,996	11,096	10,257
Montana	[5] 7,800	11,108	10,160
Nebraska	6,833	10,772	9,715
Nevada	10,036	13,287	12,854
New Hampshire	7,853	10,996	10,016
New Jersey	[8] 10,349	13,028	([9])
New Mexico	9,487	11,143	[10] 10,200
New York	11,523	13,988	15,000
North Carolina	7,365	10,620	11,275
North Dakota	6,514	9,463	9,176
Ohio	9,033	11,786	11,100
Oklahoma	8,213	9,790	9,108
Oregon	9,757	12,617	10,958
Pennsylvania	[8] 9,357	12,343	12,200
Rhode Island	9,694	12,205	12,855
South Carolina	5,082	9,600	9,770
South Dakota	6,566	9,188	8,860
Tennessee	6,926	9,998	9,878
Texas	8,299	10,290	10,136
Utah	8,983	11,038	10,150
Vermont	7,873	11,280	9,206
Virginia	[8] 7,601	11,245	11,279

Washington	9,947	13,028	12,538
West Virginia	6,967	10,765	9,124
Wisconsion	[11] 8,585	12,548	13,046
Wyoming	8,703	11,701	10,350
Outlying areas:			
American Samoa	1,502	7,035	5,100
Canal Zone	10,637	14,263	16,190
Guam	7,240	10,697	17,980
Puerto Rico	4,161	([9])	([9])
Virgin Islands	6,006	([9])	11,154

[1] Includes supervisors, principals, classroom teachers, and other instructional staff.
[2] Based on the Consumer Price Index, prepared by the Bureau of Labor Statistics, U. S. Department of Labor.
[3] Estimated.
[4] Includes professional noninstructional administrative staff.
[5] Partly estimated.
[6] Excludes kindergarten teachers.
[7] Includes clerical assistants to instructional personnel.

[8] Includes attendance personnel.
[9] Data not available.
[10] Salary data reported as median salary.
[11] Excludes vocational schools not operated as part of the regular public school system.

SOURCES: U. S. Department of Health, Education, and Welfare, National Center for Education Statistics, *Statistics of State School Systems and Statistics of Public Elementary and Secondary Day Schools*, Fall 1975.

first part of this chapter. Furthermore, when pupils feel that the teacher is in a serving status, she is less useful as a person with whom they want to identify.

Wilbur A. Yauch, Martin H. Bartels, and Emmet Morris, writing for the beginning teacher, suggest that a new teacher guard against the expectation that his or her services to the community also include guiding children in Sunday School classes, Boy or Girl Scout groups, and community playgrounds.

After spending an exhausting week of intensive devotion to children, it is only reasonable to propose that teachers be permitted to vary their efforts in after-school hours. If they are to maintain a desirable, balanced outlook on life, part of their time should be spent in activities unrelated to teaching. It is strongly urged that you seek to make your contribution to community living in adult activities.[12]

The Teacher and the Local School System

President James Garfield, describing a true teacher, said, "Give me a log hut, with only a simple bench, Mark Hopkins on one end and I on the other, and you may have all the buildings, apparatus and libraries without him."

Garfield meant, of course, that excellent teachers are all that is needed for a good education. This point of view, appealing and partially true as it is, nevertheless overlooks the importance of instructional materials, school organization, and educational leadership, especially in our complex modern society.

Of all the social forces affecting the teacher-learning process, the quality of human relations existing in the school system is by far the most important. Teaching, whether in a rural or an urban school system, is carried on in a veritable sea of human relationships. In the past teachers have been accustomed to working with other teachers, administrators, supervisors, librarians, secretaries, and custodians. But many new branches have grown on the educational tree in recent years. Some of these are school psychologists, counselors, school social workers, speech and hearing therapists, directors of research, public relations specialists, teacher aides, systems analysts, and still others. The effectiveness of the services of the new auxiliary personnel depends on how well teachers understand their functions and make use of their services in improving the teaching-learning process.

Organization and administration. Education in the United States is a responsibility of the various state governments. The states, however, generally delegate much of their authority over schools to local school districts. The people in the school districts in most states elect members of a board of education to employ personnel, establish policies, and keep the public informed about the school program. The quality of instruction in classrooms, the morale of the teaching staff, and the progress that the school system is able to make in keeping its program in line with current demands on the schools all depend to a large extent on the types of persons who serve as members of boards of education and particularly on how well they understand the functions of a board of education.

State and national associations of school board members have provided useful services during the last decade or more, particularly in developing manuals or guides for policies and procedures. There is little objective evidence, however, on how well boards of education throughout the country actually perform their functions. One study, confined to the schools of Massachusetts, provides some grounds for believing that most of them do a good job. Of the superintendents contacted, 49 per cent thought their boards of education were doing an excellent job and 33 per cent thought that they were doing a good job.[13]

The regulations established by state and local boards of education leave a great deal of freedom for the superintendent of schools, the central office staff, and building principals to initiate innovations in organization and instruction. The work of the teacher is, therefore, affected to a great extent by the quality of leadership provided by the administrative and supervisory staff of the school system.

Teacher militancy and negotiations. Evidence of increasing teacher militancy in recent years has been seen in three principal activities: strikes, sanctions, and negotiations. Many school systems, particularly in the large cities, have seen their teachers go out on strikes. Several state educational associations have invoked sanctions, notifying colleges and universities nationwide that unsatisfactory educational conditions existed in that state and that students in their institutions should be discouraged from seeking positions in the state.

Teachers, particularly in large cities, have banded together and sent representatives to negotiate with boards of education concerning salaries and working conditions. This labor-management type of arrangement bypasses the superintendent's traditional role as a representative of the teachers in dealing with the board and thus requires many adjustments; some undoubtedly will cause further controversy.

Increasing teacher militancy cannot be attributed to any single cause. Teachers in many states have become concerned upon learning that salaries are lower in their states than in other states, causing an exodus of competent young teachers. Yet, 9 of the 10 states that are lowest in average salaries have had no strikes. When teachers in one large school system were asked to list needed improvements, better salaries was far down in eleventh place, with only 5.8 per cent of the teachers listing it. Smaller classes (45.1 per cent), more planning time (35.1 per cent), relief from nonteaching chores (24.3 per cent), and other items far outranked better salaries.

The presence of more men teachers on school faculties, the desire to have more to say about school policies, greater recognition in educational associations, and time to teach seem to be important factors causing unrest among teachers. Strikes and sanctions have usually brought about slight improvements. Therefore, it is generally agreed that militant teachers must find better ways of getting their message across to the voting public before greater gains can be made.

CHANGING PATTERNS OF SCHOOL SUPPORT

Public school education has been heralded as the single most important institution for altering the social class position of a lower-class child. This theory assumes that he or she is able to receive the same quality of education as other children. During the twentieth century there has been a great increase in expenditures for both public and nonpublic education; more than three times as much of the GNP was spent on education in 1974–75 as was spent in 1929 (see Table 6). Even so, public expenditures continue to be larger for other items, such as defense, the purchase and operation of automobiles, alcoholic beverages, tobacco, and various types of recreation.

Table 5. Teacher Involvement in Work Stoppages: 1959 to 1973

Year	Number of stoppages	Workers involved	Man-days idle during year	Average no. of days idle per teacher
1959	2	210	670	3
1960	3	5,490	5,490	1
1961	1	20	20	1
1962	1	20,000	20,000	1
1963	2	2,200	2,590	1
1964	9	14,400	30,600	2
1965	5	1,720	7,880	4
1966	30	37,300	58,500	1
1967	76	92,400	969,300	10½
1968	88	145,000	2,180,000	15
1969	183	105,000	412,000	4
1970	152	94,800	935,600	10
1972	87	33,900	207,300	6
1973	117	51,400	620,700	12

NOTE: Data on stoppages and workers involved refer to stoppages beginning in the year: man-days idle refer to all stoppages in effect during the year. Because of rounding, sums of individual items may not equal totals.

SOURCES: U.S. Department of Labor, Bureau of Labor Statistics, *Work Stoppages in Government, 1958–68*, Report 348, 1970; *Work Stoppages in Government, 1973*, Report 437, 1975; *Government Work stoppages, 1960, 1969, and 1970*, 1971.

Public schools in the United States are supported by three primary sources: local, state, and federal. In 1974–75 local districts paid 53 per cent of the cost of public elementary and secondary education; the states paid 39 per cent; and the federal government paid 8 per cent. Ironically, the percentages of school revenue coming from the three levels of government are inversely related to their fund-raising abilities. It seems likely that unless fundamental changes are made in the bases of support, public school systems will not be able to meet all of the demands society places on them.[14]

Local Support

Traditionally, the chief source of support for the public schools has come from local revenues, mainly from property tax levies. A school district is the basic governmental unit through which local schools are operated. Technically, it is a unit of government created and empowered by state law to administer a public school or a public school system. There are about 16,000 separate school districts in the United States. School board members are agents of the state, elected or appointed in accordance with legal provisions, and derive their authority from the state.

School districts vary, of course, in financial support. They vary in the amounts they are willing to tax themselves and in the assessment practices on which their taxation is based: some districts value property at a low rate; others use a high rate. But these variations are relatively minor compared with the wide discrepancies in actual tax-paying ability. No matter what measuring standards are used, certain communities obviously are much less affluent than others. For instance some are high-income suburbs, others contain much low-cost housing, and others have virtually no industrial property that can be taxed. Compounding the problem is the fact that in some states legal maximum tax rates have been established; they can be exceeded, but only by a majority vote of the voters of a district. It seems hardly necessary to add that it is often difficult to persuade a majority of the residents of a district to vote to tax themselves at a higher rate.

Table 6. Gross National Product (GNP) Related to Total Expenditures for Education: 1929 to 1974

Calendar year	Gross national product (in thousands)	School year	Expenditures for education[1]	
			Total (in thousands)	As a percent of gross national product
1929	$103,095,000	1929–30	$3,233,601	3.1
1933	55,601,000	1933–34	2,294,896	4.1
1937	90,446,000	1937–38	3,014,074	3.3
1941	124,540,000	1941–42	3,203,548	2.6
1945	212,010,000	1945–46	4,167,597	2.0
1949	256,484,000	1949–50	8,795,635	3.4
1953	364,593,000	1953–54	13,949,876	3.8
1957	441,134,000	1957–58	21,119,565	4.8
1961	520,109,000	1961–62	29,366,305	5.6
1965	684,884,000	1965–66	45,397,713	6.6
1969	930,284,000	1969–70	70,077,228	7.5
1971	1,054,915,000	1971–72	[2] 82,999,062	7.9
1972	1,157,966,000	1972–73	89,100,000	7.7
1973	1,294,919,000	1973–74	[2] 98,300,000	7.6
1974	1,397,400,000	1974–75	[3] 108,700,000	7.8

[1] Includes expenditures of public and nonpublic schools at all levels of education (elementary, secondary, and higher education).
[2] Revised since originally published.
[3] Estimated.

SOURCES: U. S. Department of Health, Education, and Welfare, Office of Education, *Statistics of State School Systems*; *Financial Statistics of Institutions of Higher Education*, and unpublished data; U. S. Department of Commerce, Bureau of Economic Analysis, *Survey of Current Business*, July 1971, and July 1974.

It is quite apparent why the local property tax, as presently administered, has been called antiquated. The burden placed on homeowners, plus the growing demands made on public schools, has served to underscore the need to find other ways to secure local sources of education funds. This condition is serious for schools attended by middle- and upper-class children; it is calamitous for schools attended by lower-class children.

State Support

Most state consititutions spell out the responsibility of their state legislatures for establishing and maintaining a system of free public schools. Control over public education is also shared by the governor, the state board of education, the state department of education, and other state agencies. State departments of education are especially effective in certifying teachers, selecting textbooks, and distributing state money. State support of public education increased from one-fifth in 1920 to two-fifths in 1976. Whereas local school districts are empowered to levy only property taxes, the states have a much broader base of tax support—income and sales taxes. In order to correct inequities in school funding, most states have equalization programs that supplement local funds in order to provide minimum support for all schools. Equalization formulas require the wealthiest districts to provide the largest part of their own financial support. Conversely, the least wealthy districts receive the greatest amount of state support. The average expenditure varies widely among states, ranging from $2,251 spent for each pupil in New York during the 1974–1975 school year to $921 in Mississippi.

Some local school officials fear that increasing state funds will lead to state control. With this fear in mind, one expert has said that the most valuable contribution state funds can make towards school improvement is the release of local funds for innovative programs.[15] In the final analysis, the advantages or disadvantages of equalization programs depend largely on the terms of the funding. In any case, one study concluded that fiscally dependent and independent districts did not differ greatly in their patterns of expenditure.[16] The key consideration then becomes whether the structure adopted provides a better quality of education.

Federal Support

The federal government has always assisted in supporting public education. This tradition started, in fact, even before the adoption of the Constitution, when the Continental Congress passed two Northwest Ordinances in 1785 and 1787. The first of these acts established the policy of reserving land for the benefit of the public schools, and both acts affirmed the necessity to encourage schools and education in general. The Constitution itself does not mention education, but the federal power to aid public education is based on its general welfare clause (Article 1, section 8), which authorizes Congress to levy and collect taxes, duties, imposts, and excises and to pay the debts and provide for the common defense and the general welfare of the United States.

Federal expenditures for education are numerous. In fact, under special conditions the federal government becomes directly involved in education. Since 1804 Congress has assumed responsibility for the schools in Washington, D.C. Since 1824 the Bureau of Indian Affairs has been providing schools for Indians and natives of Alaska. In addition the federal government has established and operated schools in foreign countries where it maintains consulates, arsenals, dockyards, and other defense-related establishments. As our defense bases around the world decrease, so too do our federally operated schools for military dependents. (Dependent schools are being maintained in Europe, the British Isles, Puerto Rico, North Africa, Panama, and the Far East.)

Before 1950 federal support of education in this country was mainly concerned with vocational education. By 1965, however, broad federal programs were operating under the Vocational Education Act of 1963, the Manpower Development and Training Act, the expanded National Defense Education Act, and the Economic Opportunity Act of 1964. Even broader and more far-reaching programs were made possible by the Elementary and Secondary Education Act of 1965, which extended federal support for the first time down through elementary schools.

The case for federal support of public education is similar to the rationale for state support. Just as local school districts are limited in their revenue sources, so too are the states. Some states, for example, have higher average per capita incomes than others, ranging from Alaska with the highest to Mississippi with the lowest. Although most school districts accept state equalization plans, they nevertheless resist national equalization proposals. The federal government assists public elementary and secondary schools in the following ways:

Innovation and improvement. Money administered by the U.S. Office of Education and the National Science Foundation is used for educational research. Four major centers of research and development were founded in the early 1960s at Harvard and the Universities of Pittsburgh, Wisconsin, and Oregon. Similarly, the Elementary and Secondary Education Act of 1965 provided $100 million to start a number of regional centers for educational research and development. Twenty-nine such centers still exist.

Training of personnel. The federal government also provides money for the advanced training of various specialists. Most of this money goes for training research workers in the natural sciences, but large sums have also been provided (through the U.S. Office of Education and the National Defense Education Act) for training school counselors and for the retraining of classroom teachers in science, mathematics, foreign languages, and work with handicapped children.

Education of the underprivileged and the handicapped. The federal government is continuing its programs for the education and rehabilitation of physically handicapped

Table 7. Expenditures for Public Elementary and Secondary Education

State	Total expenditures per pupil[1]				
	1969–70	1970–71	1972–73	1973–74	1974–75
United States	$ 926	$ 1,008	$ 1,182	$ 1,281	$ 1,431
Alabama	503	572	630	790	933
Alaska	1,416	1,897	1,961	2,102	2,228
Arizona	915	985	1,291	1,439	1,546
Arkansas	632	665	731	912	1,087
California	1,067	1,060	1,129	1,318	1,373
Colorado	798	902	1,138	1,278	1,423
Connecticut	966	1,082	1,365	1,359	1,596
Delaware	1,106	1,298	1,575	1,747	1,723
District of Columbia	[2] 1,372	1,250	1,626	1,827	1,957
Florida	923	954	[3] 1,030	1,,030	1,392
Georgia	688	729	895	974	1,087
Hawaii	964	1,144	1,240	1,391	1,600
Idaho	706	761	868	942	1,232
Illinois	959	1,122	1,394	1,425	1,637
Indiana	847	1,025	1,100	1,152	1,298
Iowa	1,037	1,104	1,238	1,273	1,400
Kansas	920	860	1,025	1,114	1,607
Kentucky	693	709	788	829	960
Louisiana	746	904	1,002	1,096	1,158
Maine	816	885	952	1,033	1,130
Maryland	1,137	1,240	1,473	1,591	1,771
Massachusetts	874	980	1,234	1,279	1,504
Michigan	1,019	1,126	1,461	1,459	1,770
Minnesota	1,105	1,241	1,387	1,450	1,635
Mississippi	534	553	751	858	921
Missouri	842	843	984	1,082	1,203
Montana	982	1,000	–	1,248	1,392
Nebraska	649	837	1,074	1,188	1,378
Nevada	877	911	1,199	1,276	1,308
New Hampshire	856	918	1,073	1,036	1,173
New Jersey	1,108	1,207	1,476	1,565	[2] 1,713
New Mexico	835	912	1,105	[4] 1,220	1,282
New York	1,420	1,561	1,808	2,037	2,241
North Carolina	675	714	880	978	1,151
North Dakota	764	761	956	1,101	1,199
Ohio	804	891	1,038	1,120	1,270
Oklahoma	617	746	778	921	1,131
Oregon	1,022	1,079	1,262	1,341	1,642
Pennsylvania	1,056	1,191	1,427	1,474	1,587
Rhode Island	1,010	1,147	1,232	1,415	1,665
South Carolina	645	753	847	983	1,125
South Dakota	775	826	900	1,011	1,062
Tennessee	636	670	811	841	997
Texas	709	775	943	977	1,073
Utah	716	739	843	996	1,265
Vermont	1,034	1,162	1,360	1,308	1,267
Virginia	822	923	1,082	1,142	1,231
Washington	880	1,018	1,119	1,136	1,339

West Virginia	706	704	826	945	1,020
Wisconsin	988	1,078	1,241	1,335	1,452
Wyoming	931	1,012	1,193	1,301	1,404
Outlying areas:					
American Samoa	634	[5] 634	719	—	891
Canal Zone	1,065	1,139	([1])	—	1,603
Guam	676	854	1,047	—	1,114
Puerto Rico	[6] 312	416	483	—	[3] 483
Virgin Islands	—	—	1,433	—	2,149

[1] Includes current expenditures, capital outlay, and interest on school debt.
[2] Estimated by National Center for Education Statistics.
[3] Data for 1972–73.
[4] Excludes per-pupil expenditures for kindergarten pupils.
[5] Data for 1969–70.
[6] Data for 1968–69.

SOURCES: U. S. Department of Health, Education, and Welfare, National Center for Education Statistics, *Statistics of Public Elementary and Secondary Day Schools*, Fall 1969, Fall 1970, Fall 1972, Fall 1973, and Fall 1974.

people; the retraining of people whose jobs have been eliminated by automation; the education of adult illiterates; work experience and related education for unemployed youth; and compensatory education for disadvantaged preschool and school-age children. It also provides funds for research on the causes of mental deficiency.

EXCEPTIONAL CHILDREN

As we have seen in earlier chapters, children come to school with a wide variety of advantages and disadvantages—due to heredity, social class, group experiences, or teacher and administrator attitudes. In the jargon of education, children who differ from the normal or average characteristics are called *exceptional children*: mentally, physically, emotionally, and socially different children. Within this category we can further break them down into several groups: creative, mentally gifted, mentally retarded, physically handicapped, emotionally handicapped, and socially and culturally disadvantaged. The recent concept of "mainstreaming" (that is, placing exceptional children in regular classes) requires that all teachers be proficient in working with such students.

In previous years it was erroneously assumed that special skills were needed to teach special education classes. In reality all children are special, and therefore they all require well-trained teachers who care about them— teachers who exhibit patience, resourcefulness, and acceptance. Of course, even with teachers who care, the task of learning is more difficult for handicapped students.

Creative students. Creative students are more easy to identify in the arts—painting, drawing, dancing, and playing musical instruments or singing. Very early in life they demonstrate their ability to innovate or uniquely communicate. Often the ability does not show up in intelligence tests, and tests of creativity are generally unreliable and lack adequate validity. Consequently, countless creative students have been forced out of school because they do not build, paint, play, or write according to predetermined teacher expectations.

Mentally gifted students. While there is no common definition of mentally gifted children, the most widely accepted definition is someone whose IQ exceeds 130 on standardized tests, such as the Wechsler Intelligence Scale for Children and the Revised Stanford-Binet. (Average IQ is between 90 and 110, and superior IQ between 110 and 130.) It is also important to note that a child may be gifted in some areas but not in others.

The challenges and rewards in working with

Table 8. Educational Staff[1] Receiving Training and Expenditures for Training in Federally Aided Programs Operated by Local Education Agencies, by Source of Funds: Regular School Term 1972–73 and Summer 1973

Source of funds	Number of staff receiving training[2]	Amount of training expenditures	Percent of training expenditures
Total	[3] 344,767	$48,861,000	100.0
ESEA Title I	182,613	18,380,000	38.0
ESEA Title III	56,322	7,668,000	16.0
Follow Through	13,550	1,940,000	4.0
Emergency School Aid Act	14,644	1,517,000	3.0
Education Professions Development Act ..	15,075	7,962,000	16.0
Other Federal sources	62,563	11,394,000	23.0

[1] Includes teachers, other professional staff members, education aides, and other nonprofessional staff members.
[2] Estimated.
[3] Duplicated count; staff may receive training in more than one type of program.

SOURCE: U. S. Department of Health, Education, and Welfare, National Center for Education Statistics, Consolidated Program Information Report, 1972–73, unpublished data.

gifted students are compounded by the fact that as a group, intellectually gifted children tend to be more confident, better poised, and have higher self-concepts than other children. Studies show that gifted students are also above average in health, strength, and physical agility. Furthermore, they learn quicker than their age-mates and exhibit other characteristics that set them apart from other students— including being at ease with abstract ideas, reading rapidly and comprehensively in many fields, and excelling in independent study projects. The inquisitive nature of the gifted child, plus his or her familiarity with minute facts and intricate details, can unnerve most average-intelligence teachers, not to mention other students.

Mentally retarded students. There are at least six million mentally retarded people in the United States. Of each 1,000 persons, approximately thirty are mentally retarded. Within this category are educable, trainable, and custodial children. *Educable* children (77% of the mentally retarded students) have IQs between 50 and 75. If the standards of achievement and materials are carefully selected, educable students (or slow learners, as they are sometimes called) can master simple tasks. In terms of learning, they must be shown rather than told what to do. Much of their learning occurs through repetition.

Like other types of retarded students, educable children have extremely limited abilities of generalization, association, symbolization, comparison and comprehension. Thus their limited reading skills and vocabulary inhibit their ability to learn from experience, make sense of complex situations, form judgments, and project future behaviors and consequences. Furthermore, they are prone to "act out" in class—talk, fight, laugh, move around without permission, and cry.

Trainable students (20% of the mentally retarded students) have IQs between 25 and 50. However, despite their low IQs they are capable of some learning, reading, writing, and simple arithmetic. Contrary to popular opinion, all trainable students do not have to be institutionalized. Rather, if given appropriate instruction, they can take care of themselves and adjust socially in the community outside school. Indeed, some trainable person learn enough to become occupationally self-sufficient.

A few trainable students are housed in residential schools for the mentally handicapped. Most, however, are in neither public schools nor private institutions—they remain in their homes to vegetate. Fortunately, a growing number of public schools are assuming responsibility for the education of trainable students.

Custodial children (3% of the mentally re-

Table 9. Participation in Special Education Programs Operated by Local School Districts as a Percentage[1] of Public School Enrollment, by Category of Handicap and by Region: 1973

Region	Total	Educable mentally retarded	Trainable mentally retarded	Special disabilities[2]	Other
Total	4.04	1.58	.24	1.09	1.12
Northeast	3.48	1.32	.29	.79	1.08
Midwest	4.18	2.03	.23	1.17	.75
South	4.55	1.78	.24	1.17	1.35
West	3.17	1.00	.21	1.04	.93

[1] Percentages are based on unweighted data from 1,500 school districts, representing about 47 percent of the total national public school enrollment.

[2] Children with physical handicaps, including blind, deaf, speech impaired, orthopedically handicapped, and neurological disorders.

SOURCE: U. S. Department of Health, Education, and Welfare, Office of the Assistant Secretary for Planning and Evaluation, *Analysis of 1973 Participation of Handicapped Children in Local Education Programs*, unpublished data.

tarded students) have IQs of less than 25. Because of their extremely limited intelligence, they require constant care and supervision at home or in a mental institution. For these children daily survival and not an education is of paramount concern.

The slowness of our society to respond to the needs of mentally retarded children is evidenced in the lateness of Congress to facilitate public school education in this area. It wasn't until 1958 that Congress passed the Fogarty-McGovern Act, which authorized grants for education of teachers of the mentally retarded. In 1963 the Mental Retardation Facilities and Community Health Construction Act and the Retardation Planning Amendment were passed. The Mental Retardation Facilities Act provides funds for treatment and research facilities for the mentally retarded, while the Retardation Planning Amendment provides expanded health care for low-income mothers and others with high probability of giving birth to retarded children.

Physically handicapped students. A physically visible yet academically invisible group of students are characterized in terms of the following handicaps: visually handicapped, deaf and hard-of-hearing, speech handicaps, orthopedically handicapped, and other physical handicaps.

Approximately one-fourth of all school children need eye care and more than one million Americans suffer from glaucoma, which sometimes leads to blindness. Visually handicapped students exhibit many characteristics, including the inability to see objects and words at a distance; inflamed and watery eyes; squinting or frowning; difficulty in distinguishing colors; and redness or swelling of eye lids. All students, with or without signs of defective vision, should be examined by an eye specialist.

Partially-sighted students, those with vision of 20/70 or less after correction, need not be debilitated in the regular classroom if some adjustments are made, e.g., position partially sighted students' desks so that they receive sufficient light; locate their desks near the front of the room; cover or repaint highly reflective surfaces; schedule the work so that there is ample time to rest the eyes when close visual tasks are required; use books with large type; encourage the use of soft, dark lead pencils; allow them to make oral reports instead of demanding that all students give written reports.

Hard-of-hearing students can be taught in regular classrooms if lip reading or electronic hearing devices are available and if the students' speech is not severely retarded. (The major problem in education of the deaf, especially those who have never heard speech, is retarded speech. This is also a problem with many hard-of-hearing students.) Deaf children are best taught in special classes, since their physical handicap often leads to severe social disadvantages.

Deafness in adults is traceable to the period of early childhood. Because progressive deafness is a very gradual process, it usually is not noticed until the hearing loss is too severe to be corrected. For this reason early detection is imperative. Physical causes of deafness include malnutrition, bad teeth, inflammation of the middle ear, hardened impacted wax in the ear, hard blows to the ear, severe colds, and automobile collisions.

Within the classroom, teachers should be alert to the following symptoms of loss of hearing: failing to respond to direct questions, faulty pronounciation of common words, watching others and following their movements, frequent requests to repeat words, earaches, discharge from ears, and persistent mouth breathing.

Here too our national efforts have been late and inadequate. In 1961 Congress provided funds to educate additional teachers of deaf children and monies for schools to use speech pathologists and audiologists.

Students with speech handicaps comprise the largest group of American physically handicapped students. Generally, a speech defect is any acoustic variation from an accepted speech standard so extreme as to be evident to the speaker, confusing to the listener, or unpleasant to the speaker and/or the listener. The list of speech impairments is lengthy, including stuttering, stammering, lisping, nasality, "foreign" accents, and balking.

One of the most common and improperly diagnosed and treated perceptual and speech handicaps is dyslexia. Although more than two million children suffer from dyslexia, few are involved in reading clinics. The dyslexic student's directional perception is distorted—he reverses letters, words, and numbers: "e" becomes "c," "some" becomes "mose," and "63" becomes "36." With proper diagnosis and educational services, dyslexia—as well as speech problems which have no organic origin—can be corrected in the primary grades.

Too many parents and teachers believe that children will outgrow their speech defects. Fortunately, speech therapists are becoming integral members of a growing number of school staffs. Detection and correction are but one aspect of a speech therapist's job. Prevention is the other aspect.

Orthopedically handicapped students are the most visible because they require immediate school adjustments—in transportation, furniture, and doors. Less than one per cent of schools make the adjustments. Unfortunately, many people assume erroneously that all orthopedically handicapped children are also intellectually handicapped. Major causes of orthopedic handicaps are infantile paralysis, rheumatic fever, brain injury, spastic paralysis, and tuberculosis.

More than five million school-age children, one out of every ten, suffer from some form of brain damage—as a result of poor prenatal care, injury during birth, or a blow to the head after birth. Doctors, nurses, and physical therapists can greatly supplement school resources. To date, few teachers have been specially prepared to work with orthopedically handicapped children.

The list of students with other physical handicaps is both long and depressing—the malnourished, the underutilized, and those suffering from allergic, cardiac, diabetic, tubercular, and other diseases. These conditions did not begin in the school and, sadly, few will end in the school

Emotionally handicapped students. As our nation becomes more industrialized, affluent, and mobile, the incidence of mental illness increases. Few teachers or administrators are trained to diagnose symptoms of mental illness and fewer still are trained to provide therapy. This is the job of school psychologists and, in some instances, psychiatric social workers and counselors. Teachers can, however, provide what Carl Rogers calls "therapy for normals."

A comprehensive program of federal aid to the culturally disadvantaged began with the Economic Opportunity Act of 1964. This act provided federal funds for many activities, including community action programs, youth employment opportunities, and training of adults who are recipients or potential recipients of public welfare. Specific programs include Head Start, the Job Corps, and Work-

Figure 4. A General Working Estimate of the Number of Children Per Thousand Who Are Sufficiently Handicapped to Warrant Special Services.

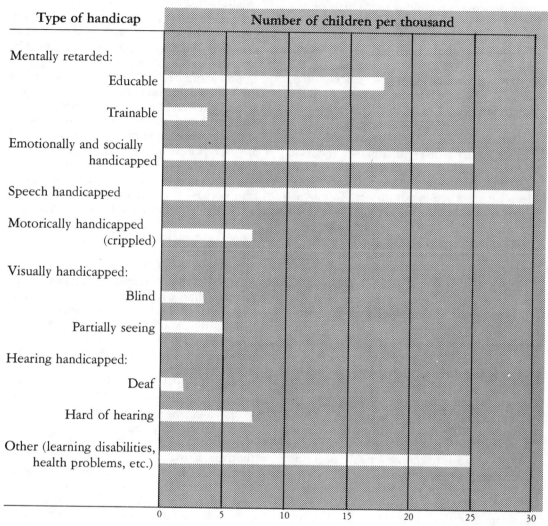

SOURCE: U.S. Office of Education

Study programs. It is mainly through these programs that cultural differences are expected to be minimized.

The American Humane Association estimates that each year at least 10,000 children are severely battered, 50,000 are sexually abused, 100,000 are emotionally neglected, and 100,000 are physically and educationally neglected. In 1976, 2,000 children died at the hands of abusive parents. Educators concerned with helping children should be aware of this type of child too.

Other chapters of this book discuss *socially* and *culturally* disadvantaged students—Blacks, Chicanos, Native Americans, poor whites, etc.

AID TO NONPUBLIC SCHOOLS

There are two types of nonpublic schools: independent (or private) and parochial. Independent schools range from vocational schools to college preparatory academies to "free" schools. While they are not limited to state certified teachers, the trend is toward independent schools recruiting individuals with at least a college degree and competency in an academic discipline. It is important to note that the independent school is not a recent phenomenon. With the exception of the junior high school, all public schools originated as private schools, i.e., nursery school, elementary school, high school, junior college, four-year college, and the university.

Despite the First Amendment to the U.S. Constitution, the first states not only endorsed but supported denominational schools. Catholic, Lutheran, and Episcopal schools are deeply entrenched in our history. To the displeasure of Catholics, the early public schools were quite sectarian with their Protestant religious exercises. In fact this condition was an important reason for the growth of Catholic schools in the late nineteenth century.

For a three-year period following 1922, when the state of Oregon enacted a statute requiring every child between the ages of six and eighteen to attend public schools, the existence of nonpublic schools was threatened. However, the U.S. Supreme Court, in *Pierce v. Society of Sisters*, invalidated the statute because it would destroy the property of private schools without the due process of law. The Court also ruled that a state could require all children to be educated and inspect all schools, but a state could not interfere with parents' or guardians' rights to choose a public or private education for their children.

Whether or not to give federal funds to private and parochial schools is a growing problem that is the subject of continuing controversy. There are valid arguments on both sides. Since Catholic schools comprise 80 per cent of the private schools, most of these comments will focus on Catholic schools and the church versus state issue.

Parochial schools educate 14 per cent of the total enrolled students in the U.S. Proponents of federal aid point out that if these schools abandoned this function, the public schools would not be able to absorb the additional students. For example, in Pittsburgh and Chicago, nearly 50 per cent and 40 per cent, respectively, of the white children are in parochial schools. Advocates of federal aid argue that since these schools perform a public service, they should receive public funds in

order to eliminate what is in effect double taxation of the parents of parochial school children.

Opponents of federal aid acknowledge the public service aspect of the issue but maintain that providing federal funds for parochial schools is unconstitutional. The U.S. Supreme Court has often reaffirmed the American tradition of keeping church and state separate, most recently in the *Abington School District* case.[17] The Court ruled that prayers and Bible reading in public schools and the laws requiring them are unconstitutional. As for double taxation, it has been justified on the ground that the cost of public education must be borne by all citizens because it is available to all citizens and because all citizens govern and control it. If citizens are dissatisfied with the way the schools are operated, they can vote to change them.

Expenditure of public funds to provide transportation and textbooks for students in private schools is based on the *child benefit theory*; that is, the rationale that such support benefits the student and not the independent school or religion that it may represent. Opponents of this view argue that aid to students receiving sectarian educational instruction is indeed aid to the institution. The U.S. Supreme Court adopted the child benefit theory in upholding the legality of using Titles I and II of the Elementary and Secondary Education Act (ESEA) of 1965. Title I of ESEA authorized assistance for the education of low-income children attending public and independent schools. Title II authorized expending funds for school library resources, textbooks, and other instructional materials to both public and independent schools. Services provided in the ESEA must be in proportion to the number of students attending public and nonpublic schools in a school district.

In 1977 the U.S. Supreme Court ruled that the following types of state aid to parochial schools are constitutional: (1) speech, hearing and some forms of diagnostic testing services, (2) textbooks and textbook supplements such as workbooks and manuals, (3) therapeutic, guidance and medical services given by public employees on sites neither physically nor educationally identified with functions of the non-public schools, and (4) academic testing services. The court prohibited states from lending parochial schools classroom equip-

Chart 4. Sectarian Activites in the Public Schools

Sectarian Activities in the Public Schools

Date	Event	Significance
1642	Massachusetts law	Made parents legally responsible for the moral and vocational education of their children.
1647	Old Deluder Satan Act	Required town government to construct schools and provide teachers.
1925	*Pierce v. The Society of Sisters of the Holy Name of Jesus and Mary*, 268 U.S. 510.	Made the private school a legal alternative to the public school.
1930	*Cochran et al. v. Louisiana State Board of Education* et al., 281 U.S. 370	Allowed the state of Louisiana to provide free textbooks for both public and parochial school students.
1947	*Everson v. Board of Education of the Township of Ewing et al.*, 330 U.S. 1	Upheld a New Jersey statute authorizing the expenditure of public funds for the transportation of parochial school students.
1948	*People of the State of Illinois exrel. McCollum v. Board of Education of School District No. 71, Champaign et al.*, 333 U.S. 203	Declared it unconstitutional to hold sectarian religious instruction on public school property.
1959	*Schempp v. School District of Abington Township, (Pa.)*, 177 F. Supp. 398 U.S. District Ct. E.D.	Declared unconstitutional the reading of the Bible and recitation of the Lord's prayer in a school assembly program.
1962	*Engel v. Vitale*, 8L ed 2d 601, 604	Declared unconstitutional the recitation of New York's nondenominational Regent's Prayer.

ment such as maps, globes, projectors, tape recorders, and record players. Nor can state aid be used for parochial school field trips. The basis of this decision is whether the aid would benefit the students, which is constitutional, or their church-run schools, which the Constitution prohibits. (See *Meek v. Pittenger*, 421 U.S. 349, 1975; and *Wolman v. Walter*, 417 F. Supp. 1113, N.D., Ohio, 1976.)

Despite unyielding opposition, federal funds are being used to assist some parochial school programs, for instance cultural enrichment for low-income students and improvement of science, mathematics, and language arts programs. When federal efforts make public school desegregation even more wide-spread, it is possible that improved parochial schools will become even more attractive to those who wish to escape racial integration. If this does happen, we will see a sadly ironic situation—highly segregated religious schools in a nation committed to desegregated public schools.

It is erroneous to label private schools per se racist. In 1971 the Council for American Private Education (CAPE) was organized. CAPE is a coalition of twelve private elementary and secondary school associations with a total enrollment of about 4.2 million students, approximately 85 per cent of all private school students. The member organizations, which have nondiscriminatory admissions policies with regard to race, color, and national origin, are: the American Lutheran Church, American Montessori Society, Association of Military Colleges and Schools in the United States, Friends Council on Education, Lutheran Church—Missouri Synod, National Association of Independent Schools, National Association of Private Schools for Exceptional Children, National Catholic Education Association, National Society for Hebrew Day Schools, National Union for Christian Schools, and the U.S. Catholic Conference.

Between the period 1970–71 and 1975–76, Catholic nonpublic schools lost nearly 22 per cent enrollment (down from 4.4 million to 3.4 million), while most non-Catholic nonpublic schools gained students. Several factors account for the increased enrollments of non-Catholic nonpublic schools, including low ethnic minority student population, the perceived higher quality of basic instruction, desire for religious and moral instruction, and more rigid discipline. The white flight out of the cities, smaller Catholic family sizes, and increased costs are but a few of the reasons for the enrollment decline in Catholic schools. Currently, this decline is slowing.

SCHOOL FACILITIES

The growing need for better educational facilities reflects insufficient expenditures for new construction, modernization, and maintenance. School buildings must change architecturally to meet changing instructional demands. Early schools consisted of only one large classroom that accommodated a single teacher with a group of ungraded students. The shift to grading brought a shift to the traditional building with an individual room for each class. In recent years the concepts of flexible scheduling and nongrading have made traditional buildings no longer functional.

Few school districts are able to keep up, structurally, with their growing populations. Though nearly $25 billion was spent on public school construction during the 1950s, schools began the 1960–1961 academic year with a shortage of 132,000 classrooms. However, this shortage is being alleviated in many districts through school desegregation—abolishing dual school systems and consolidating facilities. School construction costs are borne mainly by local districts. The local burden is compounded because the allocation of land and buildings for school use removes them from local tax rolls. As in many other areas of education, low-income communities and their students are the most seriously lacking in adequate school buildings and facilities.

HIGHER EDUCATION

The University of Santo Domingo, founded in the Dominican Republic in 1538, was the first institution of higher learning in the Western Hemisphere. The first in the North American Colonies was Harvard College, established by the Puritans in Massachusetts in 1636. Harvard, whose primary purpose was to prepare ministers for the church, remained the only institution of higher learning in North America until near the end of the seventeenth century.

The church college was the capstone of the colonial school system. Like Harvard, the next institutions all had denominational connections. William and Mary was established in Virginia in 1693, Yale in Connecticut in 1701, Princeton in New Jersey in 1746, King's College (later Columbia University) in New York in 1754, Brown in Rhode Island in 1764, Rutgers in New Jersey in 1766, and Dartmouth in New Hampshire in 1769. Other types of institutions came later. Only two states—Georgia and North Carolina—had chartered state universities by the end of the eighteenth century. In the nineteenth century, however, many new types of collegiate institutions were founded: state universities, land-grant colleges, institutions established by philanthropists, Negro colleges and universities, colleges for women, coeducational institutions, technological institutes, and many types of professional schools. The junior college did not appear until 1902.

Increasing Magnitude of Higher Education

Harvard College never had more than 20 students enrolled at one time during the first 64 years of its existence. The situation became very different in later years. There were 238,000 students enrolled in colleges and universities in 1900; 598,000 in 1920; 1,494,000 in 1940; 5,300,000 in 1964; and more than 10 million in 1976. It took about 3 centuries for this country to reach an enrollment in higher education of 1.5 million students; it took only 30 years to increase this figure to 7.1 million. The president of Harvard taught all the courses during its first 64 years; in 1975 there were 290,000 full-time college and university teachers in the United States. The U.S. Office of Education estimated that in 1975 the total cost of public and nonpublic institutions of higher education, including both current operating expenditures and capital outlay, was $40.2 billion.

Several factors have contributed to the recent rapid increase in the magnitude of the higher education enterprise: the growth in the population of the United States; the increasing percentage of high school graduates who enter colleges and universities; the increasing dependence of industry and government on institutions of higher education for research and for the preparation of specialized personnel; and the increasing recognition that the life chances of young people growing up in our kind of society are enhanced by a college education. In other words, the increases in enrollments and the expansion of programs in higher education have reflected the changes in American life.

As already noted, colonial colleges, like the common schools and grammar schools, were dominated by the religious motive; established to prepare ministers, they were controlled by denominational boards. Their programs were to a great extent patterned after the old English universities—Oxford and Cambridge—from which most of their faculties had graduated. The curricula consisted of the liberal arts, philosophy, and the classical languages. The students were listed in the order of the social rank of their parents.

Universities established in this country during the nineteenth century continued the liberal arts program, with the addition of such new subjects as biological and physical sciences, geography, history, surveying, and navigation. The professional goals of the colonial colleges were expanded to include the preparation of lawyers, physicians, teachers, engineers, and others.

Many new subjects have been added to the liberal arts curriculum in higher education since the beginning of the twentieth century; many new professional schools, such as journalism, social work, business administration, and geology, have also been established. As Figure 5 indicates, the modern university also maintains many service departments unknown in earlier universities. The student will find it interesting to examine the general catalog and the student-faculty directory of his or her own university and to compare the enterprises in which it is engaged with those listed in Figure 5.

Living in a nation whose future is both lighted by promises and clouded by threats, living in an age when the individual must pass judgment on increasingly complicated issues, every citizen has, in the words of John Erskine, "the moral obligation to be intelligent." Yet the magnitude of our higher education enterprise alone will not ensure that future citizens will be intelligent or that their intelligence will be directed toward the creation of a better tomorrow.

It is certainly true that colleges and universities have served America well. They have been a principal source of strength for government; they have provided specialized personnel, research facilities, and competent managers for industry; and they have opened the doors of opportunity to millions of American youth. Nevertheless, there is widespread concern about the ability of this huge enterprise to put into practice the principal of self-renewal so that it will be able to perform the tasks expected of it in an age of accelerated change—its ability, in fact, to bring about the internal reforms that will be needed to make it more relevant to the realities of the next few decades. The rest of this chapter considers needed reforms and promising innovations in the internal structure of institutions of higher education, as well as efforts to improve instruction and to develop a coordinated system of higher education within states and regions.

Inside the Individual Institution

Our 3000 colleges and universities have grown up independently; each has been relatively free to develop its own pattern of operation. The U.S. Office of Education has exercised less authority over higher education than has the ministry of education in any other country.

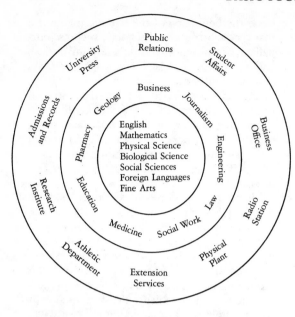

English
Mathematics
Physical Science
Biological Science
Social Sciences
Foreign Languages
Fine Arts

Figure 5. Typical Enterprises of a Modern University. The inner circle lists some typical courses generally offered in the liberal arts or general education program of a modern university. The second ring lists some of the professional schools that are frequently maintained. The outer ring represents the rapidly expanding group of service operations in which universities are engaged.

Because research relating to college and university organization and administration has been relatively neglected, we have little objective knowledge on which to base decisions about the operation of a college or a university. One observer has commented on this situation as follows:

The managerial revolution which has long been underway in business, industry, and government has been slow to start in the groves of academe. I would urge that it is high time for us to allocate more time and energy to the structural and functional problems of educational institutions and to develop a more efficient and effective system of higher education better suited to its own ends and the needs of society.[18]

It is difficult to generalize about the internal arrangements in American colleges and universities. Nevertheless, certain conditions that exist in most of them can be identified.

Administration. Colleges and universities are under the general control and supervision of boards of trustees or boards of regents. These boards generally delegate much authority to a chief administrative official, the president. The president in turn delegates much responsibility to vice-presidents, deans, chairpersons of departments, directors of various enterprises, and other administrative officers.

As colleges and universities become larger, the degree of specialization increases; as specialization increases, the task of supervision by presidents and their central office staff becomes more difficult. As another writer has aptly said, "I might pause to observe that it takes a courageous dean and fearless president to deal firmly with budgetary requests from a speciality they can neither pronounce nor spell."[19]

Many institutions have made attempts to remedy the chaos that arose from excessive diffusion of power in the area of decisionmaking. Organizations composed of representatives from the various colleges and departments have been developed for the purposes of recommending to the president and the board of trustees certain major goals and policies and of mobilizing the resources of the entire institution to achieve these goals. The faculty senate, the budget council, the council on teacher education, and the council on instruction are illustrations. Somewhat similar organizations are frequently set up within colleges and departments to provide a means for faculty participation in decisionmaking at the same time that sound policies and consistent practices are maintained. The success of these organizations in achieving coordination of the activities of a college or university varies from one institution to another. They soon degenerate into mere debating societies unless the administration has a genuine interest in their operation, provides the supervision and encouragement that is needed, and has high-level competence in human relations.

Faculty. There are many myths about college and university professors. One view holds that the comparative security and established routine of the campus provide a safe retreat from the harsh competition of other occupations. Other views are that: (1) professors live in an ivory tower and deal with abstractions that have little value for the practical man or woman, (2) they know and care little about anything outside their fields of specialization, and (3) they have little interest in students. A few individuals distrust the professor as an intellectual who disturbs the status quo by pointing out conditions in our society that call for reforms. Whatever may be said for these views, a surprising number of successful men and women in all walks of life give credit to a college or university professor who helped them to gain confidence in themselves, to respect intellectual attainments, and to develop the tools for a lifetime of learning.

The ivory tower type of professor can still be found occasionally, but the breed is almost extinct. The action intellectual is a much more prevalent type; it is this type of person who keeps the university dynamic, relevant, and significant in western culture. The action intellectual keeps well informed about a wide range of issues before the American people, is actively engaged in discussions with other members of the faculty about the mission and performance of the institution, and strives to invent ways to involve students in the learning process.

In addition to playing an active role in the academic life of the campus, many college and university professors participate in the life of the community, state, and nation. They serve on boards of education, city councils, church boards, and civic club boards and committees. They conduct important research for government and industry, provide factual information and guidance for the legislature, conduct surveys, serve as consultants for public school systems, participate actively in political campaigns, and, in some cases, are elected to important offices in government. As Woodrow Wilson, a noted example of the last category of professors, said, "We were not put into the world to sit still and know; we were put into the world to act."

Curriculum and instruction. The curriculum in most colleges and universities came into existence by historical accretion rather than by any carefully developed plan. As institutions become larger, new courses are added but few are discarded. The relative autonomy of departments has led to much duplication; it is not unusual for essentially the same course to be offered in two or more departments. The rigidity of the departmental structure makes it difficult to develop courses dealing with problems that cut across departmental lines. For example it has become common in recent decades to make teacher education a university-wide responsibility. Although it is relatively simple to develop a paper organization for this purpose, many difficulties are encountered in putting such a plan into actual operation. One typical difficulty involves students preparing to teach in elementary and secondary schools who need to learn about the content and procedures involved in the "new" mathematics and the "new" science; the courses they take in colleges and universities seldom incorporate the new content and procedures. Many college and university courses deal with conditions that existed when the professors were receiving their own education. Once professors have developed their lectures on the basis of these conditions, too often they are reluctant to change them. College students want professors to "tell it like it is." They want to know about conditions that exist now. Those who have talked with students about student unrest have found that much of what students are taught has little relevance to issues and problems which face Americans today.

Although the projects that have revolutionized instruction in elementary and secondary school have been located on university campuses and directed by university professors, universities as a whole have been slow to adopt newer teaching procedures. Involving students in the teaching-learning process, arranging learning situations so that students discover concepts and principles for themselves, making provision for individual differences, experimenting with team teaching and the use of new instructional media, discovering the use of questions—these are some of the hallmarks of effective teaching procedures. Nevertheless, the lecture method still dominates the instructional scene in most institutions of higher education (and can be effective when supplemented by other procedures).

Again student unrest can be explained, at least in part, by failure to provide classroom situations that allow students to feel that they play a significant role in their own education.

The fact that research is given greater recognition than excellent teaching, the publish or perish policy, the increasing extent to which faculty members are drawn from the classroom to work on projects financed by grants from various sources, and the increasing use of graduate students for classroom instruction also cause concern about the quality of instruction provided by colleges and universities.

These comments do not imply that no progress has been made in improving instruction in higher education. Several colleges and universities have conducted experiments designed to improve teaching arrangements and procedures. Some have made excellent provision for the use of newer instructional media, and most are engaged in self-study programs for the purpose of identifying weaknesses and developing plans for the future.

Outside the Individual Institution

As enrollments in higher education increase, as new institutions are established, and as the functions colleges and universities are expected to perform multiply, the need for coordination of programs of higher education becomes imperative. If it is difficult to coordinate the efforts of various segments within a university, it is to be expected that the task of coordinating the activities of institutions within a state or region will be even more difficult. The rationale for state, regional, and national coordination of programs of higher education is not difficult to understand. Each institution surrenders a part of its independence in order to gain greater strength by blending its activities with those of other institutions. It is more difficult to understand or defend the fact that the principle of coordination has not been more widely implemented in the United States.

State agencies for coordinating higher education. In 1965 nine states had single boards for governing all public higher education. Twelve other states had boards with more limited authority over institutions, each of which had its own board of trustees. Currently 1,200 out of 2,200 governing boards serve the private sector (2-year and 4-year institutions), 750 serve the single-campus, public 4-year, and multiple-campus systems. These master boards generally allocate a budget to each institution from the general appropriation for higher education; exercise some control over the curricula offered by each institution; issue regulations concerning admission, degree-granting standards, and reporting practices; and make studies of the future needs of higher education in the state. (The most fully developed master board for higher education is the Coordinating Council for Higher Education in California.)

Regional agencies for coordinating higher education. Agencies for accrediting institutions of higher education have been in existence for many decades. The North Central Association of Secondary Schools and Colleges, the Southern Association of Secondary Schools and Colleges, and similar associations in six regions of the United States publish standards for accreditation and periodically send visitation teams to high schools, colleges, and universities to evaluate the institutions in terms of the published criteria.

A development of the last few decades has been consortium arrangements, which have evolved in virtually every region. Their activities include procedures for exchange of student credits, joint faculty appointments, pooling of library and audiovisual resources, and coordination of extension programs. Regional compacts, such as the Southern Regional Education Board, the Western Interstate Commission for Higher Education, and the New England Board of Higher Education constitute another form of joint action in higher education. The tremendous increase in enrollments and the increasing cost of higher education in the next decade will no doubt hasten efforts to avoid the costly blunders connected with the location of new institutions, wasteful duplication of curricula, and general lack of coordination that have characterized higher education in the past.

National agencies affecting higher education. Voluntary organizations at the national level set standards for various professional schools that the local university must meet. Examples are the American Medical Association, the American Library Association, the National Commission on Teacher Education and Professional Standards, and the American Association of School Administrators. These and many similar associations serve the useful function of preventing substandard programs from springing up in institutions that lack the facilities for providing the preparation needed by members of these strategic professions. Other national organizations providing services for college and university faculty members include the American Association of University Professors, the American Council on Education, the American Chemical Society, the American Council of Learned Societies, and the American Council for the Advancement of Science. The federal government includes dozens of agencies that affect higher education; many universities receive the bulk of their research funds from these sources.

THE TWO-YEAR COLLEGE

The first junior college was established in this country in 1902. Until comparatively recent years, the principal function of this institution was to prepare students to enter four-year colleges and universities. Shortly after 1947, following the President's Commission on Higher Education Report, the name "community college" began to be applied to institutions designed to serve chiefly local community needs. Around that time many two-year colleges changed their names from junior colleges to community colleges.

Two-year colleges vary greatly in their goals, organization, and programs. Some offer the first two years of the typical four-year college curriculum, while others offer mainly vocational subjects. Some enroll only local students, while others maintain dormitories and recruit students from all over the world. Junior colleges may be regarded as institutions of higher learning which offer two years of education beyond the high school. Community colleges, on the other hand, are primarily concerned with providing higher educational services to a particular community. Most community colleges are under public control and are a part of their local school system, whereas the junior college may be privately or church controlled. Junior and community colleges confer associate degrees (Associate in Science, Associate in Arts, etc.).

The President's Commission on National Goals recommended in 1960 that two-year colleges should be within commuting distance of most high school graduates and that they should give adult education a vital role, offering new values throughout the life span.[20] In 1975 more than 897 public community colleges and 231 private junior colleges served 3,970,119 students.

The community college makes a unique contribution by admitting all students who can profit from its program; by maintaining a multiphased curriculum that provides opportunities for both the academically talented student and the nonacademic, vocationally oriented student; and by serving adults in the community who have not had an opportunity to attend college.

Summarizing the President's Commission on Higher Education, the primary functions of the two-year college are: (1) training for occupations requiring no more than two years of college, (2) general education for students who will complete their formal education after two years of college, (3) adult education, and (4) education for students who will transfer to four year colleges.

It seems likely that two-year colleges will absorb an increasingly large segment of the nation's college-bound population. This is because of several factors, especially convience of location, low tuition and expenses, availability of vocational training, and socially warm environments. As they expand two-year colleges will employ more teachers and administrators, who must have at least master's degrees and several years of related experience.

HUMAN RELATIONS SKILLS

Below are definitions for twelve human relations skills that you will be asked to comment on in the next survey. Read the definitions carefully.

1. *Listening Skills*: Works at understanding what others are saying; asks others to repeat; asks others to clarify. Tells others what he/she has heard; seems to have understood correctly what others said.

2. *Teaching Skills*: Says things clearly, using words others can understand; speaks in a way that is direct and to the point; asks what others have heard and offers to clarify; others seem to understand correctly what he/she has said.

3. *Openness*: Shares feelings and ideas spontaneously; willing to discuss own strengths and weaknesses; his/her emotions show clearly and appropriately (e.g., joy, boredom, anger, sorrow, etc.).

4. *Trust*: Willing to listen to and try out others' ideas; seeks and accepts help from others; shows that he/she expects others to be sincere and honest with him/her.

5. *Feedback*: Asks for others' impressions of him/her; shares his/her views of others with them; seems aware of whether or not others are ready to receive his/her views; presents views in a way that is helpful; lets others know when they have been helpful to him/her.

6. *Awareness of Own Behavior*: Shows he/she is aware of how others are reacting to behavior; shows he/she is aware of own reaction to the behavior of others; shows he/she is considering the implications for self; uses this awareness in considering whether or not own behavior is what is desired.

7. *Experimenting with Own Behavior*: Shows flexibility in taking different roles in the group at different times (e.g., leader, clarifier, etc.).

8. *Contributes to Class Members' Awareness of Themselves*: Helps members to be aware of what is happening as a group; raises questions about what the group is doing, feeling, heading toward; offers own views on what the group is doing, feeling, etc.

9. *Problem Solving Effectiveness*: Helps class members to make realistic progress in problem solving efforts; is effectively work oriented; aids group productivity.

10. *Helping Group Maintenance*: Works well with own and others' feelings; helps develop and maintain good relations in the class.

11. *Group Diagnostic Ability*: Able to understand why things happened as they did in class; can explain group difficulties as a basis for corrective or supportive action.

12. *Overall Effectiveness as a Group Member*: All things considered, makes effective contribution to his/her own and others' learning and work.

Put an "X" over the number that reflects your development in each human relations skill. Draw an arrow in the direction, if any, you would like for each skill to develop.

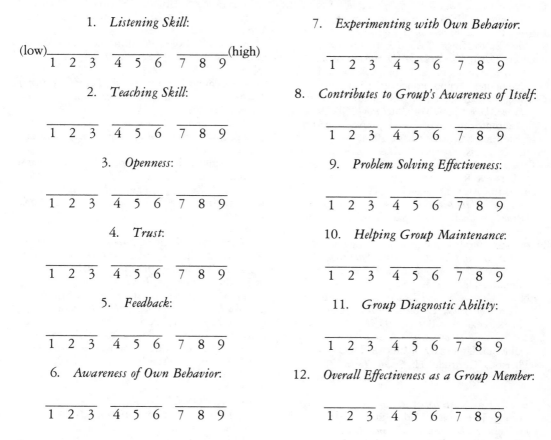

1. *Listening Skill*:

(low) _____ _____ (high)
1 2 3 4 5 6 7 8 9

2. *Teaching Skill*:

1 2 3 4 5 6 7 8 9

3. *Openness*:

1 2 3 4 5 6 7 8 9

4. *Trust*:

1 2 3 4 5 6 7 8 9

5. *Feedback*:

1 2 3 4 5 6 7 8 9

6. *Awareness of Own Behavior*:

1 2 3 4 5 6 7 8 9

7. *Experimenting with Own Behavior*:

1 2 3 4 5 6 7 8 9

8. *Contributes to Group's Awareness of Itself*:

1 2 3 4 5 6 7 8 9

9. *Problem Solving Effectiveness*:

1 2 3 4 5 6 7 8 9

10. *Helping Group Maintenance*:

1 2 3 4 5 6 7 8 9

11. *Group Diagnostic Ability*:

1 2 3 4 5 6 7 8 9

12. *Overall Effectiveness as a Group Member*:

1 2 3 4 5 6 7 8 9

ADDITIONAL READING

Brameld, Theodore B. *Education as Power*. New York, Holt, Rinehart & Winston, 1965.

Broudy, Harry S. *The Real World of the Public Schools*. New York, Harcourt Brace Jovanovich, 1972.

Burrup, Percy E. *Financing Education in a Climate for Change*. Boston, Allyn & Bacon, 1974.

Coursen, David. *Women and Minorities in Administration*. Arlington, Va., National Association of Elementary School Principals, 1975.

Gordon, Margaret S., ed. *Higher Education and the Labor Market*. New York, McGraw-Hill, 1974.

Hall, Laurence, et al. *New Colleges for New Students*. San Francisco, Jossey-Bass, 1974.

Heath, G. Louis. *The New Teacher: Changing Patterns of Authority and Responsibility*. New York, Harper & Row, 1973.

Henderson, Algo D. and Jean G. Henderson. *Higher Education in America: Problems, Priorities, and Prospects*. San Francisco, Jossey-Bass, 1974.

Herriott, Robert E. and Benjamin J. Hodgkins. *The Environment of Schooling: Formal Education as an Open Social System*, Englewood Cliffs, N.J., Prentice-Hall, 1973.

La Nove, George R. and Bruce L. R. Smith. *The Politics of School Decentralization*. Lexington, Mass., Lexington Books, 1973.

Lortie, Dan C. *Schoolteacher: A Sociological Study*. Chicago, University of Chicago Press, 1975.

McPherson, Gertrude H. *Small Town Teacher*. Cambridge, Mass., Harvard University Press, 1972.

Peters, Richard S. *Authority, Responsibility, and Education*, 3d ed. New York, Eriksson, 1973.

Piele, Philip K. *Budgets, Bonds, and Ballots: Voting Behavior in School Financial Elections*. Lexington, Mass., Lexington Books, 1973.

Sacks, Seymour, et al. *City Schools/Suburb Schools: A History of Fiscal Conflict*. Syracuse, N.Y., Syracuse University Press, 1972.

Sarason, Seymour B. *The Culture of the School and the Problem of Change*. Boston, Allyn & Bacon, 1972.

Waller, Willard, W. *The Sociology of Teaching*. New York, John Wiley & Sons, 1932.

NOTES

1. N. L. Gage (ed.), *Handbook of Research on Teaching* (Chicago, Rand McNally, 1963).

2. Jerome S. Bruner, "Needed: A Theory of Instruction," *Educational Leadership*, 20 (May, 1963), 521–527.

3. Gale W. Rose, "Performance Evaluation and Growth in Teaching," *Phi Delta Kappan*, 44 (October, 1963), 51.

4. Seymour B. Sarason et al., *The Preparation of Teachers: An Unstudied Problem in Education* (New York, John Wiley & Sons, 1962).

5. A.S. Barr et al., *Wisconsin Studies of the Measurement and Prediction of Teacher Effectiveness* (Madison, December, 1961).

6. Arthur Schlesinger, Jr., "The One Against the Many," *Saturday Review* (July 14, 1962), 55.

7. E. T. Keach, Jr., et al. (eds.), *Education and Social Crisis* (New York, John Wiley & Sons, 1967), 17.

8. *Ibid.*, 12.

9. Myron Lieberman, *Education as a Profession* (Englewood Cliffs, N.J., Prentice-Hall, 1956), 455.

10. W. W. Charters, Jr., "The Social Background of Teaching," in Gage, *Hardbook*, 764–765.

11. Based on the latest available issues of the *Research Report* and the *Research Bulletin* of the National Education Association. The reader should consult the latest issues of these bulletins for information about recent trends in teachers' salaries.

12. Wilbur A. Yauch et al., *The Beginning Teacher* (New York, Holt, Rinehart, & Winston, 1955), 247.

13. Neal Gross, *Who Runs Our Schools?* (New York, John Wiley & Sons, 1958), 90–91.

14. See for instance Orvill G. Brim, *Sociology and the Field of Education* (New York, Russell Sage Foundation, 1958), 24.

15. Arvid J. Burke, *Financing Public Schools in the United States* (New York, Harper & Row, 1957), 588.

16. H. Thomas Jones et al., *Wealth, Expenditures and Decision-Making for Education* (Stanford School of Education, Stanford University, 1963), 99.

17. *School District of Abington Township, Pennsylvania et al. v. Schempp et al.,* 374 U.S. 203 (1963).

18. Logan Wilson (ed.), *Emerging Patterns in Higher Education* (Washington, D.C., American Council on Education, (1965), 28.

19. James Perkins in *ibid.*, 10.

20. President's Commission on National Goals, *Goals for Americans* (Englewood Cliffs, N.J., Prentice-Hall, 1960), 81–100.

5.
INTRODUCTION
TO TEACHING

Professional education for teachers has undergone considerable change during the past hundred years. Research in the social and natural sciences has improved our knowledge of human learning, communication, and organizational change. There are more than 1,200 state approved higher education teacher preparation programs. Of this number, more than 450 are accredited by the National Council for Accreditation of Teacher Education (NCATE). The list of approved teacher education institutions includes public and private universities, public and private liberal arts colleges, public and private teachers colleges, technical schools, junior colleges, and unclassified schools.

Research evidence supporting formal teacher education programs is overwhelming: teachers who have had a methods course tend to rank higher in classroom performance than those who have had none. Heeding numerous criticisms, most teacher education programs are trying to improve their curricula and upgrade their faculty. Introductory education courses expose future teachers to the diverse roles and goals of education.

In considering the various education goals and roles of school personnel, Robert J. Havighurst's list of developmental tasks offers a useful illustration of the concerns of program planners:[1]

Developmental tasks of early childhood
Learning to walk
Learning to take solid foods
Learning to talk

Learning to control the elimination of body wastes
Learning sex differences and sexual modesty
Learning physiological stability
Forming simple concepts of social and physical reality
Learning to relate oneself emotionally to parents, siblings, and other people
Learning to distinguish right from wrong and developing a conscience

Developmental tasks of middle childhood
Learning physical skills necessary for ordinary games
Building wholesome attitudes toward oneself as a growing organism
Learning to get along with age-mates
Learning an appropriate masculine or feminine social role
Developing fundamental skills in reading, writing, and calculating
Developing concepts necessary for everyday living
Developing conscience, morality, and a scale of values
Achieving personal independence
Developing attitudes toward social groups and institutions

Developmental tasks of adolescence
Achieving new and more mature relations and age-mates of both sexes
Achieving a masculine or feminine social role
Accepting one's physique and using the body effectively
Achieving emotional independence of parents and other adults

Achieving assurance of economic independence

Selecting and preparing for an occupation

Preparing for marriage and family life

Developing intellectual skills and concepts
necessary for civic competence

Desiring and achieving socially responsible
behavior

Acquiring a set of values and an ethical system
as a guide to behavior

Developmental tasks of early adulthood

Selecting a mate

Learning to live with a marriage partner

Starting a family

Rearing children

Managing a home

Getting started in an occupation

Taking on civic responsibility

Finding a congenial social group

Developmental tasks of middle age

Achieving adult civic and social responsibility

Establishing and maintaining an economic
standard of living

Assisting teen-age children to become responsible and happy adults

Developing adult leisure-time activities

Relating oneself to one's spouse as a person

Accepting and adjusting to the physiological
changes of middle age

Adjusting to aging parents

Developmental tasks of later maturity

Adjusting to decreasing physical strength and
health

Adjusting to retirement and reduced income

Adjusting to death of spouse

Establishing an explicit affiliation with one's
age group

Meeting social and civic obligations

Establishing satisfactory physical living arrangements

LEVELS OF EDUCATION

The major purpose of this chapter is to expose
the reader to some of the conditions affecting
school development, curricula and teacher
preparation. Added with this information is a
brief discussion of academic teaching fields,
especially in pre-kindergarten, elementary,
and secondary schools. This data may be
supplemented by discussing education careers
with personnel officers in school systems.

Pre-elementary Education

Pre-elementary education in America owes its
existence to several factors. John Oberlin established an infant school, the forerunner of
elementary schools, in France in 1769. The
first nursery school in America was established
by Robert Owen in Harmony, Indiana, in
1826. Friedrich Froebel established the first
kindergarten in Blankenburg, Germany, in
1837. The first kindergarten in America was
founded by Mrs. Carl Schurz in her home in
Watertown, Wisconsin, in 1855. (Susan Blow
opened America's first permanent kindergarten in St. Louis in 1873.)

However the greatest push for pre-
elementary education in America came in the
1960s. By 1960 almost all states had legislation
authorizing public education below grade one.
The Social Security Act of 1961 earmarked
funds to state welfare departments for day-
care services. The Economic Opportunity
Act of 1964 contained provisions for pre-
elementary education for disadvantaged children. The Economic Opportunity Act of 1965
made Project Head Start a year-round program. The success of Head Start prompted the
Educational Policies Commission to recommend free schooling for all children when they
become four-year-olds.

A few pre-elementary schools are experimenting with "talking typewriters" that automatically pronounce the sounds of the letters typed; other schools are using computer
games. These two illustrations show the
broadened aspects of pre-elementary education.

Nursery education.   There are several types
of nursery schools: (1) those located in colleges and universities which serve as training
laboratories for nursery school teachers or
students majoring in home economics, child
development, and psychology, (2) those established within a school system's administrative
unit of early childhood education, (3) those
located within elementary schools, (4) those
located within high schools which seek to provide homemaking and social studies classes
with supervised opportunities to interact with

Chart 5. The Structure of Education

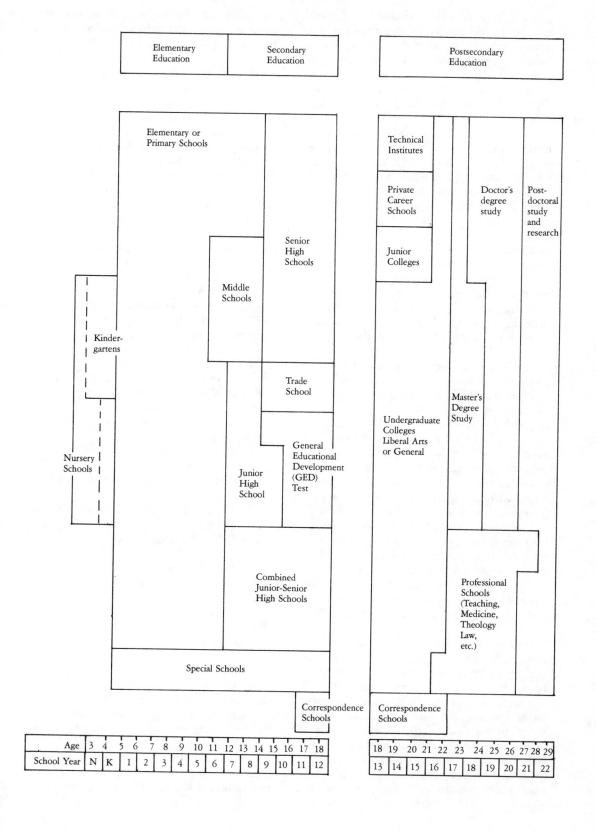

young children, (5) those located outside public schools and colleges. More than half the
nursery schools in this country are independent institutions sponsored by churches, private organizations or individuals, and welfare
agencies. In 1976 more than two million children were enrolled in pre-kindergarten
schools.

Unlike the early nursery schools, today's
institutions are not available solely to wealthy
persons who can afford to pay tuition. Rather,
the Economic Opportunity Acts resulted in
millions of low-income children being exposed for the first time to books, travel, toys,
discussions, and television programs—resources and activities that have become
routine in the lives of affluent children. Research data indicates that many children attending Head Start have had their IQs raised eight
to twelve points during an eight-week period.

Discussing "What is a Good Nursery
School?" Lillian C. Gore concluded that nursery schools should help children to:

*1. Use and manage their bodies with more skill
and a growing sense of achievement and confidence,
and develop healthful habits of play, rest, elimination, and eating;*

*2 Extend their interests and understanding of
the world about them by investigating and experimenting, and by thinking about some relationships they discover in their environment;*

*3. Work and play productively with other chil-
dren, acquire some independence, and communicate
their feelings with other children and adults;*

*4. Express themselves creatively and spontane-
ously through art (building, modeling, painting),
music (rhythms, singing), and language (conversation, storytelling, and dramatic play);*

*5. Enjoy browsing, listening, job serving,
exploring, making plans, discussing experiences,
and accomplishing tasks important to them.*[2]

Because of the many physical and intellectual needs of pre-kindergarten children, the
nursery school curriculum is necessarily
broad. Program activities vary a great deal. If
one were to seek the single most important
factor affecting the quality of a nursery school
program, it probably would be the teachers.
The more effective nursery school teachers are
well trained in child development, teaching
methods, children's literature, art, music, science (physical and social), and parent educa-

tion. Furthermore, they exhibit respect for all
children and parents, warmth, a sense of
humor, and self-insight.

Kindergarten. While few American children attend nursery schools, more than 80 per
cent of the five-year-olds in this country are
enrolled in kindergarten. Kindergartens are
either public or private; and they are financed
by federal, state or private funds or a combination of such funds. They are very similar to
nursery schools but more advanced in activities and materials. According to Lillian
Gore and Rose Koury, kindergarten education
has the following goals for children:

*1. Become aware of their physical needs; learn
healthful habits; build coordination, strength,
and physical skills; and develop sound mental and
physical health.*

*2. Gain some understanding of their social
world; learn to work and play fairly and happily
in it; grow in developing responsibility and independence; yet accept the limits present in living in a
democratic society.*

*3. Acquire interests, attitudes, and values
which aid them in becoming secure and positive in
their relationships with peers and adults.*

*4. Grow into an ever-deeper sense of ac-
complishment and self-esteem.*

*5. Grow in their understanding of their
natural environment.*

*6. Gain some understanding of spatial and
number relationships.*

7. Enjoy their literary and musical heritage.

*8. Express their thoughts and feelings more
creatively through language, movement, art, and
music.*

*9. Develop more appropriate behavior, skills,
and understandings on which their continuing
education builds.*

*10. Observe, experiment, discover, think, and
generalize at their individual levels of experience
and development.*[3]

Although kindergarten education does not
have required subjects, it does require considerable skill in teaching. Kindergarten
teachers must understand the child's learning
and development, including his or her readiness for reading, arithmetic, and specific
movement activities. This is the period when
most children are developing respect for
themselves, other people, and their property,

and learning to share common group experiences. Obviously, effective teachers are able to facilitate experimenting, clarifying ideas and values, acquiring new information, and problem solving. When kindergarten teachers do their jobs well, students moving into elementary school experience fewer failures.

Elementary Education

The first American elementary school was established in Fort Amsterdam, New Netherlands (which later become New York) in 1633. As seen in Chapter One, the earliest colonial education law was passed in Massachusetts in 1642. Most eighteenth century elementary education was conducted in reading and writing schools, which were followed by dame schools. The first dame school—a school in which a lady taught her own and neighborhood children in her home—was established in New Haven in 1651. The dame schools were followed by primary schools, the nonsectarian forerunners of elementary schools. In 1792 New Hampshire became the first state to adopt a constitutional provision prohibiting sectarian instruction.

Supporters of public elementary schools had to wait until 1834 when Pennsylvania—led by Thaddeus Stevens—became the first state to adopt a free elementary school program. The first state part-time compulsory attendance law was adopted in Massachusetts in 1852, and it was followed by Connecticut's full-time requirement in 1890.

Currently a wide variety of organizational and administrative structures and curricula make it impossible to precisely delineate elementary school from secondary education. For example, depending upon the school district, elementary school grades include one through six or one through eight. Some schools are nongraded; others embrace kindergarten; and still others only have four, five, or six grades, with middle schools comprising grades five to eight, six to eight, or seven and eight. When this happens middle school is just what the name implies—between elementary schools and secondary school. Whatever the grade range, 99 per cent of American children of elementary age are attending school. Of this number approximately 17 per cent are enrolled in private or parochial schools.

Chris A. DeYoung and Richard Wynn drew upon an Association for Supervision and Curriculum Development publication entitled *The Elementary School We Need* and summarized the major commitments of the modern elementary school thusly:

1. Health and physical development of children. *Elementary schools seek not only to maintain but also to improve the health status of children. Through planned programs of physical education, health education, as well as thorough physical examinations, elementary schools demonstrate a major concern for health and physical development. The willingness of elementary schools to adapt their programs to provide for the physical needs of children has made it possible for many pupils who have serious handicaps to enter the regular school program.*

2. Mental health and personality development of children. *The importance of helping children to achieve an adequate concept of self dominates the activities of many elementary schools. There is concern for providing opportunities for children to experience success and a sense of achievement in what they do. Efforts to provide a setting which minimizes tension for children characterize much of the teaching in the elementary school. Teachers are aware of the needs of children to be secure and to feel that they belong as worthy human beings.*

3. Development of understanding of the social and scientific worlds. *The importance of helping children to understand their environment has led to reorganization of content materials. There is a conscious effort in many elementary schools to bring the immediate world of children into a perspective that affords them a better understanding of the remote and abstract. Fundamental skills and knowledge are presented in a more functional setting in order that these concepts may lead to further learning and more effective living in the world of today.*

4. Development of the skills of effective participation in a democratic society. *The attention that many elementary schools direct to the early participation of children in group living has altered the content of instructional activities as well as the ways in which they are organized. In seeking to help children develop responsibility, self-direction, and effective communication with others, elementary schools provide a climate as well as varied opportunities for learning and practicing the responsibilities and skills of living in a democratic society.*

5. Development of values consistent with democratic living. *Closely related to the skills for participating in a democratic society are the values implied in maintaining such a society. Some of these values are honesty, respect for individual personality, personal and social responsibilities, freedom of thought and of speech, and the learning and use of methods of intelligence. Elementary schools seek to help children develop a sense of commitment to these values. Social issues and concerns are a part of these classroom experiences, and there is an emphasis on intrinsic motivation to help children aspire to worthy human roles.*

6. Creative activity. *In seeking to stimulate creativity, many elementary schools strive to achieve a program that is less rigid and sterile than the programs of some schools in past decades. Creativity is perceived as an aspect of behavior that permeates all areas of curriculum and is characteristic of all children. Creative classrooms are stimulating and supportive places in which varied approaches are used to solve problems, to express ideas, and to communicate with others.*[4]

Primary grades. The first three grades in an elementary school are most frequently called primary grades. Reading is the hub around which revolves writing, spelling, and working with numbers. Most primary classrooms are self-contained—one teacher teaches the same students each day in all subjects. The trend, however, is towards specialists for reading. A few progressive schools have introduced beginning concepts in natural and social sciences and foreign languages—especially French and Spanish. In many ways the primary grades are the most exciting and crucial of all education.

Intermediate grades. Grades four, five, and six are usually called the intermediate grades. As in the primary grades, reading is the most important subject area. However, social studies, science, language arts, fine arts, and mathematics are introduced. Also as in the primary grades, each intermediate grade teacher is expected to be able to teach all required subjects.

Middle School

While technically not elementary school teachers, middle school teachers are usually trained to teach upper-intermediate grades.

Basically the middle school is an attempt to deal in a more effective manner with the educational and emotional needs of pre-adolescent students (ages nine through thirteen). Arguments for the middle school include: (1) it groups together students in the awkward age of pubescence; (2) it avoids mixing these students with adolescents; (3) it permits a general transition of students from the regimentation of elementary school to the more independent study characterizing high school; and (4) it allows for more flexibility of curriculum.

Secondary Education

Currently more than 90 per cent of the American population between fourteen and seventeen years of age is enrolled in schools. But this has not always been the case. Until the twentieth century, relatively few youths of this age group attended school.

The history of secondary education in America can be broken down into four distinct eras: the Latin grammar school era, the tuition academy era, the free public high school era, and the reorganized high school era. The first Latin grammar school in America was founded in Boston in 1635. Philemon Pormont was appointed the first schoolmaster. The main purpose of the Latin grammar schools was to prepare students for college, and admission to these college preparatory schools was based on the applicant's social and economic rank. The schools were supported by tuition, contributions, taxes, legacies, leases, lotteries, and land grants by civil authorities or private citizens—any way that could secure funds. Since most graduates pursued careers in the ministry or professions, it was deemed proper that the clergy control the Latin grammar schools.

As the appeal of theology waned and the nation underwent economic and social changes, the Latin grammar school gave way to the tuition academy. Benjamin Franklin organized the first academy in Philadelphia in 1751. (It later became the University of Pennsylvania.) The curriculum, while including theology, was broadened to include subjects of interest to non-college-bound students, i.e., commerce and science. Also unlike the Latin grammar school, the academies permitted females to enter. The person in charge of an academy was called the headmaster or principal. Several of the original academies still exist.

The free public high school was inaugurated with the establishment of the English Classical School in Boston in 1821. This was a school for boys. The first free public high school for girls was established in Boston in 1826. These schools taught such subjects as Latin, Greek, logic, and surveying. The first coeducational high school was established in Chicago in 1856, and the first manual training school was established in Baltimore in 1884. The Michigan Supreme Court's *Kalamazoo* decision in 1874 set a legal precedent for publicly supported high schools. Along with the spread of public high schools has come a diminishing of social and economic castes.

The twentieth century saw the beginning of the vertically extended secondary school or the reorganized high school. The upward extension was begun with the first junior college, established in Joliet, Illinois, in 1902. The downward extension began with the first junior high schools, established in Berkeley, California, and Columbus, Ohio, in 1910. Junior and community colleges are discussed later in chapter four.

The objectives of secondary education were enunciated as "Seven Cardinal Principles of Secondary Education" by the Commission on the Reorganization of Secondary Education in 1918:

1. Health. *Health needs cannot be neglected during the period of secondary education without serious danger to the individual and the race. The secondary school should therefore provide health instruction, inculcate health habits, organize an effective program of physical activities, regard health needs in planning work and play, and cooperate with home and community in safeguarding and promoting health interests.*

2. Command of fundamental processes. *Much of the energy of the elementary school is properly devoted to teaching certain fundamental processes, such as reading, writing, arithmetical computations and the elements of oral and written expression. The facility that a child of twelve or fourteen may acquire in the use of these tools is not sufficient for the needs of modern life. This is particularly true of the mother tongue.*

3. Worthy home membership. *Worthy home membership as an objective calls for the development of those qualities that make the individual a worthy member of a family, both contributing to and deriving benefit from that membership. . . . The coeducational school with a faculty of men and women should, in its organization and its activities, exemplify wholesome relations between boys and girls and men and women.*

4. Vocation. *Vocational education should equip the individual to secure a livelihood for himself and those dependent on him, to serve society well through his vocation, to maintain the right relationships toward his fellow workers and society, and, as far as possible, to find in that vocation his own best development.*

5. Civic education *should develop in the individual those qualities whereby he will act his part as a member of neighborhood, town or city, State, and Nation, and give him a basis for understanding international problems.*

6. Worthy use of leisure. *Education should equip the individual to secure from his leisure the re-creation of body, mind, and spirit, and the enrichment and enlargement of his personality.*

7. Ethical character. *In a democratic society ethical character becomes paramount among the objectives of the secondary school. Among the means for developing ethical character may be mentioned the wise selection of content and methods of instruction in all subjects of study, the social contacts of pupils with one another and with their teachers, the opportunities afforded by the organization and administration of the school for the development on the part of pupils of the sense of personal responsibility and initiative, and, above all, the spirit of service and the principles of true democracy which should permeate the entire school—principal, teachers, and pupils.*[5]

In 1973 the National Commission on the Reform of Secondary Education, sponsored by the Kettering Foundation, presented the first comprehensive report of the American high school in 55 years. Composed of private citizens and educators, the commission made several recommendations, including: (1) at age fourteen students who do not want to continue their education in traditional high schools should be given opportunities to attend alternative schools—independent and specialized or publicly operated schools with different action-learning approaches to education, (2) overhaul the curriculum to improve course content and materials, (3) expand student rights, (4) abolish corporal punishment, (5) eliminate racism and sexism in schools, (6) reduce the size of high schools, (7) legalize smoking on campus, and (8) require teachers to use lavatories with students. The Kettering Commission's report speaks more directly to the late twentieth century than the National Education Association commission's 1918 seven cardinal principles.

Junior high school. Most junior high schools are composed of grades seven to nine. This educational unit was created to facilitate the transition from childhood to adolescence and to minimize articulation problems between elementary school and high school. The curriculum includes social studies, the sciences, humanities, and the arts. The usual organizational pattern is departmental, and generally teachers are subject-matter specialists well trained in methodology, curriculum, and adolescent psychology. Junior high teachers are trained in teacher education programs for secondary-school teachers.

Educational and social guidance plays an important role in the junior high school; teachers must help students assume a healthy, natural acceptance of adolescent growth patterns, so that learning will be fostered with a minimum of emotional stress and embarrassment. Junior high school teachers strive to help boys and girls grow naturally through the early adolescent years rather than risk permanent damage by forcing students through premature adult patterns.[6]

Senior high school.   Senior high school usually consists of grades ten to twelve. It is here that teachers are expected to prepare students for vocations or additional education. This results in increased emphasis on written and oral communication, increased focus on social sciences and physical sciences, plus greater self-direction in terms of physical health and social interactions. Being subject-matter specialists, senior high school teachers are expected to teach several related subjects. For example, a social studies teacher may have classes in geography, history, and sociology or human relations. Most high schools are organized into departments: physical sciences, social sciences, industrial arts, music, English, and the like.

There is a trend toward employing only high school teachers who have a master of arts degree or its equivalent. In fact an increasing number of secondary teachers are securing doctorates. As the number of jobs decreases and the number of job applicants increases, advanced degrees become an important criterion in teacher selection.

Higher Education

In addition to noting that in 1636 Harvard University became the first institution of higher education in the United States, several other events merit our listing. The University of North Carolina was the first state university (1795); the Georgia Female College (Wesleyan College at Macon) was the first chartered college for women (1836); Oberlin College was the first coeducation college (1836); Mount Holyoke College was the first liberal arts college for women (1838); Massachusetts State College established the first state normal school (1839); Lincoln University in Pennsylvania was the forerunner of the first historically Black college (1854), and Shaw University was the first school of higher education for Blacks (1865); Johns Hopkins University offered the first graduate study (1876); and the first public junior college was established at Joliet, Illinois (1902).

The Educational Policies Commission surveyed several institutions of higher education and concluded that the major purposes of American colleges and universities are:

1. To provide opportunity for individual development of able people.
2. To transmit the cultural heritage.
3. To add to existing knowledge through research and creative activity.
4. To help translate learning into equipment for living and social advancement.
5. To serve the public interest.[7]

Upon close analysis of the above statement, it is clear that colleges and universities offer four types of programs: liberal or general education, professional or vocational education, graduate study and research, and public services. With this thought in mind, it is easy to accept the American Council on Education's statement that a general education should help a college student:

1. To improve and maintain his own health and take his share of responsibility for protecting the health of others.

2. To communicate through his own language in writing and speaking at the level of expression adequate to the needs of educated people.

3. To attain a sound emotional and social adjustment through the enjoyment of a wide range of social relationships and the experience of working cooperatively with others

4. To think through the problems and to gain the basic orientation that will better enable him to make a satisfactory family and marital adjustment.

5. To do his part as an active and intelligent citizen in dealing with the interrelated social, economic, and political problems of American life and in solving the problems of postwar international reconstruction.

6. To act in the light of an understanding of the natural phenomena in his environment in its implications for human society and human welfare, to use scientific methods in the solution of his problems, and to employ useful nonverbal methods of thought and communications.

7. To find self-expression in literature and to share through literature man's experience and his motivating ideas and ideals.

8. To find a means of self-expression in music and in the various visual arts and crafts, and to understand and appreciate art and music as reflections both of individual experience and of social patterns and movements.

9. To practice clear and integrated thinking about the meaning and value of life.

10. To choose a vocation that will make optimum use of his talents and enable him to make an appropriate contribution to the needs of society.[8]

Our nation and world require that people be prepared to perform the vital professional services to society in such areas as education, law, medicine, business, communication, engineering, and transportation. Millions of students attending college are preparing for a professional career. In addition to the vocational competencies required for their respective careers, these students also need well-rounded educational backgrounds that will assist them in being good citizens.

In addition to instructional obligations, colleges and universities are mandated to contribute new knowledge through research. Accepting this responsibility, most of the larger institutions have graduate schools and research facilities to provide for training above the baccalaureate level. Although various nonuniversity research agencies have been developed in such fields as science, business, and agriculture, institutions of higher education are the major centers for research and resolution of social problems.

Adult and Continuing Education

Education has become a way of life for countless individuals driven by the need and desire to continue their mental growth. The foremost leaders in this country advocate cradle-to-grave education. Contrary to some opinions, continuous or lifelong education is not a new concept.

In the Western World, continuous education as a way of life goes back at least to Socrates and ancient Athens, and today the Socratic dialogue remains a major instrumentality of continuous education. Moving to the East, we find it going back to Judaic life, to the systematic adult study of the Scripture and the Rabbinic Commentaries. Farther to the East, continuous education as a way of life goes back, for example, to the full regimen established for the good life of the intellectually classical Hinduism.[9]

Although not organized for the primary purpose of continuing education, the town meetings in the New England colonies were the first forms of adult education. Following the American Revolution, several organizations emerged with the primary purpose of extending knowledge of the physical sciences among adults. Among these were the American Academy of Arts and Sciences in Philadelphia (1780), the Lowell Institute in Boston (1836), the Smithsonian Institute in Washington, D.C. (1846), and Cooper Union in New York City (1859). Most historians also cite the American Lyceum, founded by Josiah Holbrook in Massachusetts (1831), as an excellent example of adult education through lecture-discussion groups. Organized for the mutual benefit of their members and society, the Lyceum supported the public school movement and free libraries.

After he became president of the University of Chicago in 1891, William Rainey Harper made university extension education a part of the school's mission. Along with the State University of New York and the University of

Wisconsin, the University of Chicago's extension program was the first prototype. Basically the extension programs focused on current problems—agricultural, economic, social, political, and moral.

Other historical events include the founding of the Correspondence University (1883); founding the International Correspondence Schools at Scranton, Pennsylvania (1891); the Smith-Lever Act (1914), which provided federal funds for agricultural extension work; the recognition by law of public adult education as an integral part of free schooling (1925); the establishment by the National Home Study Council of the first educational and ethical standards for correspondence course institutions (1925); and the Manpower Development and Training Act (1962–1963), which provided occupational training and retraining for jobless youths and unschooled adults.

Public school faculty, university personnel, and various consultants comprise the teaching staff of adult education programs. All of the issues discussed in Part Two of this book are content areas for continuing education activities. These programs are found in public schools, private schools, colleges and universities, libraries, churches and synagogues, community organizations, museums, and other cultural centers. The broadest type of continuing education is the correspondence course; the discussion is the oldest medium of adult education; and the book is the most effective medium of adult learning. Several institutions are experimenting with cassette tapes, records, and television as supplements to books.

The university is the most prestigious institution sponsoring continuing education activities. The Kellogg Foundation gave continuing education a big push when it financed centers for continuing education at the University of Chicago, the University of Georgia, Michigan State University, the University of Nebraska, the University of New Hampshire, the University of Notre Dame, and the University of Oklahoma. Millions of persons—young and old—have attended workshops, classes, conferences, lectures, and forums at these centers.

The Adult Education Association of the United States believes that if adult education is to achieve its mission—to assist people to know more about themselves, to help people understand their relationships with others, and to help people learn more about their jobs—the following goals must be met:

1. There must be a national perception, especially on the part of those who control educational policy, of the essential role of continuing education in preventing human obsolescence and in preserving and further developing American society.

2. The education of children and youth must be reoriented to a conception of learning as a lifelong process. Teachers in schools and colleges must learn to teach youth so that they leave formal schooling (a) with an insatiable curiosity, (b) with a mastery of the tools of learning, and (c) with a commitment to continue learning through the rest of their life span.

3. The agencies of adult education must clarify their respective tasks of establishing between themselves orderly working arrangements and interrelated planning and to ensure that the resources of adult education are used effectively in meeting the adult educational needs of individuals, institutions, and communities.

4. A coherent curriculum of adult education must be developed that provides for the sequential development of the knowledge, understanding, skills, attitudes, and values required to maintain one's effectiveness in a changing social order.

5. The corps of leaders and teachers of adults must be enlarged and provided with the knowledge and skills required for them to help adults learn efficiently.

6. A special responsibility is placed on the universities of the country to expand the resources available for research and advanced professional training in adult education.

7. Community agencies of adult education, especially schools and colleges, must upgrade the standards of professional competence required of those guiding adult learning and employ personnel with these competencies.

8. There must be a national commitment to provide the resources and moral support necessary for the development of lifelong learning as an integral element of the American way of life.[10]

As life expectancy, standard of living, and leisure time increase, so too must the process of lifelong education. Along with this must come better designed and implemented programs. Needless to say, better teachers and administrators are also needed.

The importance of providing lifelong education for senior citizens is just beginning to be realized by American colleges and universities competing for a shrinking pool of traditional students. There are more than twenty million Americans who are sixty-five years of age or older—one-tenth of our population. With birth rates declining and life expectancy increasing, the aged will constitute a larger portion of college and university enrollments in the future.

PROFESSIONAL EDUCATION

Reacting to criticism of early normal schools that had too many methodology courses and too few subject-matter courses, twentieth century teacher preparation programs are trying to strike a balance between methodology and subject matter. However, the elementary education programs still tend to be weighted heavily on the side of methodology.

Course work for future teachers can be subdivided into three areas: general education, specialized education, and professional education. General education consists of required and elective courses in the liberal arts; specialized education consists of the areas in education (e.g., history, mathematics, English) in which a future teacher specializes; and professional education consists of courses in educational theories and methods plus a teaching practicum. Preparation for a career in education requires more than a knowledge of the field(s) of specilization and methodology.

The professional educator, while accepting the necessity for a good subject-matter background, also recognizes that prospective teachers must be taught to apply the principles of learning in a classroom situation and must acquire skills such as constructing course outlines, planning daily lessons, selecting and using the innumerable instructional materials, using audiovisual materials, and constructing and using tests to measure the extent of learning.[11]

Teachers in colleges and universities follow a significantly different preparation program than do pre-kindergarten, elementary, and secondary school teachers. With the exception of junior college teachers, there is no certification requirement for college teachers. At least a master's degree is needed for teaching in junior and community colleges and a doctorate is usually required for full-time college teaching positions. College teachers may be promoted through four ranks: instructor, assistant professor, associate professor, and full professor.

Certification

Because of the great differences among states in the certification of teachers and other school personnel, the comments in this section will be general. Specific details pertaining to certification can be secured from state departments of education. There are two other excellent resources: *Requirements for Certification: Teachers, Counselors, Librarians, Administrators for Elementary Schools, Secondary Schools*, published annually under the direction of Elizabeth H. Woellner, and *A Manual on Certification Requirements for School Personnel in the United States*, published every three years by the National Education Association.

The graduate who meets the certification requirements of her/his own state may not meet those of other states into which s/he may want to move. Reciprocity between states continues to be a problem. Most states, however, now certify graduates from any institution accredited by NCATE, even if they do not meet exact state requirements.

Most certificates issued are temporary, not permanent, licenses to teach—they require periodic (usually every five years) renewal or reissuance. Normally renewal is dependent upon completion of additional college hours. While irritating, this requirement insures that the teacher will continue to grow professionally and, hopefully, keep up with new developments in her/his own field.

In 1972 Minnesota became the first state to require human relations training for teacher certification. Wisconsin, Michigan, and Iowa have enacted similar legislation. Several public school systems, including the New York City Public Schools, also require human relations training as a component of their employment requirements. Throughout the past ten years almost every major education conference has focused on some aspect of humanistic education in general and human relations skills in particular.

SIMILARITIES AND DIFFERENCES IN ELEMENTARY AND SECONDARY SCHOOL TEACHING

Students desiring a career in elementary or secondary school teaching should make their choice on the basis of their interests, abilities, and knowledge of the jobs. The following brief discussion may add the latter dimension to the reader's decisionmaking.

Similarities

Both elementary and secondary school teachers have long work weeks, with about half of their forty-five-to-fifty-hour work week devoted to noninstructional activities such as preparing lessons, grading papers, and chaperoning school events. Administrative routines are similar in both schools, and relationships to administrators, teacher's meetings, and procedures for getting supplies are similar.

The school team consists of many persons, ranging from custodians to the principal. In some schools the team includes not only a wide array of special teachers but also paraprofessionals and teacher aides. Within each building there is both a formal and an informal structure of leadership. New teachers would do well to know who are the formal and informal leaders within their building—the two are seldom synonomous. The goals of a school team should be:

First to establish rapport and trust between school, home and child; then to create a learning environment in the school which is rich, varied and alive; next, to analyze each student's behavior within the environment so as to identify his needs, his interests, his anxieties, his goals—conscious and unconscious—his learning style, his modes of attacking a problem, his apparent feeling toward self and others. The final step in the process is to restructure the environment, while providing the medley of supportive services that are needed, as the learner meshes his strivings to an educational task which is consonant with his goals, and at the same time replete with opportunity for his growth and development.[12]

The actual process of teaching is quite similar, although elementary teachers rely more heavily on class discussion than secondary teachers, who use more lectures and reading assignments. The dropout rate is high for both elementary and secondary schools. The major difference is that the students physically drop out (or are pushed out) in secondary schools, while they mentally and socially drop out in elementary schools. Finally, there are abundant good instructional materials—textbooks, audiovisual materials, programmed material—for both levels.

Differences

Elementary schools are organized on the basis of self-contained classroom units and secondary schools are organized into departments. The elementary teacher teaches 30–40 students each day in his or her self-contained classroom, whereas the secondary school teacher teaches an average of 130–160 students daily.

The North Central Association of Colleges and Secondary Schools has recommended that each teacher be given at least one conference and preparation period daily. In schools operating on a six- or seven-period day, each teacher would be assigned not more than five classes and/or study halls; while in schools with eight or more periods teachers would not have more than six classes and/or study halls. (The American Association of University Professors recommends not more than six course preparations during the academic year— twelve hours a week for junior colleges, and nine hours a week in four-year colleges.)

Class sizes vary from eighteen to twenty children in pre-kindergarten, to twenty-six to twenty-four in industrial arts to thirty-eight to fifty in physical education. Of course private and parochial schools tend to have smaller classes. Nor should we overlook the fact that nongrading, team teaching, programmed learning, flexible scheduling, and educational television also raise the number of students teachers can handle effectively.

The elementary teacher teaches all the subject fields, while the secondary teacher is a specialist—s/he usually teaches in his or her major and minor fields of specialization. The elementary teacher also uses the unit approach in which subject matter from several fields is

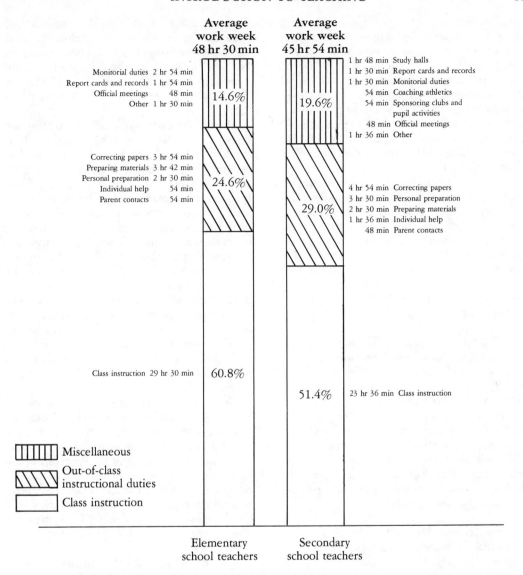

FIGURE 6. How Elementary and Secondary School Teachers Divide an Average Work Week. (*Source:* National Education Association.)

integrated. The secondary teacher focuses on specific subject-centered approaches.

In most school systems secondary school teachers have a free period each day for planning instruction, but in many systems elementary teachers teach all day without a free planning period. (In larger systems that employ special teachers in physical education, music, or art, the elementary teacher does have free planning periods.)

A good lesson plan will: (1) consist of flexible arrangements, procedures, or methods of action for achieving educational objectives which you consider to be desirable, (2) be a record of your thinking about desirable school experiences for your pupils, (3) include a description of the specific learning experiences in which pupils will participate during the time included in the plan, (4) be both long range and short range in nature, (5) give you a sense of security—of knowing where you are going and why—as well as provide a basis for appraising how well you and your pupils have succeeded.[13]

Teacher-student, teacher-parent, and teacher-community relationships tend to be closer in elementary school. As students grow older, they cease being counterdependent and seek independence from teachers. Parents also begin to exhibit less interest in their children's school activities.

One of the most pleasant or, depending on the composition of the organization, depressing school-related activities can be attending Parent-Teacher Association (PTA) meetings. Attendance is usually voluntary, but most administrators encourage teachers to attend PTA meetings. More elementary than secondary teachers attend PTA meetings. The National Congress of Parents and Teachers has the following goals:

1. *To promote the welfare of children and youth in home, school, church, and community.*
2. *To raise the standards of home life.*
3. *To secure adequate laws for the care and protection of children and youth.*
4. *To bring into closer relation the home and the school, that parents and teachers may cooperate intelligently in the training of the child.*
5. *To develop between educators and the general public such united efforts as will secure for every child the highest advantages in physical, mental, social and spiritual education.*

In some communities, PTAs have been instrumental in getting millage levies passed, schools desegregated, and needed school equipment.

Teachers have not only the right but also an obligation to become involved in community activities. As teachers they have the right to objectively discuss controversial issues in the classroom if the discussion pertains to the course work. As citizens of the United States, they may actively participate in community activities. More secondary than elementary teachers become embroiled in school-related controversial issues. When working actively in community organization, teachers should continuously make it clear that they are proceeding as citizens rather than as spokespersons of their schools. The NEA maintains the DuShane Emergency Fund and the AFT has a Defense Fund—both provide teachers with legal assistance when their rights are challenged. Other sources of support include the National Council for the Social Studies, the American Civil Liberties Union (ACLU) and the American Association of University Professors (AAUP).

Most of the homework assigned by teachers does not involve joint planning by both teacher and students. Homework is seldom assigned in pre-kindergarten and elementary schools. However, in secondary schools homework increases. (It is common in colleges, where homework usually consists of term papers.) As a rule homework is heaviest in mathematics, the sciences, and languages. William Van Til cautions: "If a teacher or professor decides to assign homework, he also assumes a responsibility—that of reading the homework, returning it promptly, and using it for educative purposes. There are few more disillusioning experiences for students than carefully preparing homework and then finding that their efforts are ignored or returned long after any possibility for reinforcement is likely."[14]

Elementary teachers have greater consensus about the educational philosophy of elementary education than secondary teachers have about the educational philosophy of secondary education. The price paid for specialization is academic discipline fragmentation. Secondary education training emphasizes depth of preparation in several fields, while elementary education emphasizes breadth. The latter approach makes it easier to embrace broad philosophical statements.

Job opportunities have historically been better for elementary than for secondary teachers. With student populations declining it is likely that the job picture will soon be bleak for both secondary and elementary teachers.

The Challenge of Teaching

A teacher must like working with young people. Few activities are more important than teaching. The more effective teacher has several characteristics, including the following:

1. *Human relations skills.* Teachers must enjoy their relationships with people within the school—students, colleagues, etc.—and

be able to deal effectively with conflict.

2. *Knowledge.* It is imperative that teachers have extensive and current knowledge of their fields. Consequently the teacher must be a lifelong learner, availing himself or herself of opportunities to attend classes, workshops, in-service training, and professional conferences.

3. *Pleasant appearance.* Both students and parents expect teachers to maintain a pleasant professional appearance. Overdressing or dressing down are frowned upon in most communities.

4. *Sense of humor.* Teachers must be able to laugh with other people and, when appropriate, at themselves. Under no circumstances should teachers ridicule their students.

5. *Good health.* In order to be optimally effective it is necessary for teachers to be in good physical and mental health. Wise use of leisure time is a factor in maintaining good health.

No matter what level one is teaching, there are some common concerns. But before listing them it is well to remember that while in college, *the student teacher does not learn how to teach but, rather, about teaching.* Usually, she spends a large part of her field experience observing classroom procedures and trying to gain insight into the teacher-student relationship.

Before one really begins to teach, he must know something about the children he is planning to teach, as well as something about the school itself. A visit to the school before the assignment begins can be helpful. A talk with the principal or his assistant will help the student teacher become familiar with the school and will give him an idea about what will be expected of him. This is also an excellent time to inquire about school rules and policies. A tour of the school building will acquaint the student teacher with the physical facilities. With permission of the cooperating teacher, or the principal, additional information may be obtained about the children in the classroom, which will involve examining cumulative records to find what they contain and how the information can be of use in teaching. A teacher's responsibilities are many, and the best time to learn them is during student teaching. [15]

Generally, the problems of teachers are many and varied. However, Frank W. Broadbent and Donald R. Cruickshank were able to identify seven recurring concerns of first year teachers:

1. Discipline
   a. Getting students to see the relationship between undesirable behaviors and their consequences
   b. Having students maintain quiet while working independently
   c. Finding ways to integrate isolated, disliked students
   d. Handling students' aggressive behavior toward each other
   e. Controlling the constantly disruptive students
2. Evaluation
   a. Learning how to evaluate personal objectives
   b. Judging students' progress in terms of stated aims
   c. Preparing classroom tests that are valid
   d. Resolving uncomfortable feelings when issuing grades
3. Methods
   a. Involving large numbers of students in group discussions
   b. Getting students to do homework
   c. Relating the subject meaningfully to students
   d. Differentiating instructional needs of the students
   e. Introducing a new topic and obtaining high interest
   f. Having independent work for some students while working with others
4. Parent Relations
   a. Discussing with parents their children's achievement and capabilities
   b. Helping students from deprived backgrounds but not causing them to reject their parents
5. Planning
   a. Adjusting to nonteaching responsibilities
   b. Planning for and working with exceptional children
6. Classroom Routines
   a. Overcoming a distaste for grading papers
   b. Keeping records and reports
7. Materials and Resources
   a. Finding out about and using special services of the school
   b. Understanding and using courses of study and instructional materials

c. *Ordering, securing, and accounting for supplies and materials* [16]

There are no foolproof techniques for coping with classroom problems. Whether beginning or experienced, each teacher must compile her own list of problems and devise her own methods of handling problems.

Perhaps no problem is more recurrent than discipline or classroom control. Katherine F. Tift suggests four practical steps in dealing effectively with students acting out in the class: (1) state clearly to the students what constituted their inappropriate behavior; (2) verbally identify your own feelings about this behavior (be honest, not cruel, but don't mince words); (3) provide a supportive structure for a change of behavior; and (4) whenever appropriate, use the participation of other students in a supportive structure.[17] First, however, when disciplinary problems arise the teacher should ask, Is anything wrong with my teaching methods? Horace Mann was correct when he said, "Teaching is the most difficult of all arts and the profoundest of all sciences."

In retrospect, the more effective teacher enjoys working with children, other teachers, administrators, and parents. The more effective teacher accepts each student for what he or she is, and realizes that there are usually good reasons for student behavior—even irritating behavior. The more effective teacher knows his or her subject and how to teach it. Nor is this knowledge limited to the course: the more effective teacher has a broad range of interests and (knowledge of different subjects.) Finally, the more effective teacher is in a continual state of intellectual and professional growth, always trying to be a better teacher.

NATIONAL EDUCATION ASSOCIATION CODE OF ETHICS OF THE EDUCATION PROFESSION

The educator believes in the worth and dignity of man. He recognizes the supreme importance of the pursuit of truth, devotion to excellence, and the nurture of democratic citizenship. He regards as essential to these goals the protection of freedom to learn and to teach and the guarantee of equal educational opportunity for all. The educator accepts his respon-

sibility to practice his profession according to the highest ethical standards.

The educator recognizes the magnitude of the responsibility he has accepted in choosing a career in education, and engages himself, individually and collectively with other educators, to judge his colleagues, and to be judged by them, in accordance with the provisions of this code.

Principle I
Commitment to the Student

The educator measures his success by the progress of each student toward realization of his potential as a worthy and effective citizen. The educator therefore works to stimulate the spirit of inquiry, the acquisition of knowledge and understanding, and the thoughtful formulation of worthy goals.

In fulfilling his obligation to the student the educator—

1. Shall not without just cause restrain the student from independent action in his pursuit of learning, and shall not without just cause deny the student access to varying points of view.

2. Shall not deliberately suppress or distort subject matter for which he bears responsibility.

3. Shall make a reasonable effort to protect the student from conditions harmful to learning or to health and safety.

4. Shall conduct professional business in such a way that he does not expose the student to unnecessary embarrassment or disparagement.

5. Shall not on the grounds of race, color, creed, or national origin exclude any student from participation in or deny him benefits under any program, nor grant any discriminatory consideration or advantage.

6. Shall not use professional relationships with students for private advantage.

7. Shall keep in confidence information that has been obtained in the course of professional service, unless disclosure serves professional purposes or is required by law.

8. Shall not tutor for remuneration students assigned to his classes, unless no other qualified teacher is reasonably available.

Principle II
Commitment to the Public

The educator believes that patriotism in its highest form required dedication to the prin-

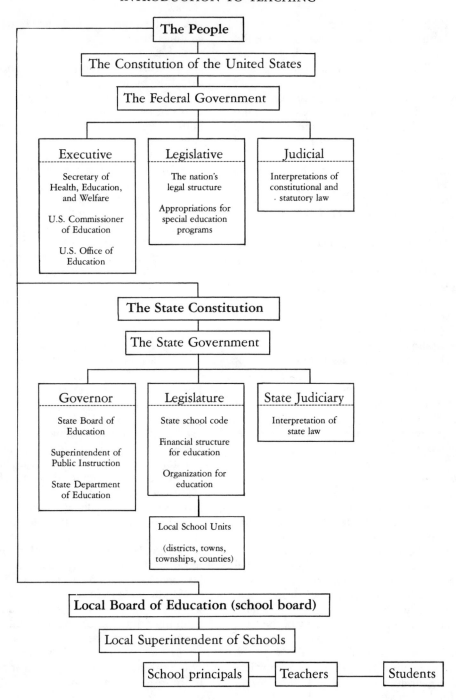

FIGURE 7. Structure of the Organization of Education in the United States.

ciples of our democratic heritage. He shares with all other citizens the responsibility for the development of sound public policy and assumes full political and citizenship responsibilities.

The educator bears particular responsibility for the development of policy relating to the extension of education opportunities for all and for interpreting educational programs and policies to the public.

In fulfilling his obligation to the public the educator—

1. Shall not misrepresent an institution or organization with which he is affiliated, and shall take adequate precautions to distinguish between his personal and institutional or organizational views.

2. Shall not knowingly distort or misrepresent the facts concerning educational matters in direct and indirect public expressions.

3. Shall not interfere with a colleague's exercise of political and citizenship rights and responsibilities.

4. Shall not use institutional privileges for private gain or promote political candidates or partisan political activities.

5. Shall accept no gratuities, gifts, or favors that might impair or appear to impair professional judgment, nor offer any favor, service, or thing of value to obtain special advantage.

Principle III
Commitment to the Profession

The educator believes that the quality of the services of the education profession directly influences the nation and its citizens. He therefore exerts every effort to raise professional standards, to improve his service, to promote a climate in which the exercise of professional judgment is encouraged, and to achieve conditions which attract persons worthy of the trust to careers in education. Aware of the value of united effort, he contributes actively to the support, planning and programs of professional organizations.

In fulfilling his obligation to the profession, the educator—

1. Shall not discriminate on grounds of race, color, creed, or national origin for membership in professional organizations, nor interfere with the free participation of colleagues in the affairs of their association.

2. Shall accord just and equitable treatment to all members of the profession in the exercise of their professional rights and responsibilities.

3. Shall not use coercive means or promise special treatment in order to influence professional decisions of colleagues.

4. Shall withhold and safeguard information acquired about colleagues in the course of employment, unless disclosure serves professional purposes.

5. Shall not refuse to participate in a professional inquiry when requested by an appropriate professional association.

6. Shall provide upon the request of the aggrieved party a written statement of specific reasons for recommendations that lead to the denial of increments, significant changes in employment, or termination of employment.

7. Shall not misrepresent his professional qualifications.

8. Shall not knowingly distort evaluation of colleagues.

Principle IV
Commitment to Professional Employment Practices

The educator regards the employment agreement as a pledge to be executed both in spirit and in fact in a manner consistent with the highest ideals of professional service. He believes that sound professional personnel relationships with governing boards are built upon personal integrity, dignity, and mutual respect. The educator discourages the practice of his profession by unqualified persons.

In fulfilling his obligation to professional employment practices, the educator—

1. Shall apply for, accept, offer, or assign a position or responsibility on the basis of professional preparation and legal qualifications.

2. Shall apply for a specific position only when it is known to be vacant, and shall refrain from underbidding or commenting adversely about other candidates.

3. Shall not knowingly withhold information regarding a position from an applicant, or misrepresent an assignment or conditions of employment.

4. Shall give prompt notice to the employing agency of any change in availability of service, and the employing agent shall give prompt notice of change in availability or nature of a position.

5. Shall not accept a position when so requested by the appropriate professional organization.

6. Shall adhere to the terms of a contract or appointment, unless these terms have been legally terminated, falsely represented, or substantially altered by unilateral action of the employing agency.

7. Shall conduct professional business through channels, when available, that have been jointly approved by the professional organization and the employing agency.

8. Shall not delegate assigned tasks to unqualified personnel.

9. Shall permit no commercial exploitation of his professional position.

10. Shall use time granted for the purpose for which it is intended.

AMERICAN FEDERATION OF TEACHERS BILL OF RIGHTS

The teacher is entitled to a life of dignity equal to the high standard of service that is justly demanded of that profession. Therefore, we hold these truths to be self-evident:

I

Teachers have the right to think freely and to express themselves openly and without fear. This includes the right to hold views contrary to the majority.

II

They shall be entitled to the free exercise of their religion. No restraint shall be put upon them in the manner, time or place of their worship.

III

They shall have the right to take part in social, civil, and political affairs. They shall have the right, outside the classroom, to participate in political campaigns and to hold office. They may assemble peacably and may petition any government agency, including their employers, for a redress of grievances. They shall have the same freedom in all things as other citizens.

IV

The right of teachers to live in places of their own choosing, to be free of restraints in their mode of living and the use of their leisure time shall not be abridged.

V

Teaching is a profession, the right to practice which is not subject to the surrender of other human rights. No one shall be deprived of professional status, or the right to practice it, or the practice thereof in any particular position, without due process of law.

VI

The right of teachers to be secure in their jobs, free from political influence or public clamor, shall be established by law. The right to teach after qualification in the manner prescribed by law is a property right, based upon the inalienable rights to life, liberty, and the pursuit of happiness.

VII

In all cases affecting the teacher's employment or professional status a full hearing by an impartial tribunal shall be afforded with the right of full judicial review. No teacher shall be deprived of employment or professional status but for specific causes established by law having a clear relation to the competence or qualification to teach, proved by the weight of the evidence. In all such cases the teacher shall enjoy the right to a speedy and public trial, to be informed of the nature and cause of the accusation, to be confronted with the accusing witnesses, to subpoena witnesses and papers, and to the assistance of counsel. No teacher shall be called upon to answer any charge affecting his employment or professional status but upon probable cause, supported by oath or affirmation.

VIII

It shall be the duty of the employer to provide culturally adequate salaries, security in illness and adequate retirement income. The teacher has the right to such a salary as will: (a) Afford a family standard of living comparable to that enjoyed by other professional people in the community; (b) Make possible freely chosen professional study; (c) Afford the opportunity for leisure and recreation common to our heritage.

IX

No teacher shall be required under penalty of reduction of salary to pursue studies beyond those required to obtain professional status. After serving a reasonable probationary period a teacher shall be entitled to permanent tenure terminable only for just cause. They shall be free as in other professions in the use of their own time. They shall not be required to perform extracurricular work against their will or without added compensation.

X

To equip people for modern life requires the most advanced educational methods. Therefore, the teacher is entitled to good classroom, adequate teaching materials, teachable class size and administrative protection and assistance in maintaining discipline.

XI

These rights are based upon the proposition that the culture of a people can rise only as its teachers improve. A teaching force accorded the highest possible professional dignity is the surest guarantee that blessings of liberty will be preserved. Therefore, the possession of these rights imposes the challenge to be worthy of their enjoyment.

XII

Since teachers must be free in order to teach freedom, the right to be members of organizations of their own choosing must be guaranteed. In all matters pertaining to their salaries and working conditions they shall be entitled to bargain collectively through representatives of their own choosing. They are entitled to have the schools administered by superintendents, boards or committees which function in a democratic manner.

SURVIVAL

Imagine that through some weird set of events it has become apparent that the entire world is about to be subjected to a violent nuclear holocaust which will spell an end to all human life on this planet. Scientists have, however, devised a special protection chamber which, although small in size, is absolutely guaranteed to keep its occupants alive through this holocaust. The chamber will hold ten persons, who have already been selected. They are:

1. A thirty year old Black homosexual female chemistry teacher
2. A twenty year old alcoholic Indian male nurse
3. A seventeen year old Chicano female retarded student
4. A twenty-nine year old white male English teacher, who has been fired for beating nonwhite students
5. A thirty-five year old Chinese male orthopedically handicapped track coach
6. A twelve year old Puerto Rican female pregnant student
7. A forty year old white female principal
8. A three year old Vietnamese male nursery school student, who does not speak English
9. A twenty-five year old white male, drug addicted high school counselor
10. A seventy year old white male vocational agriculture teacher

At the very last minute the scientists announce that, contrary to their previous calculations, only six persons can be safely life-supported in the capsule.

Which of the people listed above should be deleted from the survival list? Only six can be the sole survivors of the human race. *You* decide the four who will not survive. Ask a friend to do the same and compare your lists and reasons for keeping or deleting people from the survival list. What did you learn about yourself?

ADDITIONAL READINGS

Aiken, Lewis R., ed. *Readings in Psychological and Educational Teaching.* New York, Allyn & Bacon, 1971.

Broudy, Harry S. *The Real World of the Public Schools.* New York, Harcourt Brace Jovanovich, 1972.

Chandler, Bobby Joe. *Education and the New Teacher.* New York, Dodd, Mead, 1971.

Ehlars, Henry J. *Crucial Issues in Education.* Holt, Rinehart & Winston, 1973.

Fein, Leah G. *The Changing School Scene.* New York, John Wiley & Sons, 1974.

Foster, John M. *Creativity and the Teacher.* New York, MacMillan, 1971.

Foy, Rena. *The World of Education.* New York, MacMillan, 1968.

Goodlad, John I. *Early Schooling in the United States.* New York, McGraw-Hill, 1973.

Gorow, Frank F. *The Learning Game: Strategies for Secondary Teachers.* Columbus, Ohio, Charles Merrill, 1972.

Gross, Ronald. *The Teacher and the Taught.* New York, Dell, 1963.

Levy, Harold B. *Square Pegs, Round Holes.* Boston, Little, Brown, 1973.

Madsen, Charles H. *Teaching Discipline.* New York, Allyn & Bacon, 1974.

Wiles, Kimball. *Teaching for Better Schools.* Englewood Cliffs, N.J., Prentice-Hall, 1969.

Woodruff, A.D. *Basic Concepts of Teaching.* San Francisco, Chandler, 1963.

NOTES

1. Robert J. Havighurst, *Human Development and Education* (New York, Longmans, Green, 1953, chapters 2, 4, 9, 10, 16–18.

2. Lillian C. Gore, "What is a Good Nursery School?" *School Life,* 45 (June, 1973), 19.

3. Lillian C. Gore and Rose Koury, *Educating Children In Nursery Schools and Kindergartens* (Washington, D.C., U.S. Printing Office, 1964), 21–22.

4. Charles A. DeYoung and Richard Wynn, *American Education,* 6th ed. (New York, McGraw-Hill, 1968), 161–162.

5. Commission on the Reorganization of Secondary Education, *The Cardinal Principles of Secondary Education* (Washington, D.C., U.S. Bureau of Education, 1918), 5ff.

6. James C. Stone and Frederick W. Schneider, *Foundations of Education,* 2d ed. (New York, Thomas Y. Crowell, 1971), 70.

7. Educational Policies Commission, *Higher Education in a Decade of Decision* (Washington, D.C., National Education Association, 1957), 10.

8. T. R. McConnell, *A Design for General Education* (Washington, D.C., American Council on Education Studies, 1944), 14–15.

9. Maxwell H. Goldberg, "Continuous Education as a Way of Life," *Adult Education,* 16 (Autumn, 1965), 3.

10. *Adult Education: A New Imperative of Our Times* (Washington, D.C., Adult Education Association, 1961), 14–15.

11. John A. Green, *Fields of Teaching and Educational Services* (New York, Harper & Row, 1966), 23.

12. Gordon J. Kloph, Garda W. Bowman, and Adena Joy, *A Learning Team: Teacher and Auxiliary* (New York, Bank Street College of Education, 1969), viii.

13. Robert W. Richey, *Planning for Teaching: An Introduction to Education,* 4th ed. (New York, McGraw-Hill, 1968), 152.

14. William Van Til, *Education: A Beginning* (Boston, Houghton Mifflin, 1971), 486.

15. George Henderson and Robert F. Bibens, *Teachers Should Care: Social Perspectives of Teaching* (New York, Harper & Row, 1970), 126–127.

16. Frank W. Broadbent and Donald R. Cruickshank, "The Identification and Analysis of Problems of First Year Teachers," unpublished paper, State University of New York, College at Brockport, 1965.

17. Katherine F. Tift, "The Distrubed Child in the Classroom," *National Education Association Journal,* 57 (March, 1968), 12–14.

6.
TEACHER PREPARATION

Despite the fact that there are more qualified graduates who are currently seeking than are able to locate employment as school teachers, teaching continues to have great appeal, especially to college women, who are twice as likely as men to major in education. Furthermore this appeal continues even though in some cities garbage collectors are paid more money than beginning teachers.

During the past seventeen years the school-age population has shown a steady decline. For example, there were 15 per cent fewer children under age five in America in 1970 than in 1960. The falling birthrate is attributed to many causes, including growing economic concern among married couples and delayed marriages. Whatever the reasons, school enrollments and, concurrently, jobs are decreasing. In 1976 the NEA estimated that 233,470 new teachers competed for 94,000 available positions. Each year new graduates must compete with more than 100,000 former teachers returning to the profession, plus graduates from previous years who have been unable to get jobs. Even so, there is still a demand for special education, agricultural education, home economics, mathematics, science, and male elementary teachers.

Once the decision is made to become a teacher, considerable thought should be given to the career lines you might pursue. This chapter is but a brief survey of a few available careers in education. First it may be necessary to alter your attitude towards teaching:

Although we expect miracles from the schools, we tend to identify the classroom teacher with casual workers:

> *With the young woman just out of college who is looking for two or three years of work before marriage.*
> *With a married woman who turns to teaching temporarily to supplement family income.*
> *With a young man who uses teaching as a stepping stone to a career in another profession or business.*
> *With an older man who is retired from other employment.*

These concepts of the teacher must change rapidly and drastically. They are incompatible with efforts to staff the classroom with highly trained professional persons:

> *Who will devote a lifetime of service to teaching.*
> *Who will return to school every second or third summer to increase their knowledge.*
> *Who envision classroom teaching as important as any other profession for a college trained person.*[1]

Future teachers should know that there are eight dimensions of schooling. Regardless of the school activity, some *purpose* is being served. Developing independent thought and action is best achieved by treating students as individuals. All schools have some kind of *rules*, and they work most effectively when students are involved in determining them. There are as many different *learning styles* as there are students. Instruction should be geared to individual student styles. Permitting different learning styles necessitates individualized course *content*. Allowing students *time* to work at their own pace requires that arbitrary and rigid class periods be abandoned for flexible scheduling. Learning *space* need not be limited to within the walls of the school. In addition, internal school space should be expanded and contracted to meet group needs. Compulsory school attendance does not mean compulsory classroom *participation*. All students should be given the option of not participating in some activities. Placement, formative, and diagnostic *evaluation* are as important as summative and terminal evaluation.[2] Most of the following jobs involve all these dimensions of teaching.

EARLY CHILDHOOD EDUCATION

In an effort to insure minimum standards in programs and facilities which receive federal support under such acts as the Economic Opportunity Act or the Manpower Development and Training Act, the Federal Panel on Early Childhood Education issued a statement on *Federal Interagency Day Care Requirements*. These programs and facilities must also be licensed in the state in which they are operated.

There is a shortage of qualified professional and paraprofessional early childhood personnel at all levels. While the majority of kindergarten programs are staffed by certified teachers, many nursery schools, day care programs, and Head Start programs are not directed by persons who have a college degree in child development or early childhood education. These programs frequently do not have fully qualified teachers.

As a general rule, there is no plan for continuity between the program for children under five years of age and public school programs. Most public schools make little attempt to find out what previous school experiences a child has had or to build on these experiences. There is usually very little difference in the treatment of a child who has had two or three years of nursery school and the child who has had no prior school experience at all. In programs where there is true individualization of instruction, this may not be of great importance as far as the child's progress is concerned. Those teachers who have worked with the child during his earlier years

should be able to supply valuable and helpful information about the child and the experiences he has had, which would enable the current teacher to meet his needs better. It often happens that the programs in which a child is enrolled over a period of his preschool and primary years have conflicting purposes.[3]

While almost all states have legislation permitting the establishment of public school kindergartens, only thirty-five states provide state aid for these schools. Only one-fourth of the states authorize local boards of education to use local funds for prekindergarten children.

Administrative Responsibility

In thirty-seven states the State Department of Education is responsible for kindergarten programs, while it is responsible for prekindergarten programs in only six states. In states where the prekindergarten program is not delegated to the State Department of Welfare, it is delegated to the State Department of Social Services, or of Health. Nearly two-thirds of the states do not have legislation which provides for registration, licensing, or accreditation of nonpublic nursery schools and/or kindergartens.

Minimum Training

The preparation of personnel for early childhood education is a joint effort by local school systems, colleges and universities, and state agencies. Two committees, the Task Force on Early Childhood Education and the Ad Hoc Joint Committee on the Preparation of Nursery and Kindergarten Teachers, recommend that teacher preparation include: (1) in-depth courses in understanding children's growth and learning styles, (2) curriculum planning, and (3) knowledge of children from varied socio-economic backgrounds. Furthermore, both committees strongly endorse human relations training for teacher preparation.

At a minimum, early childhood education teachers should have a bachelor's degree in early childhood education from a college or university, or an equivalent degree from an

	Period	Monday	Tuesday	Wednesday	Thursday	Friday
8:30	1	English	English	English	English	English
	2	Mathematics	Mathematics	Mathematics	Mathematics	Mathematics
	3	Science	Science	Science	Science	Science
	4	Study hall	Study hall	Study hall	Study hall	Study hall
		Lunch	Lunch	Lunch	Lunch	Lunch
	5	Social studies	Social studies	Social studies	Social studies	Social studies
	6	Music	Music	Music	Music	Music
3:30	7	Physical education	Physical education	Physical education	Physical education	Physical education

FIGURE 8. A Traditional Secondary School Schedule.

accredited four-year teacher preparation institution. Degree requirements usually include thirty to forty semester hours in early childhood education, learning theory, growth and development, and practical teaching experiences in preschool to primary grades. Each year more colleges are moving away from traditional coursework to competency-based programs, with greater emphasis being placed on practical training.

Paraprofessionals

Early childhood education programs have been the most successful in utilizing assistant teachers—teacher's aides or paraprofessionals. Paraprofessionals may be paid personnel or volunteers. Most aides receive some basic training, including information about the school's policies and procedures, use of materials and supplies, and classroom routines. Several junior and community colleges offer certificate programs for teacher aides.

In some schools as much as one-fourth of a teacher's time is spent doing things that could be handled by paraprofessionals. The following list suggests some of the things responsible teacher aides can be employed to do:

1. Making charts, posters, and other graphic materials.
2. Cutting paper, sharpening pencils, preparing dittos, distributing supplies, and other secretarial chores.
3. Checking papers and recording daily paper and test results.
4. Supervision of playground, lunch room, library, study rooms, nurse's room, and halls.
5. Taking an inventory and making a record of the books, supplies, materials, and other media in the building.
6. Assisting the custodian.
7. Reading to individuals or groups of children.
8. Listening to children as they practice oral reading.
9. Serving as a resource person.
10. Preparing equipment and materials for art, music, science, and physical education lessons and then caring for these things upon completion of the lessons.[4]

In addition to classroom teachers, other professional careers in childhood education include: (1) administrator or director, (2) social worker, and (3) health and nutrition personnel. Key nonprofessional positions in addition to aides are secretaries, custodians, and lunchroom personnel.

BASIC SUBJECT AREAS

Several subjects taught in elementary school are required for secondary school graduation.

Some writers rank order these teaching areas, but I prefer to consider them all of equal value.

Language

The field of language focuses on verbal communication. Specifically, language study includes the processes of understanding, speaking, reading, and writing symbolic representations of ideas and recording human interaction. In elementary schools this field is called "language arts," and it includes reading, writing, spelling, and composition. Language in high school is offered as literature, grammar and composition, word study, classical and modern foreign languages, journalism, and speech.

Language is one of the most rapidly changing fields. To understand and adjust to the changes, college-level courses include (1) *linguistics*, which is research in language usage, (2) *phonetics*, which is research in language sounds, (3) *structural linguistics*, which is research in language structure, and (4) *semantics*, which is the science of meaning, as contrasted with the science of sound.[5]

Research studies show that in the English language, spelling and sound are frequently inadequately related. American children tend to spell phonetically and consequently usually spell incorrectly. The lack of attention to phonetics in many elementary school language arts programs is believed by some critics to be a major cause of reading and spelling handicaps in school-age children. Along with the trend toward teaching phonetics in elementary school is an emphasis upon current grammatical usage rather than obsolete, historical usage.

The objectives of the elementary school reading program usually include the following:

1. Primary pupils should become aware of the many purposes which reading can serve.
2. Primary pupils should gain sufficient command of essential reading skills to handle materials at their general maturity level.
3. Primary pupils should master a variety of simple reference techniques.
4. Primary pupils should begin to think critically about what they read.
5. Primary pupils should acquire simple insights into the nature of the reading process.[6]

The following objectives for high school illustrate the philosophical shift from building reading skills to using them:

1. Gaining reading stature.
2. Expanding interests and improving tastes.
3. Increasing reading fluency.
4. Establishing a different attack.[7]

The study of foreign languages uses the same type of progression from stress on skill development during the early years to increased emphasis on usage and enjoyment in later years. The younger a student begins, the more successful is the foreign language program.

Because the great majority of human communication is oral, and most learning is an oral-aural process, it stands to reason that more attention should be paid to speech communication. Unfortunately, formal instruction in speech is not offered in most schools.

To summarize, the language arts program in the elementary school focuses on reading, vocabulary, sentence structure, and complexity of concept. In the junior high or middle school and high school, the emphasis shifts to discrimination, understanding and appreciation of literature, and emphasis on creativity and originality in writing. In spite of innovative elementary and secondary schools programs, as many as two-thirds of freshmen entering college are deficient in basic reading skills needed for academic success.

The general and professional education of language teachers—English, speech, and foreign languages—is the same as that of teachers in other fields. The general education sequence consists of approximately forty semester hours in the humanities, the social sciences, mathematics, and science. The professional education sequence consists of approximately twenty semester hours in educational foundations, methods, psychology, and supervised student teaching.

Elementary school English teachers normally complete twelve to fifteen semester hours in English in addition to their general education requirements. Specific preparation for teaching of language arts consists of composition, language arts methods, and literature.

Secondary school teachers of English are

expected to have training in reading, literature, composition, speech, journalism, and dramatics. Generally the thirty to forty semester-hours in English should consist largely of courses in composition and literature, with at least an introduction to semantics, phonetics, structural linguistics, and word derivation.

Mathematics and Science Education

Mathematics, the science of numbers, includes several subdisciplines such as arithmetic, algebra, geometry, calculus, and statistics. Science, the search for order in nature, is divided into two classifications: physical sciences and biological or life sciences. Elementary and secondary teachers are mainly concerned with the scientific disciplines of biology, chemistry, physics, and geology.

Science does not attempt to explain, in the ultimate sense of that word. It does, however, attempt to give comprehensive descriptions of the universe around us. In so doing we need not detract from nor destroy any profound respect for things spiritual. Indeed, any grand view obtained through science may deepen and make secure our beliefs in a realm not reached by science.[8]

In elementary and secondary schools, both mathematics and science seek to give the students basic preparation for a variety of professions such as engineering, scientific research, and agronomy. But these courses are also of value to students who are not college-bound. In mathematics, for example, all students can benefit by learning to apply quantitative procedures effectively in dealing with such practical problems as the intelligent buying and selling of consumer goods. And with the growing debate over consumer and environmental protection, an understanding of science will make students better able to enter the debate and vote intelligently.

The elementary school mathematics program consists mainly of arithmetic, in which students learn fundamental operations with integers and decimal fractions, plus some practical applications of these computations. High school mathematics include general mathematics, algebra, and plane geometry. Several schools offer advanced mathematics, trigonometry, solid geometry, and beginning calculus.

The elementary school science program consists of general science rather than a series of science courses. High school science offerings include general science, biological science, chemistry, and physics. Most high schools require two years of science for graduation, and general science and biology are taken by most students.

Elementary teachers are not expected to complete a major in mathematics or science, but they are advised to take nine to twelve semester hours in these fields. In most colleges methods courses taught by specialists in mathematics and science are available. For high school mathematics teachers the expectations are different. It is recommended that future secondary school teachers who major in science should select mathematics as a minor, and vice versa.

Generally, colleges and universities offer undergraduates majoring in science a single major in one of the disciplines or a composite major in general science, biological science, and physical science. The composite major requires a minimum of thirty to forty semester hours in several disciplines such as chemistry, geology, and physics.

Undergraduate majors in mathematics are expected to gain proficiency in each of the branches of mathematics. Here too thirty to forty semester hours are acceptable. The American Association for the Advancement of Science suggests the course work be distributed as follows:

1. A minimum of six hours in *Math Analysis* selected from: trigonometry, plane geometry, calculus, solid geometry, advanced calculus, differential equations, infinite series.

2. A minimum of three hours in *Math Applications* selected from: mechanics, mathematical physics, astronomy, actuarial mathematics, uses in behavioral sciences.

3. A minimum of three hours in *Probability and Statistics*.

4. A minimum of three hours in *Algebra* selected from: abstract algebra, matrices, theory of numbers, theory of equations.

5. A minimum of three hours in *Geometry* selected from: metric and other geometries, non-Euclidean geometries, differential geometry, topology.

6. A minimum of three hours in *Foundation of Mathematics* selected from: theory of sets,

mathematical or symbolic logic, postulates for geometry, postulates for algebra, postulates for arithmetic, the real and complex number systems.[9]

Social Studies

Social studies is comprised of several disciplines, including history, economics, political science, geography, psychology, and sociology. History is a record of human beings' successes and failures. Economics focuses on the production and distribution of goods and services. Political science studies relationships which result from official governmental control. Geography is the study of men and women's relationships with their natural environment. Psychology studies why humans and animals behave as they do. Sociology studies lasting group interactions which govern societal living.

Social studies should not, as Horatio V. Henry pointed out, be confused with social science:

Social science is an investigation of laws governing human behavior whereby specific laws and rules governing such behavior will be established. When the laws are discovered, they are put into application by a program known as the Social Studies.[10]

There is confusion about the content and objectives of social studies. Despite Henry's clear statement, some scholars and practitioners argue that social studies should transmit citizenship concepts and values through textbooks, lectures, quizzes, and structured problem-solving exercises. Many persons support a value-neutral approach which utilizes social science methodology. Still others believe that citizenship is best promoted through reflective inquiry—rational self-analysis of individual values. Throughout the three social studies traditions (citizenship transmission, social science approach, and reflective inquiry), each emphasizes experience and knowledge of human relations for the purpose of achieving effective citizenship. Perhaps an integration of the three traditions would culminate in a comprehensive program focusing on knowledge, values, skills, social criticism, and involvement.

The first and primary objective of social studies is to develop good citizenship by helping students to: (1) develop an understanding of human relationships and the interdependence between people and nations, (2) acquire skill in critically evaluating social problems and possible solutions, and (3) acquire or maintain an attitude of respect for the dignity of all persons, without desiring to discriminate against others because of race, ethnic background, sex, creed, religion, or social class.

Social studies also has as one of its objectives to provide students with social experience, social knowledge, and social skills so that they can function effectively outside of school. Not only are the concepts of democratic government taught by democratic teaching-learning experiences, but they are also fostered through life experiences.

Elementary students get a cursory introduction to formal history, whereas it is a graduation requirement in high school. Geography may be subdivided into the physical or natural and the cultural or human. Physical geography includes studies of the land, the oceans, and the atmosphere. Human geography includes studies of population growth and change. Except in a few high schools, geography is seldom offered as a separate course.

In upper elementary and junior or middle schools, political science concepts and data are used to analyze county, state and federal government. This is an elaboration of early elementary focus on neighborhood and local government. In high school the political science focus shifts to systems of government, with major emphasis on democratic, socialistic, and communistic forms of government. Economics is offered as a separate subject only in a few high schools. Basic economic concepts integrated with other subjects include: (1) economic bases of government in political science, (2) labor and industrial problems in history, and (3) consumer economics in general mathematics.

Requirements vary, but college students majoring in social studies may, for example, elect either a thirty-hour, one-area major or a forty semester-hour composite major. Secondary school teachers are not encouraged to seek less than a major in the field, even though a provisional certificate may be obtained in some districts with a minor (eighteen to twenty semester hours) in social studies. Because secondary school teachers are often assigned to teach only one subject area, most students elect a single major with its greater depth of preparation. A composite major allows only minimal acquaintance with the five disciplines.

In both social studies and other fields, graduate work is becoming mandatory. A growing number of teachers are electing to pursue master's degree programs rather than accumulate unrelated semester hours beyond the bachelor's degree.

SPECIAL SUBJECTS

The subjects in this section are elective in secondary schools and sometimes taught by specialists in elementary schools. Generally, these subjects complement core subjects by focusing on vocational skills, physical well-being, and our cultural heritage.

Business Education

Prior to current usage of the term "business education," the terms "secretarial training" and "commercial training" were used. The private academies offered courses in bookkeeping before the Civil War, and typing was introduced into the curriculum in the 1870s. Shorthand, the oldest of business education subjects, was used by governmental recorders in ancient Greece. However, it wasn't until Robert Gregg introduced the Gregg system of shorthand into America in the 1890s that the teaching of this subject became widespread. Federal financial support for business education in the public secondary schools came mainly from three acts: the Smith-Hughes Act in 1917, the George-Deen Act in 1936, the George-Barden Act in 1946 and the Vocational Education Act of 1963. Distributive education, supervised on-the-job paid training in merchandising work, came into being with the George-Deen Act.

Secretarial training was vocationally-oriented; commercial training was broader than secretarial training since it included a wider range of vocational training; and business education is the broadest term yet, since it includes commercial training and preparation for several business careers. In addition to focusing on clerical, stenographic and secretarial, bookkeeping and recording, and sales

work, business education has four general education goals:

1. Consumer information and education.
2. Business understanding for management of personal business affairs.
3. Business and economic understanding for intelligent citizenship.
4. Common business skills for personal use.[11]

In the elementary school the focus is on consumer education, while in junior high school students learn typing and general business. In most larger high schools, the business education curriculum includes general business and vocational courses in addition to the typing, shorthand and bookkeeping courses found in small high schools. Courses such as sales, retailing, merchandising, and cooperative work experience prepare students for jobs in advertising, selling, and distribution.

Teachers of business education normally complete a major consisting of thirty to forty semester hours. This amount of coursework only minimally prepares one to teach. While most states do not require certification for business education teachers, some states require special certification for distributive education teachers. In addition to the four-year teacher education curriculum, Lloyd V. Douglas recommends that the following requirements also be met:

1. Actual business experience which should have consisted of salaried work similar to that which is to be taught and should have totaled an adequate number of hours (2,000 or more).
2. Not only full qualifications for work in the business world, but better qualifications than business trainees who are not to become business teachers. This may be at least partially assured by requiring greater depth in preparation of the teacher trainee (as by more hours of college credit or by graduate work), or by evidence of higher quality of preparatory achievement (as by maintenance of a higher academic record).
3. The inclusion of appropriate preparation for organizing and directing sound cooperative part-time programs.
4. The inclusion of appropriate preparation for teaching adult evening or continuation

classes in the teacher's own general area of preparation.

5. The inclusion of a special study of the philosophy underlying vocational education.[12]

The above requirements are becoming unofficial expectations of public school administrators as they sift through the numerous applications for a few job vacancies.

Music and Art Education

Music education was not part of the American professional education curriculum until 1760, when the "singing schools" taught music. However it was not until the last half of the nineteenth century that music teachers began to appear in great numbers. These were private music teachers, who tutored students for a fee. In 1884 Julia Crane founded the first normal school of music in Potsdam, New York. In 1907 the first professional music educators organization, the Music Supervisors Conference, was organized. (In 1934 it became the Music Educators National Conference.) The growth of music education is evidenced by the fact that almost all schools offer some of the following courses: band, chorus, orchestra, music appreciation, and music theory.

Art as a formal subject is even more recent than music. This is true even though Froebel and Pestalozzi included art work in their curricula. With the introduction of manual arts into the curriculum in the latter part of the nineteenth century, art was broadened to include arts and crafts, but little attention was given to creativity in the arts. It was not until John Dewey and his followers began encouraging early twentieth century students to express themselves through art, writing, and music that art became used for more than skill development. Elementary school art currently emphasizes creativity and freedom of expression. Only the more wealthy schools employ art specialists to help students.

The school music program seeks to provide experiences in several areas: singing, music reading, rhythm, instrumental activities, listening, and creation. The school art program seeks to provide experiences in drawing, painting, sculpture, crafts, and art appreciation. In elementary schools these areas are the joint responsibility of the classroom teacher and, when available, the specialist. In the secondary school each area is taught by a subject-matter specialist.

In addition to attending four year college programs, music teachers may also receive training in a conservatory of music, and art teachers may do additional work at an art institute. In most states the certification of music and art teachers is noted on the teaching certificate. A few states require a special certificate for elementary and secondary school fine arts teachers.

Music education preparation usually consists of the following: (1) one-third general education, (2) one-third music performances courses (voice, conducting, instrumental music, etc.), (3) twenty per cent professional education, including methods and student teaching, and (4) the rest of the program in music theory. Specifically, competencies in music education include:

1. The ability to sight read and perform well as a singer or on a major instrument.

2. The ability to play the piano, with keyboard facility developed for the playing of parts from the open score.

3. A thorough knowledge of conducting techniques, with expressive conducting as the goal.

4. A functional knowledge of local and choral technique.

5. A functional knowledge of instruments and instrumentation, including an understanding of orchestra and band scores.

6. The development of musical perception and aural ability to judge tone production, blend, balance, intonation, and rhythmic response.[13]

Art education majors can concentrate in art or arts and crafts. The art major is a minimum of thirty semester hours distributed among the following courses: drawing, art appreciation, painting, composition, water color, and design. The arts and crafts major is a minimum of forty hours (including twenty in arts courses), of which twenty hours are in the following crafts: graphic arts, art metals, and photography. Generally elementary teachers are arts and crafts majors, and secondary teachers are art

majors. A master's degree is usually required
for fine arts supervisors.

Industrial Arts

Although industrial education is sometimes
used synonymously with vocational education,
vocational education is not primarily concerned with vocational training. Technically,
industrial arts "is a phase of general education
which serves to familiarize students with tools,
products, processes, and occupations of industry as well as the social and economic
phenomena of the technological world in
which they live and work."[14]

In 1642 the Massachusetts General Court
passed a law similar to the English Poor Laws,
which required that the children of indigent
parents be apprenticed to a skilled master who
would teach them a trade in exchange for the
work they performed. Industrial arts, or manual arts as it was then called, was introduced
into a St. Louis high school by Calvin M.
Woodward in 1880. The first manual training
in elementary school was taught in Boston in
1882. The first technical high school was established in Springfield, Massachusetts, in 1898.
Frederick G. Bonser coined the term "industrial arts" in 1909.

Areas of instruction in industrial arts include
drawing, woodworking, electricity and elec-
tronics, metalworking, ceramics, leather work,
home mechanics, graphic arts, plastics, transportation and power, and textiles. General
shop is an introduction to each of these areas,
while advanced courses focus on specialization
in one or more of these areas.

The American Vocational Association supports the following objectives for a school industrial arts program:

1. To provide experience in performing
correctly operations involving basic industrial
hand tools and common machines.

2. To acquaint the students with various
fields of industry, including the materials,
products, and employment opportunities.

3. To develop desirable work habits and
ability to work cooperatively.

4. To develop safety habits with industrial
hand tools and common machines.

5. To develop an appreciation for good
craftsmanship.

6. To develop opportunities to satisfy
creative desires.

7. To develop the ability to think rationally, to plan shop work wisely, execute plans
effectively, and appraise finished products intelligently.

8. To develop the ability to select and use
wisely the products of industry.

9. To develop the ability to perform
common household repairs.

10. To develop a basic understanding of
labor-management-consumer relationships in
an industrial society.[15]

Preparation for industrial arts teaching includes two years of general education, twenty
to thirty semester hours in professional education including methods and practice teaching,
and thirty to forty semester hours in industrial
arts courses.

Physical Education

Physical education is a composite field which
subsumes physical education, health education, and recreation education. As a school
curriculum, physical education dates back to
the ancient cultures, especially the ancient
Greeks, who advocated school-directed physical training for all age groups.

In the middle nineteenth century several
German physical exercises were introduced
into American schools. These precision group
exercises gave way in the 1870s to free-flowing
Swedish gymnastics and calisthenics. Basketball and volleyball are the two American contributions to the curriculum. James A. Nai-
smith invented basketball in 1891, and William
G. Morgan invented volleyball in 1895.

Physical education is concerned with helping
each student to achieve physical fitness and be
able to optimally utilize physical skills. *Health
education* is concerned with helping students
improve the health environment, become
familiar with available health services, and understand and care for their own physical
health. *Recreation education* is concerned with
the productive use of leisure time. All schools
have some form of physical education and
health education activities.

Preparation for teaching physical education
includes the same pattern as for other teaching
fields: general education, professional educa-

tion, and special education. Most colleges offer a thirty to forty semester-hour major in physical education. Supervisors and coordinators of physical education programs are expected to take additional hours in physical education organization and administration. In fact supervisory positions usually require a master's degree.

Vocational and Technical Education

Vocational education is concerned with preparing students for nonprofessional occupations. Most of this training is offered at the high school or post-high school level. Generally, *vocational education* refers to the initial high school preparation for various occupations, while *technical education* refers to the late high school or post-high school preparation for technical occupations. Vocational and technical curricula include vocational agriculture, trades and industry, vocational home-making, and distributive education.

The Morrill Land Grant Act of 1862 provided the first important financial aid to vocational education. This act authorized financial and land grants to the states for purposes of establishing state colleges and universities in which agricultural and mechanical arts would be taught. The Smith-Hughes Act of 1917 was the first of a series of federal acts which have increased the financial support for vocational education. This act provided an annual sum of $7 million for preparing teachers and establishing secondary school programs of vocational education, especially vocational agriculture, home economics, and trades and industry.

Trade and industrial education involves both in-school and out-of-school youths and adults. In-school students are in either preparatory or cooperative work programs. Students in the preparatory program are enrolled full-time in school—they have shop, laboratory, and technical instruction for half the day and elective general education subjects for the other half. The cooperative work program involves a mix of on-the-job and in-school activities. Out-of-school students are given extension classes which are designed to improve their occupational efficiency. This is also an avenue for gaining specific skills in order to secure a job.

Distributive education prepares persons for positions in marketing or merchandising goods or retail and wholesale services. Here too there are in-school and out-of-school participants. The out-of-school program is designed to upgrade participants and qualify them for sales or junior management positions. Classroom instruction includes business management, sales management, supervision, and data processing.

Vocational agriculture education prepares students for careers in farming. Course offerings include diversified farming, dry-land farming, livestock farming, and irrigated farming. Of course, these courses include instruction in effective management.

Home economics education prepares students for home management and related occupations. While traditionally a female-oriented program, an increasing number of schools are enrolling males. Specific goals include: (1) managing time, energy, money, and other related resources for the successful attainment of family goals, (2) selecting, preparing, and serving food, and (3) applying the principles of cleanliness and orderliness in the care of the home.

Teacher preparation in these areas includes the same general and professional education required of secondary teachers in other fields. The major area of specialization involves thirty to fifty semester hours. (The highest number is in vocational agriculture.) It would be wise for future teachers to read the National Vocational Education Acts and also to check with their State Board of Vocational Education regarding certification requirements. Recently junior colleges and community colleges have become the most important institutions of vocational education.

ADMINISTRATION AND SERVICES

Many teachers find themselves moving both vertically and horizontally within their school hierarchy. All schools are supplemented by the services of specialized personnel—administrators, guidance specialists, and audiovisual experts, to mention a few. This section will discuss a few of the supportive jobs that persons in teacher preparation programs should consider.

Educational Administration

A school is a complex organization which requires many supportive staff. The period of the small administrative staff consisting of a superintendent, an assistant superintendent, and elementary and secondary principals no longer exists. School systems now employ personnel administrators, business administrators, research directors, elementary and secondary coordinators, superintendents of buildings and grounds, public relations directors, and other supervisory personnel. According to John A. Green, a good administrator possesses: "(1) human relations ability, (2) high intelligence, (3) honesty and integrity, (4) ambition and drive, (5) respect for individual competence, (6) willingness to delegate authority, (7) good health, and (8) pleasant appearance."[16]

With less time than they had in the past for general administrative activities, most superintendents delegate these reponsibilities. The designations given to high level administrative assistants of the superintendent are deputy, associate, and assistant superintendents. The assistant superintendent for instruction is responsible for instructional services, curriculum development, and staff development. The assistant superintendent for business affairs is responsible for the budget, transportation, plant maintenance, and custodial and food services. The assistant superintendent for personnel services is responsible for employment, placement, assignment, administration of the personnel office, administration of personnel rules and regulations, adjustment counseling, and salary administration. The assistant superintendent for pupil services is responsible for guidance, psychological health and social work services, attendance services, and special education; and the assistant superintendent for school-community relations (or human relations) is responsible for public relations, brochures, newsletters and house organs, school-community relations, minority recruitment, and monitoring affirmative action guidelines.

The principal is charged by the superintendent with coordinating the school's activities, personnel, and records. Furthermore he or she is expected to be a counselor, substitute teacher, disciplinarian, and secretary. Above all else the principal is the curriculum leader.

Most high schools and a few elementary schools have full-time assistant principals. The assistant principal is delegated many of the assignments that the principal does not elect to do: procuring and distributing materials and supplies; coordinating schedules, rooms, and teachers' activities; maintaining an accurate student personnel accounting system; arranging for programs, field trips, and resource persons; dealing with discipline problems; and keeping inventories of texts, materials and supplies.

Technological changes have brought about great changes in school administration. Today school administrators must be able to understand and apply systems-related technologies. One such activity is PPBS (Planning Programming Budgeting Systems). PPBS is a complex set of interrelated processes which can result in improved decision making and resource allocation.

Planning is the initial step. It involves the formulation and projection of goals and objectives towards which the organization must direct all its activities, and the development of strategies to achieve these goals and objectives. Specifically, it evolves through a systematic consideration of alternatives, using various techniques including that which is known as systems analysis.

Programming, the second state, is the devising of the means that are to be utilized to achieve the objectives. It is the more specific determination of the means that are to be utilized to achieve the objectives. It is the more specific determination of the manpower, materials, facilities, and funds necessary for carrying out agreed programs—the process of producing a long-range plan that is organized by identifiable programs and activities rather than by objects of expenditure as traditional budgets are. In other words, it is a plan classified by the outputs of the organization rather than by the inputs in which the resource requirements are identified with or related to these program outputs. It is also a process that extends far enough into the future to show to the extent practical and necessary the full resource requirements for the program outputs. It, too, to be well done, is dependent on systems analysis.

The third phase, budgeting, which in its traditional form has been described unflatteringly as a means of ensuring the uniform distribution of dissatisfaction, is the process of transforming long range programs into the terms of a periodic fiscal

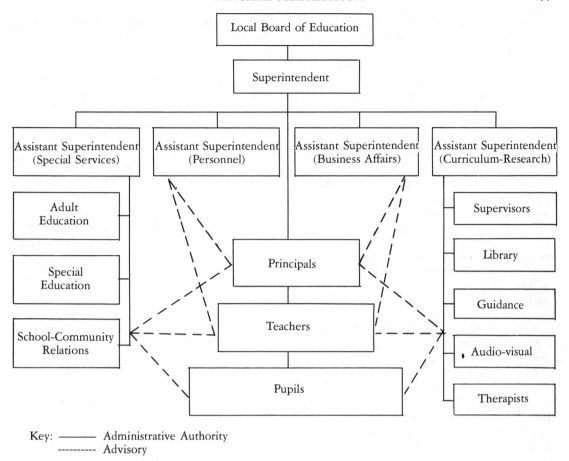

Key: —————— Administrative Authority
--------- Advisory

Figure 9. Example of Education Line and Staff Organization

budget, the process of laying down in the form of a detailed budget the financial implications of the programs and activities to achieve the agreed objectives.[17]

A fourth aspect of this activity is evaluation. Thus in many school systems the top administrators must be concerned with PPBES (Planning - Programming - Budgeting - Evaluation Systems).

Most states now require at least two years of graduate education for administrator certification. A large number of administrators have at least an educational specialist certificate, most have a master's degree, and a growing number are earning the doctor's degree. A minimum preparation for administration includes school finance, school law, and other administrative courses as well as courses in the humanities and the social sciences.

Finally, successful administrators have a variety of teaching and nonteaching experience. Ideally both elementary and secondary experience is part of the superintendent's job specification. Nor should we overlook the importance of administrative experience in industry for most education positions.

All administrative jobs are compounded by issues growing out of collective negotiations, student militancy and civil rights activities, urbanization, and modern technology.

Guidance and Pupil Personnel Services

Guidance and student personnel services staff work with teachers to enrich the quality of instruction and student adjustment. Student personnel specialists include school social workers, special education teachers, psychologists, counselors, attendance workers, and health personnel. Social work is one of the oldest of the personnel services and elementary counseling one of the newest.

School social workers assist with problem students and their parents, using the casework approach. Most of the cases are referrals from teachers, and the majority of referrals are students with discipline problems. Special education teachers work with exceptional children—the gifted, the dull, the emotionally, physically, and socially handicapped. School psychologists also work with exceptional children. They make case studies, administer the group testing program, conduct in-service education for the school staff, and supervise special education classes. Guidance counselors initiate and coordinate their school's comprehensive guidance program, which includes (1) counseling, (2) group guidance, (3) education and vocational guidance, (4) individual student test inventories, (5) student orientation, and (6) student job placement and follow-up. Attendance workers investigate cases of chronic absenteeism. School health personnel, usually a nurse and a physician, provide emergency in-school treatment. Some health personnel conduct annual health examinations for students in their district.

At least a master's degree is required in the fields of social work, guidance, and psychology. Almost all states give special certification for special education teachers as well as for guidance counselors. The trend in school psychology is toward a doctorate in counseling or clinical psychology.

Library Services

The school librarian or media-center director, is usually a trained, certified school librarian. Librarians are trained in research, the use of reference materials, the use of card catalogues and categorization systems, and liberal arts education.

Audio-Visual Coordinator

Technology has finally become a way of life in most schools. A myriad of audio-visual equipment—television, tape and cassette recorders, overhead projectors, and programmed instruction—now requires specialists to assist teachers to optimally use it. Most schools in big cities have an audio-visual department. The audio-visual director has had about five years of teaching experience, training in audio-visual education, and a master's degree (or at least a sixth year of study).

PUBLIC SCHOOL HIERARCHY

The board of education is the governing board for each school district. In most communities the board of education is elected by the citizens and its powers derive from the state. The most frequent board functions are (1) employing a district superintendent, (2) approving the system's annual budget, (3) hiring all school-district personnel, (4) levying taxes, (5) approving contracts for school-building construction, and (6) establishing school-system policy. Some boards forget that their job is to make policy but not to administer the schools; the superintendent's job is to carry out policy.

The superintendent of schools is both the executive officer of the board of education and also the school system's chief administrator. Paraphrasing Harry S. Truman, the buck stops in the superintendent's office. The superintendent's staff, frequently referred to as the central office administrative and supervisory staff, consists of assistant superintendents, divisional directors, and consultants. In carrying out her or his responsibility, the superintendent delegates building leadership responsibilities to elementary and secondary school principals. The principalship was originally a teaching position with released time for administrative duties. Today most principals (except those in small school districts) are full-time administrators. Principals are expected to maintain discipline as well as student and staff records, employ substitute teachers, supervise the instructional program, prepare schedules, assist in screening teacher applicants, provide various school reports to the central office, and encourage curriculum improvement.

The state department of education is the state agency that licenses public school teachers and issues their teaching credentials. Other functions carried out by state departments of education include preparing comprehensive plans for the state's public school programs; proposing state education legislation, establishing minimum guidelines governing curricula, building construction, and health and safety standards; and distributing state monies earmarked for local schools. Most state departments also provide consultants and materials for local districts.

There is no single most popular name for the executive officer of the state department of education. Depending on the state, she/he is called commissioner of education, state superintendent of schools, state director of education, or state superintendent of public instruction. The chief state school officer is usually elected by the citizens or appointed by the governor or the state board of education. The duties include general supervision of the state's public schools; auditing funds appropriated to public schools; reporting state school status and needs to the legislature and governor; and approving teacher-education curricula.

The state board of education has as its primary task interpreting the educational needs, practices, and trends to the state populace, and in consultation with community and educational leaders, developing the state's educational policies. Most members of state boards are either appointed by the governor (or other state officials) or elected by citizens of the state.

SCHOOL DISTRICTS

Teachers are employed by boards of education of school administrative structures of varying description. Most states have three units of administrative structure: local districts, intermediate districts, and the state department of education.

Local Districts

Local school districts, subordinate units of the state, consist of areas in which local boards of education assume responsibility for the direct administration of all schools within their purview. There are as many names for these local units as states. If the nature of the program is the determining factor, they may be called elementary or high school districts. If classified according to their local civil governmental de-

scription, they are called township school districts, town school districts, or city school districts. Other classifications include independent school districts, common school districts, and county unit districts.

Public school consolidation has eliminated many of the smaller rural school districts. In 1977 the National Institute of Education concluded that consolidation of rural schools into larger regional schools cost as much or more to operate as the old, decentralized rural systems. Furthermore, research data shows that even with the consolidation, rural parents still have not gotten what they most desired: better life chances for their children.

Intermediate School Districts

An intermediate school district is a territory comprising two or more basic administrative units. Historically these units have served as intermediaries between local school districts and the state educational agency. As rural towns and villages have grown into cities, the intermediate units have been left with the task of providing leadership mainly to rural schools. William P. McLure succinctly describes the functions of intermediate school units:

(a) to aid the state central office in exercising general supervision over schools; (b) to provide an organization whereby special supplementary services can be made available on a pooled basis to local districts which, because of small population or other reasons, cannot administer them alone economically; (c) to have responsibility for special phases of the educational program, such as certain vocational training, classes for handicapped children, and so on; and (d) to provide a program of education for post-high school youth who do not attend college.[18]

SALARY AND FRINGE BENEFITS

There is more to assessing the value of an occupation than income alone. Some of the benefits do not show up in the pay check. No matter what school unit the teacher is employed in, there are some common salary and fringe benefits. New teachers are advised to pursue each of these topics in depth with a school district before signing a contract for employment.

Salary

The single-salary schedule is used in most school districts. This type of schedule presumes equal pay for equal service and preparation. A general rule of thumb is that the maximum salary should be at least twice as much as the minimum at the bachelor's degree level. A typical city-school salary schedule contains four columns, representing bachelor's degree, master's degree, sixth-year, and doctor's degree; and it has twelve steps, representing annual increments for each year of teaching experience. A principal generally receives $1,000 to $1,500 more than the maximum for his or her level of preparation, plus $500 for each year of administrative experience up to four years.

Obviously all teachers are not equal in training or teaching abilities. Most districts do not give merit increments to outstanding teachers. They do, however, provide increments for additional college and graduate training.

The research division of the National Education Association publishes annual state minimum salary requirements for teachers holding the lowest certificate recognized, the bachelor's degree or four years of training, the master's degree or five years of training.

Most districts provide extra pay for coaching duties (football pays the most) and supervising extracurricular activities—dramatics club, yearbook, band, school newspaper. Furthermore, almost all districts provide increments for military service.

While failing to recognize individual differences, the single-salary schedule has nevertheless eliminated some discriminatory practices—lower salaries for women with the same qualifications as men and lower salaries for elementary school teachers when compared with secondary teachers.

Insurance

Most school districts provide several forms of group insurance—life, hospital, medical-surgical, major medical, and disability. At a time when inflation seems to be out of control,

this benefit is very important. Few persons could afford to bear the full cost of hospital and other medical services. When a national or state teacher's association sponsors the insurance plan, the teacher pays the entire cost of the premiums. When the school district is the sponsor, the teacher pays part or none of the premiums.

Leave Benefits

Although most school districts provide sick leave, workmen's compensation benefits are allowed only when physical disability results from injury while on the job. Leaves of absence for reasons other than illness are allowed in almost all districts. Specifically, leaves of absence are granted for the following reasons:

A. Personal and Family
   1. Personal illness or injury
   2. Maternity
   3. Religious holidays
   4. Death in immediate family
   5. Illness in immediate family (including quarantine)
   6. Wedding or birth in immediate family
   7. Moving from one domicile to another
   8. Emergencies
B. Professional
   1. Attending or participating in educational meetings
   2. Visiting other schools
   3. Studying at colleges and universities
   4. Traveling for professional improvement
   5. Exchange teaching
   6. Joining the Peace Corps
   7. Serving the organized teaching profession through a local, state, or national education association as officer, committee member, speaker, or legislative agent
C. Civic
   1. Answering a court summons
   2. Serving on a jury
   3. Voting; serving as an election official
   4. Serving in an elective office
   5. Participating in community-sponsored projects (fund drives, civic celebrations, etc.)
   6. Military duty[19]

Tenure

The teacher's contract is either an annual contract, a continuing contract, permanent tenure, or a variation of the three. The annual contract is entered into with a board of education for a period of one year and for a specified sum of money. When the contract is discharged there is no legal obligation on the part of the teacher or the school board to renew it, although fair dismissal practice dictates that the board extend an offer for renewal if the teacher performed satisfactorily. Under the terms of the annual contract, the teacher may be discharged only for cause—immorality, incompetence, or insubordination. For such a dismissal to be valid, the teacher, along with his or her legal counsel, must be given a hearing where the charges are presented.

The amount of evidence needed to justify not reemploying a probationary teacher is not as great as that needed to dismiss a permanent teacher. Generally, probationary teachers may not be reemployed at the end of a school year for any of the causes which would justify dismissal of a permanent teacher, plus any other cause related to the welfare of the students and the school. But during the school year, a probationary teacher can be dismissed only for the same causes that would apply to permanent teachers.

Causes for dismissal of permanent teachers include: immoral and unprofessional conduct, incompetency, dishonesty, refusal to obey regulations prescribed by the school board or state department of education, conviction of a felony or any crime involving moral terpitude, any act detrimental to the welfare of the students or the school.

Acts "detrimental to the welfare of the students or the school" include inability to control classes and maintain reasonable order and discipline; lack of proper knowledge of the subject matter; lack of proper self-control when disciplining students; lack of courtesy in contacts with students, co-workers, and community representatives; excessive tardiness in arriving at school or attending classes; lack of personal cleanliness or proper grooming; failure to maintain a clean and orderly classroom.

Recent court decisions do not support a teacher's right to be homosexual or transexual. Once they become known to the public— even homosexual and transexual teachers with excellent teaching records—they are fired. Nor are they granted financial relief or job reinstatement by the lower courts. While the U. S. Supreme Court has not ruled on the employment rights of transexuals, it has denied relief to homosexuals.

However, physically handicapped teachers are gaining in their struggle to achieve equal employment. The aged—the largest group of teachers seeking employment rights—are challenging mandatory retirement regulations. Additional changes seem inevitable. As the courts expand students' rights, teachers and administrators will try to improve their own conditions too.

A continuing contract with a Spring notification provision provides for automatic renewal if written notice of nonreappointment is not given by the board of education to the teacher by the date specified in the contract. Dismissal during the terms of the contract can be effected only for cause and following a hearing.

Permanent tenure may be granted in some school districts after new teachers successfully serve a probationary period of one to six years. During the probationary period the teacher has an annual contract. At the end of the probationary period, upon the recommendation of the superintendent of schools, the board of education may grant permanent tenure. Dismissal of teachers with tenure can be effected only for reasonable and just cause. However, tenure does not guarantee employment when the services of the teacher are not needed.

The NEA Committee on Tenure and Academic Freedom lists nine reasons for tenure:

1. To protect classroom teachers and other members of the teaching profession against unjust dismissal of any kind—political, religious or personal.

2. To prevent the management or domination of schools by political or noneducational groups for selfish and other improper purposes.

3. To secure for the teacher employment conditions which will encourage him to grow in the full practice of his profession, unharried by constant pressure and fear.

4. To encourage competent, independent thinkers to enter and to remain in the teaching profession.

5. To encourage school management, which

might have to sacrifice the welfare of the schools to fear and favor, to devote itself to the cause of education.

6. To set up honest, orderly, and definite procedures by which undesirable people may be removed from the teaching profession.

7. To protect educators in their efforts to promote the financial and educational interests of public school children.

8. To protect teachers in the exercise of their rights and duties of American citizenship.

9. To enable teachers, in spite of reactionary minorities, to prepare children for life in a democracy under changing conditions.[20]

Credit Unions

Through teacher credit unions, school personnel are able to save money and receive a high dividend, and borrow money at an interest rate that is much lower than most commercial rates. Other credit union benefits include life insurance and personal counseling for solving economic problems. In order to receive these benefits, the teacher must become a member of the credit union, pay a nominal entrance fee and purchase at least one share of stock.

Tax-Sheltered Annuities

Beginning in 1961 teachers and other school employees have been eligible to reduce their gross salary (and thus their federal income tax) by premiums paid for tax-sheltered annuities.

The local school board purchases annuities for the teacher with the salary withheld for this purpose. At retirement the teacher must pay federal taxes on annuity benefits received. It is wise to seek business counsel before joining an annuity plan.

Retirement

Each state has its own teacher retirement system. New Jersey adopted the first state-wide teacher retirement system in 1896. Most state plans are financed jointly by the teacher and the state and are integrated with the social security program. Teachers leaving one state school system and joining another will have difficulty in maintaining their retirement program if there is not reciprocity among the states in question. Some states transfer credits, and others allow teachers to purchase credit for years of teaching in other states. Currently the primary retirement benefits are not available until the teachers reach age 65.

Other Benefits

In addition to financial renumeration, teachers receive other benefits: (1) holidays, vacations, and breaks during the school year (Spring and Christmas), (2) the opportunity to help students of all ages to optimize their academic and social potentials, and (3) the opportunity to help communities define their goals and values.

SELF-RATING SCALE FOR DETERMINING FITNESS FOR TEACHING

	Never	Sel-dom	Some-times	Often	Al-ways
I. Leadership ability					
1. Have you served as leader in student groups; i.e., have you held an office, taken part in programs, or led discussions?	☐	☐	☐	☐	☐
2. Do your fellow students respect your opinions?	☐	☐	☐	☐	☐
3. Do they regard you as a leader?	☐	☐	☐	☐	☐
4. Do your fellow students ask you for help and advice?	☐	☐	☐	☐	☐

	Never	Sel-dom	Some-times	Often	Al-ways
5. Do you sense how others feel, i.e., whether they approve certain proposals, or like or dislike certain persons?	☐	☐	☐	☐	☐
6. Do you try to make others happy by listening to what they say, and by being courteous, friendly, and helpful?	☐	☐	☐	☐	☐
7. Do you succeed in getting others to follow your suggestions without creating friction or ill will?	☐	☐	☐	☐	☐

II. Health and physical fitness

	Never	Sel-dom	Some-times	Often	Al-ways
1. Do you have good health?	☐	☐	☐	☐	☐
2. Do you have lots of vitality? Can you stand to do hard physical tasks or nerve-racking work?	☐	☐	☐	☐	☐
3. Can you engage in activities which others in your group customarily do?	☐	☐	☐	☐	☐
4. Do you give others the impression that you are physically fit, well groomed and attractive in personal appearance?	☐	☐	☐	☐	☐
5. Do you keep cheerful and even-tempered even when tired or ill?	☐	☐	☐	☐	☐

III. Good scholarship

	Never	Sel-dom	Some-times	Often	Al-ways
1. have you maintained a better-than-average academic record?	☐	☐	☐	☐	☐
2. Are you interested in the subjects you have taken or are taking?	☐	☐	☐	☐	☐
3. Do you enjoy studying and find it easy to concentrate when you do study?	☐	☐	☐	☐	☐
4. Do you express your ideas well before a class or public group?	☐	☐	☐	☐	☐
5. Is it easy for you to explain things so that others understand and can follow your directions?	☐	☐	☐	☐	☐

IV. Intellectual traits and abilities

	Never	Sel-dom	Some-times	Often	Al-ways
1. Are school subjects easy for you?	☐	☐	☐	☐	☐
2. Do you spend time finding out more about a topic discussed in class or covered in an assignment?	☐	☐	☐	☐	☐
3. Do you read books or magazine articles on current topics?	☐	☐	☐	☐	☐
4. Do you like to work out ideas on your own?	☐	☐	☐	☐	☐
5. Do you suggest new ideas or plans which can be carried out by groups?	☐	☐	☐	☐	☐

	Never	Sel-dom	Some-times	Often	Al-ways

V. Emotional stability
  1. Are you an even-tempered, cheerful, happy sort of person? □ □ □ □ □
  2. Can you "take it" without getting angry or upset? □ □ □ □ □
  3. Do you keep from worrying and feeling depressed? □ □ □ □ □
  4. Are you naturally patient with and tolerant of others? □ □ □ □ □
  5. Are you objectively critical of yourself? □ □ □ □ □
  6. Do you see the humorous side of everyday happenings even when you yourself are involved? □ □ □ □ □

VI. Social aspirations
  1. Are you interested in the problems other people meet and do you want to help them solve them? □ □ □ □ □
  2. Are you interested in finding ways by which you can help improve human living? □ □ □ □ □
  3. Do you like people—especially children? □ □ □ □ □
  4. Do you set high social standards for yourself and seek to reach and maintain these standards? □ □ □ □ □
  5. Do you cooperate readily with other people in socially desirable activities? □ □ □ □ □
  6. Are you willing to make sacrifices and endure inconveniences to reach a goal you consider worthy? □ □ □ □ □

Source: E. E. Samuelson et al., *You'd Like Teaching*, Seattle, Wash., Craftsman Press, 1946, pp. 31–35.

ADDITIONAL READINGS

Adams, Sam, and John L. Garrett, Jr. *To Be a Teacher: An Introduction to Education.* Englewood Cliffs, N.J., Prentice-Hall, 1968.

Barr, Robert D., James L. Barth, and S. Samuel Shermis. *Defining the Social Studies.* Arlington, Va., National Council for the Social Studies, 1977.

Cann, Marjorie M., ed. *An Introduction to Education: Selected Readings.* New York, Thomas Y. Crowell, 1972.

Jordan, Thomas E. *America's Children: An Introduction to Education.* Chicago, Rand McNally, 1973.

Palardy, J. Michael. *Teaching Today.* New York, Macmillan, 1975.

Postman, Neil, and Charles Weingartner. *Teaching as a Subversive Activity.* New York, Delacorte Press, 1969.

Richey, Robert W. *Planning for a Career in Education.* New York, McGraw-Hill, 1974.

Ryan, Kevin, and James M. Cooper. *Kaleidoscope.* New York, Houghton Mifflin, 1975.

———. *Those Who Can Teach*, 2d ed. New York, Houghton Mifflin, 1975.

Silberman, Charles E. *Crisis in the Classroom.* New York, Random House, 1970.

Stone, James C., and Frederick W. Schneider, eds. *Readings in the Foundations of Education*, 2d ed. New York, Thomas Y. Crowell, 1971

Torrance, E. Paul, and R.E. Myers. *Creative Learning and Teaching.* New York, Dodd, Mead, 1970.

NOTES

1. National Education Association, *Financing the Public Schools* (Washington, D.C., NEA, 1962), 8–9.

2. William B. Ragan, John H. Wilson, and Tillman J. Ragan, *Teaching in the New Elementary School* (New York, Holt, Rinehart & Winston, 1972), 262–266.

3. Annie L. Butler, *Early Childhood Education: Planning and Administratering Programs*, (New York, D. Van Nostrand, 1974), 27–28.

4. Ragan et al., *The New Elementary School*, 143.

5. John A. Green, *Fields of Teaching and Educational Services* (New York, Harper & Row, 1966), 89.

6. Nelson B. Henry (ed.), *Development in the Schools Through Reading*, Sixtieth Yearbook for the National Society for the Study of Education (Chicago, The Society, 1961), 27–273.

7. *Ibid.*, 324–327.

8. *Ibid.*, 25.

9. Alfred B. Garrett, "Recommendations for the Preparation of High School Teachers of Science and Mathematics," *School Science and Mathematics*, 59 (1959), 282–288.

10. Horatio V. Henry, *New Social Studies Methodology* (Minneapolis, Burgess, 1961), 15.

11. Lloyd V. Douglas, James T. Blanford, and Ruth I. Anderson, *Teaching Business Subjects* (Engelwood Cliffs, N.J., Prentice-Hall, 1958), 31.

12. *Ibid.*, 36.

13. William R. Sur and Charles F. Schuller, *Music Education for Teenagers* (New York, Harper & Row, 1958), 268.

14. J. W. Giachino and Ralph O. Gallington, *Course Construction in Industrial Arts and Vocational Education* (Chicago, American Technical Society, 1961), 25.

15. See *A Guide to Improving Instruction in Vocational Arts* (Washington, D.C., American Vocational Association, 1953), 19–28.

16. Green, *Fields*, 200.

17. Herbert R. Balls, "Planning, Programming and Budgeting in Canada," *Public Administration*, 48 (Autumn, 1970), 292–293.

18. William P. McLure, *The Intermediate Administrative School District of the United States* (Urbana, College of Education, University of Illinois, 1958), 97.

19. National Education Association, *Teacher Leaves of Absence* (Washington, D.C., NEA, 1971), 2.

20. National Education Association, *Aanalysis of Teacher Tenure Provisions: State and Local* (Washington, D.C., NEA, 1954), 6–7.

7.
CURRICULUM
REFORMS
AND
INNOVATIONS

Significant curricular changes have been taking place in elementary and secondary schools and in higher education. Even more spectacular changes seem to be in the offing. Perhaps the schools of the year 2000 will differ as much from those we now know as today's schools differ from those of 1890.

Assessing the future, J. Lloyd Trump and Delmas F. Miller wrote:

We foresee even more rapid changes in curriculum content, methodology, and the educational setting. We think that schools need to make better use of the professional talents of teachers and principals, the potential talents of learners, the purchasing power of school monies, the resources of communities, and the findings of educational research.[1]

Although curriculum reform has been underway for a long time, the tempo of change increased rapidly after the launching of the first Sputnik by Soviet Russia in 1957. The massive curriculum reform movement began with mathematics, science, and foreign languages; it soon spread to other curriculum areas, such as language arts and social studies. There is abundant evidence that the need for national survival in a troubled world has been a compelling motive for curriculum reform, but this has not been the only motive. Also influential has been the need to have the schools contribute to the solution of such critical domestic problems as the urban crisis, unemployment and poverty, racial discrimination, and unequal educational opportunities. (These are treated elsewhere in this text.)

While these social and economic forces were calling for curriculum reforms, new insights into human growth and learning were undermining traditional teaching procedures. The volume of research in this field has been increasing rapidly in recent decades, and the importance of using data dealing with human development in curriculum planning has been given increasing attention. The proliferation of new programs such as those discussed below as well as declining national achievement scores have added impetus to cries for greater educational accountability.

CURRICULUM DESIGN

It is important that future teachers understand the many types of school curricula they may encounter. Curriculum refers to the total activities provided by a school for its students. In essence curricula range from those which are subject-centered to those which are student-centered, with variations in between.

Subject-Centered Curriculum

This is the oldest and most commonly used curriculum organization in America. It grew out of the ancient liberal arts *Trivium* (grammar, rhetoric, and logic) and *Quadrivium* (arithmetic, geometry, astronomy, and music). Gradually the *Trivium* was expanded to include literature and history, and the *Quadrivium* was expanded to include algebra, geometry, botany, chemistry, zoology, physics, and geography.

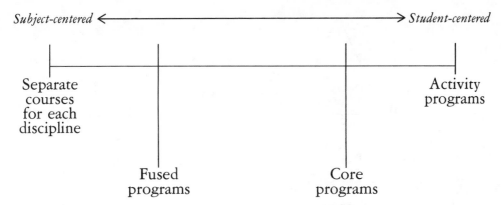

Figure 10. A Curriculum Continuum

All subjects in the subject-centered curriculum are compartmentalized—little effort is made to totally integrate them. With a primary concern being to teach ideas and facts, traditional methods of instruction in a subject-centered curriculum are lecture, discussion, question and answer, and written exercises. These methods are familiar to most parents. A major criticism of this approach is that it fosters rote learning rather than creativity.

Responding to criticism, some subject-centered programs offer a *fused* or *correlated* curriculum, in which similar subjects are combined, i.e., English or language arts (reading, writing, spelling, grammar, speech, and literature); social studies (anthropology, economics, geography, history, sociology, psychology, and political science); science (botany, geology, and zoology); and mathematics (arithmetic, algebra, and geometry). Incidentally, this curriculum approach was proposed by Johann Friedrich Herbart in the nineteenth century.

Another method of fusing separate subjects is through the unit approach: fact-centered units, project-centered units, and idea-centered units. Most elementary schools have some type of fused curriculum, while junior high or middle schools use block scheduling to provide longer periods of time for language arts and social studies. Critics of fusing activities observe that (1) the mere combining of courses does not guarantee integration; (2) the fusion usually leads to watered-down materials; and (3) an inordinate emphasis is placed on abstract as opposed to concrete learnings.

Student-Centered Curriculum.

The student in this type of curriculum is the focal point of teaching-learning activities. Core and activity curricula reflect this approach. The *core curriculum*, which may be structured or unstructured and cross broad subject area lines, stresses social values and the utilization of the problem-solving approach to learning. That is, special attention is given to facts, descriptive principles, socio-economic conditions, and moral rules of conduct. Teachers stress what ought to be in our society rather than focusing only on what is. However, each student must decide individually what s/he will do to achieve the ideal society.

The *activity curriculum* is unstructured, never completely fixed and crosses subject matter lines. Emphasis is upon doing things—observing, playing, reading, writing, and making. This is undoubtedly the most controversial and least acceptable type of curriculum. Critics sometimes refer to it as organized confusion. Its supporters counter that this is not confusion but instead allowing students—in cooperation with teachers—to grow in the areas of their interests.

Instructional Strategies

No matter what type of curriculum design is used, teachers try to maximize opportunities for students to meet learning objectives. In order to do this, three instructional strategies are commonly used: lecture-recitation, guided discovery, and inquiry.

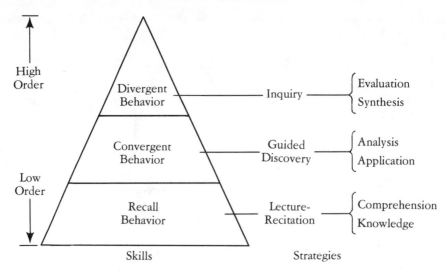

FIGURE 11. Hierarchy of Learning Skills with Instructional Strategies

In the lecture-recitation strategy, the students are not optimally active; they are expected to passively digest specific data or knowledge for recall. This is the lowest order of learning. It can be accomplished with a teacher present or by linear and/or branched programmed instruction, television, dial access equipment, and computers.

Guided discovery revolves around the analysis and application of data. In order to facilitate this type of learning, the teacher interacts with students and guides them (mainly through the use of questions) to the desired responses. This is convergent learning, a higher order of learning than lecture-recitation.

Inquiry, the highest order of instructional strategy and learning, tries to get students to make assertions and, in appropriate situations, hypotheses. This is divergent learning, since there may be many correct ways to analyze and/or solve problems. Through inquiry students are taught evaluation and synthesis skills.

Whether the learning strategy involves lecture-recitation, guided discovery, or inquiry, student learning can be enhanced through the proper use of the following instructional aids.

Programmed instruction. Programmed instruction grew out of the work of Sidney Pressey in the 1920s and 1930s, and was popularized by B.F. Skinner in the 1950s. There are two basic types of programmed instruction: linear and branch. In linear programming the student receives immediate feedback to her responses or feedback after a series of responses. In branch programming the student proceeds to additional frames for learning only after giving correct responses. If she gives incorrect responses, the student is directed along an alternate route designed to correct errors before moving to advanced learning frames.

Audio-Tutorial-IPI. Audio-tutorial and individually-prescribed instruction (IPI) provide for individual learning activities. This is the test-teach-test method. Teacher contact is held to a minimum—occurring mainly when the teacher provides enrichment and remedial services to the student. Curricular modules for individualized instruction are developed on the basis of predetermined instructional objectives. Crucial to this process is the development of a diagnostic test which measures before instruction how well each student can achieve criteria for the module objectives. Based on this diagnosis, each student proceeds through the instructional package and is tested again after completing it. The teacher monitors learning progress by means of tests. Once a student reaches expected criteria performance for the learning package, she continues in that module at her own individual rate. Audio tape recorders are part of the IPI, hence the term audio-tutorial is used.

Dial access systems. Beginning in 1961 at the University of Michigan, dial access audio and/or video systems have been used extensively for independent study. Basically, individual study carrels provide automated information retrieval facilities. Currently this method of instruction is quite popular in foreign language classes.

Learning resource centers. School libraries are being supplemented (not replaced) with learning resource centers equipped with books, programmed materials, dial access audio and/or visual tape banks, and closed circuit television. Most learning centers are found in elementary schools, but a growing number of middle schools and high schools are also employing them. Their popularity is easy to explain: teachers can program individual and group assignments into learning-resources centers.

Teachers are limited only by their imaginations and school resources. Usually it is the former condition that prevents them from improving the quality of their instruction. It would also be helpful for teachers to take a systems approach to developing appropriate learning resources: (1) assessing needs, (2) developing instructional objectives and criteria for measuring effectiveness, (3) planning alternative procedures, (4) monitoring the planned procedures to provide information on progress, and (5) evaluating and if necessary, utilizing feedback to alter the program so that it meets individual and group needs.

NEW CURRICULA

Americans have traditionally viewed the public elementary and secondary schools as belonging to the people of local communities. Indeed, the conviction was firmly held that these schools could remain truly American only so long as they remained responsive to the wishes of the people in the communities. Until recently no one seriously questioned the idea that local control of the curriculum was desirable. Curriculum reforms have therefore been initiated primarily at the state and local school district levels.

Since 1957, however, the major changes in curriculum have been initiated by curriculum improvement projects at the national level. This radical change in the direction of curriculum reform cannot be attributed entirely to the influence of the first Sputnik. For example, three years after Sputnik Myron Lieberman pointed out that mobility and interdependence had completely undermined the notion that local communities should have a free hand in educating their children.[2] Although most of the curriculum improvement projects at the national level have been initiated since Sputnik, the movement was already underway in some areas before 1957.

Salient Features of the New Curricula

The interesting story of how curriculum reform from the top down came to be the prevailing pattern during the postwar period need not be repeated in detail here. Some highlights may, however, serve as a suitable preface to the analysis of some of the new curricula that follows.

1. National curriculum improvement projects located on university campuses throughout the country have been generously supported with funds from the federal government and from private foundations.

2. Attention has been sharply focused on single subjects, so that local school systems have been left with the problem of maintaining balance in the curriculum. Many school systems have therefore found it necessary to adapt, rather than adopt, the materials produced by these projects.

3. The groups that have been responsible for directing these projects have generally included staff members from colleges of liberal arts and sciences, colleges of education, and the public schools.

4. Although the movement began with mathematics, science, and foreign languages, new courses have also been developed in English and social studies.

5. The sponsors of the new curricula gener-

ally advocate a spiral arrangement for the grade placement of content in the various curriculum areas. For example, instead of teaching geometry only in the tenth grade, elements of this subject are introduced in the elementary school, and the subject is revisited at successive grade levels. The same arrangement is used for economics, geography, and others subjects.

6. Most of the new curricula expect more of students than the mere acquisition of information. Students are expected to learn the structure of each discipline and thus to think like a scientist, a mathematician, or an economist. Something more lasting than the learning of bits of information has been sought; the new procedures emphasize concept formation, learning by discovery, and the development of the ability to think. A kind of education that will enable students to become increasingly self-propelling during a lifetime of learning is the goal.

7. There is little question that these national projects have developed vastly improved content and procedures in many curriculum areas; the questions that are raised generally deal with how these new programs can be implemented in elementary and secondary schools. Since most teachers now employed in schools have not been taught the new science and the new mathematics, the new curricula place a heavy burden on the inservice education budgets of the public school systems. Summer institutes, operating under federal grants, have helped.

8. Teaching procedures necessary to implement the new curricula involve an understanding of recent insights into the nature of the learning process. If the new programs are to achieve their maximum potential, classroom teachers must become much more proficient as practicing psychologists.

Intellectual Development

Chapter Two was devoted to the psychological and behavioral aspects of American education, but it now seems appropriate to relate new developments in learning theory to the process of curriculum planning. As curriculum specialists, principals, and teachers learn more about learning, they become more proficient in curriculum development.

Concept development. The role of concepts in intellectual development has been studied intensively for many years. Because there are several kinds of concepts, it is difficult to formulate a single definition that will fit all situations in which concepts are developed. The definition given by A. D. Woodruff is a useful one, however, in terms of the problem with which this chapter is concerned.

For purposes of talking about curriculum planning in general, a concept may be defined as some amount of meaning more or less organized in an individual mind as a result of sensory perception of external objects or events and the cognitive interpretation of the perceived data. A concept is important because it is the internal mediating variable that accounts for the direction of a person's response to a situation.[3]

One clue to an understanding of the new curricula is the emphasis placed on concept development. Observations in hundreds of traditional classrooms have revealed that the dominant activity was information-giving; the teacher presented information and the students memorized it.[4] The new curricula are designed to foster the development of concepts around which information can be organized and used in the solution of problems. Curriculum guides developed for the purpose of helping teachers implement the new curricula generally present a conceptual framework for the various subjects. The explosion of knowledge in practically every field of learning has made this arrangement necessary. The newer explanations of the learning process also support this practice. In other words, the role of the school has become increasingly that of providing students with the skills, understanding, and concepts that will make it possible for them to explore a field of knowledge on his own and to continue to educate themselves.

Woodruff has presented propositions relating to concepts that are supported by psychological research and that seem to be useful in curriculum planning. He suggests that (1) subject matter becomes more meaningful when it is presented in conceptual form; (2) students need to develop concepts in order to engage in problem-solving activities; (3) concept-forming and concept-using are interdependent; and (4) serious consideration should be given to readiness for concepts.[5]

Organizing learning experiences in any subject in terms of the basic concepts to be learned is an important step in curriculum development, but it is only the first step. The next step that confronts the classroom teacher is that of learning how the concepts of adult specialists become the concepts of students—how students come to own concepts. This involves a thorough exploration of the new research on learning, including the work of a group of psychologists who specialize in the psychology of cognition—how we know and how we teach others to know.[6] Jean Piaget, developmental psychologist at the University of Geneva, Jerome S. Bruner, director of the Center for Cognitive Studies at Harvard University, and Robert M. Gagné, director of research at the American Institute for Research, are prominent members of this group of psychologists.

Bruner called attention to an important principle of concept development when he wrote, "What is most important for teaching basic concepts is that the child be helped to pass progressively from concrete thinking to the utilization of more conceptually adequate modes of thought."[7] He has drawn upon the experimental work of Piaget and others to identify three stages of concept development: the *preoperational* stage, the stage of *concrete operations*, and the *formal operations* stage.

During the first stage, which generally ends at about age five or six, the child is concerned with manipulating objects on a trial-and-error basis. During the second stage, which begins after the child enters school, the ability to organize the data acquired through contact with concrete objects emerges, and the child learns to use organized data in the solution of problems. During the third stage, which generally begins between the ages of ten and fourteen, the child acquires the ability to operate on hypothetical propositions, without having the concrete objects visible. This process approximates the kind of intellectual activity that is the stock-in-trade of the mature scientist and the abstract thinker.

Although it is useful for those who develop curriculum guides to recognize that children generally pass through these three stages of concept development, the classroom teacher soon discovers that all children do not pass from one stage to another at the same age.

Bruner has recognized the responsibility of the classroom teacher.

Precisely what kinds of material should be used at what age with what effect is a subject for research. . . . Nor need we wait for all the research findings to be in before proceeding, for a skillful teacher can also experiment by attempting to teach what seems to be intuitively right for children of different ages, correcting as he goes.[8]

New dimensions of the readiness problem. New insights into intellectual development and information gained from curriculum improvement projects have altered traditional ideas about readiness for learning. It is no longer thought feasible to assign an absolute level of difficulty to any topic or subject; the difficulty depends on the previous learning experiences of the pupil and the methods and materials used in presenting it. The ladder system of grade placement—geometry in the tenth grade, chemistry in the eleventh grade, physics in the twelfth grade, and economics at the college level—is now regarded as out of harmony with what is known about the continuous growth of mental capabilities. As noted before, the new curricula introduce pupils to elements of these subjects as soon as they enter school, revisiting them in successively more complex and difficult forms throughout the school years (the spiral system).

A new aspect of readiness, called content or subject-matter readiness, has also become widely recognized. Gagné has explained this as follows:

The planning that precedes effective design for learning is a matter of specifying with some care what may be called the learning structure of any subject to be acquired. In order to determine what comes before what, the subject must be analyzed in terms of the types of learning involved in it.[9]

Instead of assuming that a child is not ready to begin the study of a subject until a certain age, this interpretation of readiness assumes that the child is ready to learn something new as soon as he or she has acquired the necessary capabilities through preceding learning. Curriculum workers have therefore been turning to scholars in the various disciplines for information about the structure of knowledge in their various fields.

Learning by discovery. It has been stated earlier in this chapter that the new curricula emphasize learning by discovery. John W. Renner and William B. Ragan have pointed out that (1) the act of discovery includes all forms of obtaining knowledge or insight for oneself by the use of one's own mental powers; (2) the discovery method allows students to arrive at generalizations that are truly their own; and (3) the method helps students develop their rational powers, gain understanding of content, and learn how to learn.[10] Lucile Lindberg has stated that helping children discover knowledge and ways of working for themselves eliminates the necessity of finding ways to hold their attention—that the urge to pursue learning comes from within.[11] There will always be a need for information-giving by the teacher, but teaching which consists primarily of exposition robs students of the opportunity to learn how to learn.

Games with simulated environments. The use of games that simulate real-life situations has been increasing in American classrooms. There is evidence that when this technique is used (1) students become highly motivated; (2) they learn more; (3) they learn the need for cooperation; (4) they get a more realistic understanding of how things are done in life outside the school; and (5) they gain an appreciation of the complexity of real-life situations.[12]

This review of intellectual development and some strategies in concept development should aid the reader in evaluating the following discussion of curriculum reforms. Reviewed are a few of the significant curriculum reforms that occurred during the 1950s and 1960s.

The New Mathematics Programs

The curriculum reform movement in mathematics is not new; its antecedents can be traced back at least to the 1930s. For instance William A. Brownell wrote in 1935, "The basic tenet in the proposed instructional reorganization is to make arithmetic less a challenge to the pupil's memory and more a challenge to his intelligence."[13] It has been reported that by 1953, 1,100 studies of the teaching of arithmetic had been made.[14] The

curriculum improvement projects in mathematics at the national level have, however, introduced new topics, emphasized the structure of the discipline of mathematics, and introduced elements of algebra and geometry into the elementary school program. They have given greater priority to the mathematical phases of the program and less to the social applications, fostered a more precise use of mathematical language, developed more appropriate instructional materials, and demonstrated the use of procedures designed to facilitate learning by discovery.

UICSM. In 1952 a group at the University of Illinois under the leadership of Max Beberman began to develop materials of instruction that they believed would help students understand and become enthusiastic about mathematics. They also developed methods of training high school teachers in the use of the new materials. An advisory board, the University of Illinois Committee on School Mathematics, drew its members from the colleges of education, engineering, and liberal arts and sciences. Beberman reported in 1958: "We now have courses for the four high school grades on trial in classrooms in a dozen pilot schools. Some forty teachers and over seventeen hundred students are participating."[15]

The UICSM project was the first of its kind in this country; it provided a model for other curriculum improvement projects in mathematics that started in 1957 or later. A careful examination of Beberman's description of this project reveals the extent to which it incorporated the basic principles on which the new curricula are based.[16] Kenneth B. Henderson has stated, "UICSM may properly be regarded as the progenitor of all the current curricular projects in mathematics."[17]

Since 1957 many more national curriculum improvement projects in mathematics have been set up, and several publishers have produced series of textbooks incorporating their findings. Some of the references listed at the end of this chapter give detailed descriptions of these projects. We will now therefore describe briefly only one project and merely list some others, with a few essential facts about each.

SMSG. The materials produced by the

School Mathematics Study Group are among the most widely used of all the new mathematics programs. E. G. Begle of Stanford University was director of the project, which grew out of a conference sponsored by the American Mathematical Society in February 1958. The National Science Foundation provided approximately $8 million to finance SMSG. This project prepared preliminary and revised editions of sample textbooks for grades K-12. The work of SMSG assumes that basic mathematical concepts are central to the effective teaching of mathematics; that the program should develop an awareness of the basic properties of mathematics; and that while students manipulate numbers they should move to progressively higher levels of abstraction. The basic texts are written by teams composed of college mathematicians, mathematics educators, and classroom teachers of mathematics.

Boston College Mathematics Institute's Contemporary Mathematics Program. This secondary school mathematics project is also sponsored by the National Science Foundation. It has prepared a series of textbooks that use the new terminology of mathematics and emphasize the unifying concepts. Since 1960 it has sponsored a home study program designed to strengthen the understanding of modern mathematics by elementary and secondary teachers.

Greater Cleveland Mathematics Program. This K-12 program was initiated in 1959 by the Educational Research Council of Greater Cleveland. It has prepared both teacher and pupil materials (published by Science Research Associates, Inc., Chicago). The materials emphasize the guided discovery approach and are designed to help students gain an understanding of the structure of mathematics.

Syracuse University-Webster College Madison Project. This project began at the Madison School in Syracuse, New York, with financial support from the Marcel Holzer and Alfred P. Sloan Foundations. It was sponsored by the mathematics department of Syracuse University. During its early years, the project worked with culturally deprived children; the emphasis later shifted to work with children of above-average ability living in "over-privileged" homes. A second project center was opened in Weston, Connecticut, and a third at Webster College, St. Louis, Missouri. Since 1961 the project has been supported by funds from the National Science Foundation and the U. S. Office of Education. Teacher preparation has been a central activity of the Madison project; in Chicago alone more than 18,000 teachers have been involved. The project has sought to broaden the curriculum for grades 2–8 by introducing elements of algebra, geometry, and logic.

University of Illinois Arithmetic Project. This project, started under the direction of David Page, received support from the University of Illinois, the Carnegie Corporation, and the National Science Foundation. It is now operating in connection with Educational Services, Inc. It is designed to help children develop a sense of power with respect to mathematical properties and operations. It places major emphasis on teacher preparation; some 1,000 teachers have attended the institutes sponsored by the project.

University of Maryland Mathematics Project. This project was established in 1957 with financial support from the Carnegie Corporation. It was designed to prepare experimental mathematics courses for grades seven and eight. *Mathematics for the Junior High School*, published in 1961, placed great emphasis on number systems and mathematical structure. Students in courses using these materials have scored as high in traditional standardized tests as students who used traditional materials, and they have made even better scores in tests prepared specifically to test achievement in the new courses.

New Curricula in Science

Since 1957 more attention has been given to the improvement of the curriculum in science than in any other field. Progress in science and technology has brought about drastic changes in how people live and make a living; a higher level of literacy in science than ever before is needed to make decisions about problems of living. The new programs in science place more emphasis on the processes of science and less emphasis on the products, involve more learning by discovery and less dependence on exposition, and require students to learn how a scientist thinks and acts. Curriculum improvement projects at the national level, supported by funds from the National Science Foundation and other foundations, have conducted experiments and produced materials for use in elementary and secondary schools. Local school systems have in turn developed curriculum guides that implement the principal features of these programs. Most school systems elect to adapt rather than to adopt the programs developed by these projects. The National Science Foundation, which has sponsored most of the projects, has stated, "Decisions on what to teach remain, in the healthy American tradition, the exclusive responsibility of individual schools and teachers."[18]

PSSC. Experimentation with new curricula in high school science began in the mid-1950s. Jerrold Zacharias of the Massachusetts Institute of Technology provided the leadership from which a pattern of cooperation between scientists and teachers emerged to develop new curricula in physics, biology, and chemistry. The Physical Science Study Committee, initiated in 1956, was the first of the new science programs.

The high school physics program includes a study of the universe, optics and waves, mechanics, and electricity and modern physics. The program, sponsored by the National Science Foundation, the Fund for the Advancement of Education, and the Alfred P. Sloan Foundation, emphasizes learning the structure of physics and the processes of inquiry and developing concepts through experimentation. It also stresses the interconnections between physics and other sciences.

John I. Goodlad and others state that there is no evidence that students who complete the PSSC physics courses in high school are in any way at a disadvantage when they move on to college courses based primarily on the old materials. They comment on the need for revised college courses in physics.

The Physical Science Study Committee points to the need for revising the college physics curriculum if PSSC students are to be adequately challenged, and if college courses are to keep pace with current thought in physics education. There are increasing signs that this collegiate reform has started.[19]

Other high school science projects include The Biological Sciences Curriculum Study (BSCS), the Chemical Bond Approach project (CBA), and the Earth Science Curriculum Project (ESCP).

SCIS. The Science Curriculum Improvement Study received financial support from the National Science Foundation in 1959. Instructional units for grades k-6 have been tried out in selected schools in the San Francisco Bay area and in several schools in the area of Teachers College, Columbia University, the University of California at Los Angeles, the University of Oklahoma, and the University of Hawaii.

The staff of SCIS has sponsored orientation conferences, conducted in-service education courses, and prepared instructional units for grades K-6. A teacher education package containing students' and teachers' manuals for certain topics such as "material objects" and "interaction," audiovisual aids, and kits of equipment for experiments was published by D. C. Heath and Company. A college text, *Teaching Science in the Elementary School*, provides detailed suggestions for using the SCIS approach. The authors state:

Thus, the work of the SCIS group could be thought of as being a program for elementary-school science which teaches a child science through investigation. Such experiences will, according to the SCIS group, provide a child with intellectual development (rational powers) and assist him in building a conceptual structure of the discipline.[20]

Other elementary school science projects include *Science: A Process Approach*, developed by the American Association for the Advancement of Science; the Elementary Science Study of Educational Services, Inc.; the Minnesota Mathematics and Science Teaching Project; the Elementary School Science Project of Utah State University; and the Elementary School Science Project of the University of California.

English-Language Arts Project

Project English was sponsored by the U. S. Office of Education and the National Council of Teachers of English. Sixteen universities throughout the country participated in the program, which was concerned with language arts curriculum improvement from kindergarten through the second year of college. The program, supported by National Defense Education Act funds, updated the knowledge of about 4,000 English teachers, primarily through summer institutes. Goodlad and others commented on the work of curriculum improvement centers as follows:

There is little doubt that the "new English" will be characterized by carefully structured curricula taught inductively; by literature courses that emphasize depth and analysis, and lead the student to appreciate literary craftsmanship and its relation to meaning; and by an interest in structural linguistics, in generative grammar, and in speech as an integral part of the curriculum.[21]

Projects in the Social Sciences

Very few social science disciplines receive grants from the National Science Foundation; the U. S. Office of Education began to finance social studies projects in 1962. By 1966 fourteen curriculum development centers had been established at universities. These projects had several objectives in common: (1) to clarify the scope and purposes of the social studies program, (2) to develop materials and procedures for the achievement of these objectives, (3) to submit these productions to experimentation, evaluation, and revision, and (4) to disseminate materials and information.

The Greater Cleveland Social Science Program was initiated in 1961. This program was developed around concepts from history, geography, philosophy, economics, political science, psychology, sociology, and anthropology. The program has been used by schools in the Cleveland area, enrolling some 90,000 students. The Elkhart (Indiana) Experiment in Economic Education was established in 1958; it is funded by the Elkhart Public Schools, Purdue University, and the Carnegie Corporation. Science Research Associates of Chicago has published materials produced by the project.

Obviously, only a few aspects of the massive curriculum reform movement of the 1950s and 1960s can be discussed within the limits of a single chapter. Moreover, it should come as

no surprise to learn that neither the psychological foundations of the new curricula nor the programs themselves are universally accepted.

One research psychologist examined innovations in teaching for the purpose of stating a few words of caution "that may prevent some excellent notions on teaching and learning from becoming unexamined fixtures of sacred ritual."[22] He also pointed out that some of the new programs overlook the fact that "skill in performing routine operations may be the learner's key to comprehending concepts." Moreover, "much of our faith in the discovery method of learning is based on the assumption that the student is more likely to retain insights he has developed on his own. I know of no extensive 'hard' evidence to support this view."

If the student is to evaluate these criticisms, he or she must become thoroughly familiar with the meanings of the discovery method and concept learning and with the ways these are used in the new curricula. He or she may find, for example, that these programs make adequate provision for the development of skills; that they do not depend exclusively on learning by discovery; and that the discovery method is subject to gross misinterpretations in practice.

Special Education

A growing number of schools were bridging the cultural gap between themselves and ethnic communities during the 1950s and 1960s. Unfortunately, most schools were still classifying children—especially low-income children—in ways that did not allow them to earn their rightful place in society. Indeed, special education classes had become academic graveyards for a disproportionate number of lower-class children. The Children's Defense Fund, a group seeking to reform laws dealing with children's rights, outlined the problem of student classification and labeling: Labeling is a pervasive and detrimental practice in education. In some schools a decision is made about whether a child will be a blue-collar or a white-collar worker when he or she is in the early elementary grades, and the educational opportunities for that child are designed around that decision.

During the 1950s funds from the Office of Vocational Rehabilitation stimulated the development of several model demonstration projects in special education. The most successful programs, however, were secondary level work-study programs. But these were merely a continuation of the previous decades of progress in the area of secondary vocational educational preparation programs for the retarded.

The curriculum reforms in the 1950s and 1960s had only a modest impact on education for handicapped and exceptional children. Thus unlike the previous studies cited, we must look beyond the 1950s and 1960s for significant breakthroughs in special education. In *Pennsylvania Association for Retarded Children v. Commonwealth of Pennsylvania* (1971) and in *Mills v. Board of Education of the District of Columbia* (1972), the U. S. Supreme Court confirmed that all children, regardless of handicap, are entitled to regular public school education, or the state must provide adequate alternate educational services. With these rulings it was clear that education is a right for everyone, not a privilege reserved for non-handicapped children. Nor is lack of finances an adequate reason for failure to provide services for handicapped children, the Court ruled in the *Mills* case.

Substantial catching up must be done in this area. In 1975 there were more than eight million handicapped American children. One million of them were excluded from the public schools, and more than half of those attending school did not receive adequate educational services. Currently, because of inadequate local services, many handicapped children attend private schools or public schools outside their own school district. The Education for All Handicapped Children Act of 1975 (Public Law 94–142) was designed to alter these negative situations.

The Handicapped Children Act defines handicapped children as "mentally retarded, hard of hearing, deaf, speech impaired, visually handicapped, seriously emotionally disturbed, orthopedically impaired, or other health impaired children or children with specific learning disabilities who by reason thereof require special education and related services." The phrase "children with specific learning disabilities" means "those children who have a disorder in one or more of the basic psychological processes involved in understanding or in using language, spoken or written, which disorder may manifest itself in im-

perfect ability to listen, think, speak, read, write, spell, or do mathematical calculations. Such disorders include such conditions as perceptual handicaps, brain injury, minimal brain disfunction, dyslexia, and developmental aphasia." This term does not include "children who have learning problems which are primarily the result of visual, hearing, or motor handicaps or mental retardation, or emotional disturbance, or of environmental, cultural, or economic disadvantage."

According to the Handicapped Children Act, appropriate public education will be available for all handicapped children between the ages of three and eighteen within each state not later than September 1, 1978, and for all handicapped children between the ages of three and twenty-one not later than September 1, 1980. Handicapped children of the ages three to five and eighteen to twenty-one are excluded in states where state laws do not provide for public education at these levels. Implementation of this law will require considerably more special education training than our colleges and universities are currently providing.

Summary

The innovations of the 1950s and 1960s have resulted in several curriculum trends in the 1970s, including the following.

English. There is less regimentation and more student-initiated reading and composition. Heterogeneous groupings are used to assist poor readers. There is an increase of electives and short courses.

Mathematics. Computer science and probability and statistics courses are becoming more numerous. New programs are being developed for the nonmathematically inclined or interested students.

Science. The emphasis is on new programs in environmental education and more experimentation with unified science courses.

Social Studies. Multiethnic and multicultural courses are being refined; more use of minicourses; voter registration projects are popular.

Business education.   There is a growing instruction in computer and data-processing techniques. Office practices and machine laboratories are being established in many schools. Special programs to reach potential dropouts are being developed.

Fine arts.   The trend is toward introductory general arts or music courses followed by electives and independent study. Aesthetic education, humanities, and related arts courses are increasing in popularity. Community cultural resources are being brought into the school.

Foreign language.   Foreign language study is being used to understand the cultures of peoples of the world. Many schools are moving to a balanced, less mechanical approach to teaching foreign languages.

Home economics.   Most schools are offering courses relating to education for family life. Emphasis is on specialized courses for job preparation. Occupational home economics work-experience programs are growing.

Industrial arts.   Shop-laboratories have auxiliary classrooms for media instruction. More programmed booklets are being used. Independent study projects are common.

Physical, health, and safety education. More use is being made of individualized instruction. Drug education and sex education are popular. Most programs are being designed to evoke the emotional and intellectual commitment of students.

Vocational education.   The trend is towards nongraded occupational courses. Individualized instruction is increasing. Several schools have added aeronautical and nautical courses.

INNOVATIONS IN INSTRUCTIONAL GROUPING

School organization is not an end in itself; it is a means of releasing the potential of each teacher and of facilitating the achievement of the objectives of the school. Grouping pupils for instruction is an important facet of the internal organization of a school. Innovations in grouping for instruction began in this country early in the nineteenth century; they have multiplied steadily through the years. Any history of American education is likely to include an analysis of two pioneering developments in grouping: the Lancastrian or monitorial plan, which was first established in the schools of New York City in 1806 and which spread to many other city school systems during the first decade of the nineteenth century, and the first graded elementary school in America, established at the Quincy School in Boston in 1848.

The graded school soon spread to urban school systems throughout the country and is still the type of organization used in the great majority of elementary schools. Some of the factors that have caused this form of regimentation to persist despite its obvious weaknesses are the publication of graded series of textbooks, the relative symplicity of giving the same assignment to all members of a class, the use of standardized achievement tests with norms established in terms of grade levels, the necessity to report attendance to state departments of education in terms of grades, and in general the factory-like precision made possible by the system. As the Lynds put it in their famous *Middletown*, a study of Muncie, Indiana, the typical school of 1925 was "like a factory—a thoroughly regimented affair."[23]

The consequences of the effort to regiment children became apparent many years ago: increasing dropout rates, high percentages of children not promoted, and bright students unchallenged by the standard curriculum. As a matter of fact, even before the end of the nineteenth century, some school systems began to try to break this lock step. For instance in Saint Louis, Pueblo, Portland, North Denver, and other cities, the schools adopted innovations as early as the 1890s. A few famous plans such as the Gary Plan, the Dalton Plan, and the Winnetka Plan appeared during the first few decades of this century. In general, however, the period since 1950 has been the one during which many new plans for grouping children for instruction have emerged. The rest of this chapter is devoted to an examination of the advantages and limitations of some of these plans.

The Nongraded Plan

The use of the nongraded plan for grouping pupils for instruction has been increasing since 1950. One study of a sample of 600 elementary schools (out of a total of 85,000) reported that 6 per cent were using some nongraded sequences in 1956, 12 per cent were doing so in 1961, and 26 per cent of the principals reporting said that they expected to be using the plan by 1966.[24] It is apparent that instead of centering on curriculum reform, during the 1950s, the elementary school had largely concerned itself with organizational changes designed to group children more efficiently for individual differences.[25]

The nongraded plan is primarily a development of the 1950s and 1960s—at least in terms of the number of schools using the plan and the space devoted to it in educational publications. As early in 1940, however, a Primary Unit plan was used in Pittsburgh, and an Early Elementary School system was adopted in Minneapolis. Both of these plans eliminated annual promotions during the first three years the child was in school or during the first four years in schools maintaining kindergartens.[26] The reports on these two plans indicate that they were intended to achieve more than the elimination of annual promotions. For instance the report of a survey of the Pittsburgh schools commented thus on the Primary Unit, "Combined with the activity curriculum or variations of this approach to curriculum development, it is a superior basis for advancing curriculum practice in the city."[27] A bulletin of the Minneapolis schools made this comment on the Early Elementary School, "In each year, the teacher will adapt the curriculum to the needs of each child."[28] These statements are particularly pertinent to any evaluation of nongraded plans as they exist today, for it is generally recognized that a change in the organization of a school without corresponding changes in the curriculum and in teaching may result in merely substituting one form of regimentation for another—substituting uniform materials at standards for each level for uniform materials and standards in each grade.

Motivation for developing the nongraded school has come primarily from two sources. The first source is the increasing amount of information about the wide variations that exist among children at any grade level. Students who enter the first grade generally range over a four-year spread in mental age; the longer they remain in school, the wider these variations become. Our democratic ideals demand equality of educational opportunity; they do not demand identical achievement at any age or grade level. The second source is the increasing acceptance of the philosophy of continuous growth, which holds that the school should assist each child in growing according to her natural pattern, without depriving the bright child of the opportunity of making the most of her talents or forcing the slow child to experience failure if she cannot advance as rapidly as others.

Characteristics of the nongraded plan. The nongraded plan varies from one school system to another and from one year to the next in the same school system. It is possible therefore to mention only some common characteristics that apply to most nongraded plans.

1. The plan is used most extensively in the primary division (grades 1–3 in the graded school). In some schools it has been extended to the kindergarten, the intermediate division, and the high school.

2. The content of the curriculum for the primary unit is divided into eight or nine levels, and students progress from one level to the next in terms of their rates of achievement. Each child begins in September where he or she left off the previous June, without repeating the work he or she has completed.

3. Charts are developed showing what achievement each child must attain before he or she moves from one level to the next. These charts are generally geared to reading achievement, but some schools also include levels for arithmetic and language usage.

4. A teacher is generally given a group of students who do not vary by more than two progress levels in achievement.

5. Teachers must become very proficient in the use of tests and other evaluation procedures in order to determine when a student has completed one of the levels.

6. Teachers and parents must become familiar with an entirely different form of reporting student progress.

Advantages of the nongraded plan. The nongraded plan permits each child to progress at his or her own rate of learning. It reduces the emotional tensions that develop when a child is forced into learning situations before he or she is ready. It requires teachers to become more explicit concerning objectives, materials, and procedures, and promotes cooperative planning on the part of teachers.

Limitations of the nongraded plan. The nongraded plan is not a panacea; it is merely a step in the right direction. The plan cannot achieve its greatest potential if it is merely an administrative device for regulating pupil progress through a school. It requires considerable modification in instructional materials, including both locally prepared materials and textbooks.[29] Another limitation of nongrading is that it does not give the teacher a group of students who are alike with respect to all the factors that influence their progress in school. No plan of grouping has been devised that relieves the teacher of the responsibility of recognizing and making provision for individual differences.

It is important to remember that when the plan requires all students to move through a preplanned, prescribed sequence of content and skills, it becomes merely another form of regimentation in which standards for levels are substituted for standards for grades. Some learnings are needed by all students; others are unique to the individual. Pupils therefore need opportunities to participate in the selection of some materials and the planning of some learning activities.

There is little evidence from research that the use of the nongraded plan improves the achievement of students. Some studies show a slight gain in reading for nongraded schools over graded schools; other studies do not. Although the studies were controlled for academic aptitude, they do not reveal whether the amount of time spent on reading was the same under both programs.[30] There is also the chance that since the nongraded plan is based on ability grouping, it may penalize lower-class children who are bright but not as verbal as their middle-class peers. Finally, as Goodlad and Robert H. Anderson put it in their pioneering publication on the nongraded school, "Teachers in nongraded schools who have not yet faced up to the inappropriateness of graded content for this new pattern are only beginning the process of school improvement."[31]

The Appropriate Placement School

A school using the nongraded plan combined with a multiphased curriculum is known as an *appropriate placement school*. This plan has been described as a sophisticated nongraded curriculum because it is much more than just another way of grouping students. It has been adopted in a number of high schools, notably the Melbourne (Florida) High School, which is widely known in the education profession for its pioneering and successful use of this plan.

The appropriate placement plan was developed as a result of a conference held at the Massachusetts Institute of Technology in May 1963, under the auspices of the President's Science Advisory Committee. The conference, which was headed by B. Frank Brown, sought to determine the effectiveness of the nongraded plan in salvaging the 30 per cent of American school children who become educational failures. After the meeting Brown traveled more than 100,000 miles, visiting nongraded schools throughout the nation. He spent more than a year working on a new curriculum model for nongraded schools. Brown characterized the plan as follows:

This new modus operandi can no longer be properly called a nongraded school. The nongraded school implies a change in school organization with minor curriculum adjustments. In its more sophisticated form, the nongraded school has become the Appropriate Placement School. This is a revolutionary new organization which calls for both a new organization and a corresponding revolution in curriculum.[32]

This "revolution in curriculum"—the multiphased curriculum—is described thus:

Phase 1—Subjects are provided for students who perform from 0–20th percentile on standardized achievement tests, indicating that they need special assistance in small classes.

Phase 2—Subjects are organized for students who range between the 20th and 40th percentile in achievement and who need more emphasis on fundamentals.

Phase 3—Courses are arranged for students who score between the 40th and 60th percentile on standardized achievement tests, indicating that they have an average background of accomplishment.

Phase 4—Subject matter is planned for extremely well prepared students who achieve between the 60th and 80th percentile and desire education in depth.

Phase 5—Courses are available for students who attain above the 80th percentile and are willing to assume responsibility for their own learning, pursuing college level courses while still in high school.

Phase Q—Students whose creative talents are well developed should give consideration to the Quest phase of the curriculum. This is an important dimension of the phased organization which gives thrust in the direction of individual fulfillment. In this phase a student may research any area in which he is deeply and sincerely interested.[33]

Class time in the multiphased classroom is distributed as follows:

1. Presentation of materials comprises approximately 20 per cent of the time in the course. (This includes time spent in viewing films as well as lecturing.)
2. Discussion in analysis groups constitutes approximately 40 per cent of the class time.
3. Individual work and reading encompasses roughly 40 per cent of the class time.[34]

The Dual Progress Plan

The Dual Progress Plan was initiated in 1958 in the schools of two suburban towns, Long Beach and Ossining, New York. At first it was limited to grades three through six, but by 1960 it had been extended to include grades seven and eight. The plan was developed cooperatively by the Experimental Teaching Center at New York University and the two school systems. George D. Stoddard was in general charge of the study, which received financial support from the Ford Foundation. Stoddard wrote a book that contains the most extensive description of the plan that is available.[35] As the subtitle of his book, *A New Philosophy and Program in Elementary Education*, indicates, he regards the plan as much more than a device for grouping pupils for instruction.

The Dual Progress Plan offers a semi-departmentalized arrangement as a substitute for the self-contained classroom. The self-contained classroom, which has for many years been used by most elementary schools for grouping students, is the familiar one that involves one teacher teaching all or almost all the subjects taken by one group of children in one general-purpose classroom. The propo-

nents of this plan point out that it enables the teacher to learn a great deal about each student through long association and through observation in a wide variety of situations and that it permits a more flexible use of time, since learning activities are not brought to an abrupt end because pupils must go to another classroom.[36]

The self-contained classroom plan has serious limitations, however, and it was in an effort to overcome them that the Dual Progress Plan was developed. Under it, language arts, social studies, and physical education are called *cultural imperatives*—those subjects that everyone in our society needs as a basis for effective social living. Mathematics, science, and the arts are called *cultural electives*. Students spend one-half day on the cultural imperatives with a homeroom teacher and a core specialist in physical education; they spend the other half-day on the cultural electives, taught by specialists in the various areas. The cultural imperatives portion of the program is graded; the cultural electives portion is nongraded. Promotion is generally determined by the homeroom teacher.

Advantages claimed for the dual progress plan. This plan has the advantage that every student is taught each of the curriculum areas each year by a teacher who knows the area well. The plan also makes better provision for developing the intellectual potentialities and the personalities of students than does the self-contained classroom plan. It offers a more satisfying professional role for elementary teachers as well as individualized learning programs for slow, average, and gifted students. Students profit from having several teachers, each of whom has a different personality and uses different methods, and students who have special interests and talents can progress more rapidly in the appropriate areas than they can in a conventional school.

Limitations of the dual progress plan. The division by this plan of curriculum areas into cultural imperatives and cultural electives is an arbitrary one; a more defensible position would seem to be that everything taught in an elementary school should be regarded as a cultural imperative. In addition the plan limits the opportunity for the teacher to know each student well and to make provisions for his or her individual needs; the mathematics teacher, for example, who meets a different group of students every 40 minutes (so that during the day she meets more than 150 students) has little opportunity to know each student well.

The scheduling of so many classes during the school day, each meeting with a different teacher in a different room, limits the opportunity for cultural tours and other out-of-class activities. The result is a reduction of enrichment experiences for students, and a greater adherence to a rigid, preplanned curriculum. The plan also limits the opportunities for students to see the relationship among school subjects and makes it difficult to devote time to unified learning activities that center around problems or concepts that cut across subject-matter boundaries. Perhaps the most comprehensive objection has been expressed thus: "Today's secondary schools are struggling with their problems created by over-departmentalization and subject-centeredness. It is a shame to impose the old organizational pattern of secondary education upon the elementary school."[37]

Team Teaching

Although team teaching has as its primary purpose a better utilization of the special talents of teachers, it does involve a unique procedure for grouping students for instruction. It provides for both large-group and individual learning situations.

The first experimental team teaching was done at the Franklin Elementary School in Lexington, Massachusetts, in 1957, but by 1960 more secondary schools than elementary schools were experimenting with the plan. The rationale for team teaching and an outline of the structure of teaching teams to be formed were contained in a proposal made to the Fund for the Advancement of Education by Dean Francis Keppel of Harvard's Graduate School of Education in 1956. Among the points Keppel made were that a new pattern of cooperation between universities and school systems was needed; that half the children in America were being taught by relatively inexperienced teachers; and that the difference between those who make a lifetime career of teaching and those who teach for only a few years must be recognized. The proposal resulted in a grant for the establishment of the School and University Program for Research and Develop-

ment (SUPRAD), which developed the team-teaching concept in detail, evolved methods of applying it, and directed the program in Lexington and later in Newton and Concord, Massachusetts.

The types of teaching teams vary from one school system to another. Luverne L. Cunningham has divided the teaching teams described in the literature into four categories: the team leader type, the associate type, the master teacher-beginning teacher type, and the coordinated type.[38]

The team leader type. More schools use this type than use any of the others. A large group of students is assigned to a team composed of two or more certified teachers, one or more paraprofessionals or teacher aides, and in some cases, a student teacher or two. A team leader is selected to coordinate the work of the team. The team leader presides over planning sessions, exercises varying degrees of leadership over the team, and generally does some teaching. In most cases the team leader receives a higher salary than other members of the team; she is responsible for assigning students to groups, developing a suitable curriculum, and supervising the less experienced members of the team. The paraprofessionals perform nonteaching tasks. The student teachers have an opportunity to observe more than one teacher, teach certain topics for which they have special preparation, and join in the planning and evaluation of learning activities.

The associate type. Most teaching teams of this type work with large classes. Opportunities are provided for large-group learning situations, small-group learning situations, and independent study. No teacher is designated as team leader; planning for instruction is worked out cooperatively so that the best talents of each member of the team are used. Members of the teaching team sometimes represent only one subject area and sometimes more than one. Some of the teaching teams have nonprofessional adults and student teachers assigned to them.

The master teacher-beginning teacher type. Beginning teachers and teachers who are new to the school system are sometimes teamed with one or two master teachers to share the responsibility for teaching a large group of students. This plan, which has been used most frequently in secondary schools, has not generally involved the designation of a team leader. It offers an excellent opportunity for less experienced teachers to mature under the guidance of experienced teachers.

The coordinated team type. This variation of team teaching does not assign joint responsibility for a large group of students to members of the team. Instead, teachers who have different sections of the same course meet regularly to coordinate methods and materials used in the various sections of the course. Sometimes the students in all sections of the course are brought together in an auditorium for lectures or other large-group presentations. (Cunningham and others question whether this arrangement should be called team teaching at all.)

Team teaching is not a panacea. Its success depends on the thoroughness with which administrators, teachers, and parents have been prepared for its introduction, the expertness of members of the teaching team, the availability of adequate space and materials, and the ability of the team leader to tap the talents of all members of the teaching team. Following are some of the hazards to be overcome in the operation of the plan.

1. The members of the teaching team must be able to work together harmoniously and productively; friction in interpersonal relations can destroy the effectiveness of the plan.

2. The large-group learning situations may become formal lecture sessions in which students have little opportunity to ask questions or to make contributions.

3. Unless the superior teachers who serve as team leaders do some teaching, the plan may result in the loss of expert teaching talent in the interest of the performance of semiadministrative tasks.

4. The plan can operate at its highest level of effectiveness only in a building that has been planned specifically for this type of organization.

Some Generalizations About Grouping

1. Grouping students for instruction is only one aspect of school organization. Developing the overall design of the curriculum, developing an effective organization within the individual classroom, and organizing the staff for the improvement of instruction are other important facets of organization.

2. The best type of grouping for instruction is the one that is most compatible with the major beliefs and goals of the school staff.

3. Under no type of organization yet devised can the individual teacher ignore his or her responsibility for recognizing and making provision for individual differences among students.

4. It is generally unwise for one school system to take over some package plan that has worked well in another system; the plan should be tailor-made by the local school staff within the total situation in which it must function.

5. The installation of a new plan for grouping students for instruction must also make curriculum adaptations for different types of students. Otherwise, the new plan is not likely to have much impact on the problem of meeting individual needs.

6. No organizational plan can serve as a substitute for competent teachers; the most that any plan can accomplish is to set the stage—to provide a situation in which it is possible for the teacher to perform as well as he or she is capable of performing.

The discussion of innovations in grouping students for instruction presented in this chapter is not definitive or complete. There are many other types of vertical and horizontal organizations. Enough has been said, however, to indicate the general direction that practice has been taking in the 1970s.

Despite the educational reforms of the past, we are left with this disconcerting thought.

The 1950s and 60s saw one of the largest and most sustained educational reform movements in American history, an effort that many observers . . . thought would transform the schools. Nothing of the sort has happened; the reform movement has produced innumerable changes, and yet the schools themselves are largely unchanged.[39]

LECTURE

Teach these boys and girls nothing but Facts. Facts alone are wanted in life. Plant nothing else, and root out everything else. You can only form the minds of reasoning animals upon Facts: nothing else will ever be of any service to them. This is the principle on which I bring up my own children, and this is the principle on which I bring up these children. Stick to Facts, Sir.[40]

Try to follow Thomas Gradgrind's advice and prepare a lecture of a social issue based only on *facts*, nothing else. When you select your topic, remember that a fact is something that is known with certainty.

After you have completed the lecture, compare it with a similar lecture in which you offer some subjective comments about the same social issue. Which lecture is likely to be better received by elementary or secondary school students? If you use subjective comments, what precautions should be taken?

ADDITIONAL READINGS

Bentzen, Mary M. and Associates. *Changing Schools: The Magic Feather Principle.* New York, McGraw-Hill, 1974.

Bishop, Lloyd K. *Individualizing Education Systems.* New York, Harper & Row, 1971.

Block, James H., ed. *Schools, Society, and Mastery Learning.* New York, Holt, Rinehart & Winston, 1974.

Bruner, Jerome S. *Toward a Theory of Instruction.* Cambridge, Mass., Belknap Press, 1966.

Firth, Gerald R. and Richard D. Kimpson. *The Curricular Continuum in Perspective.* Itasca, Ill., F. E. Peacock, 1973.

Friere, Paulo. *Pedagogy of the Oppressed.* New York, Heider and Heider, 1972.

Hewett, Frank M. and Steven R. Forness. *Education of Exceptional Learners.* Boston, Allyn & Bacon, 1974.

Hyman, Ronald T. *Approaches in Curriculum.* Englewood Cliffs, N. J., Prentice-Hall, 1973.

Joyce, Bruce R. and Marsha Weil. *Models of Teaching.* Englewood Cliffs, N. J., Prentice-Hall, 1972.

Leeper, Robert F., ed. *Curricular Concerns in a Revolutionary Era.* Washington, D. C., Association for Supervision and Curriculum Development, 1971.

Leeper, Sarah H., et al. *Good Schools for Young Children.* 3d ed. New York, Macmillan, 1974.

Lewis, Arthur and Alice Miel. *Supervision for Improved Curriculum and Instruction.* Belmont, Cal., Wadsworth, 1972.

Perkinson, Henry J. *The Possibilities of Error: An Approach to Education.* New York, David McKay, 1971.

Renner, John W., Gene D. Shepherd, and Robert F. Bibens. *Guiding Learning in the Elementary School.* New York, Harper & Row, 1973.

———. *Guiding Learning in the Secondary School.* New York, Harper & Row, 1972.

Rubin, Louis, ed. *Curriculum Handbook: The Disciplines, Current Movements, and Instructional Methodology.* Boston, Allyn & Bacon, 1977

Tanner, Daniel. *Secondary Education: Perspectives and Prospects.* New York, Macmillan, 1972.

Unruh, Glenys G. *Responsive Curriculum Development: Theory and Action.* Berkeley, Cal., McCutchan, 1975.

Von Haden, Herbert I. and Jean Marie King. *Innovations and Their Pros and Cons.* Worthington, Ohio, Charles A. Jones, 1971.

Walker, James E. and Thomas M. Shea. *Behavior Modification: A Practical Approach for Educators.* St. Louis, C. V. Mosby, 1976.

Watson, Bernard C. *In Spite of the System: The Individual and Educational Reform.* Cambridge, Mass., Ballinger, 1974.

Weber, Evelyn. *Early Childhood Education: Perspectives on Change.* Worthington, Ohio, Charles A. Jones, 1970.

NOTES

1. Lloyd Trump and Delmas F. Miller, *Secondary School Curriculum Improvement* (Boston, Allyn & Bacon, 1968), 16.

2. Myron Lierberman, *The Future of Public Education* (Chicago, University of Chicago Press, 1960), 34.

3. A. D. Woodruff, "The Use of Concepts in Teaching and Learning," *Journal of Teacher Education*, 15 (March, 1964), 84.

4. *Ibid.*, 81.

5. *Ibid.*, 95–96.

6. Richard C. Anderson and David P. Ausubel (eds.), *Readings in the Psychology of Cognition* (New York, Holt, Rinehart & Winston, 1965).

7. Jerome S. Bruner, *The Process of Education* (Cambridge, Mass., Harvard University Press, 1962), 38.

8. *Ibid.*, 53.

9. Robert M. Gagné, *The Conditions of Learning* (New York, Holt, Rinehart & Winston, 1965), 25.

10. John W. Renner and William B. Ragan, *Teaching Science in Elementary School* (New York, Harper & Row, 1968), 111.

11. Lucile Lindberg, "Learning Through Searching," *Childhood Education*, 38 (October, 1961), 58–60.

12. S. Boocock and James S. Coleman, "Games with Simulated Environments in Learning," *Sociology of Education*, 39 (Summer, 1966), 215–237.

13. William A. Brownell, "Psycholoyical Considerations in the Learning and Teaching of Arithmetic," in *The Teaching of Arithmetic* (Washington, D.C., National Council of the Teachers of Mathematics, 1935), 10.

14. William Van Til, *Research Affecting Education* (Washington, D.C., Association for Supervision and Curriculum Development, 1953), 120.

15. Max Beberman, "An Emerging Program of Secondary School Mathematics," in R. W. Heath (ed.), *New Curricula* (New York, Harper & Row, 1964), 10.

16. *Ibid.*, 9–11.

17. Kenneth B. Henderson, "Mathematics," in *Using Current Curriculum Developments* (Washington, D. C., Association for Supervision and Curriculum Development, 1963), 57.

18. Bowen C. Dees, *Science Course Improvement Projects* (Washington, D. C., National Science Foundation, 1962), 1.

19. John I. Goodlad et al., *The Changing Curriculum* (New York, The Fund for the Advancement of Education, 1966), 49.

20. Renner and Ragan, *Teaching Science*, 259.

21. Goodlad et al., *The Changing Curriculum*, 76.

22. Friedlander, "Today's Innovations in Teaching," *NEA Journal* (March, 1966), 11–14.

23. Robert S. Lynd and Helen Lynd, *Middletown* (New York, Harcourt, Brace & World, 1929), 188.

24. *The Look at the Schools* (Washington, D. C., National Education Association, 1962), preface and 39–40.

25. Celia B. Stendler, "Grouping Practices," in *Those First Years at School* (Washington, D. C., National Education Association, 1960), 147–148.

26. Hollis L. Caswell and Arthur W. Foshay, *Education in the Elementary School*, 3rd ed. (New York, American Book, 1957), 361–363.

27. *Ibid.*

28. *Ibid.*

29. Richard I. Miller, *The Nongraded School: Analysis and Study* (New York, Harper & Row, 1967), 13.

30. Stendler, "Grouping Practices," 155–157.

31. John I. Goodlad and Robert H. Anderson, *The Nongraded Elementary School* (New York, Harcourt, Brace & World, 1952), 214.

32. B. Frank Brown, *The Appropriate Placement School: A Sophisticated Nongraded Curriculum* (West Nyack, N. Y., Parker, 1965), 3–4.

33. *Ibid.*, 26–27.

34. *Ibid.*, 28.

35. George D. Stoddard, *The Dual Progress Plan: A New Philosophy and Program in Elementary Education* (New York, Harper & Row, 1961).

36. *The Self-Contained Classroom* (Washington, D. C., Association for Supervision and Curriculum Development, 1960).

37. Robert S. Fleming et al., "Reactions to the Dual Progress Plan," in Maurice Hillson (ed.), *Change and Innovation in Elementary School Organization* (New York, Holt, Rinehart & Winston, 1965), 262.

38. Luverne L. Cunningham, "Team Teaching: Where Do We Stand?" *The Administrator's Notebook* (Chicago, Midwest Center, University of Chicago, April, 1960).

39. Charles E. Silberman, *Crisis in the Classroom* (New York, Random House, 1970), 158–159.

40. Charles Dickens, *Hard Times* (New York, E. P. Dutton, 1966), 1.

PART II
SELECTED
ISSUES
IN AMERICAN
EDUCATION

WHAT CHICANO STUDENTS FEEL*

Frank Sotomayor

*Reprinted from *Para Los Niños—For the Children: Improving Education for Mexican Americans*, Washington, D.C.: U. S. Commission on Civil Rights, October 1974, pp. 7–9.

Parent. Teacher. Child. Each gives and receives from the educational experience. A parent watches a child grow, question, and learn. A teacher with skill imparts knowledge to her class. A youngster in the classroom accepts and responds to words and books, instructions, and attitudes. It is a universal exchange, unless the two-way street of learning—the giving and the taking—is blocked by school-made barriers that damage the student's spirit and deadens the mind.

For many of the 1.6 million Mexican American students in the Southwest, such barriers are painfully real and seemingly unavoidable. And too often, too many of these young people give up and drop out.

Statistics are shocking. Each year tens of thousands of Mexican Americans end their schooling prematurely. Four out of every 10 Chicano students do not graduate from high school. In comparison, 9 out of every 10 Anglo students do finish high school. These are people, not numbers—people who are branded as failures early in life at something that society values highly.

But are the children the failures? Or has the educational system failed them?

Mexican American parents and many educational experts believe it is the schools that have set up the pattern leading to failure, leaving only the luckiest and most adaptable to survive. They are alarmed that generally Mexican American children do less well than their Anglo classmates in school and score lower on reading and other achievement tests.

The U.S. Commission on Civil Rights, after a 5 year study of schools in the Southwest, found "a systematic failure of the educational process, which not only ignores the educational needs of Chicano students, but suppresses their culture and stifles their hopes and ambitions."

The Commission's Mexican American Education Study was the most comprehensive of its type ever conducted. It documented with facts and figures what Chicanos long have known—that Mexican Americans are being denied equal educational opportunity in the schools.

The complex process of school failure starts when the child enters the first grade.

From the beginning, many Mexican American school children are made to feel that they have some things that are not wanted—the wrong language, an accent, a different lifestyle and culture. They know they lack some things that are wanted—the right language, the right background, a Dick and Jane house, and Pilgrim ancestors.

About half of the Chicanos starting school do not have a working knowledge of English. People in this situation, such as Elena López, perhaps face the toughest time in school systems that make no provisions for non-English-speaking youngsters. For them it is sink or swim.

Yet speaking English doesn't remove all the barriers.

Even for those Chicano students whose families have lived in the Southwest for generations and who speak English as well as Anglos, the schoolmade barriers are great. They also find that they are often overlooked in class, are advised by counselors to take auto shop instead of college prep courses "because they might find them too difficult," or have to listen in history class about the settling of the Southwest by courageous Texans and stalwart Easterners.

These students and those like Elena López all know that something is wrong.

Listen to them.

"Where I come from everybody speaks Spanish and that's all you know, Spanish," says a 16-year-old. "All of a sudden they put you in this Anglo school and it's English right away, but nobody knows how to speak English. Then they try to counteract this by forbidding you to speak Spanish. 'Spanish is bad, Spanish is bad.' When I was little I had the idea Spanish was a dirty language and I felt kind of rotten."

A Tucson teenager recalls that in elementary school, "The houses in the Dick and Jane readers didn't look anything like mine. I wondered if there was something wrong with my house. And often, the things teachers discussed had no meaning in my life, but I tried to pretend they did. Teachers were always talking about getting a good breakfast—orange juice, cereal, milk, bacon and eggs. But these foods didn't mean anything to me. Our family had tortillas with beans and cheese or *chorizo*."

A young Chicano in a Texas school says, "I remember phrases from my history book such as 'Santa Anna knew that he was dealing with a superior class of men.' It is phrases like that that stay in your head until it gets to your subconscious. 'A superior class of men.' What am I—inferior or something?"

"When I was going to elementary school in Anglo middle-class West Los Angeles, there were only seven or eight Mexican Americans in the whole school," says Rachel, 21, a university student. "I spoke English, but they laughed and ridiculed me for my pronunciation of church, chair, ship. They laughed when I brought burritos for lunch, so I quit doing that. I was very uptight about what I did. I wanted to fit in.

"Then I went to live in the East Side barrio and found that many of the teachers didn't expect students there to do anything. It used to upset me to hear the teacher say, 'If I were in another school, I'd be expected to teach such and such, but not here.' The teacher was telling us in so many words that we weren't as good as students in other parts of the city.

"When I was in high school, I told my counselor I wanted to go to college, but she said, 'Don't try to achieve that. It's not for you. Instead why don't you try secretarial studies?'

"So I took secretarial studies, but still I wanted to go to college. I went to junior college for two years to try it. And then I went on to Cal. State L.A. I'll graduate this year."

Roberto, a twenty-year-old university student, says he can't forget that in his last year at a South Texas high school, "We wanted a Mexican American club on campus and Mexican American teachers, counselors, and books on Chicanos. But we ran into all kinds of trouble. We tried but we couldn't get anywhere with the principal, so we went to the district office. They told us to come back *manana* and later a bunch of us got arrested. They said we were 'parading without a permit.' Eventually they did hire one Chicano counselor, but things were pretty much the same. We were labeled 'rabble rousers' and Communists.' I can't understand it. Why do they want to destroy our language and culture?"

These young Chicano students are frustrated and angry to find that their education is not a challenge, but a battle with the odds stacked against them. It is not enough to ask anymore why Chicano students don't learn. But what should be asked is why teachers do not teach and why schools do not care.

8.
NATIONAL
ASSESSMENT

According to its original charter of 1867, one of the duties of the U.S. Office of Education (USOE) is the determination of educational progress in the states comprising the Union. Francis Keppel, U.S. Commissioner of Education from 1962 to 1965, became concerned with this responsibility and directed his attention to the problem of ascertaining how much had been learned and what progress was being made in American education. In the summer of 1963 Ralph W. Tyler, director of the Center for the Advanced Study of Behavioral Sciences, Stanford, California, was asked by leaders of education to prepare a memorandum exploring the possibility of assessing the progress of education nationally.

THE BEGINNING

Tyler's memorandum was reviewed by a conference of educational measurement personnel, who concluded that such an assessment was indeed feasible and worthwhile. In January 1964 the memorandum prepared by Tyler was placed before national educational leaders, who discussed from their perspectives the problems and benefits which might accrue in developing a procedure for national assessment. These leaders concluded that despite the potential for misuse which might inhere in such an appraisal, the need for comprehensive information was so great that the project should be undertaken. Reflecting their sentiments, Alex M. Mood wrote in *American Education*, "The schools and colleges are operating a $50 billion enterprise in ignorance of the most elemental and basic evaluative information." [1]

In July 1964, after numerous conferences and discussions, John W. Gardner, president of the Carnegie Corporation, convened a distinguished group of Americans to form an eleven-member Exploratory Committee on Assessing the Progress of Education (ECAPE), and Ralph Tyler became its chairman. The conclusions of this committee resulted in the decision to seek a plan to provide the answer to two questions: What are the current educational attainments of our population, and what change is there in the level of attainments over a period of time?

Four years of work financed by private foundations went into defining goals and developing measuring instruments to answer these questions. The Ford Foundation's Fund for Advancement of Education contributed financial support for ECAPE to continue its studies. The federal government did not provide funds for ECAPE, but it did award a $100,000 grant to the University of Wisconsin to hold conferences of educators and lay people to review and respond to the progress that had been made toward national assessment. In four years ECAPE had developed a detailed plan for assessment and had sponsored preparation of texts and exercises.

For several years lack of approval by the American Association of School Administrators hampered the progress of the assessment program. Their criticism was responsible in part for reorganization of the national assessment committee. The Committee on Assessment of Progress in Education (CAPE) became the successor to ECAPE. The chairman of the new committee was George B. Brain, dean of the College of Education, Washington State University. More in keeping with the will of the school administrators' association, this newly assembled group "had 25 members, one-third elected from major educational organizations, plus elected representatives from organizations of public officials and the general public."[2]

On July 1, 1968 the Education Commission of the States (ECS) took charge of the entire project, including the assets of the predecessor organization, CAPE (which had only been established in 1968). To advance their work, ECS employed James A. Hazlett, a former superintendent of schools in Kansas City, Missouri. The official title of the project then became National Assessment of Education Progress (NAEP). NAEP has become a continuing project of the ECS, funded principally by the National Center for Educational Research and Development. Long-range plans call for an expenditure of between four and five million dollars annually by the U.S. Office of Education for the purpose of gathering and compiling the data necessary for national assessment.

Procedures and Definitions of Terms

National assessment in education is briefly defined by Carmen J. Finley and Frances S. Berdie in *The National Assessment Approach to Exercise Development* as "a plan to systematically sample the skills, knowledges, and attitudes of youth and to report the results to all people involved directly or indirectly in the ongoing process of improving education."[3] For such a plan to be meaningful, objectives had to be written that were acceptable to three groups of people: subject matter specialists, educators, and citizens. Subject matter specialists had to consider the objectives authentic from the points of view of their respective disciplines. Educators had to recognize the objectives as desirable goals for learning, and ones which schools were actively striving to achieve. Citizens had to agree that the objectives were important for young people to know, feel, or understand.

The primary aim of national assessment is to obtain a balanced and adequate picture of how well educated our young people are and of

where the country's educational problem areas lie. NAEP exercises have been constructed to provide information by three divisions: (1) what all or almost all children are learning, (2) what the most advanced are learning, and (3) what the middle or average children are learning. The American Institute of Research, Educational Testing Service, Psychological Corporation, and Science Research Associates have participated in the development of the exercises. The accumulated results of these tests, it is hoped, will serve the purpose of differentiated assessment of the overall progress of education.

Since various populations within the country present different degrees and kinds of progress and problems, a national assessment cannot be meaningful unless testing is done in particular populations that need to be treated separately. NAEP defined 192 separate populations for testing by the following subdivisions: sex, race, geographic region, age group, community size and type, and socioeconomic level. About five per cent of the individuals in each of four age levels were determined to be sufficient to provide probability samples to represent each category. (Opinion polls have established this method as a valid means of representing large populations.) Since the exercises are intended to reflect what has been learned by representative groups within the total population rather than individual achievement, no individual will take more than a small segment of the exercises.

Taking part in the assessment will be some 120,000 to 140,000 examinees—to be selected by random sample. As a guidance it has been established that not more than 25 examinees will participate from a single school. Tapes will be used to present a large portion of the instructions and exercises, since tryouts indicated more students answered with this method than when they read the exercises themselves. Both cognitive and affective realms will be assessed.

Race is reported by white, Black and other; sex is reported by male and female. Geographic region is classified under four subdivisions—northeast, southeast, central, and west. Age groups are divided into four categories—nine year olds, thirteen year olds, seventeen year olds, and young adults. Community size and type includes extreme rural, extreme inner city, extreme affluent suburb, rest of big city, suburban fringe, medium city, and small city. Some reports include only a portion of these categories in their statistical compilations. Some reports also include parents' education, using four levels: less than or equal to eighth grade, more than eighth grade but not high school graduate, graduate from high school, and some formal education beyond high school.

Thus the national assessment procedures have been established in the hope that by assembling information about the knowledge and skills of young Americans, an index of what young people actually know will be provided. It is also hoped that through interval testing changes in skills and knowledge will be registered as they occur and that the statistical raw material will be furnished to improve the quality of education in the nation.

With the release of test data, commentaries on the national assessment of education continue to occupy a prominent place in a number of academic journals. As a result a storm of controversy continues to rage over this program. Proponents say national assessment is a necessity in the rapidly expanded systems of education existing today. Opponents say it will be an unnecessary hindrance and will create many problems throughout school systems in America.

ARGUMENTS FOR NATIONAL ASSESSMENT

Since the validity of the national assessment results is largely dependent upon the motivations and objectives which prompted the study, this section will concern itself with the arguments set forth by those who support NAEP. In the American Association of School Administrators' "Official Report," Ralph Tyler wrote of the need "to assess the educational progress of larger populations in order to provide the public with dependable information to help in the understanding of educational problems and needs and to guide in efforts to develop sound public policy regarding education."[4]

The method chosen for evaluation is also advanced as an asset by defenders of national assessment. Using the opinion poll sampling method, 192 separate populations will be evaluated. To have dependable, categorized

information—such as extreme rural, urban, Black, non-Black, Southeast, West—will assist greatly in curriculum planning and fund and material allocation decisions. Because the opinion poll sampling method will be used, each respondent will take only a fraction of the assessment exercises rather than the full battery required by the individual standardized tests now in wide use.

The NAEP method requires less time from the teacher who releases the child from his or her class for exercises and demands less time of the participating students. In "Let's Clear the Air on Assessment," Tyler commented further that "since the assessment does not require that all participants be in class, the exercises to be used are not limited to usual test items. Interviews and observational procedures are also to be employed to learn more of interests, habits, and practices that have been learned."[5] Unlike individualized test data, national assessment findings will be released to all persons interested in education. It is hoped that this knowledge will foster fuller accountability from those involved in education at all levels.

In summary, proponents of NAEP point out that the advantage to be achieved is the accumulation of dependable and differentiated national data offering new information on the youth of America. The data will be publicly available to offer help in prescriptive planning to alleviate broadly-based educational problems. To nationalize educational assessment, proponents submit, will lead to better development of human resources, resulting in a more useful and higher quality "Gross Educational Product."

CRITICISMS OF NATIONAL ASSESSMENT

Responsible critics of national assessment have leveled five major charges at the program. The first and perhaps most common charge is that NAEP will encourage teachers to teach to their test, fearing that if they do not, their district will suffer by comparison with other districts.[6] Other opponents fear that such a practice on the part of teachers will lead to the control of curriculum by the test makers themselves.[7] A corollary argument to this criticism is that since those who are responsible for educational appropriations at the local, state, and national level will look to the results of the tests as the ultimate criteria for dispensing money, the federal government, by accident or design, will control curriculum by participating, even peripherally, in such a program.[8]

Another more serious fear, if well-founded, is advanced in several articles, where it is suggested that the very objectives of American education will be modified in the process of national assessment. It is claimed that such a process, with its emphasis on machine-graded exercises, will place too high a value on those skills which lend themselves to scoring by machine.[9] As a result of this emphasis, the education of the whole child may be neglected, while the school experience becomes increasingly limited in a way which will render the traditional human values of secondary concern.[10]

Another argument against NAEP is that the assessment, no matter how well-intentioned, will produce confusing and ambiguous results.[11] Results which lend themselves to misinterpretation can easily lead to unjustified but damaging attacks on the American educational enterprise as a whole.[12] Furthermore, some critics maintain that American youngsters are already the most tested and measured students in the world. A number of existing tests, it is claimed, evaluate American education at least as well as the proposed program of national assessment.[13] Another authority has commented that many Europeans are surprised that "some critics of American education are so eager to adopt measures which they are giving up."[14]

Finally there are those who charge that the people chosen by the Carnegie Corporation to develop the objectives of national assessment were no more qualified for that task than were numerous others, of perhaps different perspectives.[15] One critic has charged that the program has been characterized by elements of secrecy on the part of those responsible for its formation, casting a shadow of doubt upon it from its inception.[16]

SCHEDULE OF ASSESSMENT

To accumulate national educational data, the following schedule was set for the Cycle I testing program. Science, writing, and citizenship exercises were administered in March 1969 and February 1970. Reading and literature exercises were administered in October 1970 and August 1971. Music and social studies exercises were administered in October 1971 and August 1972. Mathematics, science, and career and occupational development (COD) exercises were administered in October 1972 and August 1973. Reading, writing, listening, and speaking exercises were administered in October 1973 and August 1974. Citizenship, art, and consumer education exercises were administered in October 1974 and August 1975.

Cycle II began with mathematics, science, and health education exercises administered in October 1975 and August 1976. Reading, literature, and physical education exercises were administered in October 1976 and August 1977. Music, social studies, and study skills will be completed in August 1978. Mathematics, science, and COD will be administered in October 1978 and August 1979. Reading, writing, listening, and speaking exercises will be administered in October 1979 and August 1980. Citizenship, art, and consumer education exercises will be administered in October 1980 and August 1981. Schedule revisions have been necessary. Findings of tests already administered which have been evaluated will be included in later reports of test results.

NEED FOR RURAL AND INNER-CITY ASSESSMENT

The description of national assessment presented in this chapter will presumably raise the question, "Why focus a report on rural and inner-city schools?" Three factors conditioned this choice: (1) the problems which have already been identified in rural and inner-city education from past statistics make attention and remediation efforts a matter of urgency; (2) rural and inner-city education have long operated as distinct entities, with much of their data separated in a manner ideal for comparison with current findings in national assessment; and (3) tremendous appropriations are currently being made for vocational-technical education. Since vocational education is especially germane to rural and inner-city groups, early assessment of national results may be helpful in establishing need priorities.

The change in the proportion of rural and inner-city populations and the widening gap between education in urban and rural schools became so noticeable by the latter part of the nineteenth century that some educators demanded drastic curriculum changes. With the philosophy that rural and inner-city education need not be second best—that top quality education is the right of every child—changes were undertaken that brought significant rural and inner-city school improvements for the following twenty-five years. The effects of these assessments will help determine whether previous reforms had an effect.

Every major committee convened to study rural and inner-city education has shown that, while many problems in rural and inner-city schools are similar to those in suburban schools, rural and inner-city schools also have many problems unlike those of suburban schools. Some examples of the deficiencies of rural and inner-city education will support the initial thesis that remediation efforts are a matter of urgency. For instance rural teachers in general receive far fewer supportive services for administering programs designed to meet the needs of disadvantaged pupils than do their suburban colleagues. Most reports acknowledge the fact that the total size of the disadvantaged group is considerably larger in rural and inner-city areas than in suburban areas. Thus in rural and inner-city communities, the teacher's job has been made considerably more difficult by the schools' attempts to serve the emotional and physical, as well as the intellectual needs of pupils and to relate more intimately to the community served.

In a typical rural school the teacher must be prepared to guide pupils in almost every area, for the demands of school-community relations tend to be heavier in the country than in the city. Adding to this problem is the fact that rural school patrons often resist efforts to initiate curriculum innovations and new teaching techniques. Rural schools are among the slowest changing organizations in America. They are still a main bulwark of institutionalized inequality; they reflect and perpetuate the conservative elements in our social-class and racial stratification systems.[17] A further handicap of rural education is that local communities are reluctant to turn their schools over to professional educators. Trying to placate their generally conservative school

board, rural school principals frequently resist the idea of allowing teachers and students academic freedom. Many times rural principals must provide such guidance services as are available, and in small systems they sometimes double as teachers or clerks to assist their school through the academic year.

Additional evidence of the lack of sufficient funds in most rural and inner-city schools is seen in their inadequate equipment, texts, libraries, and laboratory facilities. The cost of such inadequate rural schools may be measured in terms of such items as welfare payments, juvenile delinquency, and racism. Rural and inner-city education also tends to be weak in college preparatory and vocational training courses. Continuing high unemployment and school dropout rates among the rural and inner-city populations illustrate the failure of their schools to prepare students for a productive life as adults.

With such a wealth of already accumulated data, an examination of rural and inner-city school NAEP results should afford a broad chronological base from which to view comparisons and explore solutions. However caution is in order—rural school patrons can take little comfort from NAEP data which show higher levels of achievement for rural students than for inner-city students. Both rural and inner-city students need a higher quality of education. When compared with suburban and other city students, rural and inner-city students rank low. Even though rural-urban education differences tend to diminish as students get older, the gap does not disappear.

AREAS OF ASSESSMENT

A review of selected assessment areas, test questions and results provides a basis for projecting both social implications and needed curricular changes. A danger inherent in looking at group results is the tendency to stereotype individual group members. With this caution in mind, let us briefly consider reading, writing, citizenship, science, and literature.

Reading

NAEP exercises formulated to test reading were constructed with several objectives in

Table 10. Median Per Cent Acceptable Answers for Rural and Inner-City Areas
on National Assessment Exercises

Subject	Age			
	9	13	17	Adult
Science				
Rural	57.8	47.5	37.3	45.2
Inner City	44.4	39.1	35.6	34.5
National Mediam	68.3	58.4	47.1	51.3
Citizenship				
Rural	54.9	55.8	54.6	57.3
Inner City	49.5	52.5	53.1	55.3
National Median	64.1	63.2	61.8	60.5
Reading				
Rural	67.0	66.2	76.6	*N.A.*
Inner City	56.6	60.5	72.4	N.A.
National Median	72.5	71.8	80.3	83.4
Writing				
Rural	21.5	47.1	59.7	52.3
Inner City	13.3	41.4	44.8	45.7
National Median	28.3	55.4	62.5	58.4
Literature				
Rural	39.5	51.1	59.4	N.A.
Inner City	34.1	45.4	52.4	N.A.
National Median	44.9	53.3	61.1	63.0

*N.A.: Not available.

SOURCE: Selma J. Mushkin, *National Assessment and Social Indicators, January 1973*, Washington, D.C.: U. S. Government Printing Office, 1973, pp. 34, 37.

mind. The contractors felt students should comprehend, analyze, and use what they read, and that they should have a lively interest in reading for information and for pleasure.

In the test for nine year olds, students were asked to read two passages and to answer five comprehension questions following the completion of each passage. The questions were multiple choice. As students read the entire first passage, their reading rate was recorded. Next, students marked one of four choices or "I don't know." The first passage administered was a narrative story involving a boy and a dragon. The second passage, which was similar to short accounts found in reference books or encyclopedias, gave factual information about armadillos.

Both passages for thirteen year olds were expository. The first was an essay about planting trees on sand dunes, and the second was a scientific passage regarding the flow of water. The first passage for seventeen year olds and young adults was a humorous, semiscientific article from *Reader's Digest*. The second passage was a more erudite essay on the nature and development of sociology.

Sample of test questions. To test the comprehension of nine year olds on the story of the boy and the dragon, the following question is characteristic of those asked: (1) Who does the boy ask to find out which way his home is? A seagull (a), An alley cat (b), An old sailor (c), A passing fish (d).

About the armadillo passage, the following question is a sample of those asked: (1) Armadillo young are almost always born: During the winter (a), As identical twins (b), As identical triplets (c), As identical quadruplets (d).

To test the comprehension of thirteen year olds concerning a passage on the planting of trees on sand dunes, the following question is a sample of those asked: (1) A sand dune moves: so slowly that it never does damage (a), at a very rapid rate covering houses and forests (b), when the wind blows the trees planted on the dunes (c), when the wind blows sand up one side of a bare dune and over the top (d).

In the second comprehension passage for thirteen year olds—regarding the flow of water—the following question is a sample of those asked: (1) The MOST important factor in determining water runoff is: the rate of rainfall (a), the slope of the land (b), the surrounding vegetation (c), the condition of the mantle clock (d).

Because the breakdown of exercise results furnished by NAEP for seventeen year olds and adults did not include the category "rural community" but instead was compiled by city size, results for this category are not cited.

Test results. In analyzing the test data, NAEP drew the following size and type of community distinctions: extreme rural, extreme inner-city, extreme affluent suburb, rest of the big city, suburban fringe, medium city, and small city. The statistical sampling reveals that in rural areas the percentage of students who read under one hundred words per minute is somewhat higher than the national average. Rural and inner-city students suffer more drastically in comprehension at both extremes.

Implications for educators. In nine year olds assessed for comprehension, the rural youngsters rated extremely low, with only the inner-city students falling below them. The results imply a need at an early age for available reading material with a broader vocabulary, for exercises designed to increase the use of more subtle and refined language, and for children to be read to by adults more frequently. It is insufficient to state that so long as most tests are verbally structured from middle-class, white, suburban language, the more isolated rural and inner-city students will be penalized by low standardized test ratings, unacceptable

college and vocational school entrance examinations, and inferior personnel employment test ratings. The challenge to educators is to prepare all students for educational and vocational survival today—not only tomorrow.

NAEP reading test results reveal, depending upon the particular exercise, that between 75 and 85 per cent of rural and inner-city youngsters in the thirteen year old range read at less than 200 words per minute, in contrast with only 60 per cent of youngsters from the affluent suburb group. This performance may be an indication of lack of sufficient time spent in reading. Remediation can be accomplished by apportioning more time specifically for this activity at home or at school, obtaining books more relevant to the experiences of rural and inner-city children to stimulate motivation, exploring the availability of reading materials and funds in the area of vocational technology, and increasing the expenditure of funds for community libraries or mobile book vans to serve rural and inner-city populations.

Exercise data also reveal that less than two per cent of the thirteen year olds from rural and inner-city communities could read test passages at 300 words per minute or faster and that seventeen year olds from these populations were more than three per cent below the national average. The implication here is that unless this situation is remediated by reading clinics, speed reading courses, or some other intensive emphasis in this area, these students will be severely limited by this deficiency when they try to secure a job or go to college.

As a suggested alternative, television has proved to be a mixed blessing to rural and inner-city students. Although it has served to enrich language, it has often discouraged verbal development in other areas such as reading. Reading has long been accepted as requisite to inspired imagination. The rural and inner-city students' lack of reading ability will be a handicapping factor in many job situations, and this factor can lead to an impoverishment of the personality which may have even more far-reaching effects.

In 1976 twelve states had enacted legislation or made it a policy that all students must demonstrate reading competency before they qualify for a high school diploma. In Maryland, for example, students are tested on their ability to read for survival in the adult world: ability to read medicine labels, newspaper advertisements, sales slips, charge account statements, driver manuals, job application forms, and television program listings. Unless national assessment results improve, it is likely that more states will require reading tests to supplement requirements for graduation. (See Chapter 14.)

Writing

The objectives developed to assess writing were, understandably, among the most difficult to evaluate because of the qualitative nature of the discipline. After reviewing the results of the first testing, it was announced that those objectives initially formulated in 1965 were not entirely adequate and required revision. Those objectives which governed the first battery of tests, and which are the subject of this commentary, stated that young people should write to communicate adequately in social, business, or vocational situations; write to communicate adequately in school situations; and appreciate the value of writing.

The development of articulate and proficient writers is without question a goal of education within a literate, technically advanced society. It should be noted, however, that there is extensive transfer in verbal patterns from oral to written forms—which proves a handicap to isolated or ingrown communities when they are measured by standards alien to them. Blacks, inner-city and rural communities afford three obvious examples. It is difficult to "appreciate the value of writing" when so much effort must be exerted to translate familiar feelings into unfamiliar form.

Sample of test questions. The writing exercise for nine year olds consisted of an essay. Respondents were instructed to look at a picture of a forest fire. They were then directed to write a story about what was happening in the picture. They were advised that the story was important because they would want people to know about the pictured, sad event.

Thirteen and seventeen year olds, in groups of approximately twelve each, were instructed to write an essay about someone they admired. The groups were allowed thirty minutes in which to compose and write their essays. *National Assessment Report 8* records the following oral instructions:

Most of us look up to some famous person as a representative of the things we believe in or as the kind of person we would like to be. This person may come from any part of our society. For instance, we might admire Winston Churchill or Martin Luther King, Jr., Walter Schirra or Mickey Mantle, Florence Nightingale or Barbra Streisand. No matter where this person comes from or what kind of work he or she does, however, we can recognize such traits of greatness as determination, physical courage, the ability to inspire others, and faithfulness to some worthy cause.

Think about a famous person whom you admire. Select a particularly admirable characteristic or quality of that person—such as Mickey Mantle's courage in the face of crippling physical handicaps or Florence Nightingale's determination to fight against strong governmental pressure. Write an essay of about 200–250 words describing this characteristic or quality. Be sure to provide an illustration of it from the person's life. Try to show that the person is great at least partly because of this characteristic or quality. [18]

Young adults were asked to write a letter to a public official opposing or supporting the construction of a highway interchange for their community. Each adult wrote at home, where the assessment materials were administered, with thirty minutes alloted for assignment completion. Almost one-third of the adults requested to write declined to do so, and this reluctance is reflected in the high percentage of inferior-quality papers of those who agreed to participate.

Test results. Test results revealed that rural and inner-city nine year olds have restricted vocabularies and limited ability in the construction of sentences. Simple sentence construction was used in most papers, and there was an inconsistency displayed in punctuation. Lower-quality papers were very short, with some being almost impossible to interpret.

In rural thirteen year olds, the higher-quality papers displayed a certain mastery of mechanics, but their expressions were limited in imagination and often conservative. Simple constructions and ideas were, for the most part, predominant in the writings. In rural seventeen year olds, a fairly sound grasp of the fundamentals of writing was displayed, but spelling errors were numerous. The major weaknesses were simple construction, ordinary language, and unremarkable ideas. Rural and inner-city adult writing reflected a more precise use of words, but there was minimal punctuation, and the simple sentences used were paragraphed in terse, journalistic style. The reluctance of respondents in this category to participate was reflected by a more than common number of papers of inferior quality.

Implications for educators. A comparison of the extreme rural and extreme inner-city composite statistics with those of the acceptable national median reveals a wide negative variance in writing performance. The implications of this lack of ability of students to express themselves may be more alarming than first apparent.[19] The intimacy that is inclined to humanize stems from communication. When there is an inability to communicate, a sense of isolation results, and a sense of the lack of power for self-assertion and self-expression that is a basic human need is apparent. In *Power and Innocence*, Rollo May says, "When an age is in the throes of profound transition, the first thing to disintegrate is language."[20] When language is corrupted, people lose faith in what is stated; and this leads to violence. Billy Budd is a case in point when at his trial, after he has killed the master-of-arms with his fist, he declares: "Could I have used my tongue I would not have struck him. . . . I could say it only with a blow." Since communication and violence are almost always mutually exclusive, a deficiency of the former may well increase the probability of the latter.

Minorities of whatever kind—community or racial—do not exist in isolation, and like it or not, whatever bell tolls for them tolls for us all. In the area of writing, where the psychological implications of deficiencies have been so clearly posed, rural schools and inner cities may wish to explore some dramatic measures to offset the effects of poor self-assertion that in some cases are already apparent.

Citizenship

The makers of the NAEP citizenship exercises were concerned that their assessment should mirror the achievement of nine major goals: to show concern for the welfare and dignity of others; to support rights and freedom for all individuals; to help maintain law and order; to know the main structure and functions of our government; to seek community improvement through active, democratic participation; to understand problems of international relations; to support rationality in communication, thought, and action on social problems; to take responsibility for personal development and obligations; to help and respect their own families; to nurture the development of their children as future citizens.

By far the largest percentage of respondents in the extreme rural group resided in communities with a population of less than 2,500, and a high proportion of their parents were farm workers. Results for all ages in the extreme rural groups, using the median differences on all tested, placed the respondents below the national median. The largest deviation was scored by the seventeen year old group. On most citizenship exercises, the extreme rural and extreme inner-city groups fell substantially below the national average—by 20 per cent or more in some cases.

Sample questions and test results. To test the goal of showing concern for the welfare and dignity of others, one exercise asked whether the respondent would be willing to "accept a person of a different race in most situations." Thirteen and seventeen year olds and adults from rural and inner-city areas scored below the nation as a whole. Fewer thirteen year olds from extreme rural areas indicated awareness of racial discrimination in the United States than did respondents from extreme affluent suburbs. National median differences for extreme rural students on race-related questions for thirteen year olds was −7.0 per cent; on non-race-related questions it was −4.0 per cent. For age seventeen it was −2.0 per cent on race-related questions and −9.0 per cent on non-race-related questions. For rural adults it was −3.0 per cent on race-related questions and −2.0 per cent on non-race-related questions. From 12 to 20 per cent fewer extreme rural respondents said they belonged to an organization opposing unequal opportunities than did inner-city and affluent suburb respondents.

The goal of supporting rights and freedom for all individuals assesses respondents' understanding of the value of constitutional rights and freedoms and their recognition of instances of the proper exercise or denial of constitutional rights and liberties of all people uniformly. An overview of this goal shows that extreme rural and extreme inner-city respondents showed the greatest deficit in relation to the nation as a whole, and the extreme affluent suburbs showed the greatest advantage. When asked whether a person on radio or television should be allowed to state three controversial beliefs ("Russia is better than the United States," "Some races of people are better than others," and "It is not necessary to believe in God"), fewer seventeen year olds and adults in the extreme rural and inner-city groups would allow a person on radio or television to make all three statements. When asked if they thought it was all right to tell other people that the governor or president is doing a bad job, fewer nine and thirteen year olds in rural and inner-city areas said yes than those in affluent suburbs.

On the goal of helping to maintain law and order, nearly all nine year olds in all groups indicated that rules are needed on the playground. In both the extreme rural group and the extreme affluent suburb, more nine year olds gave a reason why rules are needed on the playground than did nine year olds in the extreme inner-city. About 15 per cent fewer extreme inner-city nine year olds than those in rural areas and affluent suburbs thought adults needed rules and gave a reason. Fewer thirteen, seventeen, and adult age respondents in the rural areas stated that a dispute over money could be settled through the existing legal system than did extreme affluent suburb respondents. Fewer adults in the extreme rural and inner-city groups described an unjust or unfair law than did adults in the extreme affluent suburbs.

On the goal of knowing the main structure and functions of our government, the median difference as a whole was lower in rural and inner-city areas. Those exercises which drew more on general knowledge or experience than on information which would be learned in school showed adults in extreme rural and inner-city areas doing as well as all other adult groups. Ninety-eight per cent of adults in all types of communities knew the name of the current President of the United States, and nearly 75 per cent of adults in all types of communities could name civic groups which might want to either help accomplish or oppose a project.

On the goal of seeking community improvement through active, democratic participation, fewer nine year olds in the rural and inner-city areas as compared with the nation as a whole said they had taken part in a civic project in the past year. Fewer nine year olds in the extreme rural and inner-city groups said they had taken part in two or more projects at any time in the past. In the extreme rural groups, seventeen year olds were more likely to accomplish an assigned task in a democratic group of youngsters working together than were seventeen year olds in suburban and inner-city groups.

On the goal of understanding problems of international relations, the rural and inner-city respondents ranked below the median. The thirteen and seventeen year old and adult respondents in the extreme rural and inner-city groups showed less knowledge of wars and reasons for them than those in the extreme affluent suburbs. They were less able to name at least three countries in which fighting had occurred in the past twelve months or to give an explanation of what the fighting was about in a country.

On the goal of approaching civic decisions rationally, the deviation from the median for the rural and inner-city communities was below the national median. One of the exercises assessing recognition of problems asked respondents to choose from among four alternatives the correct answer to the question, "Which one is among the greatest problems of our large cities?" The correct answer was "inadequate transportation." Seventeen year olds in the extreme rural group were less likely to choose this alternative than were other age groups in any category.

On the goal of taking responsibility for one's own development, the deviation for rural and inner-city respondents on this goal as a whole was below the national median. Of rural adults, 20 per cent fewer said they had taken lessons or courses in the last two years. Twenty per cent fewer thirteen and seventeen year olds in the extreme rural groups than in the extreme inner-city said they had talked about plans for education or jobs with a teacher or a school counselor. Fewer rural and inner-city nine year olds than extreme affluent nine year olds named at least one magazine. Of rural and inner-city nine year olds, fewer than in the extreme affluent suburb group named at least three magazines. Of the nine year olds whose community had a library other than the school library, 20 per cent more in the extreme rural group than in the affluent suburbs or extreme inner-city said they had been to the library within the past week. Reading scores did not reflect this difference.

On the goal of helping and respecting their own families and nurturing the development of their children as future adult citizens, the deviation from the national median of these exercises as a whole was lower for rural and inner-city respondents. Of nine year olds in all types of communities, 98 per cent reported they had regular home duties. Fewer nine year olds in the extreme rural groups described something they had explained to a younger brother or sister in the last six months than did those in the extreme inner-city and extreme affluent suburb groups. Of the rural nine year olds, 15 per cent fewer than extreme affluent suburb nine year olds said that a younger brother or sister had sought their help in answer to a tough question in the past month, and 8 per cent fewer rural nine year olds than extreme inner city answered this question affirmatively. More adults in the extreme rural and extreme inner-city groups than in the extreme affluent suburb group said that they knew the favorite subject of their oldest child in school.

Implications for educators. It is immediately apparent from NAEP test results that extreme rural and inner-city groups in all age brackets fare considerably less well on exercises designed to assess their knowledge and practice of citizenship. Extreme rural and inner-city respondents do not appear to be nearly so concerned about protesting the rights of free speech and free assembly guaranteed all Americans by the Constitution as do their counterparts in most other areas of the nation. Neither do the rural and inner-city respondents seem as involved in efforts either to effect community change or to work together in civic improvement. In addition, rural and inner-city groups display a woeful lack of knowledge concerning the role of the United States in world affairs and wars in which this nation may possibly become involved. This latter fact seems particularly ironic since a disproportionate percentage of American soldiers killed or wounded in wars have been whites and nonwhites from rural and inner-city areas. Furthermore, limited rural and inner-city job opportunities make it possible that large numbers of an all-volunteer army may be drawn from these areas.

If one is to judge by the results of the NAEP assessment exercises, rural and inner-city schools are doing a seriously inadequate job in giving students formal information about the nature and goals of government at all levels. It is extremely doubtful that an individual of any age will take an interest or active part in carrying out civic duties if he or she does not know what these duties are. This lack of information can only lead to an ever-widening gulf between rural and inner-city citizens and their representatives in local, state, and national government.

A particularly startling fact is the scarcity of adequate school counseling services available to rural and inner-city adolescents. This deprivation might lead to a lack of information and a lack of encouragement on the part of authority figures, which in turn could lead to an inability to formulate and realize meaningful personal goals. No community, rural or otherwise, can long remain healthy if a large part of its youth is unmotivated because of academic failure and feels defeated at the start. The consequences to the general welfare in terms of both economics and morale are only too apparent.

Science

NAEP exercises used to assess science were constructed with specific objectives in mind. Those responsible for formulating the exercises agreed that students should know fundamental facts and principles of science and possess the abilities and skills to engage in the processes of science. Furthermore, it was thought that they should understand the investigative and explorative nature of science. Finally, students should have attitudes about and appreciation of scientists, science, and the consequences of science that stem from adequate understanding.

Sample of test questions. To test knowledge of the fundamental facts and principles of science, exercises using the following true-false questions were administered to nine year olds:

A human baby comes from its mother's body. A stick needs to be dry in order to burn. Teeth are brushed to keep them from decaying. Iron cannot be burned in an ordinary fire. Bees get their food (nectar) from flowers. Thick, dark-gray clouds are more likely than others to bring rain on a summer day. To see something, light must reach the eye. Scientists study fossils to determine what type of animals lived long ago. The sun and the penny are both made of atoms.

Similar questions, progressively more difficult, were also asked.

For age thirteen, exercises testing the ability and skills needed to engage in the processes of science contained task instructions based on such statements as the following.

From pictures showing three solids of the same size floating, determine which is heaviest. Interpret graphs showing the effect of different diets on guinea pigs. Use graphs and tabular data to determine the food needs of a dog. Time ten swings of a pendulum.

For age seventeen exercises testing understanding of the investigative nature of science required students to select the skill most useful in scientific research, and recognize that repeated measures of the same object will usually yield similar (but not exactly the same) results.

For Objective IV, having attitudes about and appreciation of scientists, science, and the consequences of science that stem from adequate understanding, young adults were asked to respond to exercise statements such as the following.

United States scientists are ahead of scientists in other countries in every field of research. If you learn about a special television program dealing with a scientific project, do you watch it?

Test results. *National Assessment Report 7, Group Results B* of the NAEP Science test were released in May 1973. Introductory comments recommended the exercise of caution in drawing conclusions from the data. The reason for this call for caution was strong evidence that a wide variety of factors might be involved which would significantly affect unadjusted findings and which were not measured by the NAEP exercises. Some examples of factors not measured are (1) attitude toward learning by family and peers, (2) innate intelligence, (3)

state of physical health and quality of nutrition, (4) school and neighborhood learning environment, and (5) personal attitude of student toward the relevance of education. Since these important variables were not measured, analysis may attribute to some factors things that are due to other factors or variables. Thus conclusive determination of causation cannot justifiably be made. Also, the factors used are measured only in course subgroupings and with certain margins of error.

Refining the category of size and type of community more precisely, the NAEP report on science defines "extreme rural" as students in schools where a high proportion of parents are farm workers. "Extreme inner-city," too, is a more refined classification. A school was classified as extreme inner-city if students' parents were (1) not regularly employed, (2) on welfare, or (3) characterized by only a small proportion holding professional or managerial positions.

In the median effect (difference between the per cent correct for the subgroup and the national per cent correct), the gap between the extreme affluent suburb and both the extreme inner-city and the extreme rural is the largest between community units compared. In the extreme rural subgroup comparisons, nine year olds test −6.3 per cent, thirteen year olds test −6.1 per cent, seventeen year olds test −3.5 per cent, and adults test −4.7 per cent when compared with the national average in per cent correct. In extreme inner city, the results are still lower. Nine year olds test −15.1 per cent, thirteen year olds test −13.7 per cent, seventeen year olds test −7.4 per cent, and adults test −10.2 per cent compared with the national average in per cent correct. While both extreme rural and extreme inner-city exhibit low scores by national comparison, some marked differences have been noted between the two. In the seventeen year old extreme inner city group, students perform relatively better in biological science, and the extreme rural students are better in physical science.

A summary chart of extreme rural comparisons for all science exercises at all four ages reveals that in 145 exercises administered to nine year old extreme rural students, their median difference was −6.3 per cent. In 122 exercises administered to seventeen year olds, their median difference was −3.5 per cent. In

119 exercises given to adults, their median difference was −4.7 per cent. Despite whatever other factors and variables may be involved, extreme inner-city and extreme rural communities display significantly lower scores on the NAEP science exercises than all others tested.

Implications for educators. Implications of the low test results of the extreme rural and inner-city segments of the population are disheartening. In a culture which is becoming increasingly technological, a poor foundation in the area of science seriously handicaps our understanding the world or seeking work within it. An analysis of the dilemma reveals that this problem, if unremediated, becomes circular. Without the academic bases to pursue a competitive career, an inferior job is acquired, keeping the economic level of the rural and inner-city population depressed. The inadequate income derived from an inferior job is a thwarting factor in pursuing post-high school vocational training and higher education for the student or young adult now, and for his children later. This results in a low level of education. A low level of parental education has been isolated as one of the factors which relates negatively to student achievement. And thus we see the dilemma perpetuate itself.

It is hoped that NAEP results will serve a purpose beyond offering a different color of band-aid for the long-recognized boil of deficient and inequitable education. Diagnosis is an important part of treatment, but unless aroused rural and inner-city communities make themselves heard in the surgical rooms of fund-slicing, their children may continue to function at fractional productivity that will ultimately have a negative effect on both the national economy and personal self-esteem.

Literature

The NAEP exercises formulated to test literature were constructed with rather broad objectives in mind: that students should read literature of excellence; that they should become engaged in, find meaning in, and evaluate works of literature; and that they should develop a continuing interest and participation in literature and literary experience.

The nine year old group was expected to recognize children's classics, such as *Mother Goose*, *Winnie the Pooh*, *Child's Garden of Verses*, *Mary Poppins*, and *Dr. Seuss* stories. Students in the age thirteen group were expected to recognize such works as *The Jungle Book*, *Tom Sawyer*, *Charlotte's Web*, and *Benet's Book of the Americans*. Age seventeen students were expected to recognize typical passages of Shakespeare, and of authors such as Pope, Swift, Whitman, Frost, e. e. cummings, and Keats. To be considered at a desirable level, students were expected to have knowledge of the major literary or cultural figures and themes from Western civilization. Nine year olds were expected to know some of the common Biblical figures. Age thirteen students were expected to know most of the common Biblical figures, Ichabod Crane, Rip van Winkle, Robin Hood, and the legends of Jason and Odysseus. Seventeen year olds were expected to have knowledge of Hamlet, Captain Ahab, Don Quixote, and the Odyssey.

The literature exercises of the NAEP program consisted of four theme sections: (1) understanding imaginative language, (2) responding to literature, (3) recognizing literary works and characters, and (4) a survey of reading habits. Exercises covered in Themes I and II related to the objective of finding meaning in and evaluating works of literature. Theme III exercises measured the objective of reading literature of excellence. Theme IV questions centered upon the objective of developing a continuing interest and participation in literature and literary experience.

Sample of test questions. Theme I exercises were of five kinds: missing-line exercises, designed to assess rudimentary skill in following rhythm or logic (or both) in poetry; pun exercises, designed to determine ability to recognize puns in passages which may or may not contain puns; metaphor exercises, which assess recognition of tenor and vehicle of specific metaphors in poems; form similarity exercises, requiring respondents to identify similar passages and choose the genre which best describes them; and inference exercises, requiring identification of the tone or mood of a passage and a written defense of the answer.

Theme II data evidently did not lend themselves to a comparison of the various groups in the categories of Size and Type of Community.

Theme III used five types of exercises to

assess different kinds of recognition of literary works. The first presented the student with a picture from a well-known nursery rhyme, story, or poem and asked what work it illustrated. The second consisted of parodies of famous poems, for example, "The Village Blacksmith," "The Charge of the Light Brigade," and "Sea Fever," with instructions to identify the source of the parody. The third type of exercise presented the respondent with an allusion to some literary work or figure and asked for identification of the allusion. The fourth presented students with a disguised myth or story pattern and asked for identification of its source. The fifth consisted of straightforward questions about specific figures and works of literature.

Theme IV contained two kinds of exercises. The first was formulated to determine attitudes toward literary instruction. The second was designed to discover how often respondents read and what types of literature they selected.

Test results. On Theme I, the extreme rural and inner-city groups scored below the national median. Theme II comparative data by size and type of community was not furnished. On Theme III, the extreme rural and inner-city median differences were below the national median. On Theme IV, the rural and inner-city groups scored below the national median.

On test results by objective, the following information was compiled. On the first objective, to read literature of excellence, rural and inner-city respondents scored below the national median. On the second objective, to become engaged in, find meaning in, and evaluate a work of literature, rural and inner-city respondents scored below the national median. On the third objective, develop a continuing interest and participation in literature and the literary experience, rural and inner-city respondents scored below the national median.

Implications for educators. It would appear from the results of the NAEP literature exercises that in the encouragement of their students to read, rural teachers of literature in nine, thirteen, and seventeen year old age groups are doing only slightly less well than their counterparts in other areas. An exception is Theme IV, in which inner-city schools ranked above rural schools in the category tested. It is also apparent from the test results that rural students spend a significant part of their time with books. This fact is borne out by information given in another part of the assessment data, which indicates that rural students visit their libraries more often than students in other types of communities in the nation.

At the same time one feels justified in concluding that teachers of literature in rural and inner-city areas are neither acquainting their students with great works of literature nor supplying them with a key to the evaluation and understanding of such universal representatives. It is a simple matter to assess the implications of the students' literary deprivation. If most extreme rural and inner-city teachers are themselves products of inadequate schools, there is the possibility that a sensitivity to great literature was not cultivated in them at an early age. It is questionable whether acquaintanceship with great literature at the university level will automatically bring with it the affective response desirable in teachers of literature. It would appear that the quality of library selection in rural and inner-city areas, in both school and community libraries, needs to be seriously reviewed and upgraded. The quality of newspapers, magazines, movies, television programs, and performing arts also affect literary expression and comprehension.

It is perhaps in great literature that our highest qualities are awakened and cultivated. Affective responses to oneself, to other human beings, and to nature and the universe are called forth through the medium of a great writer's thoughts and feelings. Often profound knowledge of and empathy with other races, other cultures, and other value systems are brought to the student by the single line of a great poet. To deprive a community of these inestimable rewards of sensitivity to fine literature is to sever it from the manifold world which comprises the life of human beings. An even more tragic result of such a deprivation is that people without empathy are somehow less than human in their callousness to others. If it is true that people define themselves by their language, then a community may be characterized by its ability to express ideas and feelings. Without a high degree of expression, meaningful communication is lost; and a community without real communication between its members is a contradiction in terms.

CONCLUSIONS

Although curriculum design and development are not a part of national assessment, "the assessment will be useful only if it provides helpful information about the progress of education that public-spirited lay citizens can understand and accept."[21] The responsibility for interpreting and using national assessment results rests with parents, educators, school board members, and professional organizations. Failure to improve the quality of education will have far-reaching social, psychological, cultural, economic, political, and military implications.

Social and Psychological Implications

NAEP test results have corroborated the conclusion that differences in education have resulted in social stratification. Rural and inner-city communities, which test below the national average in every area, are of course negatively affected by inferior education which forces their graduates into low-paying jobs and the attendant social circumstances. Two questions arise now that national assessment has separated problems by population—what social and psychological symptoms will appear, and how are they likely to be resolved?

Education is an academic sword that can be wielded to prune, to wound, to amputate, or if undrawn, to let fragile minds fend for themselves. Which of these functions, either singly or in combination, is responsible for the educational plight of rural and inner-city communities? This question must be explored at once. If steps are not taken to assure a more egalitarian result from our educational system, our democratic social structure stands to suffer.

Should this trend continue, public school education as we know it may disappear into homebound audiovisual instruction for some, vocational training to supply increasing indus-

trial demands for others, and a private-school intelligentsia created from the children of the elite. The middle class in our social structure would diminish in direct proportion to such public education attrition; class polarization would become more clearly defined. NAEP results reveal a current imbalance that holds the psychological seeds of protest. Socially and psychologically alienated persons in a state of social abuse revert to much in themselves that is animal. In *The Face of Violence,* Jacob Bronowski warns:

The love of violence is, to me, the ancient and symbolic gesture of man against the constraints of society. Vicious men can exploit the impulse, but it is a disaster to treat the impulse as vicious. For no society is strong that does not acknowledge protesting man; and no man is human who does not draw strength from the natural animal. Violence is the sphinx by the fireside, and she has a human face.[22]

Cultural Implications

One is tempted from the NAEP assessment to compare the affluent suburban school to a sun whose rays emanate with ever-diminishing strength to its satellites. Nowhere is this effect more obvious than in those subject areas dealing with the transmission of the heritage of beauty which is ours from past ages. Refinement of language, cultivation of aesthetic response, and desire to create are all objectives which the school can and should foster in order to give each student an appreciation of those values which are the glory of Western civilization. But more than just an appreciation of the past, a knowledge of the classics helps to clarify today's realities and to encourage creativity both today and tomorrow. To neglect the development of the affective responses of the young in a rapidly changing world is to invite violence, emotional disturbance, and cultural disintegration.

It would appear from the results of the NAEP assessment that many of those works of literature judged to be classics by both educational authorities and testmakers are not relevant to the experience of either the rural or the inner-city student. Of the five areas examined in this chapter, it is the literature assessment exercises which one is most likely to judge as culturally biased. Nevertheless, the fact remains that a sizeable portion of the American student population, for whatever reason, is being deprived of many of those aesthetic joys which are daily being nurtured in more fortunate youngsters.

While NAEP results show that rural students may visit their library more often and may spend more free time in reading than students in other areas of the nation, it is apparent from other NAEP assessment statistics that the quality of their reading does substantially less to broaden their horizons, develop their writing and reading skills, and cultivate their aesthetic responses than does the reading matter of students in affluent suburb areas. In fact it might be concluded that instead of contributing to their affective growth, much of their reading material makes few demands on their own thoughts and feelings. Worse still, most of the books they are inclined to read may give them a distorted view of the thoughts and feelings of others.

We do not need the NAEP assessment results to tell us that the average rural and inner-city student's opportunities to visit a great museum, hear a fine musician, converse with an inspiring poet, or enjoy a professional drama group are far fewer than for any counterpart in the rest of the nation. Plato suggested that the child's education should begin with continuous experiences of the Beautiful, so that as he develops he will associate all learning with pleasure. If we seek the cause for the comparative failure of rural and inner-city children in education, we might do well to examine seriously their affective deprivation.

Economic Implications

Few educators today would question that the period since World War II in the United States has been one of ever-increasing correlation between formal education and economic status. Current American history books still devote at least one chapter to extolling those native-born and immigrant citizens who became wealthy, influential, and beloved, though born in humble surroundings in which there was little opportunity for more than the most

rudimentary learning. That world of economic mobility is as far removed from today's reality as the world of log cabins and prairie schooners. Yet it is largely upon these same economic myths that American public education, at least at the elementary and secondary levels, still rests.

If economic status is conditioned by formal education to an appreciable degree, then it is obvious from the NAEP assessment that rural and inner-city students who are inspired by such myths compete under a crippling burden of inequality when compared to their affluent suburban counterparts. The rural or inner-city child, if one is to judge correctly from the NAEP assessment, will do well if he or she manages to secure and hold a blue-collar job, let alone find employment in the decreasing job markets of rural and inner-city America. Attempting to find work which will allow them to rise above their parents economically and give their children certain fundamental benefits, rural people often start at a place on the educational ladder only very slightly above that of the inner-city inhabitant. In the struggle for upward economic mobility, both rural and inner-city children begin, whatever their native gifts, at an educational disadvantage when compared to those in small cities, medium cities, suburban areas, and non-inner cities.

It would appear from the NAEP assessment that it is more likely that rural and inner-city students will become unskilled workers than computer programmers, and far more likely that they will work for someone else than manage their own business or pursue a profession. The prospects for their children cannot be much brighter and may be even more bleak. At a manifest disadvantage in the skills of reading and writing, relatively untutored in basic science, and less interested in civic matters than most others, they have become institutionalized failures.

Political Implications

Political writers and commentators never seem to tire of telling the American people that true democracy rests with an informed public. If this is true, the NAEP assessment should make us anxious about the future of representative government. Below the national average in reading, rural and inner-city students, one may conclude, are less likely to read those publications which can give them the facts which enable them to make informed political decisions and to work for governmental change. Deficient in writing skills, they can be expected to write few, if any, letters to their local newspaper to draw attention to a problem which affects their lives and the lives of their children. Less concerned with civic participation than other people and alarmingly willing to deny others their constitutional liberties, the average rural and inner-city respondent, according to the NAEP assessment, is a predictable target for the political candidate who promises simple solutions to complex problems. The uneducated and uninformed tend to allow others to analyze, synthesize, and make political decisions and opinions for them.

Citizens who are unaware of their rights or too unschooled in political techniques to protect them are obviously vulnerable to others who seek to manipulate them. The key to participatory democracy is found in traditional political channels; yet if these channels are not used by certain segments of our population because of lack of knowledge, the concept of democracy is at best an unfulfilled dream. Unable or unwilling to become involved in the democratic process, rural and inner-city inhabitants are more likely than their counterparts in most other areas to leave untapped their collective powers which, when exercised properly, could lead to more control of their local, state, and national governments.

The NAEP results can serve as a caution that in education all elements of our society are not being adequately served and can define those elements so that local and state agencies can seek remediation. In a democracy, where an informed constituency is requisite for stable self-government, the political implications of neglecting population pockets can readily be seen. Demagoguery, not democracy, is served by an educational system that fails in the instruction of its young. The rural pariahs of education today, as identified by NAEP, could well become the activistic malcontents of tomorrow. Those of opposing political persuasions will not ignore this data, nor dare we. Rabindranath Tagore said, "Power takes as ingratitude the writhing of its victims."[23] National assessment is serving the purpose of identifying the educational victims. Let us hope that we do not take the mistaken attitude of power.

Military Implications

An overall examination and synthesis of the NAEP data reveal that some serious military consequences may inhere. One vital force of a national government is the military troops that protect it. Test data from our armed forces have long indicated that large numbers of American young men and women are denied an opportunity to serve because of academic deficiencies, often when other forms of employment are not open to them. NAEP reports verify how profoundly true this is for those dwelling in rural and inner-city communities.

Rural and inner-city seventeen year olds, in comparison with the national median, rank low in reading, writing, science, literature, and citizenship. At the local level, the test results imply that a high status job in the military is not available because of educational deficiencies, to those youths who, by desire or because they lack other options, might choose it. At the national level, the verification by NAEP of the rural and inner-city community's unacceptable academic rating has implications that are twofold: (1) the armed forces will not be proportionately representative of national population elements, and (2) such exclusion of particular population segments tends to stratify or create caste grooves that are detrimental to a democracy.

The national assessment data can help teachers determine whether or not their expectations of educational attainment are being met on a local, regional, or national level. However, at no time should teachers feel obligated to restructure their lesson plans to accommodate national assessment test items. Basic to improving the quality of education is the ability to focus on early childhood education and to recruit and retain competent teachers. Furthermore, parents must become more involved in the entire educational process, including curriculum evaluation.

On the basis of the assessment data collected to date, several recommendations seem appropriate. First, school districts should create skills laboratories in which students are shown a clear need to learn a specific skill. Second, classroom activities should be structured to provide opportunities for communication. All teachers should encourage their students to use and develop their speaking, reading, and writing abilities. Each teacher should have fre-quent, individual conferences with students and parents. Finally, within the classroom the major emphasis should be placed upon both the affective and the cognitive dimensions of learning.

PERSONAL GROWTH GOALS

Review your human relations skills (see Exercise after Chapter 4) and select two or three goals that are important to you. Now focus on strategies for achieving these goals. Basically, the steps for achieving personal goals are:

1. Set your goals.
2. Analyze the factors that support or block your goal achievement.
3. Plan ways to lessen the effect of the blocking forces and still maintain the supporting forces. (Set realistic time targets.)
4. Experiment with new behavior and evaluate its effectiveness.

Factors That Support Your Personal Growth Goals

Factors in self:

Factors in others:

Factors in the school situation:

Factors That Block Your Personal Growth Goals

Factors in self:

Factors in others:

Factors in the school situation:

ADDITIONAL READINGS

Barr, Donald. *Who Pushed Humpty Dumpty? Dilemmas in American Education Today.* New York, Atheneum, 1971.

Banks, Olive and Douglas Finlayson. *Success and Failure in the Secondary School: An Interdisciplinary Approach to School Achievement.* New York, Harper & Row, 1973.

Bestor, Arthur E. *Educational Wastelands: The Retreat from Learning in Our Public Schools.* Urbana, University of Illinois Press, 1953.

Blackie, John H. *Transforming the Primary School.* New York, Schocken Books, 1974.

Dexter, Lewis A. *The Tyranny of Schooling: An Inquiry into the Problem of "Stupidity".* New York, Basic Books, 1964.

Dreeban, Robert. *On What Is Learned in School.* Reading, Mass., Addison-Wesley, 1968.

Ediger, Marlow. *Relevancy in the Elementary Curriculum.* Kirksville, Mo., Simpson, 1975.

Kirk, Samuel A. *Educating Exceptional Children,* 2d ed. Boston, Houghton Mifflin, 1972.

Kim, Eugene C. and Richard D. Kellough. *A Resource Guide for Secondary School Teaching: Planning for Competence.* New York, Macmillan, 1974.

Moore, Opal. *Why Johnny Can't Learn.* Milford, Mich., Mott Media, 1975.

O'Neill, William F. *Readin, Ritin, and Rafferty: A Study of Educational Fundamentalism.* Berkeley, Cal., Glendessary Press, 1969.

Schwebel, Milton. *Who Can Be Educated?* New York, Grove Press, 1968.

NOTES

1. Alex M. Mood, "National Assessment," *American Education*, 3 (April, 1967), 12.

2. Traxel Stevens, "National Assessment: Vital Need or Dirty Word?" *Texas Outlook*, 53 (April, 1969), 20.

3. Carmen J. Finley and Frances S. Berdie, *The National Assessment Approach to Exercise Development* (Ann Arbor, National Assessment of Educational Progress, 1970), 3.

4. Ralph W. Tyler, "Assessing the Progress of Education," *Science Education*, 50 (1966), 239.

5. Ralph W. Tyler, "Let's Clear the Air on Assessing Education," *Nation's Schools*, 77 (February, 1966), 69.

6. Lawrence Beymer, "Pros and Cons of the National Assessment Project," *Clearing House*, 40 (May, 1966), 540–541.

7. William H. Fisher, "National Testing—Its Correct Name," *Educational Leadership*, 23 (May, 1966), 619.

8. Galen Saylor, "National Assessment: Pro and Con," *Record*, 71 (May, 1970), 595.

9. Wayne P. Mollenberg, "National Assessment: Are We Ready?" *Clearing House*, 43 (April, 1969), 453.

10. Harold Spears, "Official Report" of the American Association of School Administrators, February 12, 1966, 28.

11. Saylor, "National Assessment," 592.

12. J. Raymond Gerberich, "Assessment: A Forward Look," *Educational Leadership*, 24 (November, 1966), 116.

13. Spears, "Official Report," 27–28.

14. Calvin Grieder, "Assess U. S. Education, But Don't Use Tests To Do It," *Nation's Schools*, 76 (November, 1965), 10.

15. Beymer, "Pros and Cons."

16. Martin Mayer, "Stop Waiting for Miracles," *PTA Magazine*, 61 (November, 1966), 23.

17. George Henderson (ed.), *America's Other Children: Public Schools Outside Surburbia* (Norman, University of Oklahoma Press 1971), 163–173.

18. National Assessment of Educational Progress, *National Assessment Report 8: Writing* (Denver, Education Commission of the States, 1972), 18.

19. Edmund J. Farrell, "Implications of National Assessment Writing Results," *English Journal*, 60 (November, 1971), 1116.

20. Rollo May, *Power and Innocence* (New York, W. W. Norton, 1972), 65.

21. Tyler, "Assessing the Progress of Education."

22. Jacob Bronowski, *The Face of Violence* (Cleveland, World, 1967), 6.

23. Rabindranath Tagore, *Collected Form of Plays of Rabindranath Tagore* (New York, Macmillan, 1966), 245.

9.
SCHOOL DESEGREGATION

As the movement of affluent whites and non-whites to the suburbs continues, many of the nation's big-city and rural school systems are being left without an adequate tax base. Instructional expenditures are distributed unequally, and less is spent on nonwhite and poor students than on other students. The most inexperienced teachers are generally found in schools attended by predominantly low-income children. Analyses of school physical plants—as measured by age of buildings, size of grounds, and presence of special facilities—suggests that the allocation of physical resources is also influenced by the economic characteristics of the neighborhood. Economic and racial desegregation are advocated as means of abating these inequities.

OVERVIEW

Although the United States was established by immigrants from many nations, it has always had minority problems. Theoretically this amalgam of disparate human components offered the promise of a truly great society, but practically it presents many divisive dilemmas.[1]

The problem for those who want to resolve these dilemmas is how to move beyond theory and into reality with specific plans for social reconstruction. The melting-pot method of acculturizing ethnic minorities has been psychologically disabling to those it endeavored to assimilate. We must overcome, as Francis T. Villemain writes, the popular belief that "democracy is held to be an ineffective conception for removing cultural disparities; presumably it is a tool for subjugating and exploiting certain ethnic groups."[2]

It was not until the latter part of the nineteenth century that Anglo-Saxon domination, which saw the absorption of other nationalities under the melting pot philosophy, was seriously questioned. One early group which took exception to this oversimplified solution to minority problems was the rebellious Catholic minority.

As the Common School movement after 1830 began to pick up impetus, it was seen as a natural facilitator of the Americanization process. The Irish and German Catholics coming into America after 1840 were immediately subject to the English linguistic and Protestant religious orthodoxy now perpetuated by the public schools. The historical result of this early clash over the issue of religious pluralism was the setting up of the Catholic parochial school system, with its eventual vindication in the famous Oregon *decision of 1925.*[3]

The obsession with superimposing Anglo-Saxon values on the new immigrants crested after 1870 and resulted in the bitter denigration of the values and cultures of newcomers arriving from southern and eastern Europe. The attitude persisted that the higher values of the Anglo-Saxons were being dissipated by the cultures of the Slavs, Poles, and Italians. Thus it is apparent that from very early times in America, human differences were not valued as enriching condiments to be preserved for variety and flavor but rather were disparaged as contrary to the homogeneity that many scholars believed a necessary prerequisite to a powerful and orderly nation.

But a few writers disagreed with the assimilationist view of melting-pot theorists. They advanced the view that democracy might be enriched by a pluralistic vision of the American ideal.

There is no such thing as humanity in general, into which the definite, heterogeneous, living creature can be melted down. . . . There is no human mould in America to which the spiritual stuff of the immigrant is to be patterned. Not only is there as yet no fixed and final type, but there never can be. . . . The very genius of democracy, moreover, must lead us to desire the widest possible range of variability, the greatest attainable differentiation of individuality, among our population. . . . The business of America is to get rid of mechanical uniformity, and by encouraging the utmost possible differentiation through mental and psychic cross-fertilization to attain a higher level of humanity. [4]

Inspired and incited to activity by this minority sense of human purpose, the leadership of various ethnic minorities came to insist upon a greater equality of cultural values in all our institutions, and most particularly in the schools.

It is almost a cliché today to state that the American educational system has largely failed in its efforts to educate the children of oppressed minority groups. The schools, as representatives of the larger society, virtually ignore the values of these groups, while embracing the perspective of the "White, Anglo-Saxon Ideal." Thus there appears to be a direct relationship between the degree to which a group's values, norms, and standards are excluded from the dominant values of the society, and the failure of the society's schools to educate its members. Apparently the schools, as subsystems of the larger societal system, reflect the dominant trends of the society vis-a-vis *its powerless minorities.* [5]

Since the late 1960s, the once tacitly agreed upon goal of assimilation for minorities has been widely disputed. From that dispute has arisen in minorities a new pride in their own ancestry, cultural contributions, and potential to enrich the emptiness growing out of modern technology and its consequent disaffection and alienation. "One of the most important recent developments in American race rela-

tions is the emerging sense of group pride that is increasingly expressed by racial minority and national origin groups," Edgar C. Epps wrote. "Black power, Chicano power and Native American power movements have stirred the ethnic consciousness of other groups." [6] In question now is the role the school can and will play in ensuring that this pride reaches fruition in the creative development of both minority—and majority—students.

It is the general consensus among educators that schools cannot be isolated from the societies that created them. Moreover if society is to escape the human losses that accrue from past class bias and racist prejudice, a new perspective of racial and cultural pluralism must become a sympathetically projected part of teachers, counselors, community, and curriculum models.

Authorities are in basic agreement that desegregation, better teaching, more equitable allocation of educational resources, and curriculum that reflects the goals of cultural pluralism are steps in the right direction if we are to cease being a segregated society. Before much progress can be made in attitude modification (which ultimately is required before such changes can be fully accepted), it is necessary to deal with the theoretical explanations of minority-group underachievement in our schools.

Minority-Group Underachievement

Most theories offered in explanation of underachievement can be subsumed under five categories: (1) biological or racial, (2) physiological, (3) demographic, (4) psychological, and (5) cultural.

Probably the oldest and most prevalent of these explanations is the biological or racial explanation of minority underachievement. This explanation, in either crude or sophisticated forms, is racist in its assertion that Black and other oppressed minority-group children tend to achieve below whites because of genetic inferiority to whites. (See the last section of Chapter 14.)

C. A. Valentine asserts that "any theory of class or racial deficits of biological inferiority is undemonstrable and scientifically untestable in an ethnically plural and structurally discriminatory so-

Table 11. Per Cent of Persons Not Enrolled in School and Not High School Graduates, by Age, Race/Ethnic Origin, and Sex: October 1974

Race/ethnic origin and sex	Total, 14 to 34 years	Age						
		14 and 15 years	16 and 17 years	18 and 19 years	20 and 21 years	22 to 24 years	25 to 29 years	30 to 34 years
All races:								
Total	14.6	2.0	9.4	16.6	15.9	15.3	16.1	21.7
Male	14.0	2.0	9.2	18.7	15.7	13.9	14.7	20.7
Female	15.2	2.0	9.6	14.7	16.0	16.5	17.5	22.6
White:								
Total	13.6	1.8	9.3	15.6	14.3	13.8	14.9	20.0
Male	13.2	1.8	9.4	17.4	14.4	12.9	13.8	19.4
Female	13.9	1.9	9.1	13.9	14.2	14.7	15.9	20.5
Black:								
Total	22.2	3.0	10.4	23.4	26.1	25.8	26.4	36.2
Male	20.6	3.9	8.3	26.9	25.1	22.6	23.9	34.0
Female	23.6	2.1	12.6	20.2	26.9	28.3	28.5	37.9
Spanish Origin:								
Total	35.2	3.9	20.2	29.8	35.1	43.8	45.9	54.4
Male	34.2	2.1	19.6	35.1	39.0	41.3	41.9	55.5
Female	36.1	5.9	20.8	25.1	31.5	46.2	50.1	53.5

SOURCE: U. S. Department of Commerce, Bureau of the Census, *Current Population Reports*, Series P–20, NO. 278.

ciety." The necessary separation of biological and socio-cultural factors is methodologically impossible in such a setting. Kenneth Clark points out a most obvious flaw not previously highlighted, namely that these theories do not explain the fact that low-income white students in the South and in urban public schools are also, on the average, consistently regarded lower in academic subjects.[7]

Physiological theories emphasize neurological and sensory deficiencies; that is, academic retardation in minority groups is a by-product of poverty and deprivation.

There is evidence . . . that even in extreme cases of obvious mental retardation and organic brain damage, when such children are taught in a supportive educational situation by teachers who accept them, they make striking gains, both educational and personal. There is danger in attributing academic retardation among oppressed minority group children to physiological causes in view of the prevalence of educational underachievement in this group and the present ambiguity in diagnosis of mental deficiencies. It is a simple matter to substitute physiological deficit for genetic inferior-

ity in day-to-day operations. In either case, low academic achievement is viewed as irremediable.[8]

In explaining educational underachievement of minorities, demographic theories focus on where children live and where they go to school. Authorities have pointed out that the academic performance of nonwhite children tends to increase after they attend previously all-white schools. It has also been asserted that Black students born in the northern part of the United States score higher on IQ tests than their newly arrived counterparts from the southern part of the country. However:

in recent years the evidence suggests that there is no difference in educational achievement between those black children who spend all their lives in northern inner-city urban schools and those who migrated from the South. However, there is still a North-South difference in average achievement scores of both black and white children.[9]

Psychological explanations stress factors such as individual motivation, self-image, delay of gratification, anxiety, and achievement expectancy. Authorities who defend psychological explanations as the reason for underachievement in minority groups emphasize that "lower-status children are low in achievement motivation, have unrealistically high aspiration levels, have incomplete or inadequate self-images, have negative self-images and a preference for things white, have an inability to delay gratification, and are frustrated when required to learn or held to high educational standards."[10] Conversely, there are those who contend that it is possible that rather than academic retardation being the consequence of motivational and behavioral handicaps that the reverse may be true: educational deprivation and social rejection precede the consequence of motivational and behavioral deficiencies.

The cultural explanation for underachievement in minority groups emphasizes cultural and social-class differences as primary factors precipitating the failure to learn. Some specific environmental features cited as inhibiting learning are neighborhood crime and delinquency, broken homes, inadequate morning meals and rest, no place to study, overcrowded living quarters, deteriorated and unsanitary housing, no books in the home, strong peer influence, and rejected linguistic patterns.

Of the five explanations for underachievement, only the biological or racial explanation lacks much credence. Physiological, demographic, psychological, and cultural factors have been sparsely documented as significantly affecting school achievement.

None of our theories, however, adequately explain the disproportionate number of low-income children who succeed as athletes despite inadequate physiological, sociocultural, and environmental conditions. If malnourished, shabbily dressed, and poorly housed students can learn to make winning touchdowns, baskets, jumps, and base hits, why can't the same proportion of them learn basic academic skills? The maintenance of cultural identity is not synonymous with perpetuation of academic or athletic superiority—all ethnic groups can be characterized by excellence in both endeavors. Therefore a culturally pluralistic school will have students of all ethnic groups performing well in all activities considered an integral part of the curriculum.

The basic factors of influence within the school that can establish and maintain cultural pluralism are administrators, teachers, counselors, curriculum and textbooks, and general ethnic programming strategies.

RACIAL DESEGREGATION IN THE PUBLIC SCHOOLS

Racial segregation parallels poverty as the most explosive issue of our time. While we are accelerating our efforts to abolish poverty, racial desegregation is taking place much more slowly. Population growth and urbanization, accompanied by the exodus of white citizens to the suburbs, have resulted in most Americans living in segregated communities where race is the major criterion for residence. This is not solely a Black versus white issue; concentrations of other groups are vividly illustrated by Mexican-American and American Indian communities in the Southwest and Puerto Rican communities in New York. These segregated communities produce racial isolation of our schools, which in turn perpetuates prejudicial attitudes and behaviors.

On May 17, 1954 the U. S. Supreme Court ruled unanimously in *Brown et al. v. the Board of Education of Topeka et al.* (347 U.S. 483) that the United States Consitution is violated when a state operates racially segregated public schools. Segregationists reacted to the decision with a combination of frustration, resentment, anger, and resignation. Civil rights advocates, on the other hand, hailed the decision as a giant step toward equal education opportunities for all people. Certain earlier Supreme Court decisions and the Civil Rights Act of 1964 also are important legal foundations for efforts to desegregate the public schools.

Supreme Court Cases

The seeds of the *Brown* case were sown in 1896 in the *Plessy v. Ferguson* (163 U.S. 537) case. Its issue was whether a state could, without violating the equal protection clause of the Consitution, require by law that passengers in railroad cars be segregated according to race. Louisiana provided "separate but equal" railroad accommodations for Black and white passengers. The Supreme Court upheld the statute, asserting that the Fourteenth Amendment had intended to accord political but not social equality to Blacks.

In the only dissenting opinion, Justice John Marshall Harlan said:

Our Constitution is color-blind, and neither knows nor tolerates classes among citizens. In respect of civil rights, all citizens are equal before the law. The humblest is the peer of the most powerful. The law regards man as man, and takes no account of his surroundings or of his color when his civil rights as guaranteed by the supreme law of the land are involved.[11]

Harlan argued that the *Plessy* decision did not merely sanction an existing practice of racial segregation but also placed the stamp of judicial approval on all types of racial segregation. Indeed, the *Plessy* doctrine did just that.

The first major departure from approval of separate but equal practices came in two key cases. In 1938 the Supreme Court ruled in *Gaines v. University of Missouri* (305 U. S. 337) that Missouri was not providing Blacks with equal professional education by paying for them to attend law school outside the state. The state responded by setting up a separate law school for Blacks in St. Louis. The Court issued a similar ruling in 1948 in *Sipuel v. Board of Regents of the University of Oklahoma.* (332 U. S. 631). Oklahoma, however, decided to admit Blacks to its regular law school rather than establish a separate Black institution.

Most jurists agree that the *Brown* decision is one of the most spectacular and significant judicial decisions of the century. In essence the Supreme Court reversed the *Plessy* decision, ruling that racial segregation of children in the public schools denies them equal protection of the laws guaranteed by the Fourteenth Amendment. Chief Justice Earl Warren wrote:

1. The history of the Fourteenth Amendment is inconclusive as to its intended effect on public education.

2. The question presented in these cases must be determined, not on the basis of conditions existing when the Fourteenth Amendment was adopted, but in the light of the full development of public education and its present place in American life throughout the Nation.

3. Where a state has undertaken to provide an opportunity for an education in its public schools,

such an opportunity is a right which must be made available to all on equal terms.

4. Segregation of children in public schools solely on the basis of race deprives children of the minority groups of equal educational opportunities, even though the physical facilities and other "tangible" factors may be equal.

5. The "separate but equal" doctrine adopted in Plessy v. Ferguson, 163 U.S. 537, has no place in the field of public education.[12]

The Court's opinion was not cluttered with legal citations. Instead it was based on the belief that human rights should transcend legal precedents. For the first time in the history of a country's highest court, a child's social growth and development overshadowed court precedents and procedures.

The period since the *Brown* decision has been sprinkled with U. S. Supreme Court rulings aimed at clarifying the school desegregation issues. In 1968 the Court ruled in *Green v. New Kent County, Virginia* (391 U. S. 430) that "the burden on a school board today is to come forward with a (desegregation) plan that promises realistically to work *now.*" In its order the Court called for a system without "white" schools or "Negro" schools, but only "schools."

In 1969 the Court ruled in *Alexander v. Holmes* (396 U. S. 19) that the "obligation of every school district is to terminate dual school systems at once and to operate now and hereafter only unitary schools." Both the *Green* and *Alexander* decisions spelled out the urgency of getting on with the task of desegregation.

In the landmark 1971 *Swann v. Charlotte-Mecklenburg Board of Education* case (402 U. S. 1), the Court considered the implications of residential segregation for school desegregation: "People gravitate toward school facilities, just as schools are located in response to the needs of people. The location of schools may thus influence the patterns of residential development of a metropolitan area and have important impact on the composition of inner city neighborhoods." To prevent residential segregation from aborting desegregation, the Court mandated the drawing of school attendance areas that "are neither compact nor contiguous; indeed they may be on opposite ends of the city." Thus through the *Green, Alexander,* and *Swann* decisions, school desegregation became a reality in the South.

The North did not become a focal point

until 1973, in *Keyes v. School District No. 1* (413 U. S. 189), when the U. S. Supreme Court ruled unconstitutional teacher and student assignments in the Denver Public Schools based on race. This removed *de facto* segregation as a legal condition of school segregation. Becuase of the late start, schools in the North are far from achieving the compliance of their southern peers. This condition is compounded by the reluctance of the courts to approve metropolitan desegregation plans.

Civil Rights Act of 1964

Title IV of the Civil Rights Act of 1964 authorizes the Commissioner of Education to provide technical assistance and financial aid for solving problems dealing with public school desegregation and authorizes the Attorney General to require desegregation in interstate commerce activities. Title VI of the same law and the regulations issued under it stipulate that no person shall, on the ground of race, color, or national origin, be subjected to discrimination in any program receiving federal financial assistance. In March 1966 the U. S. Office of Education released a "Revised Statement of Policies for School Desegragation Plans" under Title VI of the Civil Rights Act of 1964. The sections concerning desegregation of the faculties of public schools are significant.

1. Desegregation of staff. *The racial composition of the professional staff of a school system, and of the schools in the system, must be considered in determining whether students are subjected to discrimination in educational programs. Each school system is responsible for correcting the effects of all past discriminatory practices in the assignment of teachers and other professional staff.*

2. New assignments. *Race, color, or national origin may not be a factor in the hiring or assignment to schools or within schools of teachers and other professional staff, including student teachers and staff serving two or more schools, except to correct the effects of past discriminatory assignments.*

3. Dismissals. *Teachers and other professional staff may not be dismissed, demoted, or passed over for retention, promotion, or rehiring on the grounds of race, color, or national origin. In any instance where one or more teachers or other profes-*

sional staff members are to be displaced as a result of desegregation, no staff vacancy in the school system may be filled through recruitment from outside the system unless the school officials can show that no such displaced staff member is qualified to fill the vacancy. If, as a result of desegregation, there is to be a reduction in the total professional staff of the school system, the qualifications of all staff members in the system must be evaluated in selecting the staff members to be released.

4. Past assignments. *The pattern of assignment of teachers and other professional staff among the various schools of a system may not be such that schools are identifiable as intended for students of a particular race, color, or such that teachers or other professional staff of a particular race are concentrated in those schools where all, or the majority of, the students are of that race. Each school system has a positive duty to make staff assignments and reassignments necessary to eliminate past discriminatory assignment patterns.*[13]

Despite the decisions, laws and regulations applying to schools and their faculties, racial isolation in the public schools persists as a prevalent pattern throughout the United States, especially in the metropolitan areas, which include two-thirds of the population. Furthermore, as metropolitan populations increase, they are becoming more separated by race: four of every five white children live in the suburbs.[14] The picture is even bleaker in the elementary schools. Almost 50 per cent of the Black elementary students in the nation's cities are in schools with 75 to 100 per cent Black enrollments, and nearly 70 per cent of them attend predominantly Black schools. On the other hand, more than 80 per cent of the white elementary students are in all-white schools. The U. S. Commission on Civil Rights reports that in southern and border states, although the proportion of Blacks in all-Black schools has decreased since the *Brown* decision, a rising Black enrollment, combined with only slight desegregation, has produced a substantial increase in the number of all-Black schools. Another factor contributing to this problem is the increase in private, all-white schools.

COMPENSATORY EDUCATION

Compared with suburbs, cities spend a third more per capita for welfare and twice as much per capita for public safety; the suburbs, however, spend nearly twice as much in proportion for education as the cities. For a number of reasons, more disadvantaged children are nonwhite than white and these nonwhite children are more likely to live in the cities. Thus racial separation and economic factors result in more serious handicaps for nonwhite students than for white students. For instance, although both nonwhite and white children are likely to attend schools with libraries, white children attend schools that have more library volumes per student. Their schools also have better science laboratories and equipment and more advanced science and language courses.[15]

Schools are unique as social agencies working for the maximum total development of each individual's intellectual, moral, emotional, and physical potential. Although the family has the major role in this process, schools remain the primary socializing influence outside the family. There is general agreement, therefore, that in attempting to diminish and eventually abolish the academic disadvantages of Black and other minority group children, it is most practical and logical to work through the schools. There is no general agreement among educators and concerned citizens, however, on the best way. Faced with this crisis, school systems generally have taken one of two basic approaches: compensatory education, or school desegregation leading to integration.

Desegregation is accomplished by placing two or more racial groups together within the same school. *Integration*, on the other hand, requires a more intimate and lasting contact between the groups. Few schools are desegregated, and fewer still are integrated. In some desegregated schools, white and Black students voluntarily maintain caste-like cleavages. Court orders can cause various racial groups to attend the same school, but it takes great skill in human relations for school officials to bring about integration.

Compensatory education refers to programs aimed at the rehabilitation of culturally disadvantaged children. Much attention is being given to correcting conditions of poverty. Schools are being called on to provide special services to minority-group children in low-income families. These services are designed to close the gap caused by segregated schools. The public schools have developed and implemented a wide variety of compensatory education programs, but because local school funds are extremely limited, compensatory measures financed from property taxes have been unable to break the cycle of poverty significantly.

In 1965 the federal government began attacking the problem at the national level, particularly through the Elementary and Secondary Education Act of 1965 (ESEA). In Title I of ESEA, the federal government acknowledged that the special needs of children of low-income families and the impact of concentrations of low-income families on the schools necessitate additional financial assistance. By the end of its second academic year (1966–1967), Title I officials reported that 16,400 school districts had spent more than $1 billion on Title I programs involving 9.2 million children. The same officials noted, however, that only half the children needing such programs were actually involved and that the billion dollars could not, by itself, meet the educational needs of culturally disadvantaged children.[16] This is still true.

All compensatory education programs have in common dual goals—remedial work and prevention. They are remedial in that they attempt to fill gaps (whether social, cultural, or academic) in a child's total experience; they are preventive in that by doing remedial work they are trying to break the pattern of continuing failures. Compensatory education has been called "privileged education for the underprivileged." But this is an exaggeration. Although $2 billion were spent in 1976 for compensatory education, the poorer school districts actually got significantly less Title I money per pupil than affluent districts. Districts that spent less than $715 per pupil got $290 per pupil from Title I, while those that spent between $1,043 and $1,368 per pupil got $491 per pupil from Title I.

Within a relatively short time the programs for the disadvantaged began to fall into a general pattern, including:

1. preschool and early education programs aimed at compensating for early experiential deficits, primarily in language and cognitive development;

2. remedial programs in the basic skill areas;

3. individual and small-group tutoring programs conducted by professionals, paraprofessionals, and volunteers;

4. enrichment programs to overcome cul-

tural differences, enhance motivation, and otherwise widen the horizons of students from low-income areas;

5. pre-service and in-service training of teachers to familiarize them with the life styles and growth patterns of children from depressed areas;

6. special guidance programs to extend counseling and therapy services to disadvantaged children and adults;

7. lengthening of the school day and year in an effort to provide community programs;

8. work-study programs involving subsidized on-the-job training;

9. development of special remedial materials;

10. assignment of additional special service personnel (e.g., social workers, nurses, teacher aides) to schools with high ratios of disadvantaged students.

A fundamental question underlies all these efforts at rehabilitation: Can we salvage the all-Black schools? There are many schemes and proposals for upgrading and compensation, "higher horizons," keeping the schools open a few hours longer, special textbooks, appeals to the middle-class conscience, recruiting devoted teachers, and for model schools. Their main goal is to make the schools good while they remain Black or predominantly Black.[17] Joseph Alsop typified those who believe the practical solution does not lie in integration but in improving education in the ghetto schools:

The overwhelming majority of the children of the ghettos are going to be educated exclusively in ghetto schools . . . for many years to come, no matter how much politicking and patching and court ordering we may do. . . . No integration measures can ever do more than fray the fringes of the ghetto school problem in cities with school populations 50 percent Negro and above. . . . Education is the key to the whole problem, because it leads to jobs; jobs lead to achievement and achievement reduces discrimination. . . . White prejudice will surely be eroded, in every area where Negroes are enabled to achieve highly.[18]

In some communities Black parents are just as set against desegregation as white parents. Both groups argue that school distribution on the basis of race does not directly attack the educational problems found in socio-economically depressed neighborhoods. In some instances, they state, forced desegregation detracts from efforts to improve the quality of education in segregated neighborhoods. In any case we should be realistic—the reality is that our communities are becoming not less segregated, but more. Livingston L. Wingate, a Black leader, put it this way:

The greatest need today is the immediate establishment of quality education in the ghetto. We must no longer pursue the myth that integrated education is equated with quality education. Bussing a disadvantaged and isolated child out of Harlem on a segregated bus to an "integrated" classroom downtown will not give him quality education. Once in the classroom downtown, the disadvantaged Harlem pupil would find himself below the achievement level of his white classmates and suffer a more demoralizing experience of frustration than he had in the ghetto inferior school. Moreover, he would return at night to the same ghetto conditions he left in the morning.[19]

Other critics of school desegregation maintain that placing nonwhite students in white schools will (1) emphasize nonwhite pupils' low achievement, (2) suggest the superiority of whites, (3) cause nonwhite pupils to be rejected by whites, and (4) decrease the number of adult role models for nonwhites.

Advocates of compensatory education admit that the cost of establishing superior schools in the inner-cities would be high. The price, they argue, is justifiable considering the nation's social debt to disadvantaged citizens. As a matter of fact, the U. S. Office of Education study of Title I concluded that concentrated remedial assistance can help raise the level of academic achievement. However, such programs are very expensive in terms of teachers, materials, and space. Inadequate funds have resulted in what are frequently referred to as "band-aid programs" that inadequately cover what is actually a cancerous sore. The advocates of compensatory education say we simply must provide the money for really comprehensive programs. As they see it, failure to provide superior education for the culturally disadvantaged will result in continued national educational stagnation, perpetuation of conditions that lead to social disruption and political conflicts, and the continuation of cultures of poverty.

INTEGRATION

Most Americans still believe that social inequalities can be corrected through quality integrated education. This dominant ethos provides a grand formula by which they hope to perpetuate and perfect our culture. Wilbur B. Brookover, however, arguing that the American faith in the efficacy of education rests on dubious grounds, offers four discouraging propositions: (1) the control of American education is generally in the hands of conservative elements in society; (2) the control of education is exerted to prevent change except in the areas where the dominant group desires change; (3) as an integral part of the society, education can function as an agency of change only within the structure of the society, and not as an external agency; and (4) the American faith in education as the creator of a better world can be realized only as other forces also function as agencies of change.[20]

It seems likely that a number of changes in attitude are necessary. In other words, if the schools are to be effective in helping society implement integration, Americans must answer two fundamental questions: Do they agree with the preamble to the Declaration of Independence, which states that all men are created equal and that they are endowed by the Creator with certain inalienable rights? Do they believe that equal educational opportunity is an inalienable right?

Four basic reasons are usually given for supporting quality integrated education as the best way to provide equal educational opportunities. First, the amount of money needed for really far-reaching compensatory programs is vast—much more than any community (even with enormous federal aid) will agree to invest in an exclusively nonwhite network of schools. Second, the influence of other deprived children and of the ghetto culture in an all-nonwhite, lower-class school is so powerful that it largely offsets the effects of academic and technological upgrading.

A third argument is that the teachers in all-nonwhite schools often are poorly trained middle-class nonwhites (they themselves the products of an inferior education) who frequently show quite rigid and hostile attitudes toward lower-class nonwhite children. The prevailing atmosphere in these schools is often cold and authoritarian, emphasizing unthinking conformity to the values of the nonwhite bourgeoisie. Finally, it is argued that the absence in all-nonwhite schools of a mixed population of children (white, middle-class, differing national origins and religions, varied vocational status of parents) itself symbolizes the ghettoized and segregated life of nonwhite children and impresses on them constantly— no matter what the teachers do or say—that they are basically different and inferior; that they are not being brought up to take a place in the mainstream of American life.

Most proponents of school integration argue that the schools must prepare all students for life in an integrated society. They also conclude that compensatory efforts alone will not produce a significant amount of racial integration. As Clark put it, segregated schools are symbols of discrimination and make a mockery of our democratic ideals. Even if all-nonwhite schools were made equal or superior to the white schools, he surmised, they would remain visible reminders of the alleged inferiority of nonwhites; they would in fact be reminders of a situation that is incompatible with the goals of democratic education.[21] Charles E. Silberman adds this somber thought: "Failure to do *anything* about *de facto* segregation will poison the atmosphere of race relations in any community. . . . What a community does about school integration is generally regarded as the ultimate measure of white sincerity and of white willingness to share power."[22] These statements clearly reflect opposition to those who believe that there are no politically and educationally feasible alternatives to "nonwhite but better" schools. (The social effects of racial isolation are equally applicable to white students who are in all-white schools.)

RESEARCH FINDINGS

Systematic studies of the impact of desegregation and improved educational opportunity are limited, although it does seem likely that improved opportunities which include school desegregation efforts can result in improved school achievement by nonwhite pupils.[23] In general, however, the compensatory programs that have been tried have not enabled large numbers of students to reach and sustain grade-level achievement. For instance, a study of school achievement after desegregation in the Louisville Public Schools did show gains in median scores for all grades tested; furthermore, the degree of improvement in achievement levels (compared to the year before school desegregation) was greater for Black pupils than for white pupils. The Black pupils' levels of achievement nevertheless did not equal those of the white pupils.[24] In other cities studies of academic progress following desegregation of schools have showed consistent gains for the nonwhite pupils.[25] There usually are initial declines for white pupils, followed by a return to previous rates of academic achievement. The achievement level for white pupils, however, tends to remain somewhat higher than that for nonwhite pupils.

The so-called "Coleman Report" (*Equality of Educational Opportunity*) of 1966 focused on four significant issues: (1) the extent to which racial and ethnic groups are segregated in the public schools; (2) the extent to which schools offer equal educational opportunities to the various groups; (3) student academic achievement as measured by performance on standardized tests; and (4) the relationships between student achievement and the racial composition of the schools they attended. The report noted that more than two-thirds of all nonwhite first graders attended schools that were 90 per cent or more nonwhite, and about the same proportion of nonwhite twelfth graders attended schools that were 50 per cent or more nonwhite. Teachers and other staff members showed comparable racial isolation. In terms of academic achievement, the report suggested that most nonwhite students attend low-quality schools and that only through integration—not compensatory education—will they be able to raise substantially either their academic achievement or their self-conceptions.[26]

The projected picture of integration, then, is one of achievement gains for nonwhite pupils without losses for white students. Available research does not indicate clearly whether these gains result from the simple act of integration or from improved teaching techniques. Of even greater concern to those committed to equality of educational achievement is the negative fact that nonwhite pupils continue to be academically outdistanced by their white counterparts despite improvements in educational opportunities and integration efforts. A multifaceted approach probably is necessary.

One authority has summarized the components of such an approach for Black education.

1. Standards of Black schools should be raised so that integrated students will have a better chance of success.
2. Parents should be brought into school programs and their aid enlisted.
3. Integrated schools need in-service training for teachers.
4. Ability grouping within schools should be abandoned or seriously modified.
5. Desegregation should proceed from the lowest grades to the highest to optimize chances of success.[27]

Viewing desegregation of the public schools as a vital condition to resolving the nation's racial crisis, the National Advisory Commission on Civil Disorders observed that none of us can escape the consequences of the continuing economic and social decay of the central city and the closely related problem of rural poverty. Noting that overcoming segregation and racial isolation is only the first step toward equalizing education, the Commission concluded that integration should be the final goal in our schools.[28] To accomplish this end, we will need dedicated school personnel, especially teachers. Thus we now consider the role of teachers.

TEACHERS MAKE THE DIFFERENCE

The role of teachers in school integration is crucial. They help or hinder the adjustment of each child to the desegregated classroom. They also help parents form their attitudes toward school desegregation. Obviously, not all teachers respond in the same way. Some are extremely liberal in their racial views; others are quite prejudiced. As a group they are likely to be similar in attitudes to most of the residents in the communities where they teach. In many communities it is only adherence to the letter of the law that keeps the desegregation effort alive at all.

Most teachers accept assignments to desegregated schools with much anxiety. White teachers seem to be no better prepared for school desegregation than nonwhite teachers. Both exhibit what may be called a fear of the unknown. They fear that once hired they will

Table 12. Opinions of the Public on Interdistrict Busing: 1972, 1974, 1975

Question item and possible responses	Percent distribution		
	1972	1974	1975
In general do you favor or oppose the busing of Black and White school children from one school district to another?			
Total	100.0	100.0	100.0
Favor	19.5	20.1	17.2
Oppose	76.6	76.2	78.1
Don't know	3.9	3.7	4.7

SOURCE: National Opinion Research Center, University of Chicago, 6030 South Ellis Avenue, Chicago, Illinois, 60637, *General Social Survey,* 1972, 1974, 1975.

lose their jobs to better prepared individuals of the other group. Both groups are unsure about the reactions of community residents and their fellow faculty members. In addition they fear that they will be confronted by children and adults whose goals, value systems, and behaviors are different from their own.[29] This condition of temporary normlessness comes from their having learned behavior appropriate to segregated situations but inappropriate to integrated situations.[30] *Peer* relationships in desegragated schools are vastly different from *caste* relationships characterizing segregated schools. Both majority- and minority-group people must learn new roles.

As nonwhite teachers in particular move into schools with recently desegregated staffs, they carry with them intense minority sensitivities and behaviors appropriate to their past lives. This is especially true in situations centering on social activities. The slowness, reluctance, and even outright refusal of some school districts to desegregate is caused in part by a strong opinion that nonwhites in predominantly white schools would be very uncomfortable. The "concerned" community leaders erroneously believe that nonwhite Americans can only be happy with "their own kind." Fortunately, once schools actually are desegregated, anxieties tend to give way to reasonably well-defined cooperative integrated activities.

PLANS FOR PUPIL INTEGRATION

There are no sure-fire ways to integrate our schools. Faculty integration is much easier to accomplish than pupil integration. After all, most parents are not employees of school systems; therefore, the integration of pupils is not the relatively simple matter of assignment and training that it is with teachers. Quotas, redrawing attendance boundaries, reorganization of grades, open enrollment, magnet schools, and educational parks are some of the plans that have been tried. What works well in one community may not work well in another. Some communities adopt a plan and proceed gradually; others move quickly.

Quotas. Dispersing all nonwhite students to white schools on a quota basis is believed by some educators to be the only way to integrate all schools quickly. Ideally, the plan calls for some white students to be transferred to minority-group schools. Bus transportation is likely to be involved in either case. But this plan—usually referred to simply as busing—is both expensive and socially irritating. Opponents say that small children are forced to travel long distances from their homes. Proponents maintain that this method insures racial balance and is more comprehensive than any other plan.

Pupil transportation in America began in

1869 when Massachusetts, the first state to adopt compulsory education, provided pupil transportation at public expense. It is not the busing of children *per se* that most opponents of busing are fighting. In 1975 approximately 286,000 students were bused to school at a cost of $29 million per year and more than 280,000 school buses travel well over 43 million miles each year. The busing fight centers on the 3 to 5 per cent of school transportation used to desegregate the public schools. Nor is safety always the major issue—the occupant death rate per 100 million passenger-miles is considerably less for school buses than automobiles. And generally distance is not the major issue. A white mother in Richmond, Virginia, said, "It's not the distance, it's the niggers."

Redrawing attendance boundaries. Redrawing attendance boundaries to split nonwhite neighborhoods and attach them to adjoining white neighborhoods has worked in some communities. This plan does not affect as many students as the quota plan. The schools remain essentially neighborhood schools. Very little money is needed for transportation. The disadvantages are mainly two: (1) even a relatively small number of Black students in a few white schools may panic the white residents; and (2) shifts in population may necessitate a continual redrawing of boundaries.

Reorganization of grades (Princeton Plan). The Princeton Plan, in which two attendance districts not necessarily adjoining are merged, with all children in certain grades going to one school, affects more students than redrawing attendance boundaries. This plan is especially successful in small school districts. Opponents argue that when schools are not adjoining, transportation expenses generally must be borne by the parents. Proponents argue that this plan is fairer than most others because schools within both nonwhite and white districts are involved. Thus white students are also transported, breaking the usual pattern of Black students going to white schools.

Open enrollment. Open enrollment permits nonwhites in predominantly nonwhite schools to transfer to underutilized white schools until a predetermined percentage of the student body of the receiving school is nonwhite. Voluntary transfer of white students to predominantly nonwhite schools is allowed on the same basis. Proponents maintain that open enrollment will be used by highly motivated, mainly academically successful students and that the result will be the integration of highly competitive nonwhite students. Opponents note that this plan tends to drain Black schools of top scholars and articulate parents. In addition, few poverty-striken parents can pay for their children to attend out-of-district schools. This plan is one of the least effective in integrating schools.

Magnet schools. By designating various schools as centers of excellence for specific offerings (e.g., data processing, automobile mechanics, physics, and drama), some school districts have been moderately successful in their desegregation efforts. Minority-group parents frequently complain that schools in their neighborhoods are disproportionately vocation-oriented, while schools in predominantly white neighborhoods are disproportionately college-oriented.

Educational parks. Placing together on one site all schools serving an entire school district or a large section of a city is known as the educational park or "school village" plan. The costs are quite high—existing buildings must be abandoned and a campus erected. In fact, for most school districts, costs are prohibitive. Such a consolidation of school districts can, of course, lead to urban-suburban or nonwhite-white integration—or both.

Whichever plan is used, it is clear that racial integration is more than placing Black and white bodies within close proximity. *Integration is involvement.* It is white and nonwhite students and faculties interacting in a lasting and positive manner. When this happens they become participants in a common culture.

The best course to follow seems to be desegregation that leads to integration, coupled with compensatory programs so that disadvantaged students—white and nonwhite—will be better able to adjust to integrated classrooms. Once schools are racially integrated, compensatory programs should be continued as part of pupil personnel services. A major reason for this need is the fact that long after racial or ethnic differences are diminished, social class differences continue to produce different

Table 13. Opinions of White Respondents on Sending Their Children to Integrated
Schools: 1972, 1974, 1975

Question item and responses	Answers of White respondents (percentages)		
	1972	1974	1975
Objection to school where a few children are Blacks			
Total	100.0	100.0	100.0
Yes	7.1	5.2	6.8
No	91.9	94.3	91.5
Don't know	0.1	0.5	1.7
Objection to school where half of children are Blacks			
Total	100.0	100.0	100.0
Yes[1]	23.2	28.3	27.3
No	74.0	68.8	69.1
Don't know	2.8	2.9	3.6
Objection school where more than half of children are Blacks			
Total	100.0	100.0	100.0
Yes[2]	53.2	60.0	57.6
No	41.9	35.3	37.2
Don't know	4.9	4.7	5.2

[1] Includes those with an objection to sending their children to school were a few children are Black.
[2] Includes those with an objection to sending their children to school were a few children are Black or where a half of the children are Black.

SOURCE: National Opinion Research Center, University of Chicago, 6030 South Ellis Avenue, Chicago, Illinois, 60637, *General Social Survey*, 1973, 1974, 1975.

levels of educational achievement. The social class composition of a student body is more highly related to achievement than any other single characteristic. Children of middle-class or higher background tend to do well in school regardless of racial or ethnic differences.

However, attending desegregated schools does not mean that the academic achievement of nonwhite students will automatically increase. A recent study by David J. Armor of Harvard University corroborated earlier studies which concluded that academic achievement is not likely to be raised merely by placing Black and white children together in the same school.[31] Armor's analysis of busing in six northern cities stated that school desegregation had neither raised the academic

achievements, aspirations, and self-esteem of Black children nor improved race relations. On the contrary, he found that the Black children in the study exhibited heightened racial identity and a desire for racial separation.

Armor's controversial study focused on secondary school students in the cities of Ann Arbor (Mich.), Boston (Mass.), Hartford (Conn.), New Haven (Conn.), Riverside (Cal.), and White Plains (N.Y.). Critics of the study contend that educational gains will be seen only when present elementary school students enter high school. By the time students are in high school, Armor's critics contend, their attitudes and behaviors have been hardened and frozen too deeply for significant changes to occur. Furthermore, they say, school officials and school patrons created a prophecy of antagonism and failure for desegregation that fulfilled itself: when school patrons and other opinion leaders state that desegregation will not work and then engage in disruptive actions, it does not work.

In the past critics of public schools have argued, with more than a modicum of truth, that educators tend to react to community pressures for reforms and not to act to prevent the conditions which cause such pressures. Specifically, there has been a noticeable lag between school board policies and classroom practices. This has been especially true of school systems in which school board desegregation policies frequently are far ahead of school practices. In the area of racial desegregation, the net result of court pressure has been a mixture of uncoordinated programs designed to bring about minimum compliance. Separate uncoordinated programs add little to a total school effort, especially toward school desegregation. In fact, uncoordinated desegregation programs add confusion to the effort.

Although there have been setbacks, nonwhites are making gains in education and the institution of segregated schools in the South and the North is collapsing. This is happening despite the efforts by many frantic parents to move their children into segregated public and private school systems. Fearing this trend, many "liberal" school boards have abandoned their forced busing programs.

Black teachers and administrators continue to bear a disproportionate part of the financial burden of school desegregation. For example, U. S. Office of Health, Education, and Welfare statistics show that between 1968 and 1972 three-fourths of the school districts in Alabama, Georgia, Louisiana, and Mississippi had a decline of more than 2,500 Black teachers and an increase of 3,387 white teachers. Data from 70 per cent of the school districts in Florida, Georgia, Louisiana, and Mississippi showed a 20 per cent deline of Black principals and a 6 per cent gain in white principals.

Another common practice is the demotion of Blacks when school personnel are desegregated (i.e., demoting Blacks from coaches to assistant coaches, from principals to assistant principals, from superintendents to assistant superintendents and having them work under whites who keep the higher rank). The national picture is equally distressing. Although more than 10 per cent of public school teachers are nonwhite, less than 2 per cent are administrators. In higher education nonwhites comprise less than 2 per cent of college and university personnel.

It wasn't until 1972, in *Adams v. Richardson* (480 F 2d 1159), that the Office of Civil Rights of HEW was given the clout it needed to enforce higher education affirmative action plans: the power to withhold federal funds to institutions in noncompliance.

However, as we move toward eliminating unconstitutional *de jure* racial segregation in common schools and higher education, the historically Black colleges are being threatened. In 1977 HEW ordered Arkansas, Florida, Georgia, North Carolina, Oklahoma, and Virginia to eliminate segregated state colleges and universities, while enhancing educational excellence and maintaining the academic standards of these insitutions by the 1982–83 academic year. The order hit the predominantly Black institutions especially hard. It is likely that the white schools, with their better funding and diverse curricula will be able to attract more Black students. On the other hand, it is likely that, even with the additional funding and improved curricula ordered by HEW, whites will not attend most Black institutions in significantly larger numbers. Socially and psychologically, Blacks have been conditioned to believe that "if it's white, it's right," while whites have been conditioned to believe that, despite slogans to the contrary, black is not as beautiful as white.

Special Admissions Programs

Efforts to desegregate professional schools in colleges and universities have come under considerable criticism during the past few years. The battle lines were clearly drawn when Allan Bakke, a white engineer, sued the University of California in 1975 for depriving him of his constitutional protection on grounds of race under the Fourteenth Amendment.

In 1973 Bakke was one of 2,643 applicants for 100 admission places in the University of California's School of Medicine at Davis. He was rejected (as he was by ten other medical schools) and sixteen Blacks, Chicanos, Asian-Americans, and Native Americans were admitted. He tried again in 1974 and was one of 3,736 applicants. Again he was rejected (as he was by twelve other medical schools) and sixteen minority-group applicants were admitted.

The crux of Bakke's frustration grew out of the fact that all the minority-group applicants admitted to Davis' school of Medicine scored lower than he on the Medical College Admission Test (MCAT). The Caucasian applicants had to have high grade-point averages and high scores on the MCAT before being considered for an interview by one of the screening committees. On the other hand, if minority applicants appeared to have compensating strengths, their low grades were overlooked by the minority selection committee and they were considered for one of the sixteen minority places.

By a 6 to 1 decision the California State Supreme Court ruled in 1976 that the University of California had unconstitutionally discriminated against Bakke. In addition, the court declared the special admission program invalid. The university appealed to the U. S. Supreme Court. Arguing before the U. S. Supreme Court, the University of California and the U. S. Department of Justice stated that Title VI of the Civil Rights Act of 1964 supports the use of special admissions programs as a way to equalize educational opportunities for minorities. Bakke's attorneys countered that Title VI does not provide group rights, rather it explicitly says that no person shall be discriminated against on grounds of race, religion, or national origin in federally aided education programs.

This case gets to the heart of yet another issue: How can institutions select the best qualified candidates who also proportionately represent the state's major ethnic population? The California Supreme Court was unanimous in its nonsupport of the dominant use of academic criteria in selecting students for professional training, and it was equally insistent that if broader criteria are applied to one group of applicants they must be applied to all.

The significance of higher education using special enrollment programs can be seen in 1956 and 1976 national data. In 1956 colleges and universities enrolled 4.6 million whites and only 224,000 Blacks. In 1976 white enrollment was up to 6.3 million (an increase of 36%) and Black enrollment jumped to 748,000 (an increase of 234%). Even so, in 1976 there were only 836 Blacks attending 112 American medical schools other than Howard and Meharry (two predominantly Black medical schools)—an average of 8 Blacks in each school. The great increase in Black enrollment and retention has resulted in Blacks still receiving less than 3 per cent of all medical degrees. Similar conditions are true for other professional schools, including dentistry, veterinary medicine, law, and engineering.

The NEA and AFT are on opposite sides of the special admissions debate. Reflecting its own by-laws commitment to ethnic minority representation, the NEA publicly supports quotas and special admissions for ethnic minorities. On the other side, the AFT has taken the position that special admissions violate the principle of equal qualifications for appointment and quotas in a generalized manner violate the seniority rights of higher achieving students. Basically, the NEA maintains that the means justifies the end, while the AFT considers these particular means to be discriminatory and therefore do not justify the end.

No matter what the U. S. Supreme Court rules, it will be the task of well-intentioned professional schools to utilize fair and effective programs to increase the number of ethnic minority students and graduates. Broader or open admision, wider acceptance of training in non-American schools, expanded enrollments, pre-admision programs for minorities, and better teaching and career counseling in secondary schools are but a few ways in which short and long range equal opportunity goals are likely to be met. The *Bakke* case set off an international debate and will result in a U. S. Supreme Court decision but it is in the classroom where equality will be won or lost.

NEIGHBORHOOD AND HOME

In many ways where we live now affects how we want to live in the future. Complete the following sentences, in writing or orally.

1. Compared to other neighborhoods that I have seen, mine is

2. If I could live in any neighborhood in my community, I would like

3. When I take my friends home, I

4. The houses on my street are

5. The people in my neighborhood are

6. The worst thing about my neighborhood is

7. The best thing about my neighborhood is

8. The best room in my house is

9. The least desirable room in my house is

10. If I have my way, I will never live in

In what ways, if any, do you think your housing preferences will affect your ability to feel at ease in a roach-and rodent-infested slum dwelling occupied by a student in your class?

ADDITIONAL READINGS

Bagwell, William. *School Desegregation in the Carolinas*. Columbia, University of South Carolina Press, 1972.

Caughey, John. *To Kill a Child's Spirit: The Tragedy of School Segregation in Los Angeles*. Itasca, Ill, F. E. Peacock, 1973.

Chanin, Robert H. *Combatting Discrimination in the Schools: Legal Remedies and Guidelines*. Washington, D. C., National education Association, 1973.

Coleman, James S., et al. *Trends in School Segregation, 1968–73*. Washington, D. C., Urban Institute, 1975.

Gerard, Harold B. and Norman Miller. *School Desegregation*. New York, Plenum Press, 1975.

Levinsohn, Florence H. and Benjamin D. Wright, eds. *School Desegregation: Shadow and Substance*. Chicago, University of Chicago Press, 1976.

Mercer, Walter A. *Teaching in the Desegregated School*. New York, Vantage Press, 1973.

———. *Racism and American Education: A Dialogue and Agenda for Action*. New York, Harper & Row, 1970.

Rubin, Lillian E. *Busing and Backlash: White Against White in a California School District*. Berkeley, Cal., University of California Press, 1972.

Scott, J. Irving E. *The Education of Black People in Florida*. Philadelphia, Dorrance, 1975.

Smith, Al, et al. *Achieving Effective Desegregation*. Lexington, Mass., Lexington Books, 1973.

Willie, Charles. *Race Mixing in the Public Schools*. New York, Praeger, 1974.

NOTES

1. Seymour W. Itzkoff, *Cultural Pluralism and American Education* (Scranton, Pa., International Textbook, 1969), 46.

2. Francis T. Villemain, "The Significance of the Democratic Ethic for Cultural Alternatives and American Civilization," *Educational Theory*, 26 (Winter, 1976), 40.

3. Itzkoff, *Cultural Pluralism*, 48.

4. *Ibid.*, 53.

5. Edgar G. Epps (ed.), *Cultural Pluralism* (Berkeley, Cal., McCutcheon, 1974), 122.

6. *Ibid.*, 176.

7. *Ibid.*, 123.

8. *Ibid.*, 124–125.

9. *Ibid.*, 125.

10. *Ibid.*

11. *Plessy v. Ferguson*, 163 U. S. 537 (1896).

12. *Brown et al. v. Board of Education of Topeka et al.*, 347 U. S. 483 (1954).

13. U. S. Commissioner of Education, "Revised Statement of Policies for School Desegregation Plans," March, 1966, Section 181.13.

14. U. S. Commission on Civil Rights, *Racial Isolation in the Public Schools* (Washington, D. C., U. S. Government Printing Office, 1967), 260.

15. *Ibid.*, 199.

16. U. S. Office of Education, *Title I: Year II* (Washington, D. C., U. S. Government Printing Office, 1968).

17. James W. Guthrie and James A. Kelly, "Compensatory Education—Some Answers for a Skeptic," *Phi Delta Kappan*, 46 (October, 1965), 70–74.

18. Joseph Alsop, "No More Nonsense About Ghetto Education!" *New Republic*, 157 (July, 1967), 18–23.

19. Livingston L. Wingate, "Statement of Livingston L. Wingate, Executive Director of HARYOU-ACT," 25th Annual Conference for Superintendents (New York, Teachers College, July 9, 1966), 3.

20. Wilbur B. Brookover, *A Sociology of Education*, (New York, American Book, 1955), 76.

21. Kenneth B. Clark, *Prejudice and Your Child* (Boston, Beacon, 1966), 32–33.

22. Charles E. Silberman, *Crisis in Black and White* (New York, Random House, 1964), 292.

23. U. S. Commission on Civil Rights, *Racial Isolation*, chap. IV.

24. Frank H. Stallings, "A Study of the Immediate Effects of Integration on Scholastic Achievement in the Louisville Public Schools," *Journal of Negro Education*, 28 (Fall, 1959), 439–444.

25. See for example Carl F. Hansen, "The Scholastic Performance of Negro and White Pupils in the Integrated Public Schools of the District of Columbia," *Harvard Educational Review*, 30 (Summer, 1960), 216–236.

26. James S. Coleman, et al., *Equality of Educational Opportunity* (Washington, D.C., U.S. Government Printing Office, 1966). This view was supported by U. S. Commission on Civil Rights, but not by Professor Coleman, who has argued that his findings do not address the issue of whether schools should be desegregated.

27. Irwin Katz, "Review of Evidence Relating to Effects of Desegregation Performance of Negroes," *American Psychologist*, 19 (June, 1964), 381–399.

28. *Report of the National Advisory Commission on Civil Disorders* (New York, Bantam Books, 1968), 438.

29. James H. Bash, *Effective Teaching in the Desegregated School* (Bloomington, Ind., Phi Delta Kappa, 1966), 8.

30. Nebraska Mays, "Behavioral Expectations of Negro and White Teachers on Recently Desegregated Public School Faculties," *Journal of Negro Education*, 32 (Summer, 1963), 218.

31. David J. Armor, "The Evidence of Busing," *The Republic Interest*, 24 (Summer, 1972), 90–126.

10.
RACIAL
AND CULTURAL
PLURALISM

Cultural pluralism means many things, including mutual understanding and appreciation of all cultures in a society; cooperation of the various cultures in a society's civic and economic institutions; peaceful coexistence of diverse lifestyles—folkways, language patterns, religious beliefs, etc; and autonomy of each subculture to determine its own destiny.

The acceptance of cultural pluralism as a curriculum *modus operandi* does not require that schools melt away cultural differences. Rather cultural pluralism requires educators to openly affirm cultural, ethnic, and linguistic differences as being good and affirmative resources which are worthy of preserving and enhancing. James A. Banks approaches the issue thus:

Since neither the cultural pluralist nor the integrationist ideology can adequately guide curriculum reform in the common schools, we need a different ideology which reflects both of these positions and yet avoids their extremes. . . . The pluralist-assimilationist believes that the curriculum should reflect the cultures of various ethnic groups and the common culture." [1]

The importance of getting on with the task was sensitively stated by Cynthia Shepard:

Although he has not yet attended kindergarten, he can both read and write, and can accurately identify colors and forms with an acuity beyond his years. He collects American flags and pictures and ceramics of our national emblem. . . . He learned from somewhere on his own initiative the Pledge of Allegiance, which he recites with deep fervor. . . .

My precious, precocious Mark is very proud of his white, Anglo-Saxon heritage. But he is black: a beautifully carved and polished piece of black American earth. [2]

Groups whose members share a unique social and cultural heritage passed to each successive generation are known as *ethnic groups*. Social scientists tell us that ethnic groups are generally identified by distinctive patterns of family life, language, religion, and other customs which set them apart from other groups. Above all else, members of ethnic groups feel a sense of identity and common fate. While ethnicity is commonly used to mean race, it extends beyond race.

Gloria W. Grant suggests several criteria for a culturally pluralistic curriculum.

1. Reflect the pluralistic nature of our society, both past and present.
2. Present diversity of culture, ethnicity, and custom as strong positive features of our nation's heritage.
3. Present the cultural, sexual, and racial groups in our society in a manner that will build mutual respect and understanding.
4. Portray people—boys and girls, men and women—whatever their culture, as displaying various human emotions, both negative and positive. Individuals of different cultural groups should be described working and playing together.
5. Provide a balanced representation of cultural groups.
6. Present members of various cultural groups in positions of authority.

Chart 6. Levels of Activity in Multicultural Education

Level:	Activity:	For:	By:
Level 5 Integrated education	*Meshing*—Interfacing the knowledge and processes of the first four levels into a skill-sequenced program for the individual child	Students Teachers	Resource teachers in Staff Development Total district
Level 4 Implementing the curriculum through the program of instruction	*Utilize* activities related to each ethnic group: a. To achieve specific objectives of the multicultural program b. To explore and develop other curriculum models	Students Staff	Teachers Students Teacher aides
Level 3 Building curriculum models	*Integrate* materials for each ethnic group: a. Into regular Social Studies, English-Language Arts, Art, Music, Homemaking, and any other appropriate regular course of curriculum area b. Into all cocurricular activities sponsored by the school	Staff Students Paraprofessionals Community	Teachers in Staff Development activities Teachers in the classroom Consultants and teacher groups Directors of departments in subject matter areas In-service/consultants
Level 2 Acquiring information and resources for instruction	*Compile, select*, and *make available* for use: for each ethnic group: a. Books and printed materials b. Audiovisuals c. Community resource personnel d. Community environmental resources	School staff Community	Resource teachers Instructional support services Office of Community Relations In-service/consultants
Level 1 Awareness: sensitizing to characteristics, expectations, and resources	*Gain* knowledge of and feeling for each ethnic community's: a. History and ethnic experience b. Environmental impact on persons c. Expectation of the school d. Parental expectation for children e. Non-school resources for education of children	Resource teachers Administrators Community Paraprofessionals School site staff	Office of Community Relations In-service/consultants

SOURCE: Fern Kelly, "A System Approaches Multicultural Education," *Educational Leadership*, 32 (December, 1974), 186. Reprinted with permission.

7. Examine the societal forces and conditions which operate to optimize or minimize the opportunities of minority group individuals.

8. Examine real problems and real people of various cultures and not just heroes and highlights.[3]

AMERICAN INDIAN STUDIES

Educators concerned about the unfair treatment of Native Americans in textbooks are aware of several glaring omissions.

By the time white men came, the Indians had already domesticated more than 40 plants, had some 40 inventions to their credit, were great artists and craftsmen, had music, songs, dances, and poetry, used 150 medicines, surgery and drugs, had discovered rubber and invented the bulbed syringe. The mythical picture of them as cruel, primitive hunters and nomadic warriors must be replaced by the truth.[4]

Television and movies have exposed American children to the deeds—often distorted to make whites look good—of a few Indian warriors, mainly Cochise, Crazy Horse, Geronimo, Osceola, Red Cloud, and Sitting Bull. Only recently have a small number of American children become familiar with writings about other great Native Americans such as Joseph Brant, Chief Joseph, Moassasoit, John Ross, Samoset, Shawnee Prophet, Squanto, Tecumseh, Washakie, and Wovoka. This is only the beginning of a long overdue journey into a neglected and embarrassing portion of our past.

Very little is reflected in texts or in historical monuments of the cultures and histories of the diverse peoples called American Indians. Even less has been written about the suffering and degradation that Indians have endured. Only recently have more balanced historical accounts of their displacement and neglect been included in school textbooks. Traditional history books of the nineteenth and early twentieth centuries praised the heroism of white settlers in the development of the North American continent and cheered the subduing of "hostile savages." For example in the town square of Santa Fe, New Mexico, the oldest settlement in the West, there is the commemorative inscription, "To the heroes who have fallen in the various battles with savage Indians in the territory of New Mexico."

Prior to the federal government's assumption of responsibility for the welfare of Native Americans, the Society for the Propagation of the Gospel in Foreign Parts (SPG), established in 1700 by the Church of England, set up several elementary schools and more than 340 missions in the American colonies. The purpose of SPG's missionary activities were quite simple: teach Indians and Black slaves their letters and some prayers and hymns.

The first government funds for Indian schools were allocated in the early 1800s. In 1819 Congress passed a law authorizing $10,000 a year for the education of American Indians. Most of the money was given to missionary groups for support of church schools for Indians. In 1924 Congress belatedly passed a law making every Indian born in the United States a citizen. With this law came individual state responsibility for the education of Indian citizens.

The Indian Education Act

In 1972 Congress passed the Indian Education Act, creating new educational opportunities for Native American children and adults. The act was the outgrowth of three major problems of educating Indian students. They were (1) receiving an inferior quality of education, (2) excluded from management of their own education, and (3) under an imposed educational system of another culture. The act authorized the operation of three different programs (Parts A, B, and C) to meet the unmet needs of Indians from preschool to college.

Part A of the Indian Education Act provides authorization to develop and implement supplemental elementary and secondary school programs for Indian children. In 1976 more than 280,000 Indian children from 789 tribal entities in over 1,000 school districts were benefitting from Part A grants, which included bicultural-bilingual enrichment activities, guidance and counseling services, cultural awareness curricula, and transportation.

Part B of the act provides authorization to develop exemplary programs that involve Indian parents and their communities in the educational process. Part B also funds community-based early childhood programs and curriculum development projects involving Indian cultural and historical materials. The Education Amendment of 1974 added two sections to Part B. One authorizes grants for special educational programs for teachers of Indian children; the other authorizes fellowships for Indian students in graduate and professional programs in engineering, law, medicine, business, forestry, and other specializations.

Part C helps Indian tribes, organizations, institutions, and state and local agencies to plan, demonstrate, and operate programs for improving educational and employment opportunities for adult Indians. This part of the act focuses on teaching to achieve literacy, increasing the number of General Equivalency Diploma (GED) graduates, and providing a wider range of job training sites. It also supports curricula that promote self-pride based on Indian history and culture, and those which stress legal education, consumer education, vocational counseling and community education.

Part D provides for the establishment of the Office of Indian Education, within the U. S. Office of Education, to administer the projects authorized by the Indian Education Act under the direction of a Deputy Commissioner of Education. (In 1977 the Commissioner title was upgraded to Assistant Secretary for the Interior.) Part D also established the National Advisory Council on Indian Education to provide policy guidance and direction. The Advisory Council is composed of fifteen persons who are Indians or Alaskan natives appointed by the President from nominations submitted by Indian tribes and organizations.

It remains to be seen whether the Indian Education Act will do for Indian education what the Elementary and Secondary Act of 1965 has done for the general student population of America or whether this will be yet another broken promise to Native Americans.

American Indian Curricula Development Program

One of the most significant projects in Indian education has been produced by the American Indian Curricula Development Program (AICDP), a North Dakota Native American

organization. The K through 12 curriculum package includes textbooks, booklets, cassette tapes, overhead transparencies, and slide-tape programs. Other significant programs are being developed in states with large Indian populations, e.g., Wisconsin Native American Language Project at the University of Wisconsin-Milwaukee and the Juneau Indian Studies Program in Alaska. Sensitivity to Indian cultures by school staffs at all levels is a requisite to success.

The cross-cultural differences between Native American and Anglo values add to the difficulty in designing pluralistic programs for Native Americans. Lenona M. Foerster and Dale Little Soldier call to our attention the following central Indian values.[5]

Harmony with nature. Indian cultures stress reverence for and harmony with nature. This does not mean that nature should not be used. Clearly, early Indian people would not have survived if they had elected not to use their enviornment properly. However, it is the Indian way to take no more from the environment than one can use. Native Americans respected their environment, believing that if they borrowed the energy of the sun, they had to give it back to the sun to avoid breaking the Cycle of Life. Recent non-Indian programs for environmental protection would be less desperate if the early white settlers had been, like the Indians, ecology-minded.

Sharing. Native Americans share the essentials of life—food, clothing, and shelter—as well as praise and blame. Although this value has been altered somewhat because of modern life styles, sharing remains an important Indian value. Most non-Indians do not have this orientation. The cut-throat competition which characterizes school survival is in conflict with this Indian way of life.

Bravery. For a people who have been subjected to the American government's efforts to systematically destroy or emasculate them, bravery means facing a difficult situation without running away. In twentieth century terms, it means leaving one's family to go to a boarding school or obtaining a nonreservation job or retaining dignity in the face of adversity.

Indian time. Unlike Anglos, Indians look

upon time as a continuum with no beginning and no end. Thus for the Indian there is not the strong orientation toward tomorrow which characterizes many non-Indians. Most Indian children do not enter school conditioned to be clock watchers. It is important for the Indian to live each day as it comes, to do things as they need to be done. This orientation tends to irritate educators who are constantly asking children to project future goals and not to waste time.

Individual freedom. Indians are taught to rely on themselves to make wise choices. Contrary to some notions, this does not mean freedom to do whatever one wishes. Implicit in this freedom is the ability to follow the advice of others without being forced to do so. Again, the world of the school with its many rules and regulations is counter to the Indian way.

Public school education is viewed with alarm by Indians who want to maintain their ethnic identities.

To our older tribal members, education is a departure from the "Indian Way." The elderly believe that the young students are taught to be competitive where they were once taught to share and be generous. They were once taught to have a greater respect for the individual and for their elders whose wisdom guided their very existence. The young educated Indian loses his communication with nature, "mother earth," and the spirit guardians. The young educated Indian loses his "closeness" with life and his appreciation of living things. You see, our elderly believe that education and technology have caused pollution and destruction of our "mother earth"; that education is causing social disruption and less sympathy for the plight of our fellow man.[6]

The American Indian Curricula Development Program has developed materials that add Indian culture to the curriculum. AICDP, a branch of the United Tribes Education Technical Center in Bismarck, North Dakota, was organized in 1972 to develop Plains Indian social studies curricula and provide teacher training.

The AICDP senior high school "Social Conflict" unit focuses on the Bureau of Indian Affairs; federal government acts, commissions, policies, and jurisdictions relating to the Americanization of Indians; Indian education; and the nature of prejudice. The senior high school "Fine Arts" unit includes Indian art, music, drama, literature, and dance. The K through 8 curriculum focuses on a wide variety of Plains Indian cultural items: education, foods, social customs, religion, and histories. Above all else, the AICDP curricula reflect the educational philosophy and teachings of tribal elders residing in five North Dakota reservations.

Another viable approach to an ethnic studies curriculum was illustrated in 1976 by Seattle Pacific College, which offered a one-week workshop on Indian culture. Rather than learning about Indians only through written materials and films, the workshop participants lived in urban Indian homes, conversed with reservation Indians, and attended an Indian potlatch party. This type of cultural immersion has been proven successful in several places.

BLACK STUDIES

The more effective elementary and secondary schools in predominantly Black communities are accelerating their efforts to teach black pride—to help children and youth find themselves in Blackness. For example, in some schools Black pride is taught as an integral part of regular school subjects. In such schools Crispus Attucks is becoming as well known as Paul Revere, and the writings of Black writers like Langston Hughes, James Baldwin, Gwendolyn Brooks, and Ralph Ellison stand beside those of Charles Dickens, Jane Austen, and Jack London. Even bulletin board displays and school musicals and plays are taking on a Black look.

Black students are getting acquainted with nineteenth-century Black intellectuals, such as Edward Blyden, Martin Delaney, and David Walker. Furthermore, they are learning to respect the revolutionary ideals of Gabriel Prosser, Harriet Tubman, Sojourner Truth, Frederick Douglass, Marcus Garvey, W. E. B. DuBois, Malcolm X., Martin Luther King, Jr., Whitney Young, Jr., and Frantz Fanon. Gradually, Black youth are learning the importance of early twentieth-century Black musicians, including Bessie Smith, Jelly Roll Morton, King Oliver, Fats Waller, Louis Armstrong, Perry Bradford, and Duke Ellington. We can add other activities and Black persons to this growing list of Black topics. (See Chapter 17 for other illustrations).

While Black Americans and Native Americans are receiving considerably more attention, Spanish-speaking and Asian-Americans receive far less recognition in school materials. Most Anglo writers have had difficulty writing objectively about events such as the Mexican War, the Spanish-American War, and the internment of Japanese-Americans at the onset of World War II, since these events represent conflicts between American economic desires and democratic principles. For example, one author described American intervention in four countries thus: Cuba: "The United States was committed to Cuban independence." China: "American missionaries brought education, as well as the Christian religion." The Philippines: "The U. S. began to help Filipinos develop their country." Mexico: "When the U. S. sought to encourage the establishment of an orderly government, the Mexicans complained of American interference."[7]

CHICANO STUDIES

Chicano or Mexican-American children are the second largest minority group in the public schools. The word "Chicano" stems from the Mexican Indian Nahuatl word "Mechicano." The first syllable was dropped, and Chicano was left. It is an old term for the American of Mexican descent. Presently the Chicano movement (or Chicanismo) is a commitment to the improvement of life for all Spanish-speaking Americans and Americans of Mexican descent.

The lack of knowledge about cultures other than European is clearly illustrated in the fact that only a few American students learn that the first books printed in the Americas were printed in Mexico, and the first one, *Doctrina cristiana on lengua mexicana* (1540) was written in Nahuatl, the language of the Aztecs. Even fewer students learn that the *Física Speculatio* (1560) recorded the laws of gravity one hundred years before Newton, or that Mexicans pioneered the West, mapped and named many mountains, rivers and fords, and named California, Colorado, Nevada, and New Mexico. Furthermore Mexicans established numerous settlements, including Las Cruces, Los Angeles, Pueblo, San Antonio, San Diego,

San Francisco, and Santa Fe. Finally, for the sake of illustration, only a handful of students learn that most cowboy terminology is Spanish or Indo-Hispanic: adobe, arrejos, chaps, lariat, mesquite, and rodeo, among others.

It is sad that our foremost scholars have praised the significant writings of medieval Europe but not those of Latin or South America. There were bilingual dictionaries in Mexico before 1600, and teacher's guides, *Cartilla para enseñar a leer*, were trilingual—Spanish, Latin, and Nahuatl. But nothing can be done about past omissions. We can, however, prevent similar omissions in the present and the future. American students must also learn about the contributions of such persons as Juan Luis Vives, Alonso de la Vera Cruz, Octaviano Larrazolo, Miguel Hidalgo y Costilla, Rafael Ramírez, José Maria Morelos y Pavón, and Benito Juárez.

A cursory review of related literature shows that Puerto Rican history is not Mexican American history. It is imperative that American students gain an appreciation for the heroic efforts of Puerto Rican leaders such as Ramón Emeterio Betances, Ruiz Belvis, Eugenio Mariá de Hostos, and Ruis Rivera. Nor should students be unaware of the political contributions of Munnoz Rivera, Martienzo Cintron, and José Celso Barbosa. Of special significance are the writings of José de Diego, Albizu Campos, Luis Muñoz Marín, and Nicolás Guillén. Indeed, there is much more to learning about Puerto Ricans than reading Oscar Lewis' books.

In many ways Mexican-Americans and Puerto Ricans epitomize both racial integration and cultural separatism. This duality is best seen in a brief review of Mexican history. The Aztecs were intermarried with their Spanish conquerors and with Indian tribes hostile to the Aztecs. The children of these mixed matings were called *mestizos*. Also *creoles*, pure-blooded Spanish people born in Mexico, largely disappeared through intermarriage. Blacks from Africa, brought into Mexico during the colonial period as slaves, married Indians and their offsprings were called *zambos*. *Zambos* and *mestizos* later intermarried, causing the so-called "Negro blood" to disappear.

While they are a racially-mixed people, the heritage of the people called Mexican-Americans is quite similar: generally, they are highly religious (mainly Catholic); they are extended family-oriented and give allegiance to *La Raza*, "The Race"; they speak Spanish as their first language; they encourage their children to display good manners and to be especially respectful to older pesons; they train their girls for the home and motherhood, and their boys to earn their keep and to protect and honor their females.

In Arizona, California, Colorado, New Mexico, and Texas, Mexican-Americans comprise the largest minority group the public schools. Forty per cent of all Chicano students who enter the first grade do not graduate from high school. By the time they reach the twelfth grade, three out of every five Mexican-Americans students are reading below grade level. Chicanos are more likely than Anglos to have repeated a grade, and seven times more likely to be above the average age for their grade. The problems confronting most Chicano children entering school vividly illustrate the problems of other ethnic minority groups:

1. They are isolated from Anglo children.
2. Their language and culture are excluded from the curriculum.
3. Their neighborhood schools are underfinanced.
4. Teachers treat them less favorably than Anglo students.

Oral language is the most basic concern of any culturally pluralistic curriculum. This is especially true in the early elementary grades, when children depend almost entirely on their ability to communicate orally. Unfortunately for non-English-speaking subcultures, most school materials are based on the false assumption that each child has developed adequate oral language skills.

Just as Black English differs from standard English, Chicano Spanish also differs in vocabulary, grammar, and pronunciation from standard Spanish. For example, Chicano dialects often incorporate old Spanish words that were in common use during the seventeenth and eighteenth centuries. Consequently there is a need for well-designed and well-taught bilingual and bicultural instruction.

Less than 2 per cent of all Chicano students currently receive state funded bilingual education—the largest number of bilingual programs is found in Arizona and New Mexico.

This is so even though in 1974 the U.S. Supreme Court ruled that school districts are required under Title VI of the Civil Rights Act of 1964 to provide special programs for children who speak little or no English. Nationally, more than two million students do not speak English. In addition to Mexican-Americans, language minority groups include Native Americans, Puerto Ricans, Japanese-Americans, and Chinese-Americans.

The 1974 Bilingual Education Act defines a program of bilingual education as an elementary or secondary school program of instruction which uses the student's native language and English in order to allow him or her to progress effectively in the educational system, and to foster appreciation and respect for the student's cultural heritage. Bilingual education does not simply involve translation. It uses the two languages interchangeably. In addition to fostering reading, writing, and listening skills, the student is taught the history and culture associated with both languages. Thus bilingual education is not compensatory in the sense that the second language is either overtly or covertly defined as inadequate or inferior to English.

English as a Second Language (ESL) programs provide intensive instruction in English language arts skills so that students will be able to participate in monolingual classes. If it is important for non-English speaking students to appreciate English, it is equally important for English teachers to appreciate the language of their non-English speaking students.

In the past bilingual education in America was a privilege of the affluent; families that could afford a foreign governess or a private tutor could make their children minimally bilingual, if not bicultural. Broadening the base of bilingual education to include non-affluent children has not occurred smoothly. Some critics say that bilingual/bicultural education tends to polarize children of different nationalities. Implicit in this argument is the assumption that teaching in a language other than English is un-American. Other critics argue that achieving non-English language literacy is a waste of money and time since students will have few opportunities in America to use a non-English language. In addition to improving students' self-concepts and learning abilities, bilingual/bicultural programs (more appropriately called multilingual/multicultural

Table 14. Estimated Numbers Of Persons Enrolled In School Since September 1974 From Households In Which a Language Other Than English Is Usually Spoken, By Level Of Schooling and By Usual Household Language: July 1975

(In Thousands)

Non-English language usually spoken in household	Total	Nursery kindergarten	Grades 1–8	Grades 9–12	College 1–4 years
Total non-English	2,352	188	1,424	482	189
Spanish	1,685	141	1,095	336	97
Selected European languages[1]	267	(N)	147	69	(N)
Selected Asian languages[2]	220	(N)	94	(N)	(N)

[1] French, German, Greek, Italian and Porguguese.

[2] Chinese, Filipino, Japanese, Korean.

(N) The number if less than 50,000. Estimates less than 50,000 were not reported because of their large sampling error.

NOTES.—Questions on languages were supplemented to the July 1975 Current Population Survey conducted by the Bureau of the Census. The potential target group for Bilingual Education is defined in Section 731(C)(1)(A) of the Bilingual Education Act, Title VII, ESEA, as amended by P L-93-380 and includes children and adults who were born abroad, have a native language (usual language) other than English or come from an environment where a language other than English is dominant.

SOURCE: U.S. Department of Health, Education, and Welfare, National Center for Education Statistics, *Survey of Languages, 1976.*

programs) come to practical terms with the pluralistic nature of the world community.

Care must be taken to prevent bilingual education classes from becoming dumping places for low-achieving students with ethnic backgrounds. Specifically, these classes should not become but another way to segregate students while depriving them of equal educational opportunities.

Ricardo L. Garcia is an ardent supporter of the use of bicultural environmental approaches to stimulate students to read. What a student thinks, Garcia says, he or she can talk about; what student can talk about can be expressed in painting, writing, or some other form. Garcia encourages teachers to help Chicano students to use their five senses—sight, sound, touch, smell, and taste.

Calculated captures of the callous camera. *Have the reader take photographs of street and* barrio *(Chicano neighborhood) scenes. If* barrio *scenes are not available in the community, then the reader can photograph scenes from books that depict the* barrio. *The photographs can be made into slides for a multimedia presentation. The teacher should assist the reader to understand the importance in photography of balance, perspective, and*

sequence (as part of his discrimination skills introduction).

Nervous notes of notorious noisemakers. *Have the reader listen to* corridos *recorded by Chicano* musicos *(musicians), and write an English prose explanation of the* corrido *based on the English text of the* corrido. *Or have the reader describe in writing the sequence, the theme, and the figures of speech of the* corridos.

Black box of frivolous frumptions. *Have the reader touch and feel mysterious items and objects in a mystery box (without seeing the objects); then have the reader describe the objects in writing as well as orally. Objects related to the Chicano experience, such as the* huelga *symbol, should be placed in the box. Or common washers used by plumbers and carpenters could be included in the box. A game similar to penny pitching, and popular among some Chicano youngsters, is the pitching of washers into holes in the ground.*

Odoriferous hors d'oeveres of odd origins. *Have the reader smell Chicano foods with eyes closed, and describe the food in writing.* Chili or menudo *are recommended and can be prepared by the home economics teacher or by the cafeteria cook. The home economics student could benefit from the project as they will be exposed to ethnic cookery.*

Droll dishes of delicious delicacies. *Have the*

reader taste Chicano food and then describe the taste in writing. Of course, the teacher could provide the experience of having the reader prepare and then smell and taste the foods.[8]

If bilingual programs are not well-conceived, they will fail to produce students who are fluent in two languages. Instead, they will produce bilingual illiteracy on a massive scale.

One day I was walking down the street suddenly I thought if I could go to the beach. So I went. Then I saw a castle. I went inside the castle I saw a giant crying. Then I said, what happened?

The giant said I want to speak bilingual. Well that is simple I'll teach you. The giant said, when do we start? I said Right now. So we went on until the night. The giant said, Si means yes. I said now you know how to speak bilingual so much.

The next day I told my mother how it feels to speak bilingual. Well it feels good. It feels like I speak all kinds of language.[9]

ASIAN-AMERICAN STUDIES

Until recently the pattern of foreign studies in American schools was clear. In a course inappropriately called "world history" students learned that man's most significant development occurred in Europe and later in the U. S. The study of areas beyond Europe entered this version of world history only peripherally, mainly when these areas were "discovered" by Europeans. References to China were usually limited to three or four: when it was a "cradle of civilization," when it was a "discovered" by Marco Polo, when it came under European domination, and when it became an "emerging nation." In this version, Japan's "history" begins when it is "opened" by Commodore Perry.[10]

Ethnic studies curricula are teaching basic historical facts about Asian-Americans. The three largest American groups of Asian ancestry—Chinese, Japanese, and Filipinos—came to this country during the late nineteenth and early twentieth centuries. Attracted by the gold rush of the 1850s, Chinese were the first to come to America. Later, other Chinese were imported as cheap labor to help complete the transcontinental railway. Gradually overt discrimination increased until the Chinese Exclusion Act of 1882 was passed. This act denied immigration for ten years to Chinese laborers.

It was renewed in 1892, and Chinese immigration was suspended indefinitely in 1902. The Exclusion Act also denied citizenship to Chinese born outside the United States. (This act was later applied to other Orientals.)

Almost all Japanese immigration to America occurred between 1900 and 1925. Despite the fact that most Japanese duplicated the European-type immigration pattern (whole families settling in integrated communities), they were discriminated against in the same manner as the Chinese, who mainly came as single males and lived in segregated communities. The "Gentlemen's Agreement" of 1908 between the American and Japanese governments restricted the immigration of Japanese farmers and laborers to the United States.

The most infamous example of Anglo discrimination against the Japanese occurred during World War II, when by Presidential decree the total Japanese population (more than 110,000 people) in California, Oregon, and Washington was evacuated to ten relocation centers in rural areas of America. The barbed wire-encircled barracks communities were patrolled by armed guards. This aspect of American history is usually omitted in American history courses.

The Filipinos came to America in the 1920s, and like other Orientals they were ineligible for naturalization. However because the United States ruled the Philippines, the early Filipino immigrants carried U. S. passports and could not be excluded as aliens. In 1935, with the promise of freeing the Philippines, the American government set a quota of fifty Filipino immigrants per year.

After World War II alien Asians became eligible for citizenship, and in 1965 the national origin quota system was abolished. Currently, immigration from the Eastern Hemisphere and dependent areas is limited to 170,000. It is 120,000 for the Western Hemisphere. No more than 20,000 immigrants may come from any one country.

The influx into the United States between 1973 and 1975 of 50,000 school-age Vietnamese and Cambodian children has forced us to focus on the problems inherent in educating Indochinese refugees. Because of their war experiences, a significant number of these children need physical and psychological assistance as well as bilingual/bicultural education.

Culturally conditioned to be passive learners, diligent scholars, and respectful of adults, Indochinese students have difficulty adjusting to competitive classrooms, athletically-oriented students, and teacher-student peer-like relationships characterizing American schools.

Attempts to broaden educational perspectives to include cultures in Asia have helped to change the attitudes of American students towards American descendents of those cultures. As our national policies shift, so too do our feelings toward Orientals or Asians. There is, for example, a connection between our feelings toward the Chinese in Asia and Chinese-Americans. Because most Americans feel superior to other global cultures, they tend to feel superior to those ethnic representatives within the United States. Seymour Fersh observed a novel twist to this prejudice: "For some American Orientals, prejudice works the other way; teachers may believe that Chinese, for example, have superior intelligence and work harder than other students. Consequently, more is expected from them and this 'compliment' increases pressure on the learner."[11] More has been done to provide Asian-American studies in colleges and universities than in elementary and secondary schools. Even so, the higher education effort is meager.

Despite a growth in ethnic studies, most minorities are antagonistic toward and ignorant about cultures of other minorities. But so too are most Anglo children. To those who argue that ethnic minority content should only be studied by ethnic minorities, Banks gives an eloquent rebuttal:

The criterion used to determine whether [information about classical Rome and Greece, Medieval Europe, and Italian Renaissance] should be taught is not whether there are students in the class who are descendants of ancient Rome and Greece, or Italy or Medieval Europe. Such a criterion would not be intellectually sound. For the same reasons, it should not be used to select content about other cultures, such as the minority cultures in America.[12]

More than ethnic content is required if minority group students are to be successful in liberating their own communities. In addition to understanding institutionalized racism, minority students must learn strategies for social change. This can be done by involving students in social action projects in which they learn how social systems work and how they can be altered.

IMPLEMENTING CULTURAL PLURALISM STUDIES

One of the first steps in facilitating a successful racial and cultural pluralism program in the schools is to convey clearly to the community the changes that will be advocated. It is necessary to pursue aggressively steps involving the community in a culturally pluralistic approach to schooling. The community's awareness, understanding and support is most crucial to any school program's success. When designing and implementing programs focusing on cultural pluralism, the following tips are worth heeding:

1. Develop a file of community resource persons who would be willing to "rap" with classes about certain aspects of the Third World experience in American history.

2. Conduct and tape interviews with Third World and other community people (senior citizens would be a good target population) relative to their experiences in the neighborhood. The following questions might raised: What brought them there? What adjustment difficulties were experienced? What experiences do they think were unique to their cultural group? What experiences do they think were similar to those of other cultural groups? What holidays are unique to their culture? Who are the heroines and heroes of their culture? What recreational games are unique to their culture? What music do they play and appreciate? What clothing and foods are unique to their culture?

3. Develop a list of outstanding Third World people within the local community from its founding.·

4. Develop skills in evaluating instructional material relative to ethnic and sex bias so as to be able to train other community and school personnel to conduct this analysis.

5. Establish a pilot program to implement cultural pluralism in two classrooms over a one-year period with the intent of adding at least two classrooms each year thereafter to the program.

6. Conduct a survey of the community to establish a "Cultural Group Myth Distortion List"

which will be used in classroom activities to discuss "language as a murder weapon" relative to Third World groups.

7. *Identify and acquire pertinent materials (audio and printed) that reflect the dignity and worth of all people and establish a multiethnic room in each school building, local library, and community recreational facility.*

8. *Sponsor a Multiethnic Forum and Festival. This would be a major event and could be an annual activity which would be characterized by community people and students displaying and presenting their "major" works in the various disciplines of literature, art, dramatics, music, math, and science, which reflect their respective cultures.* [13]

The Role of the Teacher

When teachers and students share their respective cultures, the interaction between them tends to be positive and growth producing. Unfortunately this seldom happens; thus one of the tasks of teachers is to bridge the gap between themselves and their students. In a study of a Mexican-American community, the following suggestions were offered to teachers endeavoring to translate the goals of racial and cultural pluralism into educational plans and instruction:

1. *Teach reading and math in both English and Spanish language. Use instructional materials favorable to both cultures.*

2. *Group pupils on the basis of interests, cross-culture friendships and skill attainment. In a departure from former procedure, the memberships in groups should change frequently and give less attention to presumed aptitudes.*

3. *Add cooperative rules instead of relying solely on the practice of individual competition, e.g., all members of groups should achieve recognition when the group performance is excellent. The older procedure of rewarding those individuals who excelled over their peers is to be deemphasized. Further, at times the teacher should allow an individual child to set his/her own criteria for success on a given task.*

4. *Encourage greater parent involvement in both social and academic events. Teachers should ask parents to help plan and carry out particular lessons and activities.*

5. *Add new electives based on interests of learners from different cultures, e.g., opportunities for learning to play guitar.*

6. *Augment teaching styles to include "culture matching strategies," such as (a) giving nonverbal acceptance, e.g., tap on head and (b) giving personal experience, e.g., "I had the same problem."*

7. *Relate pupils' classroom work to their families, e.g., "You might want to make something for your home."*

8. *Develop close relations with the pupil, e.g., teacher should work side by side with child and model the behavior that is wanted.* [14]

It has also been proposed that teacher retention criteria include success operating in an open setting where ethnic group problems are explored and alternatives are considered. Teacher commitment to cultural pluralism is exemplified by those who indicate a willingness to both accept change and to change themselves. Also, teachers should be willing to attend workshops that are self-analytical in nature.

The role of the teacher in implementing racial and cultural pluralism includes the following dimensions of intergroup relations: identity consciousness, validating differences, minority group advocacy, collaborative and cooperative strategies, conflict resolution, and risk taking. Validation of differences suggests that teachers go beyond simply valuing cultural dissimilarities; they must take an active stance in protecting cultural differences. Minority-group advocacy requires "placing one's self in another's shoes; it means supporting work toward the goals identified by persons from another group; it means listening rather than telling. . . . Advocacy thinking should lead to a clarification of differences between persons, and to a recognition of when it is or is not possible to collaborate." [15]

Collaborative and cooperative strategies are required in a pluralistic setting. "Collaboration seems a more healthy means of working together—persons from different groups discover what goals they have in common and the extent to which they can collaborate in achieving them." [16]

Teachers can best serve themselves and their students when they recognize and prepare for conflict situations. Conflict is inevitable in society. It can be a destructive force that breeds bitterness, hostility, or alienation, or it can become a creative force that encourages open and constructive problem solving. It is better to vent feelings and encourage others to do so than to have unresolved conflicts that can destroy the group, not to mention the individuals.

Social change requires a risk-taking. "Risk nothing, or everything, and your commitment may be questioned. Risking something specific, in a thoughtful, calculated manner, may be the best bet. The risk should be known, that is, specifically identified. Will your actions precipitate isolation from your institutional colleagues? Is reduction in pay a factor? Will your credibility drop? Know how such factors matter to you and be prepared for the consequences."[17] The following letter written by an Indian parent to her child's non-Indian teacher illustrates these questions.

Dear ———:

Before you take charge of the classroom that contains my child, please ask yourself why you are going to teach Indian children. What are your expectations? What rewards do you anticipate? What ego-needs will our children have to meet?

Write down and examine all the information and opinions you possess about Indians. What are the stereotypes and untested assumptions that you bring with you into the classroom? What values, class prejudices and moral principles do you take for granted as universal? Please remember that different from, is not the same as "worse than" or "better than" and the yardstick you use to measure your own life satisfactorily may not be appropriate for their lives. The term culturally-deprived was invented by well-meaning middle-class whites to describe something they could not understand.

Too many teachers, unfortunately, seem to see their role as rescuer. My child does not need to be rescued; he does not consider being Indian a misfortune. He has a culture, probably older than yours; he has meaningful values and rich and varied experimental background. However strange or incomprehensible it may seem to be to you, you have no right to do or say anything that implies to him that it is less than satisfactory.

Our children's experiences have been different from those of the "typical" white middle-class child for whom most school curricula seem to have been designed. I suspect that this typical child does not exist except in the minds of curriculum writers.

Nonetheless, my child's experiences have been as intense and meaningful to him as any child's. Like most Indian children his age, he is competent. He can dress himself, prepare a meal for himself and clean up afterwards, care for a younger child. He knows his reserves like the back of his hand.

He is not accustomed to having to ask permission to do the ordinary things that are part of normal living. He is seldom forbidden to do anything; more usually the consequences of an action are explained to him and he is allowed to decide for himself whether or not to act.

His entire existence since he has been old enough to see and hear has been an experimental learning situation, arranged to provide him with the opportunity to develop his skills and confidence in his own capacities. Didactic teaching will be an alien experience for him.

He is not self-conscious in the way many white children are. Nobody has ever told him his efforts toward independence are cute. He is a young human being energetically doing his job, which is to get on with the process of learning to function as an adult human being. He will respect you and expect you to do likewise to him. He has been taught, by precept, that courtesy is an essential part of human conduct and rudeness is an action that makes another peson feel stupid or foolish. Do not mistake his patient courtesy for indifference or passivity.

He doesn't speak standard English, but he is in no way linguistically handicapped. If you will take the time and courtesy to listen and observe carefully, you will see that he and the other Indian children communicate very well. They speak functional English, very effectively augmented by their fluency in the silent language, the subtle, unspoken communication of facial expressions, gestures, body movement and the use of personal space.

You will be well advised to remember that our children are skillful interpreters of the silent language. They will know your feelings and attitudes with unerring precision no matter how carefully you arrange your smile or modulate your voice. They will learn in your classroom, because children learn involuntarily. What they learn will depend on you.

Will you help my child to learn to read or will you teach him that he has a reading problem? Will you help him to develop problem-solving skills or will you teach him that school is where you try to guess what answer the teacher wants? Will he learn that his sense of his own value and dignity is valid, or will he learn that he must forever be apologetic and trying harder because he isn't white? Can you help him acquire the intellectual skills he needs without at the same time imposing your values on top of those he already has?

Respect my child. He is a person. He has a right to be himself.

LEGAL ASPECTS

A major factor in the lack of legal suits filed in state and federal courts concerning multicultural education is that the issue itself is a relatively recent one. Bilingual education, for example, has been seen generally as a remedy for racial segregation rather than as a right of its own sake. But progress has been made, at least in state law if not in practice. Since 1968, three states (Texas, Indiana and Oregon) have repealed the requirement that English be the sole language of instruction. Criminal penalties for teaching in a language other than English have been repealed in Texas and South Dakota. Prohibitions against teaching in a "foreign" language have been modified in California, New York, Colorado, Maine, and Washington. Finally, Arizona, California, Colorado, Illinois, Maine, Michigan, New Mexico, New York, Oregon, Pennsylvania, and Texas have all passed statutes permitting or encouraging local school districts to provide bilingual education for their students. Even so, two U. S. Supreme Court decisions merit our attention.

San Antonio Independent School District v. Rodriguez, 411 U. S. 200 (1971). This is a landmark decision in the matter of equal education for minority groups in the United States, and a disappointment to advocates of bicultural education in public schools. In the summer of 1968 a class action suit was filed on behalf of school children in San Antonio, charging that the school financing system of the state of Texas, based on local property taxation, was inherently discriminatory against poor families living in school districts with a low property-tax base. A three-judge Federal District Court held that the Texas system of school financing was indeed unconstitutional and thus upheld the charge brought on behalf of the students.

However in December 1971 the U. S. Supreme Court handed down a decision on this case which seemed to set back the cause of bicultural education. The Supreme Court's majority opinion written by Justice Lewis F. Powell, Jr. said:

1. The Texas system does not disadvantage any suspect class. It has not been shown to discriminate against any definable class of "poor" people or to occasion discrimination depending on the relative wealth of the families in any district. And, insofar as the financing system disadvantages those who, disregarding their individual income characteristics, reside in comparatively poor school districts, the resulting class cannot be said to be suspect.

2. . . . the Texas school-financing system [does not] impermissibly interfere with the exercise of a "fundamental" right or liberty. Though education is one of the most important services performed by the State, it is not within the limited category of rights recognized by this Court as guaranteed by the Constitution. Even if some identifiable quantum of education is arguably entitled to constitutional protection to make meaningful the exercise of other constitutional rights, here there is no showing that the Texas system fails to provide the basic minimal skills necessary for that purpose.

3. The Texas system does not violate the Equal Protection clause of the Fourteenth Amendment. Though concededly imperfect, the system bears a rational relationship to a legitimate state purpose. While assuring basic education for every child in the State, it permits and encouarages participation in and significant control of each district's schools at the local level.[18]

At least one authority sees a clear dichotomy posed by this Supreme Court decision and the later *Goss* decision, a case dealing with the rights of students in public school suspension cases. (See Chapter 13.) Martha M. McCarthy points out that in *Rodriguez*, "the individual's interest in education was not afforded even implied constitutional protection for equal protection purposes," but in *Goss*, "the student's property interest in education was guaranteed full protection of due process of law." As McCarthy cogently points out, "it is difficult at best for one to reconcile these two decisions and ascertain the perimeters of an individual's constitutional relationship to public education."[19] The crux of the entire matter, McCarthy concludes, is that "either the rulings are contradictory or it must be concluded that the Court is determining rights in one manner for equal protection review and in another for due process analysis. Such distinctions result in a hierarchy of rights which are afforded varying degrees of judicial protection."[20]

David L. Kirp maintains that when the *Rodriguez* decision rejected the claim that education is of fundamental constitutional significance, it appeared "to foreclose all challenges to inequities in the provision of education —or, at least, inequities which are neither racial in nature nor represent complete denial of schooling."[21]

Lau v. Nichols, 414 U. S. 563 (1974). In 1974 the U. S. Supreme Court handed down another historic decision which touched directly on the issue of state responsibility for bilingual education in public schools. The *Lau* case, initiated largely by parents of Chinese children, sought to force the San Francisco Unified School District to offer bilingual instruction to non-English-speaking students. In its ruling the Court held that school districts "must take affirmative action to remedy the English language deficiencies of minority children or lose federal funds." If school districts fail to fulfill such a responsibility, they violate students' rights "to equal educational opportunities under Title VI of the U. S. Civil Rights Act." It is this decision which has impelled the U. S. Office of Civil Rights to enforce a strict timetable on school districts for compliance in instituting a bicultural program. Specifically, the Court held in its majority opinion:

Basic English skills are at the very core of what these public schools teach. Imposition of a requirement that, before a child can effectively participate in the educational program, he must already have acquired those basic skills is to make a mockery of public education. We know that those who do not understand English are certain to find their classroom experiences wholly incomprehensible and in no way meaningful.[22]

It is apparent in this decision that the U. S. Supreme Court decided to take a compassionate view of the millions of children in our land who do not use English as their primary language. The Supreme Court justices must have come to realize what a lonely time these students have in their public schools: schools which are public in the sense that parents are taxed to support them, but in which their children do not receive adequate instruction. The *Lau* decision has greatly accelerated the trend to toward bicultural programs for all of America's non-English-speaking students.

TOWARD ETHNIC AND ECONOMIC DIVERSITY

School districts which successfully design curricula for ethnic and economic diversity set in motion a memorable process. By this process their students can walk in dignity, eat a wholesome diet, sleep in a decent house, live in economic and social freedom, and, in the end, die a timely death unhurried by malnutrition and racism. Clearly, this is not much to ask of our schools; but it would be everything to refuse such an opportunity for our children.[23]

Organized education is specifically human activity. Its foremost function is to transmit culture and to develop the power and sensibility of flexible young minds. Thus it necessarily follows that in performing their functions, schools affect individual self-concepts, group processes, and ways of life for present and future generations.

Although all elements of a community should play a role in the formal education of students, it is the schools that are held accountable for children becoming functional members of our society. Indeed, it is as though parents and community leaders bring the children—kicking and screaming—to the school door, leave them, and tell school personnel, "We'll take them back when you have taught them how to be productive citizens."

In fulfilling their responsibilities, many educators are beginning to give more attention to developing a curriculum which is productive of action rather than reaction. Gradually, the importance of communication skills is being recognized—especially in schools that engender the confidence which comes from social acceptance and peer approval. In order to create a curriculum that will allow a learner to fit comfortably into a diverse society, it is necessary for teachers (1) to encourage the raising of relevant questions by all elements of the community, (2) to collect and interpret representative data, (3) to amplify consumer demands, (4) to communicate prospective producer needs, and (5) to understand the diverse values in their communities.

Of course, self-examination by those re-

Table 15. Enrollment in Public Postsecondary Area Vocational Schools, by Student Ethnic Group and Sex: 1974

Ethnic group	Total		Male		Female	
	Number	Percent	Number	Percent	Number	Percent
Total	567,476	100.0	341,755	100.0	225,721	100.0
American Indian ...	5,761	1.0	3,376	1.0	2,385	1.1
Black	63,830	11.2	34,664	10.1	29,166	12.9
Asian American	6,351	1.1	3,666	1.1	2,685	1.2
Spanish origin	23,359	4.1	15,003	4.3	8,356	3.7
Other	456,767	80.5	277,959	81.3	178,808	79.2
Unclassified	11,408	2.0	7,087	2.1	4,321	1.9

SOURCE: U.S. Department of Health, Education, and Welfare, Office of Civil Rights, *Survey of Public Postsecondary Area Vocational Schools, 1974*, unpublished data.

sponsible for designing the curriculum is necessary to make them aware of their own negative attitudes. One of the chief shortcomings of educators in bringing students to their maximum performance has been negative attitudes. When a teacher bases his or her expectations of students' performances on students' social status, children of low social status suffer an almost permanent debilitation outside of their own choice or will.

A truly functional human being cannot be transferred from school to the larger society if he or she is educated in a setting which develops or perpetuates a caste system. Assuredly, today's "classroom caste" will become tomorrow's "social class."

A Vehicle for Economic Mobility

In our highly industralized and mechanized culture, educators responsible for curriculum development are confronted with increasingly complex economic problems. For the first time since its ascendency, the United States finds itself seriously challenged as a leading economic power of the world. We have a rate of unemployment that is too high and a gross national product that is too low. In addition more of our people are engaged in services than in production and there are glaring imbalances within the service occupations—for example, an oversupply of teachers and an undersupply of doctors.

When attempting to gather data to assist in better curriculum design, educators are hampered by a national research budget which allocates 50 per cent of its resources to defense exploration but only one fifth of 1 per cent to educational research. Even so, a cursory glance at our economy makes it apparent that with increasing shortages of consumer goods, we must either produce more or consume less. Accepting the former course, national emphasis in education is being placed on vocational and technical curricula, for it is here that people are trained to produce and maintain the goods demanded for day-to-day consumption.

The practicality of this focus is apparent. Yet the task of concerned curriculum planners becomes even more complicated if they are to provide opportunities for economic mobility without sacrificing the ethnic diversity which can best derive from a liberal or broad based education

New and imaginative concepts and combinations of curricula must be explored if we are to correlate student supply with industrial demands. With the increasing emphasis on vocational and technical education, it will be the task of those committed to humanistic curriculum development to see that students trained to meet the immediate needs of industry are not programmed into employment castes from which they cannot escape. The dangling carrot of economic mobility can seduce the unwary not only toward freedom but also, under certain conditions, toward material servitude. Therefore in training students to meet the career demands of our culture, we must exercise care in planning courses that will include exposure and experience in making value judgments.

A humanistic curriculum that will contribute most conscientiously to economic mobility is one which will (1) consider and satisfy the occupational needs of both the individual student and the community, (2) present goals beyond the initial career encounter, and (3) devise educational content, methodology, and format which will build upon the strengths of students coming from several multiethnic backgrounds.

Respect for Economic and Cultural Diversity

Education should be an appreticeship for life. If the positive aspects of any society result from the cooperative efforts of it constituents, schools offer the ideal setting for communication, understanding, and consequent enrichment that all constituent elements of our culture have to offer each other. Formal education affords an opportunity for people to both learn in theory and perform in practice the creative process of accepting differences.

Institutions of learning can appeal to the highest of human values. In *The Souls of Black Folk*, W. E. B. DuBois cautioned: "We are training not isolated men but a living group of men—nay, a group within a group. And the final product of our training must be neither a psychologist nor a brickmason, but a man." [24] Those sharing the responsibility for charting the direction students will take should never lose sight of the final purpose of education: to reinforce the relevance and interlocking community of all humanhood.

Through the eyes of our children we can look at America and see an endless series of beautiful and ugly ironies. For these children, reared in predominantly affluent society which reflects a technological now-you-see-it-world, there are few places to hide either our humanity or our inhumanity. Through the mass media—television, radio, and newspapers— children are socialized in a nation torn apart by civil disorders, socio-economic deprivation, racism, and sexism. No other generation of young people has been so exposed to the totality of the nation and the world they live in.

Social critics point out that we have become a mass communication and rapid transportation society whose technology has stripped us naked and revealed our hatred, violence, and social concerns. It is these and other conditions which cause numerous humanists to conclude that the primary need of all children (and adults) is to learn to accept themselves and to have respect for themselves and others.

Some of the ways that education, through curriculum, can provide a major channel of respect for economic and cultural diversity are (1) to emphasize the dignity and satisfaction of work *per se* rather than the attainment of some high occupational level, (2) to research, compile, and present job opportunities in occupations which require both a college education and less than a full college education, (3) to acquaint students with institutions which provide quality education and training directly related to available career opportunities, (4) to counsel students more effectively so they will not develop aspirations beyond their abilities, (5) to offer vocational interest and skills courses that will enrich and supplement occupational deficits, (6) to provide remedial programs for those who suffer from failures in preschool or in-school activities, and (7) to procure and utilize teaching materials relevant to students of all backgrounds, so their differences may be understood, accepted, and respected as enriching the nation.

Urgently needed are the efforts of an understanding community working together to combine humanizing and enriching courses and experiences with those preparing students for realistic labor needs. Only then can we avoid the conflicts that are certain to arise if the edifying and unifying drives of men and women are left untended. All that is developed or left undeveloped of human resources will not only shape the essence of future generations but in fact may also affect their very existence. Therefore, educational potentiality must cease to exist in an academic vacuum.

The quality of a society stands in direct relationship to the preparation of its youth for responsibility and authority. Positive results can only be achieved by the total effort of involved communities. For instance, the depletion of oil and other material resources is serious only if we fail to develop the human resources to find solution to these problems. Ultimately if children do not learn to be humane workers, the effects for the world may not be merely serious but may also prove fatal.

THE MULTIETHNIC EDUCATION PROGRAM
EVALUATION CHECKLIST

GUIDELINES	RATING			
	Strongly			Hardly at all
1.0 Does ethnic pluralism permeate the total school environment?	☐	☐	☐	☐
1.1 Is ethnic conduct incorporated into all aspects of the curriculum, preschool through grade twelve and beyond?	☐	☐	☐	☐
1.2 Do instructional materials treat ethnic differences and groups honestly, realistically, and sensitively?	☐	☐	☐	☐
1.3 Do school libraries and resource centers have a variety of materials on the histories, experiences, and culture of many different ethnic groups?	☐	☐	☐	☐
1.4 Do school assemblies, decorations, speakers, holidays, and heroes reflect ethnic group differences?	☐	☐	☐	☐
1.5 Are extracurricular activities multiracial and multiethnic?	☐	☐	☐	☐
2.0 Do school policies and procedures foster positive interactions among the different ethnic group members of the school?	☐	☐	☐	☐
2.1 Do school policies accommodate the behavioral patterns, learning styles, and orientations of those ethnic group members actually in the school?	☐	☐	☐	☐
2.2 Does the school provide a diversity of instruments and techniques in teaching and counseling students of different ethnic groups?	☐	☐	☐	☐
2.3 Do school policies recognize the holidays and festivities of different ethnic groups?	☐	☐	☐	☐
2.4 Do school policies avoid instructional and guidance practices based on stereotyped and ethnocentric perceptions?	☐	☐	☐	☐

SOURCE: National Council for the Social Studies, 1515 Wilson Boulevard, Arlington, VA 22209

Strongly   Hardly
at all

2.5 Do school policies respect the dignity and
     worth of students as individuals *and* as
     members of ethnic groups?   ☐   ☐   ☐   ☐

3.0 Are the school staffs (administrative, in-
     struction, counseling, and supportive)
     multiethnic and multiracial?   ☐   ☐   ☐   ☐

3.1 Has the school established and enforced
     policies for for recruiting and maintaining
     multiethnic, multiracial staffs?   ☐   ☐   ☐   ☐

4.0 Does the school have systematic, com-
     prehensive, mandatory, and continuing
     multiethnic staff development programs?   ☐   ☐   ☐   ☐

4.1 Are teachers, librarians, counselors, ad-
     ministrators, and the supportive staff in-
     cluded in the staff development pro-
     grams?   ☐   ☐   ☐   ☐

4.2 Do the staff development programs in-
     clude a variety of experiences (such as
     lectures, field experiences, curriculum
     projects, etc.)?   ☐   ☐   ☐   ☐

4.3 Do the staff development programs pro-
     vide opportunities to gain knowledge
     and understanding about different ethnic
     groups?   ☐   ☐   ☐   ☐

4.4 Do the staff development programs pro-
     vide opportunities for participants to ex-
     plore their attitudes and feelings about
     their own ethnicity and others'?   ☐   ☐   ☐   ☐

4.5 Do the staff development programs ex-
     amine the verbal and nonverbal patterns
     of interethnic group interactions?   ☐   ☐   ☐   ☐

4.6 Do the staff development programs pro-
     vide opportunities for learning how to
     create and select multiethnic instructional
     materials and how to incorporate ethnic
     content into curriculum materials?   ☐   ☐   ☐   ☐

5.0 Does the curriculum reflect the ethnic
     learning styles of students within the
     school?   ☐   ☐   ☐   ☐

	Strongly			Hardly at all

5.1 Is the curriculum designed to help students learn how to function effectively in different cultural environments and master more than one cognitive style?   ☐ ☐ ☐ ☐

5.2 Do the objectives, instructional strategies, and learning materials reflect the cultures and cognitive styles of the different ethnic groups within the school?   ☐ ☐ ☐ ☐

6.0 Does the curriculum provide continuous opportunities for students to develop a better sense of self?   ☐ ☐ ☐ ☐

6.1 Does the curriculum help students strengthen their self-identities?   ☐ ☐ ☐ ☐

6.2 Is the curriculum designed to help students develop greater self-understanding?   ☐ ☐ ☐ ☐

6.3 Does the curriculum help students better understand themselves in the light of their ethnic heritages?   ☐ ☐ ☐ ☐

7.0 Does the curriculum help students to understand the wholeness of the experiences of ethnic groups?   ☐ ☐ ☐ ☐

7.1 Does the curriculum include the study of societal problems some ethnic group members experience, such as racism, prejudice, discrimination, and exploitation?   ☐ ☐ ☐ ☐

7.2 Does the curriculum include the study of historical experiences, cultural patterns, *and* social problems of different ethnic groups?   ☐ ☐ ☐ ☐

7.3 Does the curriculum include both positive and negative aspects of ethnic group experiences?   ☐ ☐ ☐ ☐

7.4 Does the curriculum present ethnics as active participants in society *and* as subjects of oppresion and exploitation?   ☐ ☐ ☐ ☐

7.5 Does the curriculum examine the diversity within each ethnic group's experience?   ☐ ☐ ☐ ☐

	Strongly			Hardly at all
7.6 Does the curriculum present ethnic group experience as dynamic and continuously changing?	☐	☐	☐	☐
7.7 Does the curriculum examine the experiences of ethnic group people instead of focusing exclusively on the "heroes"?	☐	☐	☐	☐
8.0 Does the curriculum help students identify and understand the ever-present conflict between ideals and realities in human societies?	☐	☐	☐	☐
8.1 Does the curriculum help students identify and understand the value conflicts in problematic situations?	☐	☐	☐	☐
8.2 Does the curriculum examine differing views of ideals and realities among ethnic groups.	☐	☐	☐	☐
9.0 Does the curriculum explore and clarify ethnic alaternatives and options within American society?	☐	☐	☐	☐
9.1 Does the teacher create a classroom atmosphere reflecting an acceptance of and respect for ethnic differences?	☐	☐	☐	☐
9.2 Does the teacher create a classroom atmosphere allowing realistic consideration of ethnic alternatives and options?	☐	☐	☐	☐
10.0 Does the curriculum promote values, attitudes, and behaviors which support ethnic pluralism?	☐	☐	☐	☐
10.1 Does the curriculum help students examine differences within and among ethnic groups?	☐	☐	☐	☐
10.2 Does the curriculum foster attitudes supportive of cultural democracy and other democratic ideals and values?	☐	☐	☐	☐
10.3 Does the curriculum reflect ethnic pluralism?	☐	☐	☐	☐

Strongly   Hardly
at all

10.4 Does the curriculum present ethnic pluralism as a vital societal force that encompasses both potential strength and potential conflict?

☐ ☐ ☐ ☐

11.0 Does the curriculum help students develop decision-making abilities, social participation skills, and a sense of political efficacy needed for effective citizenship?

☐ ☐ ☐ ☐

11.1 Does the curriculum help students develop the ability to distinguish facts from interpretations and opinions?

☐ ☐ ☐ ☐

11.2 Does the curriculum help students develop skills in finding and processing information?

☐ ☐ ☐ ☐

11.3 Does the curriculum help students develop sound knowledge, concepts, generalizations, and theories about issues related to ethnicity?

☐ ☐ ☐ ☐

11.4 Does the curriculum help students develop sound methods of thinking about ethnic issues?

☐ ☐ ☐ ☐

11.5 Does the curriculum help students develop skills in clarifying and justifying their values and relating them to their understanding of ethnicity?

☐ ☐ ☐ ☐

11.6 Does the curriculum include opportunities to use knowledge, valuing, and thinking in decision-making on ethnic matters?

☐ ☐ ☐ ☐

11.7 Does the curriculum provide opportunities for students to take action on social problems affecting ethnic groups?

☐ ☐ ☐ ☐

11.8 Does the curriculum help students develop a sense of efficacy?

☐ ☐ ☐ ☐

12.0 Does the curriculum help students develop skills necessary for effective interpersonal and interethnic group interactions?

☐ ☐ ☐ ☐

Strongly | | | Hardly at all

12.1 Does the curriculum help students understand ethnic reference points which influence communication? □ □ □ □

12.2 Does the curriculum help students try out cross-ethnic experiences and reflect upon them? □ □ □ □

13.0 Is the multiethnic curriculum comprehensive in scope and sequence, presenting holistic views of ethnic groups, and an integral part of the total school curriculum? □ □ □ □

13.1 Does the curriculum introduce students to the experiences of persons of widely varying backgrounds in the study of each ethnic group? □ □ □ □

13.2 Does the curriculum discuss the successes and contributions of members of some group in terms of that group's values? □ □ □ □

13.3. Does the curriculum include the role of ethnicity in the local community as well as in the nation? □ □ □ □

13.4 Does content related to ethnic groups extend beyond special units, courses, occasions, and holidays? □ □ □ □

13.5 Are materials written by and about ethnic groups used in teaching fundamental skills? □ □ □ □

13.6 Does the curriculum provide for the development of progressively more complex concepts, abilities, and values? □ □ □ □

13.7 Is the study of ethnicity incorporated in instructional plans rather than being supplementary or additive? □ □ □ □

14.0 Does the curriculum include the continuous study of the cultures, historical experiences, social realities, and existential conditions of ethnic groups with a variety of racial compositions? □ □ □ □

Strongly   Hardly
at all

14.1 Does the curriculum include study of several ethnic groups? ☐ ☐ ☐ ☐

14.2 Does the curriculum include studies of both white and nonwhite groups? ☐ ☐ ☐ ☐

14.3 Does the curriculum provide for continuity in the examination of aspects of experience affected by race? ☐ ☐ ☐ ☐

15.0 Are interdisciplinary and multidisciplinary approaches used in designing and implementing the multiethnic curriculum? ☐ ☐ ☐ ☐

15.1 Are interdisciplinary and multidisciplinary perspectives used in the study of ethnic groups and related issues? ☐ ☐ ☐ ☐

15.2 Are approaches used authentic and comprehensive explanations of ethnic issues, events, and problems? ☐ ☐ ☐ ☐

16.0 Does the curriculum use comparative approaches in the study of ethnic groups and ethnicity? ☐ ☐ ☐ ☐

16.1 Does the curriculum focus on the similarities and differences among ethnic groups? ☐ ☐ ☐ ☐

16.2 Are matters examined from comparative perspectives with fairness to all? ☐ ☐ ☐ ☐

17.0 Does the curriculum help students to view and interpret events, situations, and conflict from diverse ethnic perspectives and points of view? ☐ ☐ ☐ ☐

17.1 Are the perspectives of different ethnic groups represented in the instructional program? ☐ ☐ ☐ ☐

17.2 Are students taught why different ethnic groups often perceive the same historical event or contemporary situation differently? ☐ ☐ ☐ ☐

Strongly | | | Hardly at all

17.3 Are the perspectives of each ethnic group presented as valid ways to perceive the past and the present? □ □ □ □

18. Does the curriculum conceptualize and describe the development of the United States as a multidirectional society? □ □ □ □

18.1 Does the curriculum view the territorial and cultural growth of the United States as flowing from several directions? □ □ □ □

18.2 Does the curriculum include a parallel study of the various societies which developed in the geo-cultural United States? □ □ □ □

19.0 Does the school provide opportunities for students to participate in the aesthetic experiences of various ethnic groups? □ □ □ □

19.1 Are multethnic literature and art used to promote empathy for people of different ethnic groups? □ □ □ □

19.2 Are multiethnic literature and art used to promote self-examination and self-understanding? □ □ □ □

19.3 Do students read and hear the poetry, short stories, novels, folklore, plays, essays, and autobiographies of a variety of ethnic groups? □ □ □ □

19.4 Do students examine the music, art, architecture and dance of a variety of ethnic groups? □ □ □ □

19.5 Do students have available the artistic, musical, and literary expression of the local ethnic communities? □ □ □ □

19.6 Are opportunities provided for students to develop their own artistic, literary, and musical expression? □ □ □ □

20.0 Does the school foster the view of ethnic group languages as legitimate communication systems? □ □ □ □

Strongly   Hardly at all

20.1 Are students taught about the nature of languages and dialects? ☐ ☐ ☐ ☐

20.2 Is the student taught in his or her dominant language or dialect when needed? ☐ ☐ ☐ ☐

20.3 Does the curriculum explore the role of languages and dialects in self-understanding and within and among ethnic groups? ☐ ☐ ☐ ☐

20.4 Are the language policies and laws within the United States studied from political perspectives? ☐ ☐ ☐ ☐

21.0 Does the curriculum make maximum use of local community resources? ☐ ☐ ☐ ☐

21.1 Are students carefully involved in the continuous study of the local community? ☐ ☐ ☐ ☐

21.2 Are members of the local ethnic communities continually used as classroom resources? ☐ ☐ ☐ ☐

21.3 Are field trips to the various local ethnic communities provided for students? ☐ ☐ ☐ ☐

22.0 Do the assessment procedures used with students reflect their ethnic cultures? ☐ ☐ ☐ ☐

22.1 Do teachers use a variety of assessment procedures which reflect the ethnic diversity of the students? ☐ ☐ ☐ ☐

22.2 Do teachers' day-to-day assessment techniques take into account the ethnic diversity of the students? ☐ ☐ ☐ ☐

23.0 Does the school conduct ongoing, systematic evaluations of the goals, methods, and instructional materials used in teaching about ethnicity? ☐ ☐ ☐ ☐

23.1 Do assessment procedures draw on many sources of evidence from many sorts of people? ☐ ☐ ☐ ☐

23.2 Does the evaluation program examine school policies and procedures? ☐ ☐ ☐ ☐

	Strongly			Hardly at all
23.3 Does the evaluation program examine the everyday climate of the school?	☐	☐	☐	☐
23.4 Does the evaluation program examine the effectiveness of curricular programs, academic and non-academic?	☐	☐	☐	☐
23.5 Are the results of evaluation used to improve the school program?	☐	☐	☐	☐

ADDITIONAL READINGS

Abrahams, Roger D., and Rudolph G. Troike, eds. *Language and Cultural Diversity in America* *Education*, Englewood Cliffs, N. J., Prentice-Hall, 1972.

Allport, Gordon W. *The Nature of Prejudice.* New York, Doubleday, 1954.

Banks, James A., ed. *Teaching Ethnic Studies.* 43rd Yearbook of the National Council for the Social Studies, Washington, D. C., NCSS, 1973.

———. *Teaching Strategies for Ethnic Studies.* Boston, Allyn & Bacon, 1975.

Bereiter, Carl and Siegfried Engelmann. *Teaching Disadvantaged Children in the Preschool.* Englewood Cliffs, N. J., Prentice-Hall, 1966.

Della-Dora, Delmo, and James E. House, eds. *Education for an Open Society.* Washington, D. C., Association for Supervision and Curriculum Development, 1974.

Dworkin, Anthony G. *The Minority Report: An Introduction to Racial, Ethnic, and Gender Relations.* New York, Praeger, 1976.

Farmer, George L. *Education: The Dilemma of the Spanish-Surname American.* Los Angeles, University of Southern California, 1969.

Fasold, Ralph W. and Roger W. Shuy, eds. *Teaching Standard English in the Inner City*, Washington, D. C., Center for Applied Linguistics, 1970.

Goodwin, Mary E. *Race Awareness in Young Children*, rev. ed. New York, Collier, 1964.

Garcia, Ricardo L. *Learning in Two Languages.* Bloomington, Ind., Phi Delta Kappa, 1976.

Howard, John R., ed. *Awakening Minorities: American Indians Mexican-Americans, Puerto Ricans.* Chicago, Aldine, 1970.

Levin, Jack. *The Functions of Prejudice.* New York, Harper & Row, 1975.

Moore, John W. *Mexican Americans.* Englewood Cliffs, N. J., Prentice-Hall, 1976.

Ramirez III, Manuel, and Alfredo Castañeda. *Cultural Democracy: Bicognitive Development and Education.* New York, Academic Press, 1974.

Thompson, Frank V. *Schooling of the Immigrant.* Montclair, N. J., Patterson Smith, 1971.

———. *The What and How of Teaching Afro-American Culture and History in the Elementary Schools.* Albany, N. Y., University of the State University of New York, 1973.

United States Commission on Civil Rights. *A Better Chance to Learn: Bilingual-Bicultural Education.* Washington, D. C., U. S. Government Printing Office, 1975.

Williams, Lorraine A., and Madlyn Calbert, *A Curriculum in Black History for Secondary Schools.* Washington, D. C., Howard University, n.d.

NOTES

1. James A. Banks, "Imperative in Ethnic Minority Education," *Phi Delta Kappan*, 53 (January, 1972), 267.

2. Cynthia Shepard, "The World Through Mark's Eyes," *Saturday Review* (January 18, 1969).

3. Gloria W. Grant, "Criteria for Cultural Pluralism in the Classroom," *Educational Leadership*, 32 (December, 1974), 192.

4. Gertrude Noar, *Sensitizing Teachers to Ethnic Groups* (New York, Anti-Defamation League of B'nai B'rith, n.d.), 11.

5. Leona M. Foerster and Dale Little Soldier, "What's New—And Good—in Indian Education Today?" *Educational Leadership*, 33 (December, 1975), 194–195.

6. Philip A. LaCourse, "Personal Statement: Indian," Equal Educational Opportunity Workshop for Human Rights Workers at the Annual Meeting of the National Association of Human Rights Workers, Seattle, Washington, October 3, 1971.

7. William A. Katz, "Minorities in American History Textbooks," *Equal Opportunity Review* (June, 1973), 3.

8. Ricardo L. Garcia, "Mexican Americans Learn Through Language Experience," *Reading*

Teacher, 28 (December, 1974), 303.

9. *Para Los Ninos–For the Children* (Washington, D.C., U. S. Commission on Civil Rights, October, 1974), 23.

10. Seymour Fersh, "Orientals and Orientation," *Phi Delta Kappan*, 53 (January, 1972), 317.

11. *Ibid.*, 318.

12. James A. Banks, "Teaching for Ethnic Literacy: A Comparative Approach," *Social Education*, 37 (December, 1973), 746.

13. Edgar Epps (ed.), *Cultural Pluralism* (Berkeley, Cal., McCutcheon, 1974), 171–172.

14. John D. McNeil and Luis Laosa, "Needs Assessment and Cultural Pluralism in Schools," *Educational Technology* 15 (December, 1975), 25.

15. Richard C. Larson and Larry F. Elliott, "Planning and Pluralism: Some Dimensions of Intergroup Relations," *Journal of Negro Education*, 45 (Winter, 1976), 95.

16. *Ibid.*, 97.

17. *Ibid.*, 99.

18. See E. E. Loveless and Frank R. Krajewski, *The Teacher and School Law: Cases and Materials in Legal Foundations of Education* (Danville, Ill., Interstate, 1974), 40–42.

19. Martha M. McCarthy, "The Right to Education: From Rodriguez to Goss," *Educational Leadership*, 33 (April, 1976), 521.

20. *Ibid.*

21. David L. Kirp, "Student Classification, Public Policy and the Courts," *Harvard Educational Review*, 44 (February, 1974), 7.

22. See Bruce Beezer, "Bilingual Education and State Legislatures," *Educational Forum*, 40 (May, 1976), 539.

23. Paul Good, "To Live in Freedom, To Die a Timely Death," in George Henderson (ed.), *America's Other Children: Public Schools Outside Suburbia* (Norman, University of Oklahoma Press, 1970), 420.

24. W. E. B. DuBois, *The Souls of Black Folk* (New York, Fawcett, 1961), 72.

11.
SEXISM

More than half of the American population is female, and that is where the statistical representation ends. American females are discriminated against in almost every aspect of their institutional lives—including the schools. Ironically, more interest has been shown in freeing animals, trees, and air than women and girls. The civil rights movement that abolished racial barriers was aimed mainly at improving living conditions for ethnic minority-group males. Symbolically, females are still sitting in the back of the liberation bus. This chapter will focus on sexism both in and outside our schools. "Sexism," of course, refers to discrimination against females, especially in terms of career choices. A sexist is a person who discriminates against females—often thinking they are inferior to men and only fit for housework and child rearing.

THE EFFECTS OF SOCIALIZATION

A child is already socialized into sex-role stereotypes before she or he enters school. John Money of Johns Hopkins Medical School believes that somewhere between twelve and eighteen months, depending on its facilities with language, a child knows what sex it is.[1] Research shows that behavior conforming to sex role stereotypes appears in most children by age three.[2]

*This chapter is based on Kendyll Stansbury's monograph, *Sex Role Stereotyping in the School: A Review of the Literature*, Norman, Consultative Center, University of Oklahoma, May, 1976. Revised and reprinted with her permission.

Demands that children adhere to their sex-role stereotype are enforced earlier with boys than girls. As a result most boys try to appear masculine at age five, while girls usually don't make an effort to appear feminine until age ten. Furthermore, being a tomboy entails fewer penalties than being a sissy. Psychologist Ruth E. Harley says:

. . . more stringent demands are made on boys than on girls and at an early age, when they are least able to understand either the reasons for or the nature of the demands. Moreover, these demands are frequently enforced harshly, impressing the small boy with the danger of deviating from them, while he does not quite understand what they are. To make matters more difficult, the desired behavior is rarely defined positively as something the child should *do, but rather, undesirable behavior is indicated negatively as something he should* not *do or be. . . . Thus, very early in life the boy must either stumble on the right path or bear repeated punishment without warning when he accidentally enters into the wrong ones. This situation gives us practically a perfect combination for inducing anxiety—the demand that the child do something which is not clearly defined to him, based on reasons he cannot possibly appreciate, and enforced with threats, punishments, and anger by those who are close to him.*[3]

Anxiety induced in boys is reflected in the differential rates of referral of boys and girls to child guidance centers.

Theories concerning sex-role socialization fall generally into three categories: identification, reinforcement, and cognitive development. Freud developed the identification theory. Boys adopt masculine behavior because they wish to imitate their father; girls imitate their mother and acquire feminine behavior. Later this imitation is generalized to adults and peers of the same sex.[4]

Reinforcement theory comes from behavioral psychology. According to this theory, children are reinforced for sex-typed appropriate behavior and are punished for inappropriate behavior. Thus sex-typed behavior follows a pattern where a child (1) learns to discriminate between sex-typed behavior patterns by observation of role models, (2) generalizes from these specific learning experiences to new situations and (3) performs the sex-typed behavior.[5]

Lawrence Kohlberg's theory of cognitive development is based on Jean Piaget's writings. Kohlberg's research indicates that "children develop a conception of themselves as having an unchangeable sexual identity at the same age and through the same processes that they develop conceptions of the invariable identity of physical objects."[6] Once children realize that they are female or male, they begin to seek and value those behaviors and objects associated with their gender identities. Thus "the process of forming a constant gender identity is not a unique process determined by instinctual wishes and identifications, but a part of the general process of conceptual growth."[7]

Kohlberg observed that regardless of differences in parental behavior, there is strong agreement among young children about differences between mother and father roles. A young child's limited ability to assimilate subtle variations in concepts also explains why there is more clear-cut stereotyping of parent and sex roles in young children (5–8) than in older children or adults. Eleanor Maccoby and Carol Jacklin take exception to this thesis and maintain that sex typing of behavior occurs much earlier than children normally develop the concept of gender constancy. In essence they argue that when children label themselves boys or girls, they begin to adopt sex-typed behavior according to their limited conception of such behavior.[8]

It is virtually impossible to ascertain what qualities are uniquely innate to each sex, since differential socialization according to sex begins at birth. For example, research indicates that from the earliest age through two years old, mothers look at and talk to girls more than boys.[9] The value placed on gender in American society can be illustrated by the first question that usually is asked of new parents: Is it a boy or a girl? During the 1960s there were many complaints that new hair and clothing styles were making it difficult to tell women from men.

SCHOOL AS A CASTE-LIKE SYSTEM

If preschool children are not already inundated with examples of men in high status positions and women in low status positions, they will find ample proof in the schools. A 1970–71 nationwide survey of all school districts in the United States found that women represented 67 per cent of the public school teachers, 34 per cent of the elementary school assistant principals, 19 per cent of the elementary principals, 3.5 per cent of the junior high principals, 3 per cent of the senior high principals, 7 per cent of the deputy, associate, or assistant superintendents, and .6 per cent of the superintendents.[10] Only 2 out of 13,000 district superintendents were women.[11]

A 1974 report of the National School Boards Association found that school board members as a group were 89.9 per cent male and 10.1 per cent female, although the males and females had equal qualifications. The authors of the report believe that an informal quota of women exists on most boards: 39 per cent of school boards surveyed had no women, 34 per cent had one woman, and only 7 per cent had more than two women. Women on school boards were found to be as well or better educated than the men; more women than men had experience on boards of other organizations.[12]

While it is true that the same sorting process operates in the larger society, this is no excuse for it to operate in the schools. The Committee to Study Sex Discrimination in Kalamazoo, Michigan, found that the attitude that certain jobs were meant for women is reflected in school job application blanks, job descriptions, and contracts: cafeteria, secretarial, and clerical employees were assumed to be female, while maintenance workers were assumed to be male.[13] These are safe assumptions, since workers in such job categories are overwhelm-ingly of the specified sex. In addition media clerks, media assistants, and teacher aides are mostly women, while custodial and ground personnel and skilled tradesmen and apprentice instructors are almost all male.

The majority of elementary school teachers are female. This is partially due to the low salary and prestige of elementary teachers. In addition the elementary school division of the teaching profession has become stereotyped as feminine. One male kindergarten teacher reported that he perceived that "people . . . began to wonder about my mental stability, academic ability, moral character—or all three." [14]

Many people interested in eliminating sex-role stereotyping have applauded the increase in male elementary school teachers. However, David Woodbridge warns that male elementary school teachers might be used to actually increase stereotypic behavior. He suggests that if one reads the lines of a (usually male) principal's welcoming speech to a male teacher, one might hear:

Glad to see someone like you (that is, another male) interested in teaching. (It helps with my image problems of working in a "feminized" world.) We could use some men on the staff (a supervisor of men commands extra respect, naturally) especially in the upper grades (have to maintain the pecking order—men still on top but working down). Where we really need help is in science and P.E. (the women here are qualified, but boys know they don't have to listen to women in these subjects; can't fight that, can we?) and in social studies (women don't really understand politics, you know!). [15]

Thus a male elementary teacher may be recruited to serve as a model of male behavior and also to handle problems deemed too difficult for women, who have been coping with them for years. This attitude is reflected in Gary Peltier's suggestion that extra or "hazardous duty" pay be given to men in the female-dominated elementary school to entice them to serve as role models. [16] (If anyone has suggested combat pay for women in the male-dominated central office, it has not made it into print.)

Men and women teachers in secondary schools are frequently treated differently in terms of assignment of duties. The Kalamazoo researchers recorded the following comments

from teachers: "Men are discriminated against. Women seldom do hall, study, lunch, or riot duty." "Men are often asked to do extra physical labors to help female teachers." "Some large classes are given to men because it's believed that women can't handle them as well. Many women perpetuate the myth." [17] Discipline and control are areas where more male than female teachers are called upon for assistance by the principals. Indeed, male teachers more often than female teachers are given the school's "problem" classes. Actually, except perhaps in physical size and strength, women have as many conflict resolution resources and skills to call upon as men.

Patricia C. Sexton suggests that society is handicapped by splitting itself into a harsh dichotomy between women's and men's jobs. [18] Suzanne Taylor found in her research that all else being equal, superintendents were not as likely to hire women as administrators. Almost half the school systems she studied did not even encourage women to train or apply for administrative positions. [19] This is partially due to the popular view that administration is a man's job, requiring virility and physical strength. This view is reflected in the large number of former athletic coaches in administration. In fact there is a correlation between the height and weight of an administrator and his position in the school hierarchy. On the average, superintendents are taller and heavier than high school principals, who are in turn taller and heavier than elementary school principals. [20]

In a study of elementary principals Neal Gross and Anne Trask found that men and women principals had different career patterns: 47 per cent of the men and 79 per cent of the women were over fifty years of age, but 19 per cent of the men and 6 per cent of the women were under thirty-one years of age. [21] On the whole, men were younger than women. Men were promoted more quickly: 49 per cent of the women and 16 per cent of the men had taught in an elementary school for over sixteen years; 3 per cent of the women and 34 per cent of the men had never taught in elementary schools. [22]

Helen M. Morsink's research led her to conclude that male principals were perceived as having a greater tolerance of freedom. On the other hand, female principals were perceived to do better at speaking and acting as a representative of the teachers, reconciling conflicting demands and reducing disorder in the system, predicting outcomes accurately, maintaining a closely-knit organization and resolving intermember conflict, and maintaining cordial relations with superiors, influencing them and striving for higher status.[23]

School as a Social Environment

Given the differential evaluation of males and females, it comes as no surprise to find that teachers think of and treat students differently according to sex. Patricia Minuchin lists eight sex-linked conceptions about girls.[24]

1. Girls are not good at math and science.
2. Girls are not manually skillful or interested in or apt to respond to training in such skills.
3. Girls are less logical and analytic in the use of their minds than males.
4. Girls tend to be docile, obedient, and dependent.
5. Girls are not as aggressive or high-spirited as boys.
6. Girls are more verbal and less athletic, tidier and more interested in clothes.
7. Girls will be centered around the home and family in their adult roles.
8. Girls' careers are not apt to be serious or long term, and are apt to follow along traditional lines.

Two questions then arise: What happens to those girls who aren't like the majority? Are these traits sex-linked or learned?

School is perceived by most children as a feminine place. There is a basic conflict between what most boys are taught at home and what they are taught at school. At home a boy who fits the male stereotype is taught to be aggressive, to fight, and to stand up for his rights. At school, however, he is told to sit still, to cooperate, and to limit his physical aggression. Most girls are already conditioned to fit the school norms. It is no wonder that more girls than boys like school. Girls are more positive than boys in their attitudes toward school, relationships with their teachers, and attitudes toward their classes and the importance of doing well.

When students are anxious to receive good grades and teacher praise, they hide their academic weaknesses from the teacher and avoid situations of intellectual challenge. This hits girls particularly hard.

If we want more women to enter science, not only as teachers of science but as scientists, we must encourage the cultivation of the analytic and mathematical abilities science requires. To achieve this means encouraging independence and self-reliance instead of pleasing feminine submission in the young girl, stimulating and rewarding her efforts to satisfy her curiosity about the world to the same extent her brothers' efforts are, cultivating a probing intelligence that asks why and rejects the easy answers instead of urging her to please others and conform unthinkingly to social rules.[25]

One study found that if high school girls agree that it is appropriate for women to be leaders in politics, professions, and business, then there is a relation between their achievement motivation and their grades. If they disagree, there is no such relation.[26] James Coleman found that bright high school girls were caught in a double bind. They wish to conform to their parents' and teachers' expectations, but fear that high academic performance will hurt their chances with boys. So they do credibly, but less well than the boys. On the other hand, bright high school boys feel free to excel in scholarship.[27]

Because teachers generally expect more trouble from males, they pay more attention to boys. Not only do teachers interact with boys more than with girls, but a study of schools throughout New York indicated that two-thirds of the male dropouts had exit interviews with a counselor, teacher, or principal, while only one-half the girls received such attention. More contacts were also attempted with the boys' parents.[28]

A poll of student teachers found them ranking girls higher for rigid, conforming, orderly, dependent, passive, submissive behavior while boys were ranked higher for independent, active, assertive, flexible, nonconforming, untidy behavior. It is no surprise then that boys challenge teachers both more often and more publicly than girls do.[29] Teachers unconsciously use these stereotypes as the basis of their behavior toward their students. One grade-school teacher reported, "If a boy cries I know it's serious and I try to find out what's wrong. If a girl cries I don't pay much attention; they cry all the time."[30] A ceramics teacher confessed that while her favorite student is a male who is aggressive, sometimes to the point of being rude, she doubts that she would tolerate the same behavior in a girl.[31] Effeminate boys are particularly susceptible to both teacher and counselor concern for fear that they may become homosexuals.[32]

In spite of the fact that girls in the elementary school are as strong as or stronger than boys, when the teacher wants something heavy carried, she or he almost invariably asks a boy, reinforcing the stereotype of feminine helplessness. A girls' gym teacher berated her students for not having clean white sneakers, for forgetting handerchiefs, for not having white socks without spots—in short, for not being neat, clean, tidy little girls.[33] Dress codes requiring girls to wear dresses make it difficult for girls to participate in activities designed to develop strength, stamina, and coordination. Often the rules are different for girls and boys, raising the question of differential treatment.

Teachers sometimes assign topics according to their perceptions of a student's interests, often resulting in stereotypic assignments. Worse yet, when boys are compared to the girls and told to be nice like the girls, be quiet like the girls, or sit still like the girls, this reinforces stereotypes. Patrick Lee explains the emphasis on control as a consequence of both institutional givens and the socialization of teachers.[34] There is institutional pressure to cover too much material in too little time. In addition the public school is an institution with no control over selection of its clientele. It must socialize all students into institutional ways. Most teachers become instant professionals upon being hired, with inadequate preservice preparation. This provides for a high level of teacher self-doubt and anxiety, which in turn leads to an overly rigid insistence on control and adherence to a schedule. It also leads to conservative attitudes toward sex roles and social change because teachers are reluctant to abandon the techniques which get them through their first hectic year.

The biggest area of disadvantage for boys is in discipline. In virtually every school, boys receive a more severe punishment than girls for the same violation. In the Kalamazoo survey, "female principals felt they could and would 'spank' both boys and girls, but men principals felt that they could only 'spank' boys. This seemed especially true when there was a difference in the race of the principal and the female child."[35] Boys receive more control messages. Furthermore, boys are criticized mostly in a harsh or angry tone, while girls are criticized more often in a normal voice.

It has long been noted that boys have more trouble learning to read than girls do. Explanations are varied, ranging from "boys mature later" to "teacher discrimination." After finding that boys receive more negative comments than girls and receive less opportunity to read, John McNeal recommended that all boys be taught to read by programmed instruction.[36] Indeed, he found that boys' reading scores improved when programmed instruction was used. Research reveals, however, that the boys receive more negative comments than girls because they are perceived by teachers as greater behavior problems.[37]

Male versus Female Achievement

Rebecca Oetzel points out that elementary school girls achieve in areas which contain specific school tasks (grammar, spelling, reading, counting) while boys excel in areas which are not incorporated into elementary school (spatial, analytic, arithmetic reasoning.)[38] On achievement tests girls tend to outscore boys in reading, writing, and literature; boys tend to ourscore girls in social studies, math, and science. Girls are more verbal than boys, while boys excel at visual-spatial relations. Boys' ability in visual-spatial relations gives them an advantage in mathematics where noncomputational skills are stressed. The difference in visual-spatial relations, however, depends upon the chidren's upbringing. In cultures which stress the dependence of women, there are always dramatic differences between the scores of males and females. In cultures which stress early independence training for women too, the differences are slight.

Because boys are torn between the home and school environments, their rebellion and autonomy may be the source for their improved ability to think more critically than girls when they reach adolescence. As to whether teachers are personally free from stereotypes about males and females, one study indicates that they probably are not. A survey of San Antonio teachers in grades K through 3 found that two-thirds of the teachers agreed to some extent with the statement, "Most women have only themselves to blame for not doing better in life." One-third agreed that "children of working mothers tend to be less well adjusted than children of unemployed women." One-fourth felt that women may "best achieve full self-development" by being "good wives and mothers."[39]

A poll of 9000 teachers found that over one-third of the respondents felt that science and math were more appropriate teaching fields for men, while English and foreign languages were more appropriate for women. When asked to rank five school subjects in order of prestige for male and female teachers, the respondents ranked them in in this descending order for males: (1) science, (2) math, (3) social studies, (4) foreign language, and (5) English. The reverse order was marked for females.[40]

It is not sufficient to change only the school environment. A study was made of a free school which carried out its policy to encourage "children to free themselves from their sex roles as well as direct their own learning as they need to explore and understand their environment." The researcher concluded that while the teachers' behavior was different, the students' behavior was not different in regard to sex stereotyping.[41]

Minuchin also studied effects of different school environments on students. She classified schools into two types: conventional and modern. Conventional schools were characterized by generalized standards of achievement, mastery of a set curriculum, authority as an adult prerogative, and expecting the child to conform to social standards. Modern schools emphasized classroom process, course content, functional authority, socialization, and individual characteristics.[42] In comparing children from these two types of schools, she found that children from modern schools were less sex-typed in their test scores. Males and females in the modern schools generally were not different in problem-solving skills, while children in conventional schools showed the familiar difference favoring boys. Unlike their peers in conventional schools, boys in modern schools were high achievers and were positive in their feelings about it.

TEXTBOOKS

By far the most examined area of sex-role stereotyping in the schools is sexism in textbooks. It may be many more years before writers and book publishers reverse the sexist standard suggested by Paul Hazzard in 1944: "Girls demand books that demonstrate maternal feelings. . . . Boys demand books of valor."[43] In fairness to Hazzard, this myth—that boys and girls are interested in a limited range of totally different reading subjects because of their sex—was created and perpetuated by the earliest authors and accepted by their publishers. Thus despite a growing concern by educators to reduce sex prejudice in books written for children, girls are still typically depicted as passive, timid, dependent, and incompetent, while boys are portrayed as active, competitive, independent, and competent.

It is ironic or tragic—depending on your view—that as early as 1937 May Lazar dared to say what only recently educators have affirmed.

The girls read these books because social opinion has prescribed them. Teachers, parents, librarians, and book dealers, when asked to recommend books for girls, will probably select those that tradition has sanctioned for girls. Girls are continually exposed to such types of books. They like them because they do not know any other kind.[44]

A study of children's textbooks published in 1972 found:

The typical girl in any reader is a frilly little thing with a smile on her pretty face and a passive attitude toward life. The boy portrayed in the readers has a look of stern concentration: he is busy preparing to be a 'man'. Mothers and fathers in the readers reflect a simple, standardized existence, which becomes for the child the American Way of Life.[45]

The sex stereotyping in textbooks is particularly important because it reflects and reinforces attitudes in our society toward both males and females that are based on prejudice and custom rather than fact. Sara Zimet's study of elementary school children illustrates that children tend to readily accept the stereotypes presented in the textbooks.[46]

A recent study of children's books found females comprising from 20 to 30 per cent of the characters. There were five times as many male characters in the pictures.[47] The number of female characters actually declines from primers to fourth grade readers. If white female models are lacking, models for non-white females are even more scarce.

Strangely enough, the rationale for boys being the dominant figures in nonfiction books is because it it thought that boys are more able than girls in math, science, and statesmanship. However, boys dominate primers for the opposite reason—because they are less able than girls in learning to read. Aileen Nilson reports being advised by her colleagues to write about boys because both boys and girls will read stories about boys, but only girls will read about girls.[48] Women on Words and Images states: "We are convinced that if girls' stories were not so limp, so limited, so downright silly, even boys would cease to discriminate between boys' and girls' stories—there would only be 'good' or 'bad' stories. . . . *Harriet the Spy* and *Pippi Longstocking* have no trouble making friends among boys as well as girls."[49]

Role Models

The role models generally provided for both boys and girls in textbooks lack very important characteristics. Girls lack role models who are strong, independent, not easily frightened, and career-oriented. Boys lack role models who freely show emotion, especially uncertainty or fear, and who depend on other people for support.

Girls are mainly shown in domestic settings—baking cookies or playing with dolls. Boys are frequently shown outdoors, having adventures or solving problems. Girls shown with boys are usually shorter and younger than the boys, and they usually are accompanying, watching, and supporting the boys. Girls are rarely shown in active, adventurous roles.

Adult men are shown in significantly higher proportions engaging in constructive-productive, physically exertive, and problem-solving behaviors. Adult women are shown in significantly higher proportions engaging in passive and non-problem-solving behaviors. Consequently, males are portrayed in activities requiring aggression, physical exertion, and problem solving. Females are seen as characters developed in fantasy, carrying out directive behavior, and making both positive and negative self-statements.

Children's readers especially lack role models who are dealing with realistic problems of life in modern society, such as making new friends, dealing with conflict, and getting along with other people. Nonnuclear families are almost never shown, despite the fact that the divorce rate is climbing, increasing the chances that children will fall into this category.

In a survey of readers from 14 publishers, Women on Words and Images found that women were shown in 26 occupations, compared to 147 for men. Only 3 working mothers were found in 134 books surveyed. One receives the impression that motherhood is a full-time, life-time occupation, ignoring the more than 13 million working mothers with children under 18 years of age.

Children's readers have a number of passages in them where boys disparage girls.

"Girls are always late." (Ginn reader)

"Look at her, mother; just look at her, she's just like a girl; she gives up." (Harper and Row basic reading program)

"We don't want to play with girls, we can beat them too easily." (Scott, Foresman)[50]

Another very subtle sexist practice in textbooks is the English language itself. The language uses "he," as masculine pronoun, when the sex is unspecified. It uses words like "man" and "mankind" to stand for all people, regardless of sex. Young children are very concrete in the images they form of words. When they read "man," meaning a collection of people, they picture a collection of men. When they see "he," they think of a male. When they grow up, this perceptual pattern is well established. It requires a conscious effort to monitor one's speech and writing for this tendency, substituting "people" or "humanity" for "man", "he or she" for "he", and using gender-neutral occupational titles such as "police officer" for "policemen." Scott, Foresman and McGraw-Hill book publishers have issued guidelines to their writers and editors to assist them in nonsexist language.[51]

Women authors are rarely included in English anthologies. The main complaint about history books is their ignorance of women. The typical woman mentioned is the wife of a prominent man. Not only are individual women omitted in history books, but areas in which women made their most important contributions—fine arts and daily life—are omitted as well. Frequently history books report that women were given the right to vote, ignoring the years of struggle and demonstrations that preceded the Nineteenth Amendment.

In government textbooks most of the quotations are from men. Women are shown mainly in the role of housewife and rarely appear as active, responsible wage earners. The candidate running for office, the citizen testifying in court, the person collecting unemployment insurance are almost certain to be male. Topics of interest to women such as women's suffrage, women's employment, women and the political process, and women and the law are rarely included. The reasons for the omission of women from positions of power in our society are seldom mentioned, and almost never is it stated that this situation is changing.

One would expect mathematics and science books to be the most objective, since they deal with the natural sciences, a more-or-less objective field. Yet math books are among the most sexist offenders. In beginning mathematics books people in sets are often arranged by sex and represented in stereotypic occupations. Most males shown are mathematically competent, but some of the females have problems and are helped by boys. Actually girls out perform boys in elementary school arithmetic.

Pictures in elementary science textbooks are male-oriented. Girls in pictures are mainly observers or the objects of experiments, while boys are shown as active experimenters. In most algebra books the men are more active in word problems, more interested in financial transactions and sports, and more likely to have an occupation, while women buy things, participate socially, and sit. Elementary mathematics textbooks portray the sexes in a similar manner.

Prominent women scientists and mathematicians are rarely shown. For example Emmy Noether, a prominent twentieth-century algebraist, is omitted from most mathematical biographies. Frequently Marie Curie is treated as an assistant to her husband, even though she carried on significant research for years after his death.

Winifred T. Jay reviewed twelve mathematics textbooks for grades two, four, and six and concluded that there was definite evidence of unequal treatment of the sexes.[52] To correct this situation, she suggests several examples, exercises, and activities for use by mathematics teachers, including the following:

In the section of examples, exercises, or problems to promote learning of concepts, teachers can supplement textbook materials by featuring boys and girls in unusual nonstereotyped roles. For example:

The girls in the sixth grade need funds for the field trip to Washington, D.C. They took on paper routes in their neighborhoods. If each customer solicited means a monthly profit of $2.50, how many customers would each girl need to earn $30.00 per month?

Carol has a board 4¾ feet long. She cuts off a piece 2½ feet long. How much is left?

Martha and her mother caught 20 fish. They each caught the same number. How many did each catch?

A recipe calls for ⅔ cup of sugar. Bob wants ½ as much. How much sugar should he use?

The reverse of roles is intended to help boys and girls visualize themselves in nontraditional roles. It is important to feel comfortable while being different and to have an open-mindedness on the options in life.

Famous people are featured in quantitative situations because birthdates or anniversaries afford opportunities for arithmetical computations. Many women have made contributions towards the betterment of life, but they have been less publicized. Teacher-devised examples or narrative problems could feature birthdates of famous women. For example:

There are 90 statues in Statuary Hall in the Capitol of Washington, D.C. Four of them are in honor of women.

	Born	Died
Maria L. Sanford	1836	1920
Francies E. Willard	1839	1893
Dr. Florence R. Sabin	1871	1953
Esther Hobart Morris	1814	1902

How long did each of them live?

Amelia Earhart, the first women to cross the Atlantic by airplane, was born in 1897. In 1937 while flying over the South Pacific, her plane disappeared. If she died in the plane crash, how old was she at the time?

Madame Curie, the discoverer of uranium, was 67 years old when she died in 1934. When was she born?[53]

Notable efforts to produce and distribute non-sexist materials have been made by the National Foundation for the Improvement of Education Resource Center on Sex Roles in Education, Feminist Press, National Education Association, the Council on Interracial Books for Children, and the Foundation for Change.

THE CURRICULUM

The curriculum as a whole acts as a subtle reinforcement to sex role stereotyping. The subtleties were made more apparent in a pilot program at Wakefield Forest (Va.) Elementary School. The boys were given science materials and experiments with emphasis on building things, studies of transportation, and active games. The girls were given quiet games, fairy stories, and games and songs emphasizing feminine activities, such as sewing and housekeeping. One of the advantages cited was that the teachers could tailor the activities to the interests of the children. Thus in the study of mold, medicinal properties were emphasized for the boys and cooking properties for the girls. Even different reading series were used, since "boys don't like stories about girls" but prefer adventure tales and stories about vocations and industry.[54]

The potential of the teacher in creating and reinforcing different attitudes and abilities in students according to gender should be apparent. Even within the same classroom, teachers consciously or unconsciously support activities and interests as masculine or feminine by the students they call on or the way they talk about students. Acceptance of sex typing of activities by students only serves to discourage inerest in "inappropriate" sex roles.

Separate classes for boys and girls were once common, particularly in physical education, industrial arts, and home economics. But as the U. S. Supreme Court pointed out in 1954,

separate but equal is not equal. Consider the following comments by teachers of such classes.

"We *do* have a shop course for girls. They make crafts."

"I used to teach 'Physics for Girls.' We taught them how to put plugs together and wire toasters."

"We had to separate that class so we could teach the girls the kinds of things they'd be interested in."[55]

Even when courses are open to all students, sex-typed bias creeps in via attitudes of adults. One girl who wanted to take an advanced mathematics course was advised by her counselor that "she had already had all the math any girl needs." Comments from highly-placed people in the Ann Arbor Public Schools, reported to Marcia Federbush, included: "What do you want to take *that* course for? You just want to be with the boys." (From the principal)

"When a girl signs up for Industrial Arts, we call her in to see how serious she is."

"Girls are almost uneducable in science."[56] Boys face much the same comments when they express interest in cooking or child-care classes.

Most separate-sex classes channel girls into homemaking and motherhood, while boys are channeled into skilled occupations. Federbush found two foods classes, one for girls and one for boys. The girls received experience in organizing a tea, in preparation for jobs in catering and food service. The equivalent course for the boys prepared them for higher-paying restaurant work.

It is not enough merely to remove sex prerequisites from courses. If this is all that is done we could, for example, have a clothing class without a sex prerequisite, but with a course description saying that students will make skirts, jumpers, and dresses. Homemaking classes could benefit from focusing on household survival skills helpful to both males and females. Similarly, industrial arts courses could introduce students to trade by teaching them relevant skills to apply to their own homes. As a girl in an otherwise all-male vocational high school put it:

Also, like in Stuyvesant we have a lot of mechanical arts, all these shops and they think it's funny that I have to take them too, because they say, 'Oh, you're not gonna be a carpenter or a plumber.' They say,

'Well, maybe it's good for you to be a plumber so if your sink gets stuck washing all your dishes . . . but otherwise you're not gonna need it.' But I feel also that shops aren't gonna do them any good.[57]

Perhaps a year-long course in practical arts for junior high students, incorporating foods, fabrics, basic home repairs, money management, interpersonal relations, and care of living things, should replace the current home economics curricula. For home economics beyond an initial course to become attractive to boys, it must prepare individuals for employment as well as for homemaking.

A Self-Fulfilling Prophecy

Girls are consistently underrepresented in elective math and science courses. In his work with older elementary children, E. P. Torrance found that girls usually do not participate in science because they perceive it as a male field. When he worked with parents and teachers to change this belief, he found that participation in science by girls increased markedly. However, much to his dismay both boys and girls still valued the boys' contributions more highly.[58]

One chemistry teacher complained that the lab aprons were designed so that they cut across or continually slipped off of girls' breasts. On the other hand, a physics teacher confessed that he bent over backwards to spend extra time and effort on the girls since there were so few in his class.[59]

For years it has been noted that achievement differences in math and science appear at adolescence. The National Assessment of Educational Progress found that while male and female scores at age nine were roughly the same in social science, mathematics, and science, differences increase thereafter, until there is a dramatic difference between the performance of the sexes at the adult level. In the social science areas, girls outperformed boys on questions on care of the family. Boys did better on questions on law, government, and international problems and politics (which formed the bulk of the questions).

In mathematics males and females did about the same on exercises dealing with strict numerical computation. Males' advantages appeared in geometry, measurement, and work

problems. Females at all ages outperformed males at reading and did about the same on computational skills. Girls' achievement scores on mathematical work problems can be improved if the problems are simply reworded so that they deal with cooking and gardening, even though the logic required for solution remains the same.[60]

A recent survey found that differences in mathematics achievement in adolescence paralleled differences in the percentages of students who (1) thought that math courses were interesting, (2) thought math to be useful in making a living, and (3) talked about science with their parents and friends. Differences between boys and girls both in achievement and on these dimensions were negligible at grade seven, but increased with age.[61] Boys more than girls are trained to view mathematics as especially useful in their future occupations, and boys are encouraged more in science careers. As materials specialist Rebecca Sparling points out: "There's nothing inherently feminine about mixing a given batch of materials, exposing it to a definite temperature for a definite time and producing a cake. There's nothing inherently masculine in mixing a batch of materials, exposing it to a different temperature for a given time and producing iron casting."[62]

Males and females in school performed about the same on the biology exercises in National Assessment of Educational Progress. The difference that increases with age is on questions concerning physical science.

Why should such differences appear at early adolescence and increase with age? Do girls get dumber as they grow older? Two University of Wisconsin-Madison researchers found that girls find it just as much fun to solve problems as boys, but they consider mathematics a male domain and lack the confidence to perform adequately.[63] Some of the reasons girls gave for dropping math were fear that it would hamper relationships with boys and make them appear masculine and a feeling that math is less useful to girls than to boys.

Sex stereotypes are reflected in the distribution of males and females in high school vocational education fields. Of 136 instructional categories within the nation's vocational education program, 71 per cent of the enrollments have at least three-quarters of their students the same sex, almost half have enrollments

Table 16. Performance in Subject Areas, by Age Level and by Sex: Selected Years

Subject area, year of assessment, and sex[1]	Age level			
	9-year-olds	13-year-olds	17-year-olds	Adults
Mathematics, 1972–73				
National norm	36.7	51.3	57.1	59.3
Male	0.7	0.4	2.3	5.4
Female	−0.7	−0.4	−2.2	−5.0
Science, 1972–73				
National norm	68.2	58.3	47.0	51.2
Male	0.8	1.5	2.8	5.2
Female	−1.0	−1.4	−2.4	−4.7
Social studies, 1971–72				
National norm	72.2	66.2	73.8	72.4
Male	0.4	0.1	0.6	2.3
Female	−0.4	−0.1	−0.6	−2.2
Citizenship, 1969–70				
National norm	64.1	63.1	61.8	60.4
Male	0.1	0.3	0.4	1.4
Female	−0.2	−0.4	−0.4	−1.3
Writing, 1969–70				
National norm	28.3	55.4	62.5	58.4
Male	−4.0	−3.4	−3.4	−2.3
Female	4.1	3.2	3.0	2.1
Reading, 1970–71				
National norm	70.4	68.1	77.5	83.5
Male	−2.4−	−2.5	−2.0	0.2
Female	2.3	2.3	1.9	−0.3
Literature, 1970–71				
National norm	43.9	53.4	61.3	64.0
Male	−0.7	−1.6	−1.1	0.0
Female	0.6	1.6	1.0	−0.1
Music, 1971–72				
National norm	53.8	48.9	49.2	41.5
Male	−0.3	−0.9	−0.9	−0.9
Female	0.3	0.9	0.8	0.9

[1] Figures for sex indicate median difference in percentage points from the national norm.

SOURCE: National Assessment of Educational Progress, Education Commission of the States, Denver, Colorado, Newsletter VIII, No. 5, October 1975.

which are 90 per cent one sex, and females dominate in those programs providing preparation for lower-paying vocations such as cosmetology, typing, and sales work.[64] With such conditions, many women end up in the situation that Elizabeth Koontz describes.

A girl who is not college-bound is offered little choice in vocational training during her high school years. She may take home economics, but the skills taught are generally those that will be useful when she has her own home. Thus, unless occupational possibilities are emphasized, training in home economics is likely to make a girl dependent, not independent. . . . If secretarial training is the only vocational training available, a girl may feel trapped. Unable to go on to college and uninterested in office work, she may marry the first man who proposes, feeling that her life offers no interesting career choices. Schools should not be content to turn out graduates with such limited horizons. [65]

A program of special merit is North Carolina's New Pioneers Project, which began in 1974. It was designed to eliminate sex stereotyping in vocational education. The project has successfully increased the number of females enrolled in traditionally male-oriented trade and industrial curricula. Conversely, more males are enrolling in traditionally female-oriented home economics curricula.

Sexism in Special Education

Historically, Americans have been more tolerant of lower levels of intellectual ability in females than in males. As a rule, girls must be intellectually slower than their male peers in order to be placed in special education classes. In fact an analysis of special education curricula reveals that sex-role stereotyping is prevalent in all aspects of special education.

While secondary school vocational programs have enhanced the employability of males, they have made little or no discernible impact on the employability of females. Stated another way, the classroom training and job placement components of secondary school programs provide males with potentially higher transferable skills than females. This bias is related to traditional sexist definitions of successful employment for women: (1) housewife and supported by her husband, (2) married and working outside the home, or (3) not married but a homemaker or a housekeeper. Patricia T. Cegelka summarized the relationship of special education work-study programs to mentally handicapped females.

1. Fewer girls than boys are found in special vocational preparation programs. Girls, particularly Anglo girls, are less apt to be labeled as retarded and placed in special education classes than boys with similar intelligence quotients.

2. Once in, girls are not provided with equal vocational training opportunities. They are trained for jobs of low or no financial remuneration. The jobs for which they are trained frequently are not covered by minimum wage laws and often promise less stability than the occupations for which males are trained.

3. The field expects lower levels of adjustment for females. Girls are expected to be more dependent, as reflected by the differential criteria for success. In order to be counted as successful, a male generally must be fully employed and economically self-sufficient, while a female need not be employed, or economically self-sufficient.

4. By using nonspecific success criteria (housewife, homemaker, etc.) for girls, the field has been able to report higher success rates than would otherwise be possible. [66]

The emphasis on training girls mainly for marriage has grave implications. The soaring divorce rate suggests that women should be prepared to support themselves. Furthermore, a substantial number of married females will have to contribute to family income through employment outside the home.

In order to free the curriculum from stereotypes, males and females need not only equal access to courses but also a curriculum that combines both masculine and feminine interests. Florence Howe, a feminist educator, says: "Like the blacks, Chicanos, and other ethnic groups before them, women are saying we must build a curriculum that (1) compensates for prior deprivation, (2) allows us to raise the consciousness of many women, (3) encourages the production of useful research, (4) aims to restore the lost culture and history of women, and (5) actively works toward social change." [67]

Minority-group women are placed in double jeopardy; first as members of minority groups and second as women. For example, when we look at American jobs in the top five per cent of the income distribution, we see that Black women earn less than white women; are employed in greater numbers; and occupy a greater percentage of low-paying, low-status jobs. As recently as 1975, thirty-five per cent of Black families were headed by women who earned a median family income of less than $4,500.

Chicano women (Chicanas) earn less than all other Spanish-origin women: in 1975 their median annual income was less than $3,000. Fourteen per cent of Chicano families are supported by Chicanas, and one-half of them earn below the poverty level. The problems of Chicanas are compounded by their bilingualism and traditional religious orientation. Puerto Rican women have similar problems. Liberation may alienate them from their men and cultural heritage. Currently, more than half of the Puerto Rican women in the labor force are operative or service workers, and 70 per cent earn less than $5,000. Of the 31 per cent of Puerto Rican households headed by women in 1975, the median income was $3,889.

More American Indian women are poorly paid as workers than any other group. Almost 90 per cent of Native American women earn less than $5,000 per year. They are truly the poorest of all Americans. And more than other women, Indian women, especially those of matrilineal tribes, are not unconcerned with decision-making beyond tribal affairs. Of primary importance to most Native American women is the betterment of Indians generally rather than their status as women.

Although a larger percentage of Asian American women work outside the home than do Black and white women, the highly diversified nature of this ethnic group makes generalizatons difficult. However, one safe generalization is that even Asian American women who are highly educated tend to be employed as secretaries, bookkeepers, file clerks, and typists. This is not so much a condition of racism but, instead, sexism.

Finally, we should not attribute the plight of minority women workers to education per se. In 1974, 61 per cent of minority women workers graduated from high school, including ten per cent with four or more years of college. This compares favorably with white women, of whom 75 per cent were high school graduates, and 14 per cent had four or more years of college.

To understand the social and environmental forces impinging on the life space of ethnic minority women is to see even greater promise in the concept of cultural pluralism.

EXTRACURRICULAR ACTIVITIES

Extracurricular activities are an area where students frequently are channeled according to sex. Too often, office aides are female and audiovisual aides are male. Service organizations are differentiated into male clubs and female clubs. Girls are not trusted to assume potentially dangerous activities, such as hall monitor or school crossing guard.

School officials are reluctant to allow girls to be school crossing guards because it is believed that no one would really take a girl's orders seriously, and girls would not be safe standing alone on a corner. These views are rebutted by educators who say that if girls were permitted to exert responsibility, boys would listen to them. Furthermore if a corner is not safe for girls, it is seldom so for boys either. Also, elementary school girls are physically more mature than boys and, if properly trained, can handle most so-called "male jobs."

Honors and awards are especially reflective of sex bias. Activities such as the homecoming and sports queen, where the girl is rewarded for looks and popularity and put on display, reflect a quite different value than the outstanding athlete awards (usually male). As recently as 1965, the Division for Girls and Women of the American Association for Health, Physical Education, and Recreation recommended that "awards when given should be inexpensive tokens of a symbolic type, such as ribbons, letters, or small pins."[68] Male teams and athletes, on the other hand, are free to receive shiny trophies, letter jackets, and letters, pointing up the differences between male and female athletics.

Nonschool organizations which work with the school frequently exclude one sex. Junior Rotarians and Junior Lions are rarely female. Little League and the Junior League Football officials are allowed to come into school and recruit members, but until recently girls have not been allowed to participate. In the past employers of work-study students have employed males in higher paying jobs. Furthermore, employers still tend to sex-stereotype their work opportunities, assigning girls to sales and secretarial work and boys to mechanical and technical jobs.

The most controversial area arising from the debate preceding and following Congressional approval of the Title IX regulations has been athletics. Athletic opportunities for girls have been traditionally fewer than those for boys. In part this arises from an assumption that competition at the boys level would be harmful for girls. Boys compete in a lengthy list of sports:

football, basketball, wrestling, swimming, track, baseball, and tennis. Girls have traditionally participated in only a few sports: basketball, swimming, tennis, and volleyball. But this is not due to lack of interest. According to a survey by the National Federation of State High School Associations, participation by girls in interscholastic sports rose by 175 per cent from 1971 to 1973. Participation by boys increased by only 3 per cent in the same period.[69]

Also, in the past many state athletic associations barred girls from competing with boys, even in noncontact sports. In 1972 both the Indiana State Supreme Court and the Minnesota Supreme Court ruled that exclusion of girls from athletic teams when no alternative team was provided constituted denial of equal protection as guaranteed by the Fourteenth Amendment. After New York State rescinded its rule prohibiting girls from completing on boys' teams in noncontact sports, the New York State Board of Education conducted a study looking for evidence of psychological damage to either boys or girls playing on the same team. They concluded that there was no such evidence.[70]

In the past, girls were permitted to engage in only limited interscholastic competition. The emphasis was placed on intramural competition. One rationalization for limiting competition for girls has been a desire not to fall into the same pitfalls that plague the boys' athletic programs. If that is true, then it is time to examine closely the destructive nature of excessive emphasis on male competition and to decide whether we want the boys to suffer from it.

Even when girls are provided teams of their own, discrimination is common. Female games are often used as curtain raisers to the male events with little publicity provided for the former activity. (A notable exception is girls' basketball, which outdraws boys' basketball in Iowa, thus proving that girls' athletics can also generate income.) Cheerleaders are almost invariably female, perpetuating the old stereotype that men participate and women watch and cheer them on.

Coaches of female teams receive less money than coaches of male teams for the same or more hours of coaching. On the average girls' coaches were paid half as much as boys' coaches. Frequently female physical education teachers are asked to volunteer their coaching

services, while most male coaches are paid.

Budgets for women's and men's teams are rarely even close to equal. A survey conducted by the staff of *WomenSports* yielded an average ratio of 5:1.[71] Female athletes get the leftovers: leftover gymnasium space, leftover equipment, leftover practice times. A New Jersey woman reported "a girls' basketball team that was undefeated, but . . . couldn't use the gym on Tuesdays, Wednesdays or Fridays, and only after six on Mondays and Thursdays, when the boys were through."[72]

CAREER EDUCATION AND COUNSELING

Nearly every secondary school and an increasing number of elementary schools have counselors whose duties include career education. As noted earlier the school presents few role models in nontraditional occupations for either boys or girls. The school structure itself illustrates that occupations tend to be sex stereotyped, perpetuating the stereotypes of males as decision makers and women in positions of lower status.

One-third of all working women are concentrated in only six jobs: secretary, retail sales clerk, household worker, elementary school teacher, waitress, and nurse. Girls are taught to seek occupations of low prestige, responsibility, and salary. Thus in our society, a female college graduate working full-time can expect to earn less per year than a male high school dropout. Despite the gains made in affirmative action laws, the average salary differential between male and female workers is actually increasing.

On the other hand, boys are socialized into desiring occupations of high prestige, responsibility, and salary, which contributes to greater stress causing a higher rate of heart attacks and ulcers. Any inclination to a job involving personal contact and social service is negatively reinforced by the low salary of such positions. In the field of education, the low salary paid to teachers leads most male teachers with ability to seek either to move up the administrative ladder or to leave the profession.

Even if the counselors manage to break away from stereotyping occupations, the materials they use perpetuate this bias. There is the ubiquitous use of "he" as the third person pronoun, which transforms even sex-neuter

Table 17. Total Enrollment and Per Cent Female Participation in
Occupational Programs With 10,000 Students or More in Public
Postsecondary Area Vocational Schools: 1974

Program	Total enrolled	Percent female
Stenography	40,778	93.7
Nursing (all types)	47,939	91.7
Filing	10,345	86.5
Home economics (all types)	24,947	86.4
Accounting and bookkeeping	27,080	45.0
Data processing	22,424	38.1
Miscellaneous technology	10,812	36.9
Business office supervisory	22,751	21.3
Agriculture (all types)	17,830	15.5
Law enforcement training	12,529	14.8
Police science technology	19,429	13.9
Drafting	12,811	7.5
Electronic technology	18,380	2.9
Auto mechanics (all types)	28,500	1.3
Welding	13,233	1.3
Construction trades	11,757	.9

NOTE: These 16 programs represent 60 percent of total enrollment in all programs.
SOURCE: U.S. Department of Health, Education and Welfare, *Survey of Public Postsecondary Area Vocational Schools, 1974*, unpublished data.

occuations into masculine ones. Illustrations are frequently sex-typed. Most pictures of sex-neutral occupations are of males, leaving females little to identify with.

Until recently all forms of career interest inventories either used separate forms according to sex, or did not report the same occupations for each sex. The two more popular instruments, the Kuder Occupations Interest Survey and the Strong Vocational Interest Blank (SVIB) illustrate this bias. The Kuder compares responses of people in the selected occupations. For some occupations there are two different scales, one for men and one for women (e.g., computer programmer and lawyer). Thus a male would be compared to the male norms, and the female to the female norms. The same test would score differently on the male and female norms. Both males and females are not scored on some occupations, and males are scored on approximately two times more occupations than females.

The SVIB, on the other hand, has one form for males and another for females. Many items are identical, but each form contains items which do not appear on the other. Worse yet, the list of potential occupations are not the same. There are thirty-three occupations on which males, but not females are scored, including psychiatrist, author, and journalist. There are thirty-seven occupations on which only females are scored, including elementary teacher and medical technologist. Identical responses are interpreted to indicate potential for being a physician, phyciatrist, or psychologist on the male form and a dental assistant, physical therapist, or occupational therapist on the female form.

After the Strong Vocational Interest Blank was cited for sex bias by the American Personnel and Guidance Association, it was revised into the Strong-Campbell Interest Inventory (SCII), with a single form for both males and females and scores on all occupational scales.

The Kuder has also been revised recently. Still unresolved, however, is the controversy over the scales themselves, which are derived by comparing the respondents' responses to those of the normative sample of people in the occupation being scored. This raises the question of the stability of the normality of the responses of the standardized population over time. The SVIB norms are more than twenty years old. Certainly one can argue that attitudes must have changed from the fifties to the seventies. But what of changes from the late sixties to the middle seventies? Both men and women are entering nontraditional occupations, and ultimately this change should affect norms.

All of this paints a confusing picture for counselors who sincerely wish to be nonsexist in their approach. About the best they can do is to point out to respondents the effects of socialization and to encourage boys and girls to explore their interests without regard to sex-role stereotypes. This counseling should start as early as possible to avoid conflicting with the sexual identity crisis in the early teens that seems to cement already-formed ideas of careers.

TITLE IX

Title IX of the Education Act of 1972, a milestone instrument addressing sex discrimination in education, guarantees the right of both sexes to education without discrimination. Specifically, Title IX states, "No person in the United States shall, on the basis of sex, be excluded from participation in, be denied the benefits of, or be subjected to discrimination under any education program or activity receiving federal financial assistance."

In June 1975 HEW clarified the initial thrust of Title IX by elaborating a specific set of guidelines. Briefly, the new rules ban discrimination in admissions, employment, benefits, athletics, use of facilities, and participation in courses and extracurricular activities. Governed by these rules are all school districts or higher education institutions receiving federal funds, with the exception of some military academies and religious schools. Specifically outlawed are all-male shop classes or all-female home economics courses, sex-segregated physical education classes, and different curfews for males and females. A later clarification permits separate classes in sex education and personal hygiene.

Some facets of sex discrimination and the application of Title IX seem more germane to elementary and secondary education, and these will be the major focus of this chapter. An effort will be made to explore the policies on admissions, textbooks, and athletic programs.

Admissions

Admissions is one of the first and last areas where sexism is exercised. It prevails from kindergarten to postgraduate work. Much commentary has been made concerning the admission or exclusion by sex of kindergarteners to or from certain areas of activity. The assertion has been made that the doll corner, which is typically a female classroom area, and the block and erector building area, which is typically a male area, are the first examples of exclusion to admission practiced in many elementary schools. Vivian Paley suggests, however, that rather than fighting sexism by removing the doll corner from the educational process, "we should be more concerned about the short period of time boys spend in the doll corner rather than the long period of time spent there by girls." [73] The salient point is that even at the very earliest level of education, certain expectations and channelings pervade the educational process.

All of those engaged in education at the elementary and secondary level need to be aware of and correct such erroneous stereotyping. We must help students to overcome the pigeonholing that begins at a very early age to shape their desires and expectations for admission to institutions of higher learning and the world of work. Certain areas of education at the elementary and secondary levels have been singled out for criticism in the matter of admissions, including special education and vocational training.

In special education the designation of students who will receive special services appears to reflect biases that favor males. Boys dominate the ranks of those referred and treated in all significant areas of exceptionality—the mentally retarded, the learning disabled, the emotionally disturbed, and the gifted. Much work needs to be done to insure equal treatment in admissions by reviewing the identification process for exceptional children. It is imperative that certain questions be posed and answered. How do school personnel select children for special programs? What behavioral indices are used? To what extent are sex biases promoted by current guidelines and referral processes?

Textbooks

The federal guidelines for enforcement to Tital IX do not cover textbooks. While it acknowledges that sex bias in curriculum materials and textbooks does exist, "HEW believes that it may be unconstitutional to regulate matters relating to curriculum, given First Amendment free speech guarantees. Therefore, the Title IX regulation does not cover discrimination in curriculum materials or textbooks."[74] It is the judgment of HEW officials that school districts should deal with this problem at the local level.

Athletics

To insure that the spirit of Title IX is not violated, there must be a great deal of modification in presently existing athletic programs. Janice Pottker and Andrew Fishel list ten questions which will assist HEW's Office for Civil Rights in determining if equal athletic opportunity is present in a local school district.

1. Do the sports selected reflect the interests and abilities of each sex?
2. What is the provision of supplies and equipment?
3. What are the games and practice schedules?
4. What are the travel and per diem allowances?
5. What are the coaching and academic tutoring allowances?
6. How do the assignment and pay of coaches and tutors compare?
7. What are the locker room, practice, and competitive facilities?
8. How do medical training services compare?
9. What are the publicity provisions?

10. How do housing, dining facilities and services compare?[75]

Although these are questions likely to be posed, Title IX regulations do not specifically require identical treatment in each of these ten areas for boys' and girls' teams. They do require, however, that the overall opportunities be equal. The regulations do not require that the financial expenditure for boys' and girls' teams in the same sport be equal, nor even that the total expenditure for the entire boys' and girls' athletic programs be equal.

One consideration that will be made in assessing whether equality of opportunity exists for both sexes is whether there has been an appropriation of necessary funds to operate girls' teams. While regulations present specific characteristics which must be present if equal athletic opportunity is to be found, they do not require equivalent expenditure for each characteristic. There has been much criticism by human rights leaders concerning the failure to include an equal expenditure provision. Some civil rights leaders also deplore the fact that school districts are given the option of offering either single-sex or coed teams in contact sports and in other sports where students must compete for places on a team.

If a school district wants to have a separate boys' team in a non-contact sport, it must also offer a separate girls' team in the sport if a sufficient number of girls are interested and not otherwise accommodated. If there are not enough girls interested in a team of their own, and if the athletic opportunities for girls have previously been limited, then the school will be required to let the girls try out for the boys' team. Although few or no girls may make the "boys" team, the school has still fulfilled its obligation to them under Title IX.[76]

There is a further qualifying clause in the sexism regulations on athletics which will influence the actions school districts may elect to take:

Girls need not be given a specific team in a particular sport if the school can show that the girls' sports interests are otherwise accommodated. This could mean that if enough girls in a high school were interested in participating on a golf team, and the school did not want to offer a coed team, the school could still deny them this team if it could show that there were numerous other sports teams available to girls. Therefore, under Title IX a school could still deny a golf team to girls, even though the boys in the school were given a golf team as well as having other sports teams on which to participate. [77]

There are critics who would argue that this is not even separate opportunity, much less equal opportunity.

For individual's who encounter problems that are beyond their scope of interpretation concerning Title IX regulations, help is available from the regional offices of HEW, which are located in Boston, New York City, Philadelphia, Atlanta, Chicago, Dallas, Kansas City, Denver, San Francisco, and Seattle. Or one may write to the Director of the Office for Civil Rights, Department of Health, Education, and Welfare, Washington, D. C. 20201.

The inequities discussed in this chapter

were central issues in the 1977 National Women's Conference held in Houston, Texas. Nearly 2,000 delegates attended the $5 million, federally funded event which culminated America's International Women's Year activities. The delegates approved twenty-five resolutions, including support for the Equal Rights Amendment and reproductive freedom (abortion). The first American women's rights convention was held in Seneca Falls, New York, in 1848. At that time a small group of women adopted twelve resolutions, including one which asserted that women should have the right to vote. However it wasn't until 1920 that enfranchisement for women was guaranteed by the Nineteenth Amendment to the Constitution. Delegates who attended the 1977 conference hope that it will not take seventy-two years before their resolutions are implemented.

TEN QUICK WAYS TO ANALYZE CHILDREN'S BOOKS FOR RACISM AND SEXISM*

Both in school and out, young children are exposed to racist and sexist attitudes. These attitudes— expressed over and over in books and in other media—gradually distort their perceptions until stereotypes and myths about minorities and women are accepted as reality. It is difficult for a librarian or teacher to convince children to question society's attitudes. But if a child can be shown how to detect racism and sexism in a book, the child can proceed to transfer the perception to wider areas. The following ten guidelines are offered as a starting point in evaluating children's books from this perspective.

1. Check the Illustrations

Look for stereotypes. A stereotype is an oversimplified generalization about a particular group, race, or sex, which usually carries derogatory implications. Some infamous (overt) stereotypes of Blacks are the happy-go-lucky, watermelon-eating Sambo and the fat, eye-rolling mammy; of Chicanos, the sombrero-wearing peon or fiesta-loving, macho bandito; of Asian Americans, the inscrutable, slant-eyed Oriental; of Native Americans, the naked savage or primitive

craftsman and his squaw; of women, the completely domesticated mother, the demure, doll-loving little girl, or the wicked stepmother. While you may not always find stereotypes in the blatant forms described, look for variations which in any way demean or ridicule characters because of their race or sex.

Look for tokenism. If there are nonwhite characters in the illustrations, do they look just like whites except for being tinted or colored in? Do all minority faces look stereotypically alike, or are they depicted as genuine individuals with distinctive features?

Who's doing what? Do the illustrations depict minorities in subservient and passive roles

* SOURCE: The Council on Interracial Books for Children, 1841 Broadway, New York, N.Y. 10023

or in leadership and action roles? Are males the active doers and females the inactive observers?

2. Check the Story Line

The Civil Rights Movement has led publishers to weed out many insulting passages, particularly from stories with Black themes, but the attitudes still find expression in less obvious ways. The following checklist suggests some of the subtle (covert) forms of bias to watch for.

Standard for success. Does it take "white" behavior standards for a minority person to get ahead? Is making it in the dominant white society projected as the only ideal? To gain acceptance and approval, do nonwhite persons have to exhibit extraordinary qualities—excel in sports, get A's, etc.? In friendships between white and nonwhite children, is it the nonwhite who does most of the understanding and forgiving.

Resolution of problems. How are problems presented, conceived and resolved in the story? Are minority people considered to be the problem? Are the oppressions faced by minorities and women represented as causally related to an unjust society? As the reasons for poverty and oppression explained, or are they accepted as inevitable? Does the story line encourage passive acceptance or active resistance? Is a particular problem that is faced by a minority person resolved through the benevolent intervention of a white person?

Role of women. Are the achievements of girls and women based on their own initiative and intelligence, or are they due to their good looks or to their relationship with boys? Are sex roles incidental or critical to characterization and plot? Could the same story be told if the sex roles were reversed?

3. Look at the Lifestyles

Are minority persons and their setting depicted in such a way that they contrast unfavorably with the unstated norm of white middle-class suburbia? If the minority group in question is depicted as different, are negative value judgments implied? Are minorities depicted exclusively in ghettos, barrios or migrant camps? If the illustrations and text attempt to depict another culture, do they go beyond oversimplifications and offer genuine insights into another lifestyle? Look for inaccuracy and inappropriateness in the depiction of other cultures. Watch for instances of the "quaint-natives-in-costume" syndrome (most noticeable in areas like costume and custom, but extending to behavior and personality traits as well).

4. Weigh the Relationships Between People

Do the whites in the story possess the power, take the leadership, and make the important decisions? Do nonwhites and females function in essentially supporting roles?

How are family relationships depicted? In Black families is the mother always dominant? In Hispanic families are there always lots and lots of children? If the family is separated, are societal conditions—unemployment, poverty—cited among the reasons for the separation?

5. Note the Heroes and Heroines

For many years books showed only "safe" minority heroes and heroines—those who avoided serious conflict with the white establishment of their time. Minority groups today are insisting on the right to define their own heroes and heroines based on their own concepts and struggles for justice.

When minority heroes and heroines do appear, are they admired for the same qualities that have made white heroes and heroines famous or because what they have done has benefited white people? Ask this question: Whose interest is a particular figure really serving?

6. Consider the Effects on a Child's Self-Image

Are norms established which limit the child's aspirations and self-concept? What effect can it have on Black children to be continuously bombarded with images of the color white as the ultimate in beauty, cleanliness, virtue, etc., and the color black as evil, dirty, menacing, etc.? Does the book counteract or reinforce this positive association with the color white and negative association with black?

What happens to a girl's self-image when she reads that boys perform all of the brave and important deeds? What about a girl's self-esteem if she is not fair of skin and slim of body?

In a particular story, is there one or more persons with whom a minority child can readily identify to a positive and constructive end?

7. Consider the Author's or Illustrator's Background

Analyze the biographical material on the jacket flap or the back of the book. If a story deals with a minority theme, what qualifies the author or illustrator to deal with the subject? If the author and illustrator are not members of the minority being written about, is there anything in their background that would specifically recommend them as the creators of this book?

Similarly, a book that deals with the feelings and insights of women should be more carefully examined if it is written by a man—unless the book's avowed purpose is to present a strictly male perspective.

8. Check Out the Author's Perspective

No author can be wholly objective. All authors write out of a cultural as well as a personal context. Children's books in the past have traditionally come from authors who are white and who are members of the middle class, with one result being that a single ethnocentric perspective has dominated American children's literature. With the book in question, look carefully to determine whether the direction of the author's perspective substantially weakens or strengthens the value of his/her written work. Are omissions and distortions central to the overall character or message of the book?

9. Watch for Loaded Words

A word is loaded when it has insulting overtones. Examples of loaded adjectives (usually racist) are savage, primitive, conniving, lazy, superstitious, treacherous, wily, crafty, inscrutable, docile, and backward.

Look for sexist language and adjectives that exclude or ridicule women.   Look for use of the male pronoun to refer to both males and females. While the generic use of the word "man" was accepted in the past, its use today is outmoded. The following examples show how sexist language can be avoided: ancestors instead of forefathers, chairperson instead of chairman, community instead of brotherhood, firefighters instead of firemen, manufactured instead of manmade, the human family instead of the family of man.

10. Look at the Copyright Date

Books on minority themes—usually hastily conceived—suddenly began appearing in the mid-1960s. There followed a growing number of "minority experience" books to meet the new market demand, but most of these were still written by white authors, edited by white editors and published by white publishers. They therefore reflected a white point of view. Only very recently, in the late 1960s and early 1970s, has the children's book world begun even to remotely reflect the realities of a multiracial society. And it has just begun to reflect feminists' concerns.

The copyright dates, therefore, can be a clue as to how likely the book is to be overtly racist or sexist, although a recent copyright date, of course, is no guarantee of a book's relevance or sensitivity. The copyright date only means the year the book was published. It usually takes a minimum of one year—and often much more than that—from the time a manuscript is submitted to the publisher to the time it is actually printed and put on the market. This time lag meant very little in the past, but in a time of rapid change and changing consciousness, when children's book publishing is attempting to be relevant, it is becoming increasingly significant.

ADDITIONAL READINGS

Bernard, Jessie. *Women, Wives, Mothers: Values and Options*. Chicago, Aldine, 1975.

Frazier, Nancy and Myra Sadker. *Sexism in School and Society*. New York, Harper & Row, 1973.

Gersoni-Staun, Diane, ed. *Sexism and Youth*. New York, R.R. Bowker, 1974.

Harrison, Barbara. *Unlearning the Lie: Sexism in Schools*. New York, Liveright, 1973.

Jacobs, William Jo and Phoebe Lloyd Jacobs. *Women in History*. Beverly Hills, Cal., Benzigev, 1976.

James, Edward T., ed. *Notable American Women, 1607–1950*. Cambridge, Mass., Harvard University Press, 1971.

Johnson, Laurie O., ed. *Nonsexist Curricular Materials for Elementary Schools*. Old Westbury, N. Y., Feminist Press, 1974.

Komarousky, Mirra. *Women in the Modern World: Their Education and Their Dilemmas*. Boston, Little, Brown, 1953.

Lee, Dorothy. *Valuing the Self: What We Can Learn from Other Cultures*. Englewood Cliffs, N.J., Prentice-Hall, 1975.

Maccia, Elizabeth S., et al., eds. *Women and Education*, Springfield, Ill., Charles E. Thomas, 1975.

National Organization for Women. *Report on Sex Bias in the Public Schools*. New York, NOW, 1972.

Weitzman, Lenore and Diane Rizzo. *Biased Textbooks: The Images of Males and Females in Five Subject Areas*. Washington, D. C., The Resource Center on Sex Roles in Education, 1974.

Women on Words and Images. *Dick and Jane as Victims: Sex Stereotyping in Children's Readers*. Princeton, N.J., WOW, 1971.

NOTES

1. Pauline B. Bart, "Why Women See the Future Differently from Men," in Alvin Toffler (ed.), *Learning Tomorrow* (New York, Vintage Books, 1974).

2. Lawrence Kohlberg, "A Cognitive-Developmental Analysis of Children's Sex Role Concepts and Attitudes," in Eleanor Maccoby (ed.), *The Development of Sex Differences* (Stanford, Stanford University Press, 1966), 82–173.

3. Ruth E. Hartley, "Pressures and the Socialization of the Male Child," in Judith Stacey et al. (eds.), *And Jill Came Tumbling After: Sexism in American Education* (New York, Dell, 1974), 187.

4. Sigmund Freud, *Freud on Sex and Neurosis* (trans. by Alex Strachey et al., Garden City, New York, Garden City Publishing Co., 1949).

5. Walter Mischel, "A Social-Learning View of Sex Differences in Behavior," in Maccoby, *Sex Differences*, 57.

6. Kohlberg, "A Cognitive-Developmental Analysis," 83.

7. *Ibid.*, 98.

8. Eleanor Maccoby and Carol Jacklin, *The Psychology of Sex Differences* (Stanford, Stanford University Press, 1974).

9. Michael Lewis, "Parents and Children: Sex Role Development," *School Review*, 80 (February, 1972), 234.

10. Catherine D. Lyon and Terry N. Saario, "Women in Public Education: Sexual Discrimination in Promotions," *Phi Delta Kappan*, 55 (October, 1973), 120–123.

11. "Are You Guilty of Teaching Sex Bias?" *Instructor*, 82 (August, 1972), 80–81.

12. "Women's Record," *Integrated Education*, 12 (May/June, 1974), 49–50. See also "It's 'No Accident' That Men Outnumber Women on School Boards Nine to One," *American School Board Journal*, 161 (May, 1974), 53–55.

13. *Report of the Personnel Task Force of the Committee to Study Sex Discrimination in Kalamazoo (Mich.) Public Schools*, (June 7, 1973), 5.

14. J. M. Johnston, "A Symposium: Men in Young Children's Lives, Part 2," *Childhood Education*, 47 (December, 1970), 144.

15. David Woodbridge, "Male Teacher in the Elementary School: Image Breaker or Super-Stereotype," *California Journal of Teacher Education*, 1 (May, 1973), 42–47.

16. Gary Peltier, "Sex Differences in the Schools: Problem and Proposed Solution," *Phi Delta Kappan*, 50 (November, 1968), 182–185.

17. *Kalamazoo Public Schools*, 8.

18. Patricia C. Sexton, *The Feminized Male: Classrooms, White Collars and The Decline of Manliness* (New York, Random House, 1969).

19. Suzanne Taylor, "Educational Leadership: A

Male Domain," *Phi Delta Kappan*, 55 (October, 1973), 124–128.

20. Lindley Siles and P. Martin Nystrand, "The Politics of Sex Education," *Educational Forum*, 38 (May, 1974), 431–440.

21. Neal Gross and Anne Trask, "Men and Women as Elementary School Principals," ERIC ED 002 949.

22. *Ibid.*

23. Helen M. Morsink, "Leader Behavior of Men and Women Principals," *NASSP Bulletin*, 54 (September, 1970), 80–87. See also John Hoyle, "Who Shall be Principal—A Man or a Woman?" *National Elementary Principal*, 48 (January, 1969), 23–24.

24. Patricia Minuchin, "The Schooling of To-morrow's Women," *School Review*, 80 (February, 1972), 201.

25. Alice Rossi, "The Roots of Ambivalence in American Women," in Judith Bardwick (ed.), *Readings on the Psychology of Women* (New York, Harper & Row, 1972).

26. Peter S. Houts and Doris R. Entwisle, "Academic Achievement Effort Among Females: Achievement Attitudes and Sex-role Orientation," *Journal of Counseling Psychology*, 15 (May, 1968), 284–286.

27. James Coleman, cited in Maccoby (ed.), *Sex Differences*, 31.

28. Jack H. Pollack, "The Astonishing Truth about Girl Dropouts," *Education Digest*, 32 (November, 1966), 14–16.

29. Norma D. Feshbach, "Student Teacher Preferences for Elementary School Pupils Varying in Personality Characteristics," in Melvin L. Silberman (ed.), *The Experience of Schooling* (New York, Holt, Rinehart & Winston, 1971).

30. Nancy Pirsig, "Training the Teachers," *American Education*, 9 (June, 1973), 24–26.

31. Nella F. Weiner, "Sugar and Spice," *School Review*, 81 (November, 1972), 96–99.

32. Robert D. Myrick, "The Counselor-Consultant and the Effeminate Boy," *Personnel and Guidance Journal*, 48 (January, 1970), 355–361.

33. Kathy Mansheim, "Learning the Rules," *Changing Education*, 5 (Winter-Spring, 1974), 33.

34. Patrick Lee, "Male and Female Teachers in Elementary School: An Ecological Analysis," *Teachers College Record*, 75 (September, 1973), 79–98.

35. *Kalamazoo Public Schools*, 4.

36. John McNeal, "Programmed Instruction Versus Visual Classroom Procedures in Teaching Boys to Read," *American Eductional Research Association Journal*, 1 (March, 1964), 113–120.

37. Thomas L. Good and Jere E. Brophy, "Questioned Equality for Good Boys and Girls," *Reading Teacher*, 25 (December, 1971), 247–252.

38. Rebecca Oetzel, "Classified Summary of Re-search in Sex Differences," in Maccoby (ed.), *Sex Differences*.

39. Janet S. Chafetz, *Masculine/Feminine or Human?* (Itasca, Ill., F. E. Peacock, 1974), 90.

40. Richard L. Simpson, "Sex Stereotypes of Secondary School Teaching Subjects: Male and Female Status Gains and Losses," *Sociology of Education* 47 (Summer, 1974), 391.

41. Robert Shuter, "The Free School: A Field Study on Sex Roles and Small Group Interaction," ERIC ED 089 378.

42. Patricia Minuchin, "Sex Differences in Children: Research Findings in an Educational Context," *National Elementary Principal*, 46 (November, 1966), 48.

43. Paul Hazzard, *Books, Children and Men* (Boston, The Horn Books, 1944), 168.

44. May Lazar, *Reading Interests, Activities and Opportunities of Bright, Average, and Dull Pupils* (New York, Teachers College, Columbia University, 1937), 146.

45. Women on Words and Images, *Dick and Jane as Victims* (Princeton, N. J., 1975).

46. Sara Zimet (ed.), *What Children Read in School: Critical Analysis of Primary Textbooks* (New York, Grune and Stratton, 1972).

47. Elizabeth Fisher, "Children's Books: The Second Sex, Junior Division," in Judith Stacey, et al. (eds.), *And Jill Came Tumbling After: Sexism in American Education* (New York, Dell, 1974), 37.

48. Aileen P. Nilsen, "Women in Children's Textbooks," *College English*, 32 (May, 1971), 925.

49. Women on Word and Images, *Dick and Jane* 46.

50. "Only You, Dick Darling! Survival Report on NBA Week," *Publisher's Weekly* (March 22, 1971), 20–22.

51. "Guidelines for Improving the Image of Women in Textbooks," Scott, Foresman, 1974; "Memo from a Publisher," *New York Times Magazine* (October 20, 1974), 384.

52. Winifred T. Jay, "Sex Stereotyping in Selected Mathematics Textbooks for Grades Two, Four, and Six," Ph.D. dissertation, University of Oregon, 1973.

53. Winifred T. Jay and Clarence W. Schminke, "Sex Bias in Elementary School Mathematics Texts," *The Arithmetic Teacher*, 22 (March, 1975), 244–245.

54. Thomas B. Lyles, "Grouping by Sex," *National Elementary Principal*, 46 (November 1966), 38–41.

55. Marcia Federbush, *Let Them Aspire!* (Pittsburgh, KNOW, 1971), 14.

56. *Ibid.*, 11.

57. Nannette Rainone et al., "High School Women's Liberation," in Leslie B. Tanner (ed.), *Voices for Women's Liberation* (New York, New American Library, 1971), 222.

58. Pauline S. Sear and David Ferdman, "Teacher Interactions with Boys and with Girls," *National Elementary Principal*, 46 (November, 1966), 30–35.

59. Joy Hardin and Christopher Dede, "Even Frankenstein's Monster was Male: Discrimination Against Women in Science Education," *Science Education*, 40 (December, 1973), 18–21.

60. Sandra L. Bem and Daryl J. Bem, *Training the Woman to Know Her Place: The Social Antecedents of Women in the World of Work* (Philadelphia, Pennsylvania State Department of Education, 1975).

61. Thomas L. Hilton and Costa W. Berglund, "Sex Differences in Potential Mathematical Achievement—A Longitudinal Study," ERIC ED 069 789.

62. Rebecca Sparling, quoted in Irene Peden, "The Missing Half of Our Technical Potential: Can We Motivate the Girls?" *Mathematics Teacher*, 58 (January, 1965), 10.

63. "Girls Can Do Mathematics Problems But They'd Rather Have Dates," *Oklahoma City Times* (November 11, 1975), 6.

64. Mary Beth Kievit, "Will Jill Make Department Chairman?" *American Vocational Journal*, 49 (January, 1974), 40–43.

65. Elizabeth Koontz, quoted in Federbush, *Let Them Aspire!*, i.

66. Patricia T. Cegelka, "Sex Role Stereotyping in Special Education: A Look at Secondary Work Study Programs," *Exceptional Child*, 42 (March, 1976), 325–326.

67. Florence House, "Sexism and the Aspirations of Women," *Phi Delta Kappan*, 55 (October, 1973), 100.

68. *Journal of Health, Physical Education, and Recreation*, 36 (September, 1965), 34–37.

69. "Our Own Worst Enemies," *WomenSports*, (September, 1974), 38.

70. T. Page Johnson, "Girls on the Boys' Team: Equal Protection in School and Athletics," *NASSP Bulletin* 58 (October, 1974), 63.

71. "God Bless You, Title IX," *WomenSports*, (September, 1974), 38.

72. *Ibid.*

73. Vivian Paley, "Is the Doll Corner a Sexist Institution?" *School Review*, 81 (August, 1973), 575.

74. Alice Fins, "Sex and the School Principal: A Long Look at Title IX," *NASSP Bulletin*, 58 (September, 1974), 57.

75. Janice Pottker and Andrew Fishel, "Separate and Unequal: Sex Discrimination in Interscholastic Sports," *Integrated Education*, 14 (March/April, 1976), 4.

76. *Ibid.*

77. *Ibid.*

12.
DRUG USE AND ABUSE

One of the most urgent problems confronting contemporary society is the use and abuse of drugs by elementary and secondary school students. Although from time to time the contention is advanced that this problem is diminishing current research data do not bear out this assertion.

Many inexperienced youth still in the trial-and-error stage of adolescent life will eat, drink, smoke or sniff almost anything that promises to yield thrills. Other youth use drugs as a means of escape from our society. Still others, rebellious youth, find drugs an acceptable way of acting out.[1]

While the debate continues regarding the extent of drug abuse, the best methods of remediation, the degree of damage, and so forth, the problem has worsened to the point that many level-headed educators and representatives of the medical profession describe it as a national epidemic which, if unchecked, may destroy the nation's most valuable national resource—our children and youth. This chapter will atttempt to place some of the claims and counter claims germane to drug abuse in perspective by exploring (1) the nature of the problem, (2) the myths and misconceptions of drug abuse, (3) the causes of drug abuse, (4) the case against drug education, (5) the case for drug education, (6) specific programs designed to curb drug abuse, (7) teacher education, and (8) selected examples of effective drug education programs.

THE NATURE OF THE PROBLEM

In terms of human lives and money, alcoholism and drug addiction take an ever-increasing toll each year in the United States. A recent report of the U. S. Department of Health, Education, and Welfare to the Congress states that at least fifteen million people in this country are alcoholics or problem drinkers.[2]

The 1973 cost of alcohol consumption to the American economy, says the report, can be broken down into various categories: $9.35 billion in lost production of goods and services; $8.29 billion for health and medical care; $6.44 billion in motor vehicle accidents; $640 million in alcohol programs and research costs; $2.2 billion in welfare payments; $500 million in criminal justice costs; $135 million in social services costs; and a considerable portion of the $4.5 billion reported in 1973 as fire losses can be directly or indirectly attributed to alcohol use. The most tragic statistics are that 64 per cent of all murders, 41 per cent of assaults, and 43 per cent of nonpedestrian automobile deaths are linked each year to drinking.[3] Americans consume more than 6 billion cans and bottles of beer each year, 200 million gallons of wine, and 50 million gallons of distilled liquor. The average American will consume almost three gallons of pure alcohol per year, and during his or her lifetime will spend between $20,000 to $50,000 for alcoholic beverages.

Figures on the use and abuse of drugs other than alcohol in the United States, while not as

251

Table 18. Opinions of the Public on the Use of Drugs as a Serious Local Youth Problem, by Sex, Race, Age, Education, Community Size, and Region: 1975

Question: Is the use of drugs by young people a serious problem in this community?	Percent		
	Yes	No	Don't know no answer
National Totals	58	27	15
Sex			
Males	56	29	15
Females	60	25	15
Race			
White	57	28	15
Nonwhite	64	21	15
Age			
18 to 29 years	56	32	12
30 to 49 years	61	27	12
50 years and over	57	22	21
Education			
Elementary grades	62	21	17
High school	59	27	14
College	53	31	16
Community size			
1 million and over	54	26	20
500,000 to 999,999	57	25	18
50,000 to 499,999	62	23	15
2,500 to 49,999	69	21	10
Under 2,500	51	35	14
Region			
East	51	31	18
Midwest	63	24	13
South	59	27	14
West	60	24	16

SOURCE: Phi Delta Kappa, Inc., Bloomington, Ind., The Gallup Survey of Public Attitudes Toward the Public Schools, 1975.

reliable as those on alcohol, are nevertheless frightening. As many as 24 million Americans have used marijuana; 19 million are users of such stimulants as amphetamines and cocaine; nearly 13 million use tranquilizers and barbiturates; heroin addicts are estimated to number 800,000 and may number many more. Drug abuse costs the nation between eight and twelve billion dollars a year. The pervading dangers of drug abuse are sharply illustrated by figures recently released to the Joint Congressional Committee on Atomic Energy. Between March 1972 and February 1973, no fewer than 3,647 military and civilian employees with access to nuclear weapons were removed from their positions; 20 per cent of them because of drug problems. In addition it is reported that 39 per cent of all removals from the United States Army and 35.6 per cent of all removals from the United States Navy during the same period were the result of drug abuse.[4] There is no doubt about it:

drug abuse is killing America—mentally, morally, and physically. To understand the problem, it is helpful to review conditions of adult drug use and abuse which spill over into the schools.

GETTING HOOKED—WHAT IS ADDICTION?

Many experts agree that three steps lead to the condition commonly called drug addiction, although the particular steps may be characterized somewhat differently by various authorities. First, the individual must have developed what is labeled "tolerance"—an ability to tolerate increasing amounts of the drug before the desired effect is obtained. One of the most unfortunate aspects of opiate addiction is that tolerance to the toxic, sedative, and analgesic effects of opiates can be almost complete.[5]

Second, the individual must have become psychologically dependent on the drug. The Expert Committee on Drugs Liable to Produce Addiction of the World Health Organization has said that this step, often known as "drug habituation," includes four characteristics: a desire (but not a compulsion) to continue taking the drug for the sense of improved well-being that it engenders; little or no tendency to increase the dose; some degree of psychic dependence on the effect of the drug but absence of physical dependence and, hence, no abstinence syndrome; and a detrimental effect, if any, primarily only on the individual using the drug.[6] Several other authorities have defined this second step as a "psychic craving" for the drug[7] and as a "compulsion to continue the drug and obtain it by almost any means."[8] Obviously there is some meaningful disagreement among experts.

The Expert Committee on Drugs has listed the characteristics of the third step known as "addiction": an overpowering desire or need (compulsion) to continue taking the drug and to obtain it by any means, a tendency to increase the dose, a psychic (psychological) and generally a physical dependence on the effects of the drug, and an effect detrimental to both the user of the drug and to society. More recently, however, the Expert Committee on Drugs has recommended that the term "drug dependence" be substituted for the terms "drug addiction" and "drug habituation." The committee now defines drug dependence as a "state arising from repeated administration of a drug on a periodic or continuous basis" and asserts that the characteristics of drug dependence will vary, depending on the drug involved.[9] Morris M. Rubin prefers to use the terms "psychological dependence" and "physiological dependence" to denote the second and third stages in the making of a drug addict.[10]

Alfred R. Lindesmith, one of the most noted authorities and researchers on drug addiction, has defined addiction as "that behavior which is distinguished primarily by an intense, conscious desire for the drug, and by a tendency to relapse, evidently caused by the persistence of attitudes established in the early stages of addiction."[11] He also writes that other correlated aspects are the dependence upon the drug as a twenty-four-hour-a-day necessity, the impulse to increase the dosage far beyond bodily need, and the definition of oneself as an addict.

Johannes Biberfeld, pioneer in drug research, has posited the theory that opiate addiction involves both tolerance of and craving for a drug, and that it is the phenomenon of craving which is uniquely human.[12] It is for this reason that many writers are unwilling to use the term "addiction" when referring to animals who have developed a tolerance for a drug in laboratory experiments. Nor will it help us much in our search for a definition of drug addiction if we do not proceed further after having learned the physiological changes in the human body that a particular drug can cause. While we must bear in mind the admonition of Harris Isbell not to regard physical dependence on drugs as wholly of psychogenic origin,[13] we would still feel justified, after reading a volume on the physiological effects of drugs, in asking, "Yes, but is this what we mean by drug addiction in human beings?"

What then is the key to narcotics addiction? It is not pleasure, according to one of the most widely accepted and cogent theories of addiction. It has been pointed out that if pleasure were the ultimate goal of the addict, marijuana would be the leading addictive drug; yet it is generally admitted that marijuana is nonaddictive, at least physiologically.

Marijuana seems infinitely superior to opium as a pleasure-producing agent; its pleasures do not fade as do those of opium with continued use; its psychological effects are described with enthusiasm and hyperbole; its pleasurable effects are not counterbalanced by the extensive evil social and physical consequences which ordinarily bedevil heroin addicts. [14]

By this theory the so-called craving for drugs is determined by negative reinforcement—that is, the relief and avoidance of discomfort and pain rather than positive pleasure. The theory does not deny that individuals begin taking a particular drug because it gives positive pleasure, but it does refuse to label them as addicts until they respond to withdrawal symptoms in a particular way—by craving the drug both psychologically and physiologically. The real junkie, Jerome H. Jaffe points out, seeks a drug not because of an overwhelming desire to gain pleasure but to remain in a normal state. [15]

Lindesmith asserts that drug addiction, like almost all forms of behavior, is learned; unless the person using a drug understands the reasons for his or her withdrawal symptoms, he or she will not become addicted to that particular drug. An individual who traces the pain associated with discontinuance of a drug to some source other than its discontinuance will not become dependent on the drug. This theory, while holding that the physiological or biological effects of drugs are indispensable preconditions of addiction, maintains that they are not sufficient preconditions.

Understanding withdrawal distress means to conceptualize it, to name and categorize it, to describe and grasp it intellectually through the use of linguistic symbols. Addiction is therefore a uniquely human form of behavior which differs from the superficially comparable responses of lower animals much as human cognitive capacities differ from those of lower forms. [16]

Lindesmith adds that the habit-forming power of any drug is roughly dependent on the severity of withdrawal symptoms and not on the pleasure it produces. This theory would seem to be confirmed, at least to some extent, by Thomas de Quincey in his famous work, *The Confessions of an English Opium-Eater.*

Lord Bacon conjectures that it may be as painful to

be born as to die. That seems probable; and during the whole period of diminishing the opium, I had the torments of a man passing out of one mode of existence into another, and liable to the mixed or the alternate pains of birth and death. [17]

Lindesmith's theory has its attractions, not the least of which is that it goes far toward drawing a clear line between those who use drugs and those who are addicted to them. He appears to define drug hunger solely in terms of avoidance of withdrawal symptoms. This theory helps us understand why the narcotics addict is a pathetic, helpless creature, caught in a habit over which he or she has very little, if any, control; for his or her craving "is not a rational assessment or choice of any sort, but basically an irrational compulsion arising from the repetition of a sequence of experiences in a process like those that lead to the psychologist's conditioned response." [18]

The learning theory of drug use very well may apply also to those substances which are not considered at least phsyically addictive. Howard S. Becker says that an individual becomes a real marijuana user only if he or she learns to enjoy the sensations experienced. [19] Becker also argues that during this process the individual develops a disposition or motivation to use marijuana which was not and could not have been present when the use began. Individuals who do not go through this process fully while using the drug will not become marijuana addicts.

THE KINDS AND CHARACTERISTICS OF DRUGS

The drugs that are available to and used by elementary and secondary school students are many and varied. Hershel Thornburg classifies drugs into four basic categories: sedative-hypnotic drugs, narcotics, central nervous system stimulants, and psychedelic drugs.

Most common in the sedative-hypnotic group are alcohol and barbiturates as well as the most extensively used drug, marijuana. The narcotics include opium, heroin, morphine, codeine, and other derivatives. Nicotine and caffeine are the most widely used stimulants, although the most dangerous stimulant is the amphetamine. Within the psy-

*chedelic drugs are found LSD, PCP, and a canna-
bis ingredient known as THC.*[20]

Although the distinction between experimental or occasional drug use and drug abuse is
sometimes difficult to draw, experts in the field
cite such measurable characteristics as declining academic performance: unusual, undesirable or bizarre behavior; and blackouts as the
most obvious signs of drug-related problems.

An examination of drug abuse reveals that
three basic diagnostic types are encountered
with frequency in identifying young drug dependents: the neurotic, the behaviorally disordered, and the schizoid. The neurotic is described by Zebulon Taintor as one who is filled
with anxiety. Anxiety in turn is defined as
being afraid that something bad is going to
happen, but not knowing what it is.[21] While
able to behave in socially correct ways, the
neurotic is subject to fits of depression, which
may indicate anger with himself or herself.
"People who are suffering from anxiety, depression, or an equivalent feeling but are able
to perceive reality correctly and behave in a
socially acceptable fashion are diagnosed as
neurotic. The neurotic sub-group is a relatively small group of all drug-dependent
people that uses drugs as tranquilizers to ease
anxiety."[22]

The behavior disordered person is described by Taintor as one who experiences
feelings so fleeting that they cannot be described but must be taken care of by such
immediate action as having a fight or taking
drugs. Engaging in action without focusing on
feelings denotes a behavior disorder. Words
mean very little to people in the behavior disordered category. Explanations will not do;
they need an experience. Students with this
character disorder constitute the most frequent type of person using opiates. Such persons are described as having cynical, nihilistic,
and self-defeating behavior patterns. They
usually will take drugs for "kicks" and "to feel
high."

The third diagnostic type, which is more
than commonly vunerable to drug abuse, is the
schizoid. Young people in this category have
difficulty defining their identities; they appear
to act randomly with no particular plan in
mind. "They show no signs of distress, since
being 'cool' is their most important defense.

They try to show that nothing can shake
them."[23] Stimulants are then sought to counteract negative feelings.

*Drugs are a good way of getting away from un-
happy feelings. All abused drugs are mood-
altering. Depressants like the barbiturates and
alcohol provide relief through softening incoming
stimuli. The stimulants move one rapidly on to the
next feeling, then speed up to one beyond that so
nothing sinks in and one is preoccupied with the
phenomenon of speed itself. The opiates predictably
produce an ecstatic feeling which is a dependable
substitute for any bad feelings. The hallucinogens
help a person to get away into a different sense of
reality.*[24]

While it is readily discernible that there are
vast differences in kinds of drugs, it should also
be noted that there are vast differences in degree of danger in the drugs used by elementary
and secondary school students. Thornburg has
established a hierarchy of danger for drugs.
Heroin, the narcotic that is the strongest of the
opiates, is first on his list of dangerous drugs.
Heroin users find "the psychological effect is a
physically warm and peaceful feeling, raising
self-esteem, and confidence. Users develop a
tolerance that demands frequent and increasing doses to maintain a high. Large doses can
produce death."[25]

Second on the danger list are barbiturates,
which are commonly ingested as sleeping pills
and tranquilizers. "They do not produce a
'high'; rather, they have a sedative effect. They
can have habituating effects. Overdoses can
result in depression, often coma and death, as
well as providing strong suicidal tendencies."[26]

A close third behind barbituates are amphetamines. Drugs in this group are highly
desirable to students because they act as
stimulants to the central nervous system and
produce a high. Because of this effect, both
children and adults often become habituated
to amphetamines. They can produce physical
dependency, psychiatric disorder, and even
brain damage. Of growing concern is the trend
towards cocaine use among school-age youth.

LSD, listed fourth in the danger hierarchy,
produces "changes in perception, thought, and
sense orientation. It is a potent drug which
produces dramatic, sometimes permanent,

psychological and physical changes. Usually LSD does not possess fatal qualities directly, and rarely is there any phsycial dependence. The psychotic effects of the drug produce the greatest danger to the user and may lead to self-inflicted bodily harm or death."[27]

Marijuana, an hallucinogen, is fifth on the list. The effects produced by marijuana tend to lower inhibitions, often intensify sexual pleasure, but rarely result in violent behavior.

THE MYTHS AND MISCONCEPTIONS ABOUT ALCOHOL

When drugs are discussed, it is not uncommon for alcohol to be excluded from the list. Alcohol is, however, a drug that acts as a depressant on the central nervous system and has strong addictive power. Because it is not illegal for adults, many people—including children—harbor the popular misconception that its effects are not seriously harmful. Nothing could be farther from the truth. Patricia Cobe warns: "Since alcohol is the world's most available and socially acceptable 'drug', we often tend to forget that it is a drug at all. Because of this, alcohol has become the most widely used and abused drug in American culture. It's now the number one drug choice in teen-age circles—ahead in use over marijuana and the 'hard drugs'—and gaining all the time."[28]

Commenting in this same vein, Paul Martin wrote:

Alcohol is a drug. It is and has been the most abused drug in North America. In the United States and Canada there are probably 100 million drinkers and at least 10 million of them have substantial problems related to alcohol. Alcohol is a factor in about 50 percent of all fatalities in automobile accidents. Fifty percent of all first admissions to mental hospitals suffer from alcoholism. According to a recent report, alcoholism and related problems cost the United States more than $25 billion a year. This is more than five times the amount needed to provide food for everyone in the country afflicted with hunger. It would build 1,750,000 low-cost homes.[29]

Along with an accelerated use of alcohol, two significant developments have become apparent. First, there is an increase in the use of alcohol among women. Second, there is a lowering in the age of young people who are being identified as having alcohol problems.

Children and Youth Problems

In 1975 the National Institute on Alcohol Abuse and Alcoholism estimated that there were at least 500,000 child and teenage alcoholics in America. To counter this condition, Alcoholics Anonymous (AA) now has junior (10-to 20-year-olds) chapters scattered throughout the nation. Unlike drugs, which began primarily as an urban, ethnic minority group problem and spread to other areas and groups, alcohol has always been a national problem. The earlier children start heavy drinking, the greater probability they will be alcoholics by age 16 or 17.

The National Institute of Alcohol Abuse and Alcoholism conducted a national survey in the early 1970s and found that 28 per cent of the teenagers (thirteen to eighteen years of age) surveyed were problem drinkers. Problem drinkers were defined as youths who had been drunk at least four times during a one-year period or who admitted that their drinking resulted in problems with peers or superiors at least twice in one year. Approximately 18 per cent of girls and more than 30 per cent of boys in grades seven through twelve were heavy or moderate drinkers. Heavy drinkers consumed five to twelve alcoholic drinks on at least one occasion a week and moderately heavy drinkers consumed the same amount three or four times a month, or two to four drinks a week. Ten per cent of the students were alcoholics. A corollary study of students in the New York City Public Schools found that 12 per cent of juniors and seniors were classified as alcoholics or problem drinkers.

It is important to note that teenage alcoholism is not a new phenomenon. Studies show a long-standing and widespread acceptance of alcohol among teenagers. Although a majority of teenagers use alcohol at least occasionally, the majority of these drink moderately and responsibly. There are two major differences between drinking and taking drugs. "One is that alcohol is legal, at least for people over 18, and the other is that alcohol is far more potentially dangerous than the other abused drugs, including heroin, cocaine, amphetamines, barbiturates, and hallucinogenic drugs."[30] Children who drink heavily frequently take barbiturates and other drugs.

Numerous experts have expressed opinions concerning the causes of alcohol use and abuse among elementary and secondary school students. Most experts agree that parents' attitudes toward drinking may be the single most significant factor in whether or not their children drink excessively or abstain. Parents who drink tend to raise children who also drink, and parents who abstain are more likely to raise children who abstain. Case histories note that among patients undergoing treatment for alcoholism, more than half had at least one parent who was alcoholic.

Many youngsters view drinking as a mark of sophistication, as easily accessible coming-of-age rite. It is also believed that television advertising plays a major role in projecting drinking as an alluring sign of maturity. The sweet wines advertised on television in some areas are favorites among young drinkers. Some educators question the propriety of this apparently direct appeal to children of school age.

Commenting further regarding this problem, Albert F. Fillipps alleges that "the single most alarming recent change in motoring habits is the tremendous increase in drinking among teenagers. Even though the official speed limit is now 55 miles per hour and gas costs more, the young are 'cruising and boozing' more than ever before."[31] Because teenagers are often drinking and driving together in packed cars, teenage automobile accidents involve a high rate of multiple victims.

While much attention is focused on alcohol, marijuana, morphine, and prescription drugs, too little attention is paid to the effect of nicotine. Currently approximately one in three Americans smokes regularly, and more than 5 million people smoke two or more packs of cigarettes a day. Half the nation's teenagers are classified as habitual smokers before they graduate or drop out from high school. At least 150,000 Americans die prematurely each year because of excessive amounts of nicotine and coal tar consumption. Furthermore, each year cigarettes cause one million cases of stomach ulcers, one million cases of serious long and respiratory diseases, and 300,000 coronaries. A person smoking one pack of cigarettes a day is ten times more likely to die of lung cancer than a nonsmoker.

Americans spend more than $8 billion a year to support their deadly habit.

FACTORS THAT CONTRIBUTE TO ALCOHOL AND DRUG ABUSE

In exploring the causes for drug use, W. G. Hollister examined the ethical system of marijuana users and found that "the more the student's self-image tends to be rebellious, cynical, anti-establishment, 'hippie,' and apathetic, the more likely he is to smoke marijuana."[32] In 1975 the National Institute on Drug Abuse found that of 17,000 high school seniors surveyed, 53 per cent had tried marijuana. Hollister lists six reasons why contemporary youths use drugs: rebellion toward parents, personal feelings of inadequacy, for pleasurable thrills, to reduce boredom, as a solace for fears and doubts, and to escape from responsibility.

In an effort to determine causes, researchers classify drug users into four basic categories: (1) the experimental user, (2) the periodic or recreational user, (3) the compulsive user, and (4) the ritualistic user. The experimental users are young persons who try drugs as a result of curiosity or because they feel the need to conform to peer pressure. Since their schoolmates are on drugs, they want to experience what their friends are describing when they say they are high.

The periodic or recreational users may begin using drugs primarily for the fun and excitement, but often the use goes beyond the experimental stage and becomes a regular pattern. The compulsive users have gone beyond the periodic or recreational use of drugs and have developed either a physical or a psychological dependence on the drugs. Many compulsive users are seeking a euphoric state which will extricate them from the routine and boring details of their daily lives. The ritualistic drug user is prone to take drugs because he or she is endeavoring to reach some high spiritual or religious level.

Contrary to common belief these users are not drug abusers. They are more cultist, seeking deeper revelation through drug usage. Many even go beyond drugs and stop taking them, although they remain in a drug-oriented society.[33]

When educators are asked why all this is happening, those who answer are inclined to oversimplify the problem of youthful drug abuse by seeking either a single cause or a very few specific causes. It is the opinion of many behavioral scientists that we should look closely at societal reasons—families, the schools, peer groups—and at the individuals themselves.

There are many contributing factors that can help to explain youthful drug abuse. These involve the declining consensus about values in our society, the generation gap, the changes in the family. Peer groups are more important as parental influences decline. The spread of drugs can be formulated in public health terms. As dependency deepens, the influence of conditioning and individual psychodynamics is greater than social and group factors. Drug education is ineffectual because socializing and educative functions are confused. Since there is no one cause, but rather many contributing factors, efforts to stem the rising tide of drug abuse and dependency must proceed on many fronts.[34]

It is generally concluded that drug users as opposed to non-drug users are more likely to: (1) have drug-using friends, (2) have parents who smoke, drink, or use psychotropic drugs excessively, (3) describe themselves as worthless, helpless, impulsive and unhappy, (4) come from broken homes, and (5) participate less in school activities.

As for alcohol, one of the causes of its use among students is its legal status and the fact that there is little stigma attached, nor is there any likelihood of an extended jail sentence. However, sociability and acceptability—the initial causes for drinking—can soon degenerate into abuse if other personality problems are attendant.

DRUG EDUCATION

When drug abuse education was introduced into a few American schools in the late 1960s, the most common objective was to provide students with information about drugs. Like the early sex education program, this approach was generally unsuccessful. During this era students were frequently given erroneous or out-of-date information. It was believed that if students were given enough information, they would make the right decisions.

Effective drug education programs no longer focus exclusively on the drugs themselves, but on social attitudes and drug abusers as well. Humanistic educators suggest that open communication and trust building should be integral parts of drug education programs. In this approach affective education techniques are blended with traditional concerns, such as up-to-date information about legal, pharmacological, and social aspects of drug abuse. Harold J. Cornacchia, David J. Bentel, and David E. Smith have outlined two major arrangements for drug education.

The organizational patterns of formal drug education usually refer to the direct and correlated patterns of instruction. The direct pattern includes drug education as part of a subject that usually deals with a variety of health problems and seeks changes in the health behavior of students; this occurs in health education. The correlated pattern means that instruction is co-related to other subjects in the curriculum that generally do not focus on health matters or practices, as in social studies or biology. In health education, attitudes and behaviors are oriented toward health and are people-centered; in other curriculum areas the purposes are more likely to focus on cognitive objectives. Cognitive ends by themselves usually have little or no impact on healthful living.

In the secondary schools the direct and correlated patterns of instruction are easily distinguished. However, it is more complex at the elementary level. In elementary schools using the direct arrangement one might find drug education as a part of a subject area such as health education. Thus drug education would have status with other subjects such as language arts or social studies. The direct pattern could also refer to specific drug units that may be part of health education or entirely separated as distinct areas of instruction, provided time is allowed in the curriculum. The direct arrangement could also mean that the drug education program is related to social studies and science. In such instances drug education could be said to be co-related but often is said to be integrated into the curriculum. At the elementary level the words "correlated" and "integrated" are frequently used synonymously. Perhaps the distinction can be made that if elementary students are exposed to only one teacher daily, as in the self-contained classroom, a subject may be said to be integrated into the curriculum, whereas if students experience a variety of teachers daily in differing subject areas, a subject is said to be correlated into the curriculum. [35]

Drug and alcohol abuse programs have been separated in this book purely for discussion purposes. Strategies and tactics that work well in one program will work well in another. However, in retrospect we have advanced very little since the 1960s. There are few effective drug abuse or alcohol abuse programs.

The Case Against Drug Education

The alarming rate of drug usage by children of school age has been the impetus for the initiation of many programs to combat this insidious evil. The schools have been given the job of implementing many of these programs. Taintor criticizes the pressure to relegate this responsibility to the school.

Societal influences are getting to the individual through agencies other than the family. Schools often confuse their educative, classifactory, socializing and therapeutic functions. Some try to be all things to all students.

I recommend The Imperfect Panacea *which describes a tendency in American society for the last century to refer unsolved social problems to the schools and to blame the schools when the problems remain unsolved. . . . There is no statistical evidence to show that any drug education program has been a success. Some studies indicate it is not.* [36]

In criticizing drug education in the schools, Taintor states that "curricula are adopted that so overemphasize drugs in relation to other health issues that students are aware that something is thrilling and/or phony. Socialization and education are confused in these curricula, in that the intent is to stop drug abuse while the overt communication is that drug use is one's own decision." [37] He further suggests that drug education cannot be relegated exclusively to the schools, for drug abuse has many causes and it must be fought on many fronts. Often the initiation of drug education in the schools merely assuages the guilt feelings of parents that something should be done, and

they fail to examine the efficacy of the programs which have been instituted.

Drug education has taken many forms involving varying permutations of settings, goals, targets, methods, educators, and contents. Settings have ranged from reliance upon mass media through formalized programs in school and work institutions to individualized counseling in drug crisis in centers. The goals set typically call for either the elimination of all drug use or, failing this, the reduction of use to levels that minimize physical or emotional health hazards. [38]

In many schools drug education programs have targeted the nonusers (who are believed to be potential users) and the experimental users for remediation efforts. Various methods have been implemented, including fear induction, exhortation, authority-and entertainment-based appeals, encounter groups, role playing, and formal lectures. With such a variety of programs, it is apparent that some programs have achieved more positive results than others. Some programs exacerbate drug use by (1) providing students with sufficient information to facilitate an initiation of use, (2) providing students with facts that overcome the prejudices that had been inhibiting use, (3) desensitizing students about drugs through repeated discussions of drug concepts in environments such as schools, which have been traditionally disassociated from drug use, (4) leading students to think of themselves as potential drug users merely by virtue of their having been included in drug education programs, (5) changing attitudes that were the bastion of defense against drug use, or (6) occasionally including inaccurate or biased information which undermines the credibility of the basic educational message. [39] Since there is evidence to suggest that a relatively high knowledge about drugs is associated with higher levels of drug use, the potential for negative risks in drug education are apparent.

To expect alcohol education in the schools, for example, to deal adequately with the problem may be foolhardy because of the exposure of students to so many other influences. Too often school board members, school administrators, and other adults fail to recognize that students receive an education in alcohol usage from their parents and peers that is apart from anything their schools and their home environments teach. In contemporary society students are bombarded with alcohol information and misinformation through newspapers, magazines, radio, television, movies, billboards, books, pamphlets, and friends. When the schools attempt education regarding alcohol and drugs, too few students are reached becuase the curriculum is not broad enough or is not relevant to the way students live and think.

Most school alcohol education programs are failures—they do not reach those at whom their message is aimed: students psychologically withdrawn from school and considered problem drinkers. Steven R. Burkett and Mervin White found in their research that even when problem drinkers attend alcohol education programs, they do so with interest in the subject but not a resolve to stop drinking. Indeed, problem drinkers are likely to be more knowledgeable than nondrinkers about alcohol and alcohol abuse.

These findings suggest first that the lower knowledge of nondrinkers and the greater knowledge of the drinkers and problem drinkers may reflect the extent of interest or concern each group has in the subject matter of the alcohol education program. That is, nondrinkers may find the program irrelevant for themselves (though they consider it relevant for others) while the opposite may be true for drinkers and problem drinkers . . . Second, the findings presented earlier regarding the subcultural context of adolescent withdrawal from school and rebellion against adult controls generally suggest that experimentation with alcohol may represent a potential source of information for youngsters so involved.[40]

The Case for Drug Education

Despite the negative potential in drug education, a recent opinion poll found that teachers in schools having drug education programs generally agreed that drug education should be part of the curriculum. Nearly half of the respondents thought it should be integrated with the subject matter of one or more other subjects; about one in four thought it should be a special unit of work within another subject, and about one in ten thought it should be taught separately. This same poll, however,

indicates there is much room for improvement: 57.5 per cent rated the success of their drug education program as only fair or poor. Another criticism of drug education is that in most cases it does not begin early enough. More than half the teachers questioned thought that drug education should begin below grade four; however, only 25 per cent of these teachers said it did begin below grade four in their schools.[41]

A study involving school principals reflected these recommendations:

1. Drug education efforts should be incorporated into a comprehensive health education program and not developed as a separate, special program, unit, or curriculum.

2. The focus of the program should be on understanding oneself and others (physically, mentally, and socially). Additional emphasis should be placed on the decision-making process, an awareness of values, and the development of a values system. Drug education should not center on information about drugs *per se*, except as student interest indicates.

3. Pre-service and in-service training for educators about the nature of human living and about drugs are components of program development which must precede program implementation.

4. Teachers being asked to conduct drug education programs should be selected on their ability to relate effectively to young people.

5. Program implementation should begin at the elementary school level.

6. Learning activities should involve participation by parents and other community members as well as by students.

7. The comprehensive health education program should provide a consideration of all types of drug products and the potentially constructive consequences of drug use, instead of emphasizing only the harmful consequences of drug abuse.

8. Behavioral objectives, developed at the local level, should be developed for the drug education program and should form the basis for ongoing education.[42]

The principals in this survey believed the most effective method for dealing with suspected drug users was to set up standard procedures for handling students thought to be

Table 19. Opinions of the Public on Requiring Student Attendance at Programs on Effects of Drugs and Alcohol: 1975

Q: Should the schools in this community require students to attend a program on the effects of drugs and alcohol?	Percent			
	National totals	No children in schools	Public school parents	Parochial school parents
Yes	84	81	87	88
No	11	12	10	8
Don't know/no answer	5	7	3	4

SOURCE: Phi Delta Kappa, Inc., Bloomington, Ind., The Gallup Survey of Public Attitudes Toward the Public Schools, 1975, *Phi Delta Kappan*, December 1975.

under the influence of drugs during school hours. It was also their feeling that visitors to the school buildings and grounds during school hours should be registered for identification. These principals placed in the following rank order those school personnel who should ideally be involved in drug education: (1) selected teachers, (2) teachers in general, (3) school nurses, (4) school principals, (5) school psychologists, and (6) assistant principals.

Focusing on alcohol, Cobe offers guidelines for establishing a positive educational program for students with drinking problems. She says that generally those who are organizing a study unit need to keep in mind that students should be presented with as much accurate information as possible so they can make an informed choice based on dependable knowledge, instead of being pressured by uninformed or misinformed friends. It is also deemed important to convince students that the director of the alcohol education program believes in them by stressing that he or she agrees there is a need to know about drinking as a part of growang up and striving for self-identification. Here are some ways Cobe proposes to educate students to make informed drinking decisions:

1. Contact the State Office of Education for guidelines on alcohol education and methods of organizing units of study.
2. Establish definite objectives for your educational program. Include such goals as clarifying feelings and attitudes toward alcohol use, alerting the community to lend a hand in preventing and combating the problem, and establishing a student group to help teach other students about alcohol misuse.
3. Integrate your teaching into a logical slot in the curriculum. A family living or health education course are possibilities. Instruction should include an understanding of the different attitudes and patterns of drinking existing in the country; the physical, psychological, social and legal aspects of alcohol; and the reasons behind alcoholism.
4. Make use of open class discussions for airing views if the administration approves. Keep the discussions unbiased by interjecting opposite viewpoints here and there. Try to relate discussions to personal experience.
5. Use films, outside speakers and other information techniques to provide springboards for comment.
6. Hold panels to debate issues such as "Is Alcoholism a Disease?"; "Alcohol vs. Marijuana"; and "Should You Drive After Two Beers?" Topics also should have administration approval.
7. Attempt to establish in-service training in your school or district to keep teachers and other youth leaders up-to-date on statistics, community programs, and other information.[43]

Grace M. Barnes states that the major effort in alcohol education programs that will be productive resides in identifying the "who," "why," "how," and "what can be done" regarding alcohol misuse among teenagers.

Rather than directing most of our concern to whether teenage alcohol use and abuse have been increasing, is it not appropriate to direct prime efforts to understanding and modifying destructive behaviors such as school abuse? For example, why has this society been so unsuccessful in reducing the problems of alcohol abuse that have existed for years. Who are the teenagers with a "high risk" for the development of alcohol problems? What factors contribute to the development of problem drinking among youth? How do these drinking patterns change or progress over time? How can the teen-agers in the early stages of alcohol abuse be identified and brought to treatment? Do treatment facilities even exist in many areas? How can formal and informal education have an impact in preventing alcohol abuse? What methods and approaches are most effective with particular groups in treating and, hopefully, preventing alcohol abuse? [44]

To answer some of these questions and to act against the increasing use of alcohol and other drugs, a number of schools and researchers are conducting specific programs and studies.

TEACHER EDUCATION

Most teachers assigned responsibility for drug education do not have an adequate under-standing of the subject. One study found that most drug educators gained their own drug education from the news media and their pro-fessional associates instead of from in-service or college training.

The initial step in educating the public gen-erally, and students and teachers specifically, about alcohol abuse should be the destruction of the myths that abound concerning alcohol.

First of all, alcohol is neither a stimulant nor a food as was long believed. It is a drug that acts as a depressant or anesthetic on the central nervous system. It first affects the cerebrum causing loss of judgment and social inhibitions. Next the cerebel-lum is depressed, bringing on lack of coordination, speech, and vision. If a person continues to drink faster than his or her body is burning the alcohol, the respiratory, circulatory, and other vital systems can be harmed. [45]

Cobe dispells another popular myth. She says that once too much alcohol is consumed, the drinker must simply wait until it wears off. "Contrary to popular myth, there is no cure for a hangover except time. Neither black coffee,

cold showers, exercise, food, vitamins nor more liquor will do it!" [46] It is also erroneously thought that the amount of alcohol consumed is a primary factor in alcoholism. Few teachers know the following facts about alcohol and alcoholics:

1. It usually takes an adult drinker ten to twenty years to become an alcoholic, but chil-dren who drink may become alcoholic in six months.
2. By every medical criterion, alcohol is a drug—it induces lethargy, drowsiness, and coma; when taken in large doses, it relieves pain and numbs the senses.
3. Alcohol is an addictive drug that causes physical dependence by creating a tolerance in the body. When this happens, more and more is needed to produce the desired effect. Once a person is addicted, withdrawal symptoms occur when alcohol is not ingested. With-drawal symptoms include hangover, confu-sion, hallucinations, delirium tremens, and convulsion.
4. It takes a long time for the effects of alcohol to wear off.
5. When it is taken in large, prolonged amounts, alcohol can cause cirrhosis of the liver, brain damage, heart disease, malnutrition due to lack of appetite, and stomach trouble.
6. The National Safety Council considers 0.10 percent of alcohol in the bloodstream to be legal proof of intoxication.

Teachers should be aware that one or more of the following signs may indicate that stu-dents may have a drinking problem. An al-cohol abuser may pass out in class, look obvi-ously sick, vomit, display excessive drowsiness or restlessness, be chronically late to school or class or in turning in homework assignments when he or she previously was prompt, or have slurred speech or difficulty talking when pre-viously he or she had no difficulty in expressing himself or herself. [47]

SPECIFIC PROGRAMS TO CURB DRUG AND ALCOHOL ABUSE

Students with a drug or drinking problem need medical help. Most schools have procedures for handling medical problems. A few school districts have excellent drug and/or alcohol education prevention programs. Essie E. Lee suggests that counselors hold one-day alcohol education work shops for school staff and parents.

In one high school, the counselor and teachers of health, education and music wrote and choreographed a musical whose theme was "all about alcohol." Another counselor sought the cooperation of teachers in reaching parents who might be alcoholics. He asked teachers to refer children who came to school bruised and battered, poorly dressed, hungry, and apathetic toward learning. These referrals led to the school's affiliation with a community service agency that provided consultation services and funds to help the school produce a film and initiate a plan for a halfway house for children of alcoholics. Still another counselor trained students in outreach skills and in hot-line telephone service and agency referral so that they could provide information, clarification, and a sympathetic ear to other youths having drinking problems. [48]

Another specific program which has been developed is a new educational program funded by the Automobile Association of America's Foundation for Traffic Safety: a Preventive Curriculum Unit for high school driver education classes. This DWI (driving while intoxicated) mini-course is a comprehensive instructor's manual designed to help high school driver educators cover essential drinking/driving content in the classroom.[49] It is the purpose of this unit to teach students to cope with hazardous driving situations, including offering options intended to reduce their chances of becoming involved in DWI situations. Students are told about the influence of alcohol on driving and the potentially serious consequences of driving while drinking. In addition they are encouraged to explore and assess their own attitudes and behavior in relation to drinking. They also learn the legal penalties for DWI, receive an explanation of blood alcohol concentrations, and learn alternative ways to cope with or avoid potential DWI stiuations.

Another program called DWI Phoenix was begun as a community project for adults but has spread to more than 1,200 communities and is now being taught on a preventive basis in high schools and junior high schools. In this program films and other devices are employed to illustrate graphically the impairment in vision and judgment caused by the use of alcohol. High school students participating in this program are encouraged to work out ways they would deal with drinking on such provocative occasions as school proms, dances, and athletic contests. Some of the ways that were suggested by students and which are being put into practice are "for students to hire limousines (which is not as expensive as it sounds) to transport them in groups to and from the dance; to appoint one of their number who can be counted on not to drink as driver; or, particularly in rural communities, for high school officials to arrange for boys' and girls' dorms near the prom site to eliminate the necessity for driving while students are intoxicated or their abilities are impaired by alcohol."[50]

Parents are often the biggest stumbling block to educators trying to prevent or abate student drinking problems. "Three very common parental reactions are that they just don't want to face the problem, they don't consider their youngster's drinking dangerous or a big issue, or they don't care as long as he or she isn't taking drugs."[51] The National Parent-Teacher Association (PTA), the largest volunteer organization in America, is also involved in school alcohol prevention programs. In addition to distributing more than 500,000 copies of the pamphlet *Alcohol: A Family Affair*, the PTA has sponsored numerous programs focusing on parent enlightenment, teacher training, and student involvement.

Drug education prorams are successful when they are designed with the following observations in mind:

1. Failure of abstinence is partially related to the belief held by students that using drugs is not harmful.
2. Programs that fail to communicate with students are ineffective in preventing or abating drug use.
3. Drug effects are strongly influenced by the user's expectations, the setting, and the characteristics of the drug.
4. The primary sources of drug attitude formation are, in descending rank order: (1) personal experience, (2) close friends, (3) a youth counseling center, (4) a physician, and (5) a teacher.

Some programs fail because they erroneously tell students that there are no beneficial or pleasurable experiences associated with drug use. (Marijuana users, for example, report more positive or neutral than negative experiences.) Messages about drugs, like messages about anything else, are evaluated against what students already know from personal experience or from such trusted sources as their friends. Credibility is one of the most valuable assets of any drug education program, and to compromise it with inadequate information or fear tactics will be counterproductive.

Research concerning drug abuse reveals clearly that there is an urgent and increasing student-use problem. It is also the consensus of education, medical, and law enforcement personnel that present alcohol and drug abuse programs in the schools have not achieved the desired results. Much of the research reflects the assessment that there must be strong public commitment and involvement if future programs are to succeed.

Research also indicates that personnel within the schools who are designated to implement such programs must be specially chosen and specially trained. It is felt that past failures in drug and alcohol education have resulted from outmoded perspectives, improperly selected personnel, inadequately trained leaders, lack of emphasis on multiple contributing factors, ambiguous guidelines, and the lack of a federal program that would lend authority, support and consistency to local public school efforts.

If drug education is to be be significant, it must be relevant to the experience of students, and be structured to be responsive to each individual's needs. Therefore, the key to such education lies in (1) informing children and youth about drugs, (2) helping students identify social and personal reasons which may contribute to drug usage, and (3) structuring classroom discussions so that each individual assumes responsibility for his or her behavior with drugs.

GROUP PARTICIPATION ROLES

Through introspection you can learn how you and other people function in a group. Read the following descriptions of small group roles and try to determine how you functioned in a recent class or group activity.

Group Task Roles

Some participants try to facilitate and coordinate group efforts to select and define common problems and possible solutions. Any or all of these roles may be played by group members:

1. The *initiator-contributor* suggests or proposes group goals, defines group problems, suggests possible solutions.

2. The *information* or *opinion seeker* asks for clarification, requests facts, asks for expressions of feelings and/or values, seeks suggestions.

3. The *information* or *opinion giver* offers facts, expresses his or her feelings and/or values concerning the task, gives suggestions.

4. The *clarifier-elaborator* interprets ideas or suggestions, clears up confusion, defines terms, suggests group alternatives and issues.

5. The *summarizer* pulls together related ideas, restates suggestions after the group has discussed them, offers decisions or conclusions for group acceptance or rejection.

6. The *recorder* writes down suggestions, makes a record of group decisions, records group discuss:ons.

Group Maintenance Roles

Some participants are concerned with the group remaining active, having a good work climate, and optimizing the utilization of group member skills. Group maintenance roles include the following:

1. The *encourager* praises others, agrees with and accents the contributions of others, communicates understanding and acceptance through obvious verbal and nonverbal means.

2. The *harmonizer* tries to reconcile disagreements, reduces tension in conflict situations, gets people to explore differences in hopes that they will find more agreement than disagreement.

3. The *compromiser* often yields to his opponents, admits error, tries to maintain harmony.

4. The *gate keeper* tries to keep communica-

tion channels open, facilitates participation of other group members, suggests procedures for democratizing the group process.

5. The *standard setter* tests whether the group is satisfied with its procedures or suggested procedures, points out explicit or implicit norms which are operating.

6. The *group observer* keeps records of various aspects of group process and feeds back the data.

7. The *follower* goes along with the group movement, more or less passively accepting the ideas of others, and serves as an audience for group discussants.

Every group needs both task maintenance and group maintenance. It is important that teachers keep a balance between the two.

Self-oriented Roles

Individual members frequently have personal needs that are unrelated to the group or its tasks. If these needs go unrecognized, misunderstood, or unsuccessfully dealt with, the effectiveness of the group will be greatly impaired. Self-oriented roles include:

1. The *aggressor* deflates the status of other group members, expresses disapproval of the values and behaviors of others, ridicules individual members, demeans the group or the problems they are working on.

2. The *blocker* is stubbornly resistant, disagrees and argues without or beyond reason, attempts to bring an issue back after the group has rejected it.

3. The *recognition seeker* uses a variety of techniques to call attention to himself/herself, boasts of personal achievements, becomes a willing martyr.

4. The *self-confessor* seizes any opportunity to express non-group related feelings, insights, incidents, and ideology.

5. The *dominator* tries to assert authority or superiority in manipulating the group or certain members of the group. This domination may take the form of flattery, interpreting the contributions of others, asserting superior status, or giving orders authoritatively.

6. The *help seeker* solicits sympathy from other group members, through expressions of insecurity, personal confusion, or self-depreciation.

ADDITIONAL READINGS

Blum, Eva Maria and Richard H. Blum. *Alcoholism: Modern Psychological Approaches to Treatment.* San Francisco, Jossey-Bass, 1967.

Brecher, Edward M. and the Editors of Consumer Reports. *Licit and Illicit Drugs.* Boston, Little, Brown, 1972.

Cross, Jay N. *A Guide to the Community Control of Alcoholism.* Washington, D. C., American Public Health Association, 1968.

Fort, Joel. *Alcohol: Our Biggest Drug Problem.* New York, McGraw-Hill, 1973.

Goshen, Carles E. *Drinks, Drugs, and Do-Gooders.* New York, The Free Press, 1973.

Johnson, Bruce D. *Marihuana Users and Drug Subculture.* New York, John Wiley & Sons, 1973.

Johnson, Vernon E. *I'll Quit Tomorrow.* New York: Harper & Row, 1973.

Nelkin, Dorothy, *Methadone Maintenance: A Technological Fix.* New York, George Braziller, 1973.

Nohans, Gabriel G. *Marihuana: Deceptive Weed.* New York, Raven Press, 1973.

Pittman, David J., ed. *Alcoholism.* New York, Harper & Row, 1967.

Plaut, Thomas F. A. *Alcohol Problems: A Report to the Nation by the Cooperative Commission on the Study of Alcoholism.* New York, Oxford University Press, 1967.

Seymour, Whitney N. *The Young Die Quietly: The Narcotics Problem in America.* New York, William Morrow, 1971.

Siegel, Harvey H. *Alcohol Detoxification Programs: Treatment Instead of Jail.* Springfield, Ill., Charles C. Thomas, 1973.

Steiner, Calude. *Games Alcoholics Play: The Analysis of Life Scripts.* New York, Grove Press, 1971.

Smithsonian Institution. *Drugs in Perspective: A Fact Book on Drug Use and Misuse.* Washington, D. C., Smithsonian Press, 1972.

United States Commission on Marihuana and Drug Abuse. *Marihuana: A Signal of Misunderstanding; First Report.* Washington, D. C., U. S. Government Printing Office, 1972.

Waldorf, Dan. *Careers In Dope.* Englewood Cliffs, N. J., Prentice-Hall, 1973.

NOTES

1. Hershel Thornburg, "The Adolescent and Drugs: An Overview," *Journal of School Health*, 43 (December, 1973), 640.

2. "$25 Billion Down the Hatch," *Tulsa Tribune* (July 10, 1974).

3. Smithsonian Institution, *Drugs in Perspective: A Fact Book on Drug Use and Misuse* (Washington, D. C., Smithsonian Press, 1972), 45.

4. "3,647 Nuclear Weapons Employees Relieved of Jobs for Drug, Alcohol, Other Problems," *Drugs and Drug Abuse Education Newsletter* (January, 1974), 8.

5. Harris Isbell, "Medical Aspects of Opiate Addiction," in John A. O'Donnell and John C. Ball (eds.), *Narcotic Addiction* (New York, Harper & Row, 1966), 68–69.

6. Quoted in John R. Williams, *Narcotics and Drug Dependence* (Beverly Hills, Glencoe Press, 1974), 22–23.

7. Melvin H. Weinswig, *Use and Misuse of Drugs Subject to Abuse* (New York, Pegasus, 1973), 23.

8. Moris M. Rubin, "Panel Discussion on Drug Addiction," in James C. Bennett and George D. Demos (eds.), *Drug Abuse and What We Can Do About It* (Springfield, Ill., Charels C. Thomas, 1970), 27.

9. Williams, *Narcotics*, 22.

10. Rubin, "Panel Discussion," 27.

11. Alfred R. Lindesmith, *Addiction and Opiates* (Chicago, Aldine Press, 1968), 64.

12. Johannes Biberfield, quoted in Lindesmith, *Ibid.*, 65.

13. Isbell, "Medical Aspects," 70.

14. Alfred R. Lindesmith, "Basic Problems in the Social Psychology of Addiction and A Theory," in O'Donnell, *Narcotic Addiction*, 99.

15. Jerome H. Jaffe, "Pharmacological Approaches to the Treatment of Compulsive Opiate Use: Their Rationale and Current Status," in Perry Black (ed.), *Drugs and the Brain: Papers on the Use and Abuse of Psychotropic Agents* (Baltimore, Johns Hopkins University Press, 1969), 352.

16. Lindesmith, *Addiction and Opiates*, 95–96.

17. Thomas de Quincey, *Confessions of an English Opium Eater*, (Edinburg, Adam and Charles Black, 1862), 275.

18. Lindesmith, "Basic Problems," 103.

19. Howard S. Becker, "Become a Marijuana User," in O'Donnell, *Narcotic Addiction*, 121.

20. Thornburg, "The Adolescent."

21. Zebulon Taintor, "The 'Why' of Youthful Drug Abuse," *Journal of School Health*, 44 (January, 1974), 28.

22. *Ibid.*, 28–29.

23. *Ibid.*, 29.

24. *Ibid.*, 28.

25. Thornburg, "The Adolescent," 640.

26. *Ibid.*, 640–641.

27. *Ibid.*, 641.

28. Patricia Cobe, "The Rise in Teen-age Drinking," *Forecast for Home Economics*, 21 (March, 1976), F–24.

29. Paul Martin, "Our Teen-age Alcoholics," *The Lion*, 58 (June, 1976), 8.

30. Barbara Milbauer, "Dealing with Youngsters Who Drink," *Teacher*, 93 (February, 1976), 50.

31. Albert F. Fillipps, "Younger Driver Drinking More," *The Motorist*, 6 (July/August, 1976), 5.

32. W. G. Hollister, cited in Thornburg, "The Adolescent," 642.

33. *Ibid.*, 644.

34. Taintor, "The Why," 29.

35. Harold J. Cornacchia, David J. Bentel, and David E. Smith, *Drugs in the Classroom: A Conceptual Model for School Programs* (St. Louis, C. V. Mosby, 1973), 137.

36. Taintor, "The Why," 27–28.

37. *Ibid.*, 28.

38. Richard B. Stuart, "Teaching Facts About Drugs: Pushing or Preventing?" *Journal of Educational Psychology*, 66 (June, 1975), 189–190.

39. *Ibid.*, 190.

40. Steven R. Burkett and Mervin White, "School Adjustment, Drinking, and the Impact of Alcohol Education Programs," *Urban Education*, 11 (April, 1976), 92.

41. NEA Research, "Teacher Opinion Poll," *Today's Education*, 62 (September/October, 1973), 3.

42. Aria C. Rosner, "How We Do It: Drug and Alcohol Abuse Education: Opinions of School Principals," *Journal of School Health*, 45 (October, 1975), 469.

43. Cobe, "The Rise," 41–42.

44. Grace M. Barnes, "A Perspective on Drinking Among Teenagers with Special Reference to New York State Studies," *Journal of School Health*, 55 (September, 1975), 388.

45. Cobe, "The Rise," F–25.

46. *Ibid.*

47. Milbauer, "Dealing," 4.

48. Essie E. Lee, "The Counselor's Role in Alcohol Education Programs," *The School Counselor*, 23 (March, 1976), 292.

49. Fillipps, "Younger Drivers," 4.

50. Beth Macklin, "Teen Drinking May Double American Alcoholism Rate," *Tulsa Daily World*, (July 22, 1976), C–3.

51. Milbauer, "Dealing."

13.
STUDENT
RIGHTS

Professional educators, as well as the majority of legal scholars, would agree that in the past ten years the rights of students have been enlarged by a number of decisions handed down by state and federal courts. These decisions have resulted in a wide and often bitter disagreement between educators as to whether students' new rights will lead to a more democratic way of teaching or will foster uncontrolled student license which, in the long run, will destroy democracy itself. At the present there is simply no way to know the eventual effects of court decisions concerning such matters as suspension, corporal punishment, freedom of speech, and search and seizure, to name but a few. However, it is clear that past judicial actions will be enormously influential in shaping the future of American public schools.

THE SLOW AWAKENING

Jerry Farber shocked many persons when he charged that we treat our youth as though they are exempt from the rights of the rest of humanity.[1] Farber's thesis is supported every day by countless instances when the rights of citizens guaranteed by the Bill of Rights are set aside in public and private schools. Students' persons and lockers are subjected to unreasonable search and seizure. Students are forced to testify against themselves (a violation of the Fifth Amendment) and are held accountable for violations of school rules without confrontation with their accusers or even

awareness of the nature of the evidence held against them (a violation of the Sixth Amendment).

In addition to denial of basic rights guaranteed by our Constitution, American students are also denied rights enumerated in the "Universal Declaration of Human Rights" adopted by the United Nations in 1948. Few administrators or teachers have read the declaration and even fewer students are aware of it. The importance of helping students to understand their rights and responsibilities is evident: responsibility cannot be learned in the absence of freedom, and respect for law and order cannot be fully appreciated without experience. Thus teachers must refrain from behaviors that demean, diminish, or destroy a child's feeling of positive self-worth. Discussing student rights, Morrel J. Clute chided teachers, "It is strange, indeed, that young people who are responsible enough to walk a mile to school are not viewed as responsible enough to use the restroom properly."[2]

Beyond Puritan Ethics

Educators are caught between the authoritarianism of the early Puritan ethics and the democratic principles espoused by Thomas Jefferson and James Madison. Jefferson and Madison's notion that power resides in the people, not with the governors, is in sharp contrast to the tight, autocratic control held by the Puritan governors.

Madison believed that the best way to

counter the harmful effects of citizens' inadequate exercise of reason is to establish a government in which no one person or group has supreme authority. Jefferson viewed education not as a means of controlling the populace but instead of preparing them for governmental roles. Jefferson's system of education was designed to provide the basics (reading, writing, and arithmetic) for everyone and higher education for the cream of the student crop. Nowhere in Jefferson's plan do we find reference to the rigid control and discipline which characterized the Puritan educational system.

The concept of *in loco parentis*, standing in the place of the parent while the child is at school, gives teachers and administrators both the nurturing and the punitive aspects of the parental role. It is a double bind that creates schizophrenic-like behavior in teachers and administrators. Even so, the punishment function is as much a part of *in loco parentis* as the nurturing function. The courts have not provided clear guidance in this area of teacher/administrator responsibility. The courts do agree, however, that students have rights.

Rights. Who really has them? Rights are opinions and freedom of activities which every human is born with. You have all kinds of rights and responsibilities through the course of life, but during the education period in your life, you're pushed toward the responsibilities and denied the rights. It's like someone telling you not to lie, but never telling you the truth.

One year when I was going to high school we didn't have student rights, especially the blacks. And if one person did something against the school rules, the principal would penalize the whole school if he didn't know who did it.

I didn't feel like beating a person was a means of punishment that a student should have to suffer for being tardy for morning roll call or little petty things like talking out loud in class.

It seems as though the rules are your rights and no exceptions. I think you have to have rules to have some kind of organization, but why can they break the rules for some and not for others? It seems to me that if you have money or your parents have some sort of influence, you just don't have to go through all that crap.[3]

Due Process for Students

Perhaps the first major decision concerning juvenile rights within the past decade was the case of a fifteen-year-old boy who was convicted of making an obscene phone call and sentenced to a period of up to six years in a state reform school. His attorney pointed out that if he had been an adult when he committed such an offense, his maximum punishment would have been a fifty-dollar fine and two months in jail. Further, when convicted of the offense, the youth had been denied the right to an attorney and was unable to confront and cross-examine his accuser. The *Gault* case, as it was called, eventually made its way to the U. S. Supreme Court in 1967 and was resolved by the Court's decision to set aside the boy's conviction on the grounds that he had been denied due process. The Court ruled that juveniles must be accorded due process of law when they are faced with substantial punishment.[4] As a result of this case, it was clearly and firmly established that the Bill of Rights is not only for adults but for juveniles too.

Many educators and taxpayers believe that the *Gault* case opened a Pandora's Box of public school problems, not the least of which was the question of student discipline. After the *Gault* case, additional review by various courts clarified exactly what rights juveniles were entitled to under the Constitution when conditions which characterized the original *Gault* conviction held.[5] Juveniles now have the following adult protections in matters involving substantial punishment.

1. The right to a hearing.
2. The right to adequate notice.
3. The right to counsel.
4. The right to protection against self-incrimination.
5. The right to confrontation and cross-examination.
6. The right to the reasonable doubt rule of evidence.

However, juveniles do not yet have definitive rights concerning the compulsory process, a right which guarantees to defendants power to compel any witness to testify who could assist in their defense, nor do they have absolute protection from unreasonable search and seizure.

The question of due process for juveniles is also complicated by the fact that the U. S. Supreme Court has frequently stated that due process requires not only fairness in fact but the appearance of fairness.[6] Perhaps it is this scrupulous regard for individual rights in the due process question which has led some legal authorities to say that if the principles of due process were applied rigorously in schools, the educational organization would probably come to a halt.[7] One possible effect of such an appearance of fairness may be to make students more readily accept adverse decisions because they feel that they have had some input in the decision-making process. Those who welcome recent court decisions giving students more due process rights argue that eventually such decisions will produce a more peaceful condition in the schools than is now generally present. It is claimed that students who feel they have more input in the decision-making process will tend to work within the system rather than employ disruptive tactics to get their way.

Most educators who would not quarrel with the concept of due process for juveniles have a difficult time deciding exactly when the concept is or is not being violated. Without doubt the concept is far-ranging. "Due process is not only a fuzzy concept when used in the constitutional sense, it is also a concept used in many different senses. As a constitutional doctrine, it derives explicitly from the language of the Fourteenth Amendment (and also the Fifth Amendment), which prohibits action by government that deprives a person of life, liberty, or property without due process of law."[8]

The theoretical foundation for a claim of violation of due process rights can be summed up rather easily. "Anyone who can prove a deprivation of his rights through an action taken by the state is entitled to demand the procedural protections of constitutional due process."[9] However simple the theoretical foundation may be for a claim of due process rights violation, the practical questions and problems raised by the concept for teachers, administrators, and school boards remain complex indeed. W. Richard Brothers defines the difficulties which lie ahead.

In both federal and state proceedings the fundamental question is one of fairness for the students. All the contributing elements of due process are designed to ensure that this goal is reached. The authority of the schools to establish and enforce reasonable standards of conduct was never the issue: the process the school followed in administering discipline was. The courts did not review these cases with an inflexible standard; instead, they continually stressed that procedural due process was a pliable concept, dependent upon the local circumstances. Some elements were relatively constant, however, yielding only to local interpretation of how a right was to be granted.[10]

It does not require a legal education to surmise that if Brothers' characterization of court decisions regarding due process for students is valid, most educators would probably wish that the courts had reviewed the cases "with an inflexible standard." For if due process is a "pliable concept," how is anyone connected with the immensely difficult problem of, say, school discipline to know when he or she has or has not violated the student's right to due process? Even educators who intend to be fair will understandably live in fear, not only that they may be the target of legal action but also that such legal action could well be successful.

Educators React

Apart from the precise legal meanings, however, one fact remains undisputed: the courts have made significant changes regarding student rights during the past decade. Before 1966 courts generally granted complete authority to public school administrators, and few judges concerned themselves, except in extreme and obvious cases, with such abstract matters as how the provisions of the First Amendment applied to third-graders who wanted to publish underground school newspapers.

Perhaps no better example of the remarkable change in attitude on the part of the U.S. Supreme Court can be cited than the majority opinion written by Justice Abe Fortas in *Tinker v. Des Moines Independent School District* (1969), a case which involved First Amendment rights of students.

In our system, state-operated schools may not be enclaves of totalitarianism. School officials do not possess absolute authority over their students. Students in school as well as out of school are 'persons' under our Constitution. They are possessed of fundamental rights which the State must respect, just as they themselves must respect their obligation to the State.[11]

As if Justice Fortas' rationale for the Court's decision in *Tinker* were not enough to make school administrators unhappy, the Supreme Court is gradually rendering almost meaningless one of the theoretical bedrocks of the American public school system—the concept of *in loco parentis*. In 1975 the Supreme Court did not once mention *in loco parentis* in two related cases concerning student suspension—*Goss v. Lopez* and *Wood v. Strickland*. These decisions have led Thomas A. Shannon to write concerning *in loco parentis* that:

as a legal concept it now is applicable only in cases where school people have the responsibility of protecting the health, and safety and welfare of children. This contributes to the schizophrenic approach that some of our school people have. On the one hand, school people are charged by the courts with an increasingly high standard of care for the physical health, well being and general safety of children on the school grounds. On the other hand, their range of discretionary authority over conduct has been considerably lessened.[12]

Michael L. Berger commented rather facetiously:

The recent acceptance of affective curriculum responsibilities has in a very real sense placed the public schools in the position of serving in loco parentis. However, what recent court decisions seem to say is that the school is not an extended family, where the "teacher-parent" and/or the "administrator-parent" can discipline the "student-child" as he or she sees fit. Rather, the school is a miniature society, where all are equal citizens protected by, and subject to, a uniform legal code. In other words, there are no parents and children in the public schools, but instead a grouping of adults, some of whom happen to have more developed cognitive, affective, and psycho-motor faculties. We call the latter people "teachers" and "administrators," and assign instructional and/or leadership tasks to them based on their superior competencies.[13]

From a practical point of view, one can surely say that students had less freedom before recent court decisions, and some writers believe that not only do students now have more freedom but that the entire school climate has changed through court actions.

In the past, student behavior codes were frequently phrased in repressive and negative terms: 'students must be in their homerooms at the ringing of the second bell.' 'students may not leave the school grounds at recess or at lunch time without written permission from the main office.' Today the emphasis appears reversed, with more apparent emphasis on restructuring the authority of adults and protecting the rights of students.[14]

A number of educators welcome changes in students' rights and are quick to point out that the Supreme Court has merely awarded to students what was always rightfully theirs. The very fact that such matters had to go outside the schools for resolution seemed, at least to R. Freeman Butts, to mean that the courts "have been more faithful to the basic meaning of public education than have the profession, the critics, the reformers, and the local or state boards of education."[15] In truth what the courts have done is to spell out for the American public a relationship too often left undefined—the legal relationship between the public school and the state. Richard M. Blankenburg, an authority on school law and the civil rights of students, defines this relationship and its significance with clarity.

In looking at the difference between the public schools and the private schools relative to civil rights, it is important to look at the legal relationship between the school and the student. In a public school the relationship is one of government. The public school is an extension of the state. The relationship is one of government and citizen. This is very important in civil rights because the antithesis of civil rights is police power. Police power is defined as "that inherent and plenary power in the state over persons and property which enables the people to prohibit all things inimical to comfort, safety, health, and welfare of society."[16]

A few professional educators have been quick to brand the broadening of the civil rights of students as part of some left-wing conspiracy to disrupt American education and destroy our system of traditional values. But those who look more deeply for the causes of the great change in educational legalities see the whole process as more complex. "The rise of judicial support for student rights may be a reflection of a broader societal concern with, on the one hand, the dangers of increased conformity, authoritarianism, and uniformity and, on the other hand, a broader societal interest in the protection and nurturing of nonconformity, dissent, and the values of pluralism." [17]

Nor is it realistic to view such changes as somehow completely separate from other developments in American life. A number of events and certain changes in attitudes taking place in the United States over the last decade have called into question the sanctity of authority and the traditional role of school officials.

Consider just four of the stronger forces in our immediate past: the growing movement among educators to emphasize the process of learning rather than the content of courses; the impact of technology resulting in sudden rather than gradual changes in culture; the growing tendency of youth to create culture and often to be emulated, particularly in fashion and speech, by their elders; and the ferment in American life, related especially to issues concerning the war in Viet Nam. By the beginning of this decade, the place and influence of youth in American society were so changed that conflict with traditional authority was inevitable. [18]

Nevertheless, whatever caused the change in the courts' attitudes toward students' rights, the change has made the task of teachers and administrators enormously difficult. School officials, particularly those who are "veterans," often face a real identity crisis because of recent court decisions. The precarious position of educators in public schools everywhere in America has been well delineated by several writers. Not surprisingly, a number of educators view the restriction of official authority in the schools in favor of student rights as a most dangerous development. Still other educators see the recent court decisions as having implications far beyond the school situation.

While many educators who are genuinely concerned with the rights of students may be inclined at first to think that such warnings of disaster are quite premature, they cannot entirely disregard the fears of U.S. Supreme Court Justice Hugo Black, one of America's most distinguished legal minds and a jurist who has been one of the strongest defenders of civil liberties. In his dissent in the *Tinker* case, Justice Black wrote:

One does not need to be a prophet or the son of a prophet to know that after the Court's holding today some students in Iowa schools and indeed in all schools will be ready, able, and willing to defy their teachers on practically all orders. . . . Turned loose with lawsuits for damages and injunctions against their teachers as they are here, it is nothing but wishful thinking to imagine that young, immature students will not soon believe it is their right to control the schools rather than the right of the States that collect the taxes to hire the teachers for the benefit of the pupils. This case, therefore, wholly without constitutional reasons in my judgment, subjects all the public schools in the country to the whims and caprices of their loudest-mouthed, but maybe not their brightest students. I, for one, am not fully persuaded that school pupils are wise enough, even with this Court's expert help from Washington, to run the 23,390 public school systems in our 50 states. [19]

M. Chester Nolte, however, does not see in recent Supreme Court decisions a desire to cripple the authority of school officials. He stresses that in the *Tinker* case "the Supreme Court itself has no intention or desire of removing from school administrators the authority they need to maintain an orderly educational environment." [20] Nolte, past president of the National Organization for Legal Problems in Education, bases his belief on a passage from the majority decision in the *Tinker* case: "The Court has repeatedly emphasized the need for affirming the comprehensive authority of the States and of school officials, consistent with fundamental constitutional safeguards, to prescribe and control conduct in the schools."

Nolte says that if any further proof is required that recent U. S. Supreme Court decisions have not seriously undercut official authority in the public schools, we should read Justice Byron White's majority opinion in the case of *Wood v. Strickland.*

It is not the role of the federal courts to set aside decisions of school administrators which the court may view as lacking a basis in wisdom or compassion. Public high school students do have substantive and procedural rights while at school. But Sec. 1983 (Civil Rights Act of 1871) does not extend the right to relitigate in federal court evidentiary questions arising in school disciplinary proceedings or the proper construction of school regulations. The system of public education that has evolved in this Nation relies necessarily upon the discretion and judgment of school administrators and school board members, and Sec. 1983 was not intended to be a vehicle for federal court correction of errors in the exercise of that discretion which do not rise to the level of violations of specific constitutional guarantees.[21]

Notwithstanding Nolte's belief that Justice White's opinion protects the authority of school officials, it does appear that any school teacher or principal might still be justified in asking the Court, "Precisely what kind of error in the exercise of my discretion would or would not 'give rise to the level of violations of specific constitutional guarantees'?" If the answer is that such an error would be one involving the due process rights of students, then the average school official would still feel, it appears, quite confused and intimidated.

As stated earlier, many educators whose avowed aim is to humanize our schools have welcomed the recent extension of student rights. They believe that this development will go far toward reshaping the present environment, which they hold is conducive neither to learning nor to expressing feelings. The need for change has been vividly described by Farber.

School is where you let the dying society put its trip on you. Our schools may seem useful: to make children into doctors, sociologists, engineers—to discover things. But they're poisonous as well. They exploit and enslave students; they petrify society; they make democracy unlikely. And it's not what you're taught that does the harm but how you're taught. Our schools teach you by pushing you around, by stealing your will and your sense of power, by making timid square apathetic slaves out of you—authority addicts.[22]

FREEDOM OF SPEECH AND ASSEMBLY

The *Tinker* decision, the first significant U.S. Supreme Court recognition of student rights, involved the wearing of armbands to protest the Vietnam War. The petitioners in the suit were John F. Tinker, fifteen years old; Christopher Eckhardt, sixteen years old; and Mary Beth Tinker, thirteen years old. John and Christopher were high school students in Des Moines, Iowa, while Mary Beth was a student in junior high school. School principals in Des Moines were made aware of the plans of students to wear armbands, and on December 14, 1965 they met and decided to warn students that if they wore armbands to school, they would be asked to remove them. If they failed to remove them, they would be suspended until they returned without the armband. On December 16 Mary Beth and Christopher wore black armbands to school, and the next day John did likewise. All three were ordered to go home and were told they were suspended until they returned without their armbands. The students did not go back to classes until after New Year's Day.

Parents of the students filed a complaint in a U.S. District Court, but their complaint was dismissed. On appeal to the Court of Appeals for the Eighth Circuit, the decision of the District Court was affirmed. Finally the case was sent to the U. S. Supreme Court in 1967. The Supreme Court found that there was no evidence to substantiate the fears of the Des Moines school principals that wearing the armbands would have disrupted the orderly school process. Nor was there evidence that the students wearing armbands intended to incite their fellow students or interrupt their learning. Further the Court believed that evidence existed which showed that the principals' ban on the wearing of the armbands was based largely on their own contrary opinions concerning the Vietnam War; it was pointed out that the principals allowed students to wear other kinds of political symbols during school hours. However the Court did not deny that the principals had acted partly, at least, out of a genuine fear of disruption.

The majority opinion was perhaps one of the most important decisions the U. S. Supreme Court has rendered in this century. It laid down some specific guidelines concerning the constitutional guarantees of freedom of speech for all persons. Justice Abe Fortas, writing the majority opinion, said:

First Amendment rights, applied in light of the special characteristics of the school environment, are available to teachers and students. It can hardly be argued that either students or teachers shed their constitutional right to freedom of speech or expression at the schoolhouse gate. This has been the unmistakable holding of this Court for almost fifty years.[23]

For those who might ask exactly when school authorities have a right to prohibit such activity as that engaged in by the petitioners, Justice Fortas said:

In order for the State in the person of school officials to justify prohibition of a particular expression of opinion, it must be able to show that its action was caused by something more than a mere desire to avoid the discomfort and unpleasantness that always accompany an unpopular viewpoint. Certainly where there is no finding and no showing that engaging in the forbidden conduct would materially and substantially interfere with the requirements of appropriate discipline in the operation of the school, the prohibition cannot be sustained.[24]

Further, in what well may be called a First Amendment landmark opinion for students, Justice Fortas maintained:

In our system, students may not be regarded as closed-circuit recipients of only that which the State chooses to communicate. They may not be confined to the expression of those sentiments that are officially approved. In the absence of a specific showing of constitutionally valid reasons to regulate their speech, students are entitled to freedom of expression of their views.

Nevertheless, the Court did not uphold the opinion that freedom of expression is absolute. Where school officials can prove that such expression may lead to disruption of the learning process or cause injury to anyone, they may prohibit such expression. But the mere fear of such disruption, without some sufficient reason, is not cause to deny freedom of expression. In the words of the Court, a student's right of free speech may only be restricted where it can be demonstrated that the speech "materially and substantially interfere(s) with the requirements of appropriate discipline in the operation of the school." Richard D. Gatti and Daniel J. Gatti believe that the following rules apply to situations involving free speech for students.

1. Where the students' speech collides with the rights of others, it may be restricted.
2. Unpopular language may be allowed, but 'fighting words' and obscene language are not.
3. If the student shows gross disrespect for the principal or the teacher, it is not protected speech.
4. Discussion of all ideas relevant to the subject matter is permitted in the classroom, but this is subject to the teacher's responsibility to maintain order and right to guide the discussion.
5. Symbolic speech which is not materially disruptive must be allowed; but the equivalent spoken idea in the middle of an unrelated class discussion need not be tolerated.
6. Any speech, including spoken words, armbands, or buttons, which mock, ridicule, or are intended to disrupt the educational process because of race, religion, or national origin, are not permissible.
7. Distribution of armbands, buttons, etc. in the halls or classrooms during class may be prohibited.
8. Control of the order and direction of the class and the scope and manner of treatment of the subject matter rests with the teacher, who has a right to be free of distraction and disruption by dissident students. As a result, disruption of the classroom and insubordination may be forbidden. There ideally should exist a procedure whereby students can present their grievances about an instructor in a proper format and at a proper time.[25]

FREEDOM OF THE PRESS

Courts have held that if a school newspaper is published with school funds, the principal or other officials of the school have the power of limited review of what is in the paper, but these officials do not have broad censorship powers in such cases. Students do have a right, even in a newspaper published with school funds, to criticize or express their opinions unless such actions materially and substantially affect the discipline and operation of the school. No student has the right in an official school publication to publish obscene or libelous material. It has been suggested that two rules be followed concerning official school publications: (1) Student publications should indicate that the opinions expressed are not necessarily those of the school or of the student body. (2) There should be rules providing for a right of reply by a person who is criticized in the publication or who disagrees with its editorial policy or treatment of a given event.[26]

In the matter of so-called "underground" or unofficial papers distributed on school property, courts have ruled that students do have some rights concerning publication of such papers. They have a right to distribute them on school grounds if they do not interfere with the normal school operation, but school officials may regulate the time, place and manner of distribution of such publications. Further, school officials may require that such publications be submitted to them for prior approval. Nevertheless, "if the school enacts restrictions which are overly broad or burdensome" on such publications, "they may be seen as an impermissible prior restraint on the students' freedom of speech."[27]

According to the courts, rules concerning prior approval of underground publications in public schools must include (1) an expeditious review procedure, (2) an explanation of who has the authority to approve or disapprove of the material, and how the material may be submitted for approval, (3) a specific statement of the type of publications allowed, and (4) a clear and specific statement of the kinds of things which are prohibited and which justify censorship.[28] Some general rules regarding underground newspapers have been set down by two authorities on student rights:

In approving underground newspapers, ideological censorship must in all cases be avoided. Material which is libelous, clearly obscene, or which would reasonably lead school officials to forecast a material and substantial disruption with the educational process or the rights of others may be denied approval. . . . The courts require stricter tests to be complied with where the issue is one of prohibiting speech before it occurs. . . . Where speech has taken place, and it results in a material and substantial disruption, all courts will uphold the reasonable disciplinary measures taken to punish the responsible students.[29]

SUSPENSIONS AND EXPULSIONS

Two of the most diversely interpreted and highly controversial decisions handed down by the U.S. Supreme Court in 1975—*Goss v.*

Lopez and *Wood v. Strickland*—dealt with the right of school officials to suspend and expel students, as well as with the amount of protection the Court thought students were guaranteed under the United States Constitution. No matter what one thinks of these two decisions, it is difficult to disagree with Elliot C. Lichtman, who asserts that "the judiciary has come a long way since 1923, when an Arkansas court upheld the expulsion of a female high school student for using talcum powder on her face."[30]

Assiduous observers of court decisions regarding school matters should have expected that the U. S. Supreme Court would be called upon to hear cases involving the suspension and expulsion powers of public school officials. Most educators consider suspensions and expulsions necessary to maintain classroom control. Advocates of student rights argue that suspensions and expulsions which deprive students of education without due process of the law are in violation of property rights and of liberty under the Fifth and Fourteenth Amendments.

Courts hearing such cases have generally held that all students are entitled to be informed of what the school commands or forbids and must have a hearing in the school setting before suspension or expulsion can occur. Usually this means giving the accused student a chance to know and refute the charges brought against him or her prior to disciplinary action. But the due-process requirements vary among courts and school districts. Some courts have imposed elaborate procedural requirements, while others have given school administrators a free hand to suspend or expel students.

Goss v. Lopez, 419 U. S. 565, 95 S. Ct. 729 (1975)

High school students in Columbus, Ohio, disagreed with school officials about which community leaders should be permitted to speak at school assemblies during Black History Week. Disturbances developed, and administrators began to suspend students in mass fashion for ten days, contending that they had this right according to a 1971 Ohio state statute. The students claimed that their procedural due-process rights had been violated because they were not permitted a hearing or other necessary procedures to determine the propriety of suspension, since the statute itself did not permit such rights to a student.[31] The students were successful at the district court level and the case was appealed by the school district to the U. S. Supreme Court. It should be noted that the suit did not ask for damages but requested only declaratory relief and that the court order the record of suspension to be stricken.

Ruling in favor of the students, the Supreme Court said that a student's interest in attending public schools was protectable both as property and liberty under the Fourteenth Amendment. Further, the Court declared that the entry of suspension into the students' records might very well injure their reputations among teachers and other students. Also the future of the students could be affected because quite often colleges and future employers take into serious consideration the knowledge that an applicant has been suspended from an educational institution.[32] For these reasons, in delivering the Supreme Court's majority opinion, Justice Byron White was unusually specific in outlining recommended procedures in such cases:

At the very minimum . . . students facing suspension and the consequent interferences with a protected property interest must be given some kind of notice and afforded some kind of hearing. . . . The student must be given oral or written notice of the charges against him, and, if he denies them, an explanation of the evidence the authorities have and an opportunity to present his side of the story. There need be no delay between the time "notice" is given and the time of the hearing. In most cases, the disciplinarian may informally discuss the alleged misconduct with the student minutes after it has occurred. We hold . . . that the student first be told what he is accused of doing and what the basis of the accusation is.

Nevertheless, the *Goss* decision was not nearly as broad as many educators seem to think, for Justice White continued:

To impose in each case even truncated trial-type procedures might well overwhelm administrative facilities in many places and, by diverting resources, cost more than it would save in educational effectiveness. Moreover, further formalizing the suspension process and escalating its formality and adversary nature may not only make it too costly as

a regular disciplinary tool, but also destroy its effectiveness as part of the teaching process.

What does this mean for the school official? For one thing, students need not be given a written statement concerning the reason for their suspension; they need only receive an oral one. In addition the student has "no right to pre-disciplinary discovery proceedings, nor to representation by counsel, nor to confront and cross-examine witnesses in support of the accused student's version of the facts."[33] Or, as Thomas A. Shannon has put it: "*Goss* does not require a *Miranda* type notice. At the present stage, it is barely a hearing. . . . "[34] It should also be remembered that the Supreme Court declared that such notice and hearing as it requires can take place after the student's removal from the school if his or her presence poses a continuing danger to persons or property or there is an ongoing threat of disrupting the educational process.

A number of educators have greeted the *Goss* decision with approval because, they say, it not only signals a declaration of rights for students but also is a significant legal safeguard for teachers who face peremptory dismissal by their boards. The thrust of the Court's decision is narrow since "no issue was presented as to the due-process rights, if any, of a student threatened with a failing grade, denial of promotion, exclusion from extracurricular activities, or placement in a vocational track or in a school for students of less than average ability."[35] Nevertheless, in laying down minimum due-process safeguards for students, the Supreme Court said that its intervention would be minimal except in "unusual situations." This phrase foreshadows great trouble for public schools:

After all, what "situation" isn't "unusual" in the mind's eye of a resourceful plaintiff's attorney bent on smothering a rule with exceptions? Claims will certainly abound that the student suspended just before graduation, or just before examination time, or even before the "big game" is entitled to protections beyond those provided in the usual situation.[36]

Nor is the "unusual situations" section of the majority opinion the only one which worries both legal experts and educators. Speaking for the Court, Justice White also said: "Longer expulsions for the remainder of the school term, or permanently, may require more formal procedures. . . . There may even be situations involving only a suspension where the student is entitled to more than the rudimentary procedures outlined in this case."[37] William Buss believes that the Supreme Court "may have suggested, obliquely, that the right to present evidence (including testimony of witnesses), the right to cross examination, and the right to counsel would be required for long-term suspensions or expulsions."[38]

The General Counsel of the National Education Association noted what appears to be a beneficial result of the *Goss* ruling. "In connection with the desegregation of the schools in the South, a disproportionate number of black students have been suspended or expelled. The basic procedural safeguards now required by the Supreme Court will render it more difficult for school authorities to engage in discriminatory treatment of minority students."[39]

What should school districts do to modify their rules and regulations in the wake of the *Goss* decision? William R. Hazard suggests that school district policy and procedures:

. . . should provide for explicit notice to the student of the substance of the charges on which the suspension decision is based. The school district regulations should be clear, direct, and unambiguous as to the behavior or conduct mandated or prohibited and the specific misconduct of the pupil related directly to the officially-adopted regulations of the board. It would appear wise for the disciplinarian (usually the building principal empowered by state statute or board policy to make the suspension decision) to require direct evidence from the teacher or other school official to corroborate the oral or written account of the student's alleged misconduct. . . . Prudence suggests at least a clear, descriptive account of the incident prompting the suspension decision. Unless the incident clearly requires immediate removal of the student from the school setting, it would be wise to conduct the informal hearing at a time and under circumstances which allow corroboration of the event prior to or simultaneous with the hearing.[40]

It is clear that the *Goss* decision does much to broaden students' rights. If school board members across the nation were polled as to their interpretations of the decision, probably no consensus would be obtained. Still, as

Nolte cautions: "For all its vagueness, disjointedness, and seeming contradictions, the 'minimum' due process requirement for students which the Supreme Court now has laid down in *Goss v. Lopez* must somehow be made to work. If this turns out to be impossible (and the odds seem ominously in favor of such an outcome), the cure prescribed in a future ruling is likely to be more painful than the disease."[41]

Wood v. Strickland, 420 U. S. 308, 95 S. Ct. 992 (1975)

During a high school function in Mena, Arkansas, three female students, all sixteen years of age and all sophomores, poured three bottles of 3.2 beer into the nonalcoholic punch. There was apparently no noticeable effect on either the parents or the teachers, and it was estimated that the mixture as a whole contained no more than 0.91 per cent alcohol. The girls admitted pouring the beer into the punch and were expelled by the school board for three months (until the end of the school year), although the principal pleaded for clemency. The students claimed that since the total punch solution contained such a small amount of alcohol, they had not violated the board's rule against an intoxicating beverage at school functions. The board agreed that the final punch was not intoxicating but insisted that the meaning of the prohibition had been to exclude all alcoholic beverages, even though that was not the way the prohibition was worded. The students later filed an amended petition to include financial damages against the board members as individuals under the Civil Rights Act of 1871.

The District Court ruled for the school board, holding that its members were immune from damages, but the Court of Appeals reversed this decision and said that since the board could not produce evidence that the punch was intoxicating, it had violated the girls' constitutional rights. Finally the case reached the U. S. Supreme Court in 1975, and the 5 to 4 decision caused a great deal of controversy. The Supreme Court characterized what the students had done as a "harmless prank," which, as one writer has pointed out, was an unfortunate wording, that " . . . showed unbelievable insensitivity to the situation, the kind of insensitivity that might easily cost school people their jobs." [42]

Concerning the matter of immunity of school board members, the Court said that to secure immunity the "official must himself be acting sincerely and with a belief that he is doing right." However, the Court continued, "an act violating a student's constitutional rights can be no more justified by ignorance or disregard of settled, indisputable law on the part of one entrusted with supervision of students' daily lives than by the presence of actual malice." What this meant specifically was set forth by the Court. "A compensatory award will be appropriate only if the school board member has acted with such an impermissible motivation or with such disregard of the student's clearly established constitutional rights that his action cannot reasonably be characterized as being in good faith."

Still, the Supreme Court rejected the argument of the Appellate Court that the board had not established that the girls used an intoxicating beverage. The intent of the school district's rule was to ban all alcoholic beverages from school premises, the students had admitted that they understood the rule and that they knew they could be punished for what they did. Therefore evidence was not lacking to prove the charge against them. The Supreme Court strongly reminded the Appellate Court that the federal civil rights of students do not extend to relitigation of "evidentiary questions" or to the "proper construction of school regulations."

One important and favorable aspect of Wood *seems to have been largely ignored, at least to this point. It may be a significant step in curtailing the tendency of students to resort to* federal *court with grievances against board members. The Court in* Wood *specifically held that federal courts may not intervene in school disputes merely to correct an erroneous decision, an unwise decision or one lacking in compassion. To be properly assertable in a federal court, the student's grievance must "rise to the level of violations of specific constitutional guarantees."* [43]

Certainly the major effect of *Wood v. Strickland* has been to cause school boards to be more diligent when dealing with suspensions and expulsions. Nolte says that the Supreme Court has asserted in *Goss* and *Wood* that: (1) a school board rule must be reasonable (legislative); (2) it must apply equally to any and all students (executive); and (3) there must be fair and impartial treatment of anyone who disobeys the rule (judicial-procedural due process). [44] He goes on to say that all school boards must take cognizance of the fact that "the more serious the punishment, the more careful must the school board be to see that due process is safeguarded at *every* step of the process." [45]

It may be prudent for all boards of education to follow the example of school districts in the state of Oregon and require that students who face a possible suspension be given the rights to representation by legal counsel, to offer the testimony of witnesses and other evidence in their own behalf, to question any witnesses against them, and to have a hearing before an impartial authority.

A five-year Juvenile Justice Standards Project conducted by the American Bar Association and the Institute of Judicial Administration deals with school legal problems in a volume called *Schools and Education*. In this volume the procedures recommended in the *Goss* decision are endorsed, and it is suggested that before students are suspended for longer than a month they be given a full hearing before their board of education. This volume also recommends strongly against expulsion or suspension for more than one year, since most jobs require a high school diploma, and keeping students out longer than one year may in effect condemn them to a life of menial labor. In view of the *Goss* and *Wood* decisions, Nolte has recommended the following procedures when dealing with various student punishments.

Expulsion or Long-Term Suspensions: *The state law or board regulations are usually quite specific in what is required by way of due process; indeed in all of the states, only the board itself can expel a pupil. In absence of clear statutory or administrative requirements, it is best to accord at least the following:*

1. *written notice of the rules violated, the intention to expel, and the place, time, and circumstances of the hearing with sufficient time provided to prepare a defense.*
2. *full and fair hearing before an impartial adjudicator* (not *the person who collected the evidence*).
3. *right to legal counsel or some other adult representation.*

4. *opportunity to present witnesses or evidence in the accused pupil's behalf, and to cross-examine opposing witnesses.*

5. *some kind of written record (not necessarily verbatim) demonstrating that the decision was based on the evidence.*

Short-term Suspensions: *If nothing more is prescribed by statute or regulation, the Goss decision requires before actual suspension:*

1. *oral or written notification of the nature of the violation and the intended punishment.*

2. *"discussion" with the disciplinarian providing the pupil with an opportunity to tell his side of the story.*

3. *if the student denies the violation, an explanation of the* evidence *of the violation upon which the disciplinarian is relying. (The interview may follow by minutes the act which caused the reaction on the part of the school officials.)*

Financial Liability: *To avoid financial liability under the Civil Rights Act of 1871 (usually referred to as Section 1983 of Title 42 of the U. S. Code):*

1. *make and enforce any rule which appears to abridge civil rights only after careful consideration. If at all possible, get the advice of counsel.*

2. *if a rule or its enforcement appears to abridge a pupil's civil rights, be certain that it is necessary, reasonably related to the school's purposes, and administered without discrimination.*

3. *set up fundamentally fair disciplinary procedures which meet the standards for suspension and expulsion described above.*

4. *make a reasonable attempt to keep up with court decisions governing student conduct in your jurisdiction.*[46]

SEARCH AND SEIZURE

Although a relatively large number of suits have been filed during the past decade concerning the rights of public school students as they relate to search and seizure, the U. S. Supreme Court has not handed down a decision directly involving the Fourth Amendment rights of students. In fact only a few lower federal courts have given decisions on this matter, and where they have done so, the cases always involved college students. Since all suits involving public school students' Fourth Amendment rights have been decided by state courts, the general principles drawn from these cases are not binding precedents in all states.[47]

In no cases have school officials been criminally prosecuted for violating a student's Fourth Amendment rights, although a few decisions have found that school officials have incurred civil liability in such cases. Robert E. Phay and George T. Rogister, Jr. offer specific recommendations to school officials concerning the procedural rules for search and seizure cases in a school.

In developing regulations governing searches of students and their property, school officials should attempt to protect the students' right to privacy. Where the regulations govern searches of jointly controlled property, such as lockers or carrels, students should be made aware that the property is subject to periodic general administrative searches for contraband and rule violations. When a search focuses on a particular student because of a suspected rule violation, school officials should, if time permits, record their reasons for believing a search is justified before the search. If possible, the student's consent to the search should be obtained and he should be present when the search is made. Whenever school officials conduct a search, a witness should be present. If a major reason for a school search is to seek evidence of a criminal violation and if time permits, school officials should report their information to law enforcement officials, and allow them to conduct the search subject to standards applicable to police searches. If the police seek permission from school authorities to search a student, his property, or his locker to obtain evidence for a criminal prosecution, the school officials should require the police to obtain a search warrant unless the search comes within one of the exceptions to the Fourth Amendment's search warrant requirements. . . . Because the consequences of an unlawful search may result in the inadmissibility of evidence in criminal or school proceedings and, possibly, civil or criminal liability for school officials, incorporating these safeguards in school policies would seem prudent.[48]

REPUTATIONAL RIGHTS

As Nolte has pointed out, an individual's reputation is protected by the Fourteenth Amendment's due process clause. This protection must be extended to students as well.

If charges of misconduct are sustained and re-corded, those charges could seriously damage the student's standing with his fellow pupils and teachers as well as interfere with later oppor-tunities for higher education and employment. The state has set itself up to determine unilaterally *and without process whether that misconduct has oc-curred. Such state action collides immediately with the requirements of the Constitution.* [49]

This particular reminder is doubly relevant since the passage of the Family Educational Rights and Privacy Act of 1974, for almost all professional educators are now in a quandary about whether a suit against them on reputa-tional grounds will be successful. In order to establish a *prima facie* case, a student has only to argue that the defendant identified him in a defamatory manner by publishing the charge against him.

Thus, it may be actionable if a principal writes a letter to a newspaper describing a pupil as being "tricky and unreliable," if a college president re-ports to a prospective employer that a former stu-dent had been jailed for theft, if a teacher notes in a school register that a student was "ruined by to-bacco and whisky," or if school trustees mail an announcement to school district patrons charging that a student misbehaved during a band trip. [50]

Further, a defendant has only to communicate the defamatory statement to someone other than the defamed student to be published, and the third party could even be the student's parent. The statement, if spoken only within the hearing of the student, is not probable cause for a suit, and if the student himself published the statement, the defendant will not be held responsible.

It has not as yet been decided by a court if a critical statement spoken to a student in front of other people in order to discipline him or her constitutes a reasonable basis for a defama-tion suit. However, "if the defamation is con-veyed as gossip or if an educator otherwise exceeds his authority, an action might lie." [51] Certain communications are exempt under "conditional privilege." Obviously gossip does not constitute a conditional privilege. Ex-amples of what does constitute conditional privilege have been outlined by George E. Stevens:

A conditional privilege will also extend to reason-able communication to school officials from psychologists, physicians, and parents relating to the character, behavior, and health of particular students. Moreover, the privilege will no doubt apply to discussions of students at Parent-Teacher Association meetings, and to school conferences be-tween educators and parents and teachers if such communication relates to matters of legitimate par-ent and faculty concern. The privilege will also extend to the press and its sources of information within the school if the matter under discussion is of legitimate interest to the general public, but not if the matter relates only to a student's private character or an internal school affair of no real general or public concern. [52]

Many educators have been concerned since the passage of the Family Educational Rights and Privacy Act of 1974 about whether certain communication between the educator and another party constitutes conditional privi-lege.

It has been held that a letter of recommendation not authorized by a former student but requested by his prospective employer is conditionally privileged if the educator is discharging a legal or moral duty to the employer and the communication is pertinent to the inquiry made. If a student lists an educator as a reference or asks a teacher or administrator to write a letter of recommendation in his behalf, subsequent communication from the educator relat-ing to the student's character and ability should be at least conditionally privileged, and it could be argued that a communication authorized by a student or his parent is absolutely privileged since it has long been recognized that one may not recover damages for a publication invited by him. How-ever, a request for a letter of recommendation is not an invitation to make public something false and defamatory, unless the plaintiff knew the sub-stance of the communication beforehand and di-rectly or indirectly approved its contents. . . . An action for defamation will not lie on the theory that a person has in effect been defamed because of a refusal of another person to recommend him for employment. [53]

Stevens sums up the present situation in this area by saying:

The Family Educational Rights and Privacy Act of 1974 may result in students and parents becom-

ing more aware of their reputation rights, and hence may lead to more suits for libel or slander against school authorities. But ... decisions ... indicate that teachers and administrators are adequately protected by the defense of conditional privilege, and if the Supreme Court's decision in Gertz v. Robert Welch, Inc. *should become applicable to litigation involving school-connected defamation, the likelihood of a judgment against an educator for libelous or slanderous statements communicated as part of the legitimate performance of his duties would be even more remote.*[54]

CORPORAL PUNISHMENT

The one area in which *in loco parentis* has not been overturned is corporal punishment. This is ironic since physical punishment of mental patients and prison inmates is outlawed. To humanistic educators the use of physical violence on children is not only cruel and unusual punishment but also makes mockery of democratic values. Psychologically, the critics argue, corporal punishment is a degrading, dehumanizing, and counterproductive approach to maintaining classroom discipline.

As recently as 1977 only two states, Massachusetts and New Jersey, and a few big city school systems (including Chicago, New York, Pittsburgh, and Washington, D. C.) forbade corporal punishment in the public schools. In the majority of the states where corporal punishment is permitted, students are slapped or beaten for minor rule infractions such as arriving late, talking without permission, chewing gum, forgetting homework, or turning in late papers. One teacher described her first exposure to corporal punishment.

I was teaching in a small public school in Pittsburgh in the late 1950s when I first realized that corporal punishment was still used in the schools in the United States. One of my colleagues asked me to be her witness while she paddled a boy, just an ordinary unaffirming ten-year-old, braced himself against a desk while the teacher swung at him five times with a standard paddle the length of a baseball bat, striking him across the buttocks, or thereabouts, with all of her might. Then, puffing and winded from exertion, she explained authoritatively that this was an approved procedure, just so you had a witness.[55]

Before the U. S. Supreme Court affirmed a federal court's ruling in the case of *Baker v. Owen* in 1975, no uniform guidelines regulated corporal punishment of public school students in the United States. For example before a teacher could inflict corporal punishment on a student in the Portland School System, he or she had to obtain in advance the approval of the principal, while the Maine Department of Education Code stated "that a teacher or principal has this privilege to inflict reasonable punishment as is necessary for the child's proper education." On the other hand, the Montgomery County (Md.) Public School Student Code prohibited physical punishment in the presence of the class.[56]

Baker v. Owen, 395 F. Supp. 294 (M.D. N.C. 1975)

In this case, a mother brought suit to challenge the constitutionality of North Carolina statutes which authorized the use of corporal punishment by certain school personnel. She charged that she had told school officials beforehand not to use corporal punishment on her sixth-grade son, but that on December 6, 1973, a woman teacher struck him twice on the buttocks for an infraction of school discipline. In the suit, Mrs. Baker raised three constitutional challenges:

1. She charged that the parental right to determine discipline was violated by the administration of corporal punishment to her son over her specific objections.
2. Her son Russell charged that the North Carolina statute which had authorized corporal punishment deprived him of procedural due process.
3. Russell argued that the punishment he received in this instance constituted cruel and unusual punishment, and was thus a violation of his Eighth Amendment rights.[57]

Three federal judges were appointed to hear the case, since the plaintiffs were challenging the constitutionality of a state law. In its decision the court said that although Mrs. Baker's rights to discipline her child were guaranteed by the Constitution, school personnel also had a legitimate interest in keeping order and discipline in the schools. These competing interests must be balanced, the court said, and thus school officials are free to employ corporal punishment until they decide that its harm outweights its utility. The Bakers did not contend in their suit that corporal punishment *per se* was unconstitutional—they merely claimed that the punishment administered to Russell in this situation was unconstitutional. But the court held that such punishment in this specific case was not cruel and unusual and thus not constitutionally significant, since Russell himself testified that he felt only a "stinging sensation."

However, it was the last part of the federal court's *Baker* opinion which held by far the greatest significance for school officials and students. The court said that Russell had an "interest, protected by the concept of liberty in the Fourteenth Amendment, in avoiding corporal punishment." Thus, some procedure was due as a constitutional principle. The scope and nature of this procedure had, however, to be balanced between the student's rights and the necessity of maintaining order and discipline in the schools. At this point, the federal judges enumerated four principles governing the use of corporal punishment in public schools:

1. Corporal punishment should not be used unless the student was forewarned that specific misbehavior could cause its use.

2. Corporal punishment should never be employed as a first line of punishment for misbehavior. The court suggested that the offending student might be given extra work or detention as an alternative punishment.

3. Corporal punishment can only be administered in the company of a second staff member who has been informed beforehand and in the student's presence of the reason for the punishment. (The court said that the purpose of this requirement is to permit the student to protest, spontaneously, "an egregiously arbitrary or contrived application of punishment.")

4. If the parents so request, the official who administered the corporal punishment must furnish a written statement of the reasons for using this form of punishment. The statement must include the name of the second staff member who was present.

Nevertheless, the court qualified the first two principles in a most important way. They do not apply if the student's behavior is "so antisocial or disruptive in nature as to shock the conscience." Thus while upholding the constitutionality of the North Carolina statute, the court said that the statute could not be implemented without giving students specific procedural safeguards in order to conform with the Fourteenth Amendment. On October 20, 1975 the U. S. Supreme Court affirmed the decision with no dissents and gave no opinion in so doing.

Subsequent Cases

A more recent legal development has occurred regarding corporal punishment: the appeal in the case of *Ingraham v. Wright.* The U. S. Court of Appeals, 5th Circuit, held in this case that while the U. S. Supreme Court affirmed the decision of the lower court in the case of *Baker v. Owen*, it only affirmed the finding that the use of corporal punishment could not be prohibited by the objection of a parent and that it did not reach its ruling on procedural due process. The opinion of the Court of Appeals in the *Ingraham* case took issue with the *Baker* decision, finding that such procedural safeguards as outlined in that case are not required when corporal punishment is inflicted if such punishment is specifically permitted by state law.

The argument by the Fifth Circuit Court of Appeals in the Ingraham case presents quite another side to the corporal punishment legal picture:

While a recorded suspension can indeed have a permanent adverse impact on a person's reputation and could conceivably harm that person's chance to obtain employment or higher education, we find it difficult to contend that a paddling, a commonplace and trivial event in the lives of most children, involves any such damage to reputation.

It seems to us that the value of corporal punishment would be severely diluted by elaborate procedural process imposed by this court. . . . A hearing procedure could effectively undermine the utility of corporal punishment for the administrator who probably has little time under present procedures to handle all the disciplinary problems which beset him or her.[58]

In 1977 the U.S. Supreme Court ruled 5 to 4 that school children have no federal legal recourse when paddled by their teachers and administrators, even when the punishment is proved to be excessive. The Constitution's Eighth Amendment against cruel and unusual punishment, the court concluded, applies only to those persons convicted of a crime. Nor are hearings necessary before spankings are administered. However, teachers and administrators should take notice of the fact that in some states they are subject to possible civil and criminal liability for using excessive and unreasonable force when punishing students. Justice Byron R. White, writing for the court's dissenters, said: "The fact that a person may have a state-law cause of action against a public official who tortures him with a thumbscrew . . . has nothing to do with the fact that such official conduct is cruel and unusual punishment." The *Ingraham* issue may be dead, but the feelings are still strong.

Corporal punishment did not begin in the twentieth century; it was part of the religious philosophy of teaching under the Old Deluder Satan Act. Many teachers are still trying to beat the devil out of children. Perhaps the time has come, as the superintendent of instruction in Pittsburgh proposed in 1868, for corporal punishment to be prohibited in all schools. If students can see their teachers and administrators deal with frustration and anger without resorting to physical abuse, then they too are likely to adopt nonviolent means of coping with frustration and anger. Indeed, we teach best what we live.

BEYOND STUDENT RIGHTS

The urgency of humanizing our schools by recognizing basic student rights is not reflected merely in teacher and administrator abuses of students. Students are also violators of human rights. Consider, for example, the following student violence-related data collected from 1970 to 1973:[59]

Assaults on school teachers. . . . . .up 77.4%
Assaults on students . . . . .up 85.3%
Rapes and attempted
rapes on campus . . . . .up 40.1%
Homicides on school premises . .up 18.5%
Number of weapons confiscated .up 54.4%

A National Institute of Education survey shows that in 1976 secondary school students had one chance in nine of having something stolen, one chance in eighty of being attacked, and one chance in two hundred of being robbed.

Millions of dollars are spent each year to prevent or abate student acts of violence and vandalism. For instance the District of Columbia spends more than $600,000 a year to replace broken windows. Chicago spends nearly $3 million on school security, and New York spends nearly $10 million. The Federal Bureau of Investigation reported that in 1976 more than 70,000 teachers were assaulted and vandalism cost the nation more than $600 million. Despite massive human and economic outlays, a growing number of American elementary and secondary schools are becoming places of prostitution, drug rings, and blackmail. It seems unlikely that school officials will be able to either prevent or abate such conditions without student and community assistance. Guaranteeing student rights and demanding corresponding responsibilities will help somewhat, but other steps must be taken. The community must become a partner in humanizing the schools.

After reviewing current statistics and court cases, it would be easy to conclude that schools are battlefields or prisons in which most persons are deliberately abusing each other. This is not true. Schools are not battlefields or prisons; and only a few administrators, teachers or students intentionally violate the human rights of other people. However, victims of such violations are likely to believe that one abuse is too many. Even so, no abuse—intentional or otherwise—justifies institutionalizing violence as the means for keeping order within the schools. The problem of how to maintain order in schools effectively and humanely has become a major concern of all persons involved in the educational process.

A considerable amount of coverage has been given to students' rights. Teachers and administrators have rights, too. Teachers and administrators have the right to be appointed solely on the basis of ability and professional competence without regard to such factors as race, sex, nationality, creed, political or religious beliefs or affiliation. Once appointed, they have the right to hold and express personal opinions; establish the curriculum, subject to approval of boards of education and state departments of education; select appropriate textbooks; objectively discuss controversial issues in the classroom; express opinions on school policies and conditions; join professional associations; participate as individuals in local, state, and federal political activities; and enjoy individual and personal rights and freedom outside the school setting.

Teachers also have the following rights:

1. Teachers do not have the right to a particular position in a particular school. The right of assignment and transfer of teachers from one position to another is generally agreed to be a function of the superintendent of schools and the board of education. While school officials usually do not act in an arbitrary manner or against the interests of teachers in these matters, the law is on their side if their decisions are reasonable.

2. Teachers have the right of absence with pay during illness, the right to compensation if injured in performance of duty, the right of reasonable protection in the performance of their duties, the right of immunity from garnishment of salary, the right of immunity from personal abuse or insult, and other similar rights.

3. Although teachers are generally not denied the right of collective bargaining, they are legally and morally restricted from the right to strike because of the fact that they are public employees. [Both NEA and AFT members have, however, withheld services.]

4. Under certain conditions teachers enjoy qualified privilege in making statements concerning students. If the statements are made under obligation in the line of duty, and if the statements are made to those who have power to act on the basis of the information, it is likely that the teacher will not be liable to legal action.

5. If teachers stand ready to perform their services they may not be denied their salaries if they are prevented from teaching by acts beyond their control.

6. Teachers may be denied their salaries if they are not properly certified and if they do not keep the reports and records required by laws and regulations governing the school district.

7. Although the issue is controversial, it appears that leaves of absence for teachers are

legal. However, the courts have not followed a consistent course in deciding cases involving teachers on leave with pay. Since the teacher on such leave would be paid for a period when services are not actually being rendered, the question of expenditure of public funds for private purposes is involved.

8. Teachers being dismissed for "cause" during the duration of a contract or tenured teachers being dismissed at any time have the right to an impartial, formal, and complete hearing. The teachers involved must be made aware of the charges against them, and they should be given the opportunity to cross-examine any and all witnesses who testify against them.

9. Ordinarily, retirement rights for teachers do not become vested until the teacher retires.

10. Although some courts have held to the contrary, marriage is usually not sufficient grounds for dismissal of women teachers on permanent tenure. Women teachers not on permanent tenure may be dismissed because of marriage although the courts are not agreed on this view, either. [Title IX prohibits such dismissals unless men are dismissed for marriage too.]

11. The right of teachers to receive certain fringe benefits has not been firmly established. However, a New Mexico case in 1921 recognized the implied power of school boards to provide group and disability insurance for teachers if the boards desire. Court decisions on this problem, while very limited in number, seem to point to the fact that it is legal for boards to finance group insurance for teachers and also Workmen's Compensation.[60]

EMPATHY

Jose Sanchez crawled slowly out of his bed and stared at the tiny rays of sunlight streaming through the tattered shades hanging loosely at his window. "Damn," he mumbled, "another day of school. I wish I didn't have to go."

He could hear Mamma Sanchez coughing in the next room. It sounded as if she wanted to vomit, but she knew that she would have to clean it up herself now that Rosa was gone. He missed Rosa. She would always take care of her baby brother. She would buy him toys and tell him stories about knights and castles and wars.

Too bad she had to get married to that Alfred guy, he thought.

He thought about knights all the way to school. "Today," he decided, "I will be a knight." His heart beat faster and he ran to school, riding an imaginary horse.

Just outside the school door, Ricky Hamlet was teasing Rebecca Smith. Out of frustration, Rebecca began to cry.

"Let her go," Jose, the knight, demanded.

A startled Ricky turned to see who belonged to the intruding voice.

"Oh, it's you, Jose," he laughed. "I'll give you ten seconds to get out of here or I'll knock your butt off."

Jose straightened his back and pulled in his paunchy stomach, making his short chubby frame appear to be a couple of inches taller. He clenched his fists, balanced his weight squarely on his feet, and waited. Fights were not new or uncommon to him. But fighting for a damsel in distress was!

Ricky lunged and Jose quickly stepped aside and in the same smooth motion caught him squarely in the mouth with a left cross. A stunned Ricky found himself feebly trying to fend off Jose's fists and legs—they seemed to be coming from all directions.

Ms. Nova, a teacher, separated the boys and asked Rebecca how the fight started.

"Ricky and I were playing and Jose came and started a fight," she said.

"Go to the counselor," Ms. Nova ordered Jose.

Instruction. Close your eyes and imagine that you are Jose. What do you feel? How do you feel? Take several minutes to get into the role of Jose.

ADDITIONAL READINGS

Adams, Paul, et al. *Children's Rights: Toward the Liberation of the Child.* New York, Praeger, 1971.

Berstein, Saul W., Mary D. Cohen, and Deborah James. *Teenagers' Rights and Responsibilities.* Silver Springs, Md., The Institute for Behavioral Research, 1971.

Brant, Irving. *The Bill of Rights: Its Origin and Meaning.* Indianapolis, Bobbs-Merrill, 1965.

Chanin, Robert H. *Protecting Teacher Rights: A Summary of Constitutional Developments.* Washington, D. C., National Education Association, 1970.

Cohen, William, et al. *Equal Rights–An Intergroup Curriculum.* Harrisburg, Pennsylvania Department of Education, 1974.

Cruickshank, William M. and John B. Junkala. *Misfits in the Public Schools.* Syracuse, N. Y., Syracuse University Press, 1969.

Dollar, Barry. *Humanizing Classroom Discipline: A Behavioral Approach.* New York, Harper & Row, 1972.

Goldstein, Stephen R. *Law and Public Education: Cases and Materials.* Indianapolis, Bobbs-Merrill, 1974.

A Guide for Improving Public School Practices in Human Rights. Bloomington, Ind., Phi Delta Kappa, 1975.

Kleeman, Richard P. *Student Rights and Responsibilities: Courts Force Schools To Change.* Washington, D. C., National School Public Relations Associations, 1972.

Schofield, Dee. *Student Rights and Student Discipline.* Arlington, Va., National Association of Elementary School Principals, 1975.

Snider, Glen. *Student Rights and Responsibilities.* Washington, D. C., Department of Health, Education, and Welfare, 1972.

Strickland, Rennard, Janet Frasier Phillips and William R. Phillips. *Avoiding Teacher Malpractice.* New York, Hawthorn Books, 1976.

NOTES

1. Jerry Farber, *The Student as Nigger* (New York, Pocket Books, 1970).

2. Morrell J. Clute, "Can Human Rights Survive in the Classroom?" *Educational Leadership*, 31 (May, 1974), 682–683.

3. Anonymous student essays, quoted in Susan Kannell and Myrna Sayler, "Dropout Forum," *Educational Leadership*, 31 (May, 1974), 695–696.

4. *In re Gault*, 387 U. S. 1 (1967), cited in Richard D. Gatti and Daniel J. Gatti, *Encyclopedic Dictionary of School Law* (West Nyack, N.Y., Parker, 1975), 260.

5. *In the Matter of Winship*, 397 U. S. 358 (1970) and *McKeiver v. Pennsylvania*, cited in W. Richard Brothers, "Procedural Due Process: What is It?" *NASSP Bulletin*, 59 (January, 1975), 4.

6. William Buss, "What Procedural Due Process Means to a School Psychologist: A Dialogue," *Journal of School Psychology*, 13 (Winter, 1975), 308.

7. David Duffee, "Due Process: Can It Thrive in a Classroom?" *Education Digest*, 40 (November, 1974), 18.

8. Buss, "A Dialogue," 306.

9. M. Chester Nolte, "Why You Need a Student Grievance Plan and How You Can Have a Reasonable One," *American School Board Journal*, 162 (August, 1975), 38.

10. Brothers, "Procedural Due Process," 5.

11. *Tinker v. Des Moines, Ia., Independent School District*, 393 U. S. 503, 895. Ct. (1969), quoted in Edward C. Bolmeier, *Landmark Supreme Court Decisions on Public School Issues* (Charlottesville Va., Michie, 1973), 165.

12. Thomas A. Shannon, "*Goss* and *Wood*: Their Implications for School Practice," *Journal of Law and Education*, 4 (October, 1975), 614.

13. Michael L. Berger, "Student Rights and Affective Education: Are They Compatible?" *Educational Leadership*, 33 (March, 1976), 461.

14. Donald W. Robinson, "Is This the Right Approach to Student Rights?" *Phi Delta Kappan*, 56 (December, 1974), 234.

15. R. Freeman Butts, "The Public Purpose of the Public School," *Teachers College Record*, 74 (December, 1973), 75–208.

16. Richard M. Blankenburg, "The Rights of Children: Civil Rights of Public School Students," *Current*, (July/August, 1971), 35.

17. Richard L. Mandel, "Student Rights, Legal Principles, and Educational Policy," *Intellect*, 103 (January, 1975), 239.

18. William L. Hoyt, "Student's Rights and Responsibilities: A Point of View," *Journal of Education*, 156 (August, 1974), 16.

19. Bolmeier, *Landmark Supreme Court Decisions*, 166–67.

20. M. Chester Nolte, "Methods of Discipline: What is Allowed?" *A Legal Memorandum* (Washington, D.C., National Association of Secondary Principals, May 1976), 6.

21. *Wood v. Strickland*, 420 U. S. 308, 95 S. Ct. (1975).

22. Farber, *The Student as Nigger*, 17.

23. *Tinker v. Des Moines (IA.) Independent School District*, 393 U. S. 803 (1969).

24. See Elliot C. Lichtman, "Wood v. Strickland: A Significant Inducement for School Officials to Obey the Law," *Journal of Law and Education*, 4 (October, 1975), 591.

25. Gatti and Gatti, *Encyclopedic Dictionary*, 264–265.

26. *Ibid.*, 268.

27. *Ibid.*, 268–269.

28. *Ibid.*, 269.

29. *Ibid.*

30. Lichtman, "Wood v. Strickland,"

31. William G. Buss, "Implications of Goss v. Lopex and Wood v. Strickland for Professional Discretion and Liability in Schools," *Journal of Law and Education*, 4 (October, 1975), 567.

32. NEA General Counsel, "Let's Set the Record Straight on Student Rights," *Today's Education*, 64 (September/October, 1975), 69.

33. Arthur A. Kola, "Hard Choices in School Discipline and the Hardening of the Due Process Mold," *Journal of Law and Education*, 4 (October, 1975), 584.

34. Thomas A. Shannon, "Questions and Answers Concerning Implications for School Practice," *Journal of Law and Education*, 4 (October, 1975), 617.

35. NEA General Counsel, "Student Rights," 60.

36. Kola, "Hard Choices," 585.

37. *Goss v. Lopez*, 419 U. S. 565 (1975).

38. Buss, "Implications," 572.

39. NEA General Counsel, "Student Rights," 70.

40. William R. Hazard, "*Goss v. Lopez* and *Wood v. Strickland*: Some Implications for School Practice,"

Journal of Law and Education, 4 (October, 1975), 606.

41. M. Chester Nolte, "The Supreme Court's New Rules for Due Process," *Education Digest*, 40 (May, 1975), 42.

42. Shannon, "Qestions and Answers," 613.

43. G. Ross Smith, "*Wood v. Strickland*: An Analysis," *Journal of Law and Education*, 4 (October, 1975), 597.

44. M. Chester Nolte, "How to Survive the Supreme Court's Momentous New Strictures on School People," *American School Board Journal*, 162 (May, 1975), 51.

45. *Ibid.*, 53.

46. Nolte, "Student Discipline," 6–7.

47. See Robert E. Phay and George T. Rogister, Jr., "Searches of Students and the Fourth Amendment," *Journal of Law and Education*, 5 (January, 1976), 58.

48. *Ibid.*, 72–73.

49. Nolte, "Student Discipline," 2.

50. George E. Stevens, "The Reputation Rights of Students," *Journal of Law and Education*, 4 (October, 1975), 624–625.

51. *Ibid.*, 625–626.

52. *Ibid.*, 628–629.

53. *Ibid.*, 629–630.

54. *Ibid.*, 631.

55. Carolyn T. Schumacher, "Exit Corporal Punishment," *Educational Leadership*, 31 (May, 1974), 688.

56. Reho F. Thorum, "Codifying Student Rights and Responsibilities," *NASSP Bulletin*, 59 (January, 1975), 11–12.

57. Thomas J. Flygare, "Procedural Due Process Now Applies to Corporal Punishment," *Phi Delta Kappan*, 57 (January, 1976), 345.

58. *Ingraham v. Wright*, U. S. Circuit Court of Appeals, 5th Circuit, 525 F 2d 909 (1976).

59. "Violence and Vandalism Rise Seen by Senate Subcommittee Which Seeks Remedies," *The School Administrator*, 32 (May, 1975), 11.

60. Percy E. Burrup, *The Teacher and the Public School System* (New York, Harper & Row, 1967), 247–248.

14.
ACCOUNTABILITY

During his trial Socrates, one of the first victims of teacher accountability, characterized his teaching activity in this way:

Young men of the richer classes, who have not much to do, come about me of their own accord; they like to hear the pretenders examined, and they often imitate me, and examine others themselves; there are plenty of persons, as they soon discover, who think that they know something, but really know little or nothing; and then those who are examined by them instead of being angry with themselves are angry with me: This confounded Socrates, they say; this villainous misleader of youth![1]

Socrates taught a basic skill—perhaps the most basic of all skills—thinking. He was condemned to death not because he was an unsuccessful teacher, but because he was too successful in his mission. Today's advocates of accountability in education argue that unlike Socrates, most teachers and administrators have failed in their responsibilities toward their students.

THE CONTROVERSY IN PERSPECTIVE

The controversy over accountability in education can best be put in perspective if we remember that the demand for teacher accountability is not new. As early as the middle of the thirteenth century, professors and tutors were paid their salaries directly by their students. One distinguished historian points out that around 1250 the law students at the University of Bologna "kept their professors to the punctual observance of the lecture timetable, under threat of financial penalties, and revenged themselves on unpopular teachers by boycotts."[2] As seen in Chapter 1, the first accountability statute in America was the Old Deluder Satan Act of 1647, enacted by the Massachusetts Bay Colony, which held each town in the Colony accountable for teaching children to read the Bible. Failure to see that this was done resulted in a fine of five pounds levied against the offending town.

Without doubt the demand for accountability in education arises from many sources, each with its own particular remedy for the alleged failure. But most authorities are agreed that parents and taxpayers want a suitable explanation for what they consider the failure of the public schools. "Responsibility is the key issue in the accountability controversy."[3] But beyond the fixing of responsibility for lack of success, the public at large wants to know where the great amounts of education tax money go.

A major factor which has precipitated the reincarnation of responsibility, or accountability as it is called in the current educational vernacular, is the skyrocketing cost of education caused by inflation and the greatly needed increase in teacher salaries. Parents pour money into the public schools and are given no account of what happens to either. Now, the public is outwardly saying, "If we are paying that much, we want results."[4]

All educators would do well to examine polls reflecting what the public thinks about schools. The Fifth Annual Gallup Poll of Public Attitudes Toward Education, taken in 1973, revealed some facts which should give teachers and administrators more than a minimal amount of concern. Sixty per cent of the adults in the responding sample believed that teachers should be paid on the basis of the quality of their work and that teachers should not be paid according to standard scales. Sixty per cent were against tenure, 75 per cent wanted national testing in order to compare local student achievement with students in other communities, and 66 per cent favored a system that would hold teachers and administrators more accountable for student progress.[5]

George B. Redfern recently cautioned public school administrators that it will be more difficult each year for educators to demand larger appropriations in the face of such public distrust.[6] Leon Lessinger, a leading advocate of educational accountability, summed up the dissatisfaction of the public with its schools in terms that make good sense to the average parent and taxpayer:

What we don't know is how much student learning is produced by all these teachers, books, language laboratories, buildings, and dollars. We know a lot about input, but little about output. In terms of learning, we can't describe how close our schools come to accomplishing what they aim to accomplish—or what any state or local community expects them to accomplish. We have no measure of progress—or lack of progress—over a span of time. We cannot identify in any precise way the strengths or weaknesses of a single school or school system.[7]

While public demand for accountability persisted through the 1960s, it remained largely unfocused. However, in 1970 accountability in education became the order of the day. This is when the greatest change agent in America—the federal government—began to concern itself with the issue. In that year President Richard M. Nixon asked in his education message to Congress for an accounting of what had been accomplished in the public schools compared with dollars spent: "From these considerations we derive another concept—*accountability*. School administrators and school teachers alike are responsible for

their performance, and it is in their interest as well as in the interest of their pupils that they be held accountable."

Following President Nixon's request came the 1970 Amendments to Title I of the Elementary and Secondary Education Acts (ESEA) of 1965, which for the first time required expenditure and staff data on a school basis. Administrators of Title I money had to establish performance criteria and to evalute their programs in conformity with such criteria. Richard L. Fairley predicted that the 1970 Amendments to the ESEA would result in teachers having "a number of sets of data to work with in evaluating their own teaching—and the success or failure of the program they are involved in."[8] Other writers analyzed the 1970 Amendments and said, "Here, it is easy to see how a transfer was made in the accountability movement from evaluating the programs to evaluating the teacher."[9]

Although most educators would agree that the issue of accountability is much more complex than is generally recognized by school patrons, they cannot deny that for whatever reasons, an alarming number of public school students are failing to learn. And certainly they realize that documenting this failure is not difficult. In 1974 it was reported at the University of California at Berkeley that nearly half the entering class was unable to write a well organized three-page essay. Such a report is even more shocking when it is remembered that the Berkeley students were drawn from the top one-eighth of high school graduates in the state of California.[10]

Other instances of student failure to master basic skills are not difficult to find. For example, in several states public school students in sixth and twelfth grades ranked below national averages in writing and language arts skills.[11] In 1975 Major General Rennie L. Davis, Commander of the Air Force Recruiting Service, said that half of all Chicago high school graduates taking an Air Force test failed it. He commented that the failure was a reflection on the school system.[12] A large number of parents and taxpayers agreed with General Davis.

In some cities protests against academic failure have resulted in the refusal of city officials to ratify teacher contracts. In 1975 six Black aldermen in New Haven, Connecticut, voted not to approve a negotiated teachers' contract in protest against allegedly inadequate education offered in the schools. Alderman Eldrige Davis, one of the six, said: "I was appalled when I saw high school students—many of them in the eleventh grade—who couldn't fill out . . . applications properly and who had trouble spelling even the simplest of words. . . . But if you know that the education they received was less than adequate, then you can understand the high unemployment rate among the black youth."[13]

More than 23 million American adults, one in every five, are functionally illiterate: they cannot function effectively in a complex society. An additional 40 million adults, one in every three, have only the minimum competence required to be effective citizens, consumers, wage earners or family members. Less than half the nation's total adult population aged 18 to 65 are proficient in reading, writing, computation, and problem-solving skills. To alter this condition, the National Association of Secondary School Principals adopted a resolution in 1976 recommending that state boards of education and the separate school districts consider the establishment of minimum standards for graduation from high school to include:

1. A functional literacy in reading, writing, and speaking.
2. A competency in mathematics through decimals and percentages.
3. Knowledge of the history and culture of the United States, to include the concepts and processes of democratic governance.
4. The completion of courses and programs in other disciplines sufficient to develop competence and maturity.

In January 1977 thirty states were either planning or implementing some form of performance-based program for graduation.

Toward a Definition

It soon becomes apparent to anyone who seeks the facts concerning accountability in education that one of the main problems is the inability of experts to agree on exactly what the term "accountability" means. Allan C. Orn-stein and Harriet Talmage say that "the concept of accountability is borrowed from management. When applied to education it means holding some people (teachers or administrators), some agency (board of education or state department of education), or some organization (professional organization or private company) responsible for performing according to agreed-upon terms."[14]

Ralph D. Wray maintains that "implicit in the notion of accountability is the identification of goals that can be achieved."[15] William C. Miller says that accountability is "holding an individual or group responsible for a level of performance or accomplishment for specific pupils."[16] In yet another vein, Myron Lieberman suggests that "there is accountability when resources and efforts are related to results in ways that are useful for policy making."[17] In a more profound but equally general nature, Lessinger states that "accountability is the product of a process. At its most basic level, it means that an agent, public or private, entering into a contractual agreement to perform a service will be held answerable for performing according to agreed-upon terms, within an established time period, and with a stipulated use of resources and performance standards."[18]

In less profound but more direct terms, W. James Popham says that "in general the concept of educational accountability involves the teacher's producing evidence regarding the quality of his or her teaching, usually in terms of what happens to pupils, then standing ready to be judged on the basis of that evidence."[19] On reading this definition, the professional teacher or administrator might reply, "Oh, if it were only that simple!"

But simplicity, Glen V. Glass reminds us, unfortunately is not a basic characteristic of the accountability issue. An accountable relationship involves three components: (1) *disclosure* concerning the service being sold, (2) *performance testing*, and (3) *redress* in the event of poor performance.[20] Glass furnishes us with a cogent explanation of why the problem of defining educational accountability is so complex:

There are at least six separate activities to which the term accountability is currently applied: (1) input-output analysis relating educational re-

sources to educational outcome; (2) school accredita-
tion programs; (3) program planning and budget-
ing systems; (4) behavioral statements of objectives
and objectives-referenced testing; (5) school voucher
systems; and (6) performance contracting. None of
these activities embodies all of the elements of an
accountability relationship. Each fails in one or
more respects to hold the schools truly accountable to
the public.[21]

Finally, any attempt to give a widely accepted definition to the term "accountability" is seriously complicated by the fact that there are at least two accountability movements. One is concerned about productivity, and the other focuses on responsiveness. The latter concern includes responsiveness to race, sex, ethnic group, social class, and age differences.

WHO IS ACCOUNTABLE FOR LEARNING?

When the accountability movement began, its leaders immediately focused on classroom teachers as the individuals most responsible for educational progress or the lack of it. But teachers and their representatives were not long in answering. The educational process, they claim, is much too complex to allow the singling out of a particular group for blame or praise. Wray, a vocational educator, ventured an opinion with which virtually all teachers agree:

Implied in the notion of delegation of authority
and the coinciding creation of accountability is the
recognition that needed resources must be commen-
surate with the authority delegated. Accountabil-
ity can work only if it is seen by all involved as a
two-way street. If vocational teachers are to be
accountable for X product, they should be entitled
to Y conditions (learning resources including
equipment, software, etc.).[22]

The truth of the matter is that classroom teachers are not responsible for buying materials, hiring consultants, assigning students, and initiating new curricula; yet these steps are necessary if a change in an existing educational program is to take place.

The majority of classroom teachers would strongly assert that administrators—superintendents, principals and counselors—are just as responsible for educational progress. Still

there are those who feel that administrators are too often held accountable for factors over which they have little direct control. As Joe Huber declares:

Clearly, we should emphasize less administrator
accountability. Administrators should remain
culpable for only those tasks legitimately within
their jurisdiction. Teachers are directly responsible
for learning and, where measurable, should become
accountable for results provided that other vari-
ables have been held constant or neutralized. In
this vein we should judge administrators account-
able for providing the setting and supervision
necessary to produce desired results.[23]

Administrators who agree with Huber are often those who advocate a merit system for teachers as a way to get greater progress in learning. In order for the merit program to work, a system must be designed which will redistribute existing funds and pay bonuses to outstanding teachers. Critics of merit systems are quick to claim that this suggestion would undermine the entire teaching-learning process, encouraging even the best teachers to coach or teach to the test. Still other critics say that if faced with the merit system of pay, some teachers would use a difficult measurement or test for the pre-test and an easy one for the post-test.

In defending themselves against accountability demands, some teachers say that the school is seldom, if ever, the foremost factor in the child's ability to learn. Socioeconomic level and physical and emotional factors deriving from family life are more important than school to the child's development. Most of what students learn depends on their experiences outside of school, the argument continues. Teachers and other school personnel have little control over these community conditions. Acknowledging that social and psychological conditions are influenced by nonschool environmental conditions, Thomas J. Quirk believes that "a premise that must be accepted by teachers if they are to be responsible to their charge is that the schools are responsible for educating the pupils, regardless of the setting in which the school exists."[24]

However, Quirk points out that even if teachers are accountable to some extent, it is a difficult matter to say exactly what they are accountable for. Teachers should not be held accountable for bringing each student up to

Chart 7. Teacher Evaluation

TEACHER: *Socrates*

Rating (high to low)
1 2 3 4 5

Comments

A. PERSONAL QUALIFICATIONS

	1	2	3	4	5	Comments
1. Personal appearance	☐	☐	☐	☐	☑	Dresses in an old sheet draped about his body.
2. Self-confidence	☐	☐	☐	☐	☑	Not sure of himself—always asking questions.
3. Use of English	☐	☐	☐	☑	☐	Speaks with a heavy Greek accent.
4. Adaptability	☐	☐	☐	☐	☑	Prone to suicide by poison when under duress.

B. CLASS MANAGEMENT

	1	2	3	4	5	Comments
1. Organization	☐	☐	☐	☐	☑	Does not keep a seating chart.
2. Room appearance	☐	☐	☐	☑	☐	Does not have eye-catching bulletin boards.
3. Utilization of supplies	☐	☐	☐	☐	☑	Does not use supplies.

C. TEACHER-PUPIL RELATIONSHIPS

	1	2	3	4	5	Comments
1. Tact and consideration	☐	☐	☐	☐	☑	Places student in embarrassing situation by asking questions.
2. Attitude of class	☐	☑	☐	☐	☐	Class is friendly.

D. TECHNIQUES OF TEACHING

	1	2	3	4	5	Comments
1. Daily preparation	☐	☐	☐	☐	☑	Does not keep daily lesson plans.
2. Attention to course of study	☐	☐	☑	☐	☐	Quite flexible—allows students to wander to different topics.
3. Knowledge of subject matter	☐	☐	☐	☐	☑	Does not know material—has to question pupils to gain knowledge.

E. PROFESSIONAL ATTITUDE

	1	2	3	4	5	Comments
1. Professional ethics	☐	☐	☐	☐	☑	Does not belong to professional association or PTA.
2. In-service training	☐	☐	☐	☐	☑	Complete failure here—has not even bothered to attend college.
3. Parent relationships.	☐	☐	☐	☐	☑	Needs to improve in this area—parents are trying to get rid of him.

RECOMMENDATION: *Does not have a place in Education. Should not be rehired.*

SOURCE: John Gauss, *Phi Delta Kappan*, January 1962, back cover. Reprinted by permission.

the national norm, he cautions. Nor should they be held responsible for enabling every student to grow one grade's equivalent for each ten months in school. Quirk also says that the argument that an individual teacher should be held accountable for the achievement gains of students in his or her classes makes less sense as we progress up the grade levels.

At this point the average parent may become understandably impatient and reply, "Well, if teachers aren't responsible for all these things, just what are they responsible for?" Few professional educators would disagree with Quirk's reply:

Individual teachers must be held accountable for knowing the instructional objectives of the school program, for developing professional standards of performance, for performing according to the specifications of the programs established in the schools, and for acting to help the school perform more efficiently in the education of pupils in the light of research findings. They should also be held accountable for providing accurate information about student performance, for participating in developing a coordinated plan to influence student development, and for implementing and resolving this plan throughout the school year. This is the promise of teacher accountability.[25]

Within recent years the concept of "joint accountability" has become attractive to many teachers and administrators. In formulating an accountability plan for New York City schools, Henry S. Dyer advocated that the entire staff be held accountable to the school board for school operations, while the board in turn should be held accountable for supplying appropriate resources and facilities for each school.[26] Dyer divides his model into four variables: (1) input (characteristics of the students), (2) educational process (activities in the school organized to bring about desirable changes), (3) surrounding conditions (school, home, and community), and (4) output (characteristics of students as they emerge from a particular phase of their schooling).

Any accountability plan which is to have a possibility of success must not cause classroom teachers to feel that they are academic isolates—marked beforehand to shoulder the blame of pupil failure, while administrators receive credit for positive results. Each person should be held accountable only for those things which he or she can influence. In the end, the school staff—teachers, administrators, supervisors, counselors, aides, clerical and custodial personnel—are responsible in the aggregate for the performances of students. Sensitive observers know that upon entering most schools they can tell almost immediately, before surveying any classroom, what kind of a learning environment each furnishes its students. Quirk's questions resound prophetically: "Don't the administrators, counselors, aides and specialists all contribute to the attitudes of pupils in school? Aren't pupil attitudes related to the pupil's ability to learn in school?"[27]

Some authorities have advocated that while no single group (teachers or administrators) should be held accountable for learning, each school should be matched with similar schools and the entire staff of the school be held collectively responsible. At first reading this recommendation makes a good deal more sense than a program which pits one teacher against another like gladiators in an academic arena, cheered on by parents and other spectators. Yet comparisons between schools, even those which are similar in the socioeconomic backgrounds of students, must be made with a great deal of caution. Indeed it is best not to make an annual report of the average achievement scores of students by school in the local newspaper. Usually these data are incomplete. A school is responsible not only for how well (or poorly) its students score in subject area tests, but also for how much they have improved socially over the years.

Involving Teachers and Administrators

As the critics of the Michigan accountability plan have testified, one of the reasons for the difficulty in its implementation has been that educators, particularly classroom teachers, were only superficially consulted when the plan was formulated. This was a major reason why many Detroit teachers went on strike in 1975. Fear of the accountability plan, more than the desire for higher salaries, was the major factor in the strike. The lesson was well taught by the striking teachers: "Fear of accountability will . . . be reduced if educators are involved individually and collectively at the preplanning, decision making, implementing, evaluating, reporting and follow-up stages."[28] The same point of view is echoed in the National Education Association (NEA) Resolution on Accountability:

The Association maintains that educational excellence for each child is the objective of the education system. The Association believes that educators can be accountable only to the degree that they share responsibility in educational decision-making and to the degree that other parties who share this responsibility—legislators, other government officials, school boards, parents, students, and taxpayers—are also held accountable.[29]

Classroom teachers can hardly be expected to know the details of a complex accountability plan unless they have had some hand in its development. Vocal teachers argue—and with considerable justification—that most accountability programs are initiated, developed, and implemented by administrators, and teacher involvement is minimal or nonexistent. Ironically, the measurable and desired outcomes sought almost always have to be achieved by classroom teachers. In some cases it does seem ludicrous for school board members and administrators, who usually have been out of the classroom for several years, to formulate accountability goals and objectives. It is wise to remember that the classroom teacher is not the only one who suffers from an accountability plan based on unreasonable objectives and criteria: administrators receive their share of the blame, too.

Many principals feel that delegated responsibilities and the authority to carry them out are not commensurate. There is still too much second-guessing of the principal's actions by board members and central office superiors. . . . The proliferation of often conflicting expectations of the principal held by citizens, parents, students, teachers, central office superiors, and board members makes the principal's accountability exceedingly complex, if not impossible to fulfill.[30]

No human being can be expected to feel a duty to carry out a directive or plan which he or she thinks of as alien, or even threatening. Program planners are belatedly realizing that the best way to instill a sense of responsibility in other people is to allow them to share in program design, implementation, and evaluation. Only through ownership is lasting commitment going to be a part of school accountability programs.

STATE-MANDATED ACCOUNTABILITY PLANS

In 1973 the Cooperative Accountability Project, a seven-state, Denver-based repository for accountability projects, predicted that by the end of 1976 approximately forty-five states would have mandated some type of competency-based education. To date most states have some type of accountability legislation on the books or in legislative committee. The following summaries are overviews of a sampling of accountability plans so far mandated by state legislatures.[31]

California

In 1972 the California state legislature passed the Stull Act, which outlined the evaluation procedures to be followed by all school districts in California. The act states: "It is the intent of the Legislature to establish a uniform system of evaluation and assessment of the performance of certificated personnel within each school district of the state. The system shall involve the development and adoption by each school district of objective evaluation guidelines."[32] The Stull Act requires each board of education in the state of California to:

1. establish standards of expected student progress in each subject and to indicate techniques that will be used to assess the extent of attainment of the standards.
2. assess the competence of certificated personnel as it relates to the attainment of the standards of expected progress.
3. assess the adequacy of performance with reference to the other duties normally assigned the individual.
4. assess the degree of effectiveness with which the individual is maintaining proper control and is preserving a suitable learning environment.

Two additional requirements of the act are that (1) the advice and participation of staff members in each school district must be obtained in the development of the evaluation procedures, and (2) procedures apply to all certificated personnel, including administrators and supervisors as well as teachers.

If an employee's performance is judged less than satisfactory, follow-up counseling is required for that employee. Further, such an employee has the right to file a written dissent to his or her evaluator. If any employee is dismissed for incompetence, such a dismissal must be based on evidence produced by and through the evaluation process. In addition the act requires that written guidelines be issued to all certificated personnel each year.

George B. Redfern points out the following unique aspects of the Stull Act:

It is a competency based program with a heavy weight on the learning outcomes of students. The competence of the educational practitioner is judged in relation to predetermined standards of progress. In other words, stress is on results rather than process. Student progress is the "name of the game." In addition, employees are evaluated on the quality of their performance on other assigned duties and on their ability to create and maintain suitable learning environments for those whom they teach or direct.[33]

There can be little doubt that the Stull Act has motivated action by individual school districts throughout the state of California to set standards of their own. For example, in 1975 the Los Angeles school board decided to require every high school student who wishes a regular diploma to pass a reading proficiency test.

Oregon

In 1971 the Oregon state legislature passed a Fair Dismissal Law which mandates the annual evaluation of instructional personnel in all school districts having an average daily membership of more than 500 students. The actual text of the law relating to evaluation says: "The district superintendent of every common and union high school district having an average daily membership . . . of more than 500 students in the district shall cause to have made at least annually an evaluation of performance for each teacher employed by the district to measure the teacher's development and growth in

the teaching profession. A form shall be prescribed by the State Board of Education and completed pursuant to rules adopted by the district school board." The law makes clear that administrators as well as teachers are to be evaluated.

It should be pointed out that under the law local school districts are given freedom to devise and implement their evaluation procedures. The form mandated by the Oregon Board of Education requires the local district evaluation to indicate five items: (1) whether the teacher has met, failed to meet or exceeded his or her performance goals and objectives during the evaluation period, and an explanation of the response, (2) areas in which the teacher has shown development and growth in the teaching profession, (3) areas in which teacher needs to demonstrate additional development and growth, with suggestions for improvement, (4) additional comments, and (5) recommendations of the supervisor.

The supervisor is provided four recommendation options: (1) renewal of contract or (2) nonrenewal of contract, (3) advancement in salary or (4) nonadvancement in salary. In addition to checking the appropriate options required by the state, the supervisor may make other recommendations.

It is significant that Oregon, unlike many other states, did not stop with identifying competency criteria for teachers. A few years after passage of the Fair Dismissal Law, Oregon drew up new graduation requirements for its high school students. The Oregon minimum graduation standards provide that local school districts may waive attendance requirements and develop 11-, 12-, or even 13-year school programs based on the individual needs of the student. The local school board, advised by administrators, staff, and community, has the power to decide whether to allow credit for community service, independent study, and work experience. Further, the local school district has the authority to award a certificate of competency to the nongraduate, so that the student may have a clear understanding of his or her competency levels and what will be required by way of demonstrated performance.

Each school board is to be the judge of whether an individual student has developed "survival-level competencies." It is not necessary that the student develop all such competencies within the school, but the school system is required to ascertain whether the student does possess them. The public schools are charged by the Oregon State Board of Education with developing three major areas of minimum survival-level competencies: personal development, social responsibility, and career development.

The State Board of Education has declared that *personal development*—the survival and growth of the student—must be based on developing the following competencies: (1) basic skills—reading, writing, computing, listening, speaking, and analyzing, (2) understanding of scientific and technological processes, (3) understanding of the principles involved to maintain a healthy mind and body, and (4) the skills to remain a lifelong learner.

Social responsibility (good citizenship) can be measured by the student's ability to cope responsibly (1) with local and state government as well as national government, (2) in personal interactions with the environment, (3) on the streets and highways, and (4) as a consumer of goods and services. If the student is to survive and advance in any career area (*career development*), he or she must develop (1) entry-level skills for chosen career fields, (2) good work habits and attitudes, (3) the ability to maintain good interpersonal relationships, and (4) the ability to make appropriate career decisions.

The plan was implemented with a great deal of planning and testing. Six pilot school districts formulated guidelines and model competency statements in the three areas, and in May 1973 a state-level workshop involving local project and State Department personnel was held to synthesize the six project reports and develop guidelines for local districts. Districts were required to file their implementation plans for State Board approval by July 1, 1974. The state did not intend that the development of survival competencies should monopolize a school's learning activities; districts were encouraged to strengthen or add programs in foreign languages, fine arts, humanities, and college preparatory programs.

South Dakota

In 1969 the state legislature of South Dakota passed a South Dakota Teachers Professional Practices Act. The act authorized the formation of a Professional Practices Commission whose duty is to develop standards, criteria, and procedures for evaluation and rating of teachers. The section of the Act which relates to evaluation states that the Professional Practices Commission:

... is hereby authorized and directed, prior to January 1, 1970, to enter into a comprehensive review and evaluation of, and to establish and promulgate standards, criteria, and procedures for the evaluation of the professional performance of classroom teachers in the elementary and secondary schools of the independent school districts of the state. The Commission may provide flexible ways by which to judge performance adapted to varying local communities and differences in individuals utilizing not only experience and academic achievements but also any other factors bearing on performance, while at the same time protecting against incompetence. [34]

The act also requires that every school adopt a policy statement on supervision and evaluation. The Commission later recommended to local school districts that they adopt an approach which stressed evaluation by objectives.

Washington

In 1970 the Washington state legislature passed a law which calls for the annual evaluation of all certificated employees. The law requires that:

... every board of directors in accordance with procedures provided in RCW 28.72.030 shall establish evaluative criteria and procedures for all certificated employees. Such procedures shall require not less than annual evaluation of all employees. New employees shall be evaluated within the first ninety calendar days of their employment. Every employee whose work is judged unsatisfactory shall be notified in writing of stated areas of deficiencies along with recommendations for improvement by February 1st of each year. A probationary period shall be established from February 1 to April 15th for the employee to demonstrate improvement. [35]

Specific evaluation procedures, however, are left to the individual school systems to formulate. Traditional evaluation processes are being used by most systems.

Virginia

In 1972 the Virginia State Board of Education was ordered by the Virginia state legislature to set up standards of quality for the school divisions of the state. Five standards were established for the evaluation of teachers: (1) humanizing instruction in the classroom, (2) provision for individual differences in the classroom, (3) utilization of available instructional materials and other resources appropriate to the needs of the pupil, (4) providing a favorable psychological environment for learning, and (5) evaluation of the progress of students.

The State Board of Education suggested further that such an evaluation be by objectives. The standard that applies to the evaluation of teachers and other employees says: "The principal and his staff shall provide for the cooperative evaluation of the teachers and other employees in his school. The evaluation of teachers shall be based on the standards for classroom planning and management."

In addition it is required that teachers and other employees participate in the development of the evaluation procedures. Central office personnel and principals also will be evaluated: "The superintendent and his staff shall provide for the cooperative evaluation of central office personnel and principals and shall provide assistance to principals in the cooperative evaluation of teachers and other school employees." [36]

Michigan

During the early 1970s the Michigan Department of Education was charged with the responsibility of establishing and implementing the Michigan Accountability System. The accountability model developed by the Department has six steps:

1. Involving persons from throughout the state in defining *common goals*.
2. Translating common goals into *objectives*.
3. *Assessing needs* in relation to objectives derived from the common goals.

4. *Testing alternative delivery systems*.
5. Fostering the development of *local evaluation capability*.
6. Using *feedback* from the accountability system to guide state and local educational policy. [37]

As a further means of improving education in the state of Michigan, the State School Aid Act provides the Chapter 3 Program—a performance-based compensatory education plan which gives special funds to school districts with heavy concentrations of low achievers. An extra $200 in student aid is provided these districts for each child identified as educationally deficient—essentially, in the bottom 15 per cent on achievements tests. If a school district does not show at least three-quarters of a year gain in individual achievement scores, it is penalized part of this money. When a school district finds itself in such a situation, it must develop a different delivery system, and students are tested again to discover what funds will go to that system.

During the 1973–1974 school year, the Michigan Education Association and the National Education Association commissioned a team of experts to assess the Michigan accountability plan. The experts agreed that the accountability model:

1. Stimulated public discussion of the goals of education and provided direction for state accountability efforts.
2. Involved educators throughout the state in efforts to develop objectives and resulted in pilot forms of objectives-referenced tests that some teachers found useful.
3. Created an aura of innovation and change. [38]

The extensive criticism of the plan by the team is important to any district or state planning to implement such a program. Among the major criticisms of the Michigan model by the NEA evaluation team:

1. The common goals were not clarified.
2. The objectives were developed by relatively few people and did not represent either a consensus or minimal objectives. (The team cited the case of Bloomfield Hills School District, whose students had traditionally done better on tests than students in most other

districts in Michigan. Less than fifty per cent of the students there passed some of the objectives on an objectives-referenced test, and in one case, less than thirty per cent of them passed some of the objectives.)

3. The assessment component was too narrow in scope to serve as a state needs assessment, and it was implemented on an every-pupil basis without technical or utility justification.

4. Overall, there was no clear evidence that state and local decision making was being served by the accountability model.

5. The broad educational goals were tested for in a few cognitive areas—on basic skills at a few grade levels.

6. The objectives developed were not adequately field-tested or validated—the items used to measure those objectives had good reliability but questionable and undemonstrated validity.

7. Development of both objectives and test items was so hurried that only minimal involvement of teachers was possible.

8. The tying of test-score results to funding . . . was both unfair and quite possibly harmful.

9. No evidence was found that ethnic membership or economic levels were considered as important variables in the development of the present forms of the assessment instruments. In addition, no evidence was available that the items comprising the reading test had been field-tested or validated for use with children whose sub-cultural language styles differ from those of middle-class ethnic majority Michigan children.

10. The accountability and assessment systems risk substituting state objectives and curricula for local ones.[39]

ACCOUNTABILITY MODELS

As noted earlier, at least six types of accountability activities are used in varying degrees throughout American schools: (1) input-output analysis relating educational resources to educational outcome, (2) school accreditation programs, (3) program planning and budgeting systems, (4) behavioral statements of instructional objectives and objectives testing, (5) school voucher systems, and (6) performance contracting.[40] Each activity has its own limitations.

Input-output analysis. This activity is similar to an industrial approach to production. All efforts are aimed at getting optimum results out of financial and human resources put into schools. Given the current methods of empirical evaluation, it is impossible to measure the unique contribution of a particular teacher or administrator to the education of the students.

Accreditation. Accrediting agencies–through the use of predetermined goals, institutional records, and on-site observations—are able to evaluate institutional effectiveness. Checklists, self-study guides, and interview schedules add to the objective nature of the evaluations. However, there is little community involvement in this activity. The clandestine nature of accreditation procedures do little to democratize the accountability process.

PPBS. Program planning and budgeting systems (PPBS) focus on (1) formulating goals, objectives, and learner skills, (2) designing programs to achieve stated objectives, (3) analyzing feasible alternatives, and (4) implementing a strategy. PPBS has been criticized for excessive paperwork, overemphasis on nonrelevant testing, and curricular rigidity.

Behavioral objectives. By stating instructional objectives in behavioral terms and measuring student achievement according to these objectives, educators overcome some of the objections to PPBS. Critics of behavioral objectives say that administrators and teachers can choose their objectives so that most of them are readily achievable. Two critical questions remain: Where should we focus our objectives? Which objectives are best?

Voucher system. Allowing students or their parents to shop around and select the school that seems to best meet their needs is at best a questionable program. Until schools clearly disclose to the public their goals, operation, and effectiveness in specific areas, the concept of a free marketplace in schooling is more a long-range than a short-range solution. Once the bugs are worked out, the voucher system is an excellent means of sorting out inferior and superior services.

Performance contracting. Perhaps performance contracting is an inappropriate model of accountability, for it shifts responsibility from public school personnel onto private contractors, who make a profit only if they succeed in bringing about significant learning improvements in students. To date there is no evidence to support a massive move to performance contracting. The same issues of accountability remain whether or not the prime contractors are public school personnel or private agency personnel.

MEASURING ACHIEVEMENT

The major opposition to the concept of accountability continues to come from teachers and their organizations. The NEA Research Division estimates that teachers with negative reactions to accountability outnumber those with positive views by eleven to one. David Selden, former President of the American Federation of Teachers (AFT), angrily charged that "accountability offers ready teacher scapegoats to amateur and professional school-haters," and people who advocate accountability approach the idea "with all the insight of an irate viewer 'fixing' a television set: Give it a kick and see what happens."[41] Terry Herndon, NEA Executive Secretary, speaking at an accountability conference in Denver, May, 1973, said, "We are now finding in some states that student achievement data are being reported on a classroom basis, so the teacher's professional destiny, his standing in the community, and his relationship with the pupils become directly linked to an assumed correlation between his student's achievement and his own performance."[42]

Teachers and administrators still ask why they should be singled out for blame when so many factors other than the classroom situation play a major role in the growth and development of the child. Faced with countless uncontrollable variables, teachers are understandably apprehensive about being held directly responsible for the results outlined in accountability programs. In many instances these uncontrollable variables are not taken into consideration when teachers' performances are evaluated. The educational process is a most complex one, and teachers often point out that performance contractors themselves explain their failures by saying that test scores are not raised easily and children are difficult to teach.

Teachers have vital statistical data to offer in their argument against taking sole responsibility for student failure. A series of studies undertaken by researchers between 1966 and 1972 led to the conclusion that only a small fraction of the independent variation in student achievement is explained by school variables, and only a small part of this variation is attributable to teachers. Benjamin Bloom estimates that "33 per cent of 'general learning as based on achievement indices' takes place between birth and age four, that another 17 per cent takes place between the ages of four and six, and still another 17 per cent takes place between the ages of six and nine."[43] Thus according to these statistics, the most important period for intellectual development and academic achievement takes place before the child enters school; subsequent learning is determined by what the child has already learned.

It is small wonder that research findings in schools implementing accountability have caused many writers to assert that at the present time the responsibility of each professional toward the attainment of accountability goals cannot be adequately determined. In fact the most we can reasonably do is to hold school personnel responsible for doing what they should do even without accountability—try to provide a top quality education for all children within the limits imposed by the abilities of the students and the conditions of the school.

A second major objection to accountability in American education is that many programs exhibit a lack of concern for the human side of teaching. Clearly a constant danger exists that accountability will cause educators to focus on a narrow group of cognitive learning elements. If this occurs, the affective domain is likely to be neglected.

There is also concern that accountability encourages instruction toward narrowly defined behaviors that are immediate target outcomes and presumably form the basis of assessment. Implied is the idea that only the things we can measure are important. This view toward education is simplistic and undesirable, and overlooks the fact that there are human transactions in the classroom that cannot easily be assessed but may be equally as important as learning how to count or read. When we deal with people in a learning environment, we are dealing with feelings, emotions, and spontaneous acts. The accountability system ignores the reality of human interaction, that much of teaching and learning has little to do with intended goals and quantified outcomes. [44]

Many of the present accountability systems focus on behavioral outcomes that appear destined to produce not intelligent students but automatons. Another criticism of the accountability concept is that it seeks to quantify a process about which we know very little: the process of learning.

Accountability usually presumes that the schools know how students learn. The trouble is, we have several competing ideas about learning that introduce further difficulty in relating learning to accountability. These competing ideas range from Bereiter and Englemann's drill approach, which tends to encourage student anxiety and discourage interpersonal relations, to Skinner, who breaks down learning into behavioral conditioning motivation and programmed learning, to the progressive philosophers who frown upon drill and behavioral conditions and treat learning in terms of developing the whole child and teaching broad concepts. Also, implicit in the idea of accountability is the expectation that available tests can measure learning with sufficient precision. . . . Moreover, many of the things we are concerned with, such as conceptual thinking, creativity, and humane learning, we do not know how to measure. [45]

Furthermore, the real consumers of education—the students—define a good teacher in terms often quite different from those used by educators. Students tend to measure teacher competency in personal terms: whether the teacher cares about them, how material is presented, the classroom atmosphere, and whether the course was relevant and enjoyable.

After all is said, the issue is not whether we should have accountability but what form it will take. A related question is how we will measure the results. Standardized achievement tests—instruments designed to distinguish between different learners—are not valid instruments for measuring the success of school accountability programs. Basically, achievement tests predict future academic success; they do not measure past school learnings.

Typical achievement tests—called norm-referenced tests—provide relatively reliable and valid infor-

mation regarding where the student stands in his test performance in relation to a large norm group. But when one seeks to learn whether a student has mastered specific skills and concepts during the year, the test does not include enough questions covering the material on which he was working to furnish a dependable answer to that question—or to hold someone accountable. . . . Criterion-referenced tests can be constructed for the competencies to be learned and thus we can include a much larger sample of appropriate questions. The trouble is, most of these test types are in the infancy stages of development. Questions concerning reliability and validity are only now being discussed in psychometric literature. [46]

As more educators warm to the task of being constructively critical of accountability programs, the flaws will be removed. Anything that will improve the quality of education for students is worth educators' time and energy. There is room for all types of educators in this struggle—young and old, male and female, experienced and inexperienced.

Intelligence Tests

There is a danger that student test scores will become the major determinant of success or failure in the schools. In addition to subject area test scores (see Chapter 7), intelligence test scores are also being considered in judging the effectiveness of curricula reforms. Great care must be taken to prevent IQ tests from being blown out of proportion to their value.

The IQ debate in America has been going on since 1908, when Henry H. Goddard brought the Binet test from France, translated it into English and—like Alfred Binet—standardized it for use with retarded children in need of special education. In 1916 Lewis Terman of Stanford University published an extended version of the Stanford-Binet test, which supposedly could be used for all children and adults. Terman borrowed from Wilhelm Stern of Germany the concept of the IQ—a ratio between mental age as measured by the test and chronological age. However, it wasn't until the 1920s that paper and pencil tests of intelligence were used on a large scale to identify the intellectual capacities of public school children.

It is important to note that neither Binet nor the psychologists who revised and updated the

Stanford-Binet in 1937 and 1960 ever said that the test directly measures intelligence. Rather, they maintained that they were measuring items that would give clues to an individual's potential for learning, which in turn is influenced by environmental factors. From the beginning, then, intelligence has been a vague hypothetical construct. IQ scores have never been, as some persons believe, evidence of innate superiority or inferiority.

The hypothetical construct of intelligence, an important concept in education, can be modified by changing environmental conditions. Generally, intelligence is a term that covers a person's capacities and potentialities in a wide range of tasks involving vocabulary, numbers, problem-solving, concepts, and so on. It is measured by standardized tests which usually involve several specific abilities, often with emphasis on verbal ability. A score on an intelligence test can be converted into an intelligence quotient, or IQ, which indicates the subject's relative standing in a population, independent of his or her age. The intelligence quotient reflects several abilities, not just one, and each is fairly complex. Any intelligence test should be used with care. As Anne Anastasi concluded:

Another area of psychology in which confusions regarding heredity and environment are likely to arise is that of interpretation of psychological tests. Persons unfamiliar with the way in which psychological tests are developed and used sometimes expect such tests to measure "native intelligence," "innate capacities," "hereditary predispositions of personality," and the like. By now it should be apparent that such expectations are sheer non-sense. . . .

Every psychological test measures a sample of the individual's behavior. No test provides any special devices or "tricks" for penetrating beyond behavior or for eliminating the subject's past experiences. All conditions influencing behavior will inevitably be reflected in test scores. Insofar as performance on a given test correlates with performance in other situations the test can serve in diagnosing or predicting behavior. It is in this sense only that a psychological test can be said to measure "capacity" or "potentiality." [47]

In other words, tests and other types of psychological measuring devices are merely instruments for describing in quantitative terms a *sample* of an individual's behavior. In many school systems, unfortunately, it is still customary to administer an intelligence test and to conclude that poor performance is caused simply by low native intelligence. But test performance is influenced by cultural factors as well, and efforts are being made to eliminate cultural bias from tests.

Cultural Biases

Every intelligence test is a sample of behavior and as such reflects factors that influence behavior. It should also be apparent that every intelligence test is constructed within a specific cultural framework and that it is evaluated and standardized against practical criteria dictated by a given culture.[48] One of the faults of intelligence tests is that most such tests assume not only that the test-takers share a common cultural background but also that they have all been equally prepared, either directly or indirectly, for the tasks imposed on them by the test.[49] This usually is not the case, however. Irving Lorge noted that differences are found among individuals and groups in terms of sex, age, education, geographic origin, and occupation of father.[50] Furthermore, most existing tests emphasize middle-class concepts and information.

Critics say that intelligence tests are unfair for the simple reasons that all test-takers are *not* of the same sex, age, and geographic origin; they do *not* all have equal levels of educational achievement; they do *not* have fathers in the same occupation; and they are *not* all members of the middle class, and, therefore, have *not* all been exposed to the commonalities assumed by test-makers. It is not surprising that we find the highest IQs among children in professional families and the lowest in children in semi-skilled and unskilled families. In addition, the argument continues, extreme environmental deprivation or a depressing emotional climate can restrict the growth of even the most intellectually alert, whereas optimal intellectual stimulation and climate can improve the measured development of those with little inherent capacity.

William Turnbull documented conspicuous depressions in test performance by students in Alabama and Georgia as compared to students in New York, Iowa, Nebraska, and California.[51] Even more strikingly apparent in his results was the fact that students from large communities in all geographic regions were much more facile verbally than those from small communities, although in mathematical ability their superiority was slight, and in terms of ability to answer common-sense science questions, the two groups were equal. In a similar study of social and cultural differences and mental abilities, Gordon Fifer concluded that we have strong evidence of differential patterns of mental abilities and responses among different ethnic groups.[52] An anecdote from S. A. Kendrick succinctly illustrates this point.

Many years ago I administered an intelligence test to an adult Negro man who had spent most of his life on a cotton plantation in the South. One question on the test was, "If you found a sealed, stamped, addressed envelope on the street, what would you do with it?" His answer, "I wouldn't mess with it, boss," was not allowed for credit by the test manual, which preferred, "I would mail it," or something equivalent. It is by no means clear whether his answer was unintelligent, unsophisticated, uncooperative, or shrewdly adaptive. The poor fit between the man and the test-maker does not raise the examinee's score; it merely casts doubt on the entire evaluative enterprise.[53]

Even though numerous studies have measured extreme cultural differences and their effects on producing culturally biased test results, many school personnel using tests fail to profit from such findings. Instead they treat test scores as absolute determinations about individuals or groups. Recently, test-makers as well as test-users have become increasingly aware of the multiplicity of factors related to test performances. Individual abilities level off within a narrowly defined range as children grow older. Thus most older children and adults show little change in test performance over a period of years. This stabilization or leveling off is mainly a function of motivational and personality factors rather than any inherent qualities. Children who succeed at particular tasks are apt to maintain these skills, whereas those who are inept at them are not apt to improve. Poor readers, for example, are not likely to pursue reading exercises consciously in order to improve their skill. Rather

they will avoid or, as much as possible, abandon the task.

Arthur R. Jensen and William Shockley support a generally unacceptable view of intelligence tests: that they are valid measures of the genetic inferiority of nonwhites in general and Blacks in particular. This view has been countered by numerous behavioral scientists.[54] It is likely that the debate over genetics and intelligence will continue for a long time. Both opponents and proponents tend to become unyielding when discussing the issue.

Attempts To Eliminate Cultural Biases

For about fifty years social scientists have been revising (1) the meaning of intelligence, (2) the various tests and procedures for its estimation, and (3) the implications of the evidence from tests of intelligence. Attempts to produce unbiased tests that measure intellectual capacity rather than intelligence *per se* usually center on eliminating all individual or group differences by adding items. For example, since there are differences in verbal ability between male and female test-takers, one way to overcome the verbal superiority of females is by adding a sufficient amount of numerical reasoning items to make the average total score of males equal to that of females. The rationale is "no difference, ergo, no bias." Another method is to reduce group differences by subtracting items. This approach essentially removes the items that favor a particular group. Tests produced by subtraction, like those produced by addition, are not supposed to reflect the impact of sex, status, or culture on test performance.

Some psychometricians have attempted to produce tests that are culture-free. Beginning with the Army Beta Test, many efforts have been made to remove the differences attributable to culture, although none of these has been completely successful. Some tests that attempt to be culture-free are Dodd's International Group Mental Test, Cattell's Culture-Free Intelligence Test, Spearman's Visual Perception Test, the Multi-Mental Non-Language Test, and Rulon's Semantic Test of Intelligence. Each of these instruments attempts to measure intellectual performance by the manipulation of objects, pictured designs, or numbers that require "intelligent" behaviors of perception, selection, generalization, and organization. Each test is limited by the fact that different cultural experiences with the test materials can significantly influence test results. "Culture-common" would more accurately fit these tests than "culture-free," since performances on such tests may be free from cultural differences, but not from cultural influences.

A pertinent question that might be asked about the elimination of test items differentiating subgroups of the population is, "Where should we stop?" Should we rule out items showing socio-economic differences, sex differences, ethnic minority group differences, and educational differences? If we proceed to rule out all these, what will be left? The solution is to reduce biases in tests of intelligence, and in the interim—if they must be used—to use them with full knowledge that a wide range of differences may be produced as a result of physical endowment and cultural opportunities. This, then, is using tests as but one of many diagnostic tools to tell us where a particular child is in reference to others. When tests are supplemented with student and parent conferences, home visits, academic grades, and so forth, school personnel are better able to assist students in improving. Tests used in this manner become means to improving academic performances and not ends in themselves. Tests, in other words, should not be used by teachers as instruments for predetermining a student's interest. The more effective teachers use them as but one of many diagnostic tools.

Several issues remain unresolved in the competency debate. (1) What competencies should be required? (2) How will competencies be measured? (3) How many minimum standards should be met? (4) When should students be tested? (5) What should be done with incompetent students? (6) What should be done with students who master all competencies before finishing twelfth grade?

Testing students to determine if they have mastered certain competencies is only half the educational task. The other half consists of providing deficient students with effective coursework assistance. In short, once identified, these students need remedial teachers, smaller classes, individually-oriented instructional materials, and an extended education. It is also clear that they do not need more of the same kind of instruction that resulted in their deficiencies. Nor do they need to be pushed out of school without adequate survival skills. Successful competency-based curricula will cost the taxpayers considerably more money for education than they were willing to spend before the current national focus on basic learning skills.

Knowledgeable school officials are concerned that unless federal and state governments provide considerably more funds for schools, monies distributed for federally mandated programs will continue to be inadequate. Programs for teaching basic skills, mainstreaming handicapped students, providing bilingual instruction, assisting migrant children, and desegregating schools are but a few examples of underfunded activities which have the potential to significantly improve the quality of education for disadvantaged students. When we add to this list built-in school operational expenditures for equipment, maintenance, salaries and fringe benefits, the growing frustration of school boards and administrators is even more understandable.

LOOKING YOURSELF IN THE EYE

This exercise is designed to help you be more introspective. As you respond to the directions given below, try to be a good listener. (1) Avoid being unduly judgmental; (2) Listen carefully in order to better understand yourself; (3) Do not stray from the topic; (4) Be open and honest with yourself, and say "I" or "me" when talking about yourself.

Directions. **Respond orally to the following questions.**

1. What you think other people dislike most about you?

2. What you think other people like most about you?

3. What do you dislike most about you?

4. What do you like best about you?

5. Tell about the worst thing that ever happened to you in school.

6. Tell about the best thing that happened to you in school.

7. Complete this sentence: "It made me feel good when . . . "

8. Complete this sentence: "I made someone feel bad when I . . . "

9. If you could change one thing, what would it be?

10. What do you value most? Why?

11. Describe in as much detail as you can remember the face of someone who you love very much.

ADDITIONAL READINGS

Alberts, David S. *A Plan for Measuring the Performance of Social Programs.* New York, Praeger, 1970.

Browder, Lesley H., et al. *Developing an Educationally Accountable Program.* Berkeley, Cal., McCutchan, 1973.

Davies, Ivor K. *Competency Based Learning: Technology Management and Design.* New York, McGraw-Hill, 1973.

De Mont, Bill and Roger De Mont. *Accountability: An Action Model for the Public Schools.* Homewood, Ill, ETC, 1975.

Doll, Ronald C. *Curriculum Improvement: Decision Making and Process,* 3d ed. Boston, Allyn & Bacon, 1974.

Greenbaum, William. *Educational Progress.* New York, McGraw-Hill, 1977.

Hayman, John L., Jr. and Rodney Napier. *Evaluation in the Schools: A Human Process of Renewal.* Monterey, Cal., Brooks/Cole, 1975.

Leight, Robert L., ed. *Philosophers Speak on Accountability in Education.* Danville, Ill., Interstate, 1973.

Lessinger, Leon M. and Ralph W. Tyler, eds. *Accountability in Education.* Worthington, Ohio, Charles Jones, 1971.

Trump, J. Lloyd and Delmas F. Miller. *School Curriculum Improvement: Challenges, Humanism, Accountability,* 2d ed. Boston, Allyn & Bacon, 1973.

Wynne, Edward. *The Politics of School Accountability: Public Information About Public Schools.* Berkeley, Cal., McCutchan, 1972.

NOTES

1. Plato, *The Apology*, in *The Republic and Other Works* (trans. by Benjamin Jowett, New York, Doubleday, 1960), 452–453.

2. Friedrich Heer, quoted in Allan Ornstein, Daniel U. Levine, and Doxey A. Wilkerson (eds.), *Reforming Metropolitan Schools* (Pacific Palisades, Cal., Goodyear, 1975), 76.

3. Mohammed A. A. Shami, Martin Hershkowitz, and Khalida K. Shami, "Dimensions of Accountability," *NASSP Bulletin*, 58 (September, 1974), 14.

4. Joe Huber, "Acountability: Dangers in Misapplication," *NASSP Bulletin*, 58 (September, 1974), 14.

5. George Gallup, "Fifth Annual Gallup Poll of Public Attitudes Toward Education," quoted in Huber, *Ibid.*

6. George B. Redfern, "Accountability: Echoes from the Field," *National Elementary Principal*, 55 (March/April, 1976), 42.

7. Leon Lessinger, "It's Time for 'Accountability' in Education," *Nation's Business* (August, 1971), 54.

8. Richard L. Fairley, "Accountability's New Test," in Ornstein et al., *Reforming Metropolitan Schools*, 80.

9. *Ibid.*

10. "Chronicle of Race, Sex, and Schools—September-October, 1974," *Integrated Education*, 13 (January/February, 1975), 8.

11. "Chronicle of Race, Sex, and Schools—November-December, 1974," *Integrated Education*, 13 (March/April, 1975), 26.

12. "Chronicle of Race, Sex, and Schools—March-April, 1975," *Integrated Education*, 13 (July/August, 1975), 28.

13. "Chronicle of Race, Sex, and Schools—January-February, 1976," *Integrated Education*, 14 (May/June, 1976), 47–48.

14. Allan C. Ornstein and Harriet Talmage, "The Promise and Politics of Accountability," *NASSP Bulletin*, 58 (March, 1974), 11.

15. Ralph D. Wray, "The Accountor/Accountee Syndrome," *American Vocational Journal*, 5 (March, 1976), 34.

16. William C. Miller, "Accountabiity Demands Involvement," *Educational Leadership*, 29 (April, 1972), 613.

17. Myron Lieberman, "An Overview of Accountability," *Phi Delta Kappan*, 51 (December, 1970), 194.

18. Leon Lessinger, quoted in Shami et al., "Dimensions," 2.

19. W. James Popham, "The New World of Accountability: In the Classroom," *NASSP Bulletin*, 56 (May, 1972), 26.

20. Glen V. Glass, "The Many Faces of Educational Accountability," *Phi Delta Kappan*, 53 (June, 1972), 637.

21. *Ibid.*

22. Wray, "Syndrome," 35.

23. Charles W. Humes II, "Post-Accountability Blues," *Peabody Journal of Education*, 53 (January, 1976), 85.

24. Thomas J. Quirk, "Teacher Accountability: Negative and Positive," *NASSP Bulletin*, 57 (December, 1973), 35–36.

25. *Ibid.*, 40.

26. Henry S. Dyer, "Toward Objective Criteria of Professional Accountability in the Schools of New York City," *Phi Delta Kappan*, 51 (December, 1970), 206–211.

27. Quirk, "Teacher Accountability," 37–38.

28. Huber, "Accountability," 16.

29. NEA Resolution (73–25) on Accountability.

30. Redfern, "Accountability," 44.

31. See George B. Redfern, "Legally Mandated Evaluation," *National Elementary Principal*, 52 (February, 1973), 45–50.

32. *Evaluation and Assessment of Performance of Certified Employees*, The Stull Act, Assembly Bill No. 293, chapter 361, 635.

33. Redfern, "Legally Mandated Evaluation," 46.

34. "Standards, Criteria, and Procedures for Evaluation of and Rating of Teachers," *South Dakota Teachers Professional Practices Act*. 1969.

35. *Washington Laws of 1969*, chapter 34, section 11.

36. *Standards of Quality and Objectives for Public Schools in Virginia*, 1972–74, General Assembly of Virginia, 1972.

37. Ernest K. House, Wendell Rivers, and Daniel L. Stufflebeam, "An Assessment of the Michigan Accountability System," *Phi Delta Kappan*, 56 (June, 1974) 664.

38. See Ernest K. House, Wendell Rivers, and Daniel L. Stufflebeam, "An Assessment of the Michigan accountability System," *Phi Delta Kappan*, 55 (June, 1974), 669.

39. *Ibid.*

40. Glass, "The Many Faces," 637–638.

41. David Selden, quoted in Ornstein et al., *Reforming Metropolitan Schools*, 84.

42. Terry Herndon, quoted in Ernest R. House, "The Price of Productivity: Who Pays?" *Today's Education*, 62 (September/October, 1973), 68.

43. Benjamin Bloom, *Stability and Change in Human Characteristics* (New York, John Wiley & Sons, 1964), 68, 110.

Christopher Jencks concluded that a school's output depends largely on the characteristics of its students rather than its teachers, school budget, or administrative policy. See Jencks, *Inequality: A Reassessment of the Effect of Family and Schooling in America* (New York, Basic Books, 1972.)

44. Ornstein et al., *Reforming Metropolitan Schools*, 92.

45. *Ibid.*, 91–92.

46. Ornstein and Talmage "The Promise," 14.

47. Anne Anastasi, *Differential Psychology*, 3d ed. (New York, Macmillan, 1958), 82.

48. Anne Anastasi (ed.), *Testing Problems in Perspective* (Washington, D. C., American Council on Education, 1966), 453–457.

49. S. A. Kendrick, "College Board Scores and Cultural Bias," *College Board Review*, 57 (Winter, 1964), 7–9.

50. Irving Lorge, "Difference or Bias in Tests of Intelligence," in Anastasi (ed.), *op. cit.*, pp. 465–471.

51. William Turnbull, "Influence of Cultural Background on Predictive Test Score," in Anastasi (ed.), *Testing Problems*, 458–464.

52. Gordon Fifer, "Social Class and Cultural Group Differences in Diverse Mental Abilities," in Anastasi (ed.) *Testing Problems*, 481–490.

53. Kendrick, "College Board Scores."

54. For a review of the controversy surrounding IQ and minority groups see Arthur R. Jensen, "How Much Can We Boost IQ and Scholastic Achievement?" *Harvard Educational Review*, 39 (Winter, 1969), 1–123; William Shockley, "Dysgenics, Geneticity, Raceology: A Challenge to the Intellectual Responsibility of Educators," *Phi Delta Kappan*, 53 (January, 1972), 297–312; and the other articles in the Spring, 1969 issue of the *Harvard Educational Review*. In the May 1977 issue of *Developmental Psychology* Jensen acknowledged that environment can be traced to a progressive decline in the IQ scores of poor Black children.

PART III
HUMANIZING
AMERICAN
EDUCATION

ALL
THEY DO
IS RUN AWAY *

Kathy and Armin Beck

* Reprinted from *Civil Rights Digest*, Vol. 5, No. 2., August 1972, pp. 34–39.

The problem of the "daily racial insult," not a thing of the past, is in fact one which is the cause for much concern among some teachers and some students, particularly in desegregated schools. When black and white children get together at school, it is often under the eye of a watchful teacher who is alert to prevent or curb racial slurs or innuendos. But what if you're neither black nor white, and the teacher, in observing a restless day in the classroom of a desegregated school, says, "They're really behaving like wild Indians today, aren't they?" If you're an Indian child, what do you say now? Chances are, nothing. You go off confused, and probably cry a little, but there's nothing for a child to say. If it's brought to her attention, the teacher says something like, "I didn't mean anything personal; she's too sensitive!" Surely, those are words that have been heard before, in a different racial context. But, as many teachers have discovered in their concern over black-white relationships, they themselves are sometimes not quite sensitive enough.

We are white parents who have children in a northern school system that deliberately desegregated itself several years ago. No court involvement; just heavy community pressure. In our family, besides several white children, are a 6-year-old daughter, an Asian (Filipino) child, an 8-year-old American Indian (Chippewa) girl, and a black child, a 4-year-old boy. All are in school except our youngest son, who starts next year.

Our expected school concerns initially were with his enrollment in school because of his black skin. That may yet come. As it turned out, however, we were too complacent about our two daughters. They each are subject to almost daily racial insults from other children in the school—on the bus, on the playground, in halls, and in classrooms. Because of that, we have observed what happens in such situations.

Our Oriental child, a beautiful, bright, and delicate first grader, came home one day and said, "Why do they always run away from people like me?"

"Do you mean from little first grade girls?"

"No, they don't like Chinese-Japanese people. I don't know why."

"People don't call you names any more, do they?"

"Yes, they still do, but not all the time. Now they run away from me. I try to be nice and friendly, but all they do is run away. Why?"

Another day our youngest daughter came home from school and said, "They don't like Chinese or Japanese children; I'm Filipino, but they don't know that. Maybe if I tell them, they'll be friends." We fear, however, that once they know she is an Asian-American, they may be confused for awhile, but that won't stop the racial cruelty that brings on tears and incredulousness. The stereotypes are too deeply rooted.

Our daughters were in kindergarten when we first noticed negative actions and feelings leveled toward them. For example, as the youngest got on the bus, children would start to chant, "Ching-ching Chinaman, sitting on a fence," and she, of course, would shed some tears, if not there, then later in the safety of her own room. We have always maintained a good relationship with the school teachers and other officials. And when these incidents were brought to their attention, they were very apologetic, while vowing to develop more programs on Orientals.

Not satisfied with that answer, we mentioned the sort of cruel behavior our girls had experienced to an Oriental acquaintance of ours who also has children a bit older. Her view was, "Of course we recognize this type of situation. The same thing happens to our children. At first, we tried to do something about it in the school, but that only made matters worse. So we've stopped trying to change the school. We go to the Parent Teacher Association (PTA), we do everything we can to support them privately, but not publicly. We hope you do the same."

That discussion curtailed our vocal show of concern very much. Here were parents who had concluded that the hurts resulting from drawing attention to their children's dilemma are more painful for the children than the hurts their children receive from racial insults. Here we were, parents who had seen some progress made both in city government and in schools toward equality of educational opportunity, and who believed that this progress came about by striking at any institutions which allow lethargy and the comfort of the status quo to the detriment of its people. And we were being told to "cool it." We did, therefore, refrain from further discussion with the school officials concerning incidents involving our children. We bowed to the superior experience and knowledge of the Oriental parents; we knew very little about race relations in a nonblack, nonwhite context.

We do know now, however, that our relative silence has not improved the relationships, but we do not know if it would have been better if we had insistently raised the issue. Since these earlier discussions with our friends, we have been given a different point of view by several Orientals in the teaching profession. Their feeling is that stereotypes must be exposed regardless of the possible discomfort. Only in this way can they be dealt with by most of us. There will still be unkind remarks, but it will eventually be only the exception as practiced by many through ignorance rather than malice.

Another question we have tried to deal with is who "they" are. The girls always say "They don't like . . . ," and then finish in behavioral terms. Who are "they"? In this situation, at least, "they" are both black and white children, indiscriminately separate or together.

Could it be that black children, most of whom know so well firsthand what the "daily racial insult" is all about, have assumed some of the same insensitivity toward other minorities as many white persons have historically possessed? Could it be that children who are neither white nor black are really viewed as less acceptable, less desirable as play and work friends, or even as having less humanity or intelligence? What is the arena in which such behavior can flourish?

The public elementary school which our children attend is an exceptionally good one; perhaps one of the best in the country. It is a "laboratory" school with an outstanding biracial staff and administration, with the most exciting individualized learning programs imaginable. Our children love school with the exception of the unpleasant instances mentioned. Yet, there is the nagging thought in our minds that it should be better; that there should be a humanness about interactions that would transcend both skin color and relationships between black and white children; that the hundreds of hours over the past few years which the staff have given to the examination of their own and their students' interpersonal racial relations have not been enough. What is the problem and how could it be solved?

As many PTAs do, last year brochures were sent home urging people to attend the meetings at school. Good programs were planned; and, in my opinion, officials of the PTA are the finest people a school could have. Nevertheless, here is a description of one of the brochures. There were pictured caricatures of four children of different races, each one saying something to let the parents know that the children wanted them to attend. The white child had long hair, a nice smile, and said, "Yeah, yeah, yeah," the type of words that were often heard on the pop music stations in our area: white popular music. The black child had an Afro haircut, a nice smile, and had his fist raised in a gentle-appearing way, while he said, "Right on brother." These two caricatures were supportive of positive aspects of the culture. In all probability, neither black people nor white people would feel demeaned by these pictures. The third child was an Indian. Although he, too, had a nice smile, he wore an Indian headdress and said, "Ugh!" The Oriental child's spoken words were, "Ah soo!"

Many white children in the school have long hair and at least when they listen to their transistors, snap their fingers and sing "Yeah, yeah, yeah".

Many black children have Afros, raise their fist on occasion, and say "Right on".

These two are caricatures, but not harmful ones. But no Indian children that I know of come to school wearing a headdress, and certainly by the time they're in kindergarten, they can say more than "Ugh". A demeaning caricature, to say the least. And no Oriental children we know try to communicate with their parents, teachers, or classmates by saying "Ah soo!"

All four pictures were stereotypes with an element of truth in them. but two at least gave a positive supportive image to children. The other two were caricatures of relics of days long past.

When this was brought to the attention of the PTA, the response was one of mortification and personal apology to us. Friendly as it is, however, apology is not the answer. Somehow, we felt relationships must get beyond skin color and get into those of a common humanity.

At the height of our daughters' problems this year, a day concluded with tears and fighting. Our oldest daughter, who has already learned to take pride in being Indian, is physically what her sister is not. She plays football as well as any other second-grader and better than most. She is of necessity a good physical and ideological defender of her sister. This particular day several children were picking at our youngest daughter after school. Our oldest daughter along with her brother (an older white child in our family) intervened, and the children turned on her. By the time she got home, she had been punched and thoroughly frightened.

The problem lay again, at least partly, in the fact that the girls are neither white nor black. The school has programs and a curriculum in Indian lore, where several classes build tepees, make clothes that Indians used to wear, weave beads, and have a speaker from the nearby Indian Center. But this doesn't help an Indian child today, any more than it has helped the Sioux as a nation to regain some of the wealth and beauty of the Black Hills for their own use.

Our hunch, however, is that as the school children build the tepees and listen to the lore, they are, in their own minds, making relics of the Indians attending schools and living on reservations. Descendents of each racial group or nationality who came to this country over the past hundreds of years live in the present and in the United States. We are not viewed, for example, as running around in armor today and running people through with lances; or in wooden shoes strenuously scrubbing the roofs of our houses. Those are interesting parts of ethnic history to be read with excitement and pride. But in relating to one another, we should see ourselves as we are today, in a world of which we are now a part. The newly developing black studies programs seek to give pride in black history, while also providing a forum for black persons to define their place in today's modern world. But we still tend to hang onto a view of the Indians, Orientals, or Spanish people as we thought they were long ago and far away. It is good and important that our schools attempt to make the historical perspectives of these peoples more accurate. But we also must learn about people as they are today in order to know them.

If the schools are going to teach about reservation life, and they should, they must be willing to go beyond the romance of the peace pipe. They should examine the poverty, racism, and ethnocentrism to which today's Indians are subjected, and they must examine the people who do the subjecting. The fact, for example, that only white people are allowed to live in the towns on the Rosebud Reservation in South Dakota should be examined. It is not enough to praise the Indians for feeding Pilgrim settlers. The Indians' attitude toward early settlement in this country must be taken into account today. They willingly shared land and goods with the white men and tried to teach them to cooperate with nature instead of working to subdue it.

With that kind of understanding in the schools, white Americans will no longer look upon Indians as in the past but in modern, realistic terms. Thus, Indians of today can begin to cope with the ethnocentric behavior toward them simply because this behavior will lessen.

The school's reaction to the problems encountered by our younger daughter has been somewhat the same. "We'll take up and emphasize the study of China or Japan, their history, and their people." But our daughter isn't Chinese, she's Filipino. She doesn't live in the Orient, she lives here. We want the school to study Asian cultures, just as we want them to study African cultures and even white Anglo-Saxon Protestant cultures. However, it should not do so because the teachers think it, by itself, can help the children. It can't. It will make them cultural exhibits, perhaps, or relics, but it will not help them to be treated as flesh and blood human beings. The schools' responses, not only where we live, but generally, have been inadequate to the problem.

Is there anything that can be done about these problems? Should they be attacked? Or should we say of the children, "You're too sensitive. This is what life is all about. You'll get used to it?" We think there should be more than that. We think these are serious problems that are damaging to all children, and that schools and parents alike should be about the business of resolving them. This is especially true of desegregated schools because the writers, at least, and our colleagues and friends believe that successful participation in American life means that both the oppressor and the oppressed be aware of what's happening to them. This awareness comes about not through sublimation of the problem, but through active discussion. In fact, it will probably be necessary, at least for awhile, for parents to insist that the schools become concerned about human relations and that they work with teachers in this endeavor.

Second, in-service training programs should be broadened and extended. We note a serious deficiency developing in desegregated schools around the country. Some faculties feel that they are now experts in race relationships, having worked in desegregated schools and probably having had some in-service programs in race or human relations. Since they are now allegedly experts, the school feels that such in-service workshops can be considerably reduced or dispensed with.

We do not agree. The programs of the workshops we examined have never gone beyond black and white relationships into questions concerning people who are neither black nor white. Further, examination of the condition and treatment of nonblack-nonwhite people in all of North America has almost never been undertaken in the schools. There is a rapidly emerging wealth of material from which to draw, particularly for information and understanding about the Indian, the Puerto Rican, and Mexican-American conditions, and their relationships with the majority group.

Third, based on the sensitivity and understandings gained from such study, in-school curriculum, from pre-school through high school, should be modified and developed to bring it into line with the reality of the conditions of all people. It is no longer acceptable for Spanish-Americans to be discussed as the "manana" people; nor Oriental-Americans as quaint; nor Indian-Americans as pets or savages. They are not past or present relics; they are living today. The curriculum and other school activities should reflect this fact.

Programs in these areas should be developed by the "experts" in these fields. School personnel are surely competent at creating devices and activities in social studies or cultural studies, but just as surely the subject matter to be included belongs to the real experts. In art, for example, we turn to those artists who have taken an interest in education for their input on course content. In Jewish Studies, we turn for information to the rabbis who are devoting their lives to the understanding of Judaism and the fostering of Jewish Studies. So, in Spanish-American heritage we need content from the experts:

Spanish-American community leaders. In Indian-American heritage, we need communications with Indian leaders, both on and off the reservations. These people know about their cultural heritage as anthropologists and others outside the culture never can. They know what will give a child inner pride in his racial or ethnic background. They also know as no one else can what their heritage gave and can continue to give to the mosaic of American culture.

Again, using material from the in-service training programs mentioned earlier, community programs should be developed. They are probably best done through the PTAs, the local media, and such organizations as the League of Women Voters and the NAACP. These groups assumed considerable leadership in the examination of black-white relationships in the past, especially in preparation for desegregated schools. There is no reason why they cannot do the same now, given a real concern on the part of the schools.

A final caveat is in order here. Neither schools nor parents should use this new-found concern as an excuse to diminish the black-white problem. Too much is undone in that area to begin to ignore it now. What we are hoping for, therefore, is not a replacement of concern from black to nonblack, but an addition. Concerns should be tailored to individual schools, even to an individual child.

So that no child suffers the experience of "the daily racial slur," it is indeed time that "they stop running away."

15.
BEFORE
DESCHOOLING

In recent years the educational system in America has received a great deal of criticism—not exclusively from so-called radicals, but from responsible and respected educators and researchers, whose "values are conservative, upholding the virtues of honest, meaningful work, of community and family, and of civil human relationships."[1]

HISTORICAL OVERVIEW

The most severe critics of the existing educational system are, to use Charles Silberman's words, "part of a tradition several centuries old." Peter Schrag studied the "new critics" and concludes, "In the free-for-all of educational commentary, where the half-life of ideas is pitifully short, the ashes of fallen gods often materialize in the bodies of new critics."[2] Schrag traced the ideological lineage of contemporary critics—such as Paul Goodman, John Holt, Jules Henry and Edgar Z. Friedenberg—back through the works of John Dewey and Maria Montessori to the philosophies of Thomas Jefferson, Jean Jacques Rousseau, and Johann H. Pestalozzi.

Norman R. Bernier and Jack E. Williams verify the philosophical descendance of American education, while adding to the list of positive forces the influence of men such as

Ralph Waldo Emerson, Henry David Thoreau, and even the early Christians, i.e., Jesus and his disciples.[3] All of these philosophers share in common a respect for childhood and faith in the natural capabilities of children. Matthew 18:1-6 says that the child "is the greatest in the kingdom of heaven," and "whoso shall receive one such little child in my name receiveth me. But whoso shall offend one of these little ones . . . it were better for him that a millstone were hanged about his neck, and that he were drowned in the depth of the sea." This belief has been restated in different forms throughout history. In the eighteenth century Rousseau reiterated this principle: "The age of gaiety is spent amid tears, punishments, threats and slavery. . . . Man! Be humane! It is your first duty to all ages, to all conditions, to every creature with which man has to deal. What wisdom can there be without humanity?"[4]

In the nineteenth century Emerson advanced the idea that the child's individuality and particular variety of genius should not be violated by "the worn weeks of your [adults'] language and opinions." Emerson humorously, yet pointedly, concluded: "I suffer whenever I see the common sight of a parent or senior imposing his opinion and way of thinking and being on a young soul to which they are totally unfit. You are trying to make that man another you. One's enough."[5] Many critics say a similar process is affecting nonwhite children: they are being made into Anglo-Saxons.

In recent times Ronald D. Laing affirmed a fundamental regard for children in saying that "each child is a new being, a potential prophet,

---

*This chapter is based on portions of Ronald Berman's unpublished doctoral dissertation, "A Critical Analysis of Deschooling As a Solution to the Crisis in American Education," Norman, University of Oklahoma, 1975. Revised and reprinted with his permission.

a new spiritual prince, a new spark of light precipitated into the outer darkness."[6] Although the contemporary critics have been categorized by a variety of labels (such as progressivists, romantics, and transcendentalists), their philosophical commonality—among themselves as well as their predecessors—further revolves around a respect for children and the humanistic belief in the value, dignity, and creative potential of human existence. Schrag explains: "In many respects the new critics are more interested in the processes of growing up, in learning and experience, than they are in the formalities of educational programs, the design of curricula, or the planning of administrative conveniences. They share with Dewey a faith in the healthy capabilities of children and with Rousseau a belief that 'everything is good as it comes from the hands of the creator.'"[7]

Schrag further states that the new critics share the view that the existing institutions of education are limited in meeting the individual's needs for creative expression and self-realization. The contemporary critics, like their predecessors, view the existing educational system as an extension of a hostile society, designed to limit individual free expression in the interest of promoting conformity and preserving the societal status quo. Although many persons would argue that preservation of the status quo is precisely what the schools should promote, the humanistic critics disagree, suggesting that although it is important to teach certain fundamental skills, it is equally important to be concerned with other aspects of human existence. This position was quite adequately articulated by Emerson, who said:

It [education] does not make us brave or free. We teach boys to be such men as we are. We do not teach them to aspire to be all they can. We do not give them a training as if we believed in their noble nature. We scarce educate their bodies. We do not train the eye and the hand. We exercise their understandings to the apprehension and comparison of some facts, to a skill in numbers, in other words, we aim to make accountants, attorneys, engineers; but not to make able, earnest, greathearted men. The great object of Education should be commensurate with the object of life. It should be a moral one, to teach self-trust; to inspire the youthful man with an interest in himself; with a curiosity touching his own nature; to acquaint him with resources of his mind, and to teach him that there is all his strength.[8]

Emerson's criticism of his society and its system of education is equally appropriate to the criticism to be found in contemporary literature. Contemporary humanists restate Emerson's contentions that while the educational system may be functional in training children to adapt to the society as it currently exists, it does not teach self-trust or inspire children with a curiosity touching their own nature. The contemporary critics also argue that the current educational system is an antiquated, bureaucratic process which values administrative expediency over individual creativity and self-realization.

American children learn to recite facts and figures or to perform certain functions which will enable them to adapt at least minimally to the existing sexist and racist-oriented society. What the humanistic critics are objecting to is the inability of the educational system to meet the total needs of its students—nonwhite and white alike. The contemporary critics are questioning the very foundations on which formal education is based, and some critics are even calling for the development of a new educational process.

OUR SCHOOLS ARE IN TROUBLE

It has been suggested that the public school system as it currently exists is beyond hope. It has been suggested further that we must look beyond desegregating and reforming the schools, since past efforts have been for the most part futile. In fact a growing number of responsible educational thinkers have called for deschooling—the discontinuation of the existing system of schooling—as a first step toward a positive solution to the problem of educating all children.

Roy P. Fairfield says that it takes no seer to know that the schools are in deep crisis:

The student movement and the wide unrest on university and college campuses as well as in the high schools are symptomatic of the underlying sickness. Something is the matter with our educational system. And something drastic must be done. There is a crisis.[9]

An abundance of data supports Fairfield's contentions. The existing public school system has been, and is being, attacked on all sides. Well-known psychologist and educator Abraham H. Maslow, noting the ways in which schools tend to stifle students' creativity and limit rather than enhance human potential said, "Our conventional education looks mighty sick."[10]

Carl Rogers stated that public education in this country is the "most rigid, outdated, bureaucratic, incompetent institution in our culture."[11] Other researchers suggest that the schools, operating on antiquated traditions contrary to the realities of learning and creativity, are most successful in teaching mainly affluent white children either how to be conformists or how to play the academic game, thus enabling them to fit in the broader societal game of conformity and material consumption. Researchers, including Richard L. Berkman, have noted that the schools serve as a primary agent in teaching young citizens subservience to societal authority.[12] Traditionally, the courts have supported the schools in their function as a disciplinary agent. Furthermore, racial segregation compounds problems confronting school boards and their employees. In addition the schools have been criticized for creating and perpetuating problems relating to sex roles.

Also included in the criticism of contemporary education is the charge that the American university is a rigid and bureaucratic institution which, operating under the guise of academic freedom, functions on the principles of compartmentalism, sequentialism, essentialism, and credentialism. Another important criticism is that the existing educational system overemphasizes verbal abilities and rote memorization of irrelevant, externally-imposed subject matter, almost to the denial and exclusion of individual experience and self-motivated learning. According to Aldous Huxley, the result is that the existing educational system "turns out students of the natural sciences who are completely unaware of Nature as the primary fact of experience," and it "inflicts upon the world students of the humanities who know nothing of humanity, their own or anyone else's."[13] If this was true for the white students Huxley observed, it is also true for nonwhites whom he did not study.

The inadequacies of the educational system have in recent years led to a growing discontent which has manifested itself in widespread student reaction, including sit-ins, boycotts, vandalism, and violence as means of protest. A comprehensive study on student unrest, published by the National School Public Relations Association, hypothesized that the student unrest of the late 1960s was a general and long-range phenomenon, and that it was bound to happen.[14] Another educator, Bernard McKenna, reiterated the observation that student unrest would most likely persist until the problems of dull and irrelevant curriculum content, nonmotivating teaching methods, poor human relations between teachers and students, and lack of student involvement in the decision-making process were substantially resolved.[15]

Recent studies have confirmed the trend toward increased student unrest in the schools. In 1974 Jack Slater reported that despite efforts at curtailing student unrest (such as employing additional security personnel), vandalism and violence have become almost the norm in many of the nation's urban and suburban schools.[16] But schools are not the only culprits. Fairfield points out that it is almost impossible to watch television, listen to the radio, or even talk to one's neighbor "without encountering educational questions which threaten to overwhelm both sense and reason."[17] Regarding this point, Theodore Brameld cited headlines featured on the covers of mass-circulated magazines: "Angry Teachers—Why They Will Strike Three Hundred Times This School Year" and "Students Against the World."[18] Brameld suggested that these headlines denote the unrest that is permeating educational events.

Deficiencies in Basic Skills

As noted in earlier chapters, data has been accumulated which supports the contention that the schools are failing in their efforts to teach fundamental skills. The National Assessment of Educational Progress (NAEP) recently published its findings on a national sampling of Americans from four age groups (9, 13, 17, and 26 to 35) and their performance on a series of exercises and standardized tests.

The results were rather disquieting, since they reveal deficiencies in certain basic skills. For example the writing report (released in February 1972) revealed that in the writing exercises used in the study:

Nine-year-olds in America showed almost no mastery of basic writing mechanics.

By age 17, a considerable number still had difficulties with spelling, word choice and other skills.

In all four age groups, the writers usually chose fairly simple sentence structures and the most common punctuation marks.

Among young adults there was a strong reluctance to write at all—29 per cent of those who agreed to take part in the overall assessment refused to attempt the writing exercise. [19]

Furthermore, an essay exercise was given and graded by English teachers and scholars. Four separate analyses were made, including one by computer, and the results show a growing deficiency in all four age groups in terms of inadequate sentence structure and paragraphing, spelling and punctuation errors, and improper vocabulary usage. Deficiencies were also found in basic reading skills in all of the four age groups.

More than 40 per cent of the 17-year-olds failed to discern that a passage about Helen Keller's life, referring in almost every sentence to particular years, was organized as a chronological narrative, rather than a diary, flashback, an interview, or an eyewitness account.

Fewer than one in four 13-year-olds understood that Shakespeare in his 29th sonnet used "deaf Heaven" to refer to a God who does not hear. On the same question, more than half the 17-year-olds answered incorrectly.

Nearly half the 13-year-olds and more than 25 per cent of the 17-year-olds (and this group is only one year away from voting age) were unable to read a passage containing two conflicting statements and arrive at the conclusion that one of them has to be wrong.

More than a third of the nine-year-olds could not read two dogfood labels and determine correctly which contained more protein.

More than 15 per cent of the adults and 17-year-olds, one-third of the 13-year-olds, and nearly two-thirds of the nine-year-olds had difficulty

reading and then answering questions about a common daily TV schedule. [20]

In terms of basic social studies knowledge, a comparison of the NAEP results with satisfactory performance levels (as rated by a panel of nine social studies experts selected by the National Council of Social Studies) "shows a consistently lower level of understanding than most of the panel members would consider satisfactory." [21] For example, according to the panel, at least 80 per cent of the young citizens in America should know the procedure for nominating Presidential candidates; however, only about two out of five actually do. The data in mathematics has been analyzed in cooperation with the National Council of Teachers of Mathematics, and the results and interpretations are also discouraging. [22]

Based on the data thus far obtained by the NAEP, there is a great deal of information to support the contention that the schools are educational wastelands, not only in their inability to release creative energy but also in their failure to teach basic skills. This is especially true for lower-class children.

So why not implement deschooling?

PHILOSOPHICAL FOUNDATIONS OF DESCHOOLING

Deschooling is a philosophy of liberation; that is, liberation from the constraints of the existing system of institutionalized education. Contemporary deschooling advocates such as Ivan Illich and John Holt share, with eighteenth-century French romanticist Jean Jacques Rousseau and nineteenth-century American transcendentalists Ralph Waldo Emerson and Henry David Thoreau, the belief that society's institutionalization of education tends to limit rather than enhance the individual's experience, learning, and self-reliance. Rousseau asserted the belief that institutions corrupt human nature and enslave the minds of men and women. Thoreau, who agreed with Rousseau in his disdain for institutions, suggested that the process of formalized education is artificial and inept, since students are made to study materials which are irrelevant to their real lives. Emerson noted that institutions of education, in their quest for expediency and order, use ineffective methodologies which limit the students' experience and violate their genius.

This function of opening and feeding the human mind is not to be fulfilled by any mechanical or military method; is not to be trusted to any skill less large than nature itself. . . . It is curious how perverse and intermeddling we are, and what vast pains and cost we incur to do wrong. . . . In education our common sense fails us and we are continually trying costly machinery against nature, in patent schools and academies and in great colleges and universities . . . we sacrifice the genius of the pupil, the unknown possibilities of his nature, to a neat and safe uniformity. . . . Our modes of education aim to expedite, to save labor; to do for the masses what cannot be done reverently, one by one: say rather the whole world is needed for the tuition of each pupil.[23]

Emerson's statements embody the crux of the deschooling philosophy: the contention that schools subjugate the individual's unique creativity and intelligence to a predesigned expedient process which does not necessarily respond to the student's interests or needs. Deschooling is thus a quest to disestablish an educational system which values its own existence and its systematic perpetuation more than its individual students. Proponents of deschooling contend that schools teach children to rely on teachers, instruction, and schooling for their learning, rather than on their own experience and individual capabilities to find and internalize information.[24]

Schools, Illich contends, not only make people dependent on schooling for their learning, but also condition people to become overly dependent on institutions in other aspects of their lives. Self-reliance, individual competence, and personal values are replaced with institutional dependency. In other words people become overly dependent on schools for their learning, churches for their religion, doctors for their health, and law enforcement for their moral conduct.

To counteract this condition Illich has suggested that the deschooling of society could foreshadow a human liberation movement which would make people less dependent on institutions, and more reliant on their own energies and creative capabilities. Another fundamental aspect of the deschooling philosophy is the contention that learning is a personal activity which best occurs casually, spontaneously, and without external coercion or manipulation. Others may enhance one's learning, but they do not have the right to dictate how, when, and what another individual is to learn.

In essence the deschooling philosophy is founded on the idea that the existing process of schooling, based on authoritarian principles and rigid institutionalized values and rules, is beyond reformation and should be discontinued. This is because the system limits rather than enhances the individual's intellectual, creative, and humanistic growth and development. Inherent in the deschooling philosophy is the idea that the individual, as well as society, would benefit from the discontinuation of the existing schooling process and the creation of more imaginative, flexible, and humanistic approaches to education. This is where a great misunderstanding arises regarding the deschooling philosophy. Although the deschooling philosophy is one of negation, inasmuch as it condemns the existing system, it also has a positive side: it points toward the development of a broader, more convivial educational consciousness which places more emphasis on the individual human being.

The most significant strength of the deschooling philosophy is that it focuses attention on the limitations of the existing educational system and points out that through imagination and innovation, more effective and humanistic approaches to education can be developed. The concept of deschooling is, in a sense, misleading. Although deschooling means discontinuation of the schools as they currently exist, another premise of the philosophy is that other opportunities for learning be developed and made available and that students have a choice among a variety of educational alternatives. By a deschooled society, its proponents do not mean a society without any arrangements and resources for learning.[25]

New Resources and Networks

What deschooling advocates do propose is the development of a new set of resources and networks which offer educational opportunity based on the student's own motivation and interest. Development of libraries as learning centers offering various educational programs is one example. The development of community media centers offering access to films, records, books, videotape equipment, computers, and microscopes is another. The creation of skill development centers wherein people could learn fundamental skills such as reading, writing, basic mathematics, typing, and so forth is a possibility. Another is computer centers that direct people to educational resources, teachers, and peers with common learning interests. Educational programs built around agencies and businesses in the community, such as museums, factories, airports, laboratories, zoos, and farms could also provide opportunities for learning. The possibilities are endless, limited only by the imaginations and energies of innovative educators. As John Holt has said, "In sum, a deschooled society would be a society in which everyone should have the widest and freest possible choice to learn, whether in school or in some altogether different way."[26]

The deschooling philosophy broadens our conceptualization of education by suggesting ways in which a wide range of noncompulsory opportunities for learning may be developed. These would extend beyond the confines of the school, so that students would have the freedom to choose among many alternatives how and what they will learn. "Schools without walls" and "free schools" grew out of this quest.

In such a system it is quite possible that the amount and rate of learning would increase and discipline problems would decrease, since the motivation for learning would come from within the students themselves. Stated another way, since all learning would be centered on the interests, needs, and motivations of the students, both students and teachers would be freed from the tedium and struggle of having to deal with uninteresting or irrelevant material. Furthermore, in a noncompulsory educational system, teachers (whether authoritarian or democratic) would have as their students only those people who were attracted by their particular teaching style; thus theoretically the learning situation would be perpetually compatible with the needs of both teacher and student.

At this point some readers might suggest that the deschooling philosophy is unrealistic.

It is possible to argue that if education were not compulsory or externally motivated, most people would simply not pursue learning on their own, and given the inhumane nature of most classrooms, it is unlikely that many children would voluntarily subject themselves to schooling or deschooling. Whether one agrees or disagrees with the deschooling philosophy, it is nevertheless important in that it presents a challenge to develop a broader, more humanistic educational consciousness which encourages more flexibility, creativity, self-reliance, self-direction, and freedom of individual choice in learning.

SOCIAL REALITIES

Although the deschooling philosophy might serve as a theoretical challenge for a change in our educational consciousness, it does not at this time represent a realistic solution to the educational crisis of children. A fundamental weakness of deschooling is that the prescription is too extreme for the ills of the American educational system. Deschooling society because there are problems in the existing system would be very much like buying a new automobile because the battery in one's present car is dead. Whereas the deschooling philosophy is theoretical and tentative, the existing educational system is established, functional, and convenient. It is unrealistic to think that it would be discontinued.

Social Function of Schools

The existing system of education is a vital part of the American culture and economy, and it serves our society in a variety of ways, albeit many of them negative. One fundamental factor which must be considered, for example, is the role schools play in providing children with what Carl Bereiter has referred to as "a place to be."[27] That is, schools furnish our society with a place where young people may interact with peers, form friendships, and channel their energies into various forms of work and play. The schools currently provide a functional environment wherein some students can express their individuality and demonstrate their creativity, ability, and talents by excelling in educational and recreational activities. Although in many cases the schools might limit the students' choice of activities and options for self-expression, there are at present few other institutions in our society to which most children would have access and which allow even an opportunity for such educational, creative, and social involvement.

In providing an opportunity for peer interaction, the schools are especially important to those families living in rural areas or in urban neighborhoods devoid of suitable playmates for their children. In socioeconomically deprived areas, the positive function of schools becomes particularly apparent. Two researchers have stated that "in our rapidly polarizing society, school may be the only place where economically disadvantaged people can find friendship, acceptance, and recognition."[28] Furthermore, in many instances (particularly in economically disadvantaged areas) the schools provide a more secure and stable environment in comparison to the home. "Schools are drastic contrasts to most lower-class homes. They are relatively clean, whereas slums are dirty. Schools are sanctuaries of silence, slums are noisy. Schools smell fairly pleasant, slums stink."[29]

A deschooled society would have to undertake the monumental task of providing extensive realistic alternatives for social interaction and educational opportunity which would be readily accessible to all students who would otherwise be served in this context by the schools. At the present time, a definitive, practical plan for the nonchaotic discontinuation of schools and the establishment of an alternative educational system has yet to be designed.

Even if the schools were discontinued and alternative opportunities for learning, social interaction and creative involvement (such as skill development centers, educational media centers, educational programs in libraries and museums, and recreation centers) were established in a deschooled society, these resource centers would be noncompulsory. There would be no guarantee that people would bother to use these various facilities.[30] Many parents and educators agree with Philip W. Jackson that in our present-day society, most people would not be self-motivated to participate actively in a noncompulsory educational system. "Doubtlessly, there are children who, freed from the formal demands of schools and with a minimum of adult guidance,

would set about the laborious task of educating themselves. But whether all or most children, if pressed to do so, would turn out to be such self-motivated learners is indeed doubtful."[31]

A great many people in our society share the view that the student's "stormy genius," as Emerson said, requires direction and guidance in various educational, recreational, and social activities.[32] Some schools are attempting to provide such direction and leadership. The deschooling philosophy is highly theoretical, and in fact it may be mistaken in its assumption that students will pursue learning on their own without any external motivation. Thus, to build on Bertrand Russell's words, in spite of the evils of most existing educational institutions, the schools are currently providing our society with extremely functional settings wherein many people have the opportunity to pursue meaningful social relationships and to exercise their creative and intellectual talents and abilities.[33]

In addition to its other services, the schools perform several highly-valued nonpedagogic functions as well, such as "relieving the home, controlling delinquency, and keeping kids from competing for jobs."[34] Everett Reimer observed that custodial care is an important function of the schools in modern society.

Custodial care is now so universally provided by schools that it is hard to remember earlier arrangements. Children must, of course, be cared for—if they are children, that is, and not just young members of the community taking part in its normal productive and social affairs. Most youngsters still get along without special care, all over the world, in the tribal, peasant and urban dwellings of the poor. It is only the mothers who have been freed from the drudgery of food production and preparation who find it necessary to turn the care of their children over to others. This is because of other differences between modern and traditional societies. Older children are taken out of the house by the school, fathers go to work, and grandparents and other members of the extended family are left behind in rural or older urban settlements. Were it not for the school, child care in the modern family would fall exclusively upon the mother. Schools thus help to liberate the modern woman. Women clearly need . . . the liberation schools provide. . . . Child care costs money, and although schools provide it relatively cheaply, this is where most of the school budget goes.[35]

Therefore, another weakness of the de-schooling philosophy is that it diminishes the high value contemporary society places on providing custodial care for millions of students enrolled in our nation's schools, while offering no realistic, detailed plan for the development of alternative agencies which would equal or surpass the competency of the schools in providing such custodial care.

Even if educators or their critics wanted to set children free to learn on their own without the confines of a school and all the restrictions it implies, there is ample reason to believe that parents and other adults in our society would not stand for it. Like it or not, our schools presently perform a custodial function as well as an educational one. Parents, particularly those of young children, simply do not want their offspring to be unsupervised during much of the day. We could, of course, substitute compulsory day-care centers or neighborhood clubs for compulsory schools, but, when we consider such alternatives, they begin to look not at all that different from what used to go on in the empty schoolhouse down the block. [36]

Economic Function of Schools

The relevance of the deschooling philosophy is further diminished by the fact that the existing educational system is an elaborately established, extremely important part of the American economy. Peter Drucker concluded that education has become our largest single expenditure and is the cost center of the American economy. [37] Education is by far the largest item in the budget of state and local governments, [38] which spend approximately 40 per cent of their total fiscal budgets on education. Additional documentation of the monumental importance of the existing educational system as an economic enterprise may be found on a national scale as well. The American Enterprise Institute for Public Policy Research reported that the United States spends almost as much on education as do all of the world's other nations combined.

In sheer magnitude, America's educational establishment is truly something to behold. In 1971, one-third of all Americans were directly connected with educational institutions: 61 million as students and 6.5 million as employees. Public and private schools and colleges were scheduled to spend $85 billion in the school year 1971-1972, nearly eight per cent of our Gross National Product (GNP). This is approximately as much as the combined educational expenditures of all the other countries on earth. [39]

The purpose for citing these various statistics is simply to show that in addition to being agencies of socialization, custodial care, and education, the schools function equally (if not more so) as an important economic enterprise. Merle Curti said it well: "The school structure itself has been much less the expression of humanitarianism and democracy and much more the result of, and dependent upon, dominant economic interests than is commonly supposed." [40] The middle class is comprised of a large number of educators. Here again, whereas the deschooling philosophy is unconventional, theoretical, and by no means universally endorsed, the existing educational system is established, functional, and highly valued by the decision makers in our culture.

ABSENCE OF A VIABLE MODEL

What, then, are the most profound limitations of the deschooling concept? It is a highly Utopian theory which is largely incompatible with modern-day socio-economic realities. First, as has been shown, a tremendous economic and cultural investment has been made in the existing educational system, and it is most unlikely that deschooling will become a social reality in the near or even distant future. Second, even if there were substantial interest and support for a deschooled society, an elaborate and comprehensive plan for the relatively smooth transition from the existing system to a deschooled society would need to be developed. At this time, no such plan exists. Given the nature of the decision-making process, it is not likely that nonwhite interests would be adequately represented even if such a plan were developed. There is no real guarantee that a deschooled society would be any better for nonwhite Americans than the existing educational system. [41]

Ardent deschooling proponent Ivan Illich offers living proof that the deschooling philosophy is an extremely Utopian theory which has limited relevance to the practicalities and realities of present-day life. While propounding theories of socio-economic revolution and radical educational reform, Illich once directed an "innovative" school in Cuernavaca, Mexico. Unfortunately, traditional educational methodology and classroom structure were used in teaching the various subjects.

Howard Oxmon studied Illich's "school of deschooling," which was called the Centro Intercultural de Documentacion (CIDOC), and was disappointed in its curriculum and methods of operation. The CIDOC catalog listed over one hundred courses. Course offerings included such diverse subjects as Mexican history, encounter games, and nontraditional educational alternatives. The most heavily enrolled courses were those which taught Spanish.[42]

In 1975 all entering CIDOC students paid a registration fee of $100. Students enrolled in the Spanish language courses paid $60 per week for that program, and students who wished to participate in ICLAS (several freewheeling courses strangely dubbed Institute Contemporary for Latin American Studies) were required to pay an additional sum of $8 per week if they were not in the language program. Students who had paid their ICLAS fees were entitled to attend a special lecture program, called El Circlo, held between 11 o'clock and noon each day. During these periods instructors presented lectures designed to encourage students to enroll in their classes. If after attending El Circlo, students wanted to pursue the subject further, they then paid a fee to the instructor (generally ranging from $10 to $30 for a two-week course) and met at regularly scheduled times.

Ozman reported that while Illich has written extensively about the need for radical educational reform, the actual program at CIDOC was highly structured, very formal, and in fact was not very much different from a traditional university.

The language program . . . is highly structured with students attending set classes, repeating drills, memorizing dialogues and changing teachers at the sound of a bell. . . . Not only within the language courses, but throughout the school in general, there is an aura of strictness and control.

Many students who expected . . . a free and easy Summerhillian environment are surprised at the rules and regulations that exist. Students cannot . . . wander into lectures without paying, nor can they attend the [El Circlo] without both a registration fee and an "iclas" fee. . . . Students complained that [the language courses] consisted mostly of rote learning and that the teachers frequently become exasperated with the slowness of students in learning Spanish.

Although one can understand why the language course is so formalized, he would not expect it of the ICLAS program. . . . Yet ICLAS is not as free as one might expect . . . ICLAS courses tend to end up as either lecture or limited discussion courses.[43]

In pointing out the contradiction which seemed to exist between Illich's well-intentioned, radical educational philosophy and the realities of life, Ozman presented additional information to suggest that the deschooling philosophy has limited relevance to the educational crisis. Despite the imaginative visions of the deschooling philosophy, schooling in the United States (as well as in Cuernavaca, Mexico) appears to be a continuing fact of life. This is not to suggest that these conditions should not be abated. It is the cure, not the disease, that is in question. Jackson offers these somber thoughts:

Meanwhile, back in the classroom, there is a lot of work to be done. Our inner-city schools, particularly high schools, are disaster areas; too many of our students, particularly our adolescents, are being turned off by their school experience; the bureaucratic structure of our schools . . . is more abrasive than it needs to be; our graded system is too rigid and requires loosening up; our teacher certification laws are shamefully archaic and prevent many good people from taking their place in the classroom; our schools do need to be linked more imaginatively to the communities they serve.[44]

Improving the quality of education for children requires more than throwing the teaching and administrative rascals out. Humanistic education, along with its human relations techniques, appears to be the sturdiest bridge between what we currently have and what we ought to have in education for children.

CONVERSATION IN RETROSPECT

Think about the last important conversation that you had with a friend and left feeling either pleased or unhappy. Take three or four minutes and try to recollect what happened. Only completely candid and honest answers will be helpful. Check all responses that apply to the conversation.

1. The other person did the following things which made it difficult for me to speak freely:

☐ appeared to know more than I did.
☐ acted superior.
☐ tried to put words into my mouth.
☐ asked me personal questions.
☐ appeared to disapprove of me.
☐ tried to tell me my feelings weren't real.
☐ gave me "good advice."
☐ threatened me by his/her manner.
☐ didn't appear interested in me.
☐ was tense and fidgety.
☐ didn't pay attention.
☐ stared at me.
☐ didn't look me in the eye.
☐ cut me off.
☐ took notes.
☐ didn't smile.
☐ didn't clarify.
☐ allowed uncomfortable pauses in the conversation.
☐ disagreed with me frequently.
☐ gave no indication he/she understood.
☐ made suggestions before he/she understood.
☐ acted as if he/she understood when he/she didn't.

2. The other person did the following things which made it easier for me to speak freely:

☐ appeared to be an equal.
☐ seemed to have an open mind.
☐ let me say what I felt and meant.
☐ didn't probe with personal questions.
☐ acted as if he/she approved of me as a person.
☐ acted as if he/she trusted me.
☐ shared his/her honest thoughts and feelings with me.
☐ was not threatening or judgmental.
☐ was calm and relaxed.
☐ paid close attention.
☐ looked me in the eye occasionally.
☐ let me finish before answering.
☐ gave no "good advice."
☐ acted friendly.
☐ didn't cut me off.
☐ let me know he/she understood me.
☐ understood before he disagreed.
☐ asked helpful questions.
☐ paused, but not too long.

3. Think about your own behavior and check the appropriate responses above.

4. What have you learned about your conversation style?

ADDITIONAL READINGS

Blaze, Wayne et al. *Guide to Alternative Colleges and Universities.* Boston, Beacon Press, 1974.

Bowles, Samuel and Herbert Gintis. *Schooling in Capitalist America: Educational Reforms and Contradictions of Economic Life.* New York, Basic Books, 1976.

Curle, Adam. *Education for Liberation.* New York, John Wiley & Sons, 1973.

Eliot, Charles W. *Educational Reform.* New York, Arno Press, 1969.

Fantini, Mario D. *Public Schools of Choice.* New York, Simon and Schuster, 1974.

Glasser, William. *Schools Without Failure.* New York, Harper & Row, 1969.

Goodlad, John I. et al. *The Conventional and the Alternative in Education.* Berkeley, Cal., McCutchan, 1975.

Goodman, Paul. *Compulsory Mis-Education.* New York, Horizon Press, 1964.

Hawkins, Donald E. and Dennis A. Vinton. *The Environmental Classroom.* Englewood Cliffs, N.J., Prentice-Hall, 1973.

Hertzberg, Alvin and Edward F. Stone. *Schools are for Children: An American Approach to the Open Classroom.* New York, Schoken Books, 1971.

Holt, John. *Instead of Education: Ways to Help People do Things Better.* New York, Dutton, 1976.

Katzman, Martin T. *The Political Economy of Urban Schools.* Cambridge, Mass., Harvard University Press, 1971.

Kozol, Jonathan. *Free Schools.* Boston, Houghton Mifflin, 1972.

Ornstein, Allan C. et al. *Reforming Metropolitan Schools.* Pacific Palisades, Cal., Goodyear, 1975.

Rathbone, Charles H., ed. *Open Education: The Informal Classroom.* New York, Citation Press, 1971.

Reimer, Everett W. *School Is Dead: Alternatives in Education.* Garden City, N.Y., Doubleday, 1971.

Richmond, William K. *The Free School.* London, Methuen, 1973.

Rist, Ray C., ed. *Restructuring American Education: Innovations and Alternatives.* New York, E. P. Dutton, 1972.

Spring, Joel H. *Education and the Rise of the Corporate State.* Boston, Beacon Press, 1972.

Thelen, Herbert A. *Education and the Human Quest.* New York, Harper & Row, 1960.

Weber, Lillian. *The English Infant School and Informal Education.* Englewood Cliffs, N.J., Prentice-Hall, 1971.

NOTES

1. Ralph Waldo Emerson, "Education," in Mark Van Doren (ed.), *The Portable Emerson* (New York, Viking Press, 1946), 254–55.

2. Peter Schrag, "Education's Romantic Critics," *Saturday Review* (February 18, 1967), 80.

3. Norman R. Bernier and Jack E. William, *Beyond Beliefs: Ideological Foundations of American Education* (Englewood Cliffs, N. J., Prentice-Hall, 1973), 128–87.

4. Jean Jacques Rousseau, "Emile," in R. C. Archer (ed.), *Emile, Julie and Other Writings* (Woodbury, N.Y., Barron's Educational Series, 1964), 88–89.

5. Emerson, "Education," 256.

6. Ronald D. Laing, *The Politics of Experience* (New York, Ballantine Books, 1967), 30.

7. Schrag, "Critics."

8. Emerson, "Education," 254–55.

9. Roy P. Fairfield (ed.), *Humanistic Frontiers in American Education* (Englewood Cliffs, N. J., Prentice-Hall, 1971), 2.

10. Abraham H. Maslow, *The Farther Reaches of Human Nature* (New York, Viking Press, 1971), 170.

11. "Carl Rogers Joins the Ranks of Radical Critics of the Public Schools," *Phi Delta Kappan*, 51 (January, 1970), 294.

12. Richard L. Berkman, "Students in Court: Free Speech and the Functions of Schooling in America," *Harvard Educational Review*, 40 (November, 1970), 567–594.

13. Aldous Huxley, *The Doors of Perception* (New York, Harper & Row, 1956), 74, 77.

14. *High School Student Unrest* (Washington, D. C., National School Public Relations Association, 1969), 1.

15. Bernard McKenna, "Student Unrest: Some Causes and Cures," *Bulletin of the National Association of Secondary School Principals*, 55 (February, 1971), 54.

16. Jack Slater, "Death of a High School," *Phi Delta Kappan*, 56 (December, 1974), 251–54.

17. *Ibid.*

18. Theodore Brameld, "Illusions and Disillusions in American Education," *Phi Delta Kappan*, 50 (December, 1968), 202.

19. "Writing Test Reveals Many Lack Basic Skills," *School and Community*, 59 (October, 1972), 11.

20. Hope Justis, "Status Report on Reading," *Education Digest*, 38 (December, 1972), 12.

21. Robert Crane, "What Should They Know?"

Compact, 8 (Summer, 1974), 13.

22. Wayne H. Martin and James W. Wilson, "The Status of National Assessment in Mathematics," *Arithmetic Teacher*, 21 (January, 1974), 49.

23. Emerson, "Education," 257, 263, 267.

24. Ivan Illich, *Deschooling Society* (New York, Harper & Row, 1974), 56–57.

25. John Holt, *Freedom and Beyond* (New York, E.P. Dutton, 1972), 189.

26. *Ibid.*, 190.

27. Carl Bereiter, *Must We Educate?* (Englewood Cliffs, N. J., Prentice-Hall, 1973), 82.

28. George Henderson and Robert F. Bibens, *Teachers Should Care: Social Perspectives of Teaching* (New York, Harper & Row, 1970), 89.

29. *Ibid.*, 108.

30. Bereiter, *Must We Educate?* 70.

31. Phillip W. Jackson, "Farewell to Schools—No!," in Henry Ehlers (ed.), *Crucial Issues in Education* (New York, Holt, Rinehart, & Winston, 1973), 210.

32. Emerson, "Education," 258–59.

33. Bertrand Russell, *Education and the Good Life* (New York, Liveright, 1926), 7.

34. Paul Goodman, *Growing Up Absurd* (New York, Random House, 1960), 33.

35. Everett Reimer, *School is Dead: Alternatives in Education* (Garden City, N. Y., Doubleday, 1970), 33–34.

36. Jackson, "Farewell," 206.

37. Peter Drucker, "School Around the Bend," *Psychology Today*, 6 (1972), 50.

38. W. Vance Grant and C. George Lind, *Digest of Educational Statistics* (Washington, D. C., U. S. Government Printing Office, 1974), 26.

39. *Financing the Schools: What Should Be the Policy Towards Financing Elementary and Secondary Education in the United States?* (Washington, D. C., American Enterprise Institute for Public Policy Research, 1972), 3.

40. Merle Curti, *The Social Ideas of American Educators* (New York, Charles Scribner's Sons, 1935), 590.

41. Bereiter, *Must We Educate?*

42. Howard Ozman, "The School of Deschooling," *Phi Delta Kappan*, 55 (November, 1973), 178–79.

43. *Ibid.*

44. Jackson, "Farewell," 210.

16.
HUMANISTIC EDUCATION

The origins of humanistic education lie in the Roman-Greek tradition, especially Plato and Aristotle's objective of seeking to produce better citizens for the state.[1] Both Plato and Aristotle believed that humans have within themselves the capacity to be courageous and maganimous, just and wise, and that they can be happy only if these ideals are achieved. The first condition for this realization is self-knowledge. Aristotle's optimistic view of human behavior influenced many persons who later wrote about education. Mention should also be made of Quintilian (A.D. 35–95). He challenged tradition and advocated abolishing the whipping of students. Furthermore, he encouraged students to use their wits and creativity. Equally revolutionary for his era, he let students win in the academic game and rewarded them for their efforts. While not initially concerned about the plight of nonwhite students, humanistic education offers a new hope for an old problem—humanizing education for all children.

TOWARD HUMANISTIC EDUCATIONAL PHILOSOPHY

The Renaissance period produced an accelerated interest in humanistic values. Thomas Aquinas followed Aristotle's principles by devising an educational model based on the idea that men naturally strive toward actualization of their potential.[2] Pico della Mirandola pursued humanistic education by advocating the dignity of humans as his major premise and by proposing that each person must appreciate his or her own potentiality.[3] Desiderius Erasmus emphasized virtue as the finest quality to be inculcated into children by education.[4] Also displaying a humanistic perspective regarding education, Michel de Montaigne was one of the first writers to authoritatively advocate that a tutor should be selected for his character and intelligence, rather than for his information or knowledge.[5]

Johann A. Comenius, a major figure in the post-Renaissance period, advocated a new system of education—one that was pleasant and yet expanded the mind of the student.[6] Stating that under such a system the child would desire to learn, Comenius recognized the universal and natural inclination of all children to learn.

The eighteenth century produced a number of scholars dedicated to focusing on the needs of individual students. John Locke, for example, placed great emphasis on the child as an individual.[7] Locke, considered the father of enlightened education, viewed the child as a receptor of learning. He originated the term *tabula rasa* (blank tablet), which was unique in its concept of the child as a product of his or her environment. Some years later David Hume construed himself as having done for the inner world what Newton had done for the outer. In *A Treatise on Human Nature*, he said that the study of man is the proper foundation for all other study.[8] Jean Jacques Rousseau believed that because people are naturally good but corrupted by society, it is the function of education to prevent such corruption.[9] This thought is especially insightful for persons who are trying to teach children.

By broad definition the history of civilized society has produced three types of educational philosophies: liberal, vocational, and humanistic. The liberal educational philosophy was accentuated in the Renaissance period and derived from Greek and Roman sources. Its purpose is to produce the ethical values and mental discipline necessary for leadership. Vocational educational philosophy was institutionalized as a result of the industrial revolution. Its specific purpose is to train the nonelite for jobs. Humanistic education has mainly a twentieth-century focus and regards the experience of the student as the central concern for teachers.

In summary, although the beginnings of humanistic philosophy are found in ancient Greek and Roman writings, only in the early modern times do we find the content of what has become humanistic education. The Renaissance and post-Renaissance saw considerable narrowness and specialization in the fine arts, music, and language, with little attention to the individual needs of students. The great scientific movements following this period overshadowed any concern for the advancement of humanistic philosophy. Only after the results of industrialization and mechanization began to take their toll of people who could no longer find adequate purpose or self-fulfillment in life did a national concern for humanistic education emerge.

Present-Day Thrust

In the present day, few persons would not agree that education should be humanistic, but as the term relates specifically to education, there is disagreement in defining it. Mary Jensen suggests that humanistic education is:

. . . a value commitment toward certain educational goals. Whereas traditional education is concerned with the mastery of content, humanistic educators are committed to the growth of the whole individual. They are directly concerned with programs that foster psychological growth, including affective and motor, as well as growth in cognitive domains. They are concerned with individuals— their needs and interests, and how they relate to themselves, to others, and to society at large. In short, humanistic education is concerned with a reordering of educational priorities.[10]

Our cybernetic culture and its consequent depersonalization has been the subject of much literature. It results in both cognitive and affective alienation within individual members of the student population. There is ample documentation that affective alienation can result in the stagnation of students' intellectual growth. When this occurs students are unable to explore and discover their identity, potential and positive worth, and concurrently they are unable to fulfill their basic psychological needs.[11]

Although each proponent of humanistic education has his or her own hierarchy of goals and priorities, some goals and priorities appear on compiled lists often enough to make them representative. In assigning priorities most advocates of humanistic education seek to provide students with opportunities to come to grips with their own identity, including their value systems and self-concepts. It is commonly agreed that an understanding of self is essential in helping students comprehend and assign meaning to the various life situations they will encounter. Teachers who understand the poignant implications of the data presented in Parts One and Two of this book are better able to teach all children.

Content and Process

Those who advocate a humanistic approach are also concerned with the development of course content relevant to students' needs and interests as the students define them. It is the belief of humanistic educators that students should have greater freedom and responsibility for what they learn, how they learn, and when they learn. It is also a general tenet in humanistic education that a sense of personal effectiveness should be fostered in students so that they will develop the confidence to exercise control over the direction their learning takes.

Indeed, twentieth-century humanistic education has its historical roots in both philosophy and psychology. Forms of humanistic philosophy may be traced at least to the fifth century B.C. in the saying of Protagoras, "Man is the measure of all things, of things that are, that they are, of things that are not, that they are not."[12] In more contemporary terms, humanism may be defined as the philosophy which singles out the ultimate value and dignity of human beings and positions men and women as the point of reference for all other things. Furthermore, this particular philosophy makes human nature—recognizing both its limitations and its strengths—its central theme. In broad terms humanism may be characterized as a belief which attaches primary importance to our faculties, behaviors, aspirations, and well-being.

Of course psychology is not a philosophy but is rather a science which is basically concerned with the study of the mind and behavior. In fact the foremost aim of psychology is commonly defined as the prediction and control of behavior, and many psychologists accept the premise that humans have serious weaknesses and numerous limitations. The strong emphasis of psychology on prediction and control has resulted in the recent predominance of behavioristic and psychoanalytic schools of thought. Like philosophy, a major characteristic of psychology is its white orientation; few nonwhites are credited as being significant scholars and none are considered founders of any humanistic concepts.

In analyzing the two foregoing disparate views of humanity, a marriage of humanism and psychology would at first glance appear unlikely. However, both perspectives capture slices of life, and through the perseverance of open-minded philosophers and psychological practitioners, the new field of humanistic psychology has not only been developed, but is thriving. Labeled the "Third Force," humanistic psychology has taken its place alongside behaviorism and psychoanalysis. While advocates of humanistic psychology do not deny the validity of other psychological approaches in theory and methods, their academic content and process are sufficiently divergent to make the term Third Force an appropriate one.

HUMANISTIC PSYCHOLOGY

Humanistic education can best be understood within the context of humanistic psychology and its distinctive contributions to learning theory. At its organizational meeting, the American Association for Humanistic Psychology defined humanistic psychology as:

... the third main branch of the general field of psychology ... and as such ... primarily concerned with those human capacities and potentialities that have little or no systematic place, either in positivist or behaviorist theory or in classical psychoanalytic theory: e.g., love, creativity, self, growth, organism, basic need-gratification, self-actualization, higher values, being, becoming, spontaneity, play, humor, affection, naturalness, warmth, ego-transcendence, objectivity, autonomy, responsibility, meaning, fair-play, transcendental experience, psychological health, and related concepts. [13]

From this definition it is apparent that humanistic psychology seeks to identify and elevate human interests, values, and dignity. Through the integration of related disciplines such as sociology, psychiatry and education, humanistic psychology strives for the betterment and understanding of people, employing methods that are unswervingly anthropocentric.

Specifically, the humanistic psychology movement was founded under the guidance of Abraham H. Maslow in 1962. It was during this year that the American Association for Humanistic Psychology was established. The behavioral scientists associated with this new movement established a professional journal entitled *Journal of Humanistic Psychology*. In 1969 this organization changed its name to the Association for Humanistic Psychology. In 1971 the American Psychological Association established a division devoted principally to the study of humanistic psychology.

Major Foci

In only a few years, humanistic psychology has grown into an impressive movement. The stimulus for this growth was the fact that few other schools of psychology elected to focus on the understanding of a healthy and creatively functioning person as an achievable and ultimate product. Fewer still were concerned with healthy and creatively functioning minority-group people. Due mainly to the sponsorship of a small, dedicated group, the school of humanistic psychology has developed and expanded, and its influence has become an important factor in humanistic education. A growing number of educators believe that humanistic psychology is a firm foundation upon which to approach the child as a whole, inseparable entity. If all children can be viewed in this manner, it is likely that their teachers will be more effective in teaching them.

The past decade has witnessed the dedication of the Third Force school to the restoration of the whole-person concept in education. Although the behavioral scientists involved in humanistic education and humanistic psychology do not speak with a single voice, nor do they all specialize in the same content areas, they are united by and committed to the common goal of humanizing society. Numerous disciplines, such as gestalt psychology, existentialism, phenomenology, and personalism, as well as the newer self-theories, are utilized in this movement.

Depending upon the point of view that is emphasized, Third Force approaches to the study of human life have been designated as humanistic, existential, perceptual, transactional, and proactive. The majority of persons actively involved in this broad movement work in the applied fields of educational psychology, guidance and counseling, and clinical psychology. Nor should we overlook the sizeable number of humanistically-oriented lay persons engaged in the study of personality, social psychology, cognitive psychology, and developmental psychology.[14]

Another impetus lending dynamic force to the humanistic psychology movement was the prevailing psychological conceptualization of humans as having little freedom of choice or uniqueness among the animal species. The negative educational implications of such a perspective are at once apparent. Also, a dwindling interest in consciousness and a preoccupation with conditioned response and other physiological processes (with an implied dependence upon natural science methods) had proven inadequate to deal with the inner experience—attitudes, beliefs, and values. In addition very little attention had been devoted to the application of behavioral science theories to practical, everyday living experiences.

The humanistic psychology movement was intent upon introducing a fresh perspective to psychology rather than formulating a new basic psychology. Through constructive criticism and research, the movement endeavored to bring psychological theory into closer proximity with the understanding and perception of contemporary people—especially their needs and concerns. One authority, James F. T. Bugental, who served as the first president of the American Association for Humanistic Psychology, listed the following five basic assumptions of humanistic psychology:

Man, as man supersedes the sum of his parts.
Man has his being in a human context.
Man is aware.
Man has choice.
Man is intentional.[15]

Another authority, Frank T. Severin, offered the following three areas as deserving major emphasis in the humanistic movement: "(1) development of a concept of nature that will account for unity of personality, self-determination and primacy of self; (2) exploring techniques for dealing with immediate experience . . . conscious processes are considered valid data for scientific investigation; and (3) examining values and inner strivings related to creativity, self-actualization, and other characteristic human activities."[16]

Despite diversity of thought among the supporters of humanistic psychology (as expressed in various books and professional journal articles), most proponents embrace the foregoing assumptions and have directed their research and practical application to these concepts. From the multitude of views concerning theories and methods has emerged common support for several salient features of humanistic psychology. There is a focus on the whole person and the full range of his or her interactions. Care concerning people is a predominant theme. There is recognition that the subjective aspect of living is crucial, with stress on awareness of both self and the world. Value and meaning are key concepts. Attention is devoted to intentions, purposes, and choices. There is an underlying emphasis on the positive—on self-actualization which transcends immediate circumstances. There is more concern for the present and future than for causative factors of the past. Finally, there is a flexibility in research methods and techniques.

Humanistic psychologists insist that the goal of psychology must be a formula with which both psychologists and others can truly live, not only in the laboratory but also in the outside world. Humanistic psychology, they maintain, has not taken its place to destroy or negate what preceded it. Rather it strives to broaden the future base of psychology, to revitalize psychology's image of human beings, and to focus efforts on significant human difficulties which previously had been treated superficially or ignored.

Contributors to the Field

A number of theorists have made valuable contributions to humanistic education through psychology. Alfred Adler's individual psychology, with its stress on self and consciousness, is worthy of note. Calvin S. Hall and Gardner Lindzey stated that by attributing to man qualities such as "altruism, humanitarianism, cooperation, creativity, uniqueness, and awareness, he [Adler] restored to man a sense of dignity and worth that psychoanalysis had pretty largely destroyed. . . . Adler offered a portrait of man which was more satisfying, more hopeful, and far more complimentary. . . . "[17]

Another theorist who made a very meaningful contribution to humanistic psychology was Abraham H. Maslow, who elaborated a theory of motivation or hierarchy of needs. In ascending order of priority, Maslow's hierarchy of needs are: *physiological needs* (food, water, warmth, etc.) *safety needs* (shelter, protection from harm, etc.) *belongingness* and *love needs* (family, society membership and affection), *esteem needs* (work, accomplishments, etc.), and *self-actualization needs* (fullest development of one's capacities). Few poverty-stricken children progress beyond fulfilling physiological and safety needs, and a disproportionate number of poverty-stricken children become neurotic. Maslow defined neurosis as a failure of personal growth or an interference with the process of self-actualization. In his view it is the function of the psychologist or counselor to "help his particular client to unfold, to break through the defenses against his own self-knowledge, to recover himself and to get to know himself."[18]

There is almost unanimous agreement among educators that satisfaction of the basic needs is necessary before most students can become concerned with and perform higher level school functions. In order for students to realize their academic potential, they must be healthy. Therefore, adequate nutrition, sleep, living conditions, clothing, exercise, and medical care all contribute to increase students' capability in school. Merely meeting physical needs, however, will not necessarily lead to optimum learning. What goes on inside the classroom is as important as what goes into the students' bodies.

Bugental is another articulate leader in the humanistic psychology movement. Insisting on the desirability of subjective interaction over objective observation, he argues that humanistic psychology has as its ultimate goal the compilation of a complete description of what it means to be alive as a human being. This goal, Bugental states, is unlikely to be attained, yet even critics agree it is important to recognize the nature of the task. Such a description would necessarily include an inventory of our native endowments, our potentialities of thought, feeling, and action, our growth and decline, and our interaction with various environmental conditions. In short, it would include the range and variety of experiences possible to human beings and their meaningful place in the universe.[19] This is taking the child from where he or she is to where he or she can grow to the fullest potential.

Charlotte Buhler devoted a lifetime to helping establish and elaborate the discipline of child psychology. Her first book was a compilation of 130 diaries of young people, and she concluded that it is essential to understand the initial stages of life in order to understand the rest of human development.[20] She advanced such understanding by publishing *Childhood and Adolescence*, which is recognized as the first attempt to view childhood and adolescence together, and even more importantly to view them as a whole. Buhler's belief that the creative, healthy, active person enjoys a certain amount of tension is in contrast to Freud's relaxation theory or pleasure principle. Furthermore, her belief that infants initially expect to find "positive reality" is in conflict with Freud's "reality principle," which posits life as basically negative rather than as a positive human opportunity. Buhler's thesis that motivational processes include creativity also runs counter to Freudian concepts. She described the four basic tendencies of life as "need satisfaction, self-limiting adaptation, creative expansion, and upholding the internal order."[21] For Buhler the self is a core system within which basic tendencies are integrated. This perspective, of course, falls well within the subject matter of humanistic education, which insists that the student should be studied as a whole and cannot validly be separated into discrete parts.

Viktor E. Frankl is another leading psychologist whose research supports humanistic education. He is best known as the founder of the school of logotherapy or existential analysis. His works focus on "the existential neurosis deriving from a person's inability to find meaning in life. The goal of his logotherapy is to help the individual achieve a more authentic system of values, and to become aware of his responsibilities and his need to make choices."[22] Frankl expresses his opposition to the homeostasis theory: that individuals are basically concerned with maintaining or restoring an inner equilibrium and to this end with reducing tensions.[23] Frankl's central ideas (finding meaning in life, the importance of making choices and establishing values, and not pursuing happiness but rather permitting events to happen) are main building blocks in the theoretical foundation of humanistic education.

RELATIONSHIP BETWEEN HUMANISTIC PSYCHOLOGY AND EDUCATION

"Since psychology is basic to education in the same way that biology is to medicine," Robert Kantor wrote, "a revolution in psychology usually foreshadows a revolution in education. And to my mind, there is a revolution in psychology underway."[24] Humanistic education is the application of humanistic psychological principles to the teaching profession. In relating the influence of psychology to education, it should also be noted that Freudian psychology improved education by pointing out the role of emotions and the unconscious in human development and learning. Behavioral psychology added conceptual clarity and behavioral techniques to learning theories, especially the concept of reinforcement. Humanistic psychology added the affective domain, both as it focuses on the cognitive

domain and as it turns the attention of educators to interpersonal relations and student-centered learning.[25]

Behavioral psychology tends to focus on the act of learning rather than the conditions for learning. In contrast humanistic psychologists view learning as a condition for, rather than directly related to, the learning experience. In essence, advocates of humanistic education assert that educators must create an environment for learning.

We take the center of gravity, which has lain hitherto in the teacher, and put it firmly in the child itself, for it is our aim not to lead, but to follow, the activities of the child, using its natural interests as points upon which it can be allowed to fasten knowledge and aiding the child always to draw out and develop its native qualities. Facts and environment, we supply; such facts and such environment as will enable the children to work out for themselves, with only the spur of tutorial enthusiasm and sympathy and understanding the significance of their thoughts and deeds as they act and react upon themselves and their fellows.[26]

Applying the Principles

The principles of humanistic psychology applied to education are concerned with figuratively awakening the learner so that he or she will be conscious of the learning stimuli (lectures, readings, films, experiments, etc.). Thus humanistic learning is designed so that it occurs when one feels the truth of something as well as when he or she understands it intellectually.

Proponents of humanistic psychology contend that human beings learn by experiencing the world. Therefore, by humanistic standards it is incumbent upon educators to choose learning strategies to facilitate students in the acquisition of such experiences. In support of this position, researchers have found that students learn best: in a free environment, by relating the world to their own experiencen cooperatively, from the inside out, and in relation to their human qualities. The major concept of the humanist is that to be a fully functioning citizen, the student must come to know society in a humanistic manner in order for him or her to participate meaningfully in the interaction processes of that society. The implementation of this basic philosophy requires a well-defined strategy as well as significant community and teacher preparation.

In developing strategies compatible with the basic tenets of humanistic education, educators are advised to apply humanistic principles to themselves as well as to their students. Frankl's search for the meaning of life, Buhler's emphasis on the importance of goals and values, and Maslow's self-actualization are humanistic concepts applicable to the personal growth of educators and students alike. Ideally, the goal of education should be to enhance both student and teacher understanding, not only intellectually but also emotionally.

Learning about the world one lives in is essential to adapt successfully to the world as it is. Improving the students' capacity to experience develops the affective realm of feeling and equips them to relate more fully to other persons. While humanistic education does not provide all of the answers to the manifold problems in the educational process, conscientious application of some of the tenets of humanistic learning can improve the quality of instruction. Indeed, a trend toward humanistic learning holds within it the seeds of optimum individual growth and social betterment. But the converse is also true: humanistic learning improperly applied can be socially and psychologically damaging.

Although committed to a focus on here-and-now-behavior, humanistic educators also place a great emphasis on the future. Schools have passed the point where they can rely solely on today's knowledge and techniques to solve tomorrow's problems. Humanistic education therefore attempts to adapt students to societal change. It seeks this goal by involving students in the process of change and by helping them to learn how to learn, how to solve problems, and how to effect change in their own lives.[27] To a great extent, this means freeing young minds enslaved by traditional curricula.

Deficiencies in Traditional Classrooms

The present crisis in education, reflected particularly in the achievement of poor and minority group students, has resulted in educators scrutinizing more closely their long-accepted assumptions concerning teaching and learning. It has been discerned that so-called "disadvantaged" nonwhite pupils are not necessarily different from middle-class white children in aptitudes or interests, but as a group they are unable to excel in schools whose curricula are mainly academic, cognitively oriented, and attuned to white, middle-class cultural values.

Disadvantaged nonwhite pupils find themselves doubly handicapped when confronted with teaching styles and classroom processes utterly foreign to their environment and experience. Educators and academicians have not been very successful in responding to the needs and demands of disadvantaged pupils. The challenges these children present are not those which traditional curriculum specialists, much less scholars in colleges and universities, are accustomed to meeting. Although disadvantaged pupils may possess high levels of intellect, they are severly debilitated by lack of opportunity, years of neglect and indifference, and often racial and/or sex prejudice. For these and other reasons, the Sputnik-inspired curriculum reforms of the 1950s had little effect on the quality of instruction for these youngsters.[28]

Intent upon finding a remedy for the educational shortchanging that has occurred in public education, a number of research teams have investigated teacher classroom management (i.e., discipline and administration). They learned that often 50 per cent of the teacher's time is spent in content development—of which the greatest percentage is devoted to the giving and receiving of low-level information such as facts, definitions, and terminology. Student-centered content occupies less than 3 per cent of the time.[29] In other words, most classes are not student-centered but are instead primarily content and management-centered. Stated another way, they are teacher-centered.

Massive data bear out the assumption that the typical classroom is structured so that students can communicate seldom with each other and most often with their teachers. Communication tends to be one-way—initiated by the teacher. Elaborate rules, codes, and regulations are imposed to perpetuate the centrality of this position. As a consequence a disproportionate amount of teacher energy is expended to insure discipline and control.

Too often in the traditional classroom a seating arrangement is used which does not best serve the students. Observation has shown that certain locations in a seating arrangement result in greater amounts of interaction, in both receiving and imparting information. These locations are the central and front positions; students located at the back and on the sides (where a disproportionate number of low-achieving students are seated) are virtually left out of the mainstream of the learning that takes place from group interaction. Compounding this inequity, it has been found that most teachers seldom visit student locations, and when they do so, the locations visited are the central, front-line positions.

Bernard W. Mackler undertook a project to determine what students have to do to succeed under such conditions. In observing the progress of one thousand Black ghetto students in New York for five years, he concluded: "Observations and test scores indicated that students have to behave in a socially-acceptable or school-acceptable way to succeed. The school staff wants pupils to be passive, polite, to listen and to adhere to the rules."[30] How hopelessly circumscribing this appears when compared with the goals of humanistic education, which focus on promoting self-identity, involving the whole student, building upon student needs and interests, promoting a sense of personal effectiveness and educating for change!

Data from other research indicate that in the traditional classroom most children do not ask questions, while their teachers ask incredibly large numbers of questions. The questions teachers ask are usually factual ones, requiring a right or wrong answer that is simply a matter of memory and regurgitation of appropriate portions of textbooks. Most students are free to initiate, conduct, and evaluate their own projects only about 5 per cent of the time, while 95 per cent of school projects are teacher-precipitated, teacher-dictated, and teacher-evaluated.

Rather than meeting individual needs, most teachers teach to an aggregate. Instead of distributing their attention equally, teachers pay considerably more attention to high achievers or low achievers, neglecting the majority of average students. Instead of inculcating a sense of responsibility for their own learning, teachers and administrators demand that students be docile, polite, listen, and adhere to the rules. Instead of letting students improve their group dynamics skills, teachers dominate and direct class discussions, focusing primarily on low-level cognitive activities. Instead of being concerned with learning, most teachers and administrators are concerned with classroom control or management.[31] A disturbing inference can be drawn from analyzing research: inadequacies that are vividly apparent in educating nonwhite students are applicable to the majority of other students, who also are not achieving their full potential.

CURRICULUM CHANGES

An abundance of evidence supports the need for well-designed, humanistic education curricula, and some of the most convincing evidence comes from the widely accepted research of Jean Piaget.[32] He makes the point that because of their unique background of experience and unique internal patterning structure, students must learn for themselves; they simply cannot be "taught." For Piaget regurgitated rote memory capability does not qualify as learning in its true sense. Rather he submits that true learning occurs only after students have assimilated and accommodated new knowledge into their present schema, which is accomplished not by passive acceptance of facts but through active manipulation of their environment. Piaget also stated that the classroom should be a place where children can discuss, argue, and debate educational issues for it is such social interaction which has a tendency to move children intellectually beyond their narrow, egocentric perspectives.

While there is common agreement that our current educational results leave much to be desired, a variety of opinions exist about the degree to which change may be effected by devising new curricula. Despite differences of opinion regarding degree, most research does indicate that curriculum modification is the proper place to begin to implement humanistic education. The Sputnik-inspired curriculum reforms of the 1950s, which emphasized math and science to the detriment of the affective realm, simply do not meet the needs of today's students, who are finding it increasingly difficult to accommodate to mass alienation and the lack of close emotional ties that once characterized American family life.

Proponents of educational reform agree that no teaching procedure is apt to be effective if the course content is of little interest to the students. It has also been clearly documented that significant contact with students is effectively established and maintained if the content and method of instruction have an affective basis. Gerald Weinstein and Mario D. Fantini observed, "If educators are able to discover the feelings, fears and wishes that move pupils emotionally, they can more effectively engage pupils from any background, whether by adapting traditional methods and procedures or by developing new materials and techniques."[33]

Mobilizing for Change

Two major questions posed by those seeking educational reform are: What content will be most meaningful to students? and How can teachers convey it most effectively? In an effort to shed light on these questions, Donald Orlosky and B. Othanel Smith conducted a study for the U.S. Office of Education to determine what educational changes had been attempted over the past several decades and which ones had proven most successful. Although they found that a number of the methods that had been tried were failures, their data did show that some changes have been successfully implanted in instruction, curriculum, organization, and administration. Furthermore, their results indicate that changes in curriculum or administration have been implemented more successfully than changes in methods of instruction.[34]

Orlosky and Smith also noted that when changes in instruction were found, they were more likely to originate within the education profession than from outside it, and such changes were most often the outcome of sensitive professional perception and research. Curriculum changes involving the addition of subjects or the updating of course content are more easy to accomplish than changes in the organization or structure of the curriculum. Efforts to change the curriculum by integrating or correlating the content, or by creating new category systems into which to organize the content, are the least successful. It is a truism among some educational systems that is is easier to move a cemetery than to change a curriculum.

If there is community resistance to displacement of the existing curriculum patterns, the chances of success are greatly impaired. Conversely, if there is support, the odds for effecting change are greatly increased. There appears to be a direct correlation between the number of critical elements (community leaders, school patrons and personnel, students, etc.) involved and the chance of success.

Another impeding factor to successful curriculum change is proposals that place additional time and energy strains upon school personnel. Although such proposals may be successfully initiated and even enjoy a fair amount of faculty support, core curricula and creative education that are constant drains on the time and energy of the faculty tend to falter, dissipate, and within a short time disappear.

Because curriculum is one of the most effective vehicles for moving toward humanistic education, it is important to understand some of the past criticism that has been leveled against traditional curricula.*

One of the most common criticisms is that traditional curricula tend to be based on the requirements of the various subject disciplines rather than on content designed to assist students in dealing effectively with the problems of human conduct. Almost a decade ago John I. Goodlad made the criticism, with some justification, that "little effort has been made to determine the ultimate aims of schooling and the respective contribution each discipline can make to them. Instead, the objectives of schooling have become the composite of the objectives set for each subject. . . . The goals of today's schools do not extend beyond those subjects that have succeeded in establishing themselves in the curriculum."[35]

Enhancing Self-Images

Any curriculum that fails to enhance students' self-images, provide them with constructive relationships with other people, and allow them some control over their own future will not satisfy humanistic standards. In the words of Weinstein and Fantini: "In today's complex, precarious world a society has little choice but

*The term "traditional" is used advisedly, realizing that today's innovative curriculum could be tomorrow's traditional curriculum.

Chart 8. Contributions Various Groups Can Make in Curriculum Reform

Committee Members	Contributions
Students	React to the relevancy of content, effectiveness of presentation; provide background information on learning problems encountered, their own purposes and desires related to the subject at hand, and their concept of the continuity of the program presented to them
	React to pilot programs (graduates can provide information about the program some three or four years after they have graduated—valuable source for revisions)
Teachers	Provide sequence and placement of subject matter, and students within the subject area
	Diagnose students' backgrounds
	Provide the philosophy or purpose of their subject matter, the knowledge of alternatives in their subject fields
	Emphasize the value in a continuing focus on the learner's needs as well as the teacher's needs in relation to implementing the program
Superintendent and Board of Education	Contribute overall guiding philosophy of purpose and the various alternatives available
	Provide information on alternatives available, subject matter
Curriculum Specialists	Assist superintendent and board of education in development of overall guiding philosophy
	Provide information on alternatives available, subject matter content and organization (scope, sequence, continuity)
	Be a resource person to the council and an in-service education organizer
	Bring in resource persons
Representatives of Colleges	Assist with the development of philosophy
	Report on any recent action research their institutions may have conducted
	Provide objective evaluation/research on pilot projects
Industry and Business	Articulate their expectations of their future employees
	Provide information pertinent to the topic at hand
	Assist in fund raising for worthwhile projects
Parents and Community Groups	Contribute to the formulation of the goals and purpose of the school
	Provide valuable feedback on their aspirations for their children
	Assist in raising funds for worthwhile projects
	Point out relevant community resources

SOURCE: Shirley A. Jackson, "The Curriculum Council: New Hope, New Promise," *Educational Digest*, 29 (May 1972), 691. Reprinted with permission.

to pursue the path toward humanitarian behavior. Otherwise, no matter how successful its educational system is in teaching the specific stuff of subject matter, the society is likely to decline and decay."[36]

Since most children receive their instruction in a group, one of the first steps in determining appropriate curriculum content and teaching procedures geared to learners' needs and concerns is precise identification of students as a group. A number of criteria must be considered, some of which are the developmental level or age of the group to be taught, whether the group is of the low, middle, or upper income level, and the geographic area from which the group comes. In addition to these factors, the cultural and ethnic characteristics of the individuals comprising the group must be examined if content is to be provided which will engage them affectively. It is likely that when any group is considered compositely, more than one subgroup will emerge. It then becomes the task of curriculum planners to determine certain commonalities which can be utilized for the benefit of all children rather than to develop curriculum to satisfy the teachers' whims. "Education is always imposing, violating, constraining; the real educator is he who can best protect the child against his (the teacher's) own ideas, his peculiar whims; he who can best appeal to the child's own energies. . . . "[37]

Student Concerns

Another step in devising a humanistic curriculum is identifying the shared concerns of students. Certain specific resources will be very helpful for teachers seeking to identify the common concerns of students in the classrooms. Professional literature offers abundant sources detailing current efforts to humanize education. The folklore of various groups is helpful and discussions with colleagues can provide additional information. But most important is the teacher's own observation of the students. The most direct and potentially valuable indications of student concerns are found in what students say about their lives and relationships with their families, peers, and the rest of the world. Since most of the transactions in a classroom are either verbal or written communications, exceptional opportunities

are available for identifying individual concerns. If in the ordinary routine of the class sufficient evidence is not forthcoming, teachers can develop situations and procedures to facilitate the kinds of interaction that will elicit desired information.

In a recent research study, three major concerns were identified under which most other less permanent student concerns could be subsumed: (1) concern about self-image, (2) concern about relationships with significant other persons or society at large and (3) concern about control over one's life.[38] It has also been observed that the frequency with which clues pertaining to these concerns are expressed will reflect whether they are transient feelings or matters of deep, persistent concern. Teachers who are endeavoring to identify group concerns may find it beneficial to keep a record of reoccurrences of student concerns which are manifest in either verbal exchanges or written assignments. The concerns that continue to reappear are indicative of specific problems with which individual children are wrestling, and these are apt to be rooted in the very heart of their being. Problems centering on sex, race, age, poverty, and so forth are expressed in a wide variety of ways. Student concerns are often those that their teachers also have but in the vulnerability and plasticity of childhood they cut deep furrows and can prove difficult to extricate.

Verbal, Written, and Nonverbal Clues

One of the next steps in developing a curriculum that will facilitate humanistic education is the diagnosis of underlying factors indicated by verbal, written, and nonverbal clues. Although different children have similar concerns, the manner of expressing them may not be the same since a variety of social forces affect each child. A correct diagnosis of student concerns is a requisite for effective curriculum development. As an example, a number of students may express a feeling of powerlessness, but responsibility rests with the teacher to determine whether this concern stems from an overprotective family situation, being a member of a minority group, or a course design that does not permit student-initiated participation.

If prescriptive curriculum is to benefit the

individual student, it is necessary to know from precisely what that deficit stems. Depending upon its source, a child's sense of powerlessness may be abated by giving him or her more opportunities to make individual decisions or perhaps by placing the student in classroom situations where he or she will experience the support of a group. Failure to diagnose societal forces correctly can lead not only to misguided teaching procedures but also to the selection of inappropriate course content and objectives.

Effecting Positive Behavioral Changes

Aristotle encouraged humanistic education by endeavoring to produce better and more humane citizens for the state. Today the question at once arises: What shall determine the behavioral changes to be sought? In humanistic education it has been suggested that the behavioral changes to which curriculum and teaching procedures should be tied should be determined by a diagnosis of the students' concerns. It then follows that if, for example, a Black child's concern is for affirmative change in self-concept, procedures for achieving and evaluating this outcome must be available. However, before success can be measured it is necessary to give the student a method for organizing the ideas that derive from this concern.

Cognitive organizers. One procedure that has been proposed for organizing ideas is the use of cognitive organizers, that is:

. . . generalizations, fundamental ideas, principles, and concepts around which specific curriculum content can be developed. They are the threads with which content and procedures are woven. . . . Organizing ideas must be selected on the basis of the concerns of the learner rather than academic subject matter, and they must help the learner to cope with his concerns. . . . Organizing ideas, especially those that cut across the disciplinary lines, are the most generative and transferable item in the educational process.[39]

Ideally, these organizing ideas need to be structured by the teacher so that a larger body of knowledge can be generated from them. To achieve this objective, organizing ideas need

to help the student to draw relationships between matters that on the surface seem to be isolated from each other. Beginning with the student's concern—through the organizing ideas devised by the teacher—it is possible to lead him or her to other issues, principles, and values. In this manner the traditional approach of allowing subject matter to dictate which generalizations or ideas are most important has been reversed, and the generalizations, are made on the basis of their usefulness in linking student concerns with desired outcomes.

Content carriers. In order to link student concerns with desired educational outcomes, it is necessary for teachers to consider both types of content and what will be the most effective carriers of content. Three basic types of content that have been proposed are students' experiences, their feelings about their experiences, and what has been learned from the societal context in which the students live.

Behavioral science subject disciplines such as human relations, anthropology, sociology, and psychology are carriers of content that may be utilized by the teacher. Other content carriers are classroom situations that include significant incidents and problems. Out-of-school experiences also may be used and of course the children themselves are content carriers. Once the content carriers have been chosen by the teacher, units or lessons can be structured around them.

In formulating units or lessons, the teacher should consider what basic skills or tools it will be necessary for the student to use—such as reading or oral communications. Next it will be necessary to consider process skills, or ways of thinking, generating alternatives, analyzing, and predicting. A third area for consideration is awareness skills, which are necessary if the students are to examine themselves and others and acquire emotional intensity and effectiveness in communicating concerns.

All of these skills are interrelated. The acquisition of procedural and awareness skills depends greatly on the degree to which students can utilize basic skills, especially language skills. Students cannot express and analyze their own or others' feelings and experiences without developing at the same time more elaborate speaking, listening, reading, and, in some instances, writing skills. But such skills do not have to be developed elaborately before students begin to work with the content vehicle. They may be developed during the process or may evolve out of a teaching process that focuses on content relevant to students' feelings and concerns. Belatedly, colleges and universities are finding this to be true in teaching disadvantaged students via remedial classes.

Appropriate teaching procedures. A final consideration in structuring a humanistic education program is developing teaching procedures appropriate for moving students' concerns toward desired outcomes. Since these procedures are dependent in part on the concerns of the individuals to be instructed, they will necessarily take a variety of directions. Several things, however, are usually important in developing humanistic teacher procedures. One of these is the careful matching of teacher procedures with the learning styles of students. To accomplish this it is important to know the ways in which the child has been taught in the past and the ways in which he or she has learned best.

Valuable insights can be gained from the vast reservoir of learning theory articles and books that are presently available. The following specific learning patterns of children need to be differentiated: who learns best by concrete presentations and who by abstract presentations; who is best reached in a structured way as compared with who is most responsive to an informal approach; and who reasons more readily by moving from the general to the particular as opposed to those who reason best from the particular to the general. Good teaching procedures also require proper pacing of the students so that they are neither pressured nor permitted to become bored from lack of sufficient new material.

Teacher procedures based on affect—that is, involvement of the student in actual experience—have proven more successful than mere verbalization. Procedures that allow the learner to experiment with power roles may have considerable success. In this regard cross-age teaching—giving older children the responsibility for teaching younger students—is a procedure that uses the peer experience as a staging point for instruction. Whatever procedure is selected, it is crucial that teachers develop interaction systems that support the learners emotionally and

strengthen their feelings of self-worth.

In order to measure success and failure, evaluation procedures should be devised that will not merely appraise end results but also facilitate a continuous evaluation process. Like any other curriculum, success or failure in a humanistic curriculum should be based on the degree to which the desired outcomes are being achieved. In implementing a humanistic program, it is probable that additional student concerns will be uncovered, which in turn will necessitate the consideration of new procedures and new curriculum content. The growing interests of the students should dictate the direction instruction will take. But this is not to suggest that a core of predetermined subjects (English, mathematics, etc.) are not needed.

A CRITICAL VIEW

The potential of humanistic education to capture the interest of the student, and by its relevance to hold that attention, has been the focus of this chapter thus far. However, in order to present a balanced perspective, it would be inappropriate not to offer some of the views and objections that have been raised against humanistic education. Alton Harrison, Jr. is an eloquent spokesman for an alternative view.[40] Disenchanted with traditional education, Harrison eagerly engaged in humanistic experiments to deliver learning from the dismal, oppressive process it had become. Describing his view of the traditional classroom, Harrison stated:

Schools appeared to be repressive factories whose main purpose at the elementary level was custodial and at the upper levels utilitarian. Children were raw material that was mass processed to fit into a limited number of molds bearing the U.S. stamp of approval. Individuality was not just ignored but openly discouraged. Conformity was richly rewarded. Learning did not seem to be especially joyful, in fact, it appeared to be a grim business.[41]

Since one of the major barriers in implementing a humanistic, individualized approach appears to be that it is subject to the methods of evaluation best applied to standardized education, Harrison eliminated one major sore spot—the test. He was firmly convinced that individualization and affective development do not lend themselves to objective measurement. Proceeding on this premise, he eliminated examinations and substituted individual conferences where students were permitted to assign their own grades. Harrison informed the students that they would have full freedom to pursue topics, issues, and projects related to their own individual concerns and interests. Stress was placed on the capability of each person to make a significant contribution and on the responsibility of students to do this on their own initiative. *The results were disappointing.*

The majority clearly wanted me to give them some specific assignments. I refused to do this, and attempted to coax them into taking advantage of the opportunity to develop a meaningful course related to their own individual needs and interests. As their puzzlement and frustration increased, I agreed to throw out some suggestions and possibilities. At that point about one-third of the class immediately adopted the suggestions and began to work on them as course requirements. Another third, approximately, continued to drift, waiting for more definite directions, and the other third faded in and out doing virtually nothing. [42]

Upon beginning the project, Harrison had identified three major factors as potential causes for failure: teacher evaluation (tests, etc.), the conditioning effect of years of traditional education (freedom and responsibility), and the institutional setting (design and arrangement, or the "tell 'em and test 'em" approach). After deciding his experiment was a failure, Harrison attempted to determine the reasons. He rejected the three factors he had originally identified. He concluded, rather, that unlike himself, most of his students did not appear to have an inherent lust for learning, even when optimum environmental conditions were furnished. Discussing his own faulty projections, Harrison says, "Under a given set of conditions and circumstances I find learning to be exhilarating and extremely gratifying. I assumed that if I could create those conditions and circumstances in my classes, all or virtually all students would react in the same way. Wrong!" [43]

He found instead that a number of students wanted and needed structure, direction, and supervision. A number of others wanted neither freedom nor structure; their perspective on learning was simply to do whatever was necessary to attain the credits required for a course or a degree. And some simply tried to get through by doing as little as possible: if they could pass a course with absolutely no effort, so much the better. Harrison concluded that "there are a sizeable number of students in every school (be it free or controlled, liberal or conservative) who are there for some reason other than to learn. . . . No amount of reform will change this." [44]

Harrison's study suggests two important considerations for persons intent upon instituting humanistic education. First, a mounting body of psychological and educational reserach indicates that certain basic attitudes and behaviors are developed early in life, and all of the resources education can bring to bear seem to have a negligible effect in the modification of these basic behavior patterns. Second, research indicates that the vast majority of students perceive education as having an economic value. Harrison does concede that teacher influence is difficult to measure, and it may require many years before such influence is visible in the life of a student. Even so, he adequately challenges the illusion that all students are fuel-soaked torches, merely waiting the propitious spark of proper education to transform them into a guiding light for themselves and the world.

A review of the arguments of both supporters and critics of humanistic education indicates that there is some agreement regarding the task education faces if both the practical obligations and the personal needs of students are to be met. Both supporters and critics agree that some intervention must be made at an earlier age than is now common if detrimental behavior patterns are to be significantly curtailed. There is some agreement in both camps regarding the inordinate economic focus of our present educational system and the lack of emphasis on cooperative attitudes that must be established if humanistic education is to meet its goals.

Present studies are inconclusive in supporting the theory that the American education system can prepare its students to become useful members of the state and at the same time permit them to follow the affective trends their individual concerns dictate. For such a theory to be valid, it would necessarily follow that the concerns and needs of the state and those of its students must be alike. Abundant evidence suggests that this simply is not the case. Someone or something will have to give. Who or what shall it be? And how much?

Humanistic educators are being asked to fashion from the raw material of the real world an ideal that appears to find its two basic constituents, the student and the state, in unresolved conflict. It is a tall order—a Gordian knot of state and student that we dare not cut but must carefully unravel. Failure to accomplish this task poses alternatives that are awesome to contemplate.

MAKING IT WORK

When attempting to humanize instruction, it is of utmost importance that educators take the following steps to insure that sensitivity training is an academic boon and not a bane.

1. Carefully diagnose the current situation. What are the problems? What is prompting the priorities of need? What are the short- and long-range goals? What are the methods available for meeting objectives? What are the possible losses as well as gains which may be outcomes of each method?

2. Limit the objectives. It is tempting to use sensitivity training to try to change a whole system, both in breadth and in depth simultaneously. This seldom, if ever, works constructively. When one has unrealistic expectations he will be disappointed.

3. Specify the objective(s) as well as the depth of intervention and stick with it.

4. Specify the point of intervention and a rationale to support it. The strategy, if it is to result in a desired change, should include a rationale, based on goals and resources. Don't leave these decisions to intuition, chance, or political pressure.

5. Give each person an opportunity to choose whether or not to participate in sensitivity training. Choice should be based on adequate knowledge.

6. Do not allow sensitivity training to polarize the school.

7. Transfer of learning should be the primary concern in every training intervention.

8. Sensitivity training will not solve human problems in one part of the school system unless parallel and complementary changes are made in other parts.

9. The school system is much larger and more complex than a T-group.

10. Find and use competent human resources. Choose somebody who openly states his own values, perspectives, and criteria for decisions and who can be trusted to do whatever he can to accomplish what he states he will accomplish. His goals should be consistent with the school's defined goals.[45]

In summarizing guidelines for sensitizing students in the classroom, Max Rosenberg observed that the most important lessons students learn are those that the teacher does not pontificate, but rather the lessons in human relations which the teacher gives to the students simply be being what s/he is. These are the messages of the self that all people send and receive constantly. Self-initiated classroom messages may be conscious or unconscious, direct or indirect, obvious or subtle; they may be conveyed by word, gesture, tone of voice, or look.[46]

Rosenberg cautioned that in the critically important area of human relations, it is necessary for teachers to constantly reexamine themselves and the messages they are sending. The Human Relations Quotient (HRQ) test designed by Rosenberg can help teachers determine how well they are performing their human relations function:

1. Do I help my students accept each other on the basis of individual worth, regardless of sex or race or religion or socioeconomic background?

2. Do I help my students recognize clearly the basic similarities among all members of the human race as well as the uniqueness of every individual?

3. Do I help my students value the multicultural character of our society and reject stereotypes or derogatory caricatures of peoples of the world?

4. Do I help my students see prejudice as a wall which blocks communication, interaction, mutual understanding, and respect?

5. Do I help my students to be knowlegeable about pressures—historical and contemporary, environmental, social, political, and economic—that have been instrumental in developing group life-styles?

6. Do I help my students to honestly and objectively analyze group tension and conflict with a will to resolve these situations and to seek fairness, cooperation, and affirmative action?

7. Do I help my students appreciate the contributions of all groups—sexual, racial, religious, social class, national?

8. Do I help motivate my students to accept their responsibilities as citizens to abate injustices?

9. Do I help my students by carefully evaluating before classroom usage all curriculum materials—books, pamphlets, films, filmstrips, bulletin board pictures, charts, etc.—to insure fair and balanced treatment of all groups?

10. Do I help my students to learn the art of good human relations by providing a living model in my own treatment of people—each and every student, all members of the staff (from custodians to administrators), every parent, and other members of the community?[47]

No period of history is without its subscripts of individual efforts to humanistically leaven the whole lump of humanity. Research and evaluation are beginning to document the fact that carefully designed humanistic education activities can significantly and positively affect intrapersonal, interpersonal, and intergroup behaviors. Social acceptance is a precious human heritage, and all of us suffer when anyone in the world is denied his or her rightful share. Eradication of racial, sex, and ethnic prejudice is a foremost challenge. Marie Jean Antoine said it well many years ago:

There can be seen developing a new doctrine, which must give the final thrust to the tottering edifice of prejudice. It is the doctrine of the indefinite perfectibility of the human race. . . . Nature has set no term to the perfection of human faculties; the perfectibility, from now onwards, independent of any power that might wish to halt it, has no other limits than the duration of the globe upon which nature has cast us. The progress will doubtless vary in speed, but it will never be reversed.[48]

TEACHING STYLE

How we teach matters as much as what we teach. It is also important that teachers understand and feel comfortable with their own unique teaching styles. The following questions may have more than one answer that fits your teaching style, but you are asked to mark the one response in each question that best reflects your preference.

1. As a teacher, I would:
☐ a. be less concerned about course content than group process.
☐ b. deal more in analysis of here-and-now student behavior.
☐ c. be more concerned about course content than group process.
☐ d. not worry about students' feelings as long as they get good grades.

2. An effective teacher:
☐ a. remains detached from her/his students.
☐ b. is a member of the class who provides certain special functions.
☐ c. is mainly a resource person for the class.
☐ d. is really just an ordinary member of the class.

3. During a class project, I would guide the students by:

☐ a. staying out of the discussion most of the time.
☐ b. using occasional interventions for controlling group activity.
☐ c. influencing the behavior patterns valued by formal and informal class members.
☐ d. providing behind-the-scenes leadership.

4. I would invite student discussions of my teaching behavior in order to show:
☐ a. that I am expert in group dynamics.
☐ b. that I am a real group member.
☐ c. that the class need not be afraid of me.
☐ d. that it is safe to try out new behavior.

5. An example of teacher behavior which shows students that they are important is:

☐ a. not interrupting.
☐ b. talking very little.

☐ c. agreeing with a shy student.
☐ d. not giving negative feedback.

6. When students express feelings, I will:
☐ a. help them explore the here-and-now cause of feelings.
☐ b. keep uninvolved.
☐ c. try tactfully to indicate feelings have no place in a class discussion.
☐ d. encourage the students to withhold personal feelings until they can meet with me in private.

7. If members of the class become angry with me, I would:
☐ a. respond objectively in order to facilitate learning.
☐ b. reflect their feelings in order to help them better think them through.
☐ c. respond naturally in order to be myself.
☐ d. not respond.

8. My main goal in teaching would be to encourage students to:
☐ a. do things and analyze them.
☐ b. explore basic motivations of human behaviors.
☐ c. learn how to cope with interpersonal and intergroup problems.
☐ d. present course materials.

9. It is a help to students when the teacher:
☐ a. enforces shared leadership.
☐ b. surprises the class with unexpected assignments.

☐ c. administers her/his lesson plan efficiently.
☐ d. invites cooperative planning.

10. The basic purpose of the teacher during a class assignment is:
☐ a. to let the students practice new behaviors.
☐ b. to facilitate free activity.
☐ c. to help establish conditions for effective living.
☐ d. to keep ahead of the class.

11. If my students wanted to take over the teaching function, I would:
☐ a. clarify the teacher and student roles in order that students may remain in their proper role.
☐ b. encourage students to prepare themselves to teach a unit.
☐ c. help the students to see how inadequate they would be as teachers.
☐ d. stop teaching and let the students take over.

12. Which of the following is necessarily a characteristic of an effective teacher?
☐ a. ability to maintain consistent behavior
☐ b. unusual skill in facilitating small group interaction
☐ c. ability to handle self with minimum strain in group situations
☐ d. high persuasive talents

Note: Perhaps you would like to discuss your answers with a teacher whose behavior you believe epitomizes good teaching.

ADDITIONAL READINGS

Bernier, Norman R. and Jack E. Williams, eds. *Education for Liberation: Readings from an Ideological Perspective*. Englewood Cliffs, N.J., Prentice-Hall, 1973.

Eiben, Ray and Al Milliren, eds. *Educational Change: A Humanistic Approach*. La Jolla, Cal., University Associates, 1976.

Feather, Norman T. *Values in Education and Society*. New York, Free Press, 1975.

Featherstone, Joseph. *Schools Where Children Learn*. New York, Liveright, 1971.

Holt, John C. *Freedom and Beyond*. New York, E.P. Dutton, 1972.

Katz, Jerry. *Liberating Learning: A Manual for Individual Educational Reform*. New York, Morgan & Morgan, 1972.

Knapp, Robert H. *The Origins of American Humanistic Scholars*. Englewood Cliffs, N.J., Prentice-Hall, 1964.

Kozol, Jonathan. *The Night is Dark and I Am Far From Home*. Boston, Houghton Mifflin, 1975.

Leonard, George B. *Education and Ecstasy*. New York, Delacorte Press, 1968.

Nissman, Albert. *Operation Classroom: A Direct Experience Approach*. New York, New Voices, 1975.

Patterson, C.H. *Humanistic Education*. New York, Prentice-Hall, 1973.

Purpel, David E. and Maurice Belanger, eds. *Curriculum and the Cultural Revolution: A Book of Essays and Readings*. Berkeley, Cal., McCutchan, 1972.

Rich, John M. *Education and Human Values*. Reading, Mass., Addison-Wesley, 1968.

Ruchlis, Hyman and Belle Sharefkins. *Reality-Centered Learning*. New York, Citation Press, 1975.

Stoff, Sheldon and Herbert Schwartzberg, eds. *The Human Encounter: Readings in Education*. New York, Harper & Row, 1973.

Tyre, Kenneth A. and Jerrold M. Novotney. *Schools in Transition: The Practitioner as Change Agent*. New York, McGraw-Hill, 1975.

Weinberg, Carl. *Humanistic Foundations of Education*. Englewood Cliffs, N.J., Prentice-Hall, 1972.

NOTES

1. Francisco Ferrer, "The Modern School," in Leonard I. Krimerman and Lewis Perry (eds.), *Patterns of Anarchy* (Garden City, N. Y., Doubleday, 1966), 415.

2. Thomas Aquinas, *Treatise on Man* (trans. by James F. Anderson, Englewood Cliffs, N. J., Prentice-Hall, 1962).

3. Pico della Mirandola, *On the Dignity of Man* (trans. by Charles G. Wallis, Indianapolis, Bobbs-Merrill, 1965).

4. Desiderius Erasmus, *The Education of a Christian Prince* (trans. by Lester K. Born, New York, Columbia University Press, 1936).

5. Michel de Montaigne, *The Essays of Montaigne*, (trans. by E.J. Trechmann), London, Oxford University Press, 1927.

6. Johann A. Comenius, *John Amos Comenius on Education* (trans. by Jean Piaget, New York, Teachers College Press, 1957).

7. John Locke, *The Educational Writings of John Locke* (ed. by James L. Axtell, London, Cambridge University Press, 1968).

8. David Hume, *A Treatise on Human Nature* (London, Longmans, Green, 1898).

9. Jean Jacques Rousseau, *Emile: Or Concerning Education* (trans. by Eleanor Worthington, Boston, D. C. Heath, 1906).

10. Mary Jenson, "Humanistic Education: An Overview of Supporting Data," *High School Journal*, 56 (May, 1973), 341.

11. Richard P. Del Prete and Pearl G. Waterhouse, "Human Development Orientation Module," *NASPA Journal* 10 (April, 1973), 238.

12. Protagoras of Abdera, quoted by Plato in George Seldes (ed.), *The Great Quotations* (New York, Pocket Books, 1967), 637.

13. A. J. Sutich, "Articles of Association, American Association for Humanistic Psychology," Palo Alto, California, 1963.

14. Frank T. Severin, *Discovering Man in Psychology: A Humanistic Approach* (New York, McGraw-Hill, 1973), 5.

15. James F. T. Bugental, "The Third Force in Psychology," *Journal of Humanistic Psychology*, 4 (Spring, 1964), 19–26.

16. Frank T. Severin, *Humanistic Viewpoints in Psychology* (New York, McGraw-Hill, 1965), xv–xvii.

17. Calvin S. Hall and Gardner Lindzey, *Theories of Personality* (New York, John Wiley & Sons, 1957), 125.

18. Abraham H. Maslow, "Self-Actualization and Beyond," in James F. T. Bugental (ed.), *Challenges of Humanistic Psychology* (New York, McGraw-Hill, 1967), 7.

19. Bugental, "The Third Force in Psychology."

20. Lotte Schenk-Danziger, "Fundamental Ideas

and Theories in Charlotte Buhler's Lifework," *Journal of Humanistic Psychology*, 3 (Fall, 1963), 3–9.

21. *Ibid.*, 7.

22. Viktor Frankl, "Self-Transcendence As a Human Phenomenon," *Journal of Humanistic Psychology*, 6 (Fall, 1966), 97–106.

23. *Ibid.*

24. Robert Kantor, quoted by Thomas B. Roberts, in "Transpersonal: The New Educational Psychology," *Phi Delta Kappan*, 56 (November, 1974), 191.

25. *Ibid.*

26. Bayard Boyeson, "The Modern School: A Further Development," in Drimerman and Perry, *Patterns of Anarchy*, 417.

27. Jensen, "Humanistic Education," 343.

28. Gerald Weinstein and Mario D. Fantini, *Toward Humanistic Education* (New York, Praeger, 1970), 5.

29. Jenson, "Humanistic Education," 343.

30. Bernard W. Mackler, "WIN," *Psychology Today*, 4 (April, 1971), 61.

31. Jensen, "Humanistic Education," 344–45.

32. See Herbert Ginsburg and Sylvia Opper, *Piaget's Theory of Intellectual Development* (Englewood Cliffs, N. J., Prentice-Hall, 1969).

33. Weinstein and Fantini, *Toward Humanistic Education*, 10.

34. Donald Orlosky and B. Othanel Smith, "Educational Change: Its Origins and Characteristics," *Phi Delta Kappan*, 53 (March, 1972), 412–14.

35. John I. Goodlad, *The Changing School Curriculum* (New York, Georgian Press, 1966), 92.

36. Weinstein and Fantini, *Toward Humanistic Education*, 19.

37. Ferrer, "The Modern School," 415.

38. Weinstein and Fantini, *Toward Humanistic Education*, 39.

39. *Ibid.*, 46.

40. Alton Harrison, Jr., "Humanistic and Educational Reform: The Need for a Balanced Perspective," *Educational Forum*, 38 (March, 1974), 331.

41. *Ibid.*, 332.

42. *Ibid.*, 333.

43. *Ibid.*, 334.

44. *Ibid.*

45. Larry J. Kraft and Leland W. Howe, "Guidelines for Sensitivity Training in Your School: How To Make a Program a Boon, Not a Bane," *Phi Delta Kappan*, 53 (November, 1971), 179–180.

46. Max Rosenberg, "Test Your H. R. Q. (Human Relations Quotient)," *Teacher*, 90 (March, 1973), 28.

47. *Ibid.*

48. Marie Jean Antoine, quoted in George Seldes (ed.), *The Great Quotations*, 463.

17.
HUMANIZING THE CURRICULUM

With each passing year the cry is heard, ever more stridently, that public school curricula have little relevance to the real lives of students. Surrounded by stimuli which grow increasingly complex in their effects, most students appear to be thoroughly confused by the marked contrast between the formal subject matter presented to them in school—often in an irrelevant, prepackaged, deadly manner— and the experiences furnished them by the world outside. Schools should be exciting places which offer materials in ways that challenge—even taunt—students to use their own mental powers to synthesize interrelated fragments of reality into a coherent whole.

A growing number of educators realize that the traditional curricula, taught in the traditional way, have failed to engage the emotional resources of most students. Traditional schooling also fails to teach many students much of anything except a dislike for school. The major error which traditional educators commit, it would appear, is to view curriculum and the student as two entirely separate things, with the student imbibing from the teacher much as someone would suck milk from a straw in a soft drink container. The enormous number of intellectually and emotionally crippled students produced by traditional educational methods gives eloquent testimony that whatever learning may be, it most certainly does not correspond to a rigidly trifurcated model. John Dewey forcefully and eloquently expressed the relationship between curriculum and student.

Abandon the notion of subject-matter as something fixed and ready-made in itself, outside the child's experience; cease thinking of the child's experience as also something hard and fast; see it as something fluent, embryonic, vital; and we realize that the child and the curriculum are simply two limits which define a single process. Just as two points define a straight line, so the present standpoint of the child and the facts and truths of studies define instruction. It is continuous reconstruction, moving from the child's present experience out into that represented by the organized bodies of truth that we call studies.[1]

The following curricula and program suggestions are presented to illustrate possible ways to humanize the classroom. Ultimately, each teacher must devise his or her own methods of intervention. Just as most traditional approaches fall short in being effective, so too do many humanistic approaches.

HUMANISTIC APPROACHES IN THE SOCIAL STUDIES

Recently, William W. Crowder suggested ways to redirect the social studies curriculum in order to help children to a greater understanding of themselves and other people. For instance, focusing on similarities and differences between individuals can help students to discover the following concepts: (1) People are alike in many ways. (2) We are also unlike in many ways. (3) We are born with certain characteristics, such as brown skin, blue eyes, etc., over which we had no control. (4) From our surroundings we develop certain preferences that make us unique. (5) Each of us should try to appreciate similarities and dissimilarities in others without trying to make them like us or without feeling that we should change to be like them.[2]

Crowder lists ten activities that could help students gain a better understanding of themselves in relationship to other people:

1. *Similarities and differences.* Through discussion or composition, students should tell how they are like others in the class and how they are different. A display of photographs could be mounted with descriptions or students could start notebooks titled "Alike and Different."

2. *Self-portraits.* The students are asked to draw pictures of themselves in their favorite clothing. The teacher might then ask them to compare themselves with their friends, using their self-portraits.

3. *Who am I?* Students are asked, "Who is the *real* Mary?" (Choose the name of any class member participating.) The student whose name is called answers by describing herself or himself, including favorite foods, color preferences, etc.

4. *Who—?* Teachers might use this exercise at the beginning of the semester to help students become acquainted with one another and to make them aware of similarities and differences among themselves. The teacher should compile a list of questions which students might ask one another. Each student should be required to make an inquiry of every class member.

5. *Choosing someone like me.* A record should be selected for this activity, chairs arranged in a circle, and the following instructions given: "I want you to think very carefully of someone who is just like you in the way I say. For example, I may say, 'someone who has the same color hair as you.' When I point to your name on the board, I want you to get up, go to where this person is, and bring him or her to our circle." When the music begins, the teacher should point to the first child's name; choices continue until all students are chosen and seated in the circle. For each name, the instructions should be changed, perhaps requiring the student to select someone who is wearing the same color blouse, shirt, socks, etc.

6. *Choosing someone unlike me.* This is a variation of the above activity. The object is to select someone who is different.

7. *Using pictures.* The teacher should assemble a selection of pictures of children from magazines and newspapers. Each student should be asked to select a picture of someone approximately the same age and to describe as many ways as possible in which that child is both like and unlike himself or herself. The teacher should ask why he or she would like to resemble the other individual and also why he or she is glad to be unique.

8. *Expressing likes and dislikes in music.* The teacher should ask students to bring their favorite recording to class and to explain their choices.

9. *Stating preferences for different stories.* The teacher should collect at least six or eight different kinds of stories such as mystery, adventure, humor and read one to the class each day, always starting with a recap of earlier stories to refresh the students' memories. After the last story is read, students should be asked to state which they liked best and to compare their choices with one another.

10. *Studying the nature of likeness and differences among people.*

    a. *Heredity.* Through discussion, students can understand and perceive that some traits and characteristics are inherited, such as the color of one's skin, hair, eyes.

    b. *Environment.* The teacher should allow the students to investigate how people are alike or different because of environmental conditions.[3]

Crowder points out that teachers must give systematic and continued attention to similarities and differences at all grade levels so that an appreciation of and rapport with others cna be developed. The purpose of such attention is to pave the way for students to accept their own uniqueness. When this happens, they also realize that their culture and development will both shape and be shaped by their own individual attributes.[4]

The Living Circle

Thomas D. Yawkey and Eugene L. Aronin believe that social studies teachers, by the nature of their curriculum area, must accept responsibilities of teaching about values.[5] With this in mind, Yawkey and Aronin suggest that through the device of the "Living Circle" teachers can utilize developmental needs of students to facilitate such things as valuing behavior, self-understanding, self-worth, and ways of relating to others. Although the living circle does not appear radically different from the usual classroom discussion, there are some important differences. First, there are no restrictions on the freedom of students to voice their ideas, feelings, and experiences about personal and social concerns. Secondly, the teacher acts as a facilitator, accepting all the opinions and comments of students without criticism. When students have difficulty in specifically identifying a problem, the teacher is there to clarify the problem.[6]

All students should have the opportunity to express their opinions and observations. Analyses and solutions imposed from external sources usually are not as meaningful to students. The living circle gives them the chance to relate the subject matter of social studies to their own situations. In presenting topics for discussion, filmstrips can be used, as well as unfinished stories or stimuli pictures. At the present time multimedia kits are available to facilitate the living circle approach, and some of these offer considerable data for discussion. Generally, however, the amount of structure in the discussion depends on the teacher's personality and experience with this approach, and the readiness of the students. Finally, when used by an experienced teacher, role-playing can be a valuable technique in making the living circle an exciting and rewarding approach. In summary, the living circle offers the following benefits for students: (1) They can compare and contrast ideas, while considering alternatives. (2) They can relate the activities of adults to their own experiences and ideas. (3) They can improve their listening habits. (4) They can share their convictions with others. (5) They learn that respect and good behavior toward others is rewarding.[7]

Personal Space

In recent years the teaching of geography in the American public schools has declined in its rewards for both students and teachers, and thus a new approach to this subject is a welcome event. According to David R. Lee, there are really three geographies. The first has as its object the world—physical, empirical, spatial reality which we perceive directly through our senses. The second geography is theoretical, in which the object of study is no longer the world as it is, but as it would be given certain assumptions and constraints. The third geography is existential. Although it does have space as its unifying theme, existential geography, unlike the first two geographies, is completely and unashamedly subjective. The significance of existential geography, Lee concluded, is that "each responsible human individual possesses an existential geography of his own, his unique environmental image, his personal conception of spatial reality. Each individual attends to the space of his geography in his own subjective way."[8]

The value of making students aware of their own personal space is that they can learn to be responsible for what takes place within it, and they likewise can learn that each person in this world has his or her own space. In addition students can learn that they must be concerned with what social and physical planners do with this space. Equally important, Lee maintains, is the opportunity for each student to realize that "at the level of his country he is responsible to see that the national segment of his existential space does not become invaded by foreign foes who could ultimately threaten his town, his home, his body. He provides, therefore, for the creation of the military, and should expect that if his nation should become invaded, he himself might actively engage in repelling that invader."[9]

Another benefit of making students aware of existential geography is that they come to realize that what is harmful to others in their life space may become harmful to them too. "The ecology issue can be seen as a progressive deterioration of the quality of one's existential space. Racism can be viewed in part as the existence of pockets of anger in one's existential map, which like festering sores on the body do not vanish by ignoring them."[10] The final aim of existential geography is to personalize the material within the traditional geographies.

Intergroup Relations

Because of its content, social studies offers an excellent opportunity for teachers to focus on the historical, social, and psychological dimensions of intragroup and intergroup relationships. Instead of viewing minority groups as "social problems," social studies teachers should focus on the positive aspects of various groups. Not all humanistic lessons are to be learned from structured exercises or games. All students can be asked to present their own culture through the aesthetics of music, poetry, short stories, plays, essays, art, dance, clothing, and food. Nor must the only acceptable models be the famous Americans cited in this book and elsewhere. Local role models can also be identified and brought into the classroom. The entire community can become a laboratory for humanistic adventure and learning.

HUMANISTIC APPROACHES IN THE SCIENCES

It is only recently that a large number of educators have come to acknowledge that the subject of biology as it is generally taught has little relevance for the average student. In order to clarify the meaning of biology in a complex social structure, information and opinions were collected from lecturers and students concerned with the study of social biology in colleges at the London Institute of Education, as well as from senior students studying biology in several secondary schools in and around London. From the London study emerged a clarification of the areas covered by social biology.

Mechanisms of heredity. Human genetics.
Medical and social implications of a human genetics.
Human variation and the effects of nature and nurture on the development of man. Races of Man.
Principles of ecology; the use, management and control of natural resources.
World nutrition. Plants of economic and social importance.
Pollution and conservation.
Reproductive cycle of man and its control.
Size, growth and control of human populations.
Human behavior. Social psychology.
Basic concepts of sociology.
Social structure and organization.
Cultural evolution of Man.
Social and welfare services, Urbanization, Crime, and Delinquency.
Natures, causes and control of organic disease.
Social implications of disease. Public health.
Drug dependence; Alcoholism and smoking.[11]

With such topics offered in social biology courses, a large number of British students have become aware that biology is not the irrelevant subject it is often felt to be in modern American public schools. Social biology considers people in a much wider scope than does human biology: they are observed as "part of a community within the complexities of the total environment. In human biology courses, the individual is seen fighting for his survival in a potentially hostile world, whereas in social biology humans are seen in the context of the community which has a collective responsibility for the social and physical world which man attempts to manage and control."[12]

From the social biology curricula surveyed by the London study, it was possible to isolate four major areas of study common to most of the courses in the subject. (1) The scientific study of humans as biological organisms is studied at the level of the individual. (2) The applications of biological principles are used to augment the study of human life. (3) The structure and development of human life is related to culture and society. And (4) the relationship between humans and their total environment, particularly the interaction with their social environment and the physical world around them, is an important focus.[13] If American biology courses would incorporate some of these areas into their syllabi, more students would become aware of the interrelationships between all human beings, as well as their responsibilities in seeing that all human life is respected and cherished. Human relations training would help biology teachers to humanize their classrooms.

Sensitivity Training

E. W. Menzel described the invaluable aid which a sensitivity training group experience gave him in dealing with students in his science courses. All too often, he said, science teachers are unable or unwilling to work as encounter teachers—they fail to realize that a balance of both affective and cognitive qualities are required in today's schools.[14] Menzel believes that through sensitivity training most science teachers can learn to respond to their students in a more caring manner.

What is often lacking in science classes is the

one ingredient generally thought absolutely necessary for the student to become aware of the nature of science itself: the freedom to invent and experiment. Students must feel comfortable in the classroom if they are to allow their powers of imagination to develop and to work on the subject matter of science. Menzel stated the proposition thus: "An attitude of inventiveness can be present in the classroom which allows experiments to be created spontaneously by students and/or teachers, thus having the effect of clarifying and tightening the students' conceptual powers. Such methodology would build on the inventive notions offered by students as well as the more formal and accepted arguments."[15]

Many mathematics and science teachers in the public schools are unable to nurture and expand the imagination and inventiveness of their young students. "To be prepared for this type of teaching," Menzel wrote, "requires not only competence in science content but a feeling of comfort with spontaneity, confrontation, open-endedness, and variations in levels of understanding and language facility."[16] The T-group which Menzel joined gave him valuable insights into himself and his students, allowing him the courage to accept their freedom of invention. It also gave him the ability to show them that such freedom is a desirable goal. But a caution is in order: The T-group in which Menzel and his university colleagues participated was organized by professional educators, and a well-qualified trainer was utilized.

HUMANISTIC APPROACHES AT THE PRIMARY LEVEL

A problem which often puzzles primary grade teachers is how to bring "left-out" children into the activities of the group and how to help them be accepted by their peers. One educator has suggested various games which can be used as techniques in solving this problem. First, an observation area can be set aside so that students who do not at first want to play may have a neutral place from which to watch. The teacher might call this area "Superbase." One of the first rules of gaming for children is that no one should have to play; all children should be free to join or drop out at any time. The following activities can help students get ac-

quainted with one another and become accepted by the group:

1. *Name Catch*. The first player starts the game by rolling a ball to someone else. That player must say his or her own name and then roll the ball to a third student. The game goes on from player to player, building up a rhythm.

2. *Business Card*. The teacher gives all the players slips of paper on which they are to write their names. If thirty youngsters play, each one should have thirty slips. The object of the game is for each student to make sure that every other student has one of his or her cards. The teacher should let each player find his or her own methods for distributing his or her cards and finding ways to keep track of who has them. Students will learn names and faces by receiving cards from classmates. They will have to discover some way of getting to know each other if they don't want to get the same card twice.

3. *Formal*. The object of this game is to introduce as many people to one another as possible. The teacher should start the game off by bowing or curtsying to a child. She should explain in as exaggerated a way as possible what a great honor it is for them to have met. Although the teacher no doubt knows the child's name, she should pretend to have temporarily forgotten it. She might say something like the following: "I'm so glad you could come today. It really was so good of you to take the trouble, Ms. . . . oh, I'm terribly sorry, I seem to have forgotten your name. You are Ms. . . . This is quite embarrassing, Ms. Brown. Ah, yes, Ms. Brown! How delighted I am to see you again. But I'm afraid your first name has escaped me . . . Lisa. Lisa, of course! Lisa Brown. How could I have forgotten?" Then the teacher should introduce Lisa to someone else in the same manner. The students may then pick up the game from there.[17]

Living with Feelings

Karl R. Wullschleger suggests ways in which the primary grade teacher can encourage students to both reveal and control their feelings:

1. The teacher might allow children to role-play certain fictitious characters, such as Little Miss Muffet. A docile child may want to cast himself or herself as the vicious spider,

while an aggressive child may want to play Miss Muffet. Each one should have a chance to explore his or her feelings in an unfamiliar role.

2. If a teacher is having difficulty with students, she might allow one student to sit at her desk while she sits at the student's desk. If the youngster feels free in reversing roles to display his or her genuine feelings about the teacher, the latter will profit from being shown the student's attitudes.

3. Drama with puppets quite often offers children a safe means of self-disclosure.

4. If children become disorderly during an art project, messing with paints and clay, the teacher should place the art tables in front of a large mirror. The students can then see themselves in action and perhaps realize how unattractive their behavior is.

5. In solving conflicts between students, the teacher might suggest that two particularly hostile children pair off and sit on the floor, back to back, and hum a note. As they hum the teacher should explain that they are preparing for a quiet fight. The humming fades away and then the children "fight," back to back, without making a sound. They should be allowed to push and elbow jab for about three minutes. Usually, they will stop of their own accord, and the two who had been enemies in the classroom up to then will very probably have become friends.

6. In a game called "The Story," children divide up into three groups—the happy group, the sad group, and the angry group. For warm-up, each group practices its feelings with sounds, gestures, and dances. Then the teacher or a student reads an appropriate story, and the happy group demonstrates happiness in happy parts, the sad group acts in sad parts, and the angry group displays its proper emotion in the proper part of the story.

7. If two children have been scribbling on each other's work, give each a fresh paper and an affectionate hug. Usually the scribbling is a display of hostility, and affection can erase hostile feelings.

8. If two children are verbally assaulting one another, ask them to hold each other's hands, face to face, and see who can make the other laugh the harder.

9. If two children are throwing dirt clods at each other, ask them to hold a clod tightly, squeeze it, and growl at one another.

10. If the class is in a general uproar, the teacher should ask the children to form a circle and then lie on the floor, each child laying his or her head on the belly of the one next to him. The teacher should say a loud "Ha!" and ask the children to repeat it. Uncontrollable laughter usually results.[18]

The "Magic Box" is another exercise that is quite effective in the primary grades. The teacher asks students to sit in a circle. After they are in a circle, the students receive the following instruction from the teacher: "Imagine that you have a magic box that can be any size or any shape, and it could be anything you want that would make you happy." One at a time, the students are allowed to share what would be in their box. After students state what would be in their box, the teacher may seek further clarification by asking: "What would you do with it that would make you happy? Where would you do it? Where (in the body) would you feel happy?" Variations of this exercise include asking students to pick out of the box what they feel members of their family would have chosen.

HUMANISTIC APPROACHES TO LITERATURE AND LITERATURE-RELATED SUBJECTS

Many writers believe that the area of learning in which offers the most promise for affective teaching is literature and its related fields. One axiom of humanistic education is that students must understand and have compassion for their fellow human beings if they are to develop into caring, self-actualizing persons in later life. Carleton R. Deonanan is convinced that "literature study is definitely the study of character development as revealed in behavior throughout mankind's civilization. . . . It is indeed the most promising approach to redeem man from a stage of selfish and barbarous living to one of civilization and a concern for his fellow man."[19]

Through literature students can see how the great characters of fiction worked through their problems to a richer life. Furthermore, if guided by a caring teacher, students will open up emotionally to the beauties of language and thus the wonders of communication—especially through the medium of poetry. In an age which puts such a high price on technical efficiency and too often a low value on compassion, literature can be "the catalyst to remold the *particle man* formed by technology into the whole man so that there will be a high degree of civility, peace, and stability."[20]

Conflict Management

If the societies of the world lose their humane values, the world as we know it may very well cease to exist. It can profit a nation little to produce highly skilled robots who cannot evaluate the results of their efforts in terms of what benefits all humankind. The crucial need is to redirect our efforts toward the students' understanding of themselves and their brothers and sisters in humanity. This task may well be met first in the study of literature.

The focus on education for character development through the study of literature as a focal subject in the high school curriculum and college must be a reality in restoring the sensitivity of human values for the existence and mutual relationship of man. . . . Literature can meet each one of us on our terms and take us into the experiences and ideas of the greatest minds of all times. This is the most promising approach in civilizing man and hence the promoting of a civilization theory of education through literature. A civilizational theory in education through literature is synonymous to education for character development as a behavioral object because civilization is the manifestation of the development of character based on a value system.[21]

Norma K. Stegmaier lists specific works of literature which can facilitate the development of values in the classroom. During their years in school, most children face conflicts in four specific situations: with parents, with siblings, with members of their peer group, and intergroup conflict.[22] In dealing with conflict involving parents, an understanding teacher will try to point out that children should get along with their parents and that they cannot survive by unilateral action. Stegmaier recommends two books which can help students understand this important point: Emily Neville's *It's Like This, Cat* and Musa Nagenda's *Dogs of Fear: A Story of Modern Africa*. Both books deal with the conflict between father and son, and many

teachers will find it helpful to have students role-play characters in the stories.

Four books which may help children understand their conflicts with siblings are Jack Keats' *Peter's Chair*, Russell Hoban's *A Baby Sister for Frances*, and Doris Orgel's *Whose Turtle?* and *The Seven Wishes of Joanna Peabody*. In the latter story Joanna has a special television spirit, Aunt Thelma, who can grant her seven wishes. It is only when Joanna wishes something for someone else that her wishes are granted. It is suggested that the teacher ask students to write down their seven wishes after the story is read aloud, while telling them that their lists will be shared with other students. When the lists are collected the teacher should read each one in order to find out whether the class knows to whom it belongs. Stegmaier says that "with this activity, children discover whether they perceive themselves and others accurately. Accurate perceptions are essential to interpersonal communication."[23]

Understanding conflicts with one's peers is the subject of two books, Crosby Bonsall's *The Case of the Scaredy Cats* (for eight- to ten-year-olds) and Mary Stolz' *A Wonderful, Terrible Time*, a work especially appropriate for junior high school students. The former story deals with girls who take over a boys' clubhouse with a "No Girls" sign on it, while the latter book tells the story of two best friends, Madie and Sue Ellen, who live in a racially-mixed neighborhood.

Intergroup conflicts are well handled in five books by modern authors. Lorenz Graham's *South Town* is a story dealing with relationships between Blacks and whites; Graham's *Whose Town?* also raises the question of interracial tension. Margaret Hodges' *The Making of Joshua Cobb* is a story of rivalry between the "aristos" and the "plebes" at a public school. Emily Neville's *Berries Goodman* relates the experiences of Berries and Sidney, a Christian and a Jew, and Nathaniel Benchley's *Small Wolf* deals with the relationships between Manhattan Native Americans and the first white settlers. A teacher using any of these books will find the techniques of role-playing, group discussion, and debate most rewarding.

Children's books which deal adequately with the response of empathy are Virginia Sorenson's *Plain Girl*, a story about a public school student who comes from the single Amish family in the community, and Eleanor

Clymer's *The Spider, The Cave, and The Pottery Bowl*, a contemporary Native American story which is particularly suitable for eight- to thirteen-year-old students.

The importance of sensitivity is taken up in Mary O'Neill's *What Is That Sound!* and *Hailstones and Halibut Bones*. Both books are collections of verse. Alvin Tresselt's *Sun Up* describes sensuously a hot summer day on a farm, and it is suggested that the teacher should first have the students read the story aloud. Afterwards he or she might ask such questions as, "If you were a farm animal, a plant, or a flower, how would you feel?" The rationale for this method is that "by discussing how they would feel as another living creature or thing, children gain understanding of self and others."[24] A fourth book which deals effectively with sensitivity is Ann Nolan Clark's *Tia Maria's Garden*, a work which can help a student form judgments on the basis of his or her own perceptions.

Black Studies

Literature classes can also double as Black Studies classes. The number of books focusing on Black people is increasing at a significant rate. Despite this progress, few Black students (or their teachers) learn that *Poems on Various Subjects: Religious and Moral* (1775) by Phillis Wheatley was the first published literary work by a Black American. *Escape; Or, A Leap for Freedom* (1851), by William Wells Brown, an escaped slave, was the first play by a Black American. *The Chipwoman's Fortune* (1932) by Willis Richardson was the first Black-authored play on Broadway. *Native Son* (1940) by Richard Wright was the first Black novel to achieve classic status. *Annie Allen* (1950) by Gwendolyn Brooks, poet laureate of Illinois, was the first work by a Black poet to win a Pulitzer Prize, and *Invisible Man* (1952) by Ralph Ellison received the National Book Award. Equally revealing is the fact that few Black students (or their teachers) have read the seminal works of Frederick Douglass, Paul Lawrence Dunbar, W.E.B. DuBois, Booker T. Washington, James Weldon Johnson, and Langston Hughes, to mention a few renowned Black writers. Similar courses can be developed for Indian, Latino, and Asian studies.

It is worth repeating that teaching values through literature is effective when joined with techniques like role-playing, discussion, and creative dramatics. In this way, three major objectives are reached. (1) The children can be made aware of parent-child struggles, the love-hate dichotomy in sibling relationships, and the competition and friction between groups resulting from both a win-lose orientation and negative stereotyping of one's opponents. When they recognize the role of these elements in the breakdown in communication, most children are better able to cope with and mitigate the breakdown. (2) By becoming cognizant of their senses and responding to them, most children develop accurate perceptions enabling them not only to respond to their surroundings but also to make sound judgments. (3) By developing this awareness, these children learn to understand other people and consequently to empathize with them.

Reading Skills

Today we often hear the complaint from both teachers and parents that too many children cannot read, and it does appear that functional illiteracy is increasing at an alarming rate. George Fargo, a reading specialist, maintains that certain "cop-outs" have contributed in a major way to this problem; that is, a number of false assumptions obscure the real difficulty we face:

1. The assumption that some students just aren't educable.
2. The assumption that physical and cultural differences are deficiencies.
3. The assumption that schools still have a "melting pot" function.
4. The assumption that learning is a passive act.
5. The assumption that reading occurs the same way for every child.
6. The assumption that failure and disapproval motivates children.
7. The assumption that the answer to student failures lies in diagnosis.
8. The assumption that there must be one final cure for reading problems.
9. The assumption that solutions lie mainly in helping the child adjust to school-determined environments.

10. The assumption that more and better research and improved curriculum and teaching techniques will resolve the majority of reading problems.[25]

If we accept Fargo's reasoning, the real problem is that too often children's books are not relevant to the daily experiences of the students; they are frequently "too long, too dry, too phony, reflecting nothing of his life style or microculture and not based on any well thought out conceptualization of what people are and need in the reality of today."[26]

One of the most serious shortcomings of children's books is that most of them fail to inform the readers about cultural differences. Too many books tend to treat anything which deviates from white, middle-class, male norms as somehow undesirable or nonexistent. Perhaps many nonwhite students do not learn to read because they have little interest in reading about people and situations unrelated to their daily experiences. Authors of children's books, as well as publishers, must realize that "all children need the experience of knowing the excitement of cultural difference in the context of common human needs. All children need the experience of knowing 'their' difference as a plus rather than a minimum in the context of common human learning."[27]

VALUES CLARIFICATION

Teachers who are interested in humanizing education are often unsure as to how to go about inspiring students to think about values. As Kenneth B. Huggins puts it, a person's attitude or belief is not a true value unless he chooses it freely. "Schools," he cautions, "must teach *valuing* rather than values."[28] Of course this assertion implies that the teacher is not to force his or her own values on students. There are three general guidelines in generating alternatives for students: the alternatives must be real and feasible to the students; students who have not been exposed to alternative behavior must have additional help, and there must be a cognitive element in understanding alternatives. At the same time, it is necessary that teachers be well acquainted with the life-styles of their students. The following strategies have been effective in generating alternative values:

1. *Coat of Arms*. The teacher asks students to draw a personal coat of arms and then share it with others. Symbols on the coat of arms might represent responses to such questions as: What was the most exciting event in your life during the last year? What would you buy first if you were given a million dollars? What three words might people use to describe you if you died tomorrow? What's your favorite place on earth?

2. *Role-Playing*. The teacher asks two students to role-play a situation. After the role-play, they discuss the behavioral implications.

3. *Questions and Public Interviews*. A public interview covering various topics is conducted by the teacher with one student in front of the class. The student is allowed to pass on any question he or she doesn't want to answer, and at the end of the interview the student may ask the teacher any question the teacher asked.

4. *Other Cultures*. The teacher encourages students to put themselves in the place of individuals in other cultures. If they can learn to understand children in other cultures (even if the understanding is subconscious), they will approach an awareness that for every value choice there are other alternatives.

5. *Comparison*. Students are asked to compare their lives with those of the characters in a story, poem, or play. An easy strategy to facilitate this comparison is rank ordering. In a rank order, a problem situation is presented and three alternative responses are given for students to rank according to their preference.

6. *Twenty Loves*. When teachers are not sure what is most important to their students, they can be asked to list twenty things—trivial or important—that they love to do, indicating whether the activity requires solitude, other people, money, the outdoors, indoors, a certain season, and so forth. This strategy helps both students and teachers to identify value patterns.[29]

Sex Discrimination

An important area of values and values clarification centers on sex discrimination. A. Montgomery Johnson asked the question, "What are the more humane attitudes toward sexuality?"[30] As seen in Chapter 11, there are still too many sexist books, television programs, and texts. If this is true, the next question might be: What attitudes toward sexual identity will aid students in fully understanding what it means to be a complete human being? At least four major ones are suggested:[31]

1. Each student is a unique person with individual characteristics which transcend sex, race, color, nationality, etc. There should be no stereotyping of characteristics of either females or males.

2. Each student is a unique person free to choose any role s/he is able to play with no stereotyping of roles of females or males.

3. There should be equality of opportunity for females and males, e.g., equal pay for equal work, equal opportunity for all jobs, equal chance for promotions and leadership, equal recognition for achievements in textbooks, library books, newspapers, and television.

4. Each student, female and male, has an obligation to develop her or his talents to the fullest; no stereotype of sex characteristics should limit such talent development and use. All students should be educated to their fullest and practice their developed talents to the maximum.

Two important things which all teachers can do to change students' attitudes are to allow students to develop for themselves a clear and detailed notion of the more humane attitudes toward sexuality and to eradicate or counteract unrealistic attitudes toward sexuality. This effort might include minimizing use of books, films, and records which perpetuate less productive attitudes and eliminating use of sexist grammar.[32]

Some specific activities which have helped to bring about a change of attitude on the part of students are:[33]

1. Rethinking and changing the usual practice of having Safety Patrol for boys only.

2. Rethinking and redesigning physical education and sports programs. It is not necessary or even desirable to segregate the sexes in physical education all the time. The challenge is to develop a physical education program based on unique and individual needs, interests, and abilities rather than on sexual characteristics.

3. Rethinking the practice of classroom grouping on the basis of sex for teams, committees, and other instructional groups: "I am a person" should be more important than "I am a boy or girl."

4. Using a videotape recorder or just a plain tape recorder to record one's teaching and play it back after school. If this is done, the teacher should analyze his or her responses first to boys and then to girls in the class. The teacher should try to identify specific biases in his or her behavior and launch a program of improvement.

5. Adding to the school library books which foster more humane attitudes toward sexuality.

6. Inviting members of the sex opposite to the teacher into the classroom as resource persons to be interviewed by the class (famous persons, community leaders, experts, hobbyists, etc.), to show a group how to do something or make something, to tell about their travel or other experiences, or to tell about their hobbies or occupations.

7. Rethinking the total program for the class. Do the activities appeal largely to one personality type more than the other (sedentary, linguistic, vicarious)? Are there enough activities offered to meet the interests and needs of a wide variety of personality types (active, participatory, nonverbal, etc.)?

8. Making a survey with the students of the many different occupations women and men are pursuing in the community or a nearby larger city. The students should be encouraged to take photographs or draw pictures of each worker in his or her appropriate clothing, operating characteristic equipment. Class members should be encouraged to write to successful persons in various occupational fields for information and encouragement. Males and females should be selected.

9. Developing a unit of work on child-rearing, emphasizing the values of male and female adults both participating in the many aspects of this important task regardless of the child's sex. Teachers should help children to see the important roles that fathers as well as mothers can play at all ages for both sons and daughters.

HUMANISTIC APPROACHES IN SPECIAL EDUCATION

While much progress has been made in humanizing instruction, very little has been done to make education a really meaningful experience for the students least able to right the wrongs inflicted on them: students in special education classes. (It should be pointed out that a disproportionate number of non-white students are in special education classes.) One of the major factors which has contributed to this injustice is that special education has too often emulated the methods and goals of the natural sciences and thus has "failed to take into account the humanness of its subject, i.e., that humans are more than static objects reactively following the laws of physical nature."[34] Both the dilemma and its solution have been well stated by Constance T. Fischer and Alfonso A. Rizzo, two leading authorities on special education.

Even while we seek to address the richness of the whole person and while as practitioners we respect his structural unity, our science can accommodate him only at the level of discrete visible parts, i.e., those aspects that lend themselves to measurement. . . . The turning point which special education must take is this: Either explicitly deny that the human being is more than the billiard ball and rededicate itself to still greater precision in measurement, or *turn its efforts toward developing theories, research methods, and practices that are based on man's nature as human.*[35]

It is this latter approach which can satisfy the requirements of humanistic education in any field. Fischer and Rizzo posited seven innovative proposals to more fully humanize special education experiences:

1. *Replace diagnosis with concrete recommendations.* Assessments must be directed to particular students, with the results given in the form of recommendations that specify which persons, objects, and situations should be called into play.
2. *Eliminate test priority.* We must give priority to assessing how a student does what in which circumstances. Emphasizing life data instead of test scores puts tests in our service instead of the reverse.
3. *Provide students with access to their files.* Records should not contain references to presumably underlying traits or to esoteric interpretations of behavior, nor should they contain unexplained jargon.
4. *Shift focus from student limitations to behavioral possibilities.* Using a descriptive rather than quantitative account of each student's accomplishments, we can see both his/her experiences and how he/she does whatever he/she does.
5. *Encourage participation of significant adults.* Parents, teachers, and peers can provide perspectives and relationships that are as valid and effective as those of professional helpers. Encouraging the participation of non-professionals promotes the interpersonal sensitivity, responsibility, and hopefulness that have been critically undermined in education.
6. *Integrate classrooms.* Exceptional children can benefit from the company and surroundings of regular classrooms. Such mainstreaming will necessitate smaller class sizes for all children. Ideally, all children would come to accept differences as such rather than as "defects" or "deviations."
7. *Expand humanistic research programs.* It is time to forego the security of uncorroborated jargon. It is time to work systematically with everyday classroom events. Only through purposeful programs involving program evaluation can we establish a humanized special education that, in turn, can be supported by educators and community leaders.[36]

A HUMANISTIC APPROACH TO TEACHING MUSIC

Of all the arts, perhaps music is the one which most deeply touches our emotions, raises our aspirations, and puts us in communion with our fellow human beings. Yet too many teachers of music insist on providing not a warm, sharing experience but a rigorous, enervating course. As Meyer M. Cahn has commented, "The music appreciation class is one more place where the academic and the cognitive aspects have been emphasized at the expense of the more broadly personal and human experience that music listening can be."[37]

All human beings, and certainly the young, have an almost infinite capacity for feeling which can best be developed by exposure to great art, yet often this capacity is nearly destroyed by an overemphasis on the theoretical aspects of beauty. It should come as no surprise to learn that most students bring with them into the classroom an ability to appreciate music at the highest level and that they resent any attempt to tell them that their natural powers are not to be trusted. Cahn observed, "Any teacher will tell you of the stubborn response of students, of their insistence on listening to music with their natural powers of enjoyment, of the intransigent stance many of them take in refusing to integrate instruction with their listening."[38] Implicit in this statement is the need for music programs to include a wide range of music—classical, blues, folk, jazz, rock, and country-western—so that students will be able to appreciate their own cultural music as well as that of other cultures.

If music is to provide the healing experience so desperately needed in this impersonal world of technology, then our schools must return to their primary function: to bring forth the humane responses which enable us to feel with and for others. Surely there are better ways to discover this meaning than those provided thus far in colleges and academies. We need institutions that place human beings in high regard, that respect their socialness, and that do not denigrate their intuitive gift for mingling with their fellow humans in existentially inspiring ways. In summary, what we need is a humanistic route to music learning that will make all students feel better about themselves and that will enable them to interact with the music of their own culture as well as other cultures with the full confidence that music was meant for all people—in the warmest, broadest, and deepest sense of being human.[39]

HUMANISTIC APPROACHES IN PHYSICAL EDUCATION

In a society in which brutal competition, winning, and profit seem to have become the watchwords of so many physical education departments, it is time to take a second look at what the real function of this subject should be. Several educators, including Stratton F. Caldwell, have suggested that the theme of a new philosophy of physical education should be movement. "Movement can serve as a facilitating and actualizing medium for the experiencing of those rare and elusive moments of the most intense, overpowering human feelings of joy, supreme well-being,

ecstasy. . . ."[40] But before we can bring such joy to our public school students, we must eliminate "the jock, the throw-out-the-baller, the military martinet, the professionals who died on the vine years ago, the incompetents and uncaring who masquerade as teachers while fostering student passivity, obedience, conformity, and dependence."[41] As a group, Black students do quite well in competitive sports. However, physical education should do much more than produce athletes.

Marian E. Kneer, another authority in the field of humanizing physical education curriculum, suggests that teachers of the subject give their students the following "What Do I Value in Life?" questionnaire in order that they may clarify their major values:

Directions:

1. Read through the entire list. This is not a semantics exercise, so feel free to cross out the descriptive words in parentheses that have no meaning to your personal definition of the term capitalized; insert others if you wish. Indicate each item's level of importance to you at this time and place in your life—whether it is "not too important," "important," or "very important."

2. After completing item 1, pick out and list in the spaces provided the five items which are most important to you, and the five items that are least important to you.

Adventure (exploration, risks, danger, doing something new and/or untried)
Beauty (in the arts and in nature)
Emotional well-being (ability to recognize and handle inner conflict)
Ethical life (responsible living toward self and others, personal honor, integrity)
Family happiness (mutual caring among family members)
Forgiveness (being willing to pardon others, bearing no grudges)
Honesty (being frank and genuinely yourself with everyone)
Law and order (respect for authority, property of others)
Love (warmth, caring and receiving of respect and affection)
Meaningful work (sense of purpose, doing something that is relevant)

Money (plenty of money for things I want)

Personal freedom (independence, making own choices)

Personal power (having influence and authority over others)

Physical appearance (attractiveness—neat, clean, well-groomed)

Pleasure (excitement, satisfaction, fun, joy)

Recognition (being important, being well-liked, being accepted)

Religion (religious belief, relationship with God, meaning in life)

Service (devotion to the interests of others)

Skill (being good at doing something important to me and/or to others)

Wisdom (mature understanding, insight, application of knowledge)[42]

A few years ago a study of teachers' perceptions of student likes and dislikes in physical education was administered to a random sample of about six hundred Chicago metropolitan area high school teachers. Numbers in parentheses are the ranking given each item by the teachers in that study.

Neumann Survey of Teacher's Perception of Students'
Likes and Dislikes in Physical Education
SECTION A

Directions: Rank the items below from 1–15 on the basis of how you believe your students would rank their "most liked" class.

Praise or recognition for achievement (11)

Responsibilities you had (13)

The activity itself (1)

Good personal relationship with teacher (6)

The teacher's manner of teaching (5)

Good personal relationships with classmates (2)

Level of personal skill achieved (8)

Amount of activity in class (3)

Amount of basic knowledge and understanding you attained (9)

Method of grading (12)

Policies and routines (14)

Provided basis for out-of-school activities (10)

Feeling of accomplishment (7)

Adequate safety precautions (15)

Challenging (4)

SECTION B

Directions: Same as above but rank on the basis of their "least liked" class.

Lack of praise or recognition (13)

Lack of responsibilities (14)

The activity itself (2)

Poor personal relationship with teacher (7)

Teacher's manner of teaching (1)

Poor personal relationships with classmates (12)

Lack of personal skill achieved (9)

Amount of activity—too much—too little (3)

Little basic knowledge and understanding of the activity attained (8)

Method of grading (4)

Policies and routines (6)

No relationship to out-of-school activities (11)

No feeling of accomplishment (5)

Inadequate safety precautions (15)

Not challenging (10)[43]

Most teachers of physical education classes must change their own values and attitudes if students are to be freed from the tyranny of the philosophy that winning is the only thing. In addition professional organizations and public school systems should initiate more workshops designed to help physical educators to truly humanize the discipline and thereby achieve many of the social and emotional goals which the profession espouses. Teacher self-awareness is the first step.

HUMANIZING COUNSELING THROUGH COMMUNICATIONS GAMES

An innovative group counseling project was undertaken in a high school; it made extensive use of communications games in order to facilitate relationships between counselors and counselees. (While focusing on white students, the project is relevant for racially mixed situations.) Volunteering for the project were fifty-seven freshmen who were divided into four groups of six to eight participants of both sexes, meeting one hour weekly for eight weeks. Two of the four groups were composed of students enrolled in specially designed classes known as core classes. Students in the core classes had difficulty coping with normal classroom activity. All factors considered, they were likely candidates for dropping from school or transferring to the district's continuation high school. One of the other two groups was composed of students identified by their teachers as being academically able. The fourth group was mixed and had no distinguishable characteristics.[44]

The "Object Game" and "Positive Statements" were two of the most effective activities in facilitating communication between the participants.

The Object Game. Participants were requested to go out on the campus and pick up an object they felt represented the way they were feeling at the moment or how they felt about themselves in general. They returned with many different kinds of objects: flowers, mud, rocks, leaves, broken pencils, etc. They then placed the objects in the center of the group as each group member discussed the significance of his object.

Positive Statements. The group was asked to write something positive about each person in the group. The writer's own name and that of the group counselor were included. The positive statements could have been stimulated by any of the previous group sessions. The papers were collected, mixed, and redistributed. The counselor modeled by reading first from the paper she had. After all of the papers were read, the group engaged in a spontaneous discussion about how difficult it is to convey positive feelings and how negative or cutting statements do not seem to pose the same problem for teenagers.[45]

The more visual and action-oriented games seemed to stimulate the most communication between members of the groups. In later sessions games were not needed, for the groundwork for communication had already been laid. In reviewing the project, it is evident that the importance of having competent group leaders cannot be ignored. (Well-trained counselors use games only when required for motivating interaction and reducing tension.)

In order to evaluate the effectiveness of the project, two kinds of data were collected. First, the participants in the groups were told to write their reactions on 3 x 5 response cards at the close of each group session. The cards were then coded for group and session identification. Counselor observations, participant evaluations, and general comments from teachers, parents, and students provided another data source.

Surprisingly, the students who were expected to be the least responsive to the group procedures, the core students, were noticeably less inhibited in stating their responses. Based on participant comments, the experience seemed to have greatly benefited all the participants. The group participants were more friendly toward the counselor; they seemed inclined to be more open, less defensive, and more communicative in individual counseling sessions than students who were not involved in the project. Parents of student participants noticed positive changes in the nature of their children's remarks about school. Finally, teacher comments were generally favorable.

Because the experience might not benefit all students, participation in such programs should always be voluntary. From data compiled in this study, it appears that optimum results will occur only if the counselor leading such sessions has been well-trained in human relations techniques.

TECHNOLOGY AS AN AID TO HUMANISTIC EDUCATION

Many critics of traditional education have come to believe that it is time for educators who are humanistically oriented to stop condemning technology and begin to take a serious look at what technology has to offer. The apprehension caused by the misuse of many technological innovations has perhaps rightly generated concern among educators. As engineer Merritt A. Williamson asked, "Can we engineers in any way produce 'something' as a result of our knowledge of technology which will interject desirable (from our point of view) value judgments into the operation so that the world may be assured that the device or system can be used only to further the highest ideals of education?"[46] Whatever the qualms of humanistic educators, they must make this leap into technology, at least in some fields, if they are to truly liberate tomorrow's students. As Williamson puts it, "I think we must devise some intriguing technological device to replace an indifferent or hostile teacher for instruction in scientific and mathematical subjects."[47]

John T. Caufield, another authority in the field of educational technology, summarized a few of the innovations now available to interested teachers and administrators:

1. The Human Development Program. *This program is for use in preschool settings and the early elementary grades. It makes use of the "magic circle" approach to education. HDP materials are designed to enhance the student in the following areas: self-awareness, considerateness, eagerness, effectiveness, flexibility, interpersonal comprehension, sensitivity to others, spontaneity, stability, and tolerance.*

2. Science Research Associates. The Focus on the Self Development Program *is somewhat less structured than the* Human Development Program, *strives to achieve similar goals through the use of records, filmstrips and guided group discussion. It is designed for children in grades K-3.*

3. Argus Communications. *Argus'* Hello People, *with its emphasis on self-concept and multi-ethnic social interaction, helps the child learn to cope with today's complex society.*

4. Combined Motivation Education Systems. *This firm publishes the* Curriculum for a Developing Self, *a K-12 project. It is an experimental curriculum enabling students to maximize their full potential by focusing on six processes of human growth:*

> *learning to accept oneself, developing a better relationship with reality, becoming one's natural and creative self, viewing life in its broad perspective, expanding autonomous behavior, and developing a kinship with mankind.*[48]

In 1971 the Ford Foundation gave Gerald Weinstein and George Brown a grant of $500,000 to develop a data bank of humanistic exercises, develop and disseminate humanistic curriculum, and train teachers and evaluate the results. It seems obvious that technology has come to stay, for better or worse, in the field of education.

Combined Motivation Education Systems, one of the programs described above, has designed programs which permit and encourage personalized educational experience in order to identify and develop the unused personal strengths and potentialities of students.[49] The programs developed by this firm are based on the premise that people accomplish the most when they are doing what they want to do—when they are operating under a *want* system rather than a *should* system. The programs assume that everybody is already motivated intrinsically, and that pressures from external sources reduce rather than increase students' motivation to achieve. A student will act on his or her internal motivation more forcibly when supported, rather than pressured, by the teacher. Teachers trying to improve the cognitive and affective behavior of their students should take note of the advantages which teaching machines, audiovisual devices, programmed materials and simulation games can offer both teachers and students: They minimize the need for suppressive discipline in the classroom. Students can progress with their own interests at their own rates and on their own levels of competence. The step-by-step successes of programmed instruction tend to eliminate the frustration of failure, thereby enhancing the students' self-concept, and teachers can focus on areas requiring sensitive human interaction.[50]

In Caufield's words: "Technology-based techniques allow teachers to concentrate their attention on the personally *human* concerns of their students. Released from the tasks of maintaining classroom discipline, imparting factual information and supervising repetitive drill, they can now facilitate group meetings in which students discuss their hopes, fears, dreams and anxieties."[51] Any exercises or games a teacher selects for use in the classroom should promote the following objectives:

1. Students learn to accept a self-exploring environment in which there are no right or wrong answers.

2. Students learn to be aware of the many feelings each of us has.

3. Students learn to accept themselves as worthy subject matter for investigation.

4. Students learn to develop and accept a supportive group atmosphere in our classrooms.

5. Students learn to experience new procedures for learning.

6. Students learn to know and accept the unique response each of us has to similar experiences.

7. Students learn to describe themselves multi-dimensionally.[52]

It is important that humanistic changes in attitudes, beliefs, and values are scientifically measured. But teachers do not have to be researchers in order to get an indication of the students' perceptions of such changes. Progress can be measured by asking students to complete sentences such as "I realize that . . . ," I am pleased that . . . ," "I learned that . . . ," or "I wish. . . ." If students have difficulty writing their responses, they could use a tape recorder. Finally, the strategies and exercises presented throughout this book are only guides. Each teacher must select or devise the strategies and exercises that will best fit his or her situation and students.

A Model Program

Robert A. Anderson posed a significant question pertaining to the goals of humanistic education: "Can we design an educational system where few human beings are lost in the process?"[53] Believing that a positive response can be given to this question, Anderson designed a model secondary school for implementing humanistic approaches to education. First, it was necessary that certain philosophical considerations become operational in a model educational program focusing on the individual student:

1. The student develops at his rate and towards his potential physically, emotionally, socially, and intellectually.

2. Relationships within the school, especially between teacher-counselor and student, are sensitive, trusting, and open.

3. Because of the rapid changes in our environment, there is a need to recognize and confront new situations as they arise. Therefore, processes as well as information should be emphasized.

4. The student develops personal responsibility for his own growth and development through involvement in decision making.

5. The student develops a personal commitment to learning by learning *how to learn* and *how to decide* what is important and relevant to her.

6. The student achieves a positive self-image by being given an opportunity for optimum educational development.

7. The student participates in the evaluation of her accomplishments.

8. The commitment to the philosophy of individualized education is held by the entire staff, administration, and community and is reflected in the physical characteristics of the learning environment.[54]

Certain guidelines for the program were laid down:

1. Every student should have the opportunity for leisure, creative expression, free association with fellow students and staff, and physical as well as intellectual activities.

2. Trust and openness should form the basis for the effectiveness of the school.

3. It is imperative to provide ample opportunities for student participation in decisions about independent learning experiences.

4. Students should participate in decision making. They should determine, with the assistance of their teacher-counselors, their own activities and set their own goals.

5. To provide circumstances which enable the students' development of a personal commitment to learning, the following are recommended:

    a. Students, in conjunction with their teacher-counselors, develop a learning program specifying goals and laying out expectations (including considerations of attendance).

    b. There is no predetermined curriculum sequence or achievement level for all students at all times.

    c. A wide variety of courses of different lengths should be offered and ample resources should be available for the students' use.

6. To facilitate optimum education progress, the program should have the following features:

    a. The students have the option to choose from a set of alternatives what they want to learn.

    b. The curriculum is sectioned into small packages as a basis for continuous progress.

    c. The students are allowed to learn at their own rate.

    d. The learning program is designed so that the students usually experience success.

7. A comprehensive analysis of the stu-

dents' progress toward their own educational goals is based on achievement norms provided by the school.

8. For the school to be more effective, a total commitment to individualized, student-centered education as described above must exist. This commitment must be held not only by the staff but also by the community.

9. Once having reached a minimum performance level in each of the basic skill areas, all learning is based upon an expressed commitment by the students, not by a dictum of society or the school.[55]

A secondary school system truly devoted to humanistic education, a trust-based system, would have the following specific features:
1. Student involvement
2. Interpersonal relationships
3. Curricular reorganization
4. Administrative reorganization (multiunit concept)
5. Continuous progress
6. Comprehensive learning environment
7. Development of a positive self-concept
8. Administrative and community commitment.[56]

It is important to note that Anderson's model is also applicable to nonsecondary schools.

TIPS FOR HUMANIZING THE CLASSROOM

In order to establish a supportive classroom environment, the teacher and students may elect to adopt class norms similar to the following: (1) Everyone who is here belongs here as long as he or she does not try to hurt other people. (2) What is true for each person is determined by what is in her/him. (3) Our first purpose is to get in touch with our own feelings. (4) Our second purpose is to make contact with each other. (5) We will try to be as honest as possible and to express ourselves as we really are. (6) What we say in this classroom is confidential; no one will repeat anything said here outside the class. (7) Decisions made by the group need everyone taking part in some way.

Not all students need to be actively involved in the classroom human relations activities. Some students can be silent observers, their function being to observe activities and give feedback during debriefing sessions. For this to be an effective component of the teaching/learning process, the teacher must decide specifically what student observers shoud focus on and make certain the observers understand their role—to describe what happened, not to judge their classmates.

The teacher should not get upset when students withdraw during human relations activities. Some students feel uncomfortable in group interactions and others will use any excuse for not cooperating. There are also instances when students will be confused by an exercise and withdraw. Of course, some students will feel that an activity is not related to their needs. When this happens, the teacher should not become defensive. Instead, the teacher should ask withdrawing students to identify ways they might approach the task differently, ask the students to act as observers and give the rest of class feedback, or alter the task to accommodate these students.

Now for a discussion of specific teaching techniques and activities.

Lectures are best when they are short, less formal talks and are well organized and well delivered. Lecturers should remember that students' attention spans are short, and for this reason lectures should involve the students through interest-catching illustrations, make provision for student involvement, and not attempt to present too much information in a short period of time. Several other factors affect the quality of the lecture, including room conditions, background of the students, and the tone and voice of the speaker. Finally, when a lecture is meant to spark discussion, the lecturer should not cover the points s/he wishes the student to develop.

Generally the lecture is most effective when a teacher wants to clarify an issue, expand students' knowledge beyond available resources, share a personal experience, or give instructions. The lecture has the advantages of allowing the teacher to bring specific ideas into immediate focus and to draw on his or her own experience. It facilitates covering a large amount of material with a large number of students, helps students to develop listening skills, and can supplement other readings. Disadvantages of the lecture include the fact that it tends to be a one-way process, with students passively listening. Lectures also hinder the learning of students who have not learned to be effective listeners or note-takers, may be repetitious for some students, limit the pace of learning to the pace of the speaker, may evolve around the interest of the lecturer rather than the students, tend to cause students to accept the teacher as the final authority, and are inadequate for teaching skills and attitudes. An effective lecturer:

1. Gets the attention of the students from the beginning.
2. Makes clear the purpose of the lecture.
3. Clearly indicates the point of view from which the material is presented.
4. Periodically checks to see if the students are understanding the presentation.
5. Relates the lecture to previous learnings.
6. When possible, uses multisensory aids to clarify important points.
7. Follows a clear organizational pattern, e.g., tells students what will be told, tells them, and tells them what was told (repeats main ideas).
8. Uses helpful examples, including humor.
9. Projects interest and knowledge of subject in a warm friendly manner.
10. Allows for audience feedback.

Discussions may begin spontaneously or be planned by the teacher. In either case, sufficient time should be allowed for the discussion. It is also important for the teacher to be familiar with the subject being discussed. Groups of more than fifteen should be divided into small subgroups in order to permit each student the opportunity to actively participate. Whenever possible, students should be seated so that they can see each other. Teachers should not become unnerved by silence during discussions. Initially, the students may be reluctant to speak their feelings. If the teacher is to be an effective discussion leader, several behaviors are worth learning:

1. Encourage students to do most of the talking.
2. Provide an opportunity for all students to speak, and tactfully discourage those who are dominating the conversation.
3. Correct misunderstandings and misinformation through the use of brief, concise comments.
4. Keep the discussants on the topic.

5. Try to prevent students from physically and verbally abusing each other.
6. End the discussion while interest is still at a high peak.

Effective discussion groups have been proven to:
1. Result in above average student achievement of tests.
2. Foster positive student attitudes toward school, teachers, and the subjects of discussion.
3. Reduce anxiety levels of students.
4. Raise or maintain high levels of student self-concepts.

Advantages of discussion groups include that students can become actively involved in the process of learning; pool their individual information and gain broader insights; learn to organize facts, ask insightful questions, think reflectively on relationships with and among their personal ideas and the ideas of other persons; and test, alter, and improve their beliefs and values. Discussion groups have disadvantages also. The process can be frustrating if meetings end with questions but no agreement about solutions. Discussions can degenerate into attacks on personalities of group members. This strategy requires discussion skills on the part of all students. If the teacher or group leader does not maintain an open mind, the process is not democratic. Also, a few members of the group can dominate the discussion, causing the other members to be bored. Effective group discussions include the following teacher behaviors:

1. Assures a common knowledge base and understanding of small group discussion.
2. Does not judge student answers in terms of right or wrong.
3. Enables students to reach some positive end or purpose, e.g., alternative solutions or group consensus.
4. Provides time for student feedback to the teacher.

Similar concerns are implicit in the other strategies that follow, but these will not be spelled out in as much detail as they have been for lectures and discussions. Above all else it is important for the teacher to:
1. Know why a particular strategy is used.
2. Know the advantages and disadvantages of the strategy.

3. Provide ample instructions, material, and time for the activities.

4. Relate the activity to a class purpose of course learning.

5. Supervise carefully the students' activities.

6. Assist students in evaluating the effectiveness of their efforts.

Brainstorming is an effective way of generating ideas. In order for brainstorming to succeed, an uninhibited atmosphere, spontaneity, and teamwork are required. There are four basic principles of brainstorming:

1. Criticism is not allowed (adverse judgment of ideas is withheld until all ideas are stated).

2. "Freewheeling" is encouraged (the wilder the idea, the better).

3. Quantity is wanted.

4. Combination and improvement of previous ideas are desirable.

After all the ideas have been recorded and categorized, the students evaluate them (using group-determined criteria), and unworkable ideas are discarded.

Panel discussions are widely used but often poorly done. The teacher should:

1. Select an appropriate or relevant topic so that each panelist will be able to make a contribution.

2. Select participants with different backgrounds or experiences so that the topic will be approached from many different perspectives.

3. Select a moderator (or do it her/himself) who is able to (a) introduce the topic, (b) keep panelists on the topic, (c) prevent monopolization by any single panel member, (d) keep track of the time, (e) end the discussion in time to summarize the discussion before the question and answer period, (f) accept questions from the audience and then direct them to the appropriate panelists, and (g) stop the question-answer period in time for the final summary.

Classroom demonstrations are useful only when the teacher makes sure that the students understand the procedure. This is best accomplished in a step-by-step breakdown of the activity. Thus there should be sufficient class time for the demonstration. The demonstration should be in an area which permits all students to see and hear the demonstrator. It is important that student questions are solicited and answered. Where possible, bibliographies and other handouts should be used.

Work groups have the advantage of allowing, through a division of labor, the class members to investigate thoroughly an aspect of a subject and, by sharing their research, become familiar with the total subject. Each subgroup must be familiar with its purpose and the research steps to be taken. A team leader may be appointed by the teacher or one may emerge spontaneously. The teacher becomes a resource for the groups—s/he checks their progress and clarifies areas of confusion. Group reports should be presented in different forms so as to minimize class boredom during the show and tell period.

Buzz groups—small groups of three to six stuents—are formed for informal discussion of issues, with the teacher being available if the groups need clarification of points. Buzz groups should not be used if the students are unfamiliar with the topic. Each group may, at the teacher's discretion, have a leader and a recorder. The more effective buzz groups are thoroughly briefed on the topic—either orally or in written assignments. Furthermore, buzz groups may all be assigned the same topic or they may be given different topics. When the groups have completed their task, they should be brought together again in a large group in order to share relevant points.

Problem analysis through on-the-spot reaction works best when students feel free to share their feelings without the benefit of much time to collect their thoughts. By allowing themselves to be placed on the spot, the students are able to see a wide range of reactions and, ideally, alternative ways of viewing a situation. Answers that trigger negative reactions or laughter can serve as the basis for subsequent teacher lecturettes.

Role-playing should be done in friendly, supportive environments. Initial role-playing situations should not focus on situations that are personally threatening to the students. In most instances, it is better to let students volunteer for role-playing rather than to draft them. When possible, the teacher should give each player written instructions. In any case, instructions—written or oral—should clearly spell out who each student is to portray and how s/he is supposed to feel at the outset of role-playing. Each player should be given a few minutes alone to get into the mood of his or her role. Once the role-play begins, it should be allowed to continue until it begins to drag. After the role-play, the teacher should lead a two part discussion. Part one should focus only on the events surrounding the role-play. During part two the students are encouraged to relate the role-play to their own lives.

Dramatization—acting without rehearsal or script—differs from role-play in that in the former activity, the outcome of the situation is determined in advance. In both dramatization and role-play, the students must be at ease with each other and the teacher. In order for dramatizations to be effective, the teacher should:

1. Clearly delineate the situation to be portrayed and the outcome of the situation.

2. Allow reluctant students the option of not participating.

3. Give the actors a brief period to get themselves psychologically ready for their parts.

4. Stop the dramatization when the purpose of the activity has been realized or the students are hopelessly floundering.

5. Lead a discussion focusing on the effects of the dramatization.

Films are excellent for supplementing class presentations. Films should be planned into the lesson, and all films should be previewed. Students should know the reason why the film is to be shown, and should evaluate the film for future use.

ADDITIONAL READINGS

Beechhold, Henry F. *The Creative Classroom: Teaching Without Textbooks*. New York, Scribner, 1971.

Benne, Kenneth D., ed. *Human Relationships Curriculum Change: Selected Readings with Especial Emphasis on Group Development*. New York, Dryden Press, 1951.

Bishop, Lloyd K. *Individualizing Educational Systems, The Elementary and Secondary School*. New York, Harper & Row, 1971.

Castillo, Gloria A. *Left-Handed Teaching: Lessons in Affective Education*. New York, Praeger, 1974.

Chesler, Mark and Robert Fox. *Role-Playing Methods in the Classroom*. Chicago, Science Research Associates, 1966.

Crafty, Bryant J. *Active Learning: Games to Enhance Academic Abilities*. Englewood Cliffs, N.J., Prentice-Hall, 1971.

Harmin, Merrill, et al. *Clarifying Values Through Subject Matter: Applications for the Classroom*. Minneapolis, Winston Press, 1973.

Hendricks, Gay and Russel Wills. *The Centering Book: Awareness Activities for Children, Parents, and Teachers*. Englewood Cliffs, N.J., Prentice-Hall, 1975.

Hollaway, Otto. *Problem Solving: Toward a More Humanizing Curriculum*. Philadelphia, Franklin, 1975.

Holt, John C. *What Do I Do Monday?* New York, Dutton, 1970.

Hunter, Elizabeth. *Encounter in the Classroom: New Ways of Teaching*. New York, Holt, Rinehart & Winston, 1972.

Kniker, Charles R. *You and Values Education*. Columbus, Ohio, Charles E. Merrill, 1977.

Krupar, Karen R. *Communication Games: Participant's Manual*. New York, Free Press, 1973.

Manning, Duane. *Toward a Humanistic Curriculum*. New York, Harper & Row, 1971.

Morrow, Mary L. *Help! For Elementary School Substitutes and Beginning Teachers*. Philadelphia, Westminster Press, 1974.

Newmann, Dana. *The Teacher's Almanack: Practical Ideas for Every Day of the School Year*. New York, Center for Applied Research in Education, 1973.

Sizer, Theodore R. *Places for Learning, Places for Joy: Speculations on American School Reform*. Cambridge, Mass., Harvard University Press, 1973.

Stanford, Gene and Barbara D. Stanford. *Learning Discussion Skills Through Games*. New York, Citation Press, 1969.

Thayer, Louis, ed. *Affective Education: Strategies for Experimental Learning*. La Jolla, Cal., University Associates, 1976.

Weinstein, Gerald and Marion Fantini. *Toward Humanistic Education: A Curriculum of Affect*. New York, Praeger, 1971.

Zahorik, John and Dale Brubaker. *Toward More Humanistic Instruction*. Dubuque, Ia., Wm. C. Brown, 1972.

NOTES

1. Reginald D. Archambault (ed.), *John Dewey on Education Selected Writings* (New York, The Modern Library, 1964), 344.

2. William W. Crowder, "We're Alike, We're Different," *Teacher*, 92 (April, 1975), 83.

3. *Ibid.*, 85.

4. *Ibid.*

5. Thomas D. Yawkey and Eugene L. Aronin, "The Living Circle Approach in the Social Studies," *The Social Studies*, 65 (February, 1974), 72.

6. *Ibid.*, 72.

7. *Ibid.*, 74.

8. David R. Lee, "Existentialism in Geographic Education," *Journal of Geography*, 73 (September, 1974), 13.

9. *Ibid.*, 18.

10. *Ibid.*, 19.

11. D. M. Jeynes, "The Nature of Social Biology and Its Place in the Curriculum," *Biology and Human Affairs* 39 (1974), 21.

12. *Ibid.*, 22.

13. *Ibid.*

14. E. W. Menzel, "Science Teaching and Sensitivity Training?" *Science Teacher*, 36 (November, 1969), 18.

15. *Ibid.*

16. *Ibid.*

17. Bernard De Koven, "Finding a Way In," *Teacher*, 93 (September, 1975), 79.

18. Karl R. Wullschleger, "Facing Up to Emotions: Some Testing Methods for Primary Teachers," *Today's Education*, 62 (February, 1973), 58.

19. Carlton R. Deonanan, "Literature-Centered Approach to Humanizing Education," *Reading Improvement*, 12 (Summer, 1975), 114.

20. *Ibid.*, 115.

21. *Ibid.*, 116.

22. Norma K. Stegmaier, "Teaching Interpersonal Communication through Children's Literature," *Elementary English*, 51 (October, 1974), 927.

23. *I bid*, 928–29.

24. *Ibid.*, 930.

25. George Fargo, "It's a Possibility: Humanism in Reading," *Claremont Reading Conference*, 37 (1973), 58.

26. *Ibid.*, 61.

27. *Ibid.*, 63.

28. Kenneth B. Huggins, "Alternatives in Values Clarification," *National Elementary Principal*, 69 (November-December, 1974), 77.

29. *Ibid.*, 78–79.

30. A. Montgomery Johnston, "Teaching Humane Attitudes About Sexuality," *Tennessee Educator*, 4 (February, 1974), 41.

31. *Ibid.*, 42.

32. *Ibid.*, 43

33. *Ibid.*, 43–45.

34. Constance T. Fischer and Alfonso A. Rizzo, "A Paradigm for Humanizing Special Education," *The Journal of Special Education*, 8 (Winter, 1974), 322.

35. *Ibid.*, 324.

36. *Ibid.*, 326–28.

37. Meyer M. Cahn, "Wanted: A Humanistic Route to Great Music," *Music Educators Journal*, 60 (February, 1974), 56.

38. *Ibid.*

39. *Ibid.*, 92.

40. Stratton F. Caldwell, "Toward a Humanistic Physical Education," *Journal of Health, Physical Education, and Recreation*, 43 (May, 1972), 31.

41. *Ibid.*, 32.

42. Marian E. Kneer, "How Human Are You?: Exercises in Awareness," *Journal of Health, Physical Education, and Recreation*, 45 (June, 1974), 33.

43. Anna Neumann, cited in Kneer, *Ibid.*, 33–34.

44. Kenneth E. Blaker and Jan Samo, "Communications Games: A Group Counseling Technique," *The School Counselor*, 231 (September, 1973), 47.

45. *Ibid.*, 48.

46. Merritt A. Williamson, "Some Reservations About Humanizing Education Through Technology," *Educational Technology*, 11 (June, 1971), 27.

47. *Ibid.*

48. John T. Canfield, "Dear Machine: Don't Call Us, We'll Call You!" *Educational Technology*, 11 (June, 1971), 24.

49. *Ibid.*, 25.

50. *Ibid.*, 24.

51. *Ibid.*

52. Peter D. Cimini, "Humanizing As a Teaching Strategy," *School Health Review*, 5 (January-February, 1974), 15.

53. Robert A. Anderson, "A Humanized and Individualized Secondary School Program," *Theory Into Practice*, 11 (February, 1972), 44.

54. *Ibid.*, 45.

55. *Ibid.*, 45–46.

56. *Ibid.*, 46.

18.
THE HELPING RELATIONSHIP

Many good intentions of educators go to waste because of their lack of understanding of what is helpful to students and what constitutes a helping relationship. To the affected students, this waste of effort may be so negative that it causes them to have a revulsion against all forms of helping. When this happens, helping is seen as a process that benefits educators more than students, and educators are seen as neurotic do-gooders.

PRELUDE TO HELPING

All definitions of help are based on subjective values—something tangible or intangible discovered in a relationship between a helper and a helpee in which the helper aids the helpee in achieving a measure of self-fulfillment. In actuality help is something that a person discovers for himself or herself. Each person must accept and act on helpful information with the knowledge that the ultimate responsibility belongs to him or her. In the final analysis, help cannot be given to students; it can only be offered.

The helping relationship has qualities that are the same whether it is between therapist and client, counselor and counselee, or teacher and student. The psychological equilibrium underlying the occupational roles resides at a much deeper, more fundamental level. This is true for both the helper and the helpee. Numerous studies suggest that effective help at the emotional level is initiated not so much by technique or special knowledge of the different professions, but rather by positive attitudes of the helper. Specifically, research findings suggest that experienced helpers have a better conception of what constitutes a helping relationship than their colleagues who have mastered the theoretical concepts but have little experience. In many instances the man or woman in the street can describe a good helping relationship about as well as the so-called experts.

Some educators see the helping process as one in which they make intricate diagnoses of students and then use a wide variety of helping methods on them. Still other educators define students as being sick and themselves as being well. These are not really helping relationships. On the contrary, they are controlling relationships. When the student becomes an object rather than the subject, he or she is no longer the person who acts but instead becomes the person acted upon. Conceptually, a thin line separates wanting to help another person from wanting to change him or her to conform with our expectations.

There is an underlying assumption in the helping professions that a trained person can make a significant contribution to the lives of others if their training has instilled a commitment to effectively use oneself in the helping process. The primary technique or instrument in the helping relationship is the ability of the helper to become an instrument to be used by the helpee to achieve basic needs that must be met (at least from the helpee's perception) and to achieve some measure of self-fulfillment in doing so. From the helper's point of view, this goal of self-fulfillment means that the helpee will become more realistic, self-directing, and self-confident.

One of the most important things about helping in many school settings is that the great majority of students do not seem to want to be helped. At least they do not appear to want to be helped by administrators and teachers. Many students who ask for help are afraid of it and may try to make sure that no real helping takes place. There are many ways of asking for help. For example, acting out in the classroom may be a plea for help. Consequently, teachers must be aware of these subtle pleas and be prepared to enter into a growth-producing rather than a punitive relationship with the acting-out students.

Carl R. Rogers defined the helping relationship as "a relationship in which at least one of the parties has the intent of promoting the growth, development, maturity, improved functioning, improved coping with life of the other."[1] The characteristics that distinguish a classroom helping relationship from an unhelpful one are related primarily to the attitudes of the teacher and the perceptions of the student.

Determining what is helpful and what is not depends to a great extent on who is perceiving the situation. In other words a student may not see a situation in the same way as the teacher. An example of this would be the case of a fight between two students. A teacher may see two students fighting, with one obviously receiving much physical abuse. The teacher also may perceive that the helpful thing to do is to intervene and stop the fight. On the other hand, the student being beaten might much rather take the physical abuse than face the verbal abuse of his fellows, who in all probability will make fun of him for having to be saved by the teacher. Social humiliation can be a much greater pain than physical punishment.

Certain values in a helping relationship must be observed by educators if the relationship is to be productive in the long run. Doing a chore or making a decision for a student may help in the short run, but it will not help the student to become more self-directing in the future. Thus, some helpful values are as follows:

1. The belief that human life, happiness, and well-being are to be valued above all else.
2. The belief that each person is the master of his or her own destiny, with the right to control it in his or her own interest and in his or her own way as long as the exercise of this control does not infringe on the rights of other people.
3. The belief that the dignity and worth of each person shall be respected at all times and under all conditions.
4. The belief in the right of all people to think their own thoughts and speak their own minds.

This chapter will not attempt to provide a how-to-do-it approach with clearly outlined steps to follow. While lists will be presented, they are done so mainly to summarize various thoughts. Helping relationships do not allow a rigid structure. Therefore, this chapter presents a "be-it-yourself" approach, since teachers and administrators need an attitude of being-for-others and being-with-others in place of an attitude of doing-for-others. From this perspective, it is more important for the educator to be aware than to be an expert. To be aware and to care about the world, values, and life-styles of students is a significant aspect of the helping relationship in which teachers and administrators try to promote positive intrapersonal, interpersonal, and intergroup relationships.

CHARACTERISTICS OF A HELPING RELATIONSHIP

Carl Rogers further stated that a helping relationship is one "in which one of the participants intends that there should come about in one or both parties more appreciation of, more expression of, more functional use of the latent inner resources of the individual."[2] Relatedly, the job of the helper as seen by Alan Keith-Lucas is to provide "a medium, a situation, and an experience in which a choice is possible."[3] Ideally, through the helping relationship the fears that restrain students can to some extent be resolved, and they can find the courage to make a commitment to a course of action and learn some of the practical skills necessary to make this decision a reality. Arthur W. Combs has stated that "the helper's basic beliefs and values rather than his grand schemes, methods, techniques, or years of training are the real determiners of whether or not the helper will be effective or ineffective."[4]

In a classic article entitled "The Characteristics of a Helping Relationship," Rogers asked a series of questions that he felt revealed characteristics of a helping relationship. If a teacher or an administrator can answer these questions in the affirmative, especially most of their interactions with students, then it is likely that they will be or are helpful to their students.

Can I be in some way which will be perceived by the other person as trustworthy, as dependable or consistent in some deep sense?[5]

This is more than being rigidly consistent. It means being honest and congruent with our feelings so that we are a unified or integrated person.

Can I be expressive enough as a person that what I am will be communicated unambiguously?[6]

If we are unaware of our own feelings, a double message can be given which will confuse the situation and cause the relationship to be marred by the ambiguous communication.

Can I let myself experience positive attitudes toward this other person—attitudes of warmth, caring, liking, interest, respect?[7]

A professional attitude of aloofness is unhelpful; it creates a barrier or distance which protects scientific objectivity at the expense of establishing a helping relationship.

Can I receive him as he is? Can I communicate this attitude? Or can I only receive him conditionally, acceptant of some aspects of his feelings and silently or openly disapproving of other aspects?[8]

The helper is usually threatened when he or she cannot accept certain parts of the helpee. The helper must be able to accept those characteristics of the helpee that he or she cannot accept in himself or herself.

Can I act with sufficient sensitivity in the relationship that my behavior will not be perceived as a threat?[9]

If the other person is as free as possible from external threats, then he or she may be able to experience and to deal with the internal feelings that are threatening.

Can I let myself enter fully into the world of his feelings and personal meanings and see these as he does? Can I step into his private world so completely that I lose all desire to evaluate or judge it? Can I enter it so sensitively that I can move about in it freely, without trampling on meanings which are precious to him? Can I sense it so accurately that I can catch not only the meanings of his experience which are obvious to him, but those meanings which are only implicit, which he sees only dimly or as confusion? Can I extend this understanding without limit?[10]

Evaluative comments are not conducive to personal growth, and therefore they are not a part of a helping relationship. A positive evaluation can also be threatening because it serves notice that the helpee is being evaluated and that a negative evaluation could be forthcoming. Self-evaluation leaves the responsibility with the helpee, where it really belongs. In essence, the ultimate question becomes, "Can I meet this other individual as a person who is in the process of becoming, or will I be bound by his past and my past?"[11]

Rogers listed four subtle attitudinal characteristics necessary for constructive personality change to occur. (1) The helper manifests empathic understanding of the helpee. (2) The helper manifests unconditional positive regard toward the helpee. (3) The helper is genuine or congruent, that is, his words match his feelings. (4) The helper's responses match the helpee's statements in the intensity of affective expression. These four conditions must be communicated to the helpee. In an effort to conceptualize this process, Rogers formulated what he calls a process equation of a successful helping relationship: Genuineness plus empathy plus unconditional positive regard for the client equals successful therapy for the client. $(G+E+UPR = Success)$[12]

Keith-Lucas suggests that the helper can convey genuineness, empathy, and unconditional positive regard through four statements, including the feelings and actions that accompany them: "This is it," "I know that it must hurt," "I am here to help you if you want me and can use me," and "You don't have to face this alone."[13] These statements contain reality, empathy, and support or acceptance. It should be emphasized that the words of these statements are only one part of the communication process. As an old Indian once said about the treatment his people received from whites,

"What you do speaks so loudly I cannot hear what you say!" To be effective, reality and empathy must be conveyed to the helpee.

Reality without empathy is harsh and unhelpful. Empathy about something that is not real is clearly meaningless and can only lead the client to what we have called nonchoice. Reality and empathy together need support, both material and psychological, if decisions are to be carried out. Support in carrying out unreal plans is obviously a waste of time.[14]

Many studies on the nature of the helping relationship support the ideas of Rogers and Keith-Lucas. Various studies indicate three recurring themes as relevant to people who are considering entering the helping professions:

1. The helper's ability to sensitively and accurately understand the helpee in such a manner as to communicate deep understanding.
2. The helper's ability to project nonpossessive warmth and acceptance of the helpee.
3. The necessity for the helper to be integrated, mature, and genuine within the helping relationship.

Let us look now at three characteristics of a successful helping relationship—genuineness, empathy, and acceptance—that seem so vital to a helping relationship.

Genuineness

Lowell wrote, "Sincerity is impossible unless it pervades the whole being, and the pretense of it saps the very foundation of character." To be genuine in a student-teacher relationship requires the teacher to be aware of his or her own inner feelings. If these inner feelings are consistent with the expressed behavior, then it can be said that he or she is genuine or congruent. It is this quality of realness and honesty that allows the student needing help to keep a steady focus on reality.

To the nonhumanistic teacher, it may seem that reality is too brutal for the young student. Granted, the truth is not always painless; as the old saying goes, "The truth shall make ye free—but first it shall make ye miserable." It is also important to note that being open and honest is not a license to be brutal. A helpful, as opposed to a destructive, relationship is

very much like the difference between a fatal and a therapeutic dose of a painkiller—it is only a matter of degree.

In the process of attempting to be transparently real, it is wise for educators to evaluate their failures, their reasons for being less than honest. To protect students from the truth about their skills is to make a very serious judgment about them. It is to say that they are incapable of facing their real educational problems. However, if the teacher or administrator only provided honesty in the relationship, it probably would not be very helpful to students. The next component in the process, empathic understanding, is also needed.

Empathy

"First of all," he said, "if you can learn a simple trick, Scout, you'll get along a lot better with all kinds of folks. You never really understand a person until you consider things from his point of view—"

"Sir?"

"—until you climb into his skin and walk around in it."[15]

This passage from *To Kill a Mockingbird* accurately depicts the meaning of empathic understanding. It is literally an understanding of the emotions and feelings of another, not by the cognitive process but by a projection of one's personality into the personality of the other. It is a sort of vicarious experiencing of the feelings of the other to the degree that the helper actually feels some of the pain the person is suffering. Empathy requires the helper to leave temporarily his or her own life-space and to try to think, act, and feel as if the life-space of the other were the helper's own. The Spanish writer, Una Muno, wrote, "Suffering is the life blood that runs through us all and binds us together."

The following story demonstrates what is meant by empathic understanding.

In one of Israel's kibbutzim, or collective settlements, there was a donkey. It was a special donkey indeed with long silky ears and large shiny eyes, and all the children loved him dearly. And so when he disappeared one day, all the children were very upset. He had been the favorite attraction of the children's farm. During the morning the children used to come in two's and three's or in entire groups with their teachers to visit the donkey. The little ones would even take rides on his back. In the afternoon the children would drag their parents to the children's farm to see Shlomo, the donkey. But now he was missing, and the children were downcast. The sadness proved to be contagious, and before the day was out, all the kibbutz members had assembled in the large dining hall and, with concern written on all their faces, were trying to decide what to do next. They had looked everywhere, but Shlomo, the donkey, had not been found.

On this same kibbutz lived an old man, the father of one of the earliest settlers. He had become somewhat senile of late, and children sometimes made fun of him quite openly, although the adults were a bit more circumspect. Well when the entire kibbutz population was gathered in the large new dining hall wondering what to do next, in walked the old man dragging Shlomo, the donkey, behind him. The jubilation was great, the astonishment even greater. While the children surrounded the donkey, the adults gathered about the old man. "How is it," they asked him, "that you of all people have found the donkey? What did you do?"

Well you can imagine the embarrassment of the old man and his joy, too, for never had he been paid so much attention. He scratched his bald pate, looked at the ceiling and then at the floor, smiled, and said: "It was simple. I just asked myself, 'Shlomo,' (for that was the old man's name as well) 'if you were Shlomo, the donkey, where would you go off to?' So I went there and found him and brought him back." [16]

This story illustrates the nature and purpose of empathic understanding. The old man was able to think and feel like the donkey in order to figure out where the donkey was, but then was still separate enough to go and get him. It is important that educators maintain enough objectivity when they become empathic so that they can assist students in overcoming educational problems.

Empathic understanding does no good unless it is communicated to the student—to let him or her know that someone has a deep understanding of his or her predicament. This kind of understanding allows the student to expand and clarify his or her own self-understanding. One way of communicating this kind of understanding is through active listening. Active listening is not mere tolerance; a teacher, for instance, has to really care and feel the emotions attached to the student's

words. The following four points express what listening with empathic understanding means:

1. Empathic listening means trying to see the situation the way the other person sees it.

2. Empathic listening means one must enter actively and imaginatively into the other person's situation and try to understand a frame of reference different from our own.

3. Empathic listening does not mean maintaining a polite silence while we rehearse what we are going to say when we get a chance.

4. Empathic listening does not mean waiting alertly for the flaws in the other person's argument so that we can correct him. [17]

Once educators are behaving genuinely and have empathic understanding toward the student, the next step, which often occurs simultaneously, is acceptance.

Acceptance

In Rogerian jargon, acceptance of the student means that the teacher will feel and show unconditional positive regard for him or her. It is worth repeating that teachers and administrators must be congruent or consistent in both their feelings and expressions of acceptance for students. If educators do not really accept students yet attempt to express acceptance, they will be giving a double message—acceptance and rejection. In such a case, the best that can happen is that students will perceive these educators to be phonies. The worst that can happen is that students' self-esteem will be damaged. Double messages occur when feelings do not coincide with words. For instance a teacher's words may say, "I accept you and respect your feelings." But the nonverbal messages may be: "I don't trust you," "Poor little you," "You are disgusting," or "You must be sick." Nonverbal messages which reflect more deeply-held feelings are difficult to correct because the owner does not have as much control over them as over words. Small children know this and are perceptive enough to sense these feelings. The words of Joe Louis to one of his boxing opponents illustrate this point: "You can run but you can't hide from me."

The basic reasons for demonstrating acceptance are to build a relationship based upon trust and openness, to establish a situation in which the student is able to gain respect for self, and to develop an atmosphere through which the student can come to respect others. The process involved in this aspect of the relationship is caring, and support is given through helpful feedback. Feedback is simply the expression of reactions to a behavior. In a sense, the student will perceive the teacher's attitude of respect as an either/or thing: Either the teacher does or does not respect him or her. This may be an oversimplification, but if the student perceives it in this manner, then the consequences of that perception are real.

To the extent that educators can be themselves as persons, expressing their real selves, hopefully with empathic understanding and liking for their students, they will be helpful in promoting the growth of their students. In searching for the helping relationship, it would be wise to remember the following Zen poem:

It is too clear and so is hard to see.
A man once searched for fire with a lighted lantern.
Had he know what fire was,
He could have cooked his rice much sooner.

AND WHAT ELSE?

This section deals briefly with the various views of human beings, the healthy student, social class and poverty, and social helping—a sort of potpourri. In other words, it deals with the question asked by the little girl after being given a long list of information and data: "And what else?"

Views of Human Beings

Every human being has a totally unique inner nature. This inner self ("real self" according to Arthur Janov, "inner nature" according to Abraham H. Maslow) has characteristics which may be described in different ways. Maslow lists several ways of characterizing the inner self in *Psychology of Being*:

1. The inner self is biologically based. It is, in many ways, unchangeable or at least unchanging.
2. Each person's inner self is unique to him or her.

3. We may only discover the inner self; we cannot add to it or subtract from it.
4. The inner self is good or neutral—not bad.
5. If the inner self is allowed to develop, happiness is the result.
6. If the inner self is denied or suppressed, sickness develops.
7. Because the inner nature is not strong or overpowering, it may easily be suppressed by socialization.
8. Yet, even though denied, the inner self does not disappear. It merely persists underground forever pressing for self-actualization.[18]

Janov believes that the core of each person is the real self. The real self has real needs which must be met early in life to survive. Hunger, the need to be held, and the need to be loved are all real needs.[19] Obviously, if a child is not fed, he will die. This real need is universally recognized. The need to be held was not completely recognized until World War II, when the Nazis put infants into a room and only fed them. As a result of not being held, all the children died. The need to be loved is as universally recognized as it is misunderstood. The real self must be fed with real love—the unconditional love Eric Fromm talks about or the ok-ness Thomas A. Harris describes. If an adult does not get real love, he or she will not die but will instead split with the real self in order to survive.

Some characteristics are frequently confused with the inner self. Some of these characteristics are entrenched in political philosophy, public education, religion, and superstition. Biblical phrases such as "spare the rod and spoil the child," for example, imply some basic instinct in humans toward evil. Superstition, added to religious phrases such as these, implies that the evilness must be beaten out of the person so that "the demon won't creep out." Hence, the inner self is often considered evil.

Certain defensive feelings, such as jealousy, hate, and hostility, are often thought to be inborn in human beings. According to A. S. Neill, this is not true. Neill worked with children in his Summerhill School and found that after psychological treatment children could refrain from expressing feelings of hate, hostility, and jealousy. Because they had learned these things, they could learn to refrain from expressing them.[20]

Janov claims that primal patients do not express (or have) feelings of hate, hostility, or jealousy. According to Janov, anger may be real or unreal; fear may be real or unreal; guilt may be true guilt or socialized guilt. Hence, these feelings are not always inborn in the individual.

Defenses are not part of the real self but are added by the individual for protection, which is not protection at all. Transactional analysts say that defenses are seen in games, manipulations, ulterior transactions, and similar endeavors undertaken by children and adults. We are not born manipulators; we are taught to be manipulators. Maslow believed some defenses are desirable. He further believed that frustration, deprivation, and punishment are ways to fulfill and feed our inner selves. Whether they are expressing the real or unreal self, a disproportionate number of low-achieving students display jealousy, hate, and hostility. And an equal number become manipulators in order to survive in the academic game.

Humanistic education may be viewed as a phenomenological, personalistic, existential view of students who are engaged in a continuous process of becoming. What this jargon-loaded statement means is that students are basically good and their behavior is a function of the perceptions that they have of their world and themselves. The environment's effect on the individual is filtered through each person's perceptual apparatus. Thus, while a child may in reality be living in a ghetto, if she does not perceive herself to be a ghetto dweller, then that perception has more effect on her behavior than does her environment. While a teacher may be open, flexible, and democratic, if a student perceives him as closed, rigid, and authoritarian, then the consequences of that perception will stifle the student-teacher interaction. Humanistic education takes a relativistic view of reality. It leaves the individual at the center of decision making and responsibility. If one holds to the behavioristic or Freudian views of humanity, the individual is no longer considered the initiator of his or her acts and thus is no longer responsible. The Freudian view of the helping relationship tends to make helping a manipulative relationship, with the helpee being the object rather than the subject of the relationship.

Many basic needs affect a relationship. Maslow divided our basic needs into five major categories:

1. Physiological needs (food, water, and shelter).
2. Safety or security needs (freedom from physical and psychological attack).
3. The needs for love, affection, and belonging.
4. Esteem needs (self-concept).
5. The need for self-actualization.

Until the first four needs are met, the fifth need, which is a rather abstract concept of potentiality and self-development, is virtually unseekable.[21]

In another vein Donald Snygg defined self-concept and its development as the basis of human values, and he suggested three pertinent points for the teacher to be aware of:

1. The basic goal of all individuals is for a feeling of increased worth, of greater personal value. (This goal is never completely reached).
2. Given one success, a degree of self-enhancement, human beings will always aspire to more success.
3. Satisfaction of the need for greater personal value can be and is sought in a number of alternative ways.[22]

High grades, consumer goods, and personal experiences are of value to the student only as they contribute to the feeling of positive self-worth.

Creativity is a goal often sought by teachers for their students, but the authoritarian nature of their methods prevents most students from being creative. The key requirement for creativity is freedom. In most schools too many structural barriers block the path of personal freedom. Studies comparing the maze-learning ability of rats raised in a cage and periodically run through mazes with that of free-roaming rats concluded that the free-roaming rats outperform the caged rats in maze-learning and in more complex behavior. But rats are not people!

In a classroom that the students perceive as authoritarian, social dimensions become more than a boundary; they become barriers to openness. Students become prisoners cut off from communicating with their jailors. Under these conditions students can easily become defensive, psychological cripples. In the following passage, Earl C. Kelley describes this process and the lack of sensitivity of educators to it:

Defenses are necessary, provided they do not become so impervious that they imprison that which they defend. It often happens that defenses are inadequate for the dangers of living. This happens most often to the very young, who have tender psychological selves and inadequate protection. In these cases, which are numerous, the self becomes damaged, and in serious cases crippled. These psychological cripples have to behave as cripples do, and their actions are at wide variance with what is "expected" of them in our culture. From this group society gets its criminals, its deviates, its so-called insane. The person is crippled by conditions over which he has little control, and then because he behaves in a crippled fashion we say he is delinquent, or "insane."

This is not because we are inhuman, or devoid of human compassion. It is because we cannot see the psychological self. Our hearts go out to the physical cripple, and great deference is properly paid to him. If we could see the psychological cripple our blame, hostility, and rejection would be changed to love, and tender nurture. We would not expect him to step lively, and look out for himself. We would cease to subject him to the many forms of rejection which we have devised for those who do not conform.[23]

It should be obvious from the preceding discussion that both the teacher's and the student's frame of reference are important in understanding the classroom human relationship. The question now arises: What are the criteria for a socially and psychologically healthy student? One answer, of course is that the healthy person is mature—which is what the next section is about.

The Healthy Student

William James said, "An unlearned carpenter of my acquaintance once said in my hearing: 'There is very little difference between one man and another; but what little there is, is very important.'" We have already built a case for the assumption that the inner self is good and desirable. We may also assume that a healthy student is a person who *is* his or her inner self, and that a healthy student who is his or her inner self is self-actualizing. Or stated another way, health is self-actualization. The healthy student is one who is free to make choices. He or she is free to sift through alternatives and choose which alternative is best. He or she is free because of this awareness of alternatives. All people have options. All people make choices every day. Yet not all choices are made out of awareness. An example of making an unaware choice is losing control of one's temper and blaming others for this loss, i.e., "You *made me* angry." An example of making a choice through awareness is expression of direct anger. If anger is turned inward, it becomes depression. If anger is turned outward without responsibility, it becomes hostility. If anger is expressed outwardly with responsibility and directly at the source of anger, the result is anger with awareness. Even in extreme cases of life and death, people make choices.[24]

The healthy student is a self-regulated person. Self-regulation is learned early in life and continues to strengthen and develop as the individual matures. Self-regulation means the right to live freely, without undue outside authority. The healthy student operates in the here-and-now. He or she is primarily concerned with the present—not the past. And to repeat for emphasis, the healthy student is aware of choices and accepts responsibility for his or her behavior. What about the healthy educator?

In addition to displaying traits similar to the healthy student, the healthy educator is a perceptive person. He or she does not see everything in dichotomous terms—good or bad, childish or mature, and so forth. The healthy educator has insight into the behavior of people yet does not exploit that insight. He or she uses insight to empathize with the suffering of students. On the same note, that insight gives him or her the ability to vicariously identify with the pleasures of students as well.

Robert R. Spaulding found significant positive correlation between the height of the self-concept and the degree to which the teachers in his study were calm, accepting, supportive, and facilitative. A negative correlation was found when teachers were dominating, threatening, and sarcastic.[25] Morris L. Cogan found that students with warm, considerate teachers produced large amounts of original art and poetry,[26] while C. M. Christensen found the warmth of teachers significantly related to the vocabulary and mathematical achievement of students.[27] Horace B. Reed found that teachers characterized by students as considerate, understanding, and friendly had a favorable influence on students' interest in science.[28]

It is also important to note Frank C. Emmerling's conclusion that teachers who accept students, perceive them positively and attempt to understand them facilitate an improved learning climate.[29] Several studies have shown that if a teacher has a positive perception of the student, i.e., if he or she thinks the student is a capable learner, the student does better academically. It is extremely important that teachers be aware of their belief and value systems. Robert M. Thomas described four aspects of a teacher's value system that are important in the classroom. (1) A teacher is often unaware of his or her philosophical principles until forced to look at them. (2) Some of the teacher's values conflict with others. (3) The values teachers espouse are often different from their actions. (4) Some teacher values are impossible to realize because they are inconsistent with the facts of life.[30] Gilbert C. Wrenn made five suggestions which are both values and principles to be followed as a basic humanistic education credo:

1. I shall strive to see the positive in the other person and praise it at least as often as I notice that which is to be corrected.

2. If I am to correct or criticize someone's action, I must be sure that this is seen by the other as a criticism of a specific behavior and not as a criticism of himself as a person.

3. I shall assume that each person can see some reasonableness in his behavior, that there is meaning in it for him if not for me.

4. When I contribute to another person's self-respect, I increase his positive feelings toward me and his respect for me.

5. To at least one person, perhaps many, I am a person of significance, and he is affected vitally by my recognition of him and my good will toward him as a person.[31]

Social Class and Poverty

Educators should be aware of some other ideas about helping. Specifically, most writers suggest that four things must occur before students ask for help:

1. They must recognize that something is wrong which they can do nothing about without help.

2. They must be willing to tell someone about the problem.

3. They must give that person some right to tell them what to do.

4. They must be willing to change in some way.

All of this is very threatening to the student's equilibrium and self-concept. In schools this puts low-achieving students in a particularly difficult situation because of their relatively low self-esteem. To them, seeking help may be a degrading process. For this reason Vincent F. Calia challenged the idea that the helpee must come forward directly and ask for help before a positive relationship can be established.[32] As noted earlier, students may ask for help indirectly through various forms of acting out.

As to the actual kind of helping relationship established with students from the lower socio-economic classes, Frank Riessman warned that male adolescents from this group dislike talk and have a strong preference for action.[33] In fact adolescents in most groups tend to be secretive and afraid to talk about their inner feelings. When there is difficulty in verbalizing feelings, human relations structured exercises can be helpful as a medium for opening up communication. Group exercises can spark verbalization and the ventilation of feelings, and psychodrama and role-playing can offer opportunities for students who are less verbal to express their feelings in an action-oriented environment. Unfortunately, many of the human relations exercises are too difficult for most teachers to manage without further training.

Numerous studies have focused on the helping relationship with disadvantaged students. August B. Hollingshead and Frederick C. Redlich observed that therapists have more positive feelings toward patients whose social class standings are comparable to their own.[34] It seems reasonable, then, that teachers and administrators also tend to have more positive feelings for students of their own socio-economic class. George Banks, Bernard G. Berenson, and Robert R. Carkhuff found that helpers who are different from their helpees in terms of race and social class have the greatest difficulty effecting constructive changes, while helpers who are similar to their helpees in these respects have the greatest facility for doing so.[35]

It is important to note that culturally disadvantaged students need more (or a different kind of) attention than other students. Of course this is an over-generalization, since each child should be looked at individually in order to determine his or her personal needs. Even so, it is imperative that educators be cognizant of barriers created by racial or social class differences. If Black students are hesitant to trust a white teacher, for example, it may be because they do not trust members of that particular racial group, or it may be because the teacher's nonverbal messages say "stay away." Rather than guess, it is better to ask the students what they think the difficulty may be. If done tactfully, this will get the issue out in the open with a minimum of defensiveness. It may be that the student is not aware of his or her nontrusting behavior, or the teacher may have been projecting his or her own nontrusting attitude onto the student. In any case it is best to get and keep these feelings, perceptions, and thoughts out in the open so that trust can be built. This does not mean that helping relationships are always nice and sweet. The following interview with a student tells of a helping relationship that he had with a teacher that was not always pleasant.

He was my teacher for three years in junior high school, and I gave him hell. I was a devil then and hated the guy. That's what I thought then, but it wasn't only hate. He didn't let me get away with a thing in class, and lots of times he'd keep me in after school to talk things over. He told me exactly how he felt, and I remember I told him lots of things. . . . I don't know why exactly . . . I think, because I trusted him. Now that I think of it, that teacher never told me he was right and I was wrong. He said there were things I was doing he couldn't allow, or something like that, and he told me why. I told him how I felt about the kids in the class and how boring school was. He listened to it. We never got to see eye to eye on lots of things, but we

knew where we stood. I know now that I learned more from him in those talks than I did during four years in high school. I didn't know it then, but he taught me to think and to see what I was doing. After a while he had enough, I guess, and I don't blame him. He gave me up for lost, I suppose, and he'll never know how much he helped me. It took me years to find it out.[36]

Social Helping

Most of students' problems are rooted in their social environments. Certainly family therapy is an alternative. Another alternative is social action designed to change organizations. Donald H. Blocher observed that one of the reasons why many educators are continually frustrated is because the problems they are called upon to solve are themselves the products of other institutional or community organizations.[37] If people in the helping professions really want to be helpful, some of them will have to be active in community change. But the most significant changes that educators can make involve their own schools and neighborhoods.

Frequently a student's development depends not on his adjustment to an existing classroom situation but instead on being moved to another classroom. This kind of environmental change is not without a theoretical foundation; it is modeled after milieu therapy, preventative and community or social psychiatry. We can take as our illustration the model of milieu therapy, in which the hospital environment serves as a therapeutic instrument, and patterns of human relationships are consciously attuned to the treatment or developmental needs of the residents. When applying this model to the school, it too becomes clear that more often than not nonwhite students do not get the institutional treatment they need because school resources are not attuned to the needs of nonwhite students. Combs listed seven suggestions for what teachers can and must do if each student is to be aided and allowed to become a fully functioning person:

1. Teachers must regard each student as a vital part of the curriculum.
2. Teachers must view students positively because whatever diminishes the child's

self—humiliation, degradation, failure—has no place in education.

3. Teachers must provide for individual differences.

4. Teachers must apply the criteria of self-actualization to every education experience.

5. Teachers must learn how things are seen by their students.

6. Teachers must allow rich opportunities for individuals to explore themselves and their environment.

7. Teachers must help the young to become independent.[38]

Since sensitivity to their own feelings is a prerequisite to effective helping, it may be beneficial for teachers to undergo some type of sensitivity training. A study by Edward W. Schultz and Judith Wolf indicates that a large number of teachers are in need of some kind of experiential training.[39] A series of studies by Carkhuff and others shows extensive evidence for the idea that educators trained in such programs are more successful in helping students and have more of the characteristics of the helping relationship.

If the research studies reviewed are correct in their assertion that helping can be accomplished only on the terms of the healthier person in the relationship, then it becomes necessary to have some criteria for determining who and what a healthy person is. Rogers defined the fully functioning person as a person who lives life as an ongoing, becoming process. Such an educator is able to accept his or her present feelings and able to trust and act on feelings of what is right in a way that involves the courage to be. These educators are psychologically mature. Gordon W. Allport developed six criteria or psychological characteristics of the mature person:

1. A mature person extends his or her self-concept by caring, belonging, identifying with and working towards causes other than himself or herself.

2. A mature person accepts himself or herself.

3. A mature person is capable of intimacy and love—love that is given unconditionally.

4. A mature person functions with efficiency and accuracy in perception and cognition. He or she is able to solve problems of the real world without panic, pity, and resignation.

5. A mature person maintains balance and keeps his or her perspective through insight and humor.

6. A mature person has a clear comprehension of life's purpose.[40]

It is important that teachers get themselves together, so to speak. In an effective helping situation the helpee will ultimately be able to do everything that the helper does at nearly the same level at which the helper is functioning. Teachers who have not gotten themselves together are not able to assist students in getting themselves together.

Many studies have been conducted which indicate the importance of the interpersonal relations between the teacher and the student. The implications of these studies should be self-evident. Student-teacher relationships may be for better or worse, i.e., the development of Black students' social adjustment may be helped or retarded because of the type of relationships they have with their teachers. Helen H. Davidson and Gerhard Lang found that when students feel that teachers value and respect them, they are likely to value and respect themselves.[41]

Other researchers comparing patients' reports on the therapeutic experience with psychoanalytic, nondirective, and Adlerian therapists have found them to be more or less the same fundamental relationship. The ideal teacher is seen in almost the same way as the ideal therapist. The various helping professions are really quite similar in terms of interpersonal styles and relationships. Several researchers have noted that teachers in their study described the ideal teacher in much the same way that therapists describe the ideal therapist. This gives support to the idea that common characteristics of a helping relationship exist and that relationships that are helpful are very similar in the various helping professions.

Three major assumptions about the universality of helping should be remembered. (1) We all at times have emotional problems which we experience as unpleasant and painful. (2) We all seek help for our personal problems. (3) We all offer help to others who are experiencing emotional difficulties. When William Menninger was asked how many people suffer from emotional illness, he answered, "One out of one of us." The help we all seek may come from a spouse, a colleague, a friend, or a teacher. And it is clear that a part of our needs must be met in relation with others. The nature of this relationship was captured in the following passage:

You and I are in a relationship with each other. Yet each of us is a separate person having his own needs. I will try to be as accepting as I can of your behavior as you try to meet your own needs. I will even try to learn how to increase my capacity to be accepting of your behavior. But I can be genuinely accepting of you only as long as your behavior to meet your needs does not conflict with my meeting my own needs. Therefore, whenever I am feeling nonaccepting of you because my own needs are not being met, I will tell you as openly and honestly as I can, leaving it up to you whether you will change your behavior. I also will encourage you to do the same with me and will try to listen to your feelings and perhaps change my behavior. However, when we discover that a conflict-of-needs continues to exist in our relationship, let us both commit ourselves to try to resolve that conflict without the use of either my power or yours. I will respect your needs, but I also must respect my own. Consequently, let us strive always to search mutually for solutions to our inevitable conflicts that will be acceptable to both of us. In this way, your needs will be met but so will mine. As a result, you can continue to grow and achieve satisfaction and so can I. And, finally, our relationship can continue to be a healthy one because it will be mutually satisfying.[42]

REDUCING STUDENT ALIENATION

Four conditions characterize student alienation:[43]

1. *Powerlessness.* Alienated students believe that their own behavior cannot determine the educational outcome they seek. That is, powerless students are objects controlled and manipulated by other persons or by an impersonal education system.

2. *Meaninglessness.* The roles and actions of alienated students seem to have no relation to the broader school programs. There is a lack of understanding of the school events in which they are involved. Equally important, they are unclear as to what they ought to believe since school rules and regulations seem arbitrary.

3. *Normlessness.* Believing that rules regulating school behavior are dysfunctional for

community survival, alienated students turn to socially unapproved behaviors to achieve academic goals.

4. *Isolation.* Alienated students feel in, but not of, the school community. Thus they do not develop loyalties to the school or to their classmates.

Students who experience success are likely to feel that they can control at least some part of their educational destiny. As shown by the large number who accumulate low school achievement records or who become school dropouts or unemployed high school graduates, a disproportionate number of children in rural and urban poverty areas are familiar with failure. In terms of low-achieving students, alienation can be defined as follows. It is a general syndrome made up of a number of different objective conditions and subjective feeling states that emerge from certain relationships between students and the school setting. It exists when students are unable to control their immediate educative processes and develop a sense of purpose and function which connects their education to the overall organization of society, or to belong to integrated educational communities; and it exists when they fail to become actively involved in the process of education as a mode of personal expression.

Student Reactions to Alienation

There are many ways to adjust to feelings of alienation. Some students *retreat*—they withdraw and refuse to play the middle-class game of hard work and striving to get ahead. Dropping out of school or getting hooked on drugs are symptoms of retreating. Other techniques include tuning out teachers by day-dreaming.

Some students become dissatisfied with their deviant behaviors and seek to *conform* to school standards. This is playing the middle-class game with the expectation of winning. Conformists attend remedial or retraining courses. As a group they are highly receptive to innovative programs that seem to offer a way to school success.

In other instances students become moderately dissatisfied with the system of educational opportunities. When this happens they substitute new means to achieve the goals of the dominant culture. Cheating on examinations or extorting quiz answers from high-achieving students are ways students *innovate* to acquire passing grades.

Severe dissatisfaction with the existing school system causes a few students to *rebel* in noncriminal but nevertheless variant ways (e.g., become communists or separatists). These students have no illusions that they can succeed in the existing system, so they substitute new systems that seem to offer more hope of success.

There is also the possibility that when norms disappear or lose their holding power, a student may lose the ability to evaluate herself, to know what she is or even who she is. In *The Lonely Crowd*, David Riesman discussed alienated people who are "other-directed."[44] Even though such alienated students seem to follow the rules and regulations of the school, they actually are playing the middle-class game of life just for the sake of playing it—believing that success is beyond their grasp. Life becomes a *ritual* in which they take pride in being low academic achievers but good citizens.

The effects of failure on a child's personality have been well-documented. A much replicated 1932 study observed that students who failed reading tests had symptoms of nervous tension such as restlessness, nail-biting, and insomnia; they physically or psychologically withdrew from school; they resorted to loudness and defiance; they became cruel to other children; they were inattentive.[45] In a similar experiment students failing in reading and arithmetic tasks were studied by Ernest R. Hilgard.[46] As a result of experiencing failure some of the students appeared to be so afraid of additional failure that they set goals below past achievements, thereby trying to protect themselves from additional failure. Others were so demoralized that they set goals that were too high to be realistic, causing them to fail repeatedly.

The individual who fails in school tasks usually sets up some type of ego defense mechanism. If, for example, he believes that he will fail, he may deny the reality of school and not study at all. In this way he can tell himself and others that he could have succeeded if he had wanted to. The emphasis on high grades increases anxiety and tension in students. Furthermore, oral recitations in the classroom add to these feelings, since incorrect answers are embarrassing, causing students to

look stupid to the rest of the class. In this type of environment there may develop a comradeship between low-achieving students who have the ability to do better and those who lack such an ability. Students in the former group may altruistically refuse to achieve at a higher level so as not to embarrass their friends in public.

The deprived-student syndrome.   Much of the plight of middle-class teachers (white and nonwhite) assigned to teach students who live in depressed rural and urban areas stems from their inability to understand the educational needs of culturally different people. Many teachers erroneously think that culturally different students are alien people, having needs unlike those of normal students.

Recent studies indicate that culturally different students do not need misplaced kindness; instead, they need empathetic—but fair and firm—guidance. Teachers often attempt to make up for cultural differences. That is, with so much emphasis being placed on understanding and assisting minority-group students, some teachers fall victim to the urge to engage in overcompensatory actions. No matter how well intended, however, social promotions, watered-down curricula, and unearned rewards cause additional problems. They may, in fact, lead to the *deprived-student syndrome.*

The deprived student syndrome refers to the process by which students use their deprivations to beat the system. "When I want to get out of doing my school work," a high school student confided, "I just tell my teachers that I couldn't do it because my old man was drunk, or the light company turned off the lights." This is beating the system—getting by without doing the required work. Using their cultural differences as a crutch, they hobble through school, manipulating their perceived manipulators (school personnel). Another student, sharing a trade secret, said, "If I wants to sack in late and miss my first class, I don't worry about it. My principal says it's a miracle that I come to school at all with all the hardships that I have to put up with." Few students in this category are seeking success in school. They only seek to minimize the complications during their stay in school.

To the student who knows that he is not putting forth the required effort but receives positive sanctions, success in school is meaningless. That is, to the student who has not mastered the subject, good grades are a farce. Yet, in a way following the maxim that the shortest distance between two points is a straight line, many students are content to slide by with a minimum of effort. It is probable that most graduates who have slid by wished that their teachers had caught them. Commenting on her school performance, a high school graduate said, "I got through with no sweat, but it didn't learn me anything. . . . If I had to do it over again I'd study harder. Now the only thing that I can do is day work or something that don't call for school work." School under these conditions becomes a game in which even if one wins he still loses. Making it easy for low-achieving students to succeed in school without doing adequate work also makes it easy for them to fail in the world of work.

Capricious sanctions. Numerous studies show that the less effective teachers assume that if a child comes from a poverty-stricken home he or she is also of low intelligence. Along with this assumption goes the belief that low-income students do not know the difference between properly executed and improperly executed school tasks. Thus these teachers capriciously parcel out rewards and punishments. Unlike these who love them to their academic deaths, teachers behaving in this manner are thwarting students' desires to complete school assignments.

"Why bother?" a disgruntled student frowned. "When they feel like giving you a good grade, they will. Johnny and I turned in the same book report. I copied his. He got a 'C' and I got a 'B'." Negatively conditioned for school life, most low-income students desperately need positive sanctions to keep them in school. This does not mean that they should be given high grades for low achievement. Instead, appropriate recognition for effort and improvement is needed.

Psychologically it is less difficult for students to adjust to consistent teachers than to whimsical ones. For example the teacher who consistently marks low is better appreciated than the teacher who is a low marker on some days and high on others. "I didn't mind him giving me a 'D'," a puzzled junior high student said, "but he gave me a 'B' for the same score last week." Confused and powerless, many low-achieving students simply give up and sink

deeper into the mire of mediocrity. (Teachers who ignore individual needs for fair and consistent evaluation are given noncomplimentary nicknames.) Both bad work and good work become synonymous with wasted work. If enough teachers act this way, students do not drop out—they are pushed out!

Desired teacher qualities. Culturally different students need more teachers who will touch them, smile at them, and yes, smell them. Teachers who view them as being a group of highly contagious germs either consciously or subconsciously seek to avoid contact with them. "These teachers are as phony as a three-dollar bill," a Puerto Rican student remarked. He was specifically referring to a white teacher who habitually poured disinfectant around the classroom and wiped all books and pencils with tissues before accepting them from nonwhite students.

The methods used by the more effective teachers to gain the confidence of culturally different students usually include not only human relations lectures but also humane behaviors. The teacher who routinely schedules an "I understand your problems" lecture is suspected of being a phony. In fact students frequently test this pretense of empathy by contriving forced interactions. Many teachers fail their human relations moment-of-truth test, as did the one who jumped back violently when a shabbily-dressed girl rushed up to receive the warmth that had been promised in the lecture.

Studies indicate that lower-class students are more likely to conform to middle-class standards of cleanliness and speech if they believe that conformity is for their benefit and not that of a squeamish teacher. Sometimes the antagonism shown by low-achieving students is an attempt to gain recognition. The classroom bully illustrates this point. Unable to gain recognition under calmer conditions, a student acting out in class goads a reluctant teacher into at least touching him.

Advantaged or disadvantaged, nonwhite or white, middle class or lower class, all students need teachers who will (1) be honest in evaluating their work, (2) tell them where they are in subject matter skill development, and (3) assist them in their efforts to improve. Rebelling against the ego disintegration that comes from being an academic nobody, many low-achieving students strive to be somebody, even if delinquency seems to provide the only way.

Juvenile Delinquency

The new ethnics—Filipino, Korean, and Vietnamese—are becoming a larger percentage of juvenile delinquents. Even so, white, Black and Latino youth are by far the largest number of American juvenile delinquents. The magnitude of youthful offenses is seen in the nation's $600 million annual school vandalism cost. On a more personal level, each year more youths are arrested for violent crimes—homicide, assault, rape, and robbery. Between 1966 and 1976, juvenile arrests increased more than 120 per cent, while adult arrests increased by 15 per cent.

Most juvenile delinquents live in environments conducive to perpetuating their behaviors. Inadequate recreation facilities, overcrowded and slum housing, high adult crime rates, and unemployment are but a few of the environmental forces associated with juvenile delinquency. However, the fact that there are middle- and upper-income delinquents shows that the problem of delinquency is too complex to be attributed to a single variable such as income or a slum environment. The complexity of the problem is further shown by the fact that most boys and girls in low-income rural and urban areas are able to insulate themselves against delinquency. Nevertheless it is difficult for schools to provide this insulation if they too reflect negative environmental conditions—over-crowded classrooms, dilapidated and inadequate physical plants, and underpaid personnel.

Programs to combat delinquency. There are those, both professional and nonprofessional, who advocate punishment, strict discipline, and psychiatric clinic referral as treatment for delinquent youth. Educators who believe that punishment stops deviant behavior should heed criminologists who report that punishment *per se* has never proved an effective deterrent to crime. Nor is strict discipline a total solution. After all, many studies show that delinquent children come from a variety of home discipline situations including those in which parents are overly strict, indifferent, or inconsistent in administering discipline. As

for referral to psychiatric clinics, this is not a cure-all. Many youthful psychiatric patients become adult criminal offenders. It thus appears that solutions to student alienation must go beyond punishment, strict discipline, and psychiatric clinics.

Educators interested in positive approaches to school violence and vandalism should read *Challenge for America's Third Century: Education in a Safe Environment*, the final report of the U. S. Senate Subcommittee to Investigate Juvenile Delinquency.[47] The committee's recommendations include (1) community education and optional alternative education programs, (2) student code of rights and responsibilities (obligations), (3) inservice and preservice teacher preparation courses focusing on violence and violence prevention, (4) student and parental involvement programs, and (5) alternatives to suspension (e.g., cool-off rooms and behavior contracts).

Efforts to improve discipline in schools include the use of behavior modification techniques, students courts, early identification of and assistance for students with behavior problems, and teacher aides. The major emphasis is on organizational changes, particularly in removing blocks to learning, broadening opportunities for work and leisure-time activities, and otherwise making education a more meaningful experience for all students.

Programs in which students are the actors rather than those in which they are acted upon are the most helpful. Some school officials realize that a disproportionate number of rural and inner-city students feel powerless, and that school programs must provide them with opportunities to control successfully aspects of their school experiences by using procedures acceptable to their teachers. Programs designed primarily for the institutionalization and containment of students are inferior to those that encourage individual growth and development. Any program that is capable of helping students succeed on the basis of their own abilities is vastly superior to one in which they must passively await the capricious or paternalistic decisions of teachers and administrators.

CHANGE AGENTS

Weaknesses in the validity of attitude measurements are not adequate reasons for failing to seek ways to diminish negative student self-concepts that, in turn, impede ability to succeed in school. It is likely that until low-achieving students feel good about themselves as a reflection of their perceptions of the educational climate, they will have great difficulty learning academic concepts presented in the classroom. This premise is consistent with the view that if the perceptions of self in the educational climate are mainly derogatory, then the growing child's general attitudes toward herself will be mainly derogatory. The child toward whom the predominant attitude of significant persons has been one of hostility, disapproval, and dissatisfaction tends to view the world in similar terms. She has difficulty in seeing or learning anything better and, although she may not openly express self-depreciatory attitudes, she has a depreciatory attitude toward others and toward herself.[48]

Students' and parents' attitudes toward school can be measured by the extent to which they talk about their school experiences in favorable or unfavorable terms. Their opinions, of course, reflect how much at ease and how welcome they feel in school. And these feelings in turn reflect the extent to which administrators and teachers encourage or discourage their participation in both academic and co-curricular activities.

Administrators

School administrators are called upon to play a myriad of roles including being able to judge standards, coordinate programs, write reports, and bridge the culture gap between the school and home and community. They are placed in the unenviable position of advocates who must cut through the system's rules and regulations without being offensive. Above all, they must be able to work well with community residents, even though many residents do not desire a cooperative relationship.

W. Lloyd Warner's "Jonesville" study shows clearly that school administrators come into pre-existing sociocultural complexes where "what to do" and "what not to do" are determined by local values, beliefs, prejudices, and customs.[49] Not only must they immediately adjust to and become an integral part of these pre-existing social systems but school administrators must also organize school activities to meet the demands of people outside the community who are in power positions. August B. Hollingshead's "Elmtown" study points out that administrators must respond to the pressures from both outside and inside the system as well as to the pressures imposed by their own professional standards.[50] The role expectations emanating from these three sources often lead to conflict.

Because administrators (and teachers) typically do not serve in schools of their own neighborhoods, they are thought of as strangers. Furthermore, because of their high turnover rate, administrators usually do not remain in one community long enough to become a part of it. To a great extent they are professional gypsies, moving from one job opportunity to another. Except for superintendents, school administrators are mainly inbred and they tend to organize into formal and informal associations that protect the status quo. In the case of big-city superintendents, many grew up and first taught in small towns and gained their administrative experience in rural or suburban schools; thus they are likely to be conservative in their approach to educational changes.

Lacking intimate knowledge of their school neighborhoods, many administrators seek to compensate by becoming regulations specialists, committing school rules and regulations to memory and applying them indiscriminately. When performing as regulations specialists, they also tend to become defensive, reacting to community problems but seldom acting before problems erupt. This type of fire-fighting activity creates additional problems for other administrators who prefer to be proactive rather than reactive but instead find themselves forced to be reluctant implementers of board policies.

The principal has the key role in determining the educational climate within her building. She makes the major difference between a school that recruits and retains competent teachers and a school that has a high turnover of demoralized, dissatisfied teachers. Indeed, no one person has greater influence on every phase of school life than the principal. Although limited somewhat by external controls, each principal can initiate new school programs. This initiatory power takes on added importance in economically depressed areas where many students and their parents feel that school is a closed system and that they are outsiders. This attitude characterizes students who feel like recalcitrant prison inmates serving time while anxiously looking for ways to escape.

In times of great stress a vicious administrative self-esteem circle operates as follows. Department heads do not want their assistant (vice) principal to know that they have unresolved problems. The assistant principal does not want the principal to know that the department heads have unresolved problems. The principal does not want the assistant superintendent to know that he has unresolved problems within his school. The assistant superintendent does not want the superintendent to know that he has unresolved problems in his district. The superintendent does not want the board of education to know that she has unresolved problems within her school system. Members of the board of education do not want the voters to know that there are unresolved school problems. Failure to openly deal with problems is usually counterproductive.

Some other factors that may impede administrative action are large numbers of students who are behind the achievement level of their agemates, high student absenteeism and high yearly turnover, and teachers who are unprepared to teach low-achieving, ethnic minority students. When school administrators believe that the maintenance of discipline is their chief function, they are likely to behave in a manner that fosters negative staff attitudes toward low-achieving students and their parents. On the other hand, when administrators view their primary job as being the community's education leaders, they are likely to foster a positive school climate.

Teachers

As noted in earlier chapters, a considerable part of the socializing task performed by parents in earlier times has now been given to teachers. Teachers supervise meals and recreation, give training in hygiene and parenting, prepare students for occupations, and teach about aging and death and moral values. The importance of teachers' successfully playing their roles is underscored by the fact that they can promote or fail students, reward or punish them, encourage or discourage them. What the teacher does with this power is of great significance to the quality of education afforded students.

Role expectations for teachers, like those for administrators, are varied and conflicting. Teachers are expected to judge achievement, convey knowledge, keep discipline, give advice and receive confidences, keep records, establish a moral atmosphere, be a member of an institution, participate in community affairs, and be an exemplary member of the teaching profession.[51] Of the many roles that could be listed, two main categories emerge: director of learning and mediator between the cultures of the school and the community.

The teacher is the key figure in the entire educational process. In summary, a teacher's attitude can determine the success or failure of her students. The whole area of teacher attitudes and behavior has been the subject of an increasing amount of research in recent years. For instance Robert Rosenthal and Lenore Jacobson have reported on their study of teacher attitudes in a thought-provoking book, *Pygmalion in the Classroom.*[52] At a public elementary school in a lower-class community they led the teachers to believe that the results of a test showed that certain students would "spurt" in achievement. Actually the designated children were picked at random. Later testing showed that these children had improved in their school work to a significant degree, whereas those not designated as spurters had made for smaller gains. Achievements of minority-group children who had been designated as spurters were particularly dramatic.

Nothing was done directly for the disadvantaged children at the school—no crash programs, no tutoring, no museum trips. There was only the teachers' belief that certain children had competencies that would become apparent. If a teacher believes that a student is incapable of learning certain materials, it is likely that this belief will in some way be communicated to the student in one or more of the many student-teacher interactions and that the belief will then prove to be true. Conversely, there is impressive evidence that shows that if a teacher believes a student is capable of learning, the student gets this message, too. This, then, is the *self-fulfilling prophecy.*

In some schools teachers who have positive attitudes toward low-achieving students are themselves the subjects of ridicule and cynicism from other teachers (although they frequently are well-liked by their students). The ridiculing teachers usually are trying to escape the guilt associated with their own lack of success with these students. If nonconforming behaviors persist, the norm-violating teachers may even be ostracized. The actual reasons for ostracism are usually hidden by ostensible ones: failing to contribute to the school social fund, refusing to eat lunch with the in-crowd, or being too agressive in staff meetings. To put it bluntly, teachers who try to improve the quality of education for chronically low-achieving students often are thought of, in labor union terms, as scabs who increase their work output above the group norm.

Despite all the uncertainties in their roles most teachers accomplish a great amount of work. Perhaps more studies of successful teaching practices are needed. Teachers who feel at ease in their jobs tend to create classroom atmospheres conducive to learning; those who do not make their classrooms repressive places for themselves and for their students.

Community leaders

Educators are becoming increasingly community-conscious. Many are thus striving to eradicate the negative attitudes of parents and community leaders toward the schools. Every school-community has within it the source and power to engender positive attitudes. The need for more parents to assume leadership roles is being encouraged nationally by the Reverend Jesse Jackson's PUSH (People United To Save Humanity) for Excellence program which urges parents to visit schools, read to their children, and help the schools to curb truancy, violence, and drug addition.

If a school is to become truly a community school, its staff must do the following: (1) meet with citizens face-to-face to discuss such things as school needs, new programs, boundary changes, and complaint procedures; (2) seek ways to improve two-way communication between school and community, with special attention given to reaching parents who do not normally attend school meetings; and (3) evaluate school activities and make appropriate changes.

In final analysis the student is the living proof of how helpful school personnel have been. Eloquent speeches, attractive bulletin board displays, multicultural and non-sexist materials, and thoughtful grievance procedures are useless unless they culminate in an improved quality of education.

GROUPS

1. Check all the situations in which you feel *most* comfortable.
☐ alone
☐ in small groups of friends
☐ in small groups of people I don't know too well
☐ in large groups
☐ in meeting teenagers
☐ in meeting adults
☐ in a sports activity
☐ in a discussion
☐ in a classroom
☐ in an argument
☐ in front of a group
☐ with a special friend
☐ with a boy-friend or girl-friend

2. Check all the situations in which you feel least comfortable.
☐ alone
☐ in small groups of friends
☐ in small groups of people I don't know too well
☐ in large groups
☐ in meeting teenagers
☐ in meeting adults
☐ in a sports activity
☐ in a discussion
☐ in a classroom
☐ in an argument
☐ in front of a group
☐ with a special friend
☐ with a boy-friend or girl-friend

3. Check the one answer in each question that most nearly corresponds to your beliefs.
A. The most important problem of a teacher is:
☐ to get the job done in spite of students.
☐ to get the job done and care for students.
☐ to care for students in order to get the job done.
☐ to care for students even if the job does not get done.
B. When working in groups:
☐ I feel I am understood most of the time, but people do not agree with me.
☐ I feel I am understood most of the time, and

people agree with me but not with the way I behave.

☐ I feel I am not understood most of the time and believe it is not my fault.

☐ I feel I am not understood most of the time, and it is my fault.

C. When teachers are working with students, they should be:

☐ cooperative but out to win their point.

☐ willing to lose their point in order to cooperate with students.

☐ sensitive to the students' points.

☐ seek to share common goals.

D. Strong feelings, when expressed by students, should:

☐ be acknowledged but discouraged in subsequent meetings.

☐ be done with self-discipline.

☐ be accepted as facts.

☐ be rejected, but the students should be accepted.

E. For the most effective learning to take place:

☐ some student involvement is necessary depending on what is to be learned.

☐ intellectual, spiritual, and emotional growth are interrelated.

☐ there must be reflection on experience.

ADDITIONAL READINGS

Bennett, Neville. *Teaching Styles and Pupil Progress.* Cambridge, Mass., Harvard University Press, 1976.

Combs, Arthur W. et al. *The Professional Education of Teachers: A Humanistic Approach to Teacher Preparation*, 2d ed. Boston, Allyn and Bacon, 1974.

Cooper, James M. et al. *Teaching Skills: A Handbook.* Lexington, Mass. D. C. Heath, 1977.

Fuchs, Estelle. *Teachers Talk: Views from Inside Inner City Schools.* Garden City, N.Y., Anchor Books, 1969.

Hennelore, Wass, et al. *Humanistic Teacher Education: An Experiment in Systematic Curriculum Innovation.* Fort Collins, Colo., Shields, 1974.

Havelock, Ronald G. *Training for Change Agents: A Guide to the Design of Training Programs in Education and Other Fields.* Ann Arbor, Mich., Center for Research on Utilization of Scientific Knowledge, 1972.

Henderson, George and Robert F. Bibens. *Teachers Should Care: Social Perspectives of Teaching.* New York, Harper & Row, 1970.

Renfield, Richard. *If Teachers Were Free*, 2d rev. ed. Washington, Acropolis Books, 1972.

Rieff, Philip. *Fellow Teachers.* New York, Harper & Row, 1973.

Schmuck, Richard A. and Patricia A. Schmuck. *A Humanistic Psychology of Education: Making the School Everybody's House.* Palo Alto, Cal., National Press Books, 1974.

Simon, Sidney B. *Meeting Yourself Halfway: 31 Value Clarification Strategies for Daily Living.* Niles, Ill., Argus Communications, 1974.

Sterling, Philip, ed. *The Real Teachers.* New York, Random House, 1972.

Strom, Robert D. *The Urban Teacher: Selection, Training and Supervision.* Columbus, Ohio, Merrell, 1971.

Wilson, Charles H. *A Teacher is a Person.* New York, Holt, 1956.

NOTES

1. Carl R. Rogers, "The Characteristics of a Helping Relationship," *Personnel and Guidance Journal* 37 (September, 1958), 6.

2. *Ibid.*

3. Alan Keith-Lucas, *Giving and Taking Help*, (Chapel Hill, University of North Carolina Press, 1972), 46.

4. Arthur W. Combs, *Florida Studies in the Helping Professions* (Gainesville, University of Florida Press, 1969), 3.

5. Rogers, "Helping Relationship," 12.

6. *Ibid.*

7. *Ibid.*

8. *Ibid.*, 13–14.

9. *Ibid.*, 14.

10. *Ibid.*, 13.

11. *Ibid.*, 14.

12. See Carl R. Rogers, "The Process Equation of Psychotherapy," *American Journal of Psychotherapy*, 15 (January, 1961), 27–45.

13. Keith-Lucas, *Giving and Taking Help*, 70.

14. *Ibid.*, 88.

15. Harper Lee, *To Kill a Mockingbird* (New York, Popular Library, 1960), 34.

16. Alfred Benjamin, *The Helping Interview* (Boston, Houghton Mufflin, 1969), 47.

17. Frank H. Drause and Donald E. Hendrickson, *Counseling Techniques with Youth* (Columbus, Ohio, Charles Merrill, 1972), 39–48.

18. Abraham H. Maslow, *Toward a Psychology of Being* (New York, D. Van Nostrand, 1962), 3–5.

19. Arthur Janov, *The Primal Scream* (New York, Dell, 1970).

20. A. S. Neill, *Summerhill* (New York, Hart, 1960).

21. For a discussion of Maslow's and Rogers' concepts see George Henderson, *Human Relations: From Theory to Practice* (Norman, University of Oklahoma Press, 1974), 236–40.

22. Donald Snygg, "The Psychological Basis of Human Values," in Donald L. Avila, Arthur W. Combs, and William W. Purkey (eds.), *The Helping Relationship Sourcebook* (Boston, Allyn & Bacon, 1971), 86.

23. Earl C. Kelley, "Another Look at Individualism," in Avila, Combs, and Purkey, *Ibid.*, 315.

24. An excellent literary work focusing on suicide as a choice is found in Hermann Hesse, *Steppenwolf* (New York, Holt, Rinehart & Winston, 1963).

25. Robert R. Spaulding, "Achievement, Creativity, and Self-Concept Correlates of Teacher-Pupil Transactions in Elementary Schools," in Celia B. Stendler (ed.), *Readings in Child Behavior and Development*, 2d ed. (New York, Harcourt, Brace, 1964), 313–18.

26. Morris L. Cogan, "The Behavior of Teachers and the Productive Behavior of Their Pupils," *Journal of Experimental Education*, 27 (December, 1958), 89–124.

27. C. M. Christensen, "Relationship Between Pupil Achievement, Pupil Affect-need, Teacher Warmth and Teacher Permissiveness," *Journal of Educational Psychology*, 51 (June 1960), 169–74.

28. Horace B. Reed, "Implications for Science Education of a Teacher Competence Research," *Science Education*, 46 (1962), 473–86.

29. Frank C. Emmerling, "A Study of the Relationship Between Characteristics of Classroom Teachers and Pupil Perceptions," unpublished Ph.D. dissertation, Auburn, Alabama, Auburn University, 1961.

30. Robert M. Thomas, *Social Differences in the Classroom: Social-class, Ethnic and Religious Problems* (New York, David McKay, 1965), chapter 1.

31. Gilbert C. Wrenn, "Psychology, Religion, and Values for the Counselor," *Personnel Guidance Journal*, 36 (1958), 34.

32. Vincent F. Calia, "The Culturally Deprived Client: A Reformation of the Counselor's Role," *Journal of Counseling Psychology*, 13 (Spring, 1966), 100–105.

33. Frank Riessman, "Role Playing and the Lower Socioeconomic Group," *Group Psychotherapy*, 17 (March, 1964), 36–48.

34. August B. Hollingshead and Frederick C. Redlich, *Social Class and Mental Illness* (New York, John Wiley & Son, 1958), 176.

35. George Banks, Bernard G. Berenson, and Robert F. Carkhuff, "The Effects of Counselor Race and Training Upon Negro Clients in Initial Interviews," *Journal of Clinical Psychology*, 23 (January 1967), 70–72.

36. Benjamin, *The Helping Interview*, 92–93.

37. Donald H. Blocher, *Developmental Counseling* (New York, Ronald Press, 1966), 87–96.

38. Arthur W. Combs, "What Can Man Become?," in Avila, Combs, and Purkey, *Sourcebook*, 397–412.

39. Edward W. Schultz and Judith Wolf, "Teacher Behavior, Self-Concept and the Helping Process," *Psychology in the Schools*, 10 (January, 1973), 75–78.

40. Gordon W. Allport, *Pattern and Growth in Personality* (New York, Holt, Rinehart & Winston, 1961), 283–304.

41. Helen H. Davidson and Gerhard Lang, "Children's Perceptions of Their Teacher's Feelings Toward Them Related to Self-Perception, School Achievement, and Behavior," *Journal of Experimental Education* 29 (December, 1960), 107–18.

42. Thomas Gordon, "A Theory of Healthy Relationship and a Program of Parent Effectivenss Training," in J. T. Hart and T. M. Tomlinson (eds.), *New Directions in Client-Centered Therapy* (Boston, Houghton Mifflin, 1970), 424–25.

43. See Melvin Seeman, "On the Meaning of Alienation," *American Sociological Review*, 24 (December, 1959), 783–91.

44. David Riesman, *The Lonely Crowd* (New York, Doubleday, 1955).

45. Adolph A. Sandlin, "Social and Emotional Adjustments of Regularly Promoted and Non-Promoted Pupils," *Columbia University Monograph, No. 32*, 1932.

46. Ernest R. Hilgard, "Success in Relation to Level of Aspiration," *School and Society*, 55 (April, 1942), 423–28.

47. *Challenge for the Third Century: Education in a Safe Environment—Final Report on the Nature and Prevention of School Violence and Vandalism*, (Washington, D. C., U. S. Government Printing Office, 1977).

48. Arthur J. Jersild, *In Search of Self* (New York, Teachers College, 1960), 13

49. W. Lloyd Warner et al., *Social Class in America* (Chicago, Science Research Associates, 1949), 86.

50. August B. Hollingshead, *Elmtown's Youth* (New York, John Wiley & Sons, 1949), 128–32.

51. See Jean D. Grambs, "The Role of the Teacher," in Lindley Stiles (ed.), *The Teacher's Role in American Society* (New York, Harper & Row, 1957), 73–93.

52. Robert Rosenthal and Lenore Jacobson, *Pygmalion in the Classroom: Teacher Expectation and Pupils' Intellectual Development* (New York, Holt, Rinehart & Winston, 1968).

PART IV
THE PROMISE
OF AMERICAN
EDUCATION

WANTED:
A HUMAN
RELATIONS
APPROACH
TO EDUCATION*

Jacquelene Peters

*By Jacquelene Peters, graduate student, University of Oklahoma, 1970. Used by permission.

Although many phases of American society might fittingly be described by the phrase "man's inhumanity to man," none seems more worthy of this designation than our public schools.

Six years ago I would not have made that statement; then, I would have denied it vehemently. But then I was a young, first-year high school teacher, glossy and polished with the pride and confidence that I would be the best teacher my students had ever known. Now I am older and wiser, dulled by a system that doesn't really care but only pretends to, a system in which textbook is topdog and student is underdog, a system which dehumanizes humans.

The Past

I entered my first teaching assignment never questioning that I knew what education was all about. I had been trained to teach the English language; that was what the students needed, and that was what they were going to get. (Never did I stop to consider then that many of them had a fourth-grade reading level or a hatred for school or alcoholic parents or little money with which to buy a notebook.)

So English I taught—from informal essays to Shakespearean drama, from short stories to the medieval sonnet. I followed the traditional school rules of, "Below 70, give an F," and, "Fix all grades in an accurate curve" without question. I lowered averages for talking, for acting up in class, for failing to get homework, and for chewing gum.

One time an overweight, self-conscious sophomore girl refused to stand up in front of the class and practice our unit on etiquette (etiquette! to a class whose meals meant jelly glasses rather than china and crystal, to students whose, "May I introduce . . . ," would receive derisive laughter at home). So I *forced* her to participate, saying that it was her *duty* to the class and to me to do what the rest of the students were doing! When a freckle-faced, implike boy talked back to me, I made him stand up for fifteen minutes while the class and I sat and looked at him.

For four years I taught this way, really feeling that I was a good teacher, not knowing then that I was playing a big part in the "man's inhumanity to man" role. I liked my students, but I didn't try to get close to any of them; my main aims were to keep them relatively quiet and to finish the textbook by the end of the year. These were the criteria absorbed from my teacher-education classes, and doubting them never entered my mind.

Now I know I was wrong.

This discovery came not in the classroom, however, but as a result of my decision to become a counselor. During the course of that specialized training, I began to realize how I—and the whole educational system—have caused more hurt than help, more injury than instruction, more agony than aid. I realized for the first time that each student in every classroom is a unique individual, with hopes, dreams, problems, and needs which form the basis for his classroom behavior. (As a teacher I may have known this, but I was too wrapped up in textbooks, grades, and school rules to care.)

Through counseling I found that there was a whole human world inside that school which had never been visible to me before; in comparison, my English content became irrelevant. I had been preaching simile and metaphor to a girl whose father had been having sexual relations with her since the sixth grade. I was urging nouns and verbs on a boy who had a butcher knife hidden under his bed in wait for the right moment to kill his stepmother. I was assigning book reports to a sixteen-year-old common-law wife whose "husband" was stealing food for them at night and molesting small girls during the day. I was forcing *Julius Caesar* on a boy who believed that men from outer space were communicating with him and asking him to kill the President of the United States and anyone else in authority. These were the kids I was telling to spit out their gum, sit up straight in their seats, and practice introducing their parents to their friends properly.

The incongruity of it all was appalling.

Following my counseling training, I was again placed in an English classroom, only to find that, although I had changed, the educational system had not; now that I saw the possibilities and necessities for humanizing education, I found that rules and traditions bound me in. When I arranged my thirty-six desks in two semicircles rather than the traditional rows, the janitor complained that my room was too hard to sweep. When I used small group interaction, other teachers complained that my classes were too loud. When I suggested to the scheduling adviser that one of my students was enrolled in a course which he had already taken and passed (the boy had asked me what he should do about it), I was told to quit trying to be Jesus Christ in the classroom and to tell the boy that if he kept quiet in the course for the first semester he might get out the second semester. When a student came to me with a personal problem, I could rarely talk with him because teachers were constantly advised not to leave their classes unsupervised. As I began to be more and more student-aware, and less and less subject-aware, I found myself becoming more and more disillusioned by the little box in which I was supposed to fit, and less and less inclined to want to fit there. I found that humanizing education was not the game we were playing. So I became a teacher dropout.

The Present

Now that I am outside the public school system rather than in it, I can more clearly see what is happening: the educational system seems designed to hinder rather than help a child fulfill his basic human needs. These needs, as listed by Abraham H. Maslow in *Motivation and Personality* are:

1. *Physiological needs.* These are needs for air, food, water, and physical comfort, which must be met before the following needs can be satisfied.
2. *Safety needs.* Using children for an example, Maslow finds that they have a desire for freedom from fear and insecurity. Safety needs are needs to avoid harmful or painful incidents.
3. *Belongingness.* Needs to belong are the first of the higher-order needs. Maslow means that the human personality wants security. The human being wants to be somebody, even though in a small group.
4. *Love needs.* Man has always had and will always have the desire to love someone else and be loved in return.
5. *Self-esteeem needs.* Man wants to feel that he is worthwhile, that he can master something of his own environment, that he has a competence and an independence and a freedom and a feeling of being recognized for some kind of endeavor.
6. *Self-actualization needs.* These are the highest needs, as Maslow considers them. They involve the needs for recognition and for aesthetic reality. Man has a strong desire and need to know and understand not only himself but the world about him.

If these are the basic needs that school children, as human beings, have, then the school should, in the course of its systemization, be attempting to fulfill them. A brief analysis will indicate that it is not.

First are the *physiological needs.* Although many cities have new, showy classroom facilities and buildings, many more do not, especially in small rural towns and inner cities. A dark, gloomy hall, a moldy room with stale bathroom smells, an unappetizing cafeteria tray or a can of pork and beans brought from home (or no lunch at all), a light bulb dangling from a frayed cord in the ceiling—is this the way the most affluent society in the world meets the physiological needs of its most precious human beings, the children?

Next are the *safety needs*. Do our children feel safe in our schools? This means freedom from fear, insecurity, harmful and painful incidents. How can they? Many of them live in mortal terror (little ones and big ones alike) of threatened or actual punishment with teacher's paddle, ruler, or rubber hose. They fear being shaken, slapped, scorned, ridiculed, lambasted, and ignored. They fear those inconsistent giants called teachers who can so mercilessly mete out punishment with the flick of the wrist or a slash of the tongue. It is no wonder that assults on teachers increased 800 per cent between 1964 and 1968. The children have finally decided to show the teachers what it is like to feel a need for safety.

There is also the *belonging need*. Of course, our schools consider the belonging issue to be important—haven't we all heard teachers say, "He belongs in jail," or "She belongs in the slow group," or "I'm glad that one doesn't belong to me"? No one ever considers where the child *wants* to belong; no one helps him *feel* that he belongs. Instead, on their own bases, teachers issue out a kind of segregated belonging: "*You* belong with the rich, and *you* with the poor. *You* belong with the blacks, and *you* with the whites. *You* belong with the smart, and *you* with the dumb." In essence they are saying, "You belong where I put you and whether you like it or not, that's where you are going to stay." Since statistics show that more than one-third of all students drop out of the public schools before graduation, it is obvious that one place they feel they do *not* belong is in school.

Fourth are the *love needs*. This set of needs is truly ignored in the educational process. Who has ever heard of expressing, or feeling, love in the classroom? The formal, scientifically structured educational process seems aimed at avoiding admittance of such a need. Even when affection is displayed by students in the halls between classes, teachers—feeling that school is not the place for love—intervene.

Next are the *self-esteem needs*. These are needs that the schools seem especially adept at denying. This denial often takes the form of grading. The teacher, playing the game God in the Classroom, looks down on the efforts of the underlings below and passes a value judgment on them. He dares to say, "That is poor work—F work—even if you did do your best. You will just have to try harder." He takes an artificial yardstick and uses it to measure a human endeavor; he never gives self-esteem a chance. What the teacher is really doing is fulfilling his own self-esteem needs by playing Almighty with the gradebook. Who does the school exist for, the teacher or the student?

The highest of all human needs is *self-actualization*. Well, here is the big one, the need that theoretically does not even reveal itself until the others have been met. Then why discuss it? Because somehow the teachers and the schools are confused. They think that this need, because it is the highest, should be dealt with first. They assume that all students have, or *should* have, an intense desire to know things, a need for abstract thoughts and aesthetic experiences. Therefore, they jam textbooks in students' faces and facts down students' throats. They disregard security, belonging, love, and self-esteem in their fanatic worship of knowledge, not realizing that the needs they are so casually tossing aside must be met first.

When are our schools going to place the basic human needs first and facts second? When are they going to help a child feel secure, loved, and important, instead of afraid, unwanted, unloved, and unnecessary? When is the *child* going to come first in education? How long before it is too late?

19.
IN RETROSPECT

The foundations of humanistic education reside in the constancy of change and the need to find solutions that will permit us to survive our inhumanity. For too long the processes of education have concentrated on nonhuman questions and curricula, until it has become painfully clear that the education system is dehumanizing the very people it was created to serve: the students. And it is even more dehumanizing for nonwhite students. The traditional method of stimulus-response conditioning leaves much to be desired in developing of the humane value systems and positive self-concepts which make for order, integrity, and progress in a nation.

DESCRIPTION AND NEED

The rote learning which dominates such a large portion of traditional academic methods has failed to deal with the problem of holistic development. Being a whole person presents an intricate web of needs which goes far beyond merely preparing students to function efficiently for a lifetime as human working machines. In the complexity of our mechanized, automated, assembly-line world, students are rebelling against alienation, isolation, and plastic existence. Arthur W. Combs has pointed out that students have demonstrated—sometimes violently but largely nonviolently—their concern that learning is not a mechanical process but a human process.[1] Examples of such rebellion were seen first in areas other than education, and should have served as a forewarning to educators.

When industry developed the assembly line and other systematic techniques to increase efficiency, what happened? The workers felt dehumanized by the system and formed unions to fight it. And that is precisely what is happening with our young people today. They feel increasingly dehumanized by the system, so they are fighting it at every possible level. Applying industrial techniques to human problems just won't work.[2]

The foundations of humanistic education derive from the attempt by a few educators to redress past neglect through affective learning, which involves a student's beliefs, attitudes, feelings, and values. In endeavoring to devise a more humanistic educational system for students, one common principle has emerged as a foundation cornerstone: *the necessity that the education material presented be relevant to students.* Experience has shown that information will affect students' behavior only to the degree that they have discovered its meaning for them personally. In the past educators were intent upon making sure that students could parrot back what the textbooks said. A particular student's thoughts or feelings about the material were considered inconsequential—perhaps because it is impossible to measure this enormously important intangible by the usual testing methods.

Learning is a human problem always consisting of two parts. First, we have to provide people with some new information or some new experience, and we know how to do that very well. We are experts at it. With the aid of our new electronic gadgets, we can do it faster and more furiously than ever before in history. Second, the student must discover the meaning of the information provided him. The dropout is not a dropout because we didn't give him information. We told him, but he never discovered what the information meant.[3]

An important function of humanistic education is to bridge the great gap between educational materials and the students' life-spaces.

Another foundation undergirding humanistic education is a clear awareness of the dehumanizing effect that attends grading and grouping of students. Combs has written:

Grades motivate very few people, nor are they good as an evaluative device. Everyone knows that no two teachers evaluate people in exactly the same terms. Yet we piously regard grades as though they all mean the same thing, under the same circumstances, to all people at all times.[4]

Curve grading incites competition, which is especially deleterious since it encourages students to academically destroy their fellow students. Arbitrary grouping is another device used in traditional education that has a demoralizing effect on students and thus presents an obstacle to humanizing the classroom.

All research we have on grouping tells us that no one method of grouping is superior to any other. And yet we go right on, in the same old ways, insisting that we must have grade levels. As a result, we might have an eleven-year-old child in the sixth grade reading at the third-grade level. Every day of his life we feed him a diet of failure because we can't find a way to give a success experience to such a child.[5]

Another basic foundation of humanistic education is avoidance of reinforcing behavior patterns that are injurious to the students' self-concepts. Recognizing this need, humanistic educators propose that classrooms structured exclusively for competition do not serve the students' best interests. Only those students who believe they can win are motivated by competition, and this is a small minority of them. Students who cannot excel in academic competition become discouraged and disillusioned by the process of education itself. Or, as summarized by Combs, "When competition becomes too important, morality breaks down, and any means becomes justified to achieve the ends—the basketball team begins to use its elbows and students begin to cheat on exams."[6] This should not be interpreted to mean that all competition is bad.

Studies also indicate that students are better served when they have an active voice in the decision-making process that attends learning and when they accept responsibility for the consummation of the decisions they have made. Indeed, self-concept and personal esteem are heightened when students share in their own educational development and emotional growth.

Cooperation, mutual regard, and sensitivity to other points of view are also foundations of humanistic education. Achieving these ends can result in the increased flexibility that is a requisite for modern societies to survive the accelerating changes brought about by proliferating technology. But this is not new:

One needs to hear Job to hear lift his question into the wind; it is after all, every man's question at some time. One neds to stand by Oedipus and hold the knife at his own most terrible resolution. One needs to come out of his own Hell with Dante and to hear that voice of joy hailing the sight of his own stars returned-to. One needs to run with Falstaff, roaring in his own appetites and weeping into his own pathos. What one learns from those voices is his own humanity.[7]

Classes that are formulated and structured to bring about the greatest cross-fertilization of students from varying backgrounds afford the greatest opportunity for growth. But this means much more than taking a position at the educational workbench of America; today's students will be citizens of tomorrow's world—not a Black world or a white world, but a multiculture, multiethnic world. If understanding and compassion have not been engendered, all of the efficiency that modern technology provides will not be sufficient to save us from the holocaust that can result from indifference among ethnic groups and misunderstandings among nations. Humanistic education is visionary in its awareness that in addition to the present emphasis on efficiency and productivity which infects traditional education, an equal amount of attention must be given to the affective realm of survival.

Humanistic education holds in high regard

the role of teachers and the importance of their proper preparation if students are to gain a broader-based perspective and understanding of themselves and other people.

The humanistic foundations of education are intended to give theoretical perspective to teachers in order that they may become intelligently critical of their own and others' practice. This criticism should eventuate in better teaching and a more rational organization of schooling. But since schools both reflect and prepare for a wider culture, criticism of schooling directs criticism of other aspects of the culture and especially those aspects which serve as obstacles to equalizing and expanding educational opportunities. Study in the humanistic foundations of education, then, may direct students' critical attention to school and neighborhood segregation, the operations of local pressure groups, limitations to entry in various occupations, discrimination against women and minority groups, the role of foreign markets and military activities in the economy, and the free enterprise system itself.[8]

Teachers in traditional education have been prone to concerning themselves almost exclusively with subject matter that is amenable to standardized testing. Eunice H. Askov and Thomas J. Fischbach noted that although various researchers have emphasized the importance of studying other variables in addition to achievement in the evaluation of experimental programs, student attitudes seldom are measured.[9] Humanistic educators are concerned with the deep significance of attitudes when a comparison is made between this primarily noncognitive human characteristic and the cognitive function of intelligence. The extent to which an individual can learn or acquire a skill is related to his or her inherited potentialities or intelligence, but there is no genetic limitation on the number and kinds of likes and dislikes that students may acquire. The need for exposure to education which emphasizes the broad and varied dimensions of being cannot be overemphasized. Donald Arnstine said it quite well: "Practical skills and techniques can be directly conveyed or modeled, but the broader and more complex learnings that are focal to general education cannot be acquired so simply or directly. Learners in public schools are vastly different from one

another, and they call for very different kinds of treatment."[10]

HUMANENESS AS A FOUNDATION OF HUMANISTIC EDUCATION

In the *Decline and Fall of the Roman Empire*, Edward Gibbon said, "All that is human must retrograde if it does not advance."[11] Human beings have advanced, and the faculty that raised them from the level of the beasts is their humaneness. One of the foundations of humanistic education is the nurture of this quality. Authorities are in fairly consistent agreement that three major characteristics of humaneness are: (1) some sense of power or potency on the part of the individual, (2) self-acceptance and acceptance of each person as he or she is, and (3) intergroup, cross-cultural understanding.

Some of the most dehumanizing situations which students encounter are those that deny or limit their choices to such a degree that they are preconditioned to fail. To deny human beings choices makes of them puppets and pawns—it obviates the exercise of free will and thus, logically, exempts them from moral responsibility.

Humanistic education focuses on the individual's sense of potency. This aspect is approached from a variety of perspectives but generally focuses around the variable of what some have called "fate control," i.e., the ability of the individual to perceive himself as being able to control his own destiny. . . . This ability to make a choice of one's own style of education directly from a range of legitimate options increases the individual's sense of personal potency. The individual has the right and responsibility to choose or to reject.[12]

The process of individual decision making, and the sense of personal worth and power that accompanies it, facilitate humaneness in students. Teachers who embrace this philosophy of choice and responsibility attempt to increase students' options and exposure to various perspectives so that their decisions may be made from as broad a knowledge base as possible.

Self-acceptance and the acceptance of others as they are—with whatever differences—is another of the characteristics of humaneness that is fostered by humanistic education. As noted earlier, one deterrent to such acceptance in the traditional school or classroom is the labeling or classification system. For too long we have maintained a host of rubrics, from "gifted" to "learning disabled" which have served to place students on a continuum ranging from respected to rejected. Mario D. Fantini cautioned:

We are also reminded that a way of classifying human beings is a way of thinking about them, and this can result in a psychology of institutional expectations.... The result, research suggests, is that students perform in accordance with what is expected of them. This pattern has a negative effect on the goal of promoting individual worth.[13]

In humanistic classrooms the labeling problem is significantly reduced by the teacher's efforts to individualize the educational experience for every student. The foundations of humanistic education unequivocally prescribe the dismantling of the human classification system which in the past has proved dysfunctional in the growth and development needs of students.[14] This is especially true of the concept of race. Humaneness demands a higher and more subtle sense of value than does the labeling and recognition system Americans use for each other. It is inhumane to classify human beings like cuts of meat and accordingly pay court as we would pay prices on the basis of a sticker or a tag. Stereotypes are barriers to understanding and accepting various individuals and groups. Herman Melville said it thus: "Of all the preposterous assumptions of humanity over humanity, nothing exceeds most of the criticisms made on the habits of the poor by the well-housed, well-warmed, and well-fed."[15] Humanistic education requires that we reduce ourselves and every other human being to the ultimate common denominator—humanity. The foundations of humanistic education are compatible with the philosophy of humaneness poetically espoused by Guiseppe Mazzini:

You are men before you are either citizens or fathers. If you do not embrace the whole human family in your affections, if you do not bear witness to your belief in the Unity of that family, consequent upon the Unity of God.... If, wheresoever a fellow-creature suffers, or the dignity of human nature is violated by falsehood or tyranny—you are not ready, if able, to aid the unhappy, and do not feel called upon to combat, if able, for the redemption of the betrayed or the oppressed—you violate your law of life, you comprehend not that Religion which will be the guide and blessing of the future.[16]

Intergroup and cross-cultural understanding are also required if a humane society is to be established and maintained. The paramount importance of the school for such a shaping role is apparent when we realize that the school is a microcosmic social unit where future values are instilled. A humane value system can be accomplished only where students encounter racial, social, sexual, and cultural diversity—for understanding requires proximity, time, and committed effort. The human polarization that has taken place in our society can be ameliorated if the schools serve as places that promote positive attitudes and behaviors.[17] But we should not lose sight of the fact that humanistic education insists upon a proper plant, relevant curricula, and well-prepared teachers as basic foundation blocks for implementing this philosophy.

EXPERIENCE AS A FOUNDATION OF HUMANISTIC EDUCATION

While much of the analytical or cognitive portion of learning can be experienced vicariously, those areas that shape the direction of the affective education of students require direct, encountering experience. Humanistic education recognizes and provides in its very foundations for such exchanges. Although John Dewey and Abraham H. Maslow, two architects of humanistic education, held dissimilar views (Dewey was a pragmatist, and Maslow was a naturalistic realist), both placed great confidence in experience as a productive and creative necessity in the humanizing process of education.

To compare the importance that Dewey and Maslow placed on experience, it is necessary to understand how they defined it. Dewey used the word experience in three different ways: "First, much as it is used in general conversation to describe those everyday, routine interactions between organisms and environment; secondly, to refer to those interactions that have meaning and a thoughtful, purposive quality; and third, as an experience in particular, one which bears those marks of being an operation distinguished by a single pervasive quality, reaching the state of fulfillment or consummation."[18]

Dewey believed that the humanizing effects produced by poetry, prose, music, and painting are not confined necessarily to the arts but instead are characteristic of every genuine experience. He stated that they are more readily observable in art because the aesthetic experience which is occasioned by the arts is experience intensified. It is not, however, only with respect to art that aesthetic experiences are to be found but, according to Dewey, also in more ordinary situations and conditions not usually thought of as aesthetic. For Dewey an experience is aesthetic to the degree that the self and the object fuse to form a single, complete experience. He drew a distinction between the artistic and the aesthetic. For him artistic refers to the action that deals with materials and energies outside the body. Aesthetic refers to the delight that attends vision and hearing.

"Artistic" refers primarily to the act of production and "aesthetic" to that of perception and enjoyment. In other words, the distinction is between doing and undergoing. . . . In view of what has been said about experience in general, it is important to note that an aesthetic experience is not detached from the general stream of life. . . . Aesthetic perception, then, resides in the ability to remake past experiences so that they enter integrally into a new, a unique experience. To this extent experience is aesthetic.[19]

The foundations of humanistic education include the environment, the philosophy, and the direction which lead to the encounters that Dewey called "experience." While it is impossible to escape interaction between the self and some aspects of the environment, purposeful, intelligent action is the means by which this process is rendered significant for students. Purposeful action is the stuff of which experience is made. Dewey wrote: "Purposeful action is thus the goal of all that is truly educative,

and it is the means by which the goal is reached and its content remade. Such activity is of necessity a growth and a growing."[20] From this perspective, purposeful action does not exist outside of experience.

From Maslow's perspective the principal that posits the existence of an inner nature common to all beings is germane to humanistic education. Within all men and women is the desire for self-actualization, which includes the satisfaction of both cognitive and aesthetic needs. For Maslow the cognitive need is basically a search for meanings. "It is a desire to understand, to systematize, to organize, to analyze, to look for relations and meanings to construct a system of values."[21]

The aesthetic need, Maslow said, is much more difficult to define but has been an impulse in all cultures and all ages. It is what moves humans toward self-actualization and psychological health. Maslow stated that in order to possess a high level of aesthetic sensitivity, an individual needs to be self-actualized.[22] *Peak experiences* are encounters that are primarily subjective, but which hold value and importance to the person who has participated in them and which contribute to self-actualization. Since peak experiences are those experiences construed to lead to self-actualization (which is a basic aim of humanistic education), it seems worthwhile to explore a bit more thoroughly the distinguishing features that mark them:

1. The Universe is perceived as all of one piece, and the individual feels he belongs in it—everything seems to "hang together."

2. These moments are characterized by a particular kind of cognition which Maslow calls "Being cognition" (B-cognition). This type of perception is contrasted with D-cognition (Deficiency cognition), which is largely shaped by the individual's needs and desires. The perception here is passive and receptive. The person in a sense surrenders and submits himself to the experience.

3. Perception in the peak experience is childlike in that the experience continues to be as fresh and as beautiful as if it were the very first time.

4. The experience is felt as a self-validating moment which carries its own intrinsic value. The person, for example, may consider it so

valuable as to make life worthwhile by its occasional occurrence.

5. The experience is welcomed as an end in itself rather than a means experience. The state brought on, therefore, by such a happening is so delightful that the individual is not concerned about whether it leads to anything further or not.

6. The person undergoing the experience feels an unusual sense of timelessness and spacelessness. Reality is thus perceived "under the aspect of eternity."

7. The whole of reality in such moments is perceived as only good and desirable, with never an element of evil or pain. The person at the peak may be described as godlike in contemplating the whole of being and in seeing evil as a product of limited or selfish vision and understanding.

8. Conflicts and inconsistencies are resolved in the experience. The person himself becomes more integrated by a momentary loss of fear, anxiety, defense, and control. He becomes more his real self and feels that he is the creative center of his own universe.

9. Through continued peak experiences the individual becomes progressively more loving, honest, and motivated.[23]

From the viewpoint of the foundations of humanistic education, at issue are some of the ramifications for educators pursuing the thoughts of Dewey and Maslow. At a surface glance they would seem to be limited. Maslow expressly stated that we cannot command the peak experience, it simply happens, and Dewey said that the only way to have an aesthetic experience is simply to have it. But both drew the connections between experience as they conceived it and the educational process.

What both suggest is that education should not be solely concerned with the cognitive, with those sorts of learning experience that have immediate payoff, but that it should also allow room for the highest reaches of human experience. Maslow writes, "Aesthetic perceiving and creating, and aesthetic peak experiences are seen to be a central aspect of human life and of psychology and education rather than a peripheral one." And Dewey writes, "Without aesthetic appreciation we miss the most characteristic as well as the most precious thing in the real world." It is quite clear that both Dewey and Maslow wish to include in education this phase of
human experience. Education must make room for the private, the subjective, the affective, the ineffable, the transcendent; in short, for the aesthetic-peak experience.[24]

Philosophically and psychologically, humanistic education embodies the principle of personal experience as a requisite to humane self-actualization.

HUMAN RELATIONS PROGRAMS

Within the past ten years there has been a renascent interest in human relations education. Those persons who advocate affective learning programs have gradually gained ground against the traditionalists who still believe they can educate the cognitive portion of a person without damaging th ˙ neglected affective portion. Human relations training and application have been advanced as a viable remedy to assuage the explosion of discontent of students and parents against contemporary eduction. Few terms have been as used and abused, and as variously defined, as "human relations." Patricia P. Rosenzweig observed: "The trouble starts when you query board members, administrators, teachers, students, and John Q. Public about their individual definition of human relations. Some say it's getting along with others; others say it's improved race relations; still others say it's understanding the mood of young folks; other people say it's learning to control your prejudices; others say it's understanding the influence of your attitudes and behavior or the behavior of others."[25]

It is apparent that in the educational context there simply is no consensus definition of human relations. But if a human relations program is to be implemented to facilitate humanistic education, it will be necessary for school boards or other initiating bodies to arrive at their own meaning of the term in relationship to their overall educational goals. After a human relations program has been accepted as a requisite portion of the curricula, it is imperative that implementing bodies come to a clearly specified decision on exactly what it is that their institution proposes to accomplish.

If the board believes that the schools can't educate

unless the community is relatively free of tension, then the objective of education must be to help reduce community tensions. . . . Should the board believe the schools can't educate if the child's home environment interferes with schooltime activity, then the schools must have access to family problems and attempt to deal with them. . . . A third philosophical judgment on the part of the school board depends on the attitudes of teachers and administrators. If so, the board must implement methods designed to assess such attitudes in the assignment of teachers and bring about attitudinal changes where they are needed.[26]

These three foci by no means exhaust the possibilities that will confront a school board intent upon implementing a human relations program, nor are they necessarily mutually exclusive. It is, however, apparent that in making operative a human relations program to further humanistic education, *a school board must function within the context of its own academic policies and limitations.* All schools stand to gain something in promoting positive human relations. When they foster attitudes within their personnel that encourage learning, they will discourage destructive bigotry. When they minimize conflicts directed toward themselves, they abate conditions which interfere with their educational function.[27]

A major factor in the success of a school human relations program is the ability of the school to mobilize community agencies that have responsibility for meeting the needs of the school district. In establishing a human relations program to help humanize students, persons in authority must coordinate their activities with leaders of other community agencies. In order to accomplish this in a forthright, orderly fashion, it is necessary for the school board to (1) reach a commonly acceptable definition of human relations, (2) describe the role of the school district in respect to human relations, and (3) establish priorities and relationships within this process.

Four levels of application should be considered in designing and implementing a human relations program within an educational system: curriculum, facilities planning, personnel administration, and community relations. One perspective that has been generally accepted in the foundations of curriculum development is awareness of cultural differences between students. Rosenzweig suggested several activities, including the elimination of stereotypes from classroom stories, intercultural exchange projects between schools, and bulletin board displays having ethnic variety.[28] To this list could be added facilities planning that includes the use of buildings, pupil transfers, and busing.

Furthermore, an examination must be undertaken of the school district's equal opportunity practices concerning minority-group hiring and firing, transfer of personnel, and in-service training. Where possible, methods to counter-act negative attitudes also must be explored so that the focus of the human relations program is upon humanizing rather than alienating students and school personnel. In community relations and relations with other social agencies, plans must be devised that will result in improved communications between school and community—which will in turn result in a lessening of overall tensions.

It is clear that just as instruction for students should be individualized, so should human relations programs be tailored to fit the communities in which they will be operative. Three principles, however, are generally applicable to human relations programs in every school:

1. Planning should be centralized and formalized by the board at the highest administrative level, where all intraorganizational contacts between the human relations program and other aspects of the educational system should be carried out.

2. Inservice training and attitudinal awareness are a key part of any human relations program and should be centrally implemented at the highest level; mechanisms must exist, however, for the central office to determine specialized needs in the schools.

3. The day-to-day solving of human relations problems as they relate to individual districts and schools should be left to those local bodies, who should have the power to make their decisions stick. This is especially true of community relations functions.[29]

Failure can be expected when there exist unclear or nonexistent objectives, ill-trained or noncertificated teaching personnel, the absence of evaluative procedures, and the lack of substantive research.[30] Agreement is fairly widespread that educational programs at all levels can profit from knitting affective learning into cognitive and substantive subject matter. But the pressing need, according to Thomas W. Wiggins, is that "teachers and administrators need to improve their skills in dealing with the emotional life of their students, themselves, and their colleagues. These educators need to foster school climates which permit and encourage personal development."[31]

CRITICISM OF HUMANISTIC EDUCATION

Despite glowing endorsements of humanistic education, there are deficiencies, and this book would not be complete without summarizing some of the criticisms of humanistic education. Lloyd G. Humphreys was blunt in his criticism of attempts to humanize the phsyical and biological sciences:

Today there is a good deal of sentiment among physical and biological scientists concerning the need for a more humanistic approach to the problems of our society. It seems more reasonable to them that there should be a humanistic movement in technology and education since these disciplines deal primarily with people. As a psychologist myself and one who is intimately concerned with educational problems, I feel compelled to reject these movements because I evaluate them as dangerous, regressive trends in dealing with human problems.[32]

Humphreys goes on to say that in his opinion the foundations of humanistic education reject science and the scientific approach to the solution of human problems. This rejection of science, he feels, is a reversion to the Middle Ages, where emotions and religious biases reigned supreme. Thus, Humphreys concludes, the focus on the affective at the expense of cognitive development is dangerous for education and all those who come under its influence.

Another charge leveled by Humphreys is that a de-emphasis on measurement prevails in humanistic education, mainly because most affective learning is impossible to measure accurately. Humanistic education, he cautioned, simply does not offer the objective proof that would validate it as a proper educative approach. There is substance to this criticism, since many humanistic programs were instituted simply because of a great hue and cry that the schools of contemporary society must be drastically reformed. Indeed, Humphreys was correct when he wrote, "The facts are that objective evidence is lacking for all of the supposed defects of the schools, yet these statements have been repeated so many times that criticisms have become almost generally acknowledged as valid."[33]

When addressing unsubstantiated problems, humanistic education does nothing more than focus on problems that have been artificially manufactured. Because the means of comparing educational results have changed since the initiation of humanistic education, there is no valid way to compare the humanistic quality of schools ten years ago, for instance, with the humanistic quality of schools today.

Helen H. Franzwa was equally direct in her criticism. Although sympathetic to humanistic psychological principles, Franzwa pointed out some of the difficulties of applying them to classroom teaching. The first hazard is the freedom foisted upon the student in the open classroom.

The first of these dangers is that the teacher who would facilitate learning by allowing students to study whatever they wish, to discuss whatever they wish, and to be free to be themselves is really substituting one kind of expectation for another, and he may not be aware that he is doing so. In the teacher-centered classroom the student faces the pressure of having to know the teacher's answers; in the student-centered class the student faces the potentially more unnerving pressure of having to ask his own questions and then search for the answers. . . . The teacher who believes that he is decreasing the pressures deceives himself and his students.[34]

Franzwa believes that freedom can be a very frightening and alienating experience and that inability or ineptitude in coping with it creates a sense of aloneness and powerlessness, immobilizing students who participate in this open learning process. "Perhaps in the so-called open classroom," she concluded, "the individuals have escaped from freedom into themselves—each escape being an intensely negative emotional experience for the individual involved."[35]

Milton K. Reimer, another educator, criticized humanistic education on the grounds that it promotes confrontation. Almost overnight, Reimer observed, students at all levels seem bent on challenging all facets of the existing structure, and humanistic education has been a strong contributing factor. Specifically, Reimer points to sensitivity training and its misdirection as a means of promoting such confrontation: "There is a strong tendency for any group focus to move toward therapeutic exchange. Thus, a session intended to focus on institutional problems often ends up probing deeply into personal matters that have little, if anything, to do with the institutional function."[36] Too often facilitators of sensitivity groups are not properly prepared and while a T-group experience, even with a good trainer, may not help an individual, a T-group experience with a poor trainer can precipitate severe personal problems and be psychologically damaging to both individuals and the institutions they represent.

Another criticism which has been leveled by Reimer and others is the antirationalism or antiintellectualism and increased preoccupation with emotionalism that characterizes humanistic education in general and sensitivity training in particular:

A major objection to the use of sensitivity training as an educational device is its tendency to be irrational. Critical, reflective thinking and an intelligent analysis of problems and values represent a time-honored approach to education. But sensitivity training either ignores critical thinking as a process or is virtually hostile to it. Sensitivity training emerged as an answer to those who felt that the emotional factor was perhaps an even more important item in education than were content and skills.[37]

John H. Martin warns that "on the issue of humanizing education through technology, the present system's failure rate in the basic skills is producing large numbers of angry, alienated and unemployable youth."[38] However, Martin believes that well-designed and well-staffed humanistic education programs offer hope for human growth. He outlines these criteria as ideal: "Where the learner dominates the act of learning, where he measures his performance, where he modifies his acts as a result of his evaluation of the consequences, where he manipulates the materials of learning, and where he engages all his senses in his own style, then human growth is assured."[39]

Few humanistic educators would quarrel with the notion that while human relations training properly executed would make for better understanding and better communications, it should not be divorced from intelligence and the use of our rational faculties.

SUMMARY

Any recapitulation of the foundations of humanistic education must deal with the aims, objectives, and goals to which this educational philosophy ascribes. Cynthia G. Kruger comments precisely on this point:

The humanistic movement is a compromise between the child-centered approach of the Pragmatists and the discipline-centered approach of the Essentialists. Stressing free will, the humanists believe that the student should be allowed to select his own learning environment and curriculum. His learning schedule should be one that provides for independent research with the teacher in the capacity of guide or advisor. Educational objectives and strategies are mutually arrived at and form the framework for evaluation. The cognitive and affective domains are both emphasized in determining student progress. A thinking human being who has developed a value system and the ability to solve problems inductively and deductively is the main goal of the humanistic movement.[40]

Discussing the goals of humanistic education, Thomas Fox, Jr., and DeVault M. Vere drew a comparison between the perspectives taken by educational technology in contrast with those of educational humanism. Educational technology goals are described as having behavioral objectives that are measurable, prespecified, clearly stated, single-directed, atomistic, and focus upon mastery and skills. The goals of educational humanism, by comparison, are described as aims rather than as objectives. These are delineated as tentative or open. Many important human aims are difficult to state and some are unmeasurable. Furthermore, humanistic aims focus upon experience, related knowledge, awareness of heritage, values, inner feelings, and fantasy—they are, indeed, multidirected and complex.[41]

Several points stand out clearly in this comparison of aims or objectives between an education which emphasizes technology and an education which emphasizes humanism. Unlike technology, humanistic education gives precedence to development of the whole person, with more importance placed upon the evolution of subjective, personal judgment based upon humane values. The aim here is to produce a more flexible individual—even at the expense of either consistency or predictability. An overall goal is to emphasize the commonalities between individuals which foster understanding rather than to maximize divisive differences. Acknowledging that the world has been, now is, and probably always will be in a state of change, humanistic education assumes as its aim equipping students not merely to live with change but to become agents of humane change.

The process of change will be more humane if the stimulators for change realize that feelings and emotions are of primary importance. These prime movers must realize that the individuals they are asking to change are first of all humans; they have deep underlying feelings, wishes, and defenses, and fears that must be considered. Those involved in change must be allowed to be authentic persons, living, breathing, human beings. They must be allowed to think for themselves, to initiate, to imagine, to work without constant "over-the-shoulder" supervision; they must learn to be emphathetic; they must be willing to show concern and compassion. And they must be supported and trusted as they risk themselves in openness.[42]

Another major aim of humanistic education is the accent it places on self-realization. For the humanistic educator, a student is comprised of an aggregate of physical, mental, and spiritual needs that are met most most fully by a holistic approach. Accentuation of positive self-concept and the development of facilitative communications skills reflects an emphasis on the whole person which mandates yet other concerns.

Other concerns arising out of the humanistic movement are as follows:
1. *Create a learning environment which fosters openness, honesty and exploration.*
2. *Create a curriculum that relfects the felt needs of persons, that helps them relate to the real world, that builds on personal interests, motivation, values and goals.*
3. *Challenge students to be responsible for their own learning.*
4. *Encourage peer-teaching.*
5. *Make learning fun, emphasize joy, caring and concern for persons. . . . The intended outcome is to realize self-actualization within each individual.*[43]

In summary, the educational humanist is concerned with goals and objectives that are based on human needs. For the humanist all students are assessed to be of ultimate worth, and thus all goals and objectives should be aimed toward humanely maximizing the student's intrapersonal, interpersonal, and intergroup relationships. Fred Splittgerber and Roy Trueblood wrote: "Humanistic ends cannot be reached by dehumanizing means. Humanistic focus can be kept in mind when not only ultimate but proximate goals or objectives are established."[44] Within this perspective an aim of humanistic education is to never lose sight of the importance of the affective route when charting an educational destination. Self-realization requires that the whole person arrive at his or her educational destination and not simply the intellectual leftovers that accumulate when the affective domain is abandoned to expedite the trip.

In the midst of a modern world that is in the process of such rapid change and conflict, it is not an easy matter to turn the main direction and focus of education from purely academic development to the development of students who someday may be able to humanely change the course of society. This, however, is the goal of all educators, not just those who teach gifted students. The idea is not new, but it is one that the necessity to survive has brought out again with great force. In 1632 Comenius, a thoughtful teacher, proposed goals for education that have often been repeated but unforunately seldom heeded:

The education I propose includes all that is proper for a man, and is one in which all men who are born into this world should share. . . . Our first wish is that all men should be educated fully to full humanity, not only one individual, nor a few, nor even many, but all men together and singly, young and old, rich and poor, of high and lowly birth,

*men and women—in a word, all whose fate it is to
be born human beings; so that at least the whole of
the human race may become educated, men of all
ages, all conditions, both sexes and all nations. Our
second wish is that every man should be wholly
educated, rightly formed not only in one single
matter or in a few or even in many, but in all
things which perfect human nature....* [45]

What Comenius has stated is not a method
of education but rather an idealized goal that
offers an answer to the question which has
always plagued educators, "What are we
educating for?" The answer of Comenius—
and the answer of humanistic education—
should be the shaping force for curriculum and
for method. The overarching goal to be found
in the foundations of humanistic education and
the goal of Comenius are the same. "Simply
stated the goal is to develop children into beings who are truly human and humane. The
development of such individuals should be the
means of transforming a world society whose
chief concern is man, not scientific growth." [46]

VALUES

Am I someone who:
1. accepts opinions different from my own?
2. enjoys leisue time for creative development?
3. responds with compassion to unmarried
   pregnant women?
3. volunteers to assume leadership responsibilities?
5. thinks interracial marriage is a good thing?
6. maintains high ethical standards as a
   teacher?
7. tries to do everything as perfectly as possible?
8. would not feel uncomfortable around
   homosexuals?
9. always looks up the meaning of an unknown word?
10. is concerned about the treatment of
    minorities in movies and television?
11. would enjoy serving as a juror trying a
    rape case?
12. considers failure a bad thing?
13. prefers to conform rather than to disagree
    in public?
14. would not object to premarital sex for my
    children?
15. sets realistic life goals?
16. usually spends a lot of time worrying
    about social injustices without doing
    something about them?
17. values friendship more than money?
18. has seriously considered joining a radical
    organization?
19. would rather be alone than with strang-
    ers?
20. supports the legalization of marijuana?
21. secretly enjoys reading and looking at
    pornography?
22. has a close friend of another race?
23. feels uncomfortable in low-income neigh-
    borhoods?
24. would report to the police someone
    breaking a law, even if s/he were my
    friend?
25. invites people I don't like to my home?
26. tends to feel lonely in a crowd?
27. feels uncomfortable when in the presence
    of handicapped people?
28. believes that the Ku Klux Klan has its
    good points?
29. is conscientious about saving fuel and
    energy?
30. would rather attend a concert than an ath-
    letic contest?

ADDITIONAL READINGS

Brown, George I. *Human Teaching for Human Learning: An Introduction to Confluent Education.* New York, Viking Press, 1971.

Berman, Louise M. and Jessie A. Roderick, eds. *Feeling, Valuing, and the Art of Growing: Insight into the Affective.* Washington, D.C., Association for Supervision and Curriculum Development, 1977.

Combs, Arthur W., et al. *The Professional Education of Teachers: A Humanistic Approach to Teacher Preparation,* 2nd ed. Boston, Allyn & Bacon, 1974.

Della-Dora and James E. House, eds. *Education for an Open Society.* Washington, D.C., Association for Supervision and Curriculum Development, 1974.

Dobson, Russell and Judith S. Dobson. *Humaneness in Schools: A Neglected Force.* Dubuque, IA., Kendally/Hunt, 1976.

Hendricks, Gay and Russell Wills. *The Centering Book: Awareness Activities for Children, Parents, and Teachers.* Englewood Cliffs, N.J., Prentice-Hall, 1975.

Kurfman, Dana G., ed. *Developing Decision-Making Skills.* Arlington, VA., National Council for the Social Studies, 1977.

Schrank, Jeffrey. *Teaching Human Beings: 101 Subversive Activities for the Classroom.* Boston, Beacon Press, 1972.

Simon, Sidney B., Leland W. Howe, and Howard Kirschenbaum. *Values Clarification: A Handbook of Practical Strategies for Teachers and Students.* New York, Hart, 1972.

Weinstein, Gerald and Mario D. Fantini. *Toward Humanistic Education: A Curriculum of Affect.* New York, Praeger, 1970.

NOTES

1. Arthur W. Combs, "The Human Side of Learning," *National Elementary Principal,* 52 (January, 1973), 39.

2. *Ibid.,* 39.

3. *Ibid.,* 40.

4. *Ibid.,* 41.

5. *Ibid.,* 42.

6. *Ibid.*

7. John Ciardi, *Saturday Review* (January 31, 1959).

8. Donald Arnstine, "The Knowledge Nobody Wants: The Humanistic Foundations in Teacher Education," *Educational Theory,* 28 (Winter, 1973), 6.

9. Eunice H. Askov and Thomas J. Fischbach, "An Investigation of Primary Pupils' Attitudes Toward Reading," *The Journal of Experimental Education,* 41 (Spring, 1973), 1.

10. Arnstine, "The Knowledge Nobody Wants," 3.

11. Edward Gibbon, quoted in George Seldes (ed.), *The Great Quotations* (New York: Simon & Schuster, 1967), 484.

12. Mario D. Fantini, "Alternative Schools and Humanistic Education," *Social Education,* 38 (March, 1974), 245.

13. *Ibid.*

14. *Ibid.*

15. Herman Melville, quoted in Seldes, *Quotations,* 486.

16. Guiseppe Mazzini, quoted in Seldes, *Ibid.*

17. Fantini, "Alternative Schools," 246.

18. Lawrence J. Dennis and J. Francis Powers, "Dewey, Maslow, and Consummatory Experience," *Journal of Aesthetic Education,* 8 (October, 1974), 52.

19. *Ibid.,* 55.

20. John Dewey, "Foreward," in Albert C. Barnes and Violette de Mazia, *The Art of Renoir* (New York: Minton, Balch, 1935), vii.

21. Maslow, quoted in Dennis and Powers, "Dewey, Maslow," 58.

22. *Ibid.,* 59.

23. *Ibid.,* 60.

24. *Ibid.,* 61–62.

25. Patricia P. Rosenzweig, "Why Your District Needs a Human Relations Program," *American School Board Journal,* 159 (January, 1972), 34.

26. *Ibid.,* 34–35.

27. *Ibid.,* 35.

28. *Ibid.,* 36.

29. *Ibid.*

30. Thomas W. Wiggins, "Sensitivity Training: Salvation or Conspiracy?" *Educational Leadership,* 28 (December, 1970), 254.

31. *Ibid.,* 257.

32. Lloyd G. Humphreys, "The Humanistic Movement in Psychology and Education: Some Reservations," *Science Teacher*, 38 (September, 1971), 29.

33. *Ibid.*, 30.

34. Helen H. Franzwa, "Limitations in Applying Humanistic Psychology in the Classroom," *Today's Speech*, 21 (Winter, 1973), 31–32.

35. *Ibid.*, 32.

36. Milton K. Reimer, "Critique of Sensitivity Training," *School and Society*, 356 (October, 1971), 356.

37. *Idid.*, 357.

38. John H. Martin, "Self-Growth and Self-Enhancement Through Technology, *Educational Technology.*, 11 (June, 1971), 18.

39. *Ibid.*

40. Cynthia G. Kruger, "The Social Sciences and the Humanistic Curriculum," *The Social Studies*, 65 (November, 1974), 257.

41. Thomas Fox, Jr., and DeVault M. Vere, "Technology and Humanism in the Classroom: Frontiers of Educational Practice," *Educational Technology*, 14 (October, 1974), 8.

42. Robert L. Heichberger, "Toward a Strategy for Humanizing the Change Process in Schools," *Journal of Research and Development in Education*, 7 (Fall, 1973), 78.

43. Fred Splittgerber and Roy Trueblood, "Accountability and Humanism," *Educational Technology*, 15 (February, 1975), 25.

44. *Ibid.*, 26.

45. Comenius, quoted in Marion L. Edman, "Can Children Achieve Humaneness?" *Educational Horizons*, 51 (Spring, 1973), 108.

46. *Ibid.*

20.
PROSPECTS
FOR THE
FUTURE

This chapter constitutes both a summary and a forecast. The postmodern era in which we have been living since 1945 belongs more to the future than it does to the past. This book has tried to describe recent trends in schools and society clearly and accurately; it follows that the reader already has at least a general idea about the shape of things to come. There remains only the task of pulling the threads together and of making some general predictions about what lies ahead for future generations.

The role of the prophet has always been a hazardous one. People generally prefer to be told that all is right with the world than to be told that catastrophic changes are taking place that will require drastic changes in conventional ways of thinking, planning, and acting. Predicting some conditions likely to exist tomorrow, however, does not require the abilities of a soothsayer. The nature of life in the foreseeable future can be forecast simply by examining trends that are easily observed in the life of today.

During World War I, Vincente Blasco Ibáñez wrote the famous novel *The Four Horsemen of the Apocalypse*, taking his title from the four horsemen described in the last book of the Bible, *Revelation*, which is also called *Apocalypse*. The four horsemen identified by Blasco Ibáñez as the eternal curses of humanity were war, famine, pestilence and death.[1] A great deal of progress has been made since World War I, but though the cataclysmic effects of these scourges have been reduced, they are still with us.

The four horsemen that might be called

even greater threats to the hopes of humanity today are power, population, prejudice, and pollution. Humans have become so powerful as a result of releasing the forces of nature that it is conceivable that they will totally destroy civilization unless this power is directed toward constructive goals. The population of underdeveloped nations is increasing so rapidly that it is not possible for them to feed their people adequately, much less accumulate the savings on which a productive economy is based. Prejudice stands as the principal barrier to achieving equality of opportunity and improving the life chances of women and minority groups in our society. Air and water pollution threaten the health of citizens in every big city in the land.

GLIMPSES OF THE FUTURE

Children now enrolled in elementary school will live much of their lives in the twenty-first century. It is not possible to predict with any degree of accuracy the details of the society in which they will be living or the schools their children and grandchildren will be attending. Yet unless we assume that certain conditions are likely to exist in the society of tomorrow, there can be no intelligent planning of school programs for the future.

A careful look at current trends in school and society indicates that science and technology will continue to produce changes at a constantly accelerating rate, that new sources of energy can be used constructively to produce an age of abundance and increased leisure to an extent never before imagined, and that the right amount and kind of education can release the potential of children and adults and act as a lever to lift a nation from poverty, ignorance, and superstition to abundance, enlightenment, and cultural attainments. In brief, if persons of intelligence and good will can cultivate the science of human relationships, if they can find a way to avoid the cataclysm of a nuclear war, the world in which people will be living ten, twenty, or a hundred years from now will indeed be a fascinating one.

The Challenge of Increased Power

The word "power," of course, has many shades of meaning. It is used here in the sense of humanity's increasing control over energy— the development of other sources of energy to do the work that once depended on the muscle strength of men, women and domestic animals. Charles Frankel calls attention to the increased tempo of technical change: "It took man roughly 475,000 years to arrive at the Agricultural Revolution. It required another 25,000 years to come to the Industrial Revolution. We have arrived at the Space Age in a hundred and fifty years—and while we do not know where we go from here, we can be sure that we shall go there fast."[2]

Promises and threats. Woodrow Wilson once said that colleges should give to the nation men and women who can distinguish between promises and threats. When the invention of the printing press made it possible to provide textbooks for every pupil, the development was regarded by many as a threat to the teaching profession; textbooks, however, were instrumental in making it possible for every child, instead of a favored few, to have educational opportunities. When automobiles appeared on the scene, they were regarded as a threat to those whose livelihood depended on horse-shoeing and harness-making; instead, the event provided opportunities for employment in much more rewarding and exciting jobs. When scientists finally succeeded in releasing the energy stored in the atom and created devices for using this energy as a source of power, the destruction that followed convinced many that this would mean the end of civilization; scientists now believe that atomic power provides the only way to produce enough energy and food for the rapidly increasing population of the world. There is no longer any valid reason for half the people of the world to go to bed hungry every night; there is no longer any valid reason for forty million Americans to live at the bare subsistence level.

One technological development that has produced a great deal of uncertainty is automation. Will it provide fewer jobs or more jobs? Is it a threat to the masses, or does it promise a richer and fuller life for all humankind? Here are some facts to support those who regard automation as a threat:

1. During recent years, 300,000 production jobs have been eliminated in the aircraft industry alone because of technological change.

2. Since World War II, output per man-hour in the soft coal industry has risen 90 per cent, but employment has fallen by 300,000.

3. Steel production in 1976 was almost the same as in 1966, but employment had declined by 40 per cent.

4. In the chemical industry, the number of production jobs has fallen 10 per cent since 1956, but output has increased 30 per cent.

5. Production in the meat industry has increased 8 per cent since 1956, yet 50,000 workers have lost their jobs.

Those who see in automation the promise of more jobs and a richer life for all offer the following arguments:

1. Although machines are now doing 94 per cent of the work, there are more jobs available per 1,000 population than there were in the 1850s, when machines did but 6 per cent of the work.

2. Scholars who have studied the trends intensively foresee the time when one-fourth of the nation's labor force will be employed in semiprofessional and technical jobs that did not exist in 1930.

3. With automation taking over jobs in agriculture and material production, our society will have the potential to expand education, health, welfare, and recreation functions as well as creative efforts, including planning and research.

4. The government will surely take up the

slack in jobs for urban renewal, social welfare, beautification, and so on.[3]

The unprecedented rate at which energy has been used since 1945 has confronted our people with the necessity to make adjustments to new conditions, learn new habits and skills, and change social institutions so that they will more nearly serve the needs of a new and different age. The impact of this "Third Great Revolution of Humankind" has created new problems for labor leaders and industrial managers, for families and schools, and for city, state, and national governments. This is why this text has emphasized throughout that drastic reforms in education are demanded by the realities of the age in which we are living. As management expert Peter Drucker has pointed out, "Because we can now organize men of high skill and knowledge for joint work through the exercise of responsible judgment, the highly educated man has become the central resource of today's society, the supply of such men the true measure of its economic, its military, and even its political potential."[4]

Problems of Population Growth

Population growth and mobility can, of course, present either promises of threats. This text has discussed the population explosion in the United States, the rural-urban migration, and the relation of the population explosion to the problem of developing a productive, industrialized economy in the underdeveloped countries of the world. Particular attention has been given to the consequences of failure to provide adequate education opportunities for disadvantaged children in the cities and rural communities.

The population of the world was 1.6 billion to 1900, 2.5 billion in 1950, and 4 billion in 1975. The estimate for the year 2000 is 7.4 billion. The implications of the estimated increase in the world's population have been described as follows:

The prospect is frightening. In the span of 35 years the world population is expected to increase by 124 per cent, but the underdeveloped parts will grow 151 per cent. In contrast, the regions with an advanced economy will increase only 53 per cent. To put it another way, the underdeveloped coun-
tries which now constitute 73 per cent of the world population, will in the year 2000 comprise 81 per cent of a more than twice as numerous world population.[5]

Since World War II, seventy-seven new nations have come into existence. Most of these countries lack the stable government, the educational system, and the investment capital necessary to develop an industrialized economy which requires technically trained workers and capable managers. This situation poses both challenges and threats for the underdeveloped countries and for the human community as a whole. The Rockefeller Panel stated the situation concisely: "This panel believes that the United States has an objective that needs to be defined in new terms, broader than the old concept of national interest. This objective is to foster the development of a world order in which all peoples can live in security and realize their fullest potentialities."[6]

The Problem of Prejudice

Prejudice is now recognized as one of our nation's most dangerous threats. It can be defined in terms of attitudes or in terms of behavior. As a social problem it can best be defined as human behavior motivated by the desire to exclude certain racial, religious, sex, and ethnic groups from the attainment of equality of opportunity or status. Persons and groups who exhibit prejudiced behavior do not recognize the characteristics of an individual; rather, they treat individuals as indistinguishable parts of a stereotyped group.

Prejudiced behavior, together with rising aspirations on the part of nonwhites, has brought this country to the brink of an armed conflict, especially between Black people and white people. The most serious phases of prejudiced behavior relate to housing restrictions and discrimination in employment practices and educational opportunities. This situation represents a serious violation of our democratic ideals; it also represents a serious waste of human resources. The situation has been very well described thus:

The opportunity for every man to develop his capacities is no longer just an abstract ethical precept that attaches to democracy. It is a practical condition of a modern industrial society. Such a society can function efficiently only if opportunity for full development and participation is not arbitrarily removed from large groups of its population.[7]

The same authors described encouraging progress that has been made in desegregating the armed forces, public housing, and industries receiving contracts from the government. They also pointed out, in their section on "The Prejudiced Community," that patterns of community practices are more influential than prejudiced attitudes on the part of individuals in maintaining polarization as opposed to integration in our society; that in communities where this polarization has been broken down, prejudiced behavior has been reduced; and that it is the social situation in which individuals live that largely determines their prejudiced behavior attitudes.

This text has provided information relating to the gap that exists in our society between the life chances of the majority of Americans and those of minority groups; explained how the urban and rural crises have developed in recent years. It has examined the programs that have been initiated to remedy the situation and presented estimates of the costs of programs that are needed to deal effectively with the problems. It has also suggested steps that need to be taken to provide adequate educational opportunities for culturally disadvantaged children and youth as well as programs in intercultural education for all Americans.

The Problem of Air and Water Pollution

The cultural and economic advantages of living in an American city, the steady increase in the Gross National Product, and the rapid progress that has been made in the development of supersonic airplanes and space vehicles are widely recognized as achievements of American inventive genius and management skill. But these accomplishments have brought with them serious threats to the health of the increasing numbers of our people who live in the cities. As more people move to the cities, the demand for water increases. The industrial use of water has increased by 11 times since 1900,

and the demand for water for recreational purposes has also increased rapidly as people have had more time for leisure. The hazard of water pollution has been summarized as follows:

At the same time that our use of water is increasing, the wastes that we dump into our water are also increasing; miles of streams are being lost each year to fishing, and millions of fish are being killed because of waste products being dumped into streams; both the Gulf coast and the Atlantic coast have had epidemics of hepatitis because of polluted water; and the water pollution continues to grow as more complex waste products are finding their way into our water supplies.[8]

The health hazard of air pollution continues to grow as industrial production increases, as more people move to the cities, and as more automobiles are used. The problem of providing pure air to breathe is no longer confined to Los Angeles; it has become a problem for every large, industrialized city in the land. It is not suggested that school children can solve the problem of water and air pollution; they can, however, recognize the problem as one of the social realities existing in our nation and they can become familiar with the measures being taken to combat it.

The Fabulous Future

Despite the problems that plague us, a future bright with promise is already unfolding before our eyes. We are living in an age of revolutions. The biological revolution (which has been relatively overlooked in the shadows of the atomic revolution, the computer revolution, and the aerospace revolution) is perhaps more crucial than any of the others; indeed, it has been largely responsible for all of them. Computers, for example, are products of the biological revolution; they represent extensions of the human brain. The biological revolution has enabled humanity to increase its numbers, to manipulate its environment, and to gain a better understanding of itself.

The virtual elimination of communicable disease, the transplanting of human organs, and new cures for mental illness are already in sight. As a by-product of atomic weapon research conducted at the Oak Ridge National Laboratory, a machine has been developed for the production of a safer and more effective vaccine for influenza, other respiratory diseases, and virus-caused diseases. Scientists predict that control of some genetic characteristics, such as the sex of our offspring, may sometime be feasible, that farming of the sea will be commonplace, and that there will be a great reduction in the use of domestic food animals because plants can convert solar energy into food much more efficiently.[9]

There is no doubt that the future will glow with many devices and products that will revolutionize life in the home. The following quotation mentions only a few of these.

A new electroluminescent glass panel will heat and cool a room instantly, and the color of the wall will vary in response to the movement of a dial to the color desired. It will be possible to have cold packaged anywhere in the house, eliminating the need for a refrigerator. Clothes will be cleaned by ultrasonic waves while they hang in the closet overnight, and radio and television will be built into the wall to be tapped on and off like a wall switch.[10]

Space exploration will place more people on the moon for extended scientific research, improve weather forecasting, make it possible to view live telecasts from any place in the world, light entire cities from a mirror hung in space, and communicate messages quickly to any point on earth. Automation will make it possible for machines to perform the entire operation of bank clearinghouses with only a few workers keeping the machines in working order, will produce electronic devices for translating one language into another, and will enable libraries to swiftly tabulate and show on a screen information on any topic.

The new frontier will lie in the field of human relations. Our most eminent scientists tell us that the future of our civilization revolves around the ability of humans to learn to live together. This text has therefore emphasized the need for education for world understanding and for the lessening of intergroup tensions.

Despite the serious problems that beset our people, there are sound reasons to hope that they can be solved. Economic experts point out that there is enough strength in the American economy to make solutions possible, provided our resources are used constructively.

Long-range projections made by the United States Chamber of Commerce and the Joint Economic Committee of Congress point to greatly increased incomes for families and increased revenues for federal and local governments. They predict that by the year 2000 (1) families currently earning $8,000 a year will be earning $25,000 a year in terms of today's dollars; (2) the Gross National Proudct will be $4 trillion; (3) federal government revenues will have increased 200 per cent over 1967; (4) revenues of local governments will increase even faster, so that money will be available for jobs, housing, education, and pollution control.[11] Although money alone cannot solve all our problems, it is reassuring to have evidence that the economy is basically strong.

SCHOOLS FOR TOMORROW

Changes in American life during the next few decades will no doubt create a demand for many new kinds of educated talent which schools and colleges will be expected to provide. Indeed, there seems to be general agreement that the future of our nation in an era of unpredecented change will depend largely on the scope and quality of our educational efforts.

For several years general magazines, newspapers, television, and radio have all been describing and picturing the "revolution in the schools"—the new programs and teaching methods that have been evolved and are being used in some schools. Thus many citizens—not just those personally concerned with the schools—are now aware of the fact that the schools of tomorrow will differ in important respects from the schools of yesterday and from many of the schools of today. Although the innovations described by the mass media have so far been confined to a limited number of schools, they do provide glimpses of the shape of things to come in elementary and secondary schools. Leaders in the field of professional education have also become increasingly concerned with the changes in educational programs that the future will demand. Francis Keppel, for example, indicated the depth of his concern when he gave the title *The Necessary Revolution in American Education* to a book he wrote while he was U. S. Commissioner of Education.[12] He believes that the changes will and must be made with both quality and equality as aims.

New Directions for Teacher Education

The most serious handicap faced by school systems as they attempt both to implement the new curricula developed by projects at the national level and to adopt innovations in organization and instruction is the lack of teachers who are prepared for these new programs. No one who has been on the scene when the staff of a large school system has been struggling with these problems can fail to conclude that a new type of teacher education is the most needed reform in public education today.

More than 1,200 institutions of higher education prepare elementary and secondary teachers. At any one of them, when representatives of various academic departments meet with representatives of the college of education, the dialogue seldom gets beyond the question of whether the quality of instruction in the schools could not be improved simply by requiring teachers to take courses in the academic disciplines and few courses in education. On the other hand, when the faculty of the college of education meets to discuss its responsibilities in the preparation of teachers, the dialogue seldom gets beyond the point of how many courses in the various phases of professional education shall be required. Obviously, such discussions add very little to the solution of the critical problems confronting elementary and secondary schools.

The careful selection of candidates for teacher education is perhaps as important as the courses the students take. If a student has a firm desire to teach, a positive image of self, and a genuine interest in people, that student is quite likely to become a successful teacher, as long as he or she has had thorough preparation. If the student lacks these basic qualities, rarely will he or she become a successful teacher, no matter how thorough the education curriculum.

Thus a basic question must be faced by those responsible for formulating teacher education programs: How can an adequate proportion of the nation's most promising young people be attracted to teaching—and how can they be held in it? Committees that set up certification requirements frequently operate on the principle that a little of almost every discipline offered on the campus should be included; this results in ridiculous requirements that repel many capable young people who otherwise might enter teaching as a career. No doubt the next few decades will see drastic reform in the certification process.

Teacher education programs in the future are likely to bring students into contact with children and classrooms much earlier in their college careers than is now common. The beginning teacher who has never seen a television program used in a classroom, never seen team-teaching in action, or never seen the operation of a nongraded program is poorly prepared for teaching.

Planning a teacher education program in the future will begin with an entirely different set of questions. It will begin with an effort to identify the truly professional tasks that teachers are expected to perform in school systems. It will then plan to provide students with experiences that will help them develop the competencies needed in the performance of these tasks. The old adage, "We teach as we were taught, not as we were taught to teach," should and probably will influence teaching on college campuses more in the future than it has in the past. There is no valid reason why college students should not be given opportunities in their college courses to experience *as students* team-teaching, learning by discovery, the use of a great variety of instructional media, and participation in the planning of class activities. These, after all, are some of the methods they will be expected to use when they join the staff of a public school system.

A More Humanistic Approach to Teaching

The mechanistic concept of learning dominated educational practice for many years. The industrial age that resulted from experimentation in the physical sciences had a great impact on people's thinking about the learning process. The human organism was regarded as merely a collection of specific parts operating like a machine in response to mechanical laws. The alphabet method of teaching reading and the drill method of teaching skills flowed naturally from this explanation of learning. Mechanical laws were formulated to govern the learning process; education served as the mechanical assembly belt to transmit the cultural heritage; the end product was the patterned mind.

Earlier chapters in this text have pointed out that improvement of teacher education involves more than merely reshuffling course content and adding courses to the requirements for certification. It involves nothing less than the development of a valid theory of instruction based on our changing social needs and on the new understanding of human behavior which has emerged from research in the social sciences.

It is now widely accepted that the basic purpose of education is to help young people become fully human. The new humanistic approach has been explained as follows:

Within the past twenty years a whole series of new concepts about man and his behavior has appeared upon the scene. The social science breakthrough has resulted from the emergence in American psychology of a great new humanistic force, a new psychology deeply concerned with people, values, perceptions, and man's eternal search for being and becoming. The impact of these new ideas is powerful indeed. They promise new solutions to age-old problems. Already they have profoundly influenced the work of several other professions. Little by little as they find their way into education, they promise similar revolutions for teaching and learning.[13]

The public school that is already emerging from this humanistic philosophy-psychology will increasingly become a place where basic concepts will emerge from searching, thinking, and experimenting. School will become a place where the excitement of discovery will cause children and youth to go out on their own in search of information; it will no longer be necessary for all the impetus to come from outside forces.

The Challenge of Broader Objectives

Most people will agree that the school is not a social club, not a hospital, not a church, and not a substitute for the home. It can be expected, however, that parents in the future will continue to look to the schools for assistance in the areas of health, character development, personal finance, and appreciation for the fine arts. Despite problems with teaching basic subjects, parents are not likely to demand a return to the school of the three Rs or to the strictly academic high school. Leaders in American life will continue to expect the schools to provide education for intelligent citizenship, international understanding, intercultural harmony, and respect for legally constituted authority. The schools of the future, with the aid of instructional media, will be expected not only to teach the fundamentals more thoroughly than they now do but also to assist other educative agencies in producing adequate, fully functioning persons.

Increasing Emphasis on Concept Learning

If current trends are projected into the future, there can be little doubt that curriculum content will be organized around basic concepts or themes in the various curriculum areas. The rationale for this arrangement is not difficult to discover. One obvious reason is the explosion of knowledge in pratically every field; it has been said that knowledge in the field of science doubles every ten years. Since imparting specific information in the various fields is no longer feasible, educators have adopted the scheme of having content specialists in the various disciplines list the basic concepts essential for an understanding of that discipline. For example one publication lists fourteen themes around which the whole social studies program for grades K–12 can be organized. The geographical, historical, political, economic, and social aspects of each theme are studied at every grade level. This practice provides the pupil with a scheme for organizing bits of specific information; it provides something resembling a drawer in a file cabinet into which the student can place facts about a given topic; it helps the student see the interrelationships of information. Instead of teaching isolated facts, the schools of the future increasingly will assume the role of equipping each student with the intellectual tools and techniques of investigation that will enable him or her to investigate any field of knowledge independently during a lifetime of learning.

The Challenge of Learning by Discovery

The discovery approach to teaching is essentially a procedure by which students discover for themselves a principle, such as "metals expand when heated." It is the opposite of teaching by exposition. Learning by discovery has perhaps been best illustrated in the new programs in elementary school science. Using the discovery method requires a different conception of the role of facts in the educative process from that generally held by teachers. The facts of science are important, of course, but they are tools used in the solution of problems rather than ends in themselves. Using the discovery method emphasizes (1) helping students find answers to their questions rather than giving them ready-made answers, (2) concern for the processes of science rather than the products, (3) providing many opportunities for students to investigate, and (4) developing the ability to think.

The Need for Specialized School Personnel

This text has emphasized the urgent need for schools and colleges to make greater contributions to the strength of the nation during a period of revolutionary changes at home and abroad. It is obvious that improvements in the teaching-learning process itself are necessary, and this is one facet of educational reform that seems certain to gain momentum in coming years. It is widely recognized that one fundamental need is simply time to teach—time for the teacher to do what he or she wants to do and is supposed to do: help children grow and learn. Many methods are being tried to gain this essential time: reducing the size of classes, providing clerical help, establishing central libraries with qualified librarians, and employing special education teachers, school social workers, school psychologists, guidance workers, and playground and lunchroom supervisors. These improvements, however, have by no means materialized in all the schools. For instance, the U. S. Office of Education reported in 1975 that 50 per cent of the nation's elementary schools still had inadequate libraries and that spending for elementary school books averaged little more than $8 per pupil—an amount the U. S. Office of Education said should be quadrupled.[14]

Along with these relatively familiar ways of dealing with the problem of improving the teaching-learning situation, some new and exciting developments are beginning to appear on the educational frontier. One of the most important of these is the addition of the new types of workers to the school staff. These people who work with teachers are identified by many titles unknown to the pedagogical vocabulary of past years—teacher aides, volunteers, paraprofessionals, nonprofessionals, and auxiliary personnel. In other words "New Branches Grow on the Educational Family Tree," as one article on the topic is titled. The writer describes the role of the "new branches" thus:

People, even if they are innocent of university degrees and consider education courses a retreat from reality, are able to take over 30 per cent of what teachers now do—things that are done by people for children in homes and at parties or other places where children are found. These people are going to relieve teachers of direct and continuous involvement in such duties, and this will cause a great increase in the dignity and prestige of the teaching role. They will allow the teacher greater flexibility in using instructional resources and in responding to the whole range of each child's needs.[15]

The use of more specialized professional personnel and the use of nonprofessionals who can relieve the overburdened teacher seems likely to increase in a period of increasing abundance and liesure time.

Vertical Extension of Local School Programs

Recent research in the area of human growth and learning has highlighted the importance of the early years of a child's life in terms of subsequent achievement in school subjects, and in terms of the development of personality traits. Growth in both of these aspects takes place much more rapidly between the ages of four and eight than it does during later years. The same reserach indicates that the environment plays an important role in growth and learning during these early years. As a result it is now generally recognized that children should be admitted to the public schools at the age of four instead of six. Indeed, the National Education Association recommended such a change several years ago. This practice would help materially in narrowing the gap between the educational opportunities of children from disadvantaged homes and children from more advantaged homes. It seems likely that the schools of tomorrow will admit children at earlier ages than do schools of today.

New Organizational Structures

It is probable that the school system of tomorrow will have some type of year-round curriculum in place of the typical September to June format with a summer enrichment or remedial program. This would allow students to complete their course of studies earlier or alter their educational cycle to fit parental vacation schedules. And, of course, this plan would allow students to have more flexible work-study schedules.

Many more schools will have evening high schools. This program, like the year-round school, is currently being tried in a few places. This format will be attractive to students who must work during the day or those who prefer to break the 8:30 a.m. to 3:30 p.m. learning routine.

Still other schools—perhaps a majority if the energy crisis continues—will adopt four-day school weeks. School systems with shortened weeks will alter their curriculum to include more intensive seminars, workshops, and individualized instruction. Flexible modular scheduling is the first step towards this goal. Modular scheduling breaks up the traditional six or seven period day into modules which vary in length depending on optimum conditions for each situation.

The success of the Parkway Program, Philadelphia's School Without Walls, is also likely to influence tomorrow's schools. Organized into several units or "communities," each with less than two hundred school students, the Parkway Program has no school building. Each unit has a central headquarters with teacher offices and student lockers, but the community is the classroom. All members of the community—students, teachers, and administrators—share in the process of finding appropriate learning spaces and also in designing learning objectives. The entire community then becomes a learning resource—museums, libraries, businesses, churches and synagogues, garages, newspaper offices, etc. A few cities have already replicated and/or modified the Parkway program.

Other system-wide changes will include abolishing bells, opening the high school campus and allowing students to leave the premises when they are not scheduled for classes, initiating a school-within-school organizational arrangement in which students assume responsibility for deciding what credits they need and then contracting for a plan of study, and implementing open schools in which students of different ages (cross-age grouping) work together in programs designed to foster interdependence and creativity. Teachers will be facilitators who help students master life skills—reading skills, information gathering, problem solving, critical thinking, computation skills, physical fitness, and good mental and physical health.

The Educational Potential of Computers

Participants in a symposium on computer-assisted education sponsored by the National Academy of Science at the California Institute of Technology predicted that computers will have more of an impact on education than did the development of printing. They pointed out that today's equipment makes it possible to teach 10,000 students through computerized television consoles at a cost that would be only half that of using human teachers at a ratio of 1 to 15 students; that computers can monitor each student's progress minute by minute, correcting mistakes immediately; and that computers will soon be teaching the basic skills in reading and mathematics in one-tenth the time and at half the cost now required. They predicted that the egg-crate type of school building with each slot of the crate housing about 30 students and a teacher will disappear, that classrooms will be used many more hours a day, and that computer terminals will move into homes, where individuals of many ages will be learning together.[16]

These still rather startling predictions should not be taken to mean that the use of electronic equipment in teaching lies some distance in the future. Television teaching is not uncommon in today's schools; tape recorders and earphones enable teachers to program materials in harmony with levels of ability and rates of learning; and students in many schools know how to operate many types of electronic aids to learning with little assistance from teachers. Technology has already invaded the classroom.

The question always arises in connection with any discussion of the impact of technological aids on teaching: Will machines replace teachers? When textbooks began to appear in classrooms after the development of printing, some teachers viewed them with alarm. They have not, of course, replaced teachers. Hardware, no matter how modern, will never replace teachers. It will help the teacher get more work done and, when used properly, release the time of the teacher for the creative tasks that only a human being can perform.

Innovations in the Use of Space

The egg-crate type of school building is already being replaced in some school systems by a more functional arrangement. For example, the John F. Kennedy Elementary School in Norman, Oklahoma, has one large instructional area with approximately 16,000 square feet of floor space and no partitions. More than 400 pupils, 15 teachers, a resource director, and 2 teacher aides work in this area, which is carpeted and acoustically treated. Team-teaching and continuous progress are important features of the instructional program. Service areas include a materials center, an all-purpose room, a principal's office, a reception room, a conference room, a music room, a health room, a teachers' lounge, a supply room, and a study room used by pupils.

A visitor to this school may see one pupil reading quietly behind a screen or bookcase; a teacher working with a group of pupils in the reading, mathematics, science, or social studies center; a physical education class on the playground or in the all-purpose room; and a committee working on a special project around a table in a peripheral center. Space is allocated in terms of the function it is to serve rather than in terms of grade levels.

Glimpses of the future, coming to us from many sources, indicate that the rate of change in the future will be swifter than ever before. Human beings will need to learn faster than they have ever learned. Exciting new designs for teaching and learning are already emerging. The prospects for those who will be teaching America's children in the next few decades are indeed exhilarating.

LAST LOOK

1. Circle the number which best indicates your experience when participating as a member of this class. (1 = Low; 8 = High)

A. Do you feel you were understood?
   1   2   3   4   5   6   7   8
B. Do you feel your contributions were perceived as helpful?
   1   2   3   4   5   6   7   8
C. Do you feel you accepted the contributions of others?
   1   2   3   4   5   6   7   8
D. Estimate your tolerance of your instructor's and classmates' beliefs and values which are contrary to your own.
   1   2   3   4   5   6   7   8
E. Estimate your awareness of the feelings of others.
   1   2   3   4   5   6   7   8
F. Estimate your influence in helping the class to reach decisions and accomplish tasks.
   1   2   3   4   5   6   7   8
G. Estimate your ability to identify forces at work within the class.
   1   2   3   4   5   6   7   8
H. Estimate your skill in responding to negative forces at work within the class.
   1   2   3   4   5   6   7   8

2. Describe what you contributed to this course.

3. Describe what you have gotten from this class that will make you a more effective teacher.

4. What are some questions you still have about your teaching abilities?

5. What are the instructor's assets?

6. What are his/her liabilities?

7. How would you improve this course?

NOTE: If agreeable to the two of you, share this evaluation with your instructor.

ADDITIONAL READINGS

Anderson, Robert H. *Education in Anticipation of Tomorrow.* Worthington, Ohio, Charles A. Jones, 1973.

Faure, Edgar et al. *Learning to Be: The World of Education Today and Tomorrow.* Paris, UNESCO, 1972.

Hencley, Stephen P. and James R. Yates. *Futurism in Education: Methodology.* Berkeley, Cal., McCutchan, 1974.

Henderson, George, ed. *Education for Peace: Focus on Mankind.* 1973 Yearbook, Washington, D.C., Association for Supervision and Curriculum Development, 1973.

Hipple, Theodore W., ed. *The Future of Education: 1975–2000.* Pacific Palisades, Cal., Goodyear, 1974.

Hook, Sidney. *Education and the Taming of Power.* La Salle, Ill., Open Court, 1973.

Hostrop, Richard W., ed. *Education . . . Beyond Tomorrow.* Homewood, Ill., ETC, 1975.

Kauffman, Draper L. *Teaching the Future: A Guide to Future-Oriented Education.* Palm Springs, Cal., ETC, 1976.

Krug, Mark M., ed. *What Will be Taught—The Next Decade.* Itasca, Ill., F. E. Peacock, 1972.

Levin, Betsy, ed. *Future Directions for School Finance Reform.* Lexington Books, 1974.

Little, Dennis L. and Theodore J. Gordon. *Some Trends Likely to Affect American Society in the Next Several Decades.* Middletown, Conn., Institute for the Future, 1971.

Lloyd, Robert A. *Images of Survival.* New York, Dodd, Mead, 1975.

Morphet, Edgar L. and Charles O. Ryan. *Designing Education for the Future: An Eight State Project.* New York, Citation Press, 1967–1969.

Pulliam, John D. and Jim R. Bowman. *Educational Futurism in Pursuance of Survival.* Norman, University of Oklahoma Press, 1974.

Rogers, Carl R. *Freedom to Learn: A View of What Education Might Become.* Columbus, Ohio, Charles E. Merrill, 1969.

Silberman, Charles E. *Crisis in the Classroom: The Remaking of American Education.* New York, Random House, 1970.

Stoddard, George D. *The Outlook for American Education.* Carbondale, Southern Illinois University Press, 1974.

Theobald, Robert. *Futures Conditional.* Indianapolis, Bobbs-Merrill, 1971.

Toffler, Alvin, ed. *Learning for Tomorrow: The Role of the Future in Education.* New York, Random House, 1974.

NOTES

1. Vincente Blasco Ibáñez, *The Four Horsemen of Apocalypse* (trans. by Charlotte B. Johnson, New York, E. P. Dutton, 1919), 479–480.

2. Charles Frankel, "Third Great Revolution of Mankind," in August Kerber and Wilfred Smith (eds.), *Educational Issues in a Changing Society*, rev. ed. (Detroit, Wayne State University Press, 1964), 14.

3. Adapted from Clyde M. Campbell, "The World of Work," *The Community School and Its Administration* (Midland, Mich., Ford, 1967).

4. Peter F. Drucker, *Landmarks of Tomorrow* (New York, Harper & Row, 1957), 114.

5. Jan O. M. Broek and John W. Webb, *A Geography of Mankind* (New York, McGraw-Hill, 1968), 446.

6. The Rockefeller Panel Reports, *Prospects for America* (Garden City, N. Y., Doubleday, 1958), 21.

7. Earl Raab and Seymour M. Lipset, *Prejudice and Society* (New York, Anti-Defamation League of B'nai B'rith, 1963), 9.

8. William B. Ragan, *Modern Elementary Curriculum* 3rd ed. (New York, Holt, Rinehart & Winston, 1966), 402–403.

9. Paul R. Ehrlich, "The Biological Revolution," *Stanford Review* (September/October, 1965), 10.

10. *Ibid.*

11. John Cunliff, "Economy Inherently Strong," *Norman (OK.) Transcript* (December 18, 1968), 10.

12. Francis Keppel, *The Necessary Revolution in American Education* (New York, Harper & Row, 1966).

13. Arthur W. Combs, *The Professional Education of Teachers: A Perceptual View* (Boston, Allyn & Bacon, 1965), vi.

14. For an earlier report see Sylvia Porter, "Book Shortage Blot on Nation," *Denver Post* (August 22, 1965), 9.

15. Beatrice Boyles, "New Branches Grow on the Educational Family Tree," *National Elementary Principal*, 46 (May, 1967), 38.

16. "Computers to Replace Teachers, Experts Say," *The Daily Oklahoman* (October 28, 1968), 5.

APPENDIX

INSIDE
A POCKET
OF POVERTY

A CASE STUDY

The following case study is presented to give the reader a comprehensive view of how social forces affect the lives of people—especially lower-class children. Although the study was conducted in 1964, little has changed in the Target Area since that time. The tragic significance of this fact should be at once apparent: Despite a riot in 1967 and millions of federal, state, and private funds expended in the area, the Target Area youths of the 1970s are not much different than their predecessors in the 1960s. This is not to suggest that these efforts were wasted. There is a new Black consciousness and a few cosmetic environmental changes. Basically, however, this is a study of an American tragedy that is acted out in each successive generation. For some readers, the following pages will be a *deja vu* experience, while for others it will be a new journey into a low-income community. So let us begin.

INTRODUCTION

In his classic *The Protestant Ethic and the Spirit of Capitalism*, Max Weber described the early appearance of the American emphasis on profitable work as a goal in itself. Even though our society has undergone dramatic changes, the work ethic still survives. In recent years, however, Americans have become more consumption-oriented than work oriented. This is not to imply that we devalue work, but that more than ever it has a means orientation; work is viewed primarily as a means to consumer activities and not as assurance of one's spiritual salvation. Young children are taught

that work is good. All around them people are talking about, seeking, and engaging in work activities. Indeed, a major question that American children are continually called on to answer is, "What are you going to be when you grow up?"

Opportunities for upward social mobility through working do sometimes exist for those who are defined as lower class. Nevertheless, lower-class students are confronted with inconsistent life situations. On the one hand, they are given a work orientation in their elementary and secondary schools; on the other hand, they see chronic unemployment and underemployment in their homes. Even in good times, the unemployment and underemployment rates are proportionately higher for their parents. Quite naturally, lower-class children find it almost impossible to believe that people can ever improve their circumstances by working and saving their pennies. Besides, the social treatment accorded even the most successful nonwhites seems to prove that in order to be free, one needs something more than a bank account.

In other words, it seems very probable that most lower-class, minority-group students do not expect to achieve success within the white society. If this is true, then what is needed to give such lower-class students a sense of belonging—a sense of identity? Certainly it is not enough to add a few passages about minority groups to history books and include pictures of children of different races in other textbooks. We might make some more informed suppositions about what lower-class pupils actually do need if we first examine how they live. To be specific, what is life like inside a pocket of poverty?

THE TARGET AREA

During January and February of 1964, 200 Black young people living in what later became the core area of the 1967 Detroit riot were interviewed individually in school yards, in schools, and on sidewalks—in short, wherever it was possible to conduct an interview.[1] The respondents, 100 males and 100 females, were between 12 and 18 years old. According to the Detroit antipoverty program standards, 150 respondents were poverty-striken (annual family income less than $3,000) and 50 were middle income (annual family income between $3,000 and $10,000). (Throughout this report, the terms "lower class" and "low income" will be used interchangeably to indicate an individual from a family with an annual income of less than $3,000 and whose main wage-earner was employed in an unskilled or semi-skilled capacity.)

Although part of the time was devoted to examining objectively some of the environmental factors within the Target Area, the major emphasis was placed on exploring the youths' subjective interpretations of those factors. Partially structured field interviews, each lasting about one hour, were conducted to elicit the respondents' perceptions of their neighborhoods, families, schools, significant other factors, and, finally, their educational and occupational aspirations. Each interview was taped and later subjected to detailed content analysis.

Other studies indicate that under socially strained conditions, lower-class youths are extremely adroit in "taking the role of the other." When they do so, they say what they believe to be socially correct but not necessarily true. Thus the interviewers tried to avoid seeming to be typical well-trained, well-groomed, middle-class outsiders. Instead they dressed casually and occasionally used local jargon in an effort to gain rapport. Also, because they interviewed only those who volunteered, it is likely that defensiveness was further minimized. Before each interview the interviewer attempted to convey the feeling that he or she was aware of and respected the cultural differences of the respondents. Most interviews began this way:

Interviewer: *I'd like to interview you if I may.*
Respondent: *Interview me about what?*
Interviewer: *Oh, about you, your neighborhood school, and things like that. I'm from Wayne State University and I'm trying to find out what people in this neighborhood think about these things.*
Respondent: *I ain't so sure I can help you.*
Interviewer: *If you can't help me, I guess nobody can. One thing I've learned from going to college is that I can't get to know people by only reading books. I can spend the rest of my life reading books but never really digging people. You know, like a phony, stuck-up cat trying to save the world but not knowing how.*
Respondent: *Yeah, there's lots of cats who think they know it all 'cause they go to college. What they need is for somebody to turn them on.*

The respondents seemed to take great delight in "turning on" the interviewers to a few facts. As one girl said, they were "educating the educators."

An analysis of the data in Table 20 on both the respondents and the total Target Area population reveals that they had very similar characteristics. (The Target Area sample, however, had proportionately higher rates of welfare cases, school dropouts, and broken homes.) The degree of representativeness can be ascribed in part to an earlier pilot study that allowed the interviewers to gain neighborhood exposure and pre-interview acceptance from many respondents. Another reason was the accurate number of lower-class and middle-class youths recommended for interview by several junior high and senior high school teachers. These recommendations were convenient for the interviewers, but the fact of this kind of classifying presents a problem in itself. This report will discuss later the way such labeling by teachers can adversely affect the life chances of lower-class students.

YOUTHS' PERCEPTIONS OF THEIR NEIGHBORHOODS

Most of the youths gave unemotional, terse descriptions of their neighborhoods. Their almost observer-like descriptions created the

Table 20. Some Selected Characteristics of Households in the Target Area Sample and the Total Target Area (in percentages)

Characteristic	Target Area	
	Sample households[1]	Total households[2]
Total nonwhite	100.0	76.2
Population 13–18 years of age	10.2	8.8
Male percent of population, 13–18 years of age	47.9	49.2
Female percent of population, 13–18 years of age	52.1	50.8
Living in owner-occupied housing unit	20.5	22.7
Moved into unit since 1958	53.3	44.2
One or more persons per room	25.0	12.8
Automobile available	31.5	52.2
Adults unemployed (heads of households)	24.1	14.9
Welfare, ADC, OAA recipients	18.0	10.3
Male adults employed, (heads of households)	78.5	83.0
Professional and managerial	6.9	9.2
Clerical, sales, craftsmen, and foremen	20.8	25.0
Operatives, service workers, and laborers	72.3	65.8
Female adults employed (heads of households)	82.6	85.1
Professional and managerial	9.9	14.8
Clerical, sales, craftsmen and foremen	29.1	27.4
Operatives, service workers, and laborers	61.0	57.8
Family with annual incomes less than $5,000	80.4	14.3
16–18 year old dropout rate	35.6	28.6
Broken homes	26.0	14.3

[1] Based on information taken from interviews.
[2] Based on 1960 Census and social agency reports.

impression that one was listening to senior anthropologists quite matter-of-factly describing their field experiences. A major reason for their assuming this mannerism was that they did not, as many verbalized it, want to "lose their cool." Losing their cool, getting involved and attached to others, made them more vulnerable to disillusionments. As one boy said:

This a tough life, man . . . ain't nothin' out here but heartache. . . . No sense in losin' your cool, that's where the trouble is. . . . Don't let nobody or nothin' get close to you and you won't get hurt.

Such withholding of affection from others appeared to represent a survival motif. If they had not been able to suppress their emotions, many of the youths would have been physically and psychologically overwhelmed by their neighborhoods. This detachment from others showed up in several ways, but basically each effort was an attempt to separate self (i.e., poverty-stricken people) from nonself (i.e., middle-class people, especially social agency representatives and public school teachers). From the perspective of the lower-class respondents, people were divided into "we" and "they" categories; "we" were the lower class.

Processed (straightened) hair encased in greasy rags, slow, swaggering walks, and near-whispered conversations were extreme examples of a coolness that some low-income youths adopted in order to hide the precarious nature of their poverty-stricken existence.[2] A 15-year-old girl described her neighborhood as follows:

It's . . . kind of big in size. Lots of teenagers around every night. They go out and pick fights with boys. They pick fights and carry knives. . . . At one house party a boy got stabbed in the eye. The police couldn't find him so they just dropped the charges against the boy who gave the party.

The reasons given by the respondents for carrying knives and maintaining menacing expressions were similar to one of the adult rationalizations for nuclear stockpiling: to prevent a war, not to start one. At first glance there did appear to be a lot of fighting, but on closer analysis it was merely the noise and pushing that result wherever large groups of children and youths congregate.

Although the lower-class families in the Target Area had more children than the middle-class families, and although they were all compressed into slum neighborhoods, there were far fewer stabbings and fights than near-stabbings and near-fights. A respondent with a flair for dramatics noted that a constant war of nerves was being waged by two paradoxical opponents, one who was scared and the other who was glad that his rival was scared; thus mortal combat was averted.

Mother-Centered Homes

Over half the youths reported that their fathers were permanently absent from home and that grandparents, especially grandmothers, were present. There was a tendency for stepfathers or other father surrogates to be present. For some children this kind of extended family arrangement was psychologically more disconcerting than changing schools each year. The mother was usually perceived as being the boss in the family. The importance of the mother was further illustrated by her hierarchical ranking above the father. One youth said: "If you say that my old man [father] is a dirty bastard, I might just laugh. . . . If you say my old lady [mother] is a no good bitch, I'll try to kick your ass. . . . Nobody talk that way about my old lady."

Much of the tension centering on mother-dominated homes was vented in a game called "the dozens." The object of the game is to calmly talk about (insult) one's opponent by questioning his parentage, and not to show anger when he offers rebuttal. The youth who scores the most points is the winner of the contest. However, the first one who "blows his cool" (resorts to physical aggression or cries)

automatically loses, no matter how many points he had scored before blowing his cool. A game of the dozens between two hypothetical youths, M and G, may proceed as follows:

M: *Come here son.*
G: *I ain't your son, I'm your daddy.*
M: *Oh! You want to play the dozens, huh? Listen, son: I don't play the dozens 'cause the dozens is bad, but I can tell you how many children your mammy had. She didn't have one, she didn't have two, she had 29 bulldogs just like you.*
G: *Now son, is that any way for you to talk to your daddy? If you keep talking like that, I'm gonna tell everybody that your momma wears cast-iron drawers.*

From the interviews it was clear that in subcommunities where there are proportionately more broken homes and illegitimate children than in other sections of the city, derogatory statements about a youth's mother are crushing blows at not only the most significant other person in the home but, often, the only significant other person in the home.

The Fear

A few respondents talked about their neighborhood in such a way as to suggest that for them it had no meaning whatever. When asked, "Tell me about your neighborhood," several said, "It ain't nothin' to tell." But with a little prodding they described the violence potential. A thirteen-year-old girl noted the not-too-frequent lulls that broke the noisy routine of her slum life.

Well, it's kinda quiet. The kids get noisy sometimes. It would be a nice neighborhood if it wouldn't be too many fights around there. Kids are fussing, even the grownups and the kids. Then for a while they be quiet again.

Why, we might ask, is it that of all the problems in their neighborhoods that the youths could discuss, aggressive behavior was mentioned most often? One possible answer is that even though few wanted to lose their cool, most were anxious about and fearful of the ever-present violence potential. Other matters were of course discussed, but none approached in frequency the topics of violence and near-violence.

Friends

The most immediate answer to the question, "What do you like best about your neighborhood?" was "Nothing." They did not like the dilapidated, roach- and rat-infested buildings. Nor did they like the absence of recreational facilities or the garbage-littered alleys and streets. Positive responses were in terms of people and not surroundings. Only a few respondents mentioned a school, church, or some other community facility as being an aspect of their neighborhood that they liked best. Those who talked about people as an aspect of the community that they liked best seldom referred to teachers, social workers, or other professional people. Instead they usually talked about nonprofessional area residents, mostly peers. This was the first indication that the cool attitude was only a thin veneer.

Even though many of the youths moved from neighborhood to neighborhood, they quickly sought out friends in each new neighborhood. The lower-class respondents verbalized the same kinds of aspirations for companionship as the middle-class youths. The major difference between the two groups was the opportunity for developing and maintaining close social relationships. The higher mobility rate of the lower-class youths decreased their opportunities for interacting with a single set of peers over a prolonged period of time.

Role Models

In response to the question, "What kind of people live in your neighborhood?" the lower-class respondents described unemployed and unskilled and semiskilled adults; the middle-class youths described adults employed in higher prestige occupations, such as doctors, lawyers, teachers, and social workers. From the interviews it became evident that *the number and variety of occupations to which the lower-class Target Area youths were exposed on a day-to-day basis were extremely limited.* Most of the youths expressed a desire to engage in occupations that already had a large minority-

group representation—social worker, nurse, teacher. Missing were goals that reflected a wide range of occupational choices. Thus the economic effects of racial segregation and discrimination in job opportunities went beyond denying jobs to the poverty-stricken Target Area adults; their children were also denied adult models needed for motivating them to seek a broader range of available occupations. Equally debilitating, most of the low-income youths could not learn behavior patterns from their parents and neighbors that were functional for positive school adjustment.

Illegal Activities

When asked, "Are things going on in your neighborhood that are against the law?" answers ranged from "Definitely yes!" to "Definitely no!" Those who noted illegal activities talked about people making corn whisky, prostitutes standing on corners, pushers selling drugs, youths stealing cars, and friends playing the numbers. For many respondents these were normal activities because, as they stated, there was "some of this going on everywhere." Illegal activities were perceived by the lower-class youths as a natural part of their environment. Yet in terms of the total sample, only a small percentage engaged in or expected to engage in such occupations. For most of the respondents life was a choice between poverty and nothing. A petite twelve-year-old girl, dismissing the probability of prostitution becoming her occupational adjustment, said: "You can see people taking poison all around you . . . know where to get it, but not take it yourself. Seeing prostitution is the same way. I guess I'll always be poor." She was not aware of the many occupations lying between an illegal activity and poverty. Like several other low-income youths, she was resigned to being poor.

PERCEPTIONS OF SCHOOLS

Throughout the Target Area interviews were indications of a lack of communication between teachers and students. It was a lack and not a lag in many instances because most students felt ineffective in their efforts to communicate with their teachers. Teachers and pupils talked at each other and not to or with each other. The language of the lower-class respondents frequently did not correspond to the middle-class language patterns of their teachers. Many words such as "dig," "cool," "hip," and "busted" were not used in accordance with their nonslang dictionary definitions. One student highlighted his inability to communicate: "I told my teacher that she had a crazy dress on and she flipped [got angry] and sent me to the man [principal]. He asked me what I done and I told him. He sent me home until I apologized to the teacher." Neither the teacher nor the principal realized that when the student said it was a crazy dress, he was paying a compliment in the language of his subculture.

The other side of the communication coin was the inability of the culturally disadvantaged students to understand their teachers. As one confused and embarrassed student complained, his teachers were always cautioning him not to dangle his participle or to split his infinitives. The former warning caused him to check the zipper of his pants to see if it was open; the latter caused him sheepishly to check the seams in the seat of his pants to see if they were split.

Another example of teachers who erroneously assumed that the lower-class Target Area students understood them is taken from an interview with a 16-year-old, lower-class boy who was desperately seeking to assert his masculinity. Explaining why he dropped out of a biology course after attending only one class, he said, "That thin, funny-looking cat stood up, smiled, and said that everybody in the class was *homo sapiens*." The boy frowned and added, "It was bad enough he was a homo-[sexual], but he didn't have to be proud of it." The teacher used a word that was not correctly understood. Still another student said that she couldn't "dig" math courses where pies [π] were squared because "any fool knows that all pies are round." Finally, the communication problem was most vividly illustrated by the student who accused his English teacher of making derogatory statements about his family. Reconstructing the events leading to the allegation, the student said that the teacher called his relative pronouns "improper." And the student added, "I told her, 'So is your mama.'"

Teachers lament that once lower-class stu-

dents are outside school, they revert to the language of their contemporaries. Almost all the lower-class students stated that survival was the foremost reason they behaved in this manner. The jargon of the lower-class child is functional for survival in the subcommunity; dropping it may lead to accusations of becoming uppity or a snob. Target Area respondents who adopted "proper" English often found themselves living as true marginal people—alienated from the lower class and not completely accepted by the middle class.

Favorite Teachers

Many of the lower-class interviewees disliked their school and particularly their teachers. Their most frequent answer to the question, "What do you like best about your school?" was "Nothing" (see Table 21). The negative feelings of the students were also evident in that the most immediate answer to the question, "What do you like least about your school?" was "Everything." More lower-class than middle-class students talked about being bored with or not "hip to" school subjects. When the students talked about teachers they did not like, one could detect emotional vehemence. A sarcastic witticism expressed by a few students was: "When the last bell rings you'd better clear the halls or you'll be run over by the teachers leaving school. They're the last ones in the building and the first ones out." On the other hand, students with positive feelings about school quickly mentioned favorite teachers who seemed to care about them.

A growing community emphasis on Black nationalism caused some Target Area students to believe that Black teachers just naturally had better rapport with lower-class Black students than white teachers. However, a few students observed that their Black teachers were very middle-class in their behaviors. These teachers appeared to have a psychological need to reject or repress memories of their less successful past, including students who reminded them of it. A lower-class Black student described such rejection:

A nigger is a bitch. . . . Them stuck-up Black teachers treat us Black kids like dirt. They won't touch you and don't want you to touch them—

Table 21. The Most Frequent Reactions to School of Target Area Youth
(in percentages)

Comments	Lower-class students	Middle-class students
What the respondents liked best:		
Nothing	25	0
The students	14	10
Don't know	12	2
Going home	8	4
The subjects	5	35
The teachers	4	25
What the respondents liked least:		
Everything	20	0
The subjects	16	2
The teachers	12	6
Going to school	10	2

scared you'll dirty them up. If I want a break [fair treatment], I go to the patty [white] teachers. . . . Somebody said Mr. _____ who acts so high and mighty grew up in this neighborhood.[3]

Probing revealed that in many instances the students were using the teachers as scapegoats to cover up their own inability to pass the courses; several students did, however, cite verified instances of discriminatory treatment.

Adjusting to Failure

More lower-class than middle-class students were underachieving in school. Several low-achieving, lower-class students felt that they were not participants in the classroom dialogue. In the words of a student:

The teachers give the good kids all the attention. . . . They don't even know I'm in the class. But they know that the good kids are there. . . . They let them ask questions, answer questions, and get away with murder. Me, I just look cross-eyed and I get in trouble. So I wised up and stopped talking. . . .

Unable to succeed in school, most lower-class respondents felt that they had to attend only

until they could legally drop out. During this interim period, school was perceived by many of them as having positive attractions. It was warmer than home, it was the place where they could meet their friends, and it was cleaner than home. Nevertheless, although teachers could have provided the most immediate and direct assistance in connection with certain problems (e.g., difficulty with school subjects and knowledge of occupations), the lower-class students were likely to turn to less-qualified sources (e.g., parents and friends).

As Table 22 shows, the reasons given by the lower-class Target Area students for not getting better grades differed from the reasons given by the middle-class students who had the same grade-point averages. The low-achieving, lower-class students tended to blame others (particularly their teachers and high-achieving classmates) for their own difficulties; the low-achieveing, middle-class students tended to blame themselves. As a whole the lower-class students seemed to lack self-confidence when competing for school success symbols. The competition literally horrified most of the lower-class students in the study. One disgruntled youth said:

Sometimes I think that I know my lesson real well, but when I get to class I can't remember nothing.

Table 22. Reasons Students Gave for Not Getting Higher Grades
(in percentages)

Reasons	Lower class (N=127)	Middle class (N=46)	Total (N=173)
Working at capacity	11.8	28.2	19.1
Not working at capacity	7.3	32.6	12.7
Can't concentrate	16.5	4.4	13.3
Teachers don't like me	15.0	8.8	13.3
Acting out in class	11.9	2.2	9.3
Don't want to do better	8.7	12.2	9.8
Other students cheat	5.5	0.0	4.1
Can't think of a reason	3.9	0.0	2.9
Other reasons	19.4	10.6	15.5
Total	100.0	100.0	100.0

NOTE: N signifies number of respondents.

Lots of times I'd like to ask for help, but I don't want to look stupid in the eyes of the class. The [middle-class] kids from LaSalle Street are always ready. It's the same in all classes. They get the good grades and I get what's left.

Only a few of the lower-class students responded to failure by vowing to do better, whereas almost all of the middle-class students predicted that they would get better grades. The major difference between the lower- and the middle-class students was their expectations, not their desire for good grades. Most lower-class respondents verbalized the desire but did not expect to succeed in classroom competition; most middle-class respondents wanted and expected to succeed.

Perceptions of Jobs

There are basically two types of aspirations, ideal and real (expected). The ideal aspiration reflects what a person would most like to achieve, whereas the real aspiration reflects what a person believes he or she actually will achieve. The middle-class youths projected considerably less difference between ideal and real aspirations. On the other hand, there was a noticeable discrepancy between the lower-class respondents' ideal and real levels of occupational aspirations. The majority of both

the lower-class (78 per cent) and the middle-class (82 per cent) youths ideally aspired to professional and managerial occupations. This may have indicated either that they wanted to conform to the dominant society's educational push toward high-prestige jobs or that they sought to give socially correct ideal aspirations. Whatever the reason, the ideal aspirations of both groups indicated some internalization of the American Dream.

As for real aspirations, however, 72 per cent of the middle-class youths expected to achieve professional and managerial jobs, but only 13 per cent of the lower-class youths had such expectations. The great discrepancies between the lower-class youths' ideal and real occupational aspirations may have been caused by a "settling-down" effect; the lower-class students, in the face of their school performances and other negative environmental factors, found their aspirations settling down to a lower reality level (see Table 23). The following portion of an interview illustrates such a lowering of aspirations.

Interviewer:	*If you could be anything in the world and nothing was stopping you, what would you be?*
Respondent:	*(without hesitation) If I could be anything in the world, I'd be a nurse.*
Interviewer:	*Why do you want to be a nurse?*

Table 23. Ideal and Real Levels of Occupational Aspirations of Target Area Youths
(in percentages)

Aspiration

Occupational aspiration	Ideal			Real (expected)		
	Lower class (N=150)	Middle class (N=50)	Total (N=200)	Lower class (N=150)	Middle class (N=50)	Total (N=200)
I. Professional and managerial	78.0	82.0	79.0	13.3	72.0	28.0
II. Clerical and sales	13.3	16.0	14.0	44.7	20.0	39.5
III. Skilled	1.3	2.0	1.5	3.3	8.0	4.5
IV. Semiskilled	6.6	0.0	5.0	31.3	0.0	23.5
V. Unskilled	0.8	0.0	0.5	7.4	0.0	5.5
Total	100.0	100.0	100.0	100.0	100.0	100.0

Note: N signifies number of respondents.

Respondent: *It's a high profession and I've always wanted to be one. I could help people and earn a decent living.*

Interviewer: *What do you think you actually will be?*

Respondent: *(hesitating) I don't know. . . . Maybe I'll just work the streets or get married.*

Interviewer: *Why do you change from wanting to be a nurse to expecting to work the streets?*

Respondent: *Working the streets is easier than going to nursing school. Besides I can earn more money.*

Only a small percentage of the Black youths either ideally (1.5 per cent) or realistically (4.5 per cent) aspired to skilled trades occupations. Considering the large number of skilled jobs available, it appeared that neither the middle-class nor the lower-class Black youths were aware of or motivated to seek skilled occupations.

Job Information

On intensive probing it became evident that most of the lower-class youths could not describe the training they would need in order to achieve either their ideal or real occupational aspirations (see Table 24). It was almost as if most of them expected to go to sleep and wait until their fairy godmothers came, waved magic wands over them, and—presto! they would become occupational successes. One student all but said as much.

It don't take a lot of brains and studying to get a good job. All it takes is a little luck and you'll get it. If you ain't got no luck, you'll never get a job. Worrying about it ain't gonna change your luck.

Exceptions to this were the few lower-class respondents who expressed real aspirations to socially deviant occupations. These youths could describe in much detail the training that was required to be gamblers, pimps, prostitutes, and other types of hustlers.

As noted earlier, the adults in the families of the lower-class respondents did not, as a rule, work in occupations above the semiskilled category. When the lower-class youths aspired to middle-class occupations, they frequently sounded as misinformed as one teenager living in the Target Area:

Interviewer: *What does a stenographer do?*

Respondent: *She does plenty of things. Like she types letters and answers the phone. Most of the time she doesn't have nothing to do, that's why I wants to be one. The pay is*

Table 24. Target Area Youths' Detailed Knowledge of Skills Needed in Their Occupational Aspirations (in percentages)

| | Knowlege of needed skills | | | | | |
| | Ideal aspiration | | | Real aspiration | | |
Occupational aspiration	Lower class (N=150)	Middle class (N=50)	Total (N=200)	Lower class (N=150)	Middle class (N=50)	Total (N=200)
I. Professional and managerial	7.8	48.8	25.9	40.0	66.7	57.1
II. Clerical and sales	25.0	50.0	32.2	29.9	66.7	32.5
III. Skilled	50.0	100.0	40.0	40.0	50.0	33.3
IV. Semiskilled	40.0	0.0	40.0	53.2	0.0	53.2
V. Unskilled	100.0	0.0	100.0	63.6	0.0	63.6

Note: N signifies number of respondents.

	high, and the work is easy.
Interviewer:	*What kind of training would you need to be a stenographer?*
Respondent:	*Typing and I guess that's all except good clothes. Of course, quite naturally you need to know how to answer the phone.*
Interviewer:	*If you could not be a stenographer, what would be a suitable related job?*
Respondent:	*I guess a switchboard operator if it is a real big office. If it is a little office ain't nothing else to do.*

More middle-class than lower-class youths could name occupations that were closely related to their ideal and real occupational aspirations (see Table 24). None of the middle-class youths aspired to semiskilled or unskilled occupations. Although there was no comparison of their knowledge of these occupations, it is probable that the lower-class youths were more knowledgeable about them (see Table 25).

Unless there is a great change in their readiness to plan, to work, and to succeed, it is probable that most of the lower-class Target Area respondents will ultimately engage in semiskilled and unskilled work. It follows that as employment trends continue to move away from semiskilled and unskilled occupations toward skilled or higher occupations, the youths appear destined to perpetuate their culture of poverty.[4]

Parental Pressures

Many researchers state that lower-class children do not realistically aspire to middle-class goals because of a lack of encouragement from their parents. This was not true of the Target Area youths interviewed. As Table 26 shows, their parents did attempt to motivate them toward middle-class goals; in almost the same breath they also tried to prepare them for what appeared to be probable failure. The youths described such conditioning as follows:

My mama is always bugging me 'bout finishin' school. "Child," she say, "ain't no sense in you growin' up like me. Better git yourself a good education so you won't be no domestic like me. . . . Colored people got to be better educated then white folks just to get a job workin' for white folks."

My old man tell me to go to school and learn. Ain't nobody hiring muscles these days unless they be between your ears. . . . Need a high school diploma before they let you fill out a application for a job. . . . Like my old man says, "It's bad enough to be Black. No sense in being Black and stupid."

In summary most of the lower-class parents—conditioned by their own failures—

Table 25. Target Area Youths' Knowledge of Occupations Closely Related to Their Aspirations (in percentages)

| Occupational aspiration | Knowledge of closely related occupations | | | | | |
| | Ideal aspiration | | | Real aspiration | | |
	Lower class (N=150)	Middle class (N=50)	Total (N=200)	Lower class (N=150)	Middle class (N=50)	Total (N=200)
I. Professional and managerial	12.8	39.8	19.6	30.0	58.4	47.1
II. Clerical	15.0	50.0	25.0	22.4	40.0	24.7
III. Skilled	0.0	100.0	33.3	40.0	50.0	44.4
IV. Semiskilled	30.0	0.0	30.0	38.3	0.0	38.3
V. Unskilled	100.0	0.0	100.0	45.5	0.0	45.5

Note: N signifies number of respondents.

sought to prevent their children from absorbing undue disappointments. As a result most of the lower-class interviewees were conditioned to expect failure when performing middle-class tasks. Even so, they ideally aspired to occupations that were socially higher in prestige than their parents'. Although out of the mainstream of the dominant culture, the lower-class parents passed on high occupational aspirations to their children.

A CASE OF ILLEGAL OPPORTUNITIES

One of the respondents in the Target Area study was an eighteen-year-old Black prostitute, Toni. The youngest of five children, Toni was born and grew up in a section of Detroit's lower East Side. The adult and juvenile crime rates in her neighborhood were among the highest in Detroit. Numbers men, dope-pushers, gamblers, pimps, and prostitutes were the most successful adult role models in her neighborhood. Her parents separated shortly after she was born, and her adult male contacts were mainly with a constantly changing group of "uncles." In addition, her home consisted of one inexpensive rooming house after another in neighborhoods where the schools were old, understaffed, and over-crowded.

Toni dropped out of school at fourteen, before completing the tenth grade, to give birth to her illegitimate child. After the baby was born, determined not to live with her mother or on Aid to Dependent Children (ADC), she secured a variety of unskilled jobs, including waiting on tables and cleaning the homes of wealthy white families. From none of these jobs was she able to earn enough money to support both herself and the baby adequately.

On the block. When she was sixteen, Toni met a pimp who convinced her that he could help her earn a decent salary and not have to resort to welfare. Following a brief on-the-job training period, she began working the streets. The prostitute-pimp relationship may be described as functional and reciprocal. That is, for teaching her the profession, paying her rent, buying her clothes, and providing her with bail when she was arrested, the pimp received the major share of Toni's earnings. Many relationships in cultures of poverty embrace patterns of adjustment that differ from middle-class patterns but that nevertheless are quite functional for survival. Toni explained her socialization as follows:

Interviewer: *Toni, tell me something about the streetwalker. Is there a certain technique to this business and what are the hazards?*

Table 26. Comparison of Ideal and Real Aspirations, by Attitude of Parents Toward Choice
(in percentages)

Parents' attitude	Ideal aspiration			Real aspiration		
	Lower class (N=150)	Middle class (N=50)	Total (N=200)	Lower class (N=150)	Middle class (N=50)	Total (N=200)
Parents approve	66.7	82.0	70.1	63.3	78.0	67.0
Parents indifferent	26.7	16.0	24.0	27.3	12.0	23.5
Parents disapprove	6.6	2.0	5.9	9.4	10.0	9.5
Total	100.0	100.0	100.0	100.0	100.0	100.0

Note: N signifies number of respondents.

Toni: *Before I started working the corner, I was really a country hick, not knowing anything. My pimp taught me how to walk, talk, dress, and how to examine men for VD. The prostitute on the corner is always in constant danger of being busted [arrested] by the man [police] or being hurt by a john [customer]. You never really know who you're dealing with and what that person might do to you.*

The possibilities of being arrested, contracting a venereal disease, and being beaten by chiseling customers are normal risks a prostitute assumes. Despite the hazards, prostitution seemed to be less of a risk to Toni than trying to finish school. On the block, Toni said, the rules were clear, but in school they were always changing.

Often the system of prostitution (and other illegal occupations) is perpetuated by unofficial, cordial police-prostitute relationships. Little things, such as being on a first-name basis and teasing, act to reinforce instead of discourage prostitution. Children observing this type of interaction in their neighborhoods find it difficult to equate prostitution with bad behavior. Instead, it sometimes assumes heights of distorted altruism. Toni, for example, with tongue in cheek, referred to herself as a "lay analyst."

The payoff. Toni's response to a question about her satisfaction with her work clearly illustrated her perception of legitimate opportunity structures.

Interviewer: *How do you feel about this business? Do you enjoy your work?*
Toni: *It's not bad. It's good work.... Sometimes I don't like it, but there ain't many jobs where a high school dropout like me can earn 300 to 400 dollars a week.... I thought about applying for one of those poverty program jobs, but I just couldn't make it on 50 or 60 dollars a week.*

Prostitution may not have been the ideal occupation for Toni, but it was the only occupation she had. Equally important was her question, "What can you offer me instead?" Although Toni's condition did not begin with prostitution, it may end there. Furthermore, as she worked the streets, she became a role model for other girls in her neighborhood. Thus the cycle is self-renewing.

IMPLICATIONS OF THE STUDY

The aspirations of the youths living in the Target Area were directly related to easily discernible factors such as race, income, and education. They also were related to less discernible factors of subjective definitions of environmental situations. W.I. Thomas wrote that if people define situations as being real, they are real in their consequences.[5] This theorem also applies to children and youth. As behavioral scientists gain more insight into cognitions, motivations, and attitudes, it becomes clear that in many instances false definitions of social conditions are as important as real definitions. For example the concerned Target Area student who falsely believed that he had failed an examination in history was not less anxiety-ridden than the concerned student who correctly believed that he had failed the examination. Wattenberg, commenting on levels of aspirations of school children, concluded:

The ideal situation for normal children is for their level of aspiration to be just high enough so that they have to put forth effort to reach it, and yet, low enough for them to achieve success. In school, at least in the beginning for any subject, children tend to accept the teacher's expectation and standards as their level of aspiration. Therefore, we can influence this level quite effectively. Now, when the level favors success with effort, a number of fine things happen.

The situation itself is satisfying. The child will want to return to the type of task. So to speak now he is motivated, shows interest, and puts out effort. Moreover, unless he is emotionally disturbed, he will begin to raise his sights. After each success he will set himself a somewhat higher level of aspiration.

If the task at hand is clearly beyond his ability, he fails. What does failure do? Not only does it rob the task of interest, but it can have a depressant effect on his future level of aspiration. His ambition for himself will curve sharply downward. . . . He sets himself a level considerably below his true ability.[6]

We could compare the level of aspiration to a furnace thermostat—it protects us against cold, demoralizing, progress-slowing failures; it also keeps us to the comfortable warmth of safe, morale-building successes. When the mechanism of the level of aspiration is thrown out of balance, it fails to perform its protective function. Aspirations may then be maintained consistently above achievement; that is, the individual then experiences continual failure. On the other hand, aspirations may be maintained consistently below achievement, reflecting lack of ambition, broken morale, exaggerated caution, and cynicism.

Conflicting Data

Aspiration theories are symbolic constructs that allow us partially to account for and predict human behavior. When studied in this perspective, each theory has some potential for adding to our knowledge of human behavior. The importance of not forgetting or repressing this fact is shown by a recent college graduate who, though armed with many fine and complex theories, was much confused by the behavior of the students in his classes when he began teaching. His problem was not to acquaint the students with the relevant theories and thereby cause them to behave correctly but instead to expand his theories to account for their behavior. This situation has been vividly described as follows:

Miss B. has accepted an assignment to teach in a new school which will enroll Negroes and whites for the first time in a West Coast community. Miss B. is thrilled with her assignment. She is filled with a missionary zeal to do good for the downtrodden; she visualizes the Negroes as poor, meek children upon whom she will confer dignity and status.

Miss B. is completely unprepared for the brash, impudent, and aggressive conduct of some of her Negro (as well as white) pupils. Gone forever, after a week, is her mental picture of herself as the kindly benefactress who will help the colored children feel at ease in their new surroundings. She had visualized the victims of prejudice as being submissive; it was shocking to her middle-class mores to have them "sass" a teacher, fight, and swear. She does not realize that what she is seeing is lower-class behavior, regardless of color. She begins to think, "Give these Negroes an inch and they'll take a mile." She takes over with a firm hand and . . . is kept busy dealing with incidents which arise.[7]

Most of the Target Area respondents were in the lower socio-economic class and this, by middle-class standards, placed them in socially and economically undesirable positions. Interestingly, there are arguments both for and against the proposition that the American tradition of wanting to get ahead is shared by poverty-stricken people. The results of some research studies suggest that middle-class parents place greater emphasis on the maintenance of high levels of school and vocational success than lower-class parents; other studies conclude that the reverse is true.[8] Such studies, however, conflict only if we are looking for a single type of aspiration that can be attributed to a particular social class. There is less discrepancy if we view members of all social classes as having approximately the same aspirations, but also as having the option to choose consciously the aspiration attributed to other social classes. This would partially account for the high aspirations that the lower-class Target Area parents held for their children.

Probably most lower-class youths do not acquire real aspirations to high-status, middle-class occupations. There are enough college-graduate handymen to discourage such conditioning. Of course, there are examples of lower-class people who have managed to make it by legitimate means, but the mere fact that children see such adults does not mean that they will identify with them. Most lower-class Blacks, for example, believe that the Marian Andersons, Jackie Robinsons, Martin Luther King, Jrs., and Thurgood Marshalls would have made it if they had been polka-dotted; they are the exceptional, the gifted. (Besides, there are few white youths who expect to achieve the goals reached by these undeniably talented Blacks.)

False Assumptions

There were instances when teachers in the Target Area erroneously assumed that the poverty-stricken children could not and would not learn to master their school tasks. What seemed to be an inability on the part of lower-class students to learn their school assignments was frequently their teachers' inability to present the material so that it could be understood.

This was illustrated by a thirteen-year-old who had failed three courses in mathematics but who could explain the operation of the "numbers" (gambling):

You can play any amount you wants to from a penny on up. . . . For every penny you hit [select the winning three-number combination] you get five dollars back. . . . Like if I play for a dollar and hit, I get 500 dollars back. . . . You can box num-

bers [play all possible combinations of three numbers] but each way cost money. That is, like I think 245 is a good number and wants to play all the ways it can fall [be a winner], then I play it six ways: 245, 254, 452, 425, 542, and 524. It cost, say a dollar each. That's six dollars to box it. With two races [times numbers are selected] a day at six dollars a race to box it, I need 12 dollars a day. . . . So you got to have a whole lot of money to box numbers.

Although this boy was unable to figure out how long it would take five men to build a house if it took one man 200 hours, he could explain the very complex system of checking the daily newspapers to determine the winning numbers. There was no perceived payoff for him solving the house-building problem. He had never heard the people who were important to him talk about building a house, nor had he ever seen a house being built. All around him, however, people were talking about and playing numbers. This was an example of a latent ability that was not developed because of nonmotivating curriculum material. School assignments did not appeal to his interests, allow him to identify with some of the characters or scenes, or psychologically motivate him.

Bridging the Gap Between Theory and Practice

As a bit of academic hindsight, it seems easier for a researcher to criticize an existing educational institution than to criticize it and then if needed, offer practical alternatives for achieving more effectiveness. The latter task is psychologically disconcerting; it highlights the gaps between social theory and social practice and, equally important, it reminds the researcher of his or her own inadequacies. Yet of all the social practitioners, action researchers or social engineers have built the sturdiest bridges between theory and practice.

Bridging the gap between educational theories and practices requires a knowledge of the past, an appreciation of the present, and an eye to the future. To state merely that our schools should change is not as meaningful as to suggest some directions for change.

NOTES

1. This was an exploratory study of the formal education experiences of Black and white youths interviewed for a Detroit juvenile delinquency prevention planning project, Community Action for Detroit Youth (CADY). The data presented in this chapter are based on interviews supervised by George Henderson. For a critique of the CADY project, see Michael Schwartz, "The Sociologist in an Unsuccessful Delinquency Prevention Planning Project," in Arthur B. Shostak (ed.), *Sociology in Action: Case Studies in Social Problems and Directed Social Change* (Homewood, Ill., Dorsey Press, 1966), 166–176.

2. The trend to Black nationalism has resulted in the abandonment of hair-straightening processes and chemicals by many Black young people. They now let their hair grow into "naturals" or "Afros." The other behaviors described in this study are very much the same.

3. The same is often true for white teachers and lower-class white students. In the CADY project, low-achieving lower-class white students stated that their white teachers were unduly harsh with them, and their Black teachers tended to be more sympathetic. There is a tendency for some teachers of either race to say, "I made it without special treatment and so can they (children of my racial group)."

4. As reported in an August 5, 1967, *Business Week* article, "For Negroes, the Pie Cuts Too Thin": "For the long haul, better education is probably the answer. But unless Negroes speed up their penetration into higher-skilled, white collar jobs where employment is growing, the future looks grim. At current rates of penetration, the Labor Department esimtates, Negroes in 1975 will still suffer from twice the jobless rates of whites, and Negroes will still be over-represented in the less-skilled job." See George Henderson, "Occupation Aspirations of Poverty-Stricken Negro Students," *Vocational Guidance Quarterly*, 15 (September, 1966), 41–45.

5. For an extensive discussion of Thomas' theorem, see Robert K. Merton, *Social Theory and Social Structure*, (Glencoe, Ill., Free Press, 1957), chap. 11. See also George Henderson, "Rags to Rags: A Probable Effect of Poverty," *Teachers College Journal*, 38 (December, 1966), 105–109.

6. William W. Wattenberg, "Levels of Aspiration," *Michigan Education Journal*, 37 (November, 1959), 231.

7. Celia Burns Stendler and William E. Martin, *Intergroup Education in Kindergarten-Primary Grades* (New York, Macmillan, 1953), 32–33.

8. See Max Weiner and Walter Murray, "Another Look at the Culturally Deprived," *Journal of Educational Sociology*, 36 (March, 1963), 319–321.

INDEX

UNIVERSITY OF OKLAHOMA PRESS : NORMAN